TACITUS

TACITUS

BY

RONALD SYME

VOLUME I

OXFORD
UNIVERSITY PRESS

OXFORD

UNIVERSITY PRESS

Great Clarendon Street, Oxford OX2 6DP

Oxford University Press is a department of the University of Oxford.
It furthers the University's objective of excellence in research, scholarship,
and education by publishing worldwide in

Oxford New York

Athens Auckland Bangkok Bogotá Buenos Aires Calcutta
Cape Town Chennai Dar es Salaam Delhi Florence Hong Kong Istanbul
Karachi Kuala Lumpur Madrid Melbourne Mexico City Mumbai
Nairobi Paris São Paulo Singapore Taipei Tokyo Toronto Warsaw

with associated companies in Berlin Ibadan

Oxford is a registered trade mark of Oxford University Press
in the UK and in certain other countries

Published in the United States
by Oxford University Press Inc., New York

First published by Oxford University Press 1958
Special edition for Sandpiper Books Ltd., 1997

British Library Cataloguing in Publication Data

Data available

ISBN 0-19-814327-3 (2 volume set)

3 5 7 9 10 8 6 4 2

Printed in Great Britain by
Bookcraft Ltd.,
Midsomer Norton, Somerset

PREFACE

TACITUS has never gone short of praise for style and composition. His quality as an historian might be another matter. In the recent age the trend of study and research turned against him, producing various harsh verdicts on his performance. The time is due for a juster appraisal, a closer approach to the author and his epoch. Tacitus had been a magnificent orator, and he wrote in a proud tradition. But he was not a mere eloquent expositor. He was a Roman senator, consul, and proconsul of Asia.

Political history could not be grasped and mastered if a man was not a senator. Nor can the political historian be understood in isolation. The events must be known, his coevals registered in their careers and activities. The theme demands both a broad canvas and a mass of detail. Much of the material has never been put together, let alone properly interpreted.

Oligarchy is the supreme, central, and enduring theme in Roman history. Across the revolutionary age it links the aristocratic Republic to the monarchy of the Caesars; and the process of change in the governing order has its sequel in the century between Caesar Augustus and Trajan. In the design of the present work, Cornelius Tacitus emerges as an exponent of that process—but he is also an item in it, a personal document. It is suitable to confess in this place that the concluding section, 'The New Romans' (Chapters XLIII–V), owes something to a book begun many years ago, soon interrupted, and not yet terminated—*The Provincial at Rome*.

Diligence and accuracy (it is averred) are the only merits an historian can properly ascribe to himself. The one virtue does not always guarantee the other. The more documentation, the more chances of error. Further, time and scrutiny will reveal misconceptions as well as mistakes. The record being one of scraps and pieces, with many of the agents little better than names, and momentous transactions buried in deep obscurity, reconstruction is hazardous. But conjecture cannot be avoided, otherwise the history is not worth writing, for it does not become intelligible. And, the ultimate danger, the dominance of Tacitus himself, strong, subtle, and pervasive. Tacitus may here be found to benefit from a presentation too favourable, the *lungo studio* not impairing the *grande amore*.

The task has been long and laborious (for all that ostensible drudgery can be sheer delight). It has been hampered by various delays and vexations. Nor, in making the written text fit for publication and compiling the vast index, can aid or alleviation be recorded from any academic body, from any fund or foundation dedicated to the promotion of research in history and letters. It is therefore with alacrity and a deeper gratitude that I wish to thank Mrs. D. M. Davin, Mr. E. Birley, and Mr. G. E. F. Chilver for their help (in style, substance, and accuracy) at different stages between manuscript and final proof.

Tacitus insists on chance and hazard in the affairs of men, on the 'ludibria rerum mortalium cunctis in negotiis'. It is good fortune and a privilege if one can consort for so many years with an historian who knew the worst, discovered few reasons for ease or hope or confidence, and none the less believed in human dignity and freedom of speech.

R. S.

Oxford
26 *September* 1957

CONTENTS

PROLOGUE

THE Principate arose from usurpation. If one man seized the power, so might another. Birth or energy, chance or a horoscope would declare the ruler of the world. A hundred years after the victory at Actium the line of Caesar Augustus terminated in catastrophe. Nero's folly and a chain of accidents subverted the dynasty.

Nero feared the generals. By paradox the first move came from a provincial governor without a regular army. Julius Vindex raised rebellion among the tribes of Gaul but encountered disaster. The Roman legions on the Rhine were eager for battle against the native levies, and Verginius Rufus, commanding in Upper Germany, won a signal victory. Verginius saved the Empire for Nero, if Nero had sense or spirit. Although a large force was mustering for him in northern Italy (and there is no sign that Verginius had a mind for treason), Nero despaired too soon. Rumours threw him into confusion and panic. Intrigue did the rest. He could not hold the allegiance of the Praetorian Guard.

Gaul began the revolt against Nero, but Spain furnished his successor, an old man whom many had forgotten. Sulpicius Galba was induced by Vindex to join the movement and lend the credit of his name; and it turned out that Galba, whose cause seemed hopeless after the defeat of his ally, became emperor in the end, although not welcome everywhere. The legions of the Rhine had been slow to abandon Nero, and Verginius Rufus showed no great alacrity for Galba. Not that he would take the power himself. The soldiers solicited their victorious general, but he refused. Only Rome and the Senate, he said, were competent to confer the imperial authority. Verginius affirmed a principle and embellished his fame thereafter.

The reasons that kept Verginius loyal to Nero were still valid after Nero's death. Being the first of his family to enter the governing order, Verginius Rufus lacked prestige and alliances. The supreme power was beyond his reach.

Galba seemed the man. Galba had a pedigree of remote antiquity, and high favour with all the rulers since Caesar Augustus; his career brought military commands; and, evading various hazards, he earned a reputation for sagacity. Moreover, the destiny of Sulpicius Galba had been foretold by the stars. An expert in the science of astrology revealed it long ago, none other than Tiberius Caesar.

Thus, as was fated, the power came to Galba in his old age. Fear or senile ambition incited him to grasp what was offered, with a fair

pretext and claims that counted. Birth, office, and renown spoke for
Galba, creating a universal expectation. Galba could not fulfil it—
'omnium consensu capax imperii, nisi imperasset'.

Seven months from Nero's death were ample. Even dull Galba saw
his own predicament. He tried to avert calamity by nominating a
partner and heir whom he adopted as his son. His choice fell upon an
aristocrat, but eschewed the magnificent and superficial. Piso Licinianus was a young man of discreet and unblemished conduct,
signalized only by misfortune—both parents killed by the Caesars,
and two brothers; and he had lived long in exile. Piso knew nothing
of the imperial court, the ways of government, or the control of armies.
In that selection Sulpicius Galba looked to ancestry and the negative
virtues, advertising thereby his own incompetence. Galba was a fraud.
The wrong words had been used. Men praised him for prudence. It
was lethargy.

The adoption was no remedy, but an act of despair. It served only
to exasperate the Praetorian Guard and hasten the criminal designs
of Salvius Otho, whom Galba passed over. In any event, Piso or
another, it was too late. The armies of the Rhine already had an
emperor of their own. Anger impelled them, still indignant that Spain
with a single legion should take the profit of their victory and
produce a Caesar. On the first day of 69 the troops at Moguntiacum
refused allegiance, casting down the images of Galba. The revolt
spread at once from Upper to Lower Germany where Vitellius was
proclaimed, with 'Germanicus' for name and title.

Galba having been killed at Rome, the candidate of the Guard had
to face the onslaught of an invasion led by the generals of Vitellius.
Otho marched out to confront them in Northern Italy where he was
defeated not far from Cremona, but Vitellius was to have no long
tenancy of the power. A few months later the Danubian armies
intervened in favour of another pretender who had arisen in the East.
Intrigue had been active, and eager partisans. Swift columns crossed
the Julian Alps, the legions followed, and a second battle was fought
in the same vicinity.

In armed competition for the purple, the premium on ancestors
fell sharply. The family of Otho, municipal by origin, rose and
prospered through the patronage of the reigning house. Vitellius
belonged to the same class and type, but his father's success went
beyond all proportion—consul for the third time and chief minister
of Claudius Caesar. Otho was a courtier and a man of fashion. He
had never commanded an army before he became the Imperator, nor

had Vitellius until Galba, imprudently trusting him for that reason, sent him to be legate of Lower Germany. Vitellius had never seen a camp in his life before.

If Otho and Vitellius were eligible, the time had come for the military men to weigh their own chances. Nero's advisers made a good choice when they appointed Verginius Rufus; and they saw no harm in sending Licinius Mucianus to govern Syria, Flavius Vespasianus to crush the rebellion in Judaea. Each had known provinces and armies, but, like Verginius, they lacked the benefit of birth and renown. Neither could have risen against Nero. The surge of events now lifted them up. And since Mucianus, with various and blended capacities, ambitious yet satisfied with unobtrusive power, announced that he was ready to waive his claims in favour of one who had sons and could found a dynasty, a rival became an ally, inciting Vespasianus to accept the gift of Fortune.

A single year saw the three emperors after Nero perish in turn. Vespasian's rule, bringing order out of anarchy, gave promise of a second century of stable governance for Rome and the nations. Destiny decreed that it should not be achieved through his own line, or without hazard. The dynasty had a brief duration, ten years for Vespasian, two for Titus, and fifteen for Domitian.

Domitian's reign opened well, showing a domestic policy beyond reproach. The Emperor soon went to Gaul, marched to the Rhine and crushed the Chatti, the most formidable of all the western German tribes. The Danube, however, grew menacing. The trouble started with an incursion of the Dacians. Other peoples, Sarmatian and German, later came into conflict with Rome.

After disasters a victory was won in Dacia; but before that war ended Domitian was faced with armed treason and a pretender. Antonius Saturninus, the legate of Upper Germany, proclaimed himself emperor on the first day of January, 89. A civil war had begun. It was promptly arrested, Antonius being defeated by the commander of the other army on the Rhine.

That marked the turning point of the reign. Fear and distrust set Domitian upon a despotic course. The open clash with the Senate did not come until 93. It arose from a prosecution for high treason, and led to many deaths. The first to suffer were certain men of proud integrity (a group, and almost a party). Birth and ambition were also incriminated. The rest waited, silent and afraid—and the majority took thought only for personal safety and for advancement in the career of honours.

On September 18, A.D. 96, Domitian was assassinated in the Palace. The imperial chamberlain planned and supervised the deed. The Flavii had gone the way of the Julii and Claudii. With how close a resemblance in scene and characters was history again to be enacted— a peaceful transmission of the power or a rapid sequence of wars and proclamations?

PART I

THE POLITICAL SETTING

I. THE PRINCIPATE OF NERVA

A NEW emperor was found and produced, M. Cocceius Nerva. He was not the first choice, others had been approached, the time was short. Yet the conspirators and the court faction were not wholly at a loss. Their man had social distinction and no enemies.

The rank of the Cocceii did not go back to the Republic. It took its origin in the revolutionary period, one of the generals of Marcus Antonius being the ancestor. Now that four generations had elapsed since the Battle of Actium, the descendants of Triumviral or even of Augustan consuls were rare enough. As for the great Republican families, very few survived after Nero, himself the last of the Domitii, as well as the last Caesar in the Julian and Claudian line. With that house Nerva was connected by a slender link, not of blood but of mere propinquity. To name it is enough—a marriage contracted by a maternal uncle.[1]

In Rome of the Caesars it was perilous to have a dynastic connexion, a name known in history, or any conspicuous talent. Nerva practised that discretion which men called 'quies' if they approved, otherwise 'inertia' or 'segnitia'. Though his grandfather, a close friend of Tiberius Caesar, had been the leading jurist of the day, and his father carried on the tradition, Nerva found that the study of the law was not worth the effort and rewards. His name is absent from the roll of honour of Roman imperial jurisprudence, and the only edict preserved from the period of his rule is feeble and verbose.[2]

Nerva had never seen a province or an army. He was not a public speaker either. Instead, the arts and graces. Nerva wrote light verse and won the favour of Nero, who saluted him as the Tibullus of the age.[3] The courtier might have earned, from fidelity to his imperial patron, some other appellation. When a conspiracy was detected and

[1] For Nerva's family, App. 1.
[2] Cited in Pliny, *Epp.* x. 58. 7 ff. By contrast, the crisp rescript (ib. 10), in chancellery style.   [3] Martial viii. 70. 7, cf. ix. 26. 9 f.

defeated, the Emperor showered victory honours on friends, agents, and counsellors. Nerva, though not yet praetor, is in the forefront, his portion nothing less than the high military award of the *ornamenta triumphalia*, a statue on the Palatine, a statue in the Forum—the latter in triumphal garb.[1] Apart from Nerva, the only friend of Nero thus to be honoured with statues was the commander of the Praetorian Guard, Ofonius Tigellinus. What Nerva did to equal Tigellinus has not been disclosed.

The historian who so carefully registers that transaction can dispense with comment or epithet. It was enough to set on record the military emblems of a civilian and the bare name of Cocceius Nerva. No need to add that Nerva stood as a sublime example of that mocking paradox in all human life which was borne in ever the more upon a man when he meditated on things ancient and things modern. Rumour, conjecture, and public esteem would have designated anybody for the purple, anybody but the ruler whom Fortune was keeping in reserve behind the scenes.[2]

Nerva is not named among allies of Nero (the true or the false) in emergency at the end; and he leaves no trace in the events of the year 69. Caution and loyalty to the government, whatever the government might be, ensured the survival of Nerva, soon enhancing his station with honours more modest and conventional than the reward he had from Nero. Vespasian at once singled him out to inaugurate the years of peace as his consular colleague in 71; he shared the *fasces* with an emperor a second time, in 90; and he duly acquired several priesthoods.

A safe man and a quiet man, such were the talents and temper of the ruler who came after Domitian. There was a further advantage in Nerva. He was well on in years, being now sixty, and seeming more— and he had no children.[3]

A childless prince flattered certain prejudices which the Senate was able to parade from time to time. It was intolerable (they alleged) that Rome should be treated as the hereditary possession of a single family. The fairest of pretexts—and a miraculous temptation for plot and intrigue. It meant that the struggle for the succession to Cocceius Nerva could begin at once.

---

[1] Tacitus, *Ann.* xv. 72. 1. An inscription has the *ornamenta triumphalia*, but suppresses the other honours (*ILS* 273).

[2] *Ann.* iii. 18. 4: 'mihi quanto plura recentium seu veterum revolvo tanto magis ludibria rerum mortalium cunctis in negotiis obversantur. quippe fama spe veneratione potius omnes destinabantur imperio quam quem futurum principem fortuna in occulto tenebat.' He refers to Claudius, a forgotten nephew of Tiberius Caesar.

[3] Nerva's 'quies' was notable (Martial v. 28. 4; viii. 70. 1)—and advertised in his own edict, 'quietis meae' (*Epp.* x. 58. 7). For the date of his birth, App. 17.

When a despot is killed or a dynasty destroyed less is achieved than some expect. After the initial transports of newly won liberation men look around and discover that the system abides—and most of the people. So it was when Caesar the Dictator fell, and many times again in the history of imperial Rome. How did M. Cocceius Nerva stand with the friends of the dynasty and the holders of secret power?

That he had once been banished by Domitian is plain fiction, that his life was threatened by the tyrant, a fraudulent invention.[1] Nor was this a man whom any conspirators could approach with confidence (given his past performance) until the deed was done.[2] It is strange enough that he accepted. Nerva is more a figure at court than leader of a group or faction. He had few connexions. Despite pedigree, his relatives had forfeited rank and influence—and some perhaps were deleterious.[3] No tie of blood or marriage links Nerva with consular legates who govern the armed provinces.

If the new Princeps had no incentive to practise nepotism, there was some danger of gerontocracy. To publish a reaction and win approval, Nerva marked out for promotion certain senators whose merits, it might seem, had missed their due. The venerable Verginius Rufus survived, recalling the wars and tumults a generation past. In the eighty-third year of his life he is extracted from retirement and persuaded to take a third consulate as colleague of the Princeps in 97. Other veterans, though none quite so old as Verginius, now come back to the public scene. The amiable Arrius Antoninus becomes consul for the second time.[4] Julius Frontinus, governor of Britain twenty years before, is put in charge of the aqueducts of Rome.[5] Frontinus will soon have a second consulate, and so will Vestricius Spurinna, a healthy and athletic old gentleman.[6] Corellius Rufus, though an invalid, is chosen to serve on an agrarian commission, but prefers before long to terminate his bodily sufferings by starvation: what kept him going until now was a pertinacious resolve to survive Domitian, 'that brigand'.[7]

It was a politic device to advertise a contrast with the régime that had passed away, and Nerva turned for help to men of his own generation who had been consuls about twenty-five years previously. In

---

[1] The exile comes from a highly dubious source (Philostratus, *Vita Apollonii* VII. 8; 11). Martial shows him happy and unharmed in 93 (VIII. 70), likewise in 94 or 95 (IX. 26).

[2] The facts about a conspiracy are not always either published or ascertainable. Suetonius (who does not name Nerva) opens his account with the words 'de insidiarum caedisque genere haec fere divulgata sunt' (*Dom.* 17. 1). Dio, reporting that the commanders of the Guard and the Empress Domitia Longina knew about the plot, adds ὥς γε καὶ λέγονται (LXVII. 15. 2). Further, after sounding other persons, the conspirators approached Nerva, who consented, his life being in danger (ib. 5).

[3] App. 1.   [4] App. 10.   [5] Frontinus, *De aquis* 1. 1.
[6] For the consuls of 98, App. 11.   [7] Pliny, *Epp.* 1. 12. 8.

some he discovered tastes or a temperament like his own. Not that his physical frailty could share the robust pursuits of old Spurinna, who was addicted to country walks and ball games. Yet Spurinna was light and gay. He threw off poems both Latin and Greek, and his blameless character gave an added piquancy to the charm of convivial or erotic verse.[1]

Other personages were extant, of high repute and distinction, and one of them held the post of Prefect of the City.[2] Yet it would be hazardous to go further in quest of Nerva's following, nor is it certain that the five named consulars had been firmly associated with Nerva before now. The five have one thing in common—a lack of conspicuous favour from Domitian. Nerva, however, had his second consulate as the gift of that emperor.

Not all of the men who served the government steadily were lucky enough to keep their reputations unscathed. To be a minister of the Caesars entailed much agility and many risks. A man had to know the whims of the autocrat and guide him by compliance, to put him on guard against enemies, and also to dissuade him from outbursts of anger, sudden ideas of genius, and similar imprudences: in short, instruct, amuse, and fortify the master of the world. Palace politics might invite Caesar's friend to allay discord in the dynasty, mediate between an emperor and his consort, or exert a good influence upon the officials of the household; and he had a clear duty to hold the balance between competing groups and manipulate the traffic in honours without scandal or too much greed. Most could be done under cover, yet eloquence was requisite to expound Caesar's will softly to the high assembly and elicit the assent of senators by a show of deference—and sometimes it was necessary to quell criticism or unmask a hidden malcontent.

The art of oratory had brought wealth and fame to various bad men. Noted for eager ambition and a zealous devotion to the ruler's interests, they were feared and hated. Some, like Eprius Marcellus, were fierce and angry, but Vibius Crispus was bland, graceful, and humorous.[3] Eprius came to grief, but Vibius went on serenely and climbed to the pinnacle of a third consulate under Domitian. Vibius Crispus had recently passed away. The most astute of them all lived on—Fabricius Veiento, worthy to stand in a notable succession and be honoured,

[1] III. 1. 7. For a poet related to Spurinna and close friend of Arrius Antoninus, IV. 27. 5; for the poems of Arrius himself, IV. 3. 3 f.; 18. 1. Verginius Rufus had also written light verse (V. 3. 5).

[2] For the *praefecti urbi*, App. 13. A new ruler sometimes meant a new *praefectus*. T. Aurelius Fulvus (*suff.* ?70, *II ord.* 85) might have occupied the post in 97—if still alive (see App. 87). For the presumed second consulates in 98 of Cn. Domitius Tullus (*suff.* c. 79) and L. Julius Ursus (?84) see App. 7 and 11.

[3] p. 101.

such was his unswerving loyalty, by a statue in the Roman Forum with some suitable inscription.[1]

The irony of fate or the malice of an historian introduces Veiento in Nero's reign, gently and discreditably. He was sent into exile on a double charge—libellous writings and the sale of patronage.[2] Returning after Nero's death (or perhaps before it), Veiento so endeared himself to the Flavian dynasty that he secured the consulate from Vespasian, a second from Titus (close on the catastrophe of Eprius Marcellus), and a third from Domitian, very promptly.[3] Veiento's pasquinades made fun of senators and priests. Rising himself as high as a subject could, to a third consulate, this grand old man is decked with all the appanages of worldly success, including priesthoods to the total of four.[4] Veiento began as a dealer in petty patronage, and he ended as a merchant of honours.

Secret politics are inherent in the Principate from the beginning. The rule of the Caesars, by abolishing open debate on matters of high policy, announces the era of cabinet government. It is therefore the more remarkable that Statius, a writer who is not often given the credit for courage or originality, should have boldly versified a council of state in the days of Domitian. The poem gave him a chance to glorify the Emperor and also to bring on show the leading personages in state and society, whether senatorial or equestrian by rank. Prominent and paired together stand Fabricius Veiento and Vibius Crispus.[5]

A satirist saw the rich promise of the theme. He wrote a parody.[6] The scene is Domitian's villa at Alba Longa, where the high dignitaries muster on urgent summons, pale and afraid. It is only mockery. They are convoked to discuss what shall be done with a large fish that has been presented to the Emperor. The Prefect of the City makes his entry with Vibius Crispus close behind. Six other persons follow, among them a detestable informer, his soft voice a sentence of death. The commander of the Guard marches in; and the procession is closed by the sagacious Veiento along with a hateful man, Catullus Messallinus.

What no satire can distort, an anecdote confirms.[7] Veiento is discovered at a small dinner-party given by Nerva, reclining next to the

---

[1] Like the honouring of L. Vitellius (cos. III, 47)—'pietatis immobilis erga principem' (Suetonius, Vit. 3. 1).

[2] Ann. XIV. 50.   [3] App. 5.   [4] ILS 1010 (Moguntiacum)

[5] In the sole fragment surviving from Statius, De bello Germanico (preserved in Valla's Scholia on Juvenal IV. 94): 'lumina, Nestorei mitis prudentia Crispi | et Fabius Veiento (potentem signat utrumque | purpura), ter memores implerunt nomine fastos | et prope Caesareae confinis Acilius aulae.' The dramatic date is 83, before Domitian's expedition against the Chatti. The person named in the lost preceding line—'lumina' refers to him—must be Catullus Messallinus, who was blind (Juvenal IV. 113 f.).

[6] Juvenal IV. 37 ff. The same dramatic date can be assumed.

[7] Epp. IV. 22. 4 ff.

Emperor, and almost in his arms. The guests fell to talking about Catullus Messallinus, and much was said about his wickedness, when Nerva asked: 'what do we suppose would have happened to him if he were alive?' One of the company, Junius Mauricus, was ready with a reply—'he would be dining with us'. The story, as ingenuously reported, is meant to exemplify the courage of Mauricus, whereas the truth may be, not that Mauricus was brave and Nerva innocent, but that the Emperor, more subtle than some of the company, quietly laid a trap, elicited the answer he wanted, and extinguished a conversational topic that had often been heard before.

That a minister of despotism should survive undamaged in fame and influence might be a scandal. It could not come as a surprise to any who cast a passing glance upon the process of civil government. The five elderly consulars now in public view were commended by known integrity and sound repute, but they had been remote for many years from the conduct of affairs. If the administration was to go on, it needed counsellors who had been in the confidence of the last ruler, possessing secrets of State not yet divulged to all the world: in short, characters like Fabricius Veiento. That old man took pride and delight in his own sagacity, a new Nestor or a Fabius.[1] There is no sign that he was a powerful speaker.

In Veiento the Emperor found a congenial friend, uniting social elegance and literary gifts, a relic of the old Neronian time. More than that, a wise counsellor. Gliding onwards in the service of the Roman government and bequeathed from Domitian to Nerva, the smooth Veiento exhibited in his own person the normal continuity of high policy—and, if a change seemed imminent once again, he was no doubt vigilant to safeguard his passage from Nerva to Nerva's successor.

M. Cocceius Nerva himself could benefit from a long and devious experience in the ways of the Palace. Like Fabricius Veiento, he had survived, and survived without open disrepute; like Vibius Crispus, he had been content to go with the stream, and he was not disposed to sacrifice his life in the cause of truth.[2] Nothing debars recognition of his talents as a diplomat, soft and subtle. Capable of guiding policy by art and influence, Nerva was not equal to the task of piloting a government in a stormy season.[3]

---

[1] Veiento quotes *Iliad* VIII. 102 in the Senate (*Epp.* IX. 13. 20); and Statius (cited above, p. 5) calls him 'Fabius'.

[2] Juvenal IV. 89 ff.: 'ille igitur nunquam derexit bracchia contra | torrentem, nec civis erat qui libera posset | verba animi proferre et vitam impendere vero. | sic multas hiemes atque octogensima vidit | solstitia, his armis illa quoque tutus in aula.' Juvenal omitted Nerva from the company . . ..

[3] Compare the description of a later ruler in the *Historia Augusta*: 'blandus magis quam benignus nec umquam creditus simplex' (*Pertinax* 12. 1). For the iconography of Nerva see H. Götze, *Mitt. des d. arch. Inst.* I (1948), 139 ff.

Liberty had been restored and Rome was born anew. 'Libertas publica' and 'Roma renascens' duly appear on the currency.[1] Until now, 'libertas' and 'principatus' were incompatible. The new ruler reconciled them, it is averred, and an era of felicity was now to begin.[2] In truth, if the label seemed promising, the mixture was dangerous and likely to cause convulsions. Thoughtful men, who knew the phraseology, watched and waited, devising their plans for the event of trouble. It had also been published abroad that the armies were of one mind in allegiance to the government—'concordia exercituum'.[3] That assertion was not merely premature but sinister and suggestive. The armies had not spoken yet. It was everybody's secret that an emperor did not have to be made at Rome.[4]

The first days of the new reign were happy and tumultuous—joy, honour, and revenge. Senators exulted as they watched the statues of Domitian or the proud arches crash. Summary justice overtook slaves or freedmen who had denounced their masters, governmental spies were hunted down and killed, private enmities found scope or cover— and soon the exiles would be back.

Of the agents of despotism, only minor officials perished or men of low degree. The more important were saved by wealth and influence, by protection alertly contrived against any change of fortune. The Senate thus incurred no small unpopularity with other orders. One of the consuls, in alarm, made protest. Anarchy, he said, is worse than tyranny.[5]

Along with 'libertas' the coinage advertised the 'iustitia' and the 'aequitas' of the Princeps.[6] By temperament as by policy, Nerva was mild and easy, ill-fitted to grapple with empire. Well might his friend Arrius Antoninus commiserate.[7] Moderation became weakness when the government got into difficulties. After some months, in spring or early summer of 97, money began to run out. To make economies, the Senate set up a commission of consulars, among them Julius Frontinus and Vestricius Spurinna.[8]

[1] *BMC, R. Emp.* III (1936), 3 ff.; 15 ff. It is no surprise if types and legends emerge that had been used after the fall of Nero, cf. A. Merlin, *Les Revers monétaires de l'empereur Nerva* (1906), 14 ff. Thus LIBERTAS, LIBERTAS PVBLICA, SALVS PVBLICA, FORTVNA P.R. By paradox it is not Nerva's coins but Galba's that, with FELICITAS PVBLICA and SECVRITAS P.R., are closest to the 'felicitas temporum' and 'securitas publica' of *Agr.* 3. 1. Nerva's edict has 'ipsa felicitas temporum' and 'securitas omnium' (*Epp.* x. 58. 7).

[2] Tacitus, *Agr.* 3. 1: 'nunc demum redit animus; sed quamquam primo statim beatissimi saeculi ortu Nerva Caesar res olim dissociabilis miscuerit, principatum ac libertatem', &c.   [3] *BMC, R. Emp.* III, 1 ff. Also familiar from 68 and 69.

[4] *Hist.* I. 4. 2: 'evulgato imperii arcano posse principem alibi quam Romae fieri.'

[5] Dio LXVIII. 1. 3 (Ti. Catius Fronto, an orator of some quality, cf. App. 27).

[6] *BMC, R. Emp.* III, 1 f.   [7] Victor, *Epit.* 12. 3.

[8] Pliny, *Pan.* 62. 2, cf. 61. 6; *Epp.* II. 1. 9. Verginius Rufus was nominated but declined. On this, and kindred problems, App. 2.

Allegations that funds were scarce did not always earn credence at Rome. This time the shortage may have been genuine. At the outset the new administration had to pay, as custom prescribed, large sums to the plebs and to the troops. When it further went in for a lavish policy of public expenditure in Rome, Italy, and the provinces, designed to outbid the popularity of the Flavian House, the treasury, kept full by the careful management of Domitian, felt the strain. That stern inquisitor being removed, seductive prospects beckoned for embezzlement at home and abroad: the governors gaily exploited their new-found license.[1] And, if a civil war seemed likely to break out, it was a temptation to impound the revenues of their provinces.

In the meantime senators and groups of senators spun their webs of intrigue for office and influence. Governors came home from the provinces, others went out—and some of the consular appointments to army commands would excite comment or predictions. If a change of ruler put a stop to some ambitions, it accelerated many more. The first list of consuls tended to be a long one. Domitian's designations for 97 would be supplemented.[2] The next year might likewise be generous—yet, if the government filled several places with second consulates for elderly supporters, competition would be all the keener.

When a senator seemed vulnerable, something could be done to aggravate his discredit or block him from promotion. There were hazards in the game—and senior statesmen would be on the alert with arguments of good counsel, deprecating rancour or precipitance. The threat of a regular indictment against a man called Publicius Certus evoked a lively debate, Veiento intervening to dissuade. There was also private intercession. One of the consulars uttered his quiet warning: the action was provocative and liable to be unfavourably registered by some future emperor. Another was more precise. He pointed to the power and influence of Publicius, to the friends and allies he could command, and he named the governor of Syria, whose army was strong in numbers and prestige, whose attitude gave rise to the most alarming rumours.[3]

Speculation about a substitute for a weak ruler (and in weak health) had been going on for some time, with jobbery and ambition more in

---

[1] Suetonius, *Dom.* 8. 2: 'magistratibus quoque urbicis provinciarumque praesidibus coercendis tantum curae adhibuit, ut neque modestiores umquam neque iustiores extiterint; e quibus plerosque post illum omnium criminum reos vidimus.' Observe the proconsuls of Africa and of Baetica (pp. 70, 78).

[2] p. 70 and App. 10.

[3] *Epp.* IX. 13. 11: 'nominat quendam qui tunc ad orientem amplissimum et famosissimum exercitum non sine magnis dubiisque rumoribus obtinebat.' The incident probably belongs to the spring of the year 97 but cannot be precisely dated. Nor can the legate be identified. See further App. 3.

evidence than sound judgement or care for the public weal. There was talk of conspiracy. Calpurnius Crassus, a noble whose illustrious lineage carried names of ancient power, was denounced along with his adherents.[1] Nerva could not ignore it. He invited their presence and handed them swords to inspect, demonstrating that he did not care what happened to him. The Princeps might have added admonishment, and a melancholy truth: pedigree no longer counted.

Nerva asserted that as Princeps he had done nothing to prevent him from resigning the power and then safely receding into private life.[2] He was not granted the leisure for a free choice. It required no astrologer to predict that the emperor following Nerva would be a military man. The only question was: after a civil war, or averting a civil war?

As it happened, the storm did not break before the autumn. Despite ambiguous reports, the legate of Syria made no move, and the great armies in the provinces of the northern frontier showed no overt menace. The disturbance originated in the city of Rome.

[1] Dio LXVIII. 3. 2; Victor, *Epit.* 12. 6. To be identified as C. Calpurnius Crassus Frugi Licinianus (*PIR*[2], C 259), consul suffect in 87, presumably a nephew of the Piso Licinianus whom Galba adopted: see the stemma in *PIR*[2], vol. II, facing p. 54. These Pisones descend from the Licinii Crassi—also from Pompeius Magnus (through the Scribonii). See further p. 385.

[2] Dio LXVIII. 3. 1. For conflicting assessments of Nerva and of Nerva's rule, App. 2.

II. THE PROCLAMATION OF TRAJAN

THE Guard rose. Surging round the Palace in angry tumult, the soldiers called for vengeance on the assassins of Domitian. Nerva complied. The commander of the Guard, Casperius Aelianus, had become the accomplice of the rioters and their leader in violence. Casperius forced the Princeps to render solemn and public thanks to the soldiery.

In the annals of the Empire a constant indictment stands against the Praetorians for turbulence and rapacity. It was not always deserved. The sudden removal of Domitian surprised the Guard, with nobody to lead them when they clamoured to have their dead Imperator deified.[1] Both prefects then in office, Petronius Secundus and Norbanus, had been privy to the plot, it is said.[2] If they were not, they were quickly won over, the troops were pacified, and they kept quiet for more than a year. Norbanus slips out of historical record, and now, in October of 97, a new commander, Casperius Aelianus, exploits the trouble (if he does not instigate it), and destroys Petronius Secundus along with the assassins. Casperius had held the prefecture once before, under Domitian, late in the reign.[3] Nothing is known for certain of his origin, family, or friends.[4]

Past history with the names of Aelius Seianus and Nymphidius Sabinus showed what a commander of the Guard might hope to achieve by craft or violence. Seianus' way was stealthy—not to overthrow Tiberius Caesar but to gain control over the Princeps and the government. Nymphidius, however, having deserted Nero and supplanted Tigellinus, found himself in a position of vantage, the new emperor being far away in Spain and the allegiance of many armies still dubious. He attempted a proclamation, not without the help of senatorial allies.

Past history also showed that the provincial armies would not easily put up with a metropolitan pretender. Since Domitian's death competition for the military commands sharpened the rivalry of factions in the Senate—and vexed the government with distasteful alternatives. An elderly man should be safe with an army (and such had often been

---

[1] Suetonius, *Dom.* 23. 1.

[2] Dio LXVII. 15. 2. Observe, but not quite proving it, what Eutropius says about Petronius' role in the elevation of Nerva (VIII. 1. 1).

[3] Dio LXVIII. 3. 3, cf. LXVII. 14. 4 (two Prefects put on trial by Domitian in 95); Philostratus, *Vita Apollonii* VII. 16 ff.

[4] For a conjecture, p. 35.

favoured by suspicious emperors), but it was not certain that he would be able to curb his troops or his lieutenants, while the vigour of a youthful commander might go with dangerous aspirations.

When the Praetorians became masters of Rome, catastrophe threatened to bring the State down in ruin on the head of its hapless ruler. Nerva had forfeited all authority. There was still time to save the sum of things, if Nerva agreed, and one remedy. What passed in the secret conclave of the imperial council, and whose were the arguments that prevailed, no record survives to reveal, not even a hint; and if for once the Prefect of the Guard was perhaps absent, there were other dignitaries and other advisers. They enforced a rapid decision.[1]

The Princeps could not escape from Rome and take refuge with the legions: they did not know him. But he could forestall rebellion by an appeal or surrender to the generals. The welcome tidings of a minor victory on the Danube, won by the army of Pannonia, were opportunely published, and Nerva, mounting the Capitol, stood before the altar of Juppiter Optimus Maximus, there to announce that he took a partner in the power, adopting as his son one of the generals.[2] Not, however, the legate of Pannonia. He selected M. Ulpius Traianus, the commander of the army of Upper.Germany.[3] Other formalities followed in due course, and promptly. The storm clouds rolled away, and all disturbance subsided at once.

Nerva's discretion in the evil days was noted and praised. Empire found him out. Yet Nerva redeemed himself, whether it was fear or sagacity, wise counsellors, or a strong and crushing pressure. Nerva had relatives to choose from, and descendants could be discovered of the Republican nobility. Not many, it is true: none in the high commands, and none to touch the alleged plotter, whose line went back, not merely to the Calpurnii Pisones, but to the dynasts Pompeius and Crassus. More numerous were the candidates from families that came up and captured the consulate in the revolutionary age or under the rule of Caesar Augustus. Nerva passed them over. Whatever his own predilections, he was compelled to take Trajan and assign to a man's 'virtus' the precedence over his 'patria'.[4]

Nerva was fortunate in his choice. Two emperors to share the

---

[1] The best (and almost the only) account of this transaction comes from Pliny's consular 'actio gratiarum' of September 100 (the *Panegyricus*). Pliny attributes Nerva's action to divine inspiration.

[2] Pliny, *Pan.* 8. 2: 'adlata erat ex Pannonia laurea; id agentibus dis ut invicti imperatoris exordium victoriae insigne decoraret', &c. *ILS* 2720 shows a tribune of I Adiutrix decorated by Nerva 'bello Suebic(o)'. Hence the *cognomen* 'Germanicus' for Nerva and for his adopted son.

[3] That Trajan's command was Upper Germany is deduced from *HA, Hadr.* 2. 5 f.

[4] Dio LXVIII. 4. 2: τὴν γὰρ ἀρετὴν ἀλλ' οὐ τὴν πατρίδα τινὸς ἐξετάζειν δεῖν ᾤετο.

supreme authority, that was not altogether an idle fancy. The thing could happen, it might be a useful device if the functions were divided, with a civilian ruler at Rome to manage the Senate and superintend policy while a military man stood warden of the armed provinces. Not but what such an arrangement was hazardous unless it emerged without effort, unless it drew strength from the ties of habit and family, from concord and from forbearance. Zealous adherents and the strife of factions were likely to prove fatal. Any long survival of Nerva might only consign him to a permanent retreat on some island. Death supervened, prompt and merciful, only three months later.[1]

There was one mitigation of despotism at Rome for the senator, the historian, or the satirist. Though constrained to praise the reigning emperor, or be silent, he might often make free with his predecessor—even if that predecessor had been enrolled among the gods of the Roman State. While Trajan took Nerva's name into his titulature and made due provision for the consecration, there is no sign that he felt any special esteem or gratitude. The new emperor (it is affirmed) first wept for Nerva, as was fitting in a son, and then glorified him with a temple.[2] If the tears are a convention, the temple should be a fact, although the edifice has escaped all record. There is no coin to advertise the adoption, and none with the legend 'Divus Nerva' until a decade has elapsed.[3]

Nerva did not leave a happy memory behind him. A panegyrist, to magnify Trajan, does not disguise the gravity of the crisis. Trajan (so he avers) came to empire not in peace but in time of peril; he took over the power from one who was sorry he had ever accepted it. The State was collapsing. The adoption was tantamount to an abdication: to share the power is to surrender it.[4]

The end of the Flavian dynasty and the accession of Nerva seem to inaugurate a new era, duly to be acclaimed and celebrated. On a longer perspective of history, Nerva and 'Libertas' is but an episode. The strong and enduring tendencies resume their course. Although the proprieties are saved and respected, there is a breach in continuity between the 'principatus' of Nerva and the 'imperium' of Trajan. 'Libertas' recedes, the labels are discarded, and new men surge forward.[5]

---

[1] Victor, *Epit.* 12. 9. Trajan's 'dies imperii' is January 28; cf. now the evidence of the *Feriale Duranum*, col. i, l. 15 (*Yale Classical Studies* VII (1940), 41, cf. 77 ff.).

[2] *Pan.* 11. 1. A dedication of the year 99 celebrates Trajan's 'pietas' (*ILS* 283).

[3] *BMC, R. Emp.* III (1936), 144; and then subsequently, along with 'Divus pater Traianus' in 113 (ib. 100).

[4] *Pan.* 7. 3: 'suscepisti imperium postquam alium suscepti paenitebat'; 6. 3: 'ruens imperium super imperatorem'; 8. 4: 'nam quantum refert, deponas an partiaris imperium?'

[5] Early Trajanic coin-legends are instructive, contradicting the literary evidence, cf. P. L. Strack, *Untersuchungen zur r. Reichsprägung des zweiten Jahrhunderts* I (1931), 43 f.; H. Mattingly, *BMC. R. Emp.* III (1936), lxix.

Thus culminated the struggle for rewards and prizes, offices and commands, in the thirteen months that came after the assassination of Domitian, blending with a contest for the succession to the imperial power. Although the details of time, person, and place cannot be established and connected, the nature of the crisis and the agencies that determined its issue do not lie wholly beyond conjecture. In butchering the assassins of Domitian, Casperius and the Praetorians exacted a crude vengeance. The profit went to others. It seems accident, there may be plan and design somewhere in the transaction. The military oligarchy, aided by certain men in the background, were firm and subtle. They rescued the State from a brief interlude of 'Libertas', set it back again on a proper path of government, deposed an incompetent ruler (for such in effect was their action), and installed one of their own class as Imperator.[1]

There was a question that could not fail to be asked. It was indiscreet and subversive. Would posterity ever believe that a general who commanded a large, powerful, and devoted army was not made emperor by that army, that Rome not Germany conferred the *cognomen* of 'Germanicus'?[2]

The legions of the Rhine were heavy with prestige, carrying the memory of earlier wars and earlier proclamations. Rome lay in their power, their victories enlarged the Empire, and from them emperors derived their titles.[3] When recent history came alive again, men turned their hopes and fears towards the Rhine and the quick road over the Alps into northern Italy. It was not long ago—rebellion in Gaul and a great battle, the fall of Nero, proud and angry troops in mutiny with the civil war for sequel, the clash of armies in Italy, and the capture of Rome. And in 89 Germany again, and no less ominous, despite the failure of the legate who rose against Domitian.

Domitian had been careful to visit his troops—he took the field four times—and he reinforced their allegiance by increasing their pay. If the news of his murder provoked disturbances in some of the provincial armies, no serious trouble ensued.[4] Yet it could not be taken for granted that they would continue to acquiesce without protest in an unmilitary ruler created by a palace conspiracy, the choice of Parthenius the chamberlain. One of the generals might make a bid, noting the temper of the troops, impelled by eager lieutenants on his staff or encouraged by messages from friends at Rome. And chance could intervene with some trivial incident or a local mutiny.

---

[1] See further p. 35.   [2] *Pan.* 9. 2.
[3] *Ann.* I. 31. 5: 'sua in manu sitam rem Romanam, suis victoriis augeri rem publicam, in suum cognomentum adscisci imperatores.'
[4] An incipient mutiny at a camp on the Danube was quelled, we are told, by a sermon from Dio of Prusa (Philostratus, *Vit. Soph.* I. 7. 2). Nothing else is reported or alleged.

Trajan stood at Moguntiacum, the chief place of arms in the upper
German province, waiting perhaps while the Roman government grew
weaker, or ready to march if no summons came. Trajan was not proclaimed by the soldiers.[1] Nevertheless, the German command goes far
to explain his elevation. The friends and allies who extorted that
appointment from Nerva were not devoid of foresight.

When the purple is the prize, none but a consular can compete. Ten
legates of that rank hold the principal imperial commands. The
Roman army now comprised twenty-eight legions.[2] All except four
belong to the provinces of the ten consulars.[3]

The garrison in Spain, once among the strongest, had fallen long
since to a single legion; and the wars of Domitian against the peoples
beyond the Danube drew legions from Britain, the Rhine, and Dalmatia.[4] By the last years of his reign, Britain and the two Germanies
had each dropped from four legions to three: in Britain conquest was
carried far to the north, and intervention beyond the Rhine, now
gradual, now vigorous, won a safe and economical frontier in southern
Germany. By contrast, the reinforcement of the Danube: Pannonia,
augumented to four legions, now becomes the strongest single command, and the two provinces of Moesia lower down the river account
for five more.[5]

In the western lands, Spain, Britain, and the Rhine add up to ten
legions, balanced by nine on the Danube in the central frontier zone
of an empire that extends from the northern ocean to the river
Euphrates. In the East, facing Armenia and Mesopotamia, are two
consular commands, with two legions in Cappadocia and three in
Syria.

Legions offer a ready computation. Much of the fighting in the
Roman wars was done by auxiliary troops. By total of regiments as
by man-power for recruiting, the western lands enjoy a heavy predominance. The Rhine armies cannot be properly estimated without
the resources of their hinterland, the three Gallic provinces; while the
Danube can draw upon many fierce and populous tribes, Pannonian,
Dalmatian, and Thracian.

Though the balance of military power in the frontier zones had
recently been moving from the Rhine to the Danube, men had not

---

[1] Yet it might have come close to that, see App. 4.

[2] For details, E. Ritterling, P–W XII, 1569; 1789 f.; R. Syme, *JRS* XVIII (1928), 41 ff.

[3] The exceptions: Numidia (one legion), Judaea (one), Egypt (two).

[4] Evidence or probability indicates that II Adiutrix had gone from Britain; I Adiutrix,
XXI Rapax, and XIV Gemina in succession from the Rhine (XXI Rapax to perish in 92).
The Rhine had been reinforced by a new formation, I Minervia, early in Domitian's reign;
Dalmatia, now left without a legion, remained consular (App. 15).

[5] cf. R. Syme, o.c. 47; 50; *CAH* XI (1936), 186 f.

become used to that novel fact. Nor were the legions in Pannonia and Moesia yet ready to exploit their strength. Dispersed at wide intervals, they lacked a common tradition and the means for sudden and concerted action; and their performance in the field was variegated by disasters or by imperfect victories. The prestige of the German commands was intact and formidable: Moguntiacum and Colonia Claudia were not ready to surrender primacy of imperial esteem to the names as yet unhonoured of Carnuntum, Viminacium, or Singidunum.

The armies nearest to Moguntiacum were those of Lower Germany, Britain, and Pannonia.[1] The legions in Britain, schooled by active warfare, had a good reputation for discipline; and Britain, as previously, might be expected to wait upon events or follow the lead of the Rhine legions. Everything turned on Lower Germany. In October of 97 the legate (it appears) was either a firm ally of Trajan or ready to submit and follow.[2] Once in concert the two armies could act quickly and make their force felt. If it came to civil war, the first move was to invade northern Italy, forestalling or repelling the vanguard of the Danubian legions.

The great Pannonian command, lying athwart the routes that led from Italy and the western provinces to the armies in Moesia and to Byzantium, was strongly placed for attack or defence. The easy pass across the Julian Alps permitted an invasion of Italy even more rapid than from the Rhine—and, otherwise, the legate of Pannonia could either hold the mountain barrier or fall back upon the Moesian armies. The Danubian legions might be able to decide the contest in favour of a pretender in the East if they had no candidate of their own. It had happened once, and could be feared again. In this crisis Pannonia may have been in friendly hands; and nothing is known of any menace from distant Moesia.[3] Moreover, the adoption of Trajan, coming as it did late in the year, may have precluded troop movements in certain areas, with a respite for negotiation—if what was expedient had not already been done.

The adoption abated all disturbance, and, so far as known, repressed all rivalry. To some men's hopes the legate of Syria with three legions seemed likely to put up a claim.[4] Although the prestige of the command was high and historic, the troops were not well thought of, living at ease and seldom molested by war or discipline. Even if Cappadocia, Egypt, and Judaea could be won, with five more legions thus accruing,

---

[1] For the consular legates in 96–98 see Ch. V and App. 14.

[2] Identity unknown. Probably not Vestricius Spurinna (*Epp.* II. 7. 1 f.), cf. App. 6.

[3] Cn. Pompeius Longinus (*suff.* 90) is attested in Pannonia by a diploma bearing the date February 20, 98 (*CIL* XVI, 42): predecessor not known. Previously (in 93) legate of Moesia Superior (*CIL* XVI, 39). For Moesia, p. 51.

[4] *Epp.* IX. 13. 11.

the combined forces in the East could never compete with the mass and power of the northern frontier armies, six legions along the Rhine and nine in the Danubian provinces. Judaea was governed by a senator of praetorian rank, with one legion: the consular legate of Cappadocia was a friend of Trajan.[1]

Egypt was a factor out of all proportion to its military strength (two legions). If war threatened in the Roman world, the Prefect of Egypt could starve the capital.[2] As it happened, all went well in the eastern lands. Whatever the rumours about Syria, the mysterious consular departed from his province or was removed; and some of his legionary legates may have been compromised.[3] The record is brief and fragmentary, and not of a kind to disclose awkward facts. No written source even hints that any provincial governor was disgraced or executed when Trajan acquired the power. None the less, something happened. It is certain that there was now no consular legate in Syria. The climate, or decrepitude in the governors—elderly men being often chosen—entailed a high mortality rate. If the governor died or went away, one of the legionary commanders in the province took charge, normally of praetorian rank. This time there was a novelty. A young man called Larcius Priscus, who had been quaestor of Asia, arrived in Syria. Larcius bore the title of legate of the legion IV Scythica and deputy governor.[4] The exceptional measure denotes a state of emergency. Before long the next consular took up the command, perhaps an old man, and certainly a safe man.[3]

Trajan made no haste to show himself to Senate and People, the ostensible and legal sources of the imperial authority. The Roman People would be eager to have a glimpse of their soldier emperor.[5] That could wait. In the Senate rancour, envy, and disappointment were subdued by gratitude for peace and order, or at least overwhelmed by loud and effusive protestations. To convey the proper sentiments to the new Caesar a deputation must have gone forth with all speed. Acrimony was no doubt confined to the debate: which senators should go as delegates of the high assembly—and which be excluded because of services to Domitian.[6] To lead the mission, virtue and public renown would designate men like Frontinus or Spurinna —were it not for the veteran schemer Fabricius Veiento.[7] Yet, if

---

[1] T. Pomponius Bassus (suff. 94), cf. p. 51.

[2] M. Junius Rufus, attested by papyri from February 2, 94 to June 21, 98, cf. A. Stein, Die Präfekten von Ägypten (1950), 47 f.   [3] App. 3.

[4] ILS 1055; AE 1908, 237 (Thamugadi).   [5] Martial x. 6.

[6] Compare a scene at the end of 69 (Hist. IV. 6 f.).

[7] Veiento and his wife Attica set up a dedication at Moguntiacum (ILS 1010). Perhaps, however, there in 83, with Domitian—or even in 89. Spurinna's absence with the embassy in 97 could perhaps be deduced from Epp. II. 7. 3, cf. App. 6.

Veiento's influence availed so far, it was now close to the end.[1] Prominence among the senior statesmen passed quickly to Julius Frontinus, not perhaps without reason. In the transactions of 97 Veiento may have been defeated by the resolution of Frontinus, or outwitted by Spurinna (there could be guile beneath that surface of honest simplicity). Trajan owed these men a debt for their vigilance, if for nothing else, and he paid it with the highest of public honours.[2]

The Prefect of the Guard was not among the happy envoys who journeyed to the north. Trajan summoned him later, and he went, perhaps expecting thanks or condonation. He was put to death.[3] Trajan stayed with the legions, the true basis of his power, and confirmed or installed his adherents in their commands. The Caesar himself opened the year 98, consul as colleague of Nerva, and a brilliant sequence of *consules suffecti* served to advertise public harmony and the new turn of affairs. The news of Nerva's decease found Trajan on the lower Rhine at the principal city of the region, Colonia Claudia.[4] To take his place in the upper German command he had summoned his friend, the faithful Julius Servianus.[5]

If some looked for war and conquest in Germany, they looked in vain. There was no need or excuse for a campaign. Trajan sojourned for a time beside the Rhine, and then passed on to Pannonia, accompanied by a number of senators, to inspect the armies along the Danube frontier.[6] The Rhine commands were left in good custody;[7] and Julius Servianus, after the briefest of tenures in Upper Germany, assumed the Pannonian command—there is no evidence, however, that his predecessor in Pannonia had been disloyal or unsatisfactory.[8] Nor would Pannonia long detain the new emperor, even though the troops had conducted operations beyond the river in the previous year.[9] Trajan proceeded to Moesia. There he wintered at one of the

---

[1] Veiento was probably dead by September 100 (cf. *Pan.* 58. 1).

[2] cf. Pliny on their third consulates in 100, *Pan.* 60. 5 f.: 'bellorum istud sociis olim, periculorum consortibus, parce tamen, tribuebatur, quod tu singularibus viris ac de te quidem bene ac fortiter, sed in toga meritis praestitisti. utriusque cura, utriusque vigilantia obstrictus es.'

[3] Dio LXVIII. 5. 4.   [4] Eutropius VIII. 2. 1, cf. *HA, Hadr.* 2. 6.

[5] *Epp.* VIII. 23. 5, cf. *HA, Hadr.* 2. 5 f. For this man see App. 7.

[6] A fragmentary inscription records an eminent senator who accompanied the Emperor '[dum] exercitus suos circumit' (*ILS* 1019).

[7] The tenure of L. Licinius Sura (*suff.* ?97) in Lower Germany (*AE* 1923, 33) could have run from 98 to 100/1.

[8] Servianus (*Epp.* VIII. 23. 5) followed Cn. Pompeius Longinus (*CIL* XVI, 42), soon himself to be replaced by Q. Glitius Agricola (*ILS* 1021a).

[9] Note a *primus pilus* of I Adiutrix decorated by Trajan 'bello Germanico' (*I. l. de Tunisie* 778 f.)—perhaps in supplementation of Nerva's awards to the same legion (*ILS* 2720). No serious campaign is likely in 98.

camps, Viminacium or Singidunum, facing the land of the Dacians—
and in the strategic centre of the Empire, half-way between the northern
ocean and the river Euphrates, on or beside the highway of empire
that linked Italy and the West to the eastern provinces.

Present in Trajan's company and perhaps vocal were 'viri militares'
who fought in the various wars of Domitian, or who had seen ambition
frustrated and energy not wanted. Once again martial expectations
fell flat. After making his dispositions, with new governors in the
Danubian provinces, Trajan came to Rome. The *consules ordinarii* of
the year 99 were a pair of his younger friends, destined for the high
military commands;[1] and he proposed to inaugurate the next year,
consul himself again, with Julius Frontinus for the third time. No
danger from beyond the great rivers demanded a long residence of
Rome's Imperator in the frontier lands. The danger was internal and
political. 'Concordia exercituum' had been advertised by Nerva. It
was achieved by Trajan.

[1] Q. Sosius Senecio and A. Cornelius Palma.

III. JULIUS AGRICOLA

NERVA'S reign, and the supersession of Nerva, produced a Roman historian. When, in the course of the year 97, the aged Verginius Rufus succumbed to a long illness, the Senate voted a state funeral, and the laudation was pronounced by Cornelius Tacitus, who then held the consular *fasces*, an orator of power and repute.[1] Before many months have elapsed, Tacitus comes out with a composition of kindred nature and theme, commemorating his wife's father, Julius Agricola, who had died over four years previously. In the *Agricola* the eloquent consular announces that he will go on to write a history of his own times, as testimony to past enslavement and present felicity.[2]

The monograph itself may have something to tell about the new emperor. In the third chapter of the *Agricola* Tacitus counts the age happy because Nerva Caesar has blended 'libertas' and the 'principatus', and Nerva Traianus with every day that passes augments the 'felicitas temporum'.[3] The words convey the impression that Nerva is still alive. Later on, however, towards the end of the *Agricola*, Trajan is described as 'princeps'.[4] What is the solution? Was the book published before, or after, Nerva's death (January 28, A.D. 98)? Or was it composed before that date and published subsequently?[5] The problem hardly matters. 'Nerva Caesar' could stand in writing after Nerva had become a 'divus'—and the dominant fact is not Nerva's decease but Nerva's adoption of Trajan.

The name of Trajan occurs only twice in the *Agricola*. That work as a whole is much more than a retarded eulogy of one man's father-in-law. It stands in close relation to the training and career of the Imperator himself, to his character and his virtues.

A provincial of the better sort was often tempted to stay in his own country. Local honours and esteem, congenial neighbours, and the supervision of a patrimony ensured a dignified leisure and comfort

---

[1] Pliny, *Epp.* II. 1. 6.

[2] *Agr.* 3. 3: 'non tamen pigebit vel incondita ac rudi voce memoriam prioris servitutis ac testimonium praesentium bonorum composuisse. hic interim liber honori Agricolae soceri mei destinatus professione pietatis aut laudatus erit aut excusatus.'

[3] 3. 1.   [4] 44. 5.

[5] Compare Frontinus' treatise—'ab Nerva Augusto' (*De aquis* 1. 1), and 'imperatoris piissimi Nervae' (88. 1). Yet Nerva is twice denominated 'divus' (102. 4 and 118. 3), and the author brings in his successor as 'Imperatorem Caesarem Nervam Traianum Augustum' (93. 4).

without discredit—'honesta quies'.[1] The metropolis offered life and gaiety, and the stirring propinquity of great events. Danger also lurked there, and corruption. And there was the cost. Frugal and industrious, the men of substance in provincial Italy of the north and in the western lands got a name for good sense, and no small praise for having improved the science of agriculture.

Some put up a firm resistance against the lures of the greater world. Others were taken away by education, the impulsion of talent, and the urge to excel. One of the best was L. Julius Graecinus, who came from the colony of Forum Julii in the province Narbonensis.[2] He entered the Senate under Tiberius and reached the praetorship. Graecinus had varied accomplishments—he wrote a treatise on the cultivation of the vine, elegant as well as accurate, he acquired some note as a public speaker, and he took pleasure in the converse of philosophers. His firm principles came out in small things and in great. Two aristocrats were ready to defray the expense of the games he had to provide as praetor. He rejected the offer—they were men of infamous life.[3] Caligula ordered him to undertake a prosecution—he refused. Caligula was resentful, and, for that reason or for another, Graecinus was put to death.[4]

His son, Cn. Julius Agricola, was born in 40.[5] He pursued the higher education at Massilia, a city which at that time usefully blended provincial puritanism with the graces of Hellenic enlightenment. The only danger the young man there encountered was philosophy. In later years he was often heard to say that the ardour with which he embraced that study went beyond anything permissible in a Roman and a senator.[6] A mother's sagacity intervened. Agricola grew in years and discretion, having acquired from doctrine what few ever do, a sense of proportion.[7]

Agricola was redeemed for the service of the State. The post of military tribune brought him to Britain when Suetonius Paullinus was governor.[8] Many of the young men took their military service very

---

[1] *Epp.* I. 14. 5—referring to Minicius Macrinus of Brixia, 'equestris ordinis princeps, quia nihil altius voluit'; cf. III. 2. 4 (Arrianus Maturus of Altinum).

[2] *Agr.* 4. 1, cf. *PIR*[1] J 231 and the inscription from Rome: '[L.] Iulio L. f. Ani. / Graecino tr. pl. pr. / M. Iulius L. f. Ani. / Graecinus quaestor f.' (*AE* 1946, 94). The (elder) son Marcus was not previously known.

[3] Seneca, *De ben.* II. 21. 5 f. (Paullus Fabius Persicus and C. Caninius Rebilus, on whom, p. 571).

[4] *Agr.* 4. 1: 'namque M. Silanum accusare iussus et, quia abnuerat, interfectus est.' Not at once, however, for the death of Silanus occurred early in 38 (deduced from *CIL* VI, 2028 C, l. 35).

[5] 44. 1. For the chronology see further App. 17 (on the senatorial *cursus*).

[6] 4. 4: 'acrius, ultra quam concessum Romano ac senatori, hausisse.'

[7] 4. 5.

[8] 5. 1. In 60, the year of Boudicca's rising (not 61, the year registered in *Ann.* XIV. 29. 1,

lightly, no thought but of leave and recreation, and they learned nothing. Agricola made it his duty to find out about the province; and he kept his faculties trained and alert, avoiding the reproach of ostentation or the suspicion of timidity. There was action, also, and a chance to show his mettle, notably when the native queen, Boudicca, rose in rebellion, firing Agricola with the ambition of a military career, though the times were unpropitious, all excellence being suspect, and renown as dangerous as infamy.[1]

To make his way, a man required support and patronage. Agricola married the daughter of Domitius Decidius, a Narbonensian senator of some distinction.[2] The match contributed powerfully to his advancement. Agricola now went out as quaestor to a proconsul. The province was Asia, rich in temptations, and the governor was Salvius Titianus—whose known greed offered connivance and cover. Neither Asia nor the proconsul could contaminate Agricola.[3]

Rome was much more perilous than Asia. On his return Agricola behaved with the utmost caution during the year that passed before his next office. He had taken the measure of the times—'inertia' was 'sapientia'.[4] It was the year of the great conspiracy against Nero. Among the guilty and among the victims (terms not always synonymous) were a number of provincials, men of Agricola's own age and class.[5]

More prosecutions and judicial murders ensued in 66. Birth, talent, and independence incurred Nero's angry suspicion. Truculent advocates were at his bidding, and a compliant Senate. Ambition engrossed quick rewards, but it was no season for a young man of honourable aspirations or impetuous temper. Agricola, now tribune of the plebs, came safely through all hazards.[6] Discretion also marked his praetorship, which fell in the last year of Nero; and Galba appointed him to a commission that called for integrity and accuracy.[7] Agricola had no share in the fighting of the next year, but he promptly came over to the Flavian side, and soon found employment: he was dispatched to hold a levy in Italy, and then put in command of the Twentieth Legion, in Britain.[8]

cf. App. 69). Agricola, like others, may well have served in two campaigning seasons, cf. E. Birley, *Proc. Brit. Ac.* XXXIX (1953), 200.

[1] 5. 4: 'nec minus periculum ex magna fama quam ex mala.'   [2] 6. 1, cf. *ILS* 966.

[3] 6. 2. Otho's brother (as the author did not need to add). The next governor (64/65, summer to summer) was L. Antistius Vetus (*cos.* 55), a most upright man, prosecuted before the end of 65. It is generally held that Agricola's quaestorship would have run on into the proconsulate of Vetus. It might not be so.

[4] 6. 3: 'gnarus sub Nerone temporum quibus inertia pro sapientia fuit.'

[5] e.g. M. Annaeus Lucanus, born in 39 and recently quaestor.

[6] Another tribune, Junius Rusticus, was ready to be rash (*Ann.* XVI. 26. 4).

[7] 6. 5: 'ad dona templorum recognoscenda.'

[8] 7. 5. That Agricola should not be named in the *Historiae*, as extant, has caused surprise. Thus E. Paratore, *Tacito* (1951), 59 f.; 471 ff. Unnecessarily.

Though the initial stage in a senator's career was military by name and rank, its term was brief, the service far from exacting. If the tribunate could sort out the more useful among the young men, whose personal value might further be assessed at the metropolis and in civil offices, the post of legionary legate was decisive for the 'vir militaris'. Agricola made good the promise of his first actions a decade earlier. He was eager to be at the enemy. The legate of Britain, however, was Vettius Bolanus, a quiet man, too quiet for so bellicose a province.[1] Agricola kept his impatience under control, well schooled as he was in submission to authority. His reward came when Bolanus was replaced by Petillius Cerialis. The new governor at once attacked the Brigantes, the most powerful people in the whole island. He entrusted Agricola with a part of the army to test his capacity. Agricola knew his place, anxious that the commanding officer should have the entire credit: modesty sheltered him and earned a share of the glory.[2]

Close upon the legionary command came a high social distinction, and a provincial post which showed the straight road to the consulate: Vespasian made him a member of the patrician order and put him in charge of Aquitania, one of the three Gallic provinces.[3] There is a general belief (says Tacitus) that the military are devoid of tact and subtlety.[4] Agricola gave the lie to that opinion. And, although renown can lure the virtuous, Agricola did not pursue renown, either frankly or artfully. He was careful not to challenge in rivalry the legates of the other provinces or get drawn into disputes with the financial agents of the central government.[5]

Before three years had elapsed, Agricola came back to Rome for his consulship (77).[6] Almost at once Vespasian appointed him governor of Britain, succeeding Julius Frontinus. By the consulate Agricola won entry to the ranks of the new nobility. Furthermore, about the time of a man's consulship, there often accrued some sacerdotal honour. Agricola now became a *pontifex*.[7]

The operations of Julius Agricola in Britain (78–84) do not much concern the present inquiry.[8] They are narrated, adorned, and

---

[1] 8. 1. [2] 8. 3.

[3] 9. 1: 'deinde provinciae Aquitaniae praeposuit, splendidae inprimis dignitatis administratione ac spe consulatus, cui destinarat.' For this type of province (and career), see App. 15 f. and 18. The notion that Agricola came late, slow, and disappointed to the consulate (E. Paratore, o.c. 89 ff.) has no substance.

[4] 9. 2. [5] 9. 5.

[6] 9. 6. The year is not directly attested. Agricola's first (calendar) year in Britain must be 78, for the seventh witnessed his great victory, subsequent to Domitian's triumph over the Chatti (39. 2), which occurred late in 83 (cf. R. Syme, *CAH* xi (1936), 164), the *congiarium* being paid out in 84 (*FO* xiii s = *Inscr. It.* xiii, 1, p. 102).

[7] 9. 7: 'statim Britanniae praepositus est, adiecto pontificatus sacerdotio.' For priesthoods just before or just after the consulate cf. *ILS* 1005; 1036; 1055; 8971.

[8] Ch. XI.

magnified by his son-in-law. In the last campaign the folly of the native Caledonians, who massed their forces for a pitched battle instead of dispersing their effort in guerrilla warfare, enabled Agricola to win a victory that seemed decisive; and, if Agricola maintained that Britain was now subjugated, he had the less reason to complain about being superseded.

Domitian, who had recently celebrated his own triumph over the Chatti, gave his general the *ornamenta triumphalia*—and something was said about Syria.[1] Returning to Rome, the conqueror of Britain made a discreet arrival, and subsided quietly into private life. He was now only forty-four, mortifyingly young to retire from affairs—the penalty for rapid success, an early consulate, and a command twice as long as Cerialis or Frontinus had. And what further honours awaited a 'vir triumphalis'? To be a senior statesman under the monarchy was thankless and empty, unless a man had the gift of speech or favour with the court faction. Agricola was not an orator or an intriguer—and the best places were already occupied.

In due course a second consulate might come, for the Flavian emperors had not been ungenerous hitherto;[2] and the passage of years would admit Agricola's name to the ballot for the proconsulates of Asia and Africa. There was nothing else. Nothing more was heard about Syria. Domitian and his advisers might have argued that any claim for a second consular province was offset by the abnormally long tenure of Britain.

Nor was there a command for Agricola when war broke out on the Danube with a series of Roman defeats caused by rashness or incapacity in the generals.[3] According to Tacitus there arose a popular clamour for Agricola: everybody compared his energy, resolution, and experience with the torpor and timidity of the other military men. It will be doubted whether foreign affairs aroused much concern among a populace which the historian elsewhere indicts for its vile and frivolous habits, with a sole preoccupation, the price of foodstuffs.[4] If the merits of Agricola were canvassed, it was only in the clubs and circles where talk against the government was ever the fashionable pastime—and public misfortune a chance for private malice. While Agricola was away in Britain, other consulars and other groups had been building up positions of advantage. The Prefect of the Guard, the impetuous Cornelius Fuscus, was chosen by the Emperor to conduct

[1] 40. 1.   [2] Several precisely in 85 (App. 12).
[3] 41. 2: 'tot exercitus in Moesia Daciaque et Germania et Pannonia temeritate aut per ignaviam ducum amissi,' &c. The trouble began in 85 with the disaster of Oppius Sabinus, the legate of Moesia.
[4] *Hist.* I. 4. 3: 'plebs sordida et circo ac theatris sueta' ; IV. 38. 2: 'vulgus cui una ex re publica annonae cura.'

an invasion of Dacia (which failed);[1] and the managers of patronage were able to produce the men to hold the great Danubian commands—one general perhaps a little elderly for active warfare, but another with Balkan experience, who won a great victory at Tapae in the land of the Dacians.[2]

They also cheated Agricola of his proconsulate. Men who knew the thoughts of the Emperor made a tactful approach to Agricola, inquired about his intentions, praised the advantages of leisure, and promised their diplomatic offices if he wished to decline. Menace was added to exhortation; and these men of good will conducted Agricola into the presence of Domitian, who assented to a subject's prayer—and graciously accepted a subject's thanks.[3]

The behaviour of Agricola was exemplary, now and all through the dull stretch of enforced inactivity, nine years from his return to his death (August 23, A.D. 93).[4] When a 'vir militaris' came back to Rome, with all the weight and conscious habit of authority, he might become a burden and a nuisance in polite society. Agricola was easy, modest, affable. The majority, who measure fame by pomp and ostentation, were disconcerted when they saw Agricola. Was Agricola in truth a great man?[5]

More delicate was the adjustment between a famous general and a jealous emperor, with enmity often ensuing, or disgrace and death. Domitian had wronged Agricola, and Domitian therefore hated Agricola. The Emperor was swift to anger, implacable in revenge, but Agricola showed no resentment for shabby treatment. Defiance and a provocative exhibition of 'libertas' would have earned him ruin and renown. He chose prudence and escaped harm.[6]

Agricola's demeanour was far from heroic. It might easily have been misconstrued while he lived, and no doubt it was so subsequently—by those whom Tacitus condemns for 'admiring what is wrong'.

Tacitus has a sharp answer. 'Let me tell them', he says, 'that there can be great men even under bad emperors, that duty and discretion, if coupled with energy of character and a career of action, will bring

---

[1] For Fuscus, App. 33.

[2] L. Funisulanus Vettonianus (*suff.* ?78), passing from Pannonia to the newly created Moesia Superior in 85/86 (*ILS* 1005, cf. *CIL* xvi, 30 f.), and L. Tettius Julianus (*suff.* 83), victor at Tapae in 88 (Dio LXVII. 10. 1, cf. Statius, *Silvae* III. 3. 115 ff.). Julianus had been legate (quaestorian) of VII Claudia in 69 (*Hist.* I. 79. 5; IV. 40. 2). For the link between the two generals, note that Funisulana Vettulla was married to C. Tettius Africanus, the Prefect of Egypt (*ILS* 8759c), an Umbrian (cf. *CIL* xi, 5382).

[3] 42. 1 ff. Presumably early in 90, for the proconsulate of 90/91. What helped to deter Agricola was the fate of a proconsul of Asia in 88/89, 'occiso Civica nuper' (cf. *ILS* 1374).

[4] 44. 1. [5] 40. 4.

[6] 42. 4: 'non contumacia neque inani iactatione libertatis famam fatumque provocabat.'

a man to no less glorious summits than are attained by perilous paths and ostentatious deaths, with no advantage to the Commonwealth.'[1]

The fervour and acerbity in this outburst belies the normal gravity of the Roman and the senator. His anger can be explained. After the assassination of Domitian the friends and relatives of those who had suffered exile or death were loud for vengeance—and many whose tie or claim was tenuous took up the cry. However, the needs of ordered government impose bars and limits. That soon became apparent, and sagacious senators would support a plea for moderation. Although the greater criminals duly secured protection, although the men of principle and the eager careerists were alike baffled in their cravings for revenge or advancement, they were by no means reduced to silence; and some would later exhibit the propriety of their sentiments and seek approbation in the world of letters by composing pamphlets on the deaths of illustrious men.[2]

Tacitus proclaims his scorn for the brave enemies of dead tyrants, the noisy advocates of the heroes and martyrs. They had not confined their reprobation to evil men, the willing agents of despotism, but had gone much further. The rule of the Caesars depended not only on political managers or venal prosecutors. It had the support of administrators; and the whole senatorial order was acquiescent. Tacitus goes out of his way to make a passionate confession of collective guilt—'our hands dragged Helvidius off to prison, our countenances felt shame at the sight of Mauricus and Rusticus, it was we whom Senecio bespattered with his innocent blood'.[3]

Tacitus refers to the sudden sequence of prosecutions in the autumn of the year 93.[4] Agricola was dead at the time of these transactions, and Tacitus himself may have still been absent from Rome.[5] No matter, Tacitus puts himself among the majority that witnessed and condoned the worst acts of tyranny. It does not follow that Tacitus would have quietly concurred when anybody else arraigned Agricola's conduct, or his own, for cowardice and subservience.

Attacking those who admired the martyrs unduly, Tacitus defends his father-in-law—and shields his own conduct under the tyranny of Domitian. Tacitus may have spoken in the Senate, deprecating the excesses of faction and fanatics. When the time came, he was to show how well he could demonstrate that theme—'it was all very well to

---

[1] ib. 5: 'sciant, quibus moris est inlicita mirari, posse etiam sub malis principibus magnos viros esse, obsequiumque ac modestiam, si industria ac vigor adsint, eo laudis excedere quo plerique per abrupta sed in nullum rei publicae usum ⟨enisi⟩ ambitiosa morte inclaruerunt.'

[2] p. 92.   [3] 45. 1.

[4] For the chronology of these events, Ch. VII and App. 19.   [5] 45. 5.

emulate Brutus and Cato in fortitude: one was only a senator, and
they had all been slaves together'.[1]

Tacitus speaks not only for Agricola or for himself. The *Agricola*
expounds the moral and political ideals of the new aristocracy, not
systematically formulated but emerging gradually in the portrayal of
an individual and in the stages of a senator's career.

The provincial magnates, as depicted in the *Agricola* and discoverable elsewhere, bear a strong resemblance to their predecessors in the
invasion of the Roman State, the men of substance and repute from
the Italian towns: the categories are inherited, the labels often conventional, and the general portrayal is highly flattering.[2]

In the first place, wealth and the use to which it is put. Some provincial fortunes were enormous. Agricola had adequate means.[3] The
new-comers were good farmers and keen men for gain. Financial
ability commended them as procurators to the imperial government,
and money was needed to carry the next generation forward in the
career of honours. The habit of parsimony endured even in the
opulent, and, with other antique virtues, kept its dominance in
the provinces, as in the remoter tracts of Italy, when it had long since
fled from the capital.[4] Fashion was not allowed to wreak its ravages
among the womenfolk, though some might acquire the rudiments of
a polished education; and the alacrity of youth in the pursuit of 'bonae
artes' was curbed and preserved from dangerous thoughts by native
shrewdness or domestic pressure.

The Caesars had need of loyal and capable servants, at home and
abroad. Provincials were alert and ready.[5] Neither rancour nor idealism
could be permitted to interfere. Many of them had all the robust
patriotism of a frontier zone and a fervid devotion to the great past
of Rome, but they did not take the name for the thing. Unobtrusive
in performing the flat and regular duties of the urban magistracy, and
firmly treading a middle path between economy and display, a man
intent on the highest honours was careful to show deference towards
seniority. Military training was valued, but did not have to be lengthy;
and military ways would not always blunt a senator's capacity for civil
business. Disdaining to be showy and competitive, he established by
subordination his right to be promoted.

The sum of meritorious qualities falls a long way short of the heroic
or the spectacular. It evokes the sober virtues which in ancient days
won the hegemony in Italy and dominion over the nations—according

---

[1] *Hist.* IV. 8. 3 (the oration of Eprius Marcellus).
[2] cf. R. Syme, *Rom. Rev.* (1939), 81 ff.; 359 ff.; 449 ff.
[3] 44. 4.   [4] *Ann.* XVI. 5. 1, cf. *Epp.* I. 14. 4.   [5] Ch. XLIII.

to what was believed or advertised under the rule of Caesar Augustus by the writers of improving prose or verse.

In their manner of thought the Romans were addicted to tradition. If a person, quality, or thing could be styled 'antiquus' or 'priscus', all was well. The provincial notables not infrequently embodied the antique notions of frugal merit or rustic valour. And some were assiduous in preaching the theme. Roman opinion, when confronted with upstarts who were often not conservative but innovatory, and who combined frugality with great possessions, was muzzled and disarmed by its own most cherished conventions.

The generals of old and the empire-builders became ideal and legendary figures. Very different were the *nobiles* as men had known them in their own time or by recent examples. In the last epoch of the Free State the pursuit of honour and the lust for power engendered the monarchic aristocrat, ruinous to the Commonwealth. 'Libertas' was the badge and device of the ruling order. Asserting privilege to the limit, the nobles competed, gladly and ruthlessly. To incur a feud was a title of distinction, and an intractable character became a glorious virtue. If the struggles in which the old order perished be taken on a broad view as the battle between Republic and Monarchy, it will be well to recall that the principal contestants belonged to the same class in society, professing the same aristocratic ideals, though at odds about their interpretation: they paraded 'dignitas' and 'magnitudo animi'.

If Cato failed, and Brutus, so did Caesar and Antonius. And, although the prestige of the *nobiles* was refurbished by Caesar Augustus, he yoked them to the monarchy: they had to share their privilege and lower their pretensions. The true victory went to the new men and to the non-political classes.[1] For a season the Republican façade of the dynasty, the aristocratic temper of Tiberius Caesar, and the prominence of the noble families might keep up a semblance of the old pride and dignity. The day of the great men and the splendid virtues was over. To succeed, or even to survive, modesty was requisite, and discretion; while 'quies', previously the mark of the Roman knight, became honourable in a senator.[2] 'Libertas' itself, the dearest virtue of the noble, had to recede and surrender to 'obsequium'.

The fall of the Republic demonstrated that liberty and the Empire were incompatible. It was now evident that the maintenance of the Empire called for subordination and obedience in the governing class. Compromise was distasteful to the independent spirit of the Roman

---

[1] R. Syme, o.c. 513 ff.
[2] ib. 13 f.; 517. Observe the contrast between Republic and Principate—'ipsa inimicitiarum gloria' (Tacitus, *Dial.* 40. 1) and 'quietis gloria' (Pliny, *Pan.* 86. 2).

aristocrat. Yet in ancient days (if history was to be believed), not only in the struggle of the orders but even in the strife of noble factions, compromise had been invoked to preserve stability, and private feuds abated for the Commonwealth. If the Commonwealth survived only as a name, the Empire was a fact; and, to keep the Empire intact, a compromise was needed between the Emperor and the Senate. For Rome, anarchy and despotism were equally intolerable. The notion of the middle path—liberty without licence and order without despotism—is inherent in the Principate from the beginning. Men might be found who understood that ideal and put it into their conduct long before it was formulated by any orator or theorist: it might be possible to steer a safe course amid the temptations of public life and all the perils.[1]

As the destiny of the Empire worked itself out, and the power grew ever more concentrated in the hands of the ruler, the emphasis fell more heavily on order and subordination. The notion of 'obsequium' is put on show in the exposition of Agricola's career.[2] The word denotes rational deference to authority—the obedience which an officer owes to his commander, a senator to the Senate, an emperor to the gods of the Roman State.[3]

In the process of adjustment between the Emperor and the Senate two battles had to be fought. In the first the old governing order, the families who claimed to be the 'res publica', were tamed, broken, and almost annihilated. In the second 'Libertas', surviving as the habit of free speech and free criticism, and incorporated in the men of principle who withstood the autocratic rule of Nero and of Domitian, was reduced to obedience. The Republic died hard. It was not until the accession of Trajan that the ghost of Cato was laid at last.

If the glories of the Free State were far behind, so too the shams and pretences of the early Principate. If pride and contumacy were abolished, political wisdom now prevailed. In their ideal of service to the Roman State the new aristocracy could assert a firm claim. It was not a foreign enemy that endangered the Empire, but internal weakness—a wicked ruler, an irresponsible opposition. Patience and sagacity held the structure together.

To the eye of romance or sentiment a dreary period dawned upon the world, inimical to excellence and murderous to renown. The great men belonged to the past, to an epic age. They were 'ingentes viri'.[4]

---

[1] *Ann.* IV. 20. 3 (M. Lepidus).

[2] 42. 5 (cited above). Compare his conduct as a legionary legate, 'peritus obsequi' (8. 1); 'virtute in obsequendo' (8. 3).

[3] The following examples of 'obsequium' in Pliny will be instructive: *Epp.* VIII. 23. 5; X. 3a. 3; 100; *Pan.* 9. 3 and 5; 78. 1.

[4] *Pan.* 69. 5.

On a sober estimation those heroes were too large for the Commonwealth, with virtues no less ruinous than their vices. They were
portents to admire, not models to imitate. The new Romans had an
answer, deriving not from books but from their lives, not from the city
but from the Empire. There could still be great men, even under a
bad emperor.

It is the mark of political literature under the Empire, especially
when it happens to be written by Cornelius Tacitus, that it should
not carry its meaning on its face.[1] The *Agricola* purports to be a composition in praise of Tacitus' father-in-law. Being that, it cannot fail
to be an attack on Domitian. Violent language shows that it is also an
attack on other persons, on political extremists.[2] Something further
is implied—a vindication of the new men from the provinces, setting
them up against effete aristocrats and the parochial Italians.

A happy artifice conveys the link between Agricola and Trajan.
Fortunate in the season of his death, Agricola was spared the sight of
many tribulations. Of one felicity he was frustrated—the accession of
Trajan. That was what he prayed for, and prophesied.[3]

[1] Mommsen was premature when he denied that there was any political literature in
Rome of the Empire (*Reden u. Aufsätze* (1905), 149).

[2] This political element in his *Agricola* has generally been recognized. Compare
Anderson in his edition (Oxford, 1922), xxxviii ff., who, however, minimizes the strain of
apologia. For the literary genre of the treatise, its honesty, and its veracity, see Ch. XI.

[3] 44. 5: 'quod augurio votisque apud nostras auris ominabatur.'

IV. THE NEW EMPEROR

TRAJAN'S family came from the far part of Spain, from Italica in the province of Baetica, where Scipio Africanus had settled veterans from his army during the second war against the Carthaginians. Italica lay in the opulent region, at an equal distance from Gades and from Corduba. It is a fair assumption that the Ulpii took a high place among the notables of the province for wealth, dignity, and alliances.[1]

The first Ulpius known to history is M. Ulpius Traianus, who commanded the legion X Fretensis under Vespasian in the Jewish War. After subjugating the territories east of Jordan he brought his army to join Vespasian at Jericho in the spring of 68. The campaign now slowed down on news of sudden events in Gaul and Spain. Men began to guess and to intrigue. In July of the next year the eastern armies proclaimed an emperor. Traianus, who is not reported among the legionary legates at the council of war before the final assault was launched on Jerusalem, may have gone from Palestine to Egypt in the company of the new ruler. The name of this trusty adherent no doubt stood among the earliest of the Flavian consulates.[2] Vespasian also signalized him by adlection into the patriciate.

A surer mark of confidence was the Syrian command, which Traianus assumed in 73 or 74 and held for at least three years.[3] And in due course he reached the pinnacle of a senator's career, the proconsulate of Asia.[4] While Traianus was legate of Syria, the king of the Parthians conceived annoyance with the Roman government for a failure to acknowledge the common interests of the two empires, or for some minor act of stealthy aggression. The threat of war, if it went as far as that, was dispelled by a prompt move.[5] A 'Parthian laurel' dispatched to the capital advertised a diplomatic success (such laurels had been seen before at Rome), and Traianus received the triumphal ornaments, likewise not without precedent in the bloodless victories of the Empire.[6] Panegyric or gossip, the annals of imperial

---

[1] Ch. XLIV.

[2] Presumably in 70, cf. R. Syme, *JRS* XLIII (1953), 154. Add the argument of J. Morris (ib. 79 f.), who adduces ']ius Tr[' as a reading in the fragment *FO* XI, which he plausibly assigns to this year, instead of 72 (*Inscr. It.* XIII, 1, p. 190).

[3] *ILS* 8970. The governorship of Syria runs not merely from 75 (*AE* 1933, 205), but from 73/74, cf. the inscription from Antioch reported by L. Robert in *CRAI* 1951, 255.

[4] *ILS* 8797, &c. Dated to 79/80 (*IGR* IV, 845).

[5] Victor, *Epit.* 9. 12; *De Caes.* 9. 10. Cf. *CAH* XI (1936), 143.

[6] Pliny, *Pan.* 14. 1.

Rome set on record all too often the casual and the trivial, neglecting or obscuring matters of great moment. Traianus may have been Vespasian's principal agent in the ordering of the whole frontier and its defences, from the Armenian mountains to the desert of Arabia.[1]

About the early career of his son nothing is known save what derives from the oration which the consul Plinius Secundus delivered in September of the year 100. The young Trajan was a military tribune in the Syrian army, powerfully augmenting the renown of his father, if Pliny is to be believed; and in his prolonged service as a tribune Trajan visited the most widely distant of lands, linking Rhine to Euphrates in the admiration of his valour. 'Stipendia decem', such is Pliny's figure (surely all too generous).[2]

A brief spell in Britain fired Agricola with the passion for a military career. The concentration of ambition and the total of experience denoted by ten years as a tribune would baffle all imagining, for there is no parallel, and nothing to approach such a record.[3] The orator (it seems) is using and exploiting the ancient and consecrated term for the interval between manhood and the first magisterial office.[4] No exact definition can be given of the beginning or the end of Trajan's period with the armies. He may have served in several of the legions on Rhine, Danube, and Euphrates; perhaps taking the field in the modest and pedestrian operations that Vespasian held adequate to secure the frontiers of the Roman Empire and impress the barbarians along the periphery with the majesty of the Roman name.

For the next decade Trajan is lost to view. He became quaestor, presumably about 78, and in due course praetor.[5] He missed (so it appears) the Dacian campaigns, which began in 85.[6] He is next heard

[1] Instead of '[pro pra]et.' before 'provinciae Syriae' (*ILS* 8970), Dessau in *Milet* I, 5, 53 (1919) suggested '] et'—i.e. evidence for a previous imperial province. It must be recalled that the inscription is built up from six small fragments (see plates 24 f.). Traianus might have governed the new province Cappadocia-Galatia before Syria.

[2] 15. 3: 'cognovisti per stipendia decem mores gentium, regionum situs', &c.

[3] Some *tribuni laticlavii* must have spent more than a year with their legion; service in two is exceptional, in three attested only twice, namely for P. Aelius Hadrianus (*HA, Hadr.* 2. 2 ff.; *ILS* 308), and for the son of L. Minicius Natalis (*suff.* 106) c. 115–17 (*ILS* 1061, cf. 1029).

[4] Namely the 'decem stipendia' once held requisite before a man could stand for senatorial office (Polybius VI. 19. 2; Plutarch, *C. Gracchus* 2). For Trajan it corresponds to the interval between *toga virilis* (at fifteen) and quaestorship (?68–78). The age of the *laticlavius* is about nineteen or twenty, but could be lower (even sixteen, cf. Statius, *Silvae* v. 2. 8 ff.).

[5] Trajan's birthday was September 18 (*Pan.* 92. 4; *Epp.* x. 17. 2), there are discrepancies about the year (cf. *PIR¹*, V 575). If 53 be accepted, the quaestorship could fall in 78: note (what is otherwise inexplicable) Trajan's choice of Q. Articuleius Paetus (son of a *suffectus* of 78), to share the *fasces* in 101: his last partner was Julius Frontinus (*tertio* in 100), his next M'. Laberius Maximus (*iterum* in 103). Being a patrician, Trajan was excused the next stage (aedileship or tribunate of the plebs): his praetorship should go c. 84.

[6] Peculiar, given his ostensible military record. Speculation is baffled.

of as commander of the legion in Hispania Tarraconensis, a few years after his praetorship. The facts have to be disentangled from the luxuriant laudations and incomplete avowals of the official orator. Pliny tells how Domitian summoned Trajan as his surest aid for the wars of Germany, how Trajan conducted the legions with miraculous rapidity.[1] There was only one legion in Spain, and the war was a civil war.

Antonius Saturninus proclaimed himself emperor at Moguntiacum on January 1 of the year 89. The tidings travelled quickly. Domitian was prompt—delay and indecision had ruined Nero. He left Rome with the Guard on January 12, making for the north, and ordering his armies to meet him. By January 25, however, a victory was known and celebrated in Rome. The legate of Lower Germany, Lappius Maximus, stood loyal to Domitian and defeated the usurper in a pitched battle beside the Rhine.[2]

Domitian proceeded on his march, came to the German frontier, punished the accomplices of Saturninus, and took measures for future security. From the Rhine he went to the Danube in the spring of the year and sent a punitive expedition against the Suebic Germans of Bohemia, the Marcomanni and Quadi, who, neglecting the terms of their treaty, had failed to provide help to the Romans in the war against Dacia. He then superintended the final settlement with the Dacians (a victory had been won in the previous year by Tettius Julianus), and returned to Rome to celebrate his triumph.[3]

Whether Trajan in dutiful response to the Emperor's summons came as far as the Rhine (and went with him to the Danubian armies), or led the legion back to Spain when the victory was announced, there is no means of telling. At this high peak and important juncture in his hero's life, the panegyrist flags and fails—nothing but a vague reference to 'other expeditions' after the march from Spain.[4]

In the year 89 the rule of Domitian, in its relation to the senatorial class, had taken a decisive and evil turn: one of the army commanders rose in rebellion, and it was asserted that he had called to his aid the Germans beyond the frontier. There were perhaps accomplices in other armies, or partisans in the West or the East, malcontents at

[1] 14. 3: 'cum legiones duceres seu potius (tanta velocitas erat) raperes,' &c. It could be argued that the 'Celer' of Martial VII. 52. 3 f. was governor of Tarraconensis at this time and identical with L. Pompeius Vopiscus C. Arruntius Catellius Celer (*PIR*[1], P 501), consul suffect presumably in 77; and that Q. Glitius Agricola (*suff.* 97) was the *iuridicus* (*ILS* 1021).

[2] cf. the reconstruction of E. Ritterling, depending on dates furnished by the *Acta Fratrum Arvalium* (*CIL* VI, 2066): followed in *CAH* XI (1936), 172 ff.

[3] For the chronology of Domitian's Dacian Wars see R. Syme, *CAH* XI, 168; A. Stein, *Die Legaten von Moesien* (1940), 34 ff.

[4] 14. 5: 'cum aliis super alias expeditionibus itinere illo dignus invenireris.'

Rome. In the eastern lands a false Nero arose about this time;[1] and a proconsul of Asia was put to death.[2]

If sharp punishment overtook the authors of treason, rewards and honours attended upon loyalty to dynasty and Empire. For the legionary legates the due recompense was patent and palpable—the consulate, but not at once. In the most rapid of such careers, a praetorian province (the normal tenure is three years), intervenes.[3] Trajan, however, legate of a legion in the month of January 89, becomes *consul ordinarius* only two years later, with a relic of the Republican *nobilitas* for colleague, an Acilius Glabrio, of no personal talent, but ill-starred and doomed to destruction.

As the son of a consular who had been made a patrician and became a 'vir triumphalis', Trajan already stood high. The quick consulate confirmed his rank. To such eminence, whether military or civil, a priesthood would properly belong. Of consulate, or of any sacerdotal distinction, there is no word in Pliny's oration.[4] The silence is suspect. Nor is any consular command noted.

The Danube flared up again in 92. Sarmatians were the enemy this time, not Dacians—the vassal kingdom of Decebalus remained loyal and proved its value as a barrier, separating the tribes of the Hungarian plain, the Jazyges, from their kinsmen the Rhoxolani towards the mouth of the Danube. The Jazyges made an irruption into Pannonia. A legion met them and was cut to pieces. The disaster brought Domitian to Pannonia. He fought a campaign and, after an absence of eight months, returned to Rome in January of 93.[5]

Not a single particular about Trajan's career under Domitian, subsequent to the year 89, is recorded by Pliny. What happened to him during the years of silence and oppression? 'You shared our life', exclaims Pliny, 'our perils, our fears.'[6] In spite of the perils and the fears, while delation prospered and prosecutions raged, with exile or death for enemies of the government, the administration went on, senators held offices and provinces and rose in the service of the State, some by scandalous and rapid leaps, others persistent, unobtrusive, and unblamed. Later on, these things had to be explained away. Conventional forms of apologia were to hand, and the audience avowed its own complicity by the toleration and esteem that attended upon political alertness. One could argue that a man was not really the Emperor's friend but his enemy, menaced already and destined soon to perish if the Emperor lived; that his career had in fact been

---

[1] Suetonius, *Nero* 57. 2.   [2] *Agr.* 42. 1, cf. *ILS* 1374.   [3] App. 15 f. and 18.

[4] His father was *sodalis Flavialis* and *XVvir sacris faciundis* (*ILS* 8970)—and perhaps died too soon to have a second consulate.

[5] For this campaign (the Germans of Bohemia were also involved) see *CAH* XI, 175 ff.

[6] *Pan.* 44. 1.

retarded through the jealous malevolence of the tyrant; that, although he had benefited from promotions before an 'insidiosissimus princeps' manifested his true nature, he voluntarily called a halt when Domitian published his hostility towards all good men.[1]

Did Trajan incur disfavour or danger? Apparently not. He must have been under the protection of the divine power: Domitian failed to harm him, just as Nerva could not fail to honour him.[2]

The alternatives are clear. Either Trajan received consular employment from Domitian or he did not. If not, it was a slight and an affront, given Trajan's station and merit: it showed that Domitian was envious. Pliny neglects to crown his elaborate structure of contrasts and antitheses. The mere thought of Trajan's setback filled him with horror, stifled his indignation, and constrained him to be silent.

The alternative is perhaps easier: Pliny suppresses Trajan's province as he suppresses Trajan's consulship. It may well be that the ex-consul held a staff appointment as one of the imperial 'comites' when Domitian went to Pannonia in 92. Furthermore, there are some grounds (but no certainty) for the belief that Trajan governed a province in the last years of Domitian, perhaps one of the Danubian provinces. He may have stood at the head of an army on September 18 of the year 96. A casual fact suggests that one member at least of Trajan's family circle was a consular legate on the Danube towards the end of Domitian's reign. Military tribunes commonly serve in armies that their kinsmen command. Aelius Hadrianus, the son of a cousin of Trajan, was tribune in three legions in succession.[3] The first two were Danubian. When serving in the second of these, he was chosen to convey to Trajan the congratulations of the army of Lower Moesia on his adoption, and was transferred to a legion of Upper Germany, at Moguntiacum; and from Moguntiacum only a few months later (his commanding officer being his sister's husband Julius Servianus) he carried to Trajan, now in Lower Germany, the news that Nerva was dead.[4]

The father of Trajan was a friend and adherent of Vespasian: the emperor was his patron, 'pietas' his duty. Nothing suggests that Trajan himself was deficient in loyalty towards the son of Vespasian. Trajan kept out of critical or rebellious company. With the enemies of the government he had no ties of family or friendship, and few tastes in common. While courage might be admired in the men who

---

[1] 90. 5; 95. 3.

[2] 94. 3: 'praeteritus est a pessimo principe qui ab optimo praeteriri non poterat.'

[3] *ILS* 308: 'trib. leg. II / Adiutricis p.f. item legionis V Macedonicae item legionis XXII Primigeniae p.f.', cf. *HA, Hadr.* 2. 2 ff. The position of the first of these legions is not certain (probably Moesia Superior), the second was in Moesia Inferior, the third in Germania Superior.   [4] *HA, Hadr.* 2. 5 f.

fortified their character with precept or doctrine, and constancy in evil days, their virtue was useless, for it could render no service to the Commonwealth.

There is no reason to fancy that Trajan was anything other than a firm adherent of the Flavian dynasty. If some persons held that against him after Domitian's death, their objections were soon quelled when the Praetorians rose and the government began to totter. And indeed, there was an easy retort. If an anecdote can be trusted, Trajan himself once pointed out that Domitian was the wickedest of emperors—but he had good friends.[1]

The elevation of Trajan was approved by two of the senior consulars commanding influence under Nerva, Julius Frontinus and Vestricius Spurinna—and it may have been furthered by them. Such at least is the suggestion conveyed by the public honours they had from Trajan.[2] It does not suffice to explain the transaction. The covert operations of other persons might be surmised, heralding a resurgence of men who had held office and commands recently, in the last years of Domitian. The consular marshals would have a word to say. Julius Servianus may have been in the game, with a group of Trajan's friends, involving various agents at Rome or abroad with the armies.[3] The whole thing could have begun as a conspiracy, designed not to rescue Nerva but to supplant him.[4]

Although so much must remain obscure, one name that crops up in history is significant, with a strong hint about what really happened: it was through the agency of Licinius Sura that Trajan was induced to seize the power.[5] Brief and fragmentary, the notice cannot be exploited to the full—neither the date of Sura's consulship is attested, nor the position he held in the year 97.[6] Even were those facts established, much would remain enigmatic about Licinius Sura. Odd items suggest the orator and friend of letters rather than the soldier; and all inquiry about parentage and relatives is baffled.[7]

---

[1] *HA, Alexander Severus* 65. 5.

[2] *Pan.* 60. 5 f., cf. p. 17. Probably friends of Trajan's father, their coeval. Note also the splendid honours of Q. Sosius Senecio (*cos.* II 107), who married Frontinus' daughter.

[3] e.g. Q. Glitius Agricola, the retiring legate of Belgica (*ILS* 1021), or L. Julius Ursus, who probably acquires a second consulate in 98 (cf. App. 7).

[4] Indeed, nothing proves that Trajan was not the candidate of the Prefect of the Guard. Casperius Aelianus had been a tribune under Vespasian in Judaea, if Philostratus can be trusted, and went with him to Egypt (*Vita Apollonii* VII. 18): hence known to Trajan's father. Tacitus emphasizes a Casperius centurion in the eastern legions under Corbulo (*Ann.* XII. 45 f.; XV. 5. 2). The *nomen* is not common (Schulze, *LE* 270). Aelianus might come from Amisus in Pontus (*IGR* III, 98, cf. *PIR*², C 462).

[5] Victor, *Epit.* 13. 6: 'ob honorem Surae, cuius studio imperium arripuerat, lavacra condidit.'

[6] It becomes more and more likely that 97 is the year of his consulate (App. 10).

[7] App. 85.

Trajan's allies had done their work well. Design collaborated with chance. In what measure, who could tell thereafter? Truth was inexpedient, and the necessary pretences could be safely left to the public pronouncements of reputable senators.[1]

Credulity helped. In the persuasions of the vulgar (and often of the learned) the advent of a ruler of the world could not fail to be foreshadowed or foretold. Various doctrines contributed or clashed. Pliny in the *Panegyricus* proclaims that the ruler may be ordained by God and not by fate or chance. Rome's emperor was discovered, not by the inscrutable power of destiny, but in the open light of day and before the sight of men.[2] Pliny, as was proper, denies destiny—he appeals to the supreme deity of the Roman People. Yet the last word need not be left with divine providence. Whether Juppiter had guided Nerva in his decision, as was duly announced, or, as the populace believed, omens and portents advertised the decrees of fate, a Roman senator who regarded with equal contempt both official truth and the opinions of the mob, and, knowing the 'res publica', knew how an emperor was made, would discern the will and act of certain men.

The fame of Trajan is secure in the select company of the virtuous Caesars.[3] The appellation 'Optimus', emerging soon after his accession, finally won its way into his titulature.[4] Trajan's excellence became canonical, paired with the good fortune of Augustus. 'Felicior Augusto, melior Traiano', such was the joyous asseveration with which the Senate centuries later dutifully welcomed the new emperor that fate or the soldiers had given them.[5] Trajan, as the event was to show, had the luck of Augustus, the audacity of Alexander, and the benevolence of Pompeius.[6] It would be worth knowing how soon it became apparent that Nerva's choice was indeed the best. Hitherto all that a prudent man allowed was to pray for an emperor

---

[1] The mutiny of the Guard was providential, for it led to the adoption of Trajan (*Pan.* 5. 7 ff.); he had done nothing himself, only obeyed (9. 2 f.); he was chosen 'absens et ignarus' (9. 3); reluctant, he had to be compelled, 'igitur cogendus fuisti' (5. 6).

[2] 1. 4 f.

[3] See Cassius Dio's panegyric (LXVIII. 6. 2 ff.).

[4] In the late summer of 114, cf. F. A. Lepper, *Trajan's Parthian War* (1948), 46. For the three stages in the application of 'optimus' to Trajan see M. Durry in his edition of the *Panegyricus* (1938), 12; 231 f. The term was not novel—applied to Claudius in a *senatus consultum* (Pliny, *Epp.* VIII. 6. 13), and to Nerva (Frontinus, *De aquis* 64. 1).

[5] Eutropius VIII. 5. 3—a statement, not a prayer. For the type of ritual acclamation cf. *ILS* 451 (for Caracalla, from the *Acta Fratrum Arvalium*): 'iuvenis triumphis, senex imp., maior Aug.' This helps to explain the grotesque allegation produced by the *Historia Augusta*—'et Traianus senex ad imperium venit' (*Tacitus* 5. 1).

[6] cf. Augustus' prayer for his adopted son Gaius: ᾔτειτο παρὰ τῶν θεῶν εὔνοιαν αὐτῷ τὴν Πομπηΐου, τόλμαν δὲ τὴν Ἀλεξάνδρου, τύχην δὲ τὴν ἑαυτοῦ παρακολουθῆσαι (Plutarch, *Apophth. reg. et imp.* 207e).

better than the worst;[1] and it stood as a notable exception if a ruler improved.[2]

The eloquent Pliny salutes the Emperor as 'castus et sanctus et dis simillimus'.[3] Disclosing to the Senate the fruit of his silent thoughts, the orator avows a frank amazement. Much as he had meditated upon the capacities requisite in the lord of earth and sea, of peace and war, he had never in his imagination been able to create a prince like Trajan. With each one of the Caesars (he continues) some essence of virtue was outweighed by a contrary defect. One ruler was splendid in war but mouldered away in peace, another won repute in the toga but not in arms; and so on, through a catalogue of predictable antitheses. No virtue but with a vice for neighbour—save only in Trajan, where perfection abode, and harmony. The panegyrist, after a powerful recital of noble and amiable qualities all blended together, concludes with the Emperor's advantages of build and body, and the majesty of hair grown prematurely grey.[4]

Signal merits commend Trajan's administration of Rome, Italy, and the provinces.[5] He showed tact in his dealings with the Senate, and an indulgence perhaps excessive in the first years. He was patient under ceremonial, civil and gracious to the individual senator. Splendour and benevolence won the citizens, while tolerance and good sense prevailed everywhere, although the governmental power grew steadily more strong and more concentrated. In the Emperor's management of the high assembly his path was prescribed, and it was easy to tread—he had only to avoid all that rendered Domitian odious and unbearable. The senatorial order could submit to guidance with the better grace for it had been severely chastened under the despotism of Domitian, abruptly sobered by the prospect of civil war. 'You bid us be free', says Pliny to his imperial master, 'and we will be free.'[6]

If Domitian's conduct was a warning, his rule of the Empire might be a model and a challenge. The letters that passed between Trajan and the governor of Bithynia disclose the best side of the Emperor and the worst of the senator.[7] Trajan is firm and sagacious, his mandatory timid and pedantic. The letters of Trajan, along with his edicts, display a proper concern for justice, equity, and sound government; and some are tempted to discover in these documents the character of the man and even his language.[8] Certainty is precluded. The central

---

[1] Pliny, *Pan.* 44. 2: 'summa votorum melior pessimo princeps'.
[2] Tacitus, *Hist.* I. 50. 4: 'et ambigua de Vespasiano fama, solusque omnium ante se principum in melius mutatus est.'
[3] I. 3.   [4] 4. 4 ff.   [5] cf. R. P. Longden, *CAH* XI, 205 ff.
[6] 66. 4: 'iubes esse liberos: erimus.'
[7] The volume *Epistulae ad Traianum* (here referred to as *Epp.* X).
[8] A. Hennemann, *Der äussere u. innere Stil in Trajans Briefen* (Diss. Giessen, 1935).

administration had a long history behind it. Despite the Roman distaste for rules and categories, it had evolved formulas and even principles. A standard chancellery style was to hand, crisp, clean, and
unpretentious. In earlier days, with the friends of the Princeps and
the officials of his household managing imperial business, the ministers and secretaries tended to survive the demise of a ruler, and sometimes to dominate his successor. Now that bureaucracy existed as a
fact, with the system continuous as well as the personnel, the higher
civil servant did not have to transform his habits and prose style when
the source of authority became Nerva after Domitian, and Trajan
after Nerva.[1]

Some adaptation there might be. The acute stylistic perceptions of
the sophisticated secretariat could be suitably invoked to alleviate the
labours of an emperor and simulate his authentic utterance in the
shape of a phrase or the choice of a word. It is not wholly fanciful to
discover traces of Trajan in the letters to Bithynia. He several times
refers to the troops as 'comrades in arms', a practice that Caesar
Augustus was glad to drop once the civil wars were over.[2] The term
also occurs in a rescript. The Imperator, trusting the integrity of his
own sentiments, robustly overrides all legal pedantry. He proclaims
that soldiers' testaments must be held valid in any event. Let them
make what wills they like, what wills they can![3]

Trajan affirms that it is right to protect his 'commilitones' in their
'simplicitas'. The relationship between the Roman Emperor and his
soldiers was conceived as personal and paternal. Happily varying the
'imperator' with the 'commilito', Trajan knew them by name, he
knew each man's exploits.[4] Trajan spoke like a soldier, and he looked
like a soldier even to the way he wore his hair: Nero and Domitian
had affected a structure of locks elaborately curled and waved.[5] The
plebs of Rome easily consigned their favours to the youth and grace
of princes born in the purple, detesting old, scraggy, or squalid rulers.[6]
Furthermore, a large, military, and majestic physique was an enormous asset to impress the plebs, and the army as well, to inspire venera-

---

[1] Thus Cn. Octavius Titinius Capito, in continuous employment as *ab epistulis*
(*ILS* 1448). Nerva's edict, however (cited in *Epp.* x. 58. 7 ff.), looks like his own product.
[2] *Epp.* x. 53; 101; 103. Cf. Suetonius, *Divus Aug.* 25. 1.
[3] Dig. xxix. 1. 1: 'secutus animi mei integritudinem erga optimos fidelissimosque
commilitones simplicitati eorum consulendum existimavi, ut quoquomodo testati fuissent,
rata esset eorum voluntas. faciant igitur testamenta quo modo volent, faciant quo modo
poterint sufficiatque ad bonorum suorum divisionem nuda voluntas testatoris.' He had to
elucidate this later (ib. 24).
[4] *Pan.* 15. 5, cf. 19. 3.
[5] cf. J. M. C. Toynbee, *Num. Chron.*[6] vii (1947), 126 ff. For the iconography of Trajan
see W. H. Gross, *Bildnisse Traians* (1940).
[6] *Hist.* i. 7. 3: 'ipsa aetas Galbae inrisui ac fastidio erat', &c.

tion in provincials and foreigners.[1] The Senate had become unpopular with other orders in Rome; and, after the tumult of the Praetorians, a stern Imperator was required. The governmental class generously belauded Trajan as the restorer of ancient discipline in the army;[2] and they had cause to be thankful for merciless punishment falling on spies and informers.[3]

Pliny pictures the consternation of the enemy when they behold a Roman of the old stamp who embodies the victories of the martial Republic.[4] What were the sentiments of the more refined among the Roman senators?

While aspirants to public distinction frequented the schools of rhetoric and heard the lectures of professors, winning already their first oratorical triumphs in the courts of law, Trajan passed from army to army. If there was little scope for liberal studies in the frontier garrisons of Cappadocia or Moesia, the ancient cities in Syria offered all the diversions of leisure, from the discourse of sages to the pleasure groves at Antioch. The young officer repelled temptation in either guise, it will be assumed.

In his mature age, ex-consul and Emperor, Trajan kept up the military exercises of his early prime, vying with the common soldier in feats of skill and endurance.[5] Manly and laudable also were his recreations—hunting and boating—in sharp contrast to the vices or inertia of other rulers, born as princes or nurtured in the entourage of the Caesars.[6]

Of men who in past ages broke into the governing class through capacity in the arts of war it was often alleged that they were crude, uncouth, uneducated. The reproach was sometimes justified: Caesar Augustus dismissed a legate of consular standing who was weak in orthography.[7] On the other hand, a certain disdain for arts and letters flattered the prejudices of the Roman People, recalling the ancient ideals of rustic simplicity and rustic valour. Alert politicians and hardened careerists knew how to exploit the Roman tradition. They looked stupid, and were believed honest.[8]

---

[1] Thus Domitius Corbulo, 'corpore ingens, verbis magnificis' (*Ann.* XIII. 8. 3).

[2] *Pan.* 18. Trajan's successor also restored discipline (Dio LXIX. 9. 2; *HA, Hadr.* 10. 3).

[3] 34 f. A whole convoy of these criminals was dispatched to the mercy of wind and wave—'memoranda facies, delatorum classis', &c. (35. 1).

[4] 12. 1: 'vident enim Romanum ducem unum ex illis veteribus et priscis.' Cf. 13. 4: 'inter Fabricios et Scipiones et Camillos.'

[5] 13. 1 ff.

[6] 81 f.

[7] Suetonius, *Divus Aug.* 88: 'legato eum consulari successorem dedisse ut rudi et indocto, cuius manu *ixi* pro *ipsi* scriptum animadverterit.'

[8] A great orator will feign total ignorance of Hellenic culture (Cicero, *De oratore* II. 4); and some politicians put on a rustic accent (*Brutus* 137). The type and device is known in other ages.

C. Marius paraded as a plain blunt soldier, savage against the privileges of birth and fashion. If his guile became patent at the time, it was covered up in patriotic and ethical literature, and posterity was left to admire the conventional model of plebeian integrity. The type recurs. Vespasian was the first *novus homo* on the throne. A rough appearance, frugal habits, and a coarse sense of humour accorded well with the soldier and the disciplinarian. Men duly compared him with the generals of the old Republic.[1] Vespasian also possessed many of the qualities for success under the Caesars. His career owed decisive advancement to court influences—an imperial freedman is named—and Nero chose to have his company when he made a tour in Hellas.[2] The unpretentious and reassuring exterior of Vespasian covered subtlety and tenacity.

Some of the Caesars professed an attachment to letters and made a showing in authorship. The most hated of all. Though Claudius by his antiquarian erudition came in for ridicule rather than detestation, aesthetic taste in Nero and in Domitian (extravagant in the one but restrained in the other) was paired with cruelty and vice. Nor were the imperial women any better. In Trajan Rome witnessed the novel spectacle of a ruler whose family life was decorous and orderly, with an exemplary consort.[3] Parents and husbands could breathe again.

Trajan had little to show in the way of intellectual pursuits. He left such things to his wife, Pompeia Plotina; and he was content that his friend Licinius Sura should compose the necessary orations.[4] Pliny extols the Emperor for the honour he confers on eloquence and philosophy: the arts and the sciences had come back from exile.[5] Nor had Trajan any excuse for hostility towards the professors. An anecdote is instructive. The Emperor, with Dio of Prusa in his triumphal car beside him, observes amiably: 'I do not understand what you say, but I love you as myself.'[6]

Trajan perhaps exaggerated his role of plain man. In what the sophist preached there was nothing to exceed the Emperor's understanding, try his patience, or fail his approbation. Dio delivered sermons about an ideal monarch who was chosen by Providence for his high estate, who passed a dedicated life in toil and service, who loved the citizens and the soldiers, who took none but good men for his associates in government.[7]

---

[1] *Hist.* II. 5. 1: 'prorsus, si avaritia abesset, antiquis ducibus par.'
[2] He went in for adulation of Caligula (Suetonius, *Divus Vesp.* 2. 3); Narcissus and the legionary command (4. 1); the Hellenic tour (4. 4).
[3] *Pan.* 83. 5: 'quid enim illa sanctius, quid antiquius?'
[4] Julian, *Caesares* 327b.   [5] *Pan.* 47.
[6] Philostratus, *Vit. soph.* I. 7. 2.
[7] Notably in his two speeches Περὶ βασιλείας (I and III).

The public and official façade exhibits a soldier emperor of the nobler sort, firm, just, and courteous.[1] Behind it is something elusive and perhaps discordant, not easily to be estimated in words.[2] Discipline and modesty concealed a devouring ambition that in youth made him eager for the military career—sharpened by frustration, and later breaking out fiercely and proudly in wars of conquest. It might all end in anger, conceit, and obstinacy. The service of Rome meant less than the love of battle and the pursuit of fame. Ostentatious frugality in the conduct of the Emperor's personal establishment did not preclude official pomp, with games and gladiators and pageantry, with the majesty of great constructions to emulate Nero and Domitian.[3]

One of the principal functions of an aristocracy, so grave inquirers concede, is to exhibit to the plebs a spectacle of splendour, power, and iniquity beyond their reach and beyond their envy. At Rome the 'principes' had been ousted by the Princeps as purveyor to the eyes and appetites of the mob. He was in truth their 'patronus'. Caesar had a plain duty to be a great showman, and Nero in his dying breath exclaimed that he had kept his word: 'qualis artifex pereo!'[4]

Pride and magnificence are not to be disdained or deprecated in a Caesar. Such was the nature of great men. If odd scraps of scandal combine to disclose sundry human frailties, the robust conscience of an imperial people need not have endured discomfort. The habits of Trajan had been formed in the camps. He liked strong drink[5]—and he was addicted to one of the grosser vices.[6] Nor is it certain that all his friends could have stood close scrutiny. A splendid cohort of civil and military dignitaries encompassed the Emperor, and there were men of taste and refinement among the marshals, notably Licinius Sura, erudite, inquiring, and eloquent. Moral transgressions are not likely to be heard of unless one of Caesar's friends happened to clash or incurred disgrace.[7]

The private vices of men who hold power and privilege are a source of reprobation to the moralist, of malignant pleasure to the vulgar

---

[1] The busts are stylized to express 'imperial dignity and a virile, heroic beauty' (G. M. A. Hanfmann, *Observations on Roman Portraiture*. Coll. Latomus XI (1953), 45).

[2] cf. W. Weber, *Rom: Herrschertum u. Reich im zweiten Jahrhundert* (1937), 35.

[3] cf. Fronto on Trajan: 'ut qui sciret populum Romanum duabus praecipue rebus, annona et spectaculis, teneri; imperium non minus ludicris quam seriis probari; maiore damno seria, graviore invidia ludicra neglegi' (p. 210 N = Haines II, p. 216).

[4] Suetonius, *Nero* 49. 1.

[5] Fronto, p. 226 N = Haines II, p. 8: 'potavit satis strenue.' Cf. Dio LXVIII. 7. 4; *HA, Hadr.* 3. 2; Julian, *Caesares* 327c.

[6] Dio LXVIII. 7. 4, cf. 10. 2 (the dancer Pylades); Julian, *Caesares* 333b; *HA, Hadr.* 2. 7; 4, 5 (the imperial page-boys).

[7] Thus C. Vibius Maximus, the Prefect of Egypt (*P.Oxy.* 471). Note, however, what Epictetus could say about Sura, adducing the dancer Philostorgus—ἤθελες ἂν σὺ μετὰ Σούρα κοιμᾶσθαι; (Arrian, *Diss. Epicteti* III. 17. 4.)

and superficial. A Roman historian, sceptical and contemptuous of received opinions, and acutely aware of the debatable frontier between good and bad, dwells with predilection on the apparent paradox of senators who passed their leisure among the frivolous or vicious but displayed integrity when governing a province and energy at the head of armies.[1]

In Trajan any minor and personal shortcomings, known or surmised, were for the moment barely relevant. How would the new emperor, whom necessity imposed, face the social test of birth and origin?

The name 'Ulpius' was of recent emergence on the consular *Fasti*, and highly unprepossessing. Moreover, it labelled the first provincial among the Caesars. Though vigilance is requisite when claims and pedigrees in the new nobility are investigated, whether their origin lies within the borders of Italy or outside, it is clear that the Ulpii are not an enfranchised Spanish family but Italian ultimately, of ancient colonial extraction.[2] Whether a family of the provincial notables derived from Italian or native stock mattered little at this late epoch, nor would it always have been easy to sift and catalogue the different strains in the racial amalgam of the new Romans from the western lands. None the less, the first immigrant to wear the purple is a large and startling fact. Pliny, it might seem, is blind to the splendour of his subject—he missed the chance to expound the imperial destiny of Rome. Not at all. The orator was alert and circumspect, managing a theme both painful and perilous. For indeed the accession of Trajan is not merely the emergence of a military man, sent by Providence to save a government in collapse. It publishes the triumph of the provincial aristocrats.

With what sentiments the Roman from Spain subdued himself to the eloquence of Pliny and surveyed the company before him, it would take a Tacitus to divine. Tacitus might also have penetrated behind the pageantry to depict the varying emotions of the Senate. The thing must have come as a shock to some at least in the upper order, to the remnant of the *nobilitas*, to the senators of suburban Italy. When confronted with the wealth and resources of the provinces, Italy now seemed impoverished, but Italy should not be utterly devoid of virtue and vitality. 'Non adeo aegram Italiam', they must have murmured.[3] Too late to hope for an emperor from the old ruling families—the

Note in margin: FIRST PROVINCIAL IN PURPLE

---

[1] *Ann.* VI. 32. 4 (L. Vitellius); XIII. 46. 3 (Otho); XVI. 18. 2 (Petronius). By contrast, the verdict on Galba—'magis extra vitia quam cum virtutibus' (*Hist.* I. 49. 2).

[2] Despite the allegation of Dio (LXVIII. 4. 1). See App. 81.

[3] Like the counsellors of Claudius Caesar (*Ann.* XI. 23. 2).

Caesars had broken and all but annihilated them. In Rome's hour of need a ruler might still have come out of the ancient and kindred races of the land, perhaps from the Sabine country, or at least from the North which, though provincial in origin and character, was proud and fervent in its claim to be Italy.

If the truth so abruptly revealed to the sons of Italy was a surprise as well as a vexation, the fault was their own. They had only to look about them and ponder upon the recruitment of the military oligarchy. For the edification of the dull *nobilitas* or the more pretentious among the municipal senators, a powerful sermon on the Empire was waiting to be delivered. If the succession lapsed, or if it threw up a flagrantly incompetent ruler, what claims and qualities would be decisive in the choice of the new emperor?

When men cast their minds back to Neronian times and reflected upon the old nobility, its ruin consummated by that ruler, yet failing also through its own incapacity, they might have been impelled to ask whether too high a value had not been set upon birth and pedigree, whether the energy and patriotism of newer stocks had not been too long scorned and neglected. There were great men under Nero as under Domitian. While Nero sat at Rome and, passing from boy to man, passed only from frivolity to vice and murder, Domitius Corbulo, a general worthy of the conquering Republic, led the Roman legions beyond the river Euphrates, vindicated the majesty of the Empire— and preserved the dynasty. Corbulo had been cheated of conquests in Germany by the timid jealousy of Claudius Caesar. From Nero he earned the recompense of duty, the command to die.

The Flavian dynasty developed like the Julii and Claudii, degenerate and intolerable, with a bloodthirsty Nero, but worse than Nero, for Domitian kept the armies under control and knew how to govern an empire. Although the chance and prospect of his overthrow might seem remote enough, speculation could no longer be confined to the names illustrious in history. It would have to take into reckoning the new aristocracy, in its wider extent.

Who, indeed, were the Flavii? Small people from Reate in the Sabine country—Vespasian's grandfather had been a soldier, his father a tax-gatherer.[1] Vespasian himself was a utilitarian rather than a decorative figure. To be pelted with turnips when proconsul of Africa is no sign of dignity.[2] Nor was his wife any credit.[3] The social distinction of the Flavii, for what it was worth, came from Vespasian's

---

[1] Suetonius, *Divus Vesp.* 1. 2 f. [2] 4. 3.
[3] 3. 1. Flavia Domitilla was originally not of full citizen status, but only Latin—and she had been the mistress of a Roman knight from Sabrata. On her death Vespasian lived in concubinage with Caenis, the freedwoman of Antonia.

mother, who belonged to a reputable family of local consequence at Nursia.[1] On that score there were provincial magnates who had nothing to fear from the comparison, men of old colonial stock or descendants of native dynasts in the western lands.[2] When one of them grasped the power, the moral was plain.

---

[1] I. 3.   [2] Ch. XLIII.

V. *CAPAX IMPERII*

TRAJAN, the candidate of the generals, was neither able nor eager to announce forthwith a dynastic heir to the power from his own family circle, even though he gave to Aelius Hadrianus the hand of his grand-niece Vibia Sabina.[1] If Trajan were to die before long, the decision would rest with the marshals—and he may have felt (but could hardly enforce) a preference for Licinius Sura. But Trajan was not thinking about death. If the fortune of Rome held, the Imperator might enjoy a reign unsurpassed in length since Caesar Augustus.

Trajan was still young, in the prime of life. When adopted by Nerva he was just forty-four.[2] The Caesars since Augustus ran to extremes—young princes wild and unteachable, old men sad and sorry, imprisoned by their experience or debilitated by various infirmities. Galba at seventy was quite incapable of learning the trade or art, and Nerva at sixty was too fragile. The subtle Vespasian was in his sixtieth year when the armies proclaimed him. Only two of the Caesars hitherto had the right age along with a safe and dynastic succession. Destiny converted them into types of contrast. Tiberius was forty-four when Augustus adopted him; but Tiberius had to wait ten years—and then he lived on for twenty-three more. Titus succeeded his father in his fortieth year, and the world was happy; but Titus died after a rule of two years and two months, secure in his unfulfilled renown. The favourites of the Roman People died young. Popularity and long life were hardly compatible.

Of all the Caesars since Tiberius, with the exception of Galba and Vespasian, only Trajan passed through the regular stages of a senator's promotion, rising to the consular command of an army. Galba had military repute behind him when he became Princeps, cheaply acquired or enhanced by the ignorant. Vespasian's achievement seemed solid and unimpeachable—active warfare when legionary legate during the invasion of Britain, and the arduous subjugation of Judaea. Vespasian had never been tempted by splendour or risks. The new emperor, however, young, energetic, and a soldier by training, seemed likely to bring a change from the foreign policy of the Flavian dynasty with its timid advances or equivocal compromises. The war might come at once, to enhance the glory of Trajan, to blot out the memory of the Praetorians' rising and the threat of open strife for the power.

---

[1] *HA, Hadr.* 2. 10 (before 101).
[2] Assuming him born in 53 (p. 31).

Trajan was still on the Rhine when Tacitus wrote his second monograph, an essay on the land and people of Germany. In the *Germania*
he is mentioned once, and only as a date, the second consulate in 98,
so it might seem at first sight.[1] In itself the treatise carried a clear
appeal to the lettered public. It was no long or exacting task to compile: almost every item derives from written sources.[2] None the less,
in the midst of an ethnographical catalogue, style, passion, and prejudice betray the preoccupations of the author.

A native tribe across the lower Rhine, the Bructeri, had been wiped
out by a coalition of their neighbours. Resentment at their arrogance
was the cause, or greed for booty—or an especial grace of the gods towards the Roman People. A Roman army contemplated the massacre.
More than sixty thousand of the Bructeri perished—and not by Roman
weapons but, what is more splendid, to gladden Roman eyes.[3]

The incident was either recent, belonging to the year 97, or recently
brought to conspicuous notoriety at Rome.[4] The language of Tacitus
is ferocious and exultant, heavily charged with moralizing. No less
fervent is what follows. He utters a solemn prayer. May the nations
persist, since they cannot love the Romans, in hating one another: as
fate bears remorselessly on Rome, fortune can offer no greater boon
now than the disunion of Rome's enemies.[5]

The passage is not a little enigmatic, and has been much debated
in its interpretation. The present condition of Rome and of the Empire,
it should seem, gave no cause for fear and foreboding, with Trajan
emperor. Yet the reference is clearly to the present.[6] Moreover, the
phrase 'urgentibus imperii fatis' is most ominous. It evokes the age-
old menace to Rome from the northern peoples, with a clear echo of
the tone and language in which the classic historian of the Republic
prepared his readers for the capture of Rome by the Gallic invaders.[7]

[1] *Germ.* 37. 2.
[2] Ch. XI.
[3] 33. 1 f.: 'nam ne spectaculo quidem proelii invidere. super sexaginta milia non armis
telisque Romanis, sed, quod magnificentius est, oblectationi oculisque ceciderunt.'
[4] Spurinna's exploit might be another aspect of the same episode—he intimidated the
Bructeri and made them take back their king (Pliny, *Epp.* II. 7. 2). Probably not, cf. App. 6.
[5] 33. 2: 'maneat quaeso duretque gentibus, si non amor nostri, at certe odium sui,
quando urgentibus imperii fatis nihil iam praestare fortuna maius potest quam hostium
discordiam.'
[6] G. Andresen, *Wochenschr. für cl. Phil.* 1915, 756; R. Heinze, *Vom Geist des Römertums*
(1938), 255 ff.; J. G. C. Anderson in his edition (Oxford, 1938), 163, and in his review
(*JRS* XXVI (1936), 274) of the text of R. P. Robinson (*Am. Phil. Ass., Phil. Monographs*
V (1935)). See further, reinforcing Heinze, V. Pöschl, *Wiener Studien* LXIX (1956),310 ff.
[7] Livy v. 36. 6: 'iam urgentibus Romanam urbem fatis', echoing the doom of another
city, Veii, 'postremo iam fato quoque urgente' (ib. 22. 8). The note of fate is also
enhanced by another verb, 'deorum monita ingruente fato spreta' (32. 7). Compare also
Lucan on Alexander, 'perque Asiae populos fatis urgentibus actus' (x. 30)—that is, the
doom of Asia.

From that catastrophe the Romans emerged to vigour and empire. When they had at last defeated the Gauls in Italy they were ready to engage any adversary.[1] The mastery of the world ensued. No rival remained, and no threat to the dominion of Rome—only civil war, letting the vanquished rise again and the outer peoples break in.

Though Rome, in the opinion consecrated since the time of Augustus, was built to endure for ever, though 'aeternitas' was predicated of the Empire and of the imperial peace,[2] sombre thoughts might invade a reflective man. Past history declared that empires were transient— internal discord, the decline of energy, new and vigorous competitors.[3] The civil wars of 68 and 69 were fresh in mind—rebellion among the nations, the burning of the Capitol, and prophecies of doom.[4] And only a few months earlier a catastrophe threatened. Even now, stability was precarious.

Rome and the Germans, it was a story of two hundred and ten years since the first conflict of arms. 'Tam diu Germania vincitur.'[5] Tacitus gives a date. He may have hoped it would be the end of an era. In that long period of the German wars many disasters had befallen the Romans, yet the Roman invasions brought no conquest. Peace came, or rather warfare lapsed, yet the Germans intervened in 69, and Domitian (it was asserted) celebrated triumphs without gaining victories.[6] The free peoples of Germany were a deadlier enemy than any monarch of Parthia.[7]

It was not for the consular Cornelius Tacitus to play the mentor to a military emperor. None the less, there may be anger brooding beneath the exultant thanks rendered to fortune for the extinction of a German tribe, and fierce resentment that Roman arms should never be employed for a war of conquest and revenge. In the days of Caesar Augustus the Roman legions traversed Germany as far as the Elbe. In the time of Tacitus that river was only a name.[8]

The author of the *Germania* confutes Domitian's claim that Germany had been conquered.[9] He also implies a hope, if he may not utter the expectation, that Trajan, being now on the Rhine, will settle the German question by methods altogether different from those of the

---

[1] Polybius I. 6. 6; II. 20. 8 ff.

[2] Virgil, *Aen.* I. 278 f.; Tibullus II. 5. 23; Livy IV. 3. 4; XXVIII. 28. 10. Compare, though not yet so positive, Cicero, *Pro C. Rabirio perduellionis reo* 33. For the notion of 'aeternitas' see further p. 208.

[3] cf. Sallust, *Cat.* 2. 4 ff.   [4] *Hist.* IV. 54. 2.

[5] *Germ.* 37. 2.   [6] ib. 6: 'triumphati magis quam victi.'

[7] ib. 3: 'non Samnis, non Poeni, non Hispaniae Galliaeve, ne Parthi quidem saepius admonuere: quippe regno Arsacis acrior est Germanorum libertas.'

[8] 41. 2: 'flumen inclutum et notum olim; nunc tantum auditur.'

[9] cf. H. Nesselhauf, *Hermes* LXXX (1952), 122 ff.

Flavian emperors.[1] In truth, the Danube had become the more important frontier; and Trajan soon went there. If Tacitus had composed an ethnographical essay a year later, he would have been tempted, if not compelled, to write about the peoples beyond the Danube—with ample detail about the Suebi in Bohemia, the Sarmatae Jazyges of the great plains, the Dacians of Transylvania, and more Sarmatians, the Rhoxolani. It would not be at all easy. For Germany he had full and valuable sources: knowledge about Sarmatians was probably traditional and obsolete, and nobody perhaps had recently written upon Dacia.

The career and character of the new emperor, the presumed ambitions of a military man, and the cautious policy of the Flavian rulers made it a fair guess that Trajan proposed to launch forth on a war of conquest. No prediction of Tacitus about Trajan, whether made by him or merely reported, would be crude and obtrusive. He was saved by good sense—and by scepticism.

It was better for a senator to refrain altogether from forecasts about foreign and military policy. He might fall into errors of tact or judgement or both. On the Rhine and beyond the Rhine nothing remained to be done, so it appears. Domitian devised a large operation which he carried out felicitously despite all the malice against him then and later, with talk of spurious triumphs, with recurrent fables. Domitian subjugated the Chatti and bound them by a treaty of vassalage, with the result that a wide region south and south-east from the Chatti was covered and secure. Other measures followed (force or diplomacy), the whole frontier was organized, and the strength of the two armies could be reduced from eight legions to six.[2]

The Danube showed disturbance all the way from Bohemia to the Black Sea, and a national kingdom emerged among the Dacian tribes. Their ruler Decebalus after the vicissitudes of war won recognition, as a friend and ally of the Roman People, from Domitian. That emperor, in conflict with Germans and Sarmatians, required support beyond the frontier; and he also got into touch with certain powerful peoples of inner Germany, behind Bohemia.[3]

---

[1] Extreme opinions have been held about the 'purpose' of the *Germania*—a moralizing satire or a political pamphlet; and, as a pamphlet that reveals the German menace, designed either to incite Trajan to action or indirectly to commend him for having done nothing rash. For a sagacious exposition see J. G. C. Anderson, o.c. IX ff.; also J. Perret in his edition (Budé, 1949), 6 ff. For the literary genre to which the treatise belongs, Ch. XI. The violent language in the digressions on the Bructeri (*Germ.* 33) and on the whole history of the relations between Romans and Germans (37) can fairly be taken as a clue to the author's own sentiments. Observe also the contemptuous note in Tacitus' reference to the natives of the 'decumates agri' (29. 4), annexed by the Flavians.

[2] For the purpose and success of Domitian's operations see *CAH* XI (1936), 162 ff.

[3] Dio LXVII. 5. 2 f. (the Semnones and the Lugii).

The device of a treaty with the king of the Dacians, which was evoked by military emergency, could be defended as traditional, and it worked well, so far as known. No menace to the Roman dominion, but a centre of stability in the Danubian lands to curb and separate the nomad peoples on either side of Dacia. Moreover, time or accident might decide, the Dacian monarchy perhaps collapsing as suddenly as it had arisen. The like had happened before.[1]

Not but what an arrangement of that kind could easily be deplored as damaging to the prestige of an imperial people, and easily be disowned. Trajan spent a winter on the lower Danube. Nothing happened. Pliny praises his emperor for a resolute stand on the river, nobly disdaining to force war upon a reluctant adversary.[2] It would not perhaps have strained the orator's agility to combine therewith some intimation of battle and victory, with a genuine triumph at last.[3]

Martial themes were generously advertised in the early years of Trajan's rule.[4] The show and will to war does not always issue in action. Some of Trajan's counsellors (it may be surmised) took a sober view of Danubian policy, quietly deprecating the things said about Domitian. Others were eager and buoyant, not least those 'viri militares' who lacked experience in the field. Trajan himself, it may be, had been thwarted all the time of blood and battle.

If the Imperator insisted, it might not be calamitous. There was a greater danger, perhaps, lest he seek adventure in the eastern lands, lured by fame and legend, and by various fallacies. Dacia offered, and no need anxiously to look for a pretext.

Trajan would pay heed to some at least of the leading consulars. Notably the imperial legates past and present. From the body of the senators no questions arose when they heard instructions about peace or war, happy enough that faction strife had ceased and prosecutions for treason, even though no liberties were regained. It was a relief that the Imperator should turn to provinces and armies as his chief concern. Trajan, although imposed by necessity, was 'civilis'. Not a tyrant but a citizen, not a master but a parent, and comporting himself, as Pliny says, 'like one of us'.[5] The senior statesmen, Frontinus

---

[1] Burebistas the Dacian, whose empire disappeared with his death soon after 44 B.C., and Maroboduus in Bohemia, attacked by Rome, converted into an ally under emergency, and finally subverted by Tiberius Caesar. For a defence of Domitian's Danubian policy see *CAH* xi, 176; 185 f.

[2] *Pan.* 16. 1 f.

[3] 16. 3–17. 4 (probably added, however, when the Dacian War had begun).

[4] Notably Victoria, Hercules, and Mars as types or legends, cf. P. L. Strack, *Untersuchungen zur r. Reichsprägung des zweiten Jahrhunderts* I (1931), 67 ff.; H. Mattingly, *BMC, R. Emp.* III (1936), lxvii f. There was even a triumphal arch by the year 100 (Strack, o.c. 92 ff.).

[5] *Pan.* 2. 3; 63. 2.

and Spurinna, may have reinforced those prepossessions, with a firm hint of their own foresight and sagacity, from time to time.

Not impairing the general amity, but beneficial, was the fact that Trajan had been away from the capital for a large part of his career. At any given moment the provinces of Caesar detain about forty praetorian senators and ten consulars.[1] The high assembly is therefore weakened by the absence of active members in their best years; and the 'vir militaris', successful but not abnormal, who becomes consul quickly after two posts abroad, and who holds two commands after his consulship, will have spent altogether in the provinces something like a dozen years of his lifetime between thirty and fifty.

The Senate comprised about six hundred members. In the last epoch of the Republic, weight and consequence belonged to the ex-consuls. With the Empire the consulate alters in character and function, and a paramount oligarchy emerges—though of a new complexion—drawn in the main from the men who govern the armed provinces of Caesar. More consuls and praetors now, it is true, but the Senate harbours a mass of nonentities, as before.

If Trajan was an unfamiliar figure to many of the minor senators, the chief men in the military oligarchy knew him: exploits of active warfare were not required. It was evident from the beginning (and sometimes admitted) that, though the Empire needed a single head, it could not be governed by one man alone. Caesar Augustus had trusty allies and many subordinates of value. Each ruler would need a cluster of friends—it was his principal duty to acquire them.[2] Trajan was well provided. He enjoyed a further advantage denied to most of the Caesars. Several consular legates with whom his career ran level, or whom it even overtook, were his seniors in age, and he could profit from their guidance.[3]

There was an inner circle of Trajan's adherents. In the first place, his own kinsfolk and those of his wife, his father's friends and his own.[4] Apart from persons related by blood or marriage, Trajan's most powerful allies will be sought among the consuls of the last decade of Domitian's reign. A man marked out for prominence in the military hierarchy might expect to hold one of the great commands within five

---

[1] The total of praetorians comprises the legionary legates, three *iuridici*, and eight provincial governors. Fewer senators in the public provinces, the term is annual, the persons not commensurate in rank and value (only two ex-consuls). The grand total for both categories is about eighty.

[2] *Pan.* 85. 6: 'praecipuum est principis opus amicos parare.'

[3] e.g. Ser. Julius Servianus (*suff.* 90), born about 47 (App. 7), and Cn. Pompeius Longinus (*suff.* 90).

[4] Ch. XLIV, with App. 87.

years of his consulate, if not sooner. Promotions had been rapid. Next after the recent consuls come the men of praetorian rank, commanding legions or governing provinces in the last years of Domitian or in 97, eager for advancement and pinning their hopes to influential consulars. From the large company of the legionary legates emerge the governors of the eight praetorian provinces who proceed at once, and almost inevitably, to the consulate; and hence, in due season, the consular legates.[1]

Nothing less than a catalogue of governors, registering the appointments made in turn by Domitian, by Nerva, and by Trajan, would suffice to indicate the shifts and hazards in the transmission of the imperial power. What can be recovered is imperfect, some items are ambiguous, but several names offer guidance.[2]

Of Domitian's consular legates a number were now dead, others in seclusion or decay. Some had earned the right to be distrusted. Silence envelops Tettius Julianus after his victory over the Dacians. His was an exceptional glory, yet overshadowed by Lappius Maximus, who had won a civil war and saved the dynasty. Domitian gave Lappius a second consulate in 95, a distinction that had become preternaturally rare in the course of the previous decade.[3] Neither of those generals could with safety have been put in charge of Syria.

It would be worth knowing who was sent to Syria in that late and suspicious epoch of the reign[4], or, for that matter, which of the consulars held the two commands on the Rhine, the three on the Danube. As it happens, only three of the legates in office at Domitian's death can be certified. Two were replaced—the governors of Britain and of Moesia Inferior—though not all at once.[5] The third, Pomponius Bassus, who had been appointed to Cappadocia in 95, continued for five years, passing thence to a civilian employment in Italy.[6]

One of Trajan's first acts was to bring his ally Julius Servianus to the Upper German command: his previous occupations elude inquiry.[7] Pompeius Longinus, an experienced person, who is discovered in Pannonia at the beginning of 98, might have been there for some time.[8] The new legate of Britain was Avidius Quietus, noted for refined taste

---

[1] App. 15 f.; 18.　　　　　　　　　　[2] For details and persons, App. 14 f.

[3] Since 85, only Nerva in 90 (App. 12).

[4] Ch. II, with App. 3.

[5] A diploma issued in 98 (*CIL* XVI, 43) shows that the predecessor of T. Avidius Quietus had been a certain Nepos: i.e. P. Metilius Nepos (*suff.* 91). In January of 97 (?L.) Julius Marinus (*suff.* ? 93) is attested in Moesia Inferior (*CIL* XVI, 41): perhaps replaced by Q. Pomponius Rufus (*suff.* 95), who is there in 99 (ib. 44 f.).

[6] For his tenure, evidence cited in *PIR*[1], P 530. After this, the charge of the *alimenta* (*ILS* 6106; 6675). He had been legate under Trajan's father in Asia in 79/80 (*ILS* 8797).

[7] Perhaps a Danubian command (p. 34).

[8] *CIL* XVI, 42, cf. p. 15.

and much approved by men of principle and learning.[1] Avidius had come to manhood before the end of Nero's reign.[2] Pomponius Rufus (attested in Lower Moesia in 99) began his fortunes long ago with a command from Galba in the rebellion against Nero, but suffered delay or vicissitudes in his career.[3] Further, Trajan's first legate of Syria: he may be Javolenus Priscus, whom posterity knows as an eminent lawyer. Not a young man either. Javolenus possessed abundant acquaintance with the provinces—before his consulate he had seen Dalmatia, Numidia, and Britain; and Domitian had used him to govern Upper Germany shortly after the civil war.[4]

The legates thus recorded or surmised in office early in Trajan's reign seem to form a heterogeneous company. One thing they have in common, the lack of consular parentage; and only one of them, Julius Servianus, earns from Trajan the distinction of a second consulate. New figures also emerge (merit or favour), notably Licinius Sura, Glitius Agricola, and Laberius Maximus, and the period of Trajan's first war discloses a whole group of marshals, but an interval must pass before Trajan and his friends can decisively modify the complexion of the military oligarchy.

The Emperor did not choose to tarry long in Rome. The legions called, and glory. In 101 he invaded the land of the Dacians, girt by mountain and forest, and defended with fanatical valour. The first campaign suffered a check, with heavy losses in a pitched battle.[5] The whole enterprise was now seen to be very arduous, and the victory won in the next year did not result in total conquest. Decebalus kept his kingdom as a vassal, surrendering a tract of territory as penalty or guarantee.[6]

There is no means of assessing the quality of the high command. Trajan had his chief adherents with him, Servianus and Sura;[7] and the governors of the three Danubian provinces all found employment— Glitius Agricola holding Pannonia, Cilnius Proculus and Laberius Maximus in the Moesian commands.[8] Some of the generals may

---

[1] CIL XVI, 43. A friend of Thrasea Paetus and of Plutarch (PIR², A1410). Perhaps appointed by Nerva, not by Trajan.

[2] As emerges from Epp. VI. 29. 1. He had been a legionary legate not later than 82 (ILS 6105).

[3] CIL XVI, 44 f.; IRT 537 (Lepcis).

[4] ILS 1015, cf. CIL XVI, 36. For Syria, App. 3.

[5] Dio LXVIII. 8. 2, cf. (perhaps exaggerating) P. L. Strack, Untersuchungen zur r. Reichsprägung des zweiten Jahrhunderts I (1931), 123 ff.

[6] Dio LXVIII. 9. 5.

[7] For Sura, Dio LXVIII. 9. 2. For Servianus, Pliny, Epp. III. 17. 3: 'exspectantem in horas timentemque pro capite amicissimo.' Not perhaps both there at the same time.

[8] Consular dona are recorded for the first two (ILS 1021a; Not. Scav. 1925, 224). Laberius had splendid exploits to his credit in 102 (Dio LXVIII. 9. 4). Further, the man left in charge of occupied Dacia might be Cn. Pompeius Longinus (suff. 90), cf. App. 14.

previously have known warfare in the field as legionary legates, some had certainly not.[1] Trajan duly conferred military decorations, and four iterated consulates advertised a successful war—two before it was over—Servianus and Sura in 102, and two at the conclusion—Glitius Agricola and Laberius Maximus in 103.

The other armies were in safe control. From Britain to Syria the list is almost complete.[2] It exhibits contrasts and one apparent anomaly. Julius Quadratus, the legate of Syria, was an elderly man and totally devoid of military training. Political reasons operated and personal favour—a friend of Trajan.[3]

In the meantime the younger men had been coming on, the legionary commanders of the period 94–97. Prompt access offered to the consulate—and some abbreviation might be assumed in the normal stages and intervals.[4] In the forefront stand the *ordinarii* of 99, Cornelius Palma and Sosius Senecio. Neither was of consular parentage, but Sosius had married the daughter of Julius Frontinus.[5] Both Palma and Sosius are soon discovered in consular commands.[6]

A steady succession follows. Fabius Justus and Publilius Celsus are not far behind, consuls in 102.[7] Fabius, like Sosius, was a cultivated person, a friend of the orators and men of letters: Publilius remains intangible.[8]

After a brief lull hostilities broke out again on the Danube in 105. In the next year Dacia was annexed and converted into a province of consular rank with a garrison of several legions.[9] Nor had the government lost sight of the eastern frontier. Cornelius Palma, the legate of Syria, added to the Empire the land of the Nabataean Arabs.[10] When Palma left to assume his second consulship, Fabius Justus took his place.[11] Sosius Senecio (it will be presumed) held a high command in the conquest of Dacia—consul for the second time he opens the year 107, sharing the *fasces* with Licinius Sura, who now reaches the pinnacle of 'consul tertio'.

---

[1] e.g. Glitius Agricola.   [2] App. 14 f.

[3] viz. A. Julius Quadratus (*suff.* 94, *II ord.* 105). Legate in Asia for two years c. 80 (*ILS* 8881), perhaps there with Trajan's father. A friend of Trajan, cf. the inscription (bilingual) found near the *Traianeum* at Pergamum and referring to 'Iuppiter amicalis' (*IGR* IV, 336).

[4] As had happened for Trajan himself (p. 33).   [5] *ILS* 1104 f.

[6] Palma in Tarraconensis in 100 or 101 (Martial XII. 9. 1); Sosius in an unknown military province c. 103 (*Epp.* IV. 4. 1).

[7] Also D. Terentius Scaurianus (*suff.* 102 or 104) and the *Ignotus* honoured at Nemausus (*CIL* XII, 3169).

[8] For L. Fabius Justus, p. 74; about L. Publilius Celsus in the reign of Trajan nothing is known save the second consulate in 113—and a 'statua triumphalis' (Dio LXVIII. 16. 2).

[9] Probably three legions, cf. R. Syme, *Laureae Aquincenses* I (1938), 267 ff. The first legate was D. Terentius Scaurianus, cf. *CIL* XVI, 57; 160; 163.

[10] Either in 105 or 106, cf. p. 222.   [11] *AE* 1940, 210 (nr. Palmyra).

Last in sequence among the Trajanic marshals may be discerned the legionary legates from the period of the wars, some with service and decorations, and one who came in time to lead a victorious army in Dacia soon after his consulate.[1] Abundant testimony is available. The names reveal the true younger generation of Trajan's principate.[2] When their seniors have died or receded, their influence will be in the ascendant a decade later, and some will hope to fight in another war, earning the decorations of a consular command.

Such, in outline, is the system of rank and promotion superintended by Trajan and his allies. Some of Trajan's friendships began not at Rome but in the provinces, local magnates as well as senators in public employment. He had also come to know the leading dignitaries among the knights.[3]

From its inception the monarchy held out splendid rewards to members of the equestrian order. While the provinces of Caesar have senators to govern them, knights administer the revenues; the ruler of Egypt under Caesar in the place of the kings is a prefect of equestrian rank; and other territories (though none comparable to Egypt) are administered by knights. Before the reign of Augustus ends, three posts are created in the city of Rome—to manage the Praetorian Guard, the fire-brigade, and the food-supply. The path is open for education, talent, and loyalty to rise under the patronage of the dynasty. And the system develops. After the end of the Julii and Claudii, knights gradually supersede freedmen of the household in the imperial secretariat.[4]

Various avenues led to the coveted post of 'procurator Augusti', which ranked high in official status, quite apart from social prestige already owned or thereby acquired: it is rated parallel and equivalent to what the consulate is in the senatorial career.[5]

Of prime value among the procuratorships are the two posts in the wealthy provinces of Gaul. The one embraced Lugdunensis and Aquitania. The other took in along with Belgica the territory of the German commands. This procurator managed the disbursements for

---

[1] C. Julius Quadratus Bassus (suff. 105), general in the Second Dacian War, cf. the inscription from Pergamum, A. v. Premerstein, Bayerische S-B, 1934, Heft 3, 15 f. See App. 14.

[2] For the younger marshals, App. 16.

[3] To be safely assumed, even if Pliny did not affirm how happy people were 'quod equestris ordinis decora honore nominum sine monitore signares' (Pan. 23. 1).

[4] For the development of the equestrian offices cf. H. M. Last, CAH xi, 426 ff.; A. N. Sherwin-White, BSR Papers xv (1939), 11 ff.; H. G. Pflaum, Les Procurateurs équestres sous le Haut-Empire romain (1950).

[5] Agr. 4. 1: 'utrumque avum procuratorem Caesarum habuit, quae equestris nobilitas est.'

two huge armies (about eighty thousand men all told). In a season of civil war he counted for much more than the senator who was legate of Belgica, and the alternatives confronting him might well be death or hazard and high promotion.[1] The normal process, if it did not carry a procurator to the splendid posts in the metropolis (and these were liable to be intercepted by court favourites), none the less ensured that his son would be a senator if he wished, and probably consul.

Merely to become a senator was no adequate recompense for an equestrian magnate, or testimony of his weight. It might look more like supersession. Though such a man might have risen from the lower grades, having served as a centurion in the army, many knights belonged to families of solid repute, at social parity with senators or connected by blood or marriage. There were visible and vestimentary distinctions. It is public status, 'dignitas', that marks the senator, not a genuine difference of rank in society.[2]

In real power the men who governed Egypt or commanded the imperial Guard had long since come to equal, and sometimes to surpass, the consular legates. Their secret influence could be exorbitant. Domitian's reign showed formidable examples. Julius Ursus rose to be Prefect of Egypt and Prefect of the Guard. It is the same Ursus whom a mysterious incident imperfectly reveals. When the Emperor, at variance with his consort, would have put her to death, Ursus by diplomatic arts established concord in the Palace. Although he soon incurred Domitian's displeasure, he was saved by the intervention of Julia, the daughter of Titus, and was elevated to the consulate. Julius Ursus is suitably discovered holding the *fasces* for the second time in 98.[3]

Trajan had various useful allies in this class. At his accession a certain Junius Rufus was governing Egypt, whom Domitian had appointed and Nerva did not recall. Trajan kept him until the summer of 98.[4] The next prefect was Pompeius Planta, a veteran procurator.[5] To replace Planta after three years Trajan sent Minicius Italus, whose

[1] The procurator in 69 was put to death (*Hist.* I. 58. 1). In 97 the procurator may have been Sex. Attius Suburanus (*AE* 1939, 60: Heliopolis).

[2] *Ann.* II. 33. 3: 'distinctos senatus et equitum census, non quia diversi natura', &c.; Suetonius, *Divus Vesp.* 9. 2: 'utrumque ordinem non tam libertate inter se quam dignitate differre.' Cf. Josephus, *AJ* XIX. 3. For social parities, A. Stein, *Der r. Ritterstand* (1927), 195 ff. A continuance of conditions in the late Republic, cf. R. Syme, *Rom. Rev.* (1939), 13 f., 81 ff., 357 f., 384 f.

[3] For this complicated (and hazardous) reconstruction see App. 7. Kinsman (it is to be presumed) and adopting parent of Julius Servianus. Ursus was succeeded by L. Laberius Maximus, brought from Egypt to be colleague of Cornelius Fuscus (as can be deduced from *P. Berol.* 8334).

[4] For dates and details see A. Stein, *Die Präfekten von Ägypten* (1950), 47 ff.

[5] Procurator of Lycia under Vespasian (*IGR* III, 466).

career, beginning with equestrian military posts under Vespasian, exhibited a decisive act of fidelity to Domitian when he was procurator of Asia: he suppressed a disloyal proconsul and took charge of the province.[1] Upon Minicius followed in 103 Vibius Maximus, benefiting by a rapid advancement.[2] Vibius, who had senatorial connexions and literary tastes, was later impugned for dubious morality.[3] His successor was a man promoted from the centurionate.[4]

In the station of supreme trust at the Emperor's flank stood the commander of the Guard.[5] Installing his prefect, Trajan uttered a noble pronouncement. He handed him the sword of office, to use in the Emperor's protection—or against him, if duty to the Commonwealth should so enjoin.[6] This was Attius Suburanus, who first emerged in the troubles of 68 and 69, and who soon attached himself to two persons of influence (Vibius Crispus and Julius Ursus). A long series of employments brought him to the procuratorship of Gallia Belgica, which post he was holding (it could be conjectured) in the crisis of 97.[7]

Another prefect early in the reign (perhaps the colleague of Suburanus) soon asked for his release. The Emperor complied with reluctance, and, in touching and ceremonial farewell to his old friend, went down to the coast and watched the ship recede on the horizon.[8] Suburanus' command over the Guard was also very brief: promoted to the Senate, he became consul in 101, and again in 104, this time as *ordinarius*.[9]

A Caesar in the dynastic succession inherited the devotion of plebs and soldiers, and a usurper need not fail if ready with cash and pageantry. Nor was the effort arduous to win the goodwill of the senatorial order in the first days. The exacting test came from the personal adherents of a new emperor, with multifarious claims to satisfy, not all open and avowed. Hence lengthy consular lists,

---

[1] *ILS* 1374: 'proc. provinciae Asiae quam / mandatu principis vice defuncti procos. rexit.' The reference is to the proconsul put to death in 88/89, C. Vettulenus Civica Cerialis (*suff.* c. 76), cf. *Agr.* 42. 1.

[2] Two conjectures could fill out his career. First, a post in Rome in December, 96 (cf. Martial xi. 106), perhaps the command of the *vigiles*; second, a post in 101 (Pliny, *Epp.* iii. 2. 5), i.e. perhaps the *annona*. Cf. R. Syme, *Historia* vi (1957), 480 ff.

[3] For a (presumably) senatorial relative, Statius, *Silvae* iv. 7. 49 ff.; his literary tastes, ib. 52 ff., also perhaps Pliny, *Epp.* ix. 1. 1; his moral transgressions, *P.Oxy.* 471, cf. H. A. Musurillo, *The Acts of the Pagan Martyrs* (1954), 150 ff.

[4] Ser. Sulpicius Similis (Dio LXIX. 19. 1).

[5] Martial vi. 76. 1: 'ille sacri lateris custos' (Cornelius Fuscus).

[6] *Pan.* 67. 8; Dio LXVIII. 16. 1²; Victor, *De Caes.* 13. 9.

[7] *AE* 1939, 60 (Heliopolis).

[8] *Pan.* 86. His identity evades inquiry.

[9] The commander of the Guard with Trajan in Dacia in 102 was Ti. Claudius Livianus (Dio LXVIII. 9. 2, cf. *PIR*², C 913).

unforeseen promotions, and some honours that can hardly have evaded sharp comment.

Trajan, it appears, was firm and sagacious in managing his entourage. No ruler could abolish the competition of groups and factions— and the campaigns in Dacia might easily engender rivalry or friction among the generals. If some were set back and disappointed, overt scandal was avoided. Trajan's prime allies were Julius Servianus and Licinius Sura, with strong claims upon his gratitude. At first the two ran level in public honours (and perhaps in the Imperator's esteem), sharing a second consulate in 102. Then, in 107, Sura with his third consulate leaves Servianus far behind. There is no hint of what Servianus thought. The marshals continue in ostensible concord.[1]

The military emperor entered upon the tenth year of his rule in warranted pride. His vigour had brought Rome back to the mission and habit of conquest. Caesar Augustus, by winning Illyricum, advanced the frontier to the Danube, binding province to province and army to army. That was the principal achievement of his long reign.[2] Trajan's Dacia, projecting across the river like a strong bastion, dominated wide territories on its flanks. Another advance was not out of the question. The German peoples faced the Danube as well as the Rhine: to occupy Bohemia would round off the conquest of the Danubian basin and ensure complete mastery over central Europe. The means were available. Trajan had raised two new legions, making a total strength of thirty. No fewer than twelve were now stationed in the Danubian lands.[3]

Trajan was the emperor produced and designated by the Empire. Not merely in virtue of his Spanish origin or through the command in Upper Germany, but because he knew the provinces and had personal ties with senators, knights, and soldiers. Trajan went on from land to land and from task to task. Later ages would tell of his glory and point out the traces of his passage.[4] He was like Hercules in athletic pursuits, and in something more: strength of body is not of much account in itself, unless the mind rules and directs.[5]

[1] The sole known exception, undated and unexplained, is M'. Laberius Maximus (*suff.* 89, *II ord.* with the Emperor in 103): in 117 he is discovered in exile on an island (*HA, Hadr.* 5. 5). [2] For this conception cf. R. Syme, *CAH* x (1934), 380 f.

[3] The legions II Traiana Fortis and XXX Ulpia Victrix were presumably enrolled before or during the Second Dacian War; while two taken from the Rhine (X Gemina and XI Claudia) did not go back there. That would give thirteen in the Danubian armies; but, Arabia having been annexed, an extra legion would be needed in the East; cf. R. Syme, *Laureae Aquincenses* I (1938), 267 ff.

[4] *Pan.* 15. 4 (where the phrase 'magnus hospes' deserves attention).

[5] 82. 6: 'nec vero per se magnopere laudaverim duritiam corporis ac lacertorum.' Hercules is alluded to in the next section—'maritos dearum ac deorum liberos.'

The parallel with Hercules is not mere ornament or clever flattery of an emperor who came from the vicinity of Gades on the far edge of the western world.[1] Pliny in the *Panegyricus* lays especial emphasis on Trajan's career of service—and subordination. Trajan did nothing to make himself emperor: obedience brought him to the Principate.[2] The word is 'obsequium'. Tacitus insisted on this quality in Agricola: duty and discretion can produce a great man still, if he has 'vigor' and 'industria'.[3]

Trajan was heralded by Agricola, and manifested as 'capax imperii'. Though that phrase is not used by Tacitus in his *Agricola* or by Pliny in his *Panegyricus*, it is implicit in both works. And the notion is highly significant. It runs through all the historical writings of Tacitus and imparts a unity to the record of dynastic politics and civil wars.[4]

[1] That a ruler be compared to Hercules is nothing new. On Trajan as the new Hercules see W. Weber, *Untersuchungen zur Gesch. des Kaisers Hadrianus* (1907), 9 ff. However, the type appearing for the first time on coins of 100 looks like the 'Hercules Gaditanus', cf. P. L. Strack, *Untersuchungen zur r. Reichsprägung des zweiten Jahrhunderts* I (1931), 95 ff. See also J. Gagé, *Rev. ét. anc.* XLII (1940), 425 ff.; *Rev. hist.* CCV (1951), 189 ff.

[2] *Pan.* 9. 3: 'ad principatum obsequio pervenisti'; 5: 'obsequii gloria.' Compare Trajan, in obedience to Domitian, paralleled by 'ille genitus Iove' to his 'rex' (14. 5).

[3] *Agr.* 42. 5 (p. 24).

[4] He uses the phrase of Galba (*Hist.* I. 49. 4) and of Titus (II. 77. 1, cf. II. 1. 2). Note also *Ann.* I. 11. 1: 'solam divi Augusti mentem tantae molis capacem'; 13. 2: 'capacem sed aspernantem.' For the Greek equivalent note Plutarch, *Galba* 29: τοὺς μὲν οὐδεὶς ἠξίωσε τῆς ἡγεμονίας, οἱ δ' ⟨οὐδ'⟩ ἑαυτοὺς ἠξίωσαν, also *Otho* 15: εἰ τῆς τῶν Ῥωμαίων ἡγεμονίας ἄξιος γέγονα. Similarly, Dio LXIX. 17. 3 (with Boissevain's note): τῆς αὐταρχίας ἄξιον (Trajan's estimate of Julius Servianus). Also, on the events after the assassination of Caligula, Josephus *BJ* II. 205: κρινεῖν ψήφῳ τὸν ἄξιον τῆς ἡγεμονίας.

PART II

TACITUS AND PLINY

VI. THE CAREER OF TACITUS

CORNELIUS TACITUS speaks for the emperor and for provincial Romans. Yet he is chary of information about his own life and career. Neither family nor birthplace stands on record. Even the *praenomen* seems to admit a doubt—was he Gaius or Publius?[1]

Ignorance has fed upon fable. The ingenious author of the *Historia Augusta* comes out with an engaging item. The Emperor Claudius Tacitus (so he alleges) claimed the historian for an ancestor and demonstrated his piety by governmental enactment: statues of Cornelius Tacitus should be set up in all public libraries, and ten copies of the writings should be produced every year.[2]

The fiction may be dismissed. A way of inquiry offers, though not without its hazards. The parsimony of the historian has been providentially compensated by Pliny, who was never tired of talking about himself and his friends. His correspondence serves to put Cornelius Tacitus in a clear social and literary setting. Not only that. What is known of the character and pursuits of Pliny may shed light on Tacitus—and not least by contrast. Pliny exemplifies the cultivated senator of the day in a happy combination of moral endeavour and deliberate frivolity. Tacitus had something more. Pliny's generous revelations about his own activities are supplemented by the epigraphic record of an official career.[3] Comparison may begin with the facts and details, how the two senators passed from office to office in the service of the State.

---

[1] Sidonius Apollinaris twice calls him 'Gaius' (*Epp.* IV. 14. 1; 22. 2). However, the *Codex Mediceus I* has 'P. Corneli' at the subscriptions to Books I and III of the *Annales*. It is preferable to neglect the 'P. Corneli' in small capitals on the top right-hand margin of the first page, with 'Taciti' added by a Renaissance hand: cf. now R. P. Oliver, *TAPA* LXXXII (1951), 234.

[2] *HA, Tacitus* 10. 3. Fiction, cf. App. 88.

[3] *ILS* 2927 (Comum).

The friendship between their families went back to the previous generation. It probably originated either in the schools at Rome or abroad in the imperial service: a certain Cornelius Tacitus, financial agent of the government in Gallia Belgica, was known to Pliny's uncle.[1] The promotion and success of a new senator depends very much upon talent and energy in the family when it is still equestrian in rank. Pliny's family, the Caecilii, were a reputable stock from early days at the town of Comum in the Transpadane zone of Italy.[2] It may be taken without question that their means were comfortable.[3] Pliny's own father did nothing of note.[4] The true author of his 'dignitas' is his mother's brother, C. Plinius Secundus.

That remarkable character deserves more than a casual tribute.[5] Born in 23 or 24, he entered the 'militia equestris' in his early twenties and spent the greater part of the next twelve years in three officer positions (? 46–58). His terms of service were all passed with the armies of the Rhine.[6] The frontier was tranquil, with plenty of leisure, and the officer was passionately addicted to study. He composed various treatises, among them a manual on the use of the javelin for cavalry and a biography of his friend and patron P. Pomponius Secundus—not only an illustrious tragic poet but governor of Upper Germany.[7] Pliny also began an historical work, embracing all the wars between the Romans and the Germans, in twenty books.

Military service concluded, a civil post might have been waiting for this energetic person. No procuratorship fell to Pliny when he re-

---

[1] *NH* VII. 76 (discussing children of abnormal physical growth): 'ipsi non pridem vidimus eadem ferme omnia praeter pubertatem in filio Corneli Taciti equitis Romani Belgicae Galliae rationes procurantis.' The context implies that the creature died.

[2] Note the poet from Comum (Catullus 35).

[3] cf. Pliny on some of his friends, *Epp.* I. 14. 9: 'nescio an adiciam esse patri eius amplas facultates'; VII. 22. 2: 'natus splendide, abundat facultatibus' (equestrian families at Brixia and at Bergomum).

[4] Perhaps L. Caecilius C. f. Secundus, a local magistrate (*CIL, Supp. It.* 745). Another magistrate, L. Caecilius L. f. Cilo (*ILS* 6728), might be a relative. The *nomen*, however, is common.

[5] The letter to Baebius Macer (III. 5) chronicles his writings and his habits. The fundamental inquiry (drawing copiously on details in the *NH*) is that of F. Münzer, *Bonner Jahrbücher* CIV (1899), 67 ff. The recent article of K. Ziegler (P-W XXI, 271 ff.) adds nothing. A *phalera* found at the legionary camp of Vetera is inscribed 'Plinio praefec.' (*CIL* XIII, 10026²²). The inscription from Aradus (*OGIS* 586), recording]ίνιον Σεκοῦν[δον], an equestrian officer and deputy of Ti. Julius Alexander in Judaea (69/70), cannot be assigned to Pliny (for a renewed attempt, P-W XXI, 277 ff.).

[6] F. Münzer, o.c. 73 ff. On Münzer's showing, under Domitius Corbulo (Germania Inferior) and under Pomponius Secundus (Germania Superior); then, after an interval (?52–55), again on the lower Rhine, under Pompeius Paullinus and Duvius Avitus (till late 57 or early 58).

[7] On whom cf. C. Cichorius, *Römische Studien* (1922), 423 ff. Attested in 50, *Ann.* XII. 27. 2. By his full nomenclature, '[? P. Calv]isius Sabinus Pomponius Secundus', cf. *CIL* XIII, 5201 and 5237; 11515 (of the year 51).

turned to Italy in 58, so far as can be established.[1] His failure might prompt speculation—the loss of a patron, some minor indiscretion in the society of the capital, a sudden distaste for affairs, or a prescience of the dangers that lurked in the path of industry and integrity. Pliny lapsed into retirement. The Neronian tyranny, and such catastrophes as the Pisonian conspiracy (which involved a large number of knights as well as senators), confirmed his luck or judgement. Senators might invoke the evil times as a cover for inertia. To Pliny there could never be an excuse for idleness. He adopted an exacting task, to write about Latin grammar.

A decade passed. It terminated in civil war. Pliny, emerging opportunely as a partisan of Vespasian, took up his career again in fine style. He ran through a sequence of procuratorships, ending with Gallia Belgica, which made him paymaster general for the armies of the Rhine.[2]

Leaving Belgica about 76, Pliny is discovered at the capital, holding a post that involved daily visits to Vespasian.[3] The title is not specified: the fire-brigade or the corn-supply would have gone well with his methodical habits. The former is not unlikely, the latter is excluded, for three known tenants of the office of *praefectus annonae* will account for the period 76–82. One of the three had previously been *praefectus vigilum*, and all of them passed in turn to the governorship of Egypt.[4]

Belgica ranked very high, but if it brought Pliny to the post of *praefectus vigilum*, that was all. His next appointment is not as important or promising as its title would seem to imply. It was the command of one of the two imperial fleets stationed in Italian waters. The month of August 79 found Pliny in charge at Misenum on the bay of Naples.[5] When the volcano erupted, Pliny was eager to inspect the phenomenon and succour the distressed. He perished in the attempt. His

---

[1] Such a post is not excluded, to be sure. Of his procuratorships only Tarraconensis is directly attested—or convincingly to be dated (c. 73).

[2] Suetonius (ed. Roth, p. 300): 'procurationes quoque splendidissimas et continuas summa integritate administravit.' Münzer (o.c. 103 ff.) argues for Narbonensis, Africa, Tarraconensis, and Belgica. The sequence might well seem too rapid. Narbonensis seems the least secure. For Tarraconensis (conjecturally 73/74), observe the census statistics cited in *NH* III. 28. The consular legate was Vibius Crispus (*AE* 1939, 60). Cf. R. Syme, *Rev. ét. anc.* LVIII (1956), 236 ff.

[3] *Epp.* III. 5. 9: 'ante lucem ibat ad Vespasianum imperatorem (nam ille quoque noctibus utebatur), inde ad delegatum sibi officium.'

[4] The three *praefecti annonae* are C. Tettius Africanus (*CIL* XI, 5382), L. Julius Ursus (*AE* 1939, 60), and L. Laberius Maximus (*ILS* 5049). Tettius had previously held the *vigiles*. For their tenure of Egypt, see A. Stein, *Die Präfekten von Ägypten in r. Zeit* (1950), 41 ff.; R. Syme *JRS* XLIV (1954), 116 f. For Ursus, App. 7.

[5] *Epp.* VI. 16. 4: 'erat Miseni classemque imperio praesens regebat.' The adjective 'praesens' could suggest that the commander was not regularly there; hence his 'officium' at Rome might not be what is conjectured above, the charge of the *vigiles*.

nephew stayed behind, reading Livy and making excerpts from that author.[1]

Duty and curiosity set their stamp on the life of the elder Pliny from first to last. Habits of learning once acquired by a conscientious boy may be difficult to discard. Pliny held all time wasted that went not to study.[2] He read at meals, in the bath, and when carried in the litter. No book, he said, could be wholly bad. Apart from his published works, he left 160 volumes of extracts to attest the variety of his reading and the strength of his convictions. That vast erudition was not sought as an escape from the concerns of active life or designed for ostentation. A sceptic about the gods, and harshly contemptuous of personal immortality, Pliny proclaimed that man's help to man is true divinity.[3] To this end he laboured. History was surely useful. In addition to the *Bella Germaniae* he composed the annals of his own times. Scrupulous for the truth and avoiding the imputation that he might have flattered the dynasty, Pliny aspired to a higher fame and refused to publish that history.[4] There was no reason to hold back the supreme monument of his labours. It was an encyclopedia of all human knowledge, a work unattempted before by Greek or Roman, the *Naturalis Historia*.

The aristocratic ideal of leisure, inherited from the Greeks, led by an easy decline to the disdain of serious effort, to the advertising of elegant accomplishments as a pretext for sloth or emptiness. Pliny's gospel, that work is a good thing, is a typically Roman manifestation.[5] The energy, the tenacity, and the devotion of equestrian officials go far to explain the success of the imperial system.[6] Nothing guaranteed that a Caesar would possess the taste or endurance for hard tasks, that an indolent voluptuary might turn into a model proconsul. Nor was it likely that the initial impulse from an equestrian ancestry would persist for many generations when a family assumed the gilded pride and decorative pretensions of the governing class.

Pliny was a personal friend of Vespasian. Always an early riser, he would go and visit the Emperor before daybreak to discuss the busi-

---

[1] VI. 20. 5.

[2] III. 5. 16: 'nam perire omne tempus arbitrabatur quod studiis non impertiretur.'

[3] *NH* II. 18: 'deus est mortali iuvare mortalem, et haec ad aeternam gloriam via. hac proceres iere Romani, hac nunc caelesti passu cum liberis suis vadit maximus omnis aevi rector Vespasianus Augustus fessis rebus subveniens.'

[4] *NH, praef.* 20. For the historical writings, Ch. XVI; XXIII.

[5] ib. 18: 'profecto omnis vita vigilia est'; cf. Seneca, *Epp.* 96. 5: 'atqui vivere, Lucili, militare est'; 82. 3: 'otium sine litteris mors est et hominis vivi sepultura.' Compare Pliny's complaints about the decline of arts and sciences, of invention and discovery, because men love ease and wealth (*NH* II. 117 f.; XIV. 2 ff.).

[6] Observe Turranius, who, dismissed 'post annum nonagesimum', took it as a death sentence, 'nec finivit ante tristitiam quam labor illi suus restitutus est' (Seneca, *De brevitate vitae* 20. 3).

ness of his post at Rome.[1] His acquaintance with Titus went back to the latter's service as military tribune on the Rhine, and to Titus he dedicated the encyclopedia, in 77.[2] For the nephew, whom he adopted as his son, the *latus clavus* was ready on request and a senator's career under the Flavian dynasty.

The antecedents of Cornelius Tacitus are closely comparable. Tacitus nowhere has occasion to say anything about his father, and he mentions his own entry to the senatorial order only because it is strictly relevant—an assertion that the historian will be frank and honest despite benefits owed to the dynasty.[3] The decease of a parent or relative might easily impair a young man's prospects.[4] The procurator of Belgica may no longer have been alive, but his rank guaranteed a good start for the young Tacitus—better indeed than for many born in the senatorial order.[5]

The birth of Cornelius Tacitus may be assigned to 56 or 57.[6] Vespasian granted the *latus clavus*. Between adolescence and the age of twenty ensued the interlude of social probation. The aspirant to honours held one or other of the twenty appointments in the four minor magistracies: duties were negligible, but the post allotted gave some sign of a man's future prospects and career.[7] These were the impressionable years, just before military service, and sometimes influenced by it.[8] Tacitus went in for the study of public speaking, assiduous in the company of senior practitioners. A quarter of a century later, when composing a dialogue on the decline of oratory, Tacitus laid the scene in the sixth year of Vespasian's rule (75).[9] Four characters participate—two orators (the most celebrated forensic

---

[1] *Epp.* III. 5. 9.

[2] *NH, praef.* 3: 'et nobis quidem qualis in castrensi contubernio.' Cf. Suetonius, *Divus Titus* 4. 1.

[3] *Hist.* I. 1. 3: 'dignitatem nostram a Vespasiano inchoatam, a Tito auctam, a Domitiano longius provectam haud abnuerim; sed incorruptam fidem professis neque amore quisquam et sine odio dicendus est.'

[4] cf. Julius Naso, a friend of Tacitus and of Pliny (*Epp.* VI. 6. 4).

[5] Among sons of procurators observe M'. Laberius Maximus (*suff.* 89, *II ord.* 103), the orator (? Cn.) Lucceius Albinus (consul before 103), and C. Valerius Paullinus (*suff.* 107). There is no reason for doubting that Tacitus was the son (or possibly nephew) of the procurator of Belgica: cf. further Ch. XLV.

[6] Borghesi suggested 55 or 56 (*Œuvres* VII (1872), 321 ff.). There are no new data—but much of the evidence accruing about the senatorial *cursus honorum* has never been properly exploited. For the normal and differential consular ages, and for the various types of careers, cf. App. 17 f.

[7] See valuable hints in E. Birley, *Roman Britain and the Roman Army* (1953), 3. More fully, *Proc. Brit. Ac.* XXXIX (1953), 201 ff.

[8] Tacitus was now 'iuvenis admodum' (*Dial.* 1. 2). Compare Helvidius Priscus—'ingenium inlustre altioribus studiis iuvenis admodum dedit' (*Hist.* IV. 5. 1). Agricola nearly succumbed to philosophy at this season (*Agr.* 4. 4).

[9] *Dial.* 17. 3, cf. App. 28.

speakers of the day), a senator who preferred poetry, and a young man of family and distinction, aged about twenty-five.[1]

Political eloquence at this time was dominated by Vibius Crispus and Eprius Marcellus. Two other consulars, the last *ordinarii* of Nero's reign, claim a passing notice: Galerius Trachalus, who had volume and resonance beyond equal, and Silius Italicus, a man of many parts. The season itself was not unpropitious to civilian attainments. Of those who trod the path shortly before Tacitus, some had been hampered by the last Neronian years (the orator's talent seldom went with good reputation or survival), others were cut off by the civil wars, others again benefited, passing swiftly into an administrative career. Few are known by name among the predecessors and the rivals of Tacitus. Before he reached the consular age, he challenged his seniors, and none of his juniors (so far as known) surpassed him.[2]

Meanwhile, the stages of advancement: some fixed by an inevitable prescription, others modified by birth or patronage, by personal choice or by already proved aptitudes.[3]

In Rome of the aristocracy, *leges annales* ordained the limits of age and status within which ambition might compete for honours without wrecking the 'res publica'. The renovated oligarchy which Caesar and his ministers directed also had need of regulations. For mere magistracies and proconsulates they were easy to devise and operate. The creation of sequence and hierarchy in the imperial service took longer; and for the consular army commands merit, favour, or emergency are inimical to routine and seniority. None the less, under the Flavian emperors the code acquires remarkable precision and stability.

The government had twenty-seven military tribunates to fill.[4] The holders of the vigintivirate make up the total, supplemented by some iterations.[5] The age of the *tribunus laticlavius* was twenty or thereabouts.[6] Army or legion (or both) might be commanded by relatives and friends of the family. Matrimony strengthened such ties. Returning from service, the young man looked for a suitable bride in some consular or rising family. Tacitus won the approbation of Julius Agricola, to whose daughter he was betrothed in 77.[7] Marriage in the early twenties was common, for a precise reason—the law according privileges to candidates with children.

---

[1] M. Aper, Julius Secundus, Curiatius Maternus, and Vipstanus Messalla, cf. Ch. IX; also App. 90 (Maternus); 91 (Aper).

[2] For orators, senior and coeval, see App. 26 f.

[3] For three types of career see E. Birley, *Proc. Brit. Ac.* xxxix (1953), 198 f.

[4] There were now, it appears, twenty-nine legions—but two were in Egypt, without *laticlavii*.

[5] Not all aspirants, however, seem to have been required to serve (E. Birley, o.c. 200).

[6] cf. p. 20 (Agricola); p. 31 (Trajan).   [7] *Agr.* 9. 7.

The quaestorship came in 81 or 82, with the odds equal for service abroad. Ten of the twenty quaestors go out with the proconsuls of the provinces in the Senate's portion (two consular and eight praetorian). Two are allotted to attendance upon the Princeps, and some of the remainder to the consuls: birth or special favour selects the *quaestores Augusti*.[1]

Two or three years later, the tribunate of the plebs or the aedileship. Altogether, sixteen posts, senators of patrician family being excused. Next, after a short interval, one of the praetorships (the total was normally eighteen).[2] Cornelius Tacitus became praetor in 88. The magistracy he mentions casually in reference to the Secular Games celebrated in that year, when he was a member of the sacerdotal college concerned therewith, the *quindecimviri sacris faciundis*.[3]

Pageantry appealed to the Emperor Domitian, and ritual even more. As head of the state religion he enforced the traditional observances with pedantic rigour. Several of the sacred virgins of Vesta who had neglected their vows were punished, the senior delinquent being entombed alive in the primeval fashion.[4] And, although Domitian permitted the *flamen Dialis* to divorce his wife, the thing could not be done without horrid rites and incantations.[5]

The *quindecimviri* had custody of the Sibylline oracles and super-intended cults of extraneous origin, some very ancient, others quite recent, such as the worship of Isis and Serapis, which the Flavian emperors regarded with favour. The archives of the college contained documents of immemorial antiquity, or believed such. To interpret them called for scholarship and good sense among the priestly experts when the government required supernatural sanction for its projects or quietly altered the date of some stated ceremony. The cycle of recurrence for the Secular Games had already been revised more than once. The calculation that suited Domitian was not the weakest in the series. There is no sign that it was impugned by Cornelius Tacitus.[6]

---

[1] Patricians will normally hold this post, cf. S. Brassloff, *Hermes* XXXIX (1904), 618. Furthermore, all of the epigraphically attested *quaestores Augusti* in the period 70–120 except two (*ILS* 1000; 1003) are known to have reached the consulate: mostly patrician, but also some later commanders of military provinces (e.g. *ILS* 1021; 1040; 1053). A *novus homo* of literary talent might stand a chance, however.

[2] *Dig.* I. 2. 2. 32. Titus abolished one place, but Nerva restored it.

[3] *Ann.* XI. 11. 1: 'nam is quoque edidit ludos saeculares iisque intentius adfui sacerdotio quindecimvirali praeditus ac tum praetor.'

[4] Suetonius, *Dom.* 8. 3 f.; Pliny, *Epp.* IV. 11. 5 ff.

[5] Plutarch, *Quaest. Rom.* 50: οἱ δ' ἱερεῖς παρεγένοντο τῇ τοῦ γάμου διαλύσει, πολλὰ φρικώδη καὶ ἀλλόκοτα καὶ σκυθρωπὰ δρῶντες.

[6] The stated 110 years take one back from A.D. 88 to 23 B.C.; and, according to Zosimus (II. 4), Domitian followed the Augustan computation. Various reasons suggest that Augustus originally intended to hold the *Ludi Saeculares* in 23 or 22 B.C., cf. O. Hirschfeld, *Kl. Schr.* (1913), 444; M. P. Nilsson, P-W I A, 1710. When, however, Augustus

In rank and honour the sacerdotal colleges exhibit a wide divergence. The four inherited by the Principate from the last age of the
Republic kept their primacy, namely pontiffs, augurs, *quindecimviri*,
and *epulones*. Nobody could belong to more than one of them. Next
came the priests to whom the Senate had consigned the official worship of Divus Augustus, the *sodales Augustales*.[1] Lowest in estimation
were certain confraternities which Caesar Augustus had revived by
artifice from long desuetude: the *fetiales*, the *sodales Titii*, and the
fratres arvales. He had not been able to install them beside the 'quat-
tuor amplissima sacerdotia'.[2]

Nonentities now tend to congregate among the Arval Brethren
(fairly full registers are extant for the Flavian period), and their
activities (apart from banquets) are largely taken up with anniver-
saries or events that concern the dynasty.[3] The *quindecimviri* embrace
a superior selection—fashionable young men, with literary talent at a
premium, and certain wise old politicians.[4] To be of the company was
delight and instruction—who could fail to benefit from Fabricius
Veiento? It was also a promise (seldom delusive) of further honours.[5]
That Tacitus acquired this priesthood so early in his career is a noteworthy fact, indicating high favour with the managers of patronage.
Many senators had to wait until the consulate or later. Save in an
aristocrat, an early priesthood easily carried the imputation of base
arts or undue influence.[6] Tacitus had perhaps already earned repute
as a speaker—in the Senate, not merely in the courts of law or the
schools of rhetoric. Some resounding success may mark the years 86
or 87.[7] Further, he would now augment his own following among the
aspirants to oratorical distinction.[8]

decided to postpone and needed justification for 17 B.C., a series of earlier *Ludi* (at the
proper intervals) was duly produced from the *commentarii* of the *XVviri* (Censorinus,
De die natali XVII. 8; 10 f.).

[1] For their status, *Ann.* III. 64. 3 f.; Dio LVIII. 12. 5.

[2] For the different *sacerdotia*, M. W. Hoffman Lewis, *The Official Priests of Rome under
the Julio-Claudians* (1955). The *arvales* of the period are persons of some distinction for
the most part (o.c. 121 ff.).

[3] *ILS* 5034 (from the *Acta* of 87). A social decline can be discovered by comparing
the *arvales* of 78 (*ILS* 5027) with those of 58 and 59 (229 f.).

[4] See the fifteen other names discoverable between 70 and 120 (App. 22). Among them,
Trajan's father, Fabricius Veiento, the poet Valerius Flaccus, the highly presentable
Arruntius Stella.

[5] App. 22.

[6] cf. *Hist.* IV. 42. 4 (in the speech denouncing the young Aquillius Regulus). For the
importance of birth, cf. *Hist.* I. 77. 3—priesthoods for 'honorati iam senes' and for 'nobiles
adulescentuli.'

[7] The *Acta Fratrum Arvalium*, by thanksgivings on September 22, 87, 'ob detecta
scelera nefariorum' (*CIL* VI, 2165, l. 62), indicate the unmasking of a conspiracy.

[8] *Epp.* VII. 20. 4: 'equidem adulescentulus, cum iam tu gloria famaque floreres, te sequi,
tibi *longo sed proximus intervallo* et esse et haberi concupiscebam.'

In the *Agricola* Tacitus musters all the resources of an advocate's art, mature in its command of innuendo, to demonstrate how an evil emperor visited upon the conqueror of Britain his envy, his hatred, and his fears. Good sense and personal dignity saved Tacitus from dishonesty about himself. He does not hint that his own advancement had been impaired by the ostensible disgrace of his wife's father; and he may have had other friends and patrons, active while Agricola was away in Britain, and after his return.[1] The ministers and counsellors of Domitian stand on record.[2] It would be worth knowing more about the operations of Fabricius Veiento or Vibius Crispus—or the influence exerted by Pegasus, the Prefect of the City, and by Cornelius Fuscus, commander of the Guard.[3]

The posts after the praetorship, by number, quality, and duration, decide a man's ultimate success. The standard consular year is the forty-third, but not all have to wait so long. A scion of the primeval nobility of Rome (the patriciate) may omit the praetorian posts, thus coming to the consulate as young as thirty-two; and other aristocrats benefit from birth and privilege, with little or no constraint to seek active employment abroad.[4] For a man of talent and ambition, honour accrues through the service of Caesar. The provinces of the Senate are in minor esteem.[5] They will seldom see him again after the quaestorship until, a senior consular, he qualifies for Asia or Africa— which an eminent 'vir militaris' may well forgo.[6]

It was expedient to command a legion. With a triennial tenure eight of the praetors of each year normally become legionary legates. The field of promotion narrows. With six consuls in a normal year, not every legionary legate can hope to crown his ambitions.[7]

In the career of the imperial commands a legion followed by a praetorian province takes a man in a clear run to the consulate, which

[1] The notion that Tacitus owed everything to Agricola (E. Paratore, *Tacito* (1951), 52, cf. 73) cannot be accepted.

[2] Juvenal IV. 75 ff. Cf. G. Highet, *Juvenal the Satirist* (1954), 259 ff.; J. Crook, *Consilium Principis* (1955), 50 f. Add presumably M. Cocceius Nerva; but the enigmatic Julius Ursus had not yet become joint commander of the Guard with Cornelius Fuscus (App. 7). Ursus was succeeded by L. Laberius Maximus (cf. *P. Berol.* 8334).

[3] Pegasus (App. 68; 94); Fuscus (App. 33).

[4] For patricians (old or new) with no post between praetorship and consulate, *ILS* 999; 1044; 1049; *AE* 1914, 267.

[5] Of about fifty discoverable proconsuls of praetorian rank between 70 and 120, not more than half a dozen are known to have governed later a military province. Nor does the post of legate to a proconsul (except in Asia or Africa) indicate promise.

[6] Hence the suggestion made to the conqueror of Britain (*Agr.* 42. 1) was not wholly outrageous. See also the list of proconsuls of Asia from 103/4 to 120/1 (App. 23). Only three known legates of consular provinces. Conversely, only five proconsuls among the thirty-seven consular legates registered in App. 14.

[7] Three pairs (89, 91, 94, 96) or the Emperor and six other consuls (87, 92, 95) can be taken as 'normal'.

he can hold four or five years short of the standard age, with a firm prospect of later distinction in charge of an army.[1] Not all of the 'viri militares' are so fortunate; and other senators (especially the sons of knights) must wait until forty-two, sometimes longer. A variety of posts occupies the interval, at Rome, in Italy, or abroad.

Cornelius Tacitus, not long after his praetorship, departed to an employment in the provinces. When Julius Agricola died (August 23, A.D. 93) Tacitus was still absent: he had been away for a 'quadriennium'.[2] The nature of Tacitus' occupations permits only a wide conjecture. A decision between civil or military might be prompted by opinions about the experience of affairs which his historical writings are deemed to disclose. It could never claim validity. The consular Julius Frontinus compiled several volumes of *Strategemata*: for the most part, literary and antiquated. The reader would never guess that Frontinus had once governed the province of Britain and subdued a refractory region.[3]

It is a fair assumption that Tacitus commanded a legion, as did almost every *novus homo* ambitious to see his name on the *Fasti*.[4] Moreover, the recent wars accelerated the promotion of legates, leaving places to be filled. Otherwise a civilian employment might be surmised, though not with any confidence, at this stage. In three of the consular provinces (Hispania Citerior, Britain, and Cappadocia) the Flavian emperors created a new post, that of *iuridicus*, to assist the governor.[5] If Tacitus' sojourn abroad comprised four full years, it might have terminated with a year as proconsul somewhere, in a minor province, nor is a proconsulate after a short interval excluded. Certain senators offer parallels, but no certainty.[6]

There was still a period to be spent, with or without some further post. A dozen years could easily elapse after a man's praetorship if no signal merits intervened.

Various hazards could help or hinder. Vespasian took a number of new men into the Senate by adlection, in 69 and in 73, some being

---

[1] For this type of promotion cf. Agricola's career. Further, App. 18.

[2] *Agr.* 45. 5, cf. 44. 1.

[3] No reference at all to Britain—but three to Domitian's German operations in 83 (*Strat.* 1. 1. 8; 3. 10; II. 11. 7).

[4] Of the complete and detailed *cursus* of consulars (other than patricians) between 70 and 120 only three fail to show that post, viz. *ILS* 8819 (A. Julius Quadratus); 2927 (Pliny); 1024 (Cornutus Tertullus).

[5] The epigraphic instances in the Flavio-Trajanic period are, for Hispania, *ILS* 1021; 1016; Britain, 1011; 1015; Cappadocia, 8971; 8819; 1017. Add Larcius Licinus (*PIR*[1], L 54), in Spain c. 73. The title *iuridicus* is not applied to the praetorian legates in the Cappadocian province.

[6] e.g. P. Tullius Varro (*ILS* 1002), or C. Salvius Liberalis, proconsul of Macedonia after his legionary command (*ILS* 1011).

given praetorian rank.[1] After ten years the competition grew intense; after fifteen, intolerable. An expanded consular list from time to time brought alleviation—one or two may be presumed early in Domitian's reign, the year 86 shows eight consuls, while 90 is portentous, after the civil war.[2] The subsequent years (except perhaps for 93) are regular and conventional.[3]

The civil war produced a number of gaps, and four years later party strife in the Senate provoked a chain of prosecutions for treason, with many deaths and exiles. Moreover the period exhibited a sequence of unhealthy seasons. Some deadly infection was going about. It excited suspicion of maleficence or crime, and strange rumours.[4] Death from natural causes might easily overtake the governor of an insalubrious province;[5] and it was not unusual for a consular to pass away in his early fifties.[6] This time the young were extinguished with the old: senators of high promise in society and letters, for whom the consulate could confidently have been predicted, were carried off in their prime.[7]

Yet there was no lack of rivals in the race. A group of aristocrats encumbered the course. Their ancestry commanded a preference.[8] Nor should the members of more recent consular families have to wait until the standard age. The son of Silius Italicus would come in ahead of any coeval *novus homo*, and so would the two Neratii, Marcellus and Priscus (a favoured pair who belonged to the new patricians).[9] At the other extreme were older men without benefit of birth, some tardy in their advancement but hoping to exploit the hazards of influence, the caprice of the emperor, or his need of loyal agents.[10]

A variegated company stood in prospect of the consulate. Some

[1] A. W. Braithwaite in his edition of Suetonius, *Divus Vespasianus* (Oxford, 1927), 51 f. Add presumably L. Javolenus Priscus (*ILS* 1015), and also Sex. Lucilius Bassus (cf. *PIR*[1], L 283).

[2] Twelve names, besides the Emperor's.

[3] For 93 (imperfect on the *Fasti Potentini*) see App. 8.

[4] Observe the peculiar story in Dio—malefactors with poisoned needles causing many deaths at Rome and throughout the world (LXVII. 11. 6, under 90 or 91).

[5] e.g. C. Ummidius Quadratus (Syria) in 60 (*Ann.* XIV. 26. 2); T. Atilius Rufus (Syria) in 84 (*Agr.* 40. 1); L. Antistius Rusticus (Cappadocia) c. 93 (Martial IX. 30, cf. *AE* 1925, 126: his *cursus*, and his edict in a season of famine).

[6] In 93 Agricola—and, about the same time, Cn. Domitius Lucanus (*suff.* c. 79), cf. Martial IX. 51. Also T. Aurelius Fulvus (*cos.* 89), cf. App. 87. M. Otacilius Catulus (*suff.* 88) died in or before 95 (cf. *Dig.* XXXI. 29 *praef.*). For a *suffectus* dying in 93, p. 638.

[7] e.g. Valerius Flaccus (Quintilian X. 1. 90), and Severus, the (younger) son of Silius Italicus (Martial VIII. 66, cf. IX. 86; Pliny, *Epp.* III. 7. 2).

[8] App. 24.

[9] The son of Silius (Martial VIII. 66. 4) may be identified as L. Silius Decianus (*suff.* 94); the consulates of the Neratii are in 95 and 97.

[10] e.g. Q. Pomponius Rufus (*IRT* 537), *suffectus* in 95, or A. Julius Quadratus (*ILS* 8819) in 94.

were closely calculable by reasons of age, standing, and employment. Ten triennial posts stand as direct designations—with the eight legates of imperial provinces go the collegiate pair of prefects, who manage the Senate's treasury, the *aerarium Saturni*.[1] On an average three of the consuls in each year derive from this type of promotion. For praetorian legates in the period 94–97 the evidence is scanty, but sufficient to dispel the notion that Cornelius Tacitus governed Gallia Belgica.[2] The legate of Belgica was Glitius Agricola, who returned to hold the *fasces* in 97.[3]

The consulate of Tacitus fell in the second half of that year. He was one of a long list.[4] A strong persuasion is sometimes expressed that Tacitus came late to the consulship.[5] That is false. Some hold that he owed the supreme dignity to Nerva or the friends of Nerva. That is far from certain. One would have to know when consuls were designated. Now some of the consuls who held office in 69 had in fact been designated by Nero.[6] Nero committed suicide on June 9 of the previous year. As likely as not, Cornelius Tacitus had been marked out for promotion before the assassination of Domitian. For a knight's son not aspiring to the army commands he had made a good career.[7]

The consul's only known action is a funeral oration.[8] His next public appearance is at the trial of Marius Priscus, as advocate for the prosecution along with his friend Pliny.[9] Priscus, proconsul of Africa under Nerva, set himself to exploit the 'felicitas temporum', rapacious, oppressive, and condoning murder for money. After some delays the case was terminated in January of the year 100.[10] The Princeps presided in the Senate. It was one of the first duties that fell to him after his arrival. Trajan comported himself with tact and discretion, solicitous for the dignity of senators, even when a flagrant offender was involved. The indictment of a senator might evoke signal manifestations of class solidarity and eloquent appeals to compassion. On behalf of Priscus the attempt was made to let him off with mere restitution of the monies he had extorted. The prosecution, however, insisted and prevailed. Priscus had to go into exile. The interests of the government

---

[1] For this post, and for the pair in office in 97, having been appointed by Domitian, see p. 78 and App. 19. One of their predecessors will have been L. Neratius Priscus (*ILS* 1033 f.), suffect in 97.

[2] The notion that Tacitus might have governed Belgica, common since Borghesi (*Œuvres* VII (1872), 323), and believed helpful for the *Germania*, was invoked to explain his absence from Rome in the period 89–93 (*Agr.* 45. 4). Belgica, however, is not the kind of province a junior ex-praetor can govern.

[3] *ILS* 1021.   [4] App. 10.   [5] See the writers cited in App. 17.
[6] *Hist.* I. 77. 2.   [7] For careers to compare, App. 18.   [8] *Epp.* II. 1. 6.

[9] II. 11. 2 ff. The defence had good advocates, namely C. Salvius Liberalis and Ti. Catius Fronto: presumably among the best of the time (cf. App. 27).

[10] Priscus was probably proconsul in 97/98. For the delay cf. Pompeius Silvanus, proconsul of Africa in 53/54 (*IRT* 338), prosecuted in 58 (*Ann.* XIII. 52. 2).

were safeguarded, and the honour of the Senate, with an enhanced reputation for Tacitus and for Pliny. The Africans were not so happy.[1]

In 101 began the first war against the Dacians, prosecuted and terminated in the next year. Of Cornelius Tacitus there is no trace in the correspondence of Pliny for several years after the trial of Marius Priscus. He was now eligible for a consular post in Rome, Italy, or the provinces; and certain of his coevals were holding important commands. Pride and duty carried a strong appeal. And, although Tacitus now renounced oratory for history, an official occupation might be less inimical to studious leisure than were the busy futilities of the capital— receptions, recitations, and senatorial debates.[2] A letter of Pliny in 104 or 105 welcomes Tacitus' arrival in Rome.[3] He may have been absent somewhere in the service of the government.

Various posts offered. At Rome, the superintendence of temples and other public buildings, of the river Tiber, or of the aqueducts.[4] In Italy the new system of poor relief (the *alimenta*) was at this time being administered by commissioners of consular rank;[5] and a consular could be put in charge of an important road.[6] There was also the periodic census of Tres Galliae.[7]

To govern an imperial province did not always demand the training or habits of the military. The command of the army was only one among the functions of Caesar's legate: civilian tact and knowledge of the law would be requisite. And some regions declined in military

[1] Juvenal 1. 49 f.: 'exul ab octava Marius bibit et fruitur dis | iratis, at tu victrix provincia ploras.'

[2] When Cicero, incited to write history, spoke of the need for leisure, Atticus came out with an appropriate suggestion—'legationem aliquam nimirum ista oratio postulat aut eius modi quampiam cessationem liberam atque otiosam' (*De legibus* 1. 10). The amount of time given by senatorial Romans to administrative duties tends to be overestimated by modern inquirers.

[3] *Epp.* IV. 13. 1: 'salvum in urbem venisse gaudeo.' The Ciceronian examples of this formula imply a journey of some distance. The letter refers to Pliny's visit to Comum (ib. 3), and therefore is of late 104 at the earliest (App. 19). Tacitus' absence is also alluded to in VI. 9. 1.: 'si te Romae morante ipse afuissem.'

[4] For the *curatores operum publicorum* see the list drawn up by A. E. Gordon, *Univ. of California Pub. in Class. Arch.* II, 5 (1952), 279 ff. The *curatores* as a collegiate consular pair are not attested before the last years of Hadrian. Nearest in date to Tacitus are Ti. Julius Celsus Polemaeanus (*ILS* 8971), Q. Pomponius Rufus (*IRT* 537), and C. Julius Proculus (*ILS* 1040), consuls suffect in 92, 95, and 109. The Tiber Conservancy was held by Ti. Julius Ferox (*suff.* ?99), attested in 101 and 103 (*CIL* VI, 31549 f.). The *cura aquarum* was a more senior post. The next holders after Julius Frontinus (appointed by Nerva) were L. Silius Decianus (*CIL* XV, 7302) and L. Neratius Marcellus (*ILS* 1032), *suffecti* in 94 and 95.

[5] C. Cornelius Gallicanus (*suff.* 84), under Trajan (*ILS* 6675), followed by T. Pomponius Bassus (*suff.* 94), before the end of 102 (*ILS* 6106, cf. 6675).

[6] Thus P. Calvisius Ruso (*suff.* 79) in charge of an unnamed road subsequent to his proconsulate of Asia (*AE* 1914, 267). Cornutus Tertullus (*suff.* 100) was appointed to the Aemilia c. 104 (*ILS* 1024, cf. *Epp.* V. 14. 1), perhaps in connexion with the *alimenta*.

[7] e.g. *ILS* 1024 and 1040, cf. p. 81.

importance: the Rhine armies, reduced by Domitian, now surrendered two more legions for the needs of the Danube. Nothing debarred Cornelius Tacitus from governing the Upper or the Lower Germany in these years (101–4).[1] Syria, indeed, was held by a man who had never seen an army, even as a young tribune.[2] That was not altogether normal. Other legates, however, were more than mere soldiers. They found no incompatibility between a military career and literary tastes or accomplishment.[3]

Even when the books of the *Historiae* had been completed and given to the world, with the certitude of an immortal renown, the consular did not disdain to submit his name to the ballot for the two provinces of highest dignity in the senatorial career, Asia and Africa. The interval since a man's consulship, fixed originally by Caesar Augustus at five years, increased when more and more ex-consuls became eligible, and, although from time to time an attempt seems to have been made to keep it at ten or twelve years, the exclusion of eminent senators was invidious. Extending to fourteen and to fifteen years under Trajan, the interval reaches seventeen before the death of that emperor. An inscription shows that Cornelius Tacitus was proconsul of Asia. His term of office ran from summer to summer, almost certainly 112/13.[4]

So far the official career of Cornelius Tacitus. For the rest the sole testimony is the *Annales*. How soon he began the work there is no evidence, and the larger portion may have been composed after the death of Trajan. Had Tacitus belonged to the group of families in close alliance with Trajan's successor, he might have hoped for a second consulate before long. The quality of his historical writings would not alone have sufficed, even were they to the liking of the new emperor—a hazardous assumption.

The men of Tacitus' consular year exhibit the vicissitudes of fame and survival. Introduced by Cocceius Nerva and Verginius Rufus, that year throws up another paradox, a second consulate for the amiable Arrius Antoninus (his first was in 69).[5] Other consuls on that list are bare names, or not much better. Annius Verus leaves no trace in Trajan's reign. His prominence comes only when Trajan is dead.[6]

---

[1] That is, unless the roll of consular provinces is full at this time (cf. p. 53). No legate of Germania Superior is attested. The other Germania appears to have been held by Q. Acutius Nerva (*suff.* 100), cf. App. 14. Note also that Sosius Senecio (*cos.* 99) is holding an army command c. 103 (*Epp.* IV. 4. 1).

[2] A. Julius Quadratus (*suff.* 94, *II ord.* 105), cf. *ILS* 8819.

[3] Thus Licinius Sura, Sosius Senecio, and Fabius Justus.

[4] App. 23. The inscription (*OGIS* 437) was found at Mylasa: revised by R. Meister, *Jahreshefte* XXVII (1932), Beiblatt 242.

[5] App. 10.

[6] App. 86. Pure chance shows that he was a *frater arvalis* in 105 (*CIL* VI, 2075).

No conspicuous actions explain it. His colleague in 97 was Neratius Priscus, a jurist of superior attainments. Like Annius, Neratius would outlive Trajan.[1]

Only for Glitius Agricola is the full and precise register of an official career to be had.[2] The earlier stages are not at all rapid. Military tribune in a Moesian legion and already quaestor before the death of Vespasian, Glitius held three provincial posts after his praetorship, being *iuridicus* in Hispania Citerior, commander of the legion VI Ferrata in Syria, and legate of Gallia Belgica. From Belgica he passed straight to the consulship. At the time of the Dacian War Glitius was governor of Pannonia, with military decorations and a second consulate thereupon in 103; and he subsequently became Prefect of the City.[3]

No writer notices even the name of Glitius Agricola. More is disclosed about Licinius Sura, but fragmentary and perplexing. His consular year is not anywhere directly attested.[4] Nor is it clear by what path he came to that office, and to military ambitions. The earliest signs provide no hint. About the year 85 Sura is named as a speaker and advocate by the poet Martial; in 90 he is among the high patrons of literature; in 92 he falls ill and nearly dies.[5] Martial never mentions Licinius Sura again—the man whose act or counsel proved momentous in the making of an emperor, whose station was soon beside Caesar in war and peace, consul again in 102, and for the third time in 107.

Sura duly turns up among the correspondents of Pliny, but not with the earliest. He receives a pair of letters. Not about war or government—they concern curiosities of nature, and the things beyond nature.[6] Pliny alludes to the erudition of Sura, and implies that his judgement is cool and sceptical.[7]

The circle of Pliny will repay inspection. About Tacitus the facts are scanty. It would be needful to have knowledge about various groups and categories—his father's friends and the Narbonensian allies acquired through the family of his wife; the members of his sacerdotal college; the orators and the masters of jurisprudence; the men of birth and fashion.[8] Curiosity asks in vain how Tacitus stood with the five elder statesmen who emerged under Nerva—or with the personages most prominent during the first decade of Trajan's rule.

There could be no end to speculation, and little profit. Apart from

---

[1] For L. Neratius Priscus (*ILS* 1033 f.) see App. 68.
[2] *ILS* 1021a.   [3] *CIL* v, 6980.   [4] App. 10.
[5] Martial I. 49. 40; VI. 64. 13; VII. 47.   [6] *Epp.* IV. 30 (not before 104); VII. 27.
[7] IV. 30. 11: 'scrutare tu causas (potes enim)'; VII. 27. 15: 'eruditionem tuam'; 16: 'licet etiam utramque in partem, ut soles, disputes.'
[8] For some of these categories see App. 22, 24, 26, 68.

Pliny, only one of the Trajanic consulars can be invoked with certitude, Fabius Justus, the friend to whom Tacitus dedicated a literary treatise in dialogue form.

Fabius was at Rome in December of the year 96.[1] Not long afterwards he is absent abroad in one of the military zones.[2] Furthermore, his consulate early in 102 proves active merit—when Licinius Sura resigns after a brief tenure, it is Fabius who takes his place. Fabius is again with the armies in 106, perhaps governing one of the Danubian provinces or a general under Trajan in the second war against the Dacians.[3] Two years later he accedes to the governorship of Syria, with which his known employments end.[4]

---

[1] I. 5. 8.

[2] I. 11. 2: 'fac sciam quid agas, quod sine sollicitudine summa nescire non possum.' Perhaps a legionary legate.

[3] VII. 2. 2: 'patiar ergo aestatem inquietam vobis exercitamque transcurrere.' The possibility that the 'Iustus' to whom the letter is addressed might be the elderly knight Minicius Justus (Groag in *PIR²*, F 41) need not detain.

[4] *AE* 1940, 210 (nr. Palmyra). For his career, R. Syme, *JRS* XLVII (1957), 131 ff.

VII. THE CAREER OF PLINY

PLINY was some half-dozen years junior to Cornelius Tacitus.[1] He inherited from his uncle in 79, held a minor magistracy, and went out to Syria as military tribune. Of the condition of the army at this time (about 82) he was later to draw a deplorable and a conventional picture—energy came under suspicion, and inaction was prized, there was no authority, no discipline.[2] In the prevalent corruption, the modest talents of the young officer were put to good use. He audited the accounts of the auxiliary regiments.[3] He also applied himself to the company of philosophers, with proper selection. Not any showy sophist, and still less one of the street preachers whose diatribes might provoke unrest in the cities and call for police measures; but only the wise and the good. Euphrates of the mighty beard and majestic demeanour united sanctity and social advantages, being connected with the leading family in the province,[4] while the virtuous Artemidorus earned the admiration of a Roman knight, Musonius Rufus, and was rewarded with the hand of his daughter.[5]

Even before his brief spell of service Pliny had begun to practise at the bar, adopting his seniors for model and guidance.[6] He soon undertook one case at least of some importance, advocate for the defence against the most influential men in the State, even against the friends of Caesar, so he proclaims.[7] Pliny came to no harm.

When Pliny held the quaestorship, he enjoyed favour and confidence: he was one of the two quaestors attached to the Emperor with the duty of reading out the ruler's communications to the high assembly. The year could be 87, 88, or 89.[8] Caesar's quaestor would have had exacting employment in 89. Opening with the rebellion of Antonius Saturninus, that year witnessed Domitian's departure to the

---

[1] Pliny's birth must fall in 61 or 62 (*Epp.* VI. 20. 5). His *cursus* is provided by *ILS* 2927. For the chronology Mommsen remains most useful, *Hermes* III (1869), 31 ff. = *Ges. Schr.* IV (1906), 366 ff. Subsequent argument was mainly sterile. For the quaestorship, App. 17; later posts, App. 19; the dating of the *Letters*, App. 21.

[2] VIII. 14. 7. The governor was probably T. Atilius Rufus (*suff.* c. 75), attested in Pannonia on June 13, 80 (*CIL* XVI, 26), in Syria in 83 (*AE* 1925, 95), where he died the next year (*Agr.* 40. 1). Possibly from Transpadane Italy, where Atilii are very common.

[3] VII. 31. 2.

[4] I. 10. 2 f. A 'princeps provinciae' gave Euphrates his daughter. For this philosopher see P. Grimal, *Latomus* XIV (1955), 370 ff.

[5] III. 11. 5.   [6] V. 8. 8.

[7] I. 18. 3 f. (defending a certain Junius Pastor).

[8] App. 17. The *quaestores Augusti* tend to be men of birth: important for the estimation of Pliny—and of Domitian.

Rhine, his campaign on the middle Danube, the peace with Dacia, and the ostentatious pomp of the double triumph. To the danger on the frontiers was added treason in the army and discontent in the governing class.

When the quaestor recited the imperial dispatches to the sad submissive senators, they endured the hollow phrases of deference, the dishonest asseveration of their collective loyalty and patriotism; and they heard the authentic language of anger, of irony, of exultation. Pliny has not chosen to tell how he fared during his uncomfortable apprenticeship in the arts and hypocrisies of public life. It was no bad training for one who hoped in due course to compose and deliver his own speech of thanksgiving to Caesar.

The next stage was the tribunate of the plebs. That office was a name and a shadow. Pliny, indulging in a solemn make-believe, impresses upon one of his young friends an important truth—the protectors of the plebs enjoy sacrosanctity. Not to impair which, Pliny pushed scruple to extremities and abstained from practising as an advocate.[1] It may be assumed that his comportment in the Senate was discreet and decorous. The Emperor by special grace accelerated his praetorship.

The year 93 saw him praetor, and charged with a public prosecution. On complaint from the province of Baetica against the proconsul Baebius Massa, the Senate instituted a trial, appointing Pliny and Herennius Senecio to prepare and conduct the indictment.[2] Massa was found guilty. But Massa artfully impeached Herennius Senecio for high treason. At this delicate juncture Pliny showed courage and resource. He protested: if Massa was honest, he should not have named Senecio only, but both prosecutors. Pliny's words were noted and approved. The venerable consular Cocceius Nerva wrote to congratulate him on an action worthy of the ancient days.

Pliny's intervention had no effect. Herennius Senecio was put on trial and condemned. Other prosecutions followed, with death for Helvidius Priscus (the younger of that name) and for Junius Rusticus likewise, while his brother Junius Mauricus and certain women of the group were sent into exile.[3] Theirs was a family tradition of hostility to despotism, and they continued the line of the martyrs. Thus did Domitian, in his Neronian development, deal with disaffection among senators. At the same time he banished from the city their adherents among the professional philosophers. Artemidorus went to a house in the suburbs, and Pliny the praetor visited him there, supplying him with funds.[4]

---

[1] I. 23 (to Pompeius Falco, presumably the same person as the Murena tribune in 97, IX. 13. 19: that is, Q. Roscius Coelius Murena Pompeius Falco, *suff*. 108).
[2] VII. 33. 4 ff.   [3] *Agr*. 45. 1, cf. App. 19.   [4] III. 11. 2.

Pliny is not reticent about his own courage—and his own peril. All around him fell the thunderbolts, striking down his friends.[1] Yet Pliny was serene and unscathed. In fact, he prospered.

With scarcely any delay, Pliny is discovered in possession of a fresh office, as one of the three prefects in charge of the *aerarium militare* (not a word about this anywhere in his letters). The post was praetorian in rank, triennial in tenure. Few senators were fortunate enough to obtain it straight from the praetorship. Several stages generally intervened, among them the command of a legion.[2]

In the last years of Domitian Pliny bounded forward in his official career. The fall of the tyrant, so far from prejudicing a man's prospects, might offer the most brilliant chances for daring allied with discretion. Pliny meditated an attack upon the great barrister, Aquillius Regulus, who, conscious of the disapprobation of good men, found that he now had to tread warily.[3] Regulus, it is averred, went in fear of his young rival's enmity. He made anxious exploration of Pliny's intentions, approached mutual friends (among them old Spurinna), and solicited an interview, which was inconclusive. Pliny held his hand, waiting (so he professed) until one of the exiles, Junius Mauricus, should return—and nothing happened.

It would not have been easy to bring down a man equipped with all Regulus' resources.[4] Moreover, while the prime and overt iniquities of Regulus went back to the Neronian age—merciless prosecutions and a scandalously rapid reward[5]—his subsequent conduct, though highly objectionable, had not involved him in the prosecution of any notable members of the senatorial opposition.

Those illustrious victims clamoured to be avenged. Pliny at once discerned an admirable incentive: to punish the wicked, vindicate the innocent, and acquire distinction for himself.[6] He set his aim on Publicius Certus, who had prosecuted Helvidius Priscus. He consulted the widow and other ladies of the group, but did not go into action until some months had elapsed. It would be valuable to know the reasons for the delay, what turn of events now made Certus seem vulnerable. Pliny was not a rash man.

Pliny never embarked on any enterprise without taking counsel of his elderly mentor, Corellius Rufus. This time he had not asked

Rufus

---

[1] *Pan.* 90. 5.

[2] Note, in the period 70–120, *ILS* 8971; 1041; *IGR* III, 558; *CIL* VI, 31678+XIV, 4444. Furthermore, Ti. Caepio Hispo (*suff. c.* 101) might have commanded a legion (*ILS* 1027 is selective, not complete); and the *Ignotus* of *ILS* 1020 (*suff.* ? c. 108) had been *leg. leg.* as quaestorian, anomalously.   [3] I. 5. 1 ff.

[4] ib. 15: 'est enim locuples, factiosus, curatur a multis, timetur a pluribus.'

[5] ib. 3, cf. *Hist.* IV. 42. 3.

[6] IX. 13. 2: 'occiso Domitiano statui mecum ac deliberavi esse magnam pulchramque materiam insectandi nocentes, miseros vindicandi, se proferendi.'

Corellius.[1] Nerva in a conversation with Corellius once described Pliny as one of the 'boni iuvenes'.[2] But Nerva did not approve of these activities, and some of Pliny's consular friends urged him to be careful. Certus, they said, had powerful allies.[3] Yet Pliny's conduct may have been not so much dangerous as inopportune. One of his letters (written a decade later) gives a full and lively account of the whole transaction, with names and details—but not the name of the consul presiding in the Senate.[4] The attack was not pushed to a conclusion, but Pliny's intervention was not the failure it might seem. Publicius Certus was one of the two prefects who managed the other treasury, the *aerarium Saturni*. That office normally led straight to the consulate. As the result of Pliny's efforts the colleague of Certus secured designation, but not Certus.[5]

The *praefecti* who took their place turn out to be none other than Pliny and his closest friend, Cornutus Tertullus.[6] They kept the post for a triennium.[7] The consulship was now in sight. They held it during September and October of 100.

In the meantime Pliny had signalized himself as a prosecutor at the bidding of the Senate. He undertook, with Tacitus, the case against Marius Priscus.[8] That affair took some time to terminate, and he had accepted another commission, to indict Caecilius Classicus, proconsul of Baetica in the year when Marius Priscus governed and plundered the province of Africa.[9]

To crown the dignity of his station, the successful consular still lacked one thing, a priesthood. A petition to the Emperor attests his anxious zeal.[10] The answer has not been preserved. Not that his friends had been inactive. Years before, the aged Verginius Rufus was wont to issue from retirement and push his claims repeatedly.[11] In vain. Nor had Julius Frontinus availed, urging Pliny's nomination year after year.[12] At last Frontinus died. They co-opted Pliny into the vacant place (probably in 103). It was an augurship. A peculiar satisfaction to Pliny, succeeding to so eminent a man. Cicero too had become an augur, he pointed out, though not as early as Pliny.[13] Cicero was compelled to wait a very long time indeed for the rightful reward of eloquence and high ideals.

---

[1] IX. 13. 6.   [2] IV. 17. 8.

[3] IX. 13. 11 (i.e. the legate of Syria, above, pp. 8, 16, and App. 3).

[4] ib. 9. His tactics were very able—and Nerva took no cognisance of the attack on Publicius Certus. Nine senators are named in this debate.

[5] ib. 23, cf. App. 19. The colleague is Q. Fulvius Gillo Bittius Proculus (*PIR*[2], F 544), *suffectus* possibly at the end of 97, but better in the last two months of 98 (cf. App. 11). He was married to the mother of Pliny's recently deceased (second) wife (ib. 13, cf. 4)— i.e. Pompeia Celerina (1. 4, &c.). He is not honoured with a letter from Pliny.

[6] X. 3a. 1, cf. 8. 3; *Pan.* 91. 1. Cf. App. 19.   [7] *Pan.* 91. 1.   [8] p. 70.

[9] III. 4. 2, cf. 8; 9. 1 ff.   [10] X. 13.   [11] II. 1. 8.   [12] IV. 8. 3.   [13] ib. 4.

So far Pliny had won credit by three trials before the Senate, vindicating the wrongs of provinces and exacting retribution from criminal proconsuls. The next case is for the defence.[1] Julius Bassus was an aged man, of many tribulations. Under Vespasian he was accused but finally acquitted. Titus he feared, because he was a friend of Titus' brother. That brother banished him. Returning with other exiles under Nerva, Bassus recovered senatorial rank. His proconsulate of Bithynia brought him into danger once more.

The defence of Julius Bassus called for singular proficiency in all the arts of high-minded equivocation. The proconsul had taken money. A simple and candid person, he was not aware that he was doing wrong. The provincials knew him, and loved him—and he had only accepted some little presents on his birthday and in the festive season.[2] But the law was clear. Hence a dilemma for the advocate. He could not deny the charges: to admit them ruined his client. Pliny resolved to steer a middle course, and he kept to it through five hours of oratory. Nor was the feeling of the high assembly in doubt. The misfortunes of Julius Bassus inclined the senators to mercy, reinforcing a natural prepossession. In the upshot Bassus did not have to forfeit his rank, while the pecuniary reparation due to the Bithynians was fixed by a panel of assessors.

The year 104 brought a consular post—not provincial but urban and suburban. Pliny became president of the Curators of the Tiber.[3] The duties of such an employment might, or might not, prove exacting. Much depended upon the man. When Julius Frontinus was put in charge of the Roman aqueducts, he took his function most seriously, effecting repairs, repressing fraud, and composing a manual on the whole subject. Pliny has not chosen to say anything about operations carried out under his supervision: he did not wish to burden his letters with technicalities. Instead, a vivid and ornate description of the devastation ensuing when the river overflowed its banks.[4]

Pliny was able to visit Comum in 104,[5] which he had not seen for at least eight years. Then Bithynia again burst into notoriety. The prosecution of the proconsul Varenus Rufus began in 106.[6] Pliny, who was among the advocates for the defence, delivered a speech at the initial hearing, but took little part as the case dragged on into the next year, becoming more and more complicated. Trajan, who had returned to Rome in the autumn of 106 after the conquest of Dacia, was compelled to give some attention. Then the thing took a strange

---

[1] IV. 9. 1 ff. (in the winter of 102/3). [2] ib. 7 f.
[3] V. 14. 2, cf. III. 6. 6. Pliny does not name the post. [4] VIII. 17.
[5] V. 14, cf. App. 19.
[6] V. 20. 1 ff. For the date, App. 21. For the later stages, VI. 5 and 13; VII. 6 and 10.

course. Envoys turned up from Bithynia with a decree of the provincial assembly, dropping the indictment. The Emperor undertook to find out the true sentiments of the province. How it all ended is not told anywhere.

Pliny will have continued in his presidency of the Tiber Board for some three years. That office did not exhaust energy or ambition. A consular occupation in foreign parts could suitably engage his merits. Character, tastes, and career did not mark him out for governor of an armed province. Yet a jurist or an orator could qualify. Pliny, though not at all an expert in the law, had acquired fame as an advocate; and his financial ability was superlative. If Pliny did not get one of the normal commands, he might yet have seemed destined to serve as one of the three consulars who supervised the census in Tres Galliae.

Further prospects were opening in the imperial administration. Now that the wars were over, Trajan gave thought to the welfare of the senatorial provinces. In 108 he sent out a special commissioner, a certain Maximus, to investigate and regulate the affairs of the free cities in Achaia.[1] Pliny, with gentle admonishment, reminds Maximus how noble is his task and how delicate—Hellas is the home and the mother of arts, letters, and civilized life; he must honour the great past of the Greeks, their history and their fables, not infringing dignity, freedom, or even vanity; he will remember that he has been entrusted with authority over Athens and over Lacedaemon, that it were barbarous to take away the last vestiges of ancient liberty; to insult others is the wrong use of power, intimidation does not win respect, and love is a more effective agent than fear.

Pliny's words of counsel to Maximus furnish an unobtrusive testimonial to his own possession of the requisite tact and judgement. Nor is it an isolated hint. About the same time (in 107) Calestrius Tiro went out as proconsul of Baetica.[2] Pliny, who had not shown much interest in Calestrius hitherto, despite collegiality in their early career, was alert and helpful. Before the proconsul departed, he warned him to be careful what friends he took in his company, with pointed reference to a recent scandal.[3] For the conduct of his office, the proconsul earned Pliny's commendation—and more advice, and a sharp admonition. He ought to apply himself to the society of the notables and avoid encouraging men of low degree; it is necessary to preserve the distinctions of rank and station; nothing is more unjust than equality.[4]

Were Pliny himself denied scope for the exercise of sound principles in government, it would have been highly regrettable. In 108 or 109

---

[1] VIII. 24.   [2] VII. 16, 23, and 32 (his journey).   [3] VI. 22. I.
[4] IX. 5. I: 'honestissimum quemque complecti atque ita a minoribus amari ut simul a principibus diligare'; 3: 'nihil est ipsa aequalitate inaequalius.'

he seems to conceive a firm expectation of employment: his friend Voconius Romanus, who belonged to one of the leading municipal families in Hispania Tarraconensis, was to join him, when the matter was settled, and serve on his staff.[1]

Pliny's hopes may have been disappointed, or at least deferred. The call may indeed have come in 109 or 110. Perhaps he had to wait until 111. It took the form of a special commission. Not, however, for the census in Tres Galliae, where an appointment fell to Cornutus Tertullus.[2] Pliny was to go to Bithynia-Pontus as Caesar's legate, in place of the praetorian proconsul. The delinquencies of Roman magistrates were patent, and the prosecutions had shown up grave disorders in the cities; while Pliny had been able to acquire some familiarity with Bithynian affairs.

After the voyage to Ephesus and a delay at Pergamum caused by heat and by fever, Pliny set foot in his province on September 17. He spent a winter there, a summer, and another winter.[3] Before the second year of office terminated, the governor's correspondence with the Emperor ceases abruptly. Death may be surmised. Pliny's frame was delicate, he has been ill in his middle thirties, and the climate of the province might prove fatal even to the robust. To aggravate the governor's ailments, cares and worries came thick and fast. They preyed upon his conscience, they multiplied his dispatches—municipal finance and peculation, aqueducts, fire-brigades, and foreign religions.[4]

After Pliny, the governor of Bithynia-Pontus is Cornutus Tertullus, also bearing the title of imperial legate.[5] Cornutus survived into the next reign, and so did the great consular historian. Tacitus' proconsulate of Asia may have been concurrent with a part of Pliny's tenure in Bithynia, and his experiences comparable, for he cannot have been spared the frauds and vanities of the Greeks in their cities—and sundry other vexations.[6]

The official career of Pliny is variously notable. First of all, speed and success between praetorship and consulate. While certain of his close coevals, praetors in the period 90–94, go abroad to command

---

[1] IX. 28. 4, cf. App. 20.

[2] ILS 1024, for Aquitania. The colleagues in Belgica and in Lugdunensis are surely the Ignotus of ILS 1020 (suff. ? c. 108), and C. Julius Proculus (ILS 1040), suff. in 109.

[3] App. 20. For the details of his movements, U. Wilcken, Hermes XLIX (1914), 120 ff.; O. Cuntz, ib. LXI (1926), 19 ff.

[4] For his activities and policy cf. especially W. Weber, Festgabe für K. Müller (Tübingen, 1922), 24 ff.

[5] ILS 1024, which also shows him proconsul, 'provinci[ae Asiae]'. It could be 'Africae' (cf. App. 23).

[6] Ch. XXXV.

legions, or supervise minor roads in Italy,[1] Pliny at once acquires an advantageous post at the capital. The chance survival of authentic evidence, disclosing the prefecture of the *aerarium militare*, blows away the orator's assertion that he called a halt in his career.[2] No more tangible is the notion that Pliny would infallibly have been prosecuted but for the providential assassination of the tyrant, even though he supports it by alleging that a notorious 'delator' had laid an information: the document was found among Domitian's papers.[3]

Details about two of Pliny's friends furnish a sharp contrast. With Calestrius Tiro he shared military service as a tribune, he was quaestor in the same year and praetor likewise.[4] Henceforth their paths diverge. Calestrius is next discovered, tardily, and still of praetorian rank, when he becomes proconsul of Baetica fourteen years later. Calestrius failed to move forward—perhaps from a deplorable tendency to disregard social distinctions.[5]

Pliny meanwhile was consul, seven years from his praetorship. Cornelius Tacitus took nine years. Other *novi homines*, not wholly lacking protection and kinship, had to wait longer. With Pliny, his friend Cornutus Tertullus assumed the *fasces* in 100. Pliny was still under forty. Cornutus was a good twenty years his senior.

Cornutus Tertullus, a senator already, acquired praetorian rank from Vespasian in his censorship.[6] Through the next twenty-four years, until he became prefect of the *aerarium Saturni* with Pliny for colleague, Cornutus held two offices only—legate to a proconsul, and proconsul himself. Not posts of high promise. In the estimation of Pliny, Cornutus was a man of principle and integrity, a genuine specimen of antique virtue.[7] They had the same friends, and both were menaced by the tyrant's anger.[8] Caution as well as conscience may

---

[1] App. 25.

[2] *Pan.* 95. 3 f.: 'vos modo favete huic proposito et credite, si cursu quodam provectus ab illo insidiosissimo principe, ante quam profiteretur odium bonorum, postquam professus est, substiti; si, cum viderem quae ad honores compendia paterent, longius iter malui', &c.

[3] VII. 27. 14. The 'delator' was Mettius Carus, who prosecuted Herennius Senecio (VII. 19. 5). Pliny's friend Cn. Octavius Titinius Capito was secretary *ab epistulis* at this time (*ILS* 1448). [4] VII. 16. 2.

[5] cf. the strong hint in IX. 5. Calestrius' own local origin cannot be discovered. The *nomen*, very rare, is of an Etruscan type.

[6] *ILS* 1024. The inscription reveals a part of his full nomenclature 'C. Julio P. f. Hor. [......] / Cornuto Tertul[lo /', to which the *gentilicium* 'Plancius' might belong, cf. the dedicator 'C. Iulius Pla[n]cius Varus Cornutus'. Origin mysterious, cf. E. Groag, P–W x, 571. But observe the Plancii Vari of Perge in Pamphylia (p. 509, n. 4), which city can also show a C. Julius Cornutus (*IGR* III, 789).

[7] V. 14. 3: 'Cornuto autem quid melius, quid sanctius, quid in omni genere laudis ad exemplar antiquitatis expressius?'

[8] *Pan.* 90. 5. Cornutus was guardian of the daughter of the younger Helvidius Priscus (*Epp.* IX. 13. 16).

have deterred Cornutus from an intensive pursuit of public honours. There is no sign that he was an active malcontent, as was Herennius Senecio, who had written a political biography.[1] However, even the practice of 'quies' might be culpable under the inquisitive despotism of Domitian. It was alleged among the treasonable charges against Senecio that he chose, wantonly and ostentatiously, not to rise higher than the quaestorship.[2] Yet two other members of the group became consuls, Helvidius Priscus and Junius Rusticus.[3] As for Cornutus, Domitian may have distrusted his capacities as well as his sentiments.

Honours and office gave Pliny every cause for pride and contentment. The decisive stages came between praetorship and consulate. The first treasury post he acquired by favour of Domitian, the second not without some exertions of his own, after the attack on Publicius Certus. Among the praetors of Pliny's epoch were men not lacking in birth or talent. Several orators can be discerned, among them an elegant and versatile member of a new patrician family, or an exemplary *novus homo* with a consular connexion.[4] Most of them were outstripped by Pliny. The crisis of 97 had been propitious for legionary legates in certain provinces. Pliny with the second treasury post gains a promotion comparable to theirs, and through civilian employments he equals the most favoured class of 'viri militares'.

Later, when Trajan ruled, he may have felt a slight frustration. Though Pliny numbered venerable senators among his patrons (notably those influential under Nerva), the alert young orator did not excite the enthusiasm of all the military men. Trajan could not refuse the consulate. But the consular was kept out of a priesthood for some time; and the provincial command may have seemed slow in coming. Nor were Pliny's eager efforts to secure promotion for his friends invariably rewarded.[5] Some of them lacked ambition or had lost favour.[6]

Pliny's employments were mainly civilian and urban. When the elder statesman gave Calestrius and Maximus the benefit of his reflec-

---

[1] *Agr.* 2. 1.

[2] Dio LXVII. 13. 2.

[3] Priscus before 87 (despite his father's fate), Rusticus in 92 (by his full nomenclature 'Q. Arulenus Iunius Rusticus'). Also T. Avidius Quietus, in 93.

[4] App. 25. Note especially L. Arruntius Stella, poet and patron of poets, and M. Vitorius Marcellus, to whom Quintilian dedicated his work (*Inst. or., praef.* 6).

[5] Two examples may suffice. The attempt to get Voconius Romanus into the Senate (x. 4) fails—and there is no evidence that he received an equestrian post under the army commander Priscus (II. 13). These letters emphasize his local distinction. By full nomenclature 'C. Licinius Marinus Voconius Romanus', from Saguntum, cf. *PIR*[1], L 144 and the inscriptions there cited. Secondly, Rosianus Geminus, Pliny's quaestor in 100, and warmly commended to Trajan (x. 26): he did not reach the consulate until twenty-five or more years had elapsed since 100 (as may be deduced from *ILS* 1067).

[6] Thus Erucius Clarus and Bruttius Praesens (p. 242).

tions on the conduct seemly in a governor of provinces, an ingenuous reader might suppose that personal experience informed the language of that sagacious discourse. In fact Pliny had never been abroad save for a few months as tribune in a Syrian legion. He told Maximus how to behave towards Greeks. Maximus may have been born in a Roman colony of the eastern lands, at Alexandria in the Troad.[1]

Posterity knows Pliny the consul as an orator and a man of letters. For all his fame in the Senate, his main field was forensic, the law of property. The centumviral court was the arena of his triumphs.[2] Juries clamoured their enthusiasm, and fanciers flocked.[3] Moreover, the two treasury posts and the mission to Bithynia suggest that his principal capacity in the eyes of the government was financial.[4]

Pliny was a wealthy landowner with estates at Comum in the North and at Tifernum Tiberinum on the borders of Etruria and Umbria; and he had four country houses in the vicinity of the capital.[5] He was generous with his money, subsidizing friends or old retainers and handsomely endowing the city of his birth. Comum received more than a million and a half sesterces, including a library and a trust fund for the children of the poor; and Pliny's will produced nearly two millions more, for baths and for the maintenance of a hundred of his freed slaves.[6] Pliny's patrimony was mainly in land. He is not averse from explaining that the rich are not really well-off, what with bad seasons, poor vintages, and tiresome tenants;[7] and the business of agricultural exploitation seems alien or distasteful to a person of refined and literary pursuits. He will wander through the fields, nibble a grape, or cast a cursory glance at account books—nothing more.[8] The appearance is delusive. The nephew had his share of the old Pliny's accuracy and acumen. The mother of Pliny's second wife owned much real estate. She allowed Pliny to employ and invest her funds anywhere, at discretion.[9] It is not likely that her confidence was misplaced or abused.

---

[1] If identical with Sex. Quinctilius Valerius Maximus, given the *latus clavus* by Nerva, quaestor of Bithynia-Pontus (*ILS* 1018). Cf. E. Groag, *Jahreshefte* XXI/XXII (1924), Beiblatt 435 ff.; M. N. Tod, *Anatolian Studies Presented to William Hepburn Buckler* (1939), 333 ff. The identity cannot quite be taken as proved. For an anecdote about Maximus, described as διορθωτής, see Arrian, *Diss. Epicteti* III. 7. 1 ff.

[2] VI. 12. 2.

[3] IV. 16; VI. 33. 4; IX. 23. 1.

[4] Elsewhere judgement and decision were sometimes deficient. There is some impatience in Trajan's answers, e.g. X. 38. 2; 82. 1; 99.

[5] Apart from the famous Laurentum, villas at Tusculum, Tibur, and Praeneste (v. 6. 45).

[6] cf. the details in *ILS* 2927.

[7] II. 4. 3; 15. 2; IV. 6. 1; VIII. 2; IX. 37. 2 ff.

[8] V. 14. 8; IX. 20. 2.

[9] III. 19. 8. Pompeia Celerina had estates at Ocriculum, Narnia, Carsulae, and Perusia (I. 4. 1).

The correspondence presents to the world a carefully arranged and tinted picture of the author, his pursuits, and his friends. About Pliny, the letters sometimes tell more than he intended, and supplementary evidence corrects the simple and surface impression. About Cornelius Tacitus, they do not offer much direct information. But they reveal him in the ambit of the literary life of that epoch—not a little in contrast, and perhaps in wilful opposition.

VIII. LITERATURE UNDER TRAJAN

BEGINNING with his own town and region, the circle of Pliny grew ever wider through associations that formed and ripened in the schools of Rome and in the law-courts, in salons and in the Senate. Though the North for many of its sons held out no fairer prospect than the highroad to the capital, the emigrants did not all forswear the country of their birth. Transpadane men might be absent for long years or never return, but they dutifully acknowledged a vigorous sentiment of local patriotism.[1]

Not that the whole region was a unit. Italy beyond the river Po had a wide extension, some three hundred miles from the western Alps to the Istrian peninsula. Estimated by the names of cities, it went all the way from Augusta Taurinorum to Aquileia, Tergeste, and Pola. Italia Transpadana showed common features but local diversities, with old racial or tribal boundaries still perceptible. Mediolanium had once been the town of the Insubres, a Gallic people, whereas Patavium was Venetic. Pliny's own city was Comum, a Roman colony, but of no great weight or prestige. Mediolanium was the dominant place in the neighbourhood—the convergence of roads had already made it the capital of a large district. Pliny's closer attachments belong to the old Insubrian territory and to adjacent cities like Brixia and Bergomum; they take in Vercellae and Ticinum, and go eastwards to embrace Verona, but are not quite so strong at Patavium or Ateste.[2]

Pliny could benefit from the friendship and the support of illustrious consulars. Verginius Rufus, his guardian, came from Mediolanium.[3] Also northern is Corellius Rufus, whose family became linked with his own.[4] Probably also Vestricius Spurinna.[5] Pliny in his turn

[1] *Epp.* I. 14. 4: 'ex illa nostra Italia' (referring to a Brixian family). His uncle described Catullus as 'conterraneus meus' (*NH, praef.* 1). For northern solidarity, G. E. F. Chilver, *Cisalpine Gaul* (1941), 86 ff. The dynamic zone, in late Republic and early Empire, is clearly the tract north of the Po. The Cispadana seems to count much less—at least no persons of note from cities like Placentia, Parma, Mutina.

[2] That is to say, the 'Pliny country' corresponds closely to the eastern part of the *Regio XI* in the Augustan classification of Italy, but includes Verona in *Regio X*. Verona and Brixia had an ancient link, cf. Catullus 67. 34: 'Brixia Veronae mater amata meae.' An eminent second-century family, the Nonii, seems attached to both cities, cf. P-W XVII, 864 f.; 897 f. [3] II. 1. 8, cf. *ILS* 982.

[4] The *nomen* 'Corellius' is very rare. *CIL* v shows one instance, Q. Corellius Q. f. Paulinus, a *decurio* at Laus Pompeia (6366). Note, however, an *eques Romanus* at Ateste (*NH* XVII. 122) and inscriptions of *liberti* found there (*Not. Scav.* 1930, 281). Corellius Rufus married a woman called Hispulla (*Epp.* I. 12. 9): observe Calpurnia Hispulla (*PIR²*, C 329), daughter of Calpurnius Fabatus (the grandfather of Pliny's third wife).

[5] App. 6.

lent enthusiastic suffrage to younger friends in the career of honours, or gave solid help to aspirants of lower station—to one the financial subsidy requisite for attaining equestrian rank,[1] to others commendation for posts in the army.[2]

More than a hundred persons receive epistles from Pliny. How complete is the picture of Roman society under Trajan? A full catalogue would be instructive, and tedious. Not a few of the correspondents betray the marks of mediocrity, whether rank or accomplishment be regarded—family retainers, school friends, local bards and small-town snobs, admirers of eloquence, devotees of culture, some who had fallen behind in the race, and some who never started. Instead, profit may accrue from an indirect computation, from reviewing the categories that happen not to be strongly in evidence.

First of all, the men of power in the entourage of Trajan. Julius Servianus can count as an acquaintance before the Emperor's accession;[3] Licinius Sura is there with missives to his address, likewise Sosius Senecio and Fabius Justus.[4] Yet a number of the senior marshals have no entry, even a general of high honour from the North, Glitius Agricola from the city of Augusta Taurinorum.[5] Pliny's career and tastes help to explain the gaps. Some of the younger military men are also absent.[6]

If the military hierarchy was not all and at once accessible, nobles with their prestige of birth seemed to invite cultivation. A frank and open predilection for the aristocracy might have been surmised in the alert parvenu. However, not a single descendant either of the Republican *nobilitas* or of the Augustan consular houses is discovered on the list of Pliny's correspondents.[7] The oriental grandees, the descendants of kings and tetrarchs, are also missing;[8] and the equestrian dignitaries of weightiest moment, prefects of Egypt and commanders of the Praetorian Guard, display a solitary specimen. This is Vibius Maximus, a man not lacking in social rank and literary pretensions.[9] Septicius Clarus, to whom the correspondence is dedicated, did not earn high promotion until much later.[10]

---

[1] I. 19.   [2] IV. 4; VI. 25. 2; VII. 22.   [3] X. 2. 1 (of 98), cf. III. 17. 3.

[4] IV. 30; VII. 27 (Sura); I. 13; IV. 4 (Senecio); I. 11; VII. 2 (Justus).

[5] *ILS* 1021. Others who have no letters are M'. Laberius Maximus, A. Cornelius Palma, and L. Publilius Celsus—all, like Glitius Agricola, rising to second consulates.

[6] Thus D. Terentius Scaurianus (*suff.* ? 102 or 104); and some of the younger marshals (App. 16), consuls between 105 and 112.

[7] For some of these personages see App. 24.   [8] Ch. XXXVIII.

[9] *PIR*, V 389, cf. p. 56. Add that he perhaps comes from Verona, *Epp.* VI. 34. 1; Martial I. 7 (a reference to 'tuus Catullus').

[10] Appointed Prefect of the Guard in 119 (*HA, Hadr.* 9. 4). He could perhaps have been *praefectus vigilum* at an earlier stage. Local origin not established. Uncle of Sex. Erucius Clarus (*suff.* 117).

Though Trajan cared not even to put up a pretence, his wife was benevolently disposed towards literary pursuits. To the Empress Pliny has not ventured to dedicate any composition of his own, but he promises that the epistles of a friend in Spain will be forwarded for her perusal.[1] More remarkable, since it was Pliny's habit to encourage talent or promise in the younger generation, there is no letter to Aelius Hadrianus, no trace of him anywhere in the collection.[2] Silence also envelops certain of Hadrianus' kinsmen and friends, already persons of consequence or later prominent on the family tree of the dynasty.[3]

The world of letters in the last years of Domitian comprised several groups, notably those associated with the names of Statius and Martial. The two poets, neither of whom deigns to mention the other, praised the Emperor in eager emulation and competed for the favour of various patrons. Some of those patrons were of Pliny's own age or rank, and might appear to share his literary tastes. Hardly any of them turn up again in Pliny's circle, not even Arruntius Stella, high-born and wealthy though he be, gifted, eloquent, and poetical.[4] Stella came from Patavium.[5] Previous generations knew bad Transpadani as well as good, for example Vibius Crispus.[6] Not all of Pliny's seniors from the northern towns are enrolled in the category of Pliny's friends. The eminent Silius Italicus received no letter.[7] The sons are also absent.[8]

To new groups and rising talent the time of Trajan offered a clear field of endeavour, for the Flavian poets went out in rapid sequence, with hardly anybody left to compete or impede. Statius, whose efforts did not stop at the elaborate occasional verse of the *Silvae*, duly

[1] IX. 28. I (Voconius Romanus, of Saguntum).

[2] He comes very close with Pedanius Fuscus (IX. 36 and 40). That young man's promise is extolled (VI. 11. 1 ff.), and Julius Servianus is congratulated for choosing him as bridegroom for his daughter (VI. 26. 1)—i.e. Julia, the niece of Hadrian.

[3] Notably M. Annius Verus (*suff.* 97) and, coeval with Pedanius Fuscus, the young T. Aurelius Fulvus (*cos.* 120); but also Cn. Domitius Tullus (*suff.* c. 79, *II* 98), L. Dasumius (?93), and L. Ceionius Commodus (*cos.* 106). See App. 87.

[4] L. Arruntius Stella (*suff.* ?101). For details, *PIR²*, A 1151. Another absentee is M. Vitorius Marcellus (*suff.* 105). On these men, App. 25.

[5] Martial I. 61. 4. Presumably related to 'M. Arruntius [' and to M. Arruntius Aquila, *suffecti* in 66 and 77. For the latter, *ILS* 980 (Patavium).

[6] From Vercellae (*Dial.* 8. 1): governor of Hispania Citerior when Pliny's uncle was procurator, cf. p. 61.

[7] By his full nomenclature, 'Ti. Catius Asconius Silius Italicus', cf. the inscription from Aphrodisias (published in *CR* XLIX (1935), 217). The *nomen* 'Asconius' inevitably suggests Patavium, whence came the scholarly Asconius, whom Silius himself evokes (*Pun.* XII. 212 ff.). The claims of Mediolanium or Ticinum will not be omitted—note the Insubrian Ti. Catius, an Epicurean philosopher, from the same town as Cornelius Nepos (Cicero, *Ad fam.* XV. 16. 1, cf. Pliny, *Epp.* IV. 28. 1).

[8] e.g. L. Silius Decianus (*suff.* 94); or Ti. Catius Caesius Fronto (*suff.* 96), who may be related to Silius Italicus. Fronto was an orator, cf. App. 27.

delivered one mythological epic of standard proportions and began another, but was carried off before he could acclaim Nerva and Trajan with congenial enthusiasm and familiar artifice. And Valerius Flaccus died before Domitian's removal, his *Argonautica* unfinished. If Silius Italicus persisted, it was for a task to complete, not because he was disposed to sacrifice his leisure and decorate the new government—or be decorated by it. His public life belonged to the past—one of the prosecutors under Nero and consul in 68, but redeemed by discreet conduct subsequently; and fame accrued from his governorship of Asia. Letters claimed him, his art collections, and the cult of Cicero and Virgil. The old consular stayed in his Campanian villas, not stirring even to witness the advent of Trajan. He was hard at work, 'maiore cura quam ingenio'. When he heroically terminated the seventeen books of the *Punica*, but still had to struggle with an incurable malady, he ended his life by voluntary starvation at the age of seventy-five.[1]

The extinction of Silius, closing a line of epic poets, seems to mark the end of a period in literature. Within a year or so Rome had the loss to chronicle of a less pretentious talent. The epigrammatist Valerius Martialis, though willing to pay brief tribute to the felicity of the times, soon found that the changed atmosphere was not altogether exhilarating, while affection for the land of his birth—he had not seen it for a third of a century—grew stronger and reinforced distaste for the metropolis. Martial returned to Spain, where he died not long after.[2]

Silius belongs to the lower slopes of Parnassus—industry rather than talent—but Valerius Flaccus knows how to write with elegant precision and make a narrative move; Statius is a pleasing and accomplished poet; and Martial refines the vigour and clarity of Latin with Attic point and elegance. Such in brief is what the poets of the Flavian age achieved. The names of two prose authors will be added, of high and classical rank—Fabius Rusticus (an historian whose works are lost) and Fabius Quintilianus. After a successful career of teaching (he held the first endowed chair of rhetoric at Rome, whence came wealth and official honours), Quintilian in his retirement wrote the *Institutio Oratoria*. Published shortly before the death of Domitian, it is a general treatise on education—clear, eloquent, sagacious.[3]

---

[1] For his career and habits cf. the necrological letter III. 7 (of 101). Add the inscription *CR* XLIX (1935), 217, showing a blameless action when proconsul: an edict to prevent people from interfering with the sacred doves of Aphrodite.

[2] III. 21 (probably of 102). Martial departed in 98, and after a 'triennium' published his last book (XII, *praef.*). He alludes to the consulate of Arruntius Stella (XII. 2. 10), which fell in an October (*ILS* 6106): presumably in 101, cf. App. 18.

[3] Compare the firm and cordial appreciation of Mommsen, concluding Roman Spain, in *The Provinces of the Roman Empire* I (1886), 77.

The government lent encouragement to literature, not merely from the personal caprice of a prince whose tastes inclined towards poetry and the arts, but of set policy. Official patronage need not always be harmful to poetry, to education, to erudition. Oratory or history is another matter. An uneasy and suspicious emperor inhibited free comment about present conditions, and soon about the past even, with espionage, delation, and the burning of books. The evil was not novel. It seemed to grow inevitably out of the system of government. Yet tyrants passed away and were consigned to eternal infamy, not least because they attempted to abrogate the traditional privilege of free speech which senators under the Caesars inherited from the aristocracy of the Republic. What was to follow after Domitian in the happier years when 'libertas' and 'principatus' joined in unwonted amity and concord?

Liberation from despotism brought relief to Cornelius Tacitus, but any transports of enthusiasm were chilled by sober reflection. Genius and learning, once curbed and repressed, cannot easily be revived; inactivity, at first resented as a penalty, grows congenial, and may slip into complacent sloth.[1] Tacitus' friend did not allow himself to doubt. Polite studies, so Pliny avers, flourish as never before.[2] Pliny acclaims a genuine renascence, with handsome credit to his own efforts and orations, to the multifarious talents of friends and clients. Any year might now bring forth a whole crop of poets, any month be given over almost wholly to daily recitations.[3]

All modes were practised, including lyric and drama, and some that had been seldom or never attempted in Latin.[4] Versification not only frivolous but even scabrous embellished the quiet years of consular statesmen such as Vestricius Spurinna and Arrius Antoninus, in well-earned repose after the cares of office.[5] The young men took up the challenge, emulating in hendecasyllables the fame of Catullus. Some of them had the poet's town and region for an excuse. A specimen has been preserved, emanating from a relative and protégé of Spurinna, and it suffices—not the grace and spirit of Verona's poet, but triviality and flatness.[6] The versatility of these people was disquieting, and so was their conceit. One of Pliny's northern friends was not content to throw off poems elegantly and easily, another veritable Catullus. He was a fluent and sonorous orator, commanding all fashions of public discourse; he honoured history with his attentions; and he would

---

[1] *Agr.* 3. 1: 'ingenia studiaque facilius oppresseris quam revocaveris. subit quippe etiam ipsius inertiae dulcedo, et invisa primo desidia postremo amatur.'

[2] I. 10. 1; III. 18. 5.   [3] I. 13. 1.

[4] One man, Vergilius Romanus, even essayed both 'mimiambi' and the 'vetus comoedia' (VI. 21. 2 ff.).   [5] p. 4.

[6] IV. 27. 4: 'canto carmina versibus minutis / his olim quibus et meus Catullus', &c.

recite epistles of a studied archaic manner, ostensibly his wife's but perhaps his own.[1]

Under the specious garb of mutual criticism, mutual flattery paraded unashamed. A composition seldom reached the book-market before it had circulated among admirers or got advertisement in the salons. Social constraint and reciprocal needs generally sufficed to muster an audience and preserve the decencies. Yet a soldier, a lawyer, or a scholar might well become restive. When a poet from Asisium in Umbria, who numbered Propertius among his ancestors, began to recite some elegiacs, invoking the command of his friend Javolenus Priscus with the words 'Prisce iubes', that person at once retorted 'ego vero non iubeo'. There was much laughter. Pliny, reporting the matter to a distant correspondent, expresses grave doubts about the sanity of Javolenus, who was a jurist of classic attainments.[2]

Another stray detail is of interest. By paradox one of Pliny's comrades has to be rebuked for diffidence, for a culpable reluctance to publish.[3] This honorable exception is not a bard or a declaimer but a learned antiquarian: Suetonius Tranquillus, the son of an equestrian tribune. His quest for a career had been plagued by doubts and fancies. Having to plead a suit, he took alarm from a dream: he begged Pliny to intervene and have the hearing postponed.[4] Then there was military service. Mere superstition should not have kept a man out of the Roman army, yet when Pliny secured him a tribunate in Britain, he drew back.[5] Literary researches had attracted others as a refuge and consolation. Suetonius could know that the prime exponent of Latin textual criticism, Valerius Probus, failed to get the post of centurion.[6] He might also read a challenge in the performances of Pliny's uncle. He dedicated his life to scholarship. Not until many years had passed, when the vicissitudes of favour and patronage brought an employment in the Palace, with access to the archives, did Suetonius embark on the *Lives of the Caesars*.[7]

Biography offers the easy approach to history, and some go no further than biography. To this form of writing the establishment of the monarchy and the long duration of a dynasty might have seemed not a little propitious. Yet the earlier theme in imperial Rome is not so much the Caesars as their victims. If the practice took its origin

---

[1] I. 16 (Pompeius Saturninus). As for Voconius Romanus 'epistulas quidem scribit ut Musas ipsas Latine loqui credas' (II. 13. 7).

[2] VI. 15. 3: 'est omnino Priscus dubiae sanitatis, interest tamen officiis, adhibetur consiliis atque etiam ius civile publice respondet.' The date is about 106. There was nothing wrong with Javolenus, for he taught P. Salvius Julianus (*Dig.* XL. 2. 5), the consul of 148. The poet is C. Passennus Paullus Propertius Blaesus (*ILS* 2925: Asisium).

[3] V. 10.   [4] I. 18. 1.

[5] III. 8. 1. The commander was L. Neratius Marcellus (cf. App. 14).

[6] Suetonius, *De gram.* 24.   [7] p. 501 and App. 76.

from the funeral oration, it was soon exploited by persons extraneous to the deceased, avowedly as a genre intermediate between oratory and history. A certain C. Fannius resolved to write about those whom Nero killed or banished.[1] He composed three volumes. Then the author was vouchsafed a vision of Nero. The spectre came and sat on his bed, read the scrolls one by one, and went away. Fannius divined that it was not his destiny to write any more; and Fannius died.

The Domitianic persecution supplied fresh matter. It was put to abundant use. Pliny hastened to elaborate his invective against Publicius Certus, which he put out expressly as the avenging of Helvidius Priscus. Pliny was in the habit of commending the speech for imitation, to young men of rank and promise, in their oratorical exercises; and some thought Demosthenes the only comparison.[2]

Fannius in his choice of a subject may have been encouraged by ties of kinship,[3] but Pliny's relations with the circle of Helvidius Priscus were not perhaps as close and continuous as his professions imply. The behaviour of Titinius Capito, who set down in writing the deaths of illustrious men, is instructive and salutary.

Titinius multiplied his activities, not only an author but a friend, a patron, a champion.[4] Literature was in a decline; Titinius arrested the decline.[5] He never missed a recitation, and his own house was generously lent for those performances. Titinius (so Pliny affirms) stood out among the especial ornaments of the age. What else is known about Titinius and the age will be held to strengthen that amiable pre-possession. In his mansion this man exhibited the consecrated effigies of Cato, of Brutus, of Cassius, so genuine was his devotion to the great names of the Republican past; and he asked permission of the Emperor to erect in the Roman Forum the statue of a nobleman who had been put to death by Nero.[6]

No suspicion of Republican sentiments incriminates the life and career of Titinius Capito, nor does any link of propinquity with the aristocratic houses explain or extenuate his behaviour. Not a noble, not even a senator, but merely a Roman knight, Titinius is a document of social mimicry. Undue subservience to the prestige of rank and station transforms imitation into parody, involuntarily exposing the inner falsity of conventional beliefs and pious observances.

---

[1] V. 5.   [2] IV. 21. 3; VII. 30. 4 f.; IX. 13. 1, cf. I. 2. 2.

[3] Perhaps related to Fannia (*PIR*[2], F 118), daughter of Thrasea Paetus and wife of the elder Helvidius Priscus.

[4] VIII. 12, cf. V. 8.

[5] VIII. 12. 1: 'ipsarum denique litterarum iam senescentium reductor ac reformator.' Anticipated in this beneficent function by a patron of Statius—'Manilius certe Vopiscus, vir eruditissimus et qui praecipue vindicat a situ litteras iam paene fugientis' (*Silvae* I, *praef.*).   [6] I. 17.

The record of Titinius' career substantiates the revelation.[1] An officer on some campaign or other, he attracted the notice of Domitian through pleasing gifts, elegance of style, or some act of loyal service. Rewarded with military decorations, he was taken out of the army to become the Emperor's confidential secretary. Nerva kept him, and so did Trajan, with promotion from the secretariat to the charge of the *vigiles*, a post which likewise called for discretion and loyalty. Knights illustrate the permanence of officialdom when rulers change, and the higher knights are often literary celebrities.

Such was the Maecenas of Trajan's Rome, writer and patron both. Pliny also sustained the double role, with an assiduity that recalled his uncle and an exuberance all his own. No kind of writing was immune from his solicitations. A votary of the Muses from early youth, Pliny composed a Greek tragedy when only fourteen; and Latin verses beguiled an interval of delay on the voyage home from service in Syria.[2] Copious and varied productivity came much later. One day during the hour of the siesta inspiration descended upon Pliny.[3] He discovered that he could write hexameters. Then he passed to elegiacs, with no less facility, and soon other metres invited a trial. A whole series of hendecasyllables emerged and gained wide esteem. Greeks adored the slim volume—it made them love the Latin language—and they set the poems to music. Some of Pliny's intimates, however, were unable to conceal their distress: the productions were not only frankly immoral, they were unseemly in a person of his station.[4] Pliny is at great pains to justify his incursion into the realms of conventional frivolity. Men unimpeachable in the purity and the dignity of their days had ever been addicted to light verse—why, all the great orators and statesmen, a whole catalogue, and emperors even, like Nerva, and some classical authors, though they were not (he concedes) of senatorial rank.[5]

Roman tradition did not regard serious poetical endeavours, like the epic or didactic compositions, as proper or predominant occupation for a senator, still less as any basis for enduring fame. Only oratory or history would do, as being each a form of political activity. From early youth Pliny aspired to excellence in public speech, put himself to the best masters, and made a successful début in the courts. The glory of Cicero was ever before his eyes. He avowed emulation of the great exemplar, and thereby exposed himself to flattery from Martial,

---

[1] *ILS* 1448.   [2] VII. 4. 2 f.
[3] ib. 4 ff., with the hexameters quoted. He produces some prosaic elegiacs in VII. 9. 11. Two lines deserve to be quoted—'utque sacri fontes non sola incendia sistunt | saepe etiam flores vernaque prata lavant.'
[4] IV. 14. 4 ff.; V. 3. 1 ff.
[5] V. 3. 6: 'non quidem hi senatores, sed sanctitas morum non distat ordinibus.'

a sneer from Aquillius Regulus.[1] Of his manifold production, Pliny in the correspondence refers by name to several speeches which he worked up and published, notable among them the harangue to the town council of Comum preliminary to dedicating the library, and the invective against Publicius Certus.[2]

Pliny formed a general habit of reciting his speeches to an audience. That was an innovation at Rome. Not everybody liked it. Pliny offers a defence: if histories can be recited (and the goal of history is veracity and honesty), if drama and lyric poetry, then why not an oration?[3]

Pliny's especial pride was the consular 'actio gratiarum'. The *Panegyricus* in the shape that has survived to posterity would take something like three hours to declaim. When the head of the government is also the leader of society, ceremonial observances become strict and insidious. The demeanour of the Caesars at a banquet, a religious rite, or a session of the Senate was jealously watched for the faintest betrayal of intolerance or fatigue. Trajan sustained nobly the role of a 'civilis princeps' with consummate dignity, condescension, and good humour when he presided as consul in the Senate.[4] Outward form, however false or tedious, had to be respected. Yet three hours of intensive glorification would be an inhuman ordeal for the most patient of rulers.

In fact, the normal 'actio gratiarum' was tolerably brief. The proud author of the *Panegyricus* subsequently expanded the oration.[5] Pliny not only circulated the manuscript among his friends for admiration or improvements, but invited them to hear it read. They came without urgent summons in all weathers, and some asked for more.[6]

Amplification was congenial. In a lengthy epistle, Pliny takes his stand against brevity, and proclaims that the best speech is the biggest.[7] He makes appeal to the orators of the past, and reiterates his own practice as an advocate, with metaphorical elaborations in support. Nor is he afraid to quote adverse criticism, namely the comment of Aquillius Regulus, when once they shared a case. Pliny would leave nothing out: Regulus went at once to the heart of the matter.[8]

Moreover, the theme asked for it. An encomium of the Emperor, once as loathsome as it was dishonest, had now become pleasing because of its sincerity.[9] Pliny revels in his task. Enlarging upon the

---

[1] Martial x. 20. 12 ff. (cited in *Epp.* III. 21); *Epp.* I. 5. 11: 'Satrius Rufus, cui non est cum Cicerone aemulatio.'

[2] The invective, VII. 30. 4 f.; IX. 13. 1; the library speech, I. 8. 2.

[3] VII. 17. 3.   [4] *Pan.* 76.

[5] III. 18. 1, cf. J. Mesk, *Wiener Studien* XXXII (1910), 239 ff.; M. Durry in his edition (Paris, 1938), 6 ff.   [6] III. 13; 18.

[7] I. 20. 4: 'bonus liber melior est quo quisque maior.'

[8] ib. 14.   [9] III. 18. 7.

virtues of Trajan, he proposes not merely to applaud the character and conduct of his emperor, but to create a model for all posterity, guiding future rulers in the path of duty and glory.[1] They could also be warned by the recent past. To enhance Trajan and exhibit his own virtuosity, Pliny evokes at great length the tyranny of Domitian. The facts were bad enough to tell their own tale. Such is the regularity with which he distorts them, that the reality underlying the rhetoric can often be surmised or disinterred.

An official orator need not confine his loyal efforts to distorting the truth. It may sometimes be expedient to suppress it entirely. Pliny passes rapidly over Trajan's career subsequent to Trajan's consulship; he has no word about the comportment of other generals during the reign of Nerva; and he omits the provincial origin of the new emperor. In the *Panegyricus* the type of discourse devoted to flattering the supreme power has come to perfection, with few tricks left for later practitioners to learn. The way to it led from Cicero's *Pro Marcello*, praising the glory and the clemency of Caesar the Dictator, through the *De clementia* which Seneca dedicated to Nero.[2]

Pliny is aware that his theme is far from novel—'nota vulgata dicta sunt omnia'.[3] Eloquent consuls there had been before, artists in adulation, managing an identical technique whether the Emperor was good or bad; Pliny had listened to the thanksgivings of senators in the days of Domitian; and he may have helped, as a proper and pious duty, to compose the speech delivered by Verginius Rufus in his third consulate under Nerva. What is exceptional about the *Panegyricus* is the fact that the author chose to publish his 'actio gratiarum'.

It is in the letters that originality will be discovered, and by paradox, for their contents appear to be extremely conventional. There was an ancient tradition to cast all manner of literary themes into the form of a speech or a letter; and genuine correspondence, after suitable editing, was sometimes given to the world. When Seneca had already turned out a number of ethical treatises, he went on to compose a whole series of short sermons in the guise of epistles, all addressed to a single friend. Seneca's style had gone out of fashion; and, though moral fervour necessarily extorted approbation from serious men, though enormous tribute was publicly rendered to the profession of philosophy, gentlemen of taste now found that Seneca was declamatory

---

[1] ib. 2 f. Cf. M. Durry, o.c. 21 ff.

[2] J. Mesk, *Wiener Studien* XXXIII (1911), 71 ff. Also M. Durry on 'les idées et leurs sources' (o.c. 27 ff.) and 'les lieux communs', with a catalogue (33 ff.). On the kindred topic of Pliny's views about government cf. M. Hammond, *Harvard Studies* XLIX (1938), 115 ff.

[3] III. 13. 2.

and boring. It was Pliny's design to make moralizing a delicate art, emerging unobtrusively from the portrayal of men and manners.

He displays people in their daily pursuits or confronting the important events of upper and middle class life in a stable society characterized by ease and refinement. Betrothal and matrimony, wills and bequests, the illness of a friend or bereavement in a family, the first flowering of poetical or oratorical genius, the early stages of youthful ambition in the career of honours, the multifarious occupations enjoined by metropolitan life, the ceremonial obsequies of illustrious men—such are among the subjects of Pliny's epistolary essays. Rome is at the centre of the stage. Yet pictures are vouchsafed of life in the country—the comprehensive description of a villa, the management of an estate, the cares of a landowner, the pastimes of retired statesmen, or the habits of those municipal worthies whom 'honesta quies' enfolded in dignified leisure. ·Law, politics, and administration are incidental, being brought in because they concern public morals, the progress of the arts—and the vicissitudes of individuals, especially the author. The only prosecutions in the high assembly recorded by Pliny are those in which he took a leading part.

Genuine epistles preserved and solicitously edited, or little essays specially fabricated, sometimes after an interval: such is the skill of Pliny that it is difficult to draw a distinction.[1] A suspicious feature may be noted: with hardly an exception each missive is confined to a single subject. Detail tends to be pruned away, as in the instructions sent to an architect;[2] and, when Pliny writes to a consular army commander, he never seems to specify the province or region of his activity.[3] Careful attention is given to the choice of correspondents and to the arrangement of letters where the order in time is relevant.[4]

For grace and neatness of style, for variety of topic and tone, for delicacy and for tact, the correspondence of Pliny has no rival. There is some risk that the portrayal of contemporary manners may engender satire and malice, if indeed it does not derive from that unkind propensity of the human heart. Pliny kept vigilant watch upon himself. The general colouring of the letters is amiable, sympathetic, improving. Censure of the living is the mildest imaginable, as when the writer adverts on social lapses, admonishes a proconsul for disregard of class distinctions, or evinces pained surprise at rebellious

---

[1] Opinions vary. For the predominance of artifice cf. W. Kroll, *Studien zum Verständnis der r. Literatur* (1924), 238 ff.; A.-M. Guillemin, *Pline et la vie littéraire de son temps* (1929), 128 ff.

[2] IX. 39.

[3] II. 13 (Priscus); III. 17 (Julius Servianus); IV. 4 (Sosius Senecio); IV. 26 (Metilius Nepos); VII. 2 (Justus); IX. 2 (Sabinus); IX. 16 and 25 (Mamilianus).

[4] For slips and inadvertences, App. 21.

tendencies among the younger generation.[1] It is generally anonymous. Exceptions are so rare as to be remarkable. The author in manifest relish fills several letters with scandalous stories about the behaviour, past and present, of Aquillius Regulus.[2] And his comment on a consular jurist, Javolenus Priscus, excites wonder and tempts speculation.[3]

Martial and Statius extol with eager devotion their patrons and benefactors among the eminent. Martial celebrating the eloquence, the splendour, and the munificence of Regulus might almost be Pliny on one of Pliny's friends; while phrases from the *Panegyricus* resemble Statius' laudations of Domitian.[4] The resemblance goes beyond language. It is seen in the choice of subjects. When Statius describes a villa at Tibur, chants the nuptials of Arruntius Stella, condoles in his bereavement with Claudius Etruscus, and offers up vows that Rutilius Gallicus be restored to health, not without details about the life and career of that high personage, he is anticipating several of Pliny's themes.[5] Conversely, some of the Plinian essays might have been versified and put into a collection of *Silvae*, without much change or loss.

Statius and Martial left a gap behind them. It is not fanciful to discover in Pliny their successor as a social commentator. The third book of Pliny's collection concludes with a necrological notice of Martial. The letter quotes verses from Martial in praise of his patron's eloquence, with a suitable reference to Cicero; and the letter ends with a compliment to talent and industry that deserve immortality but perhaps will not achieve it—'at non erunt aeterna quae scripsit? non erunt fortasse, ille tamen scripsit tamquam essent futura.'[6]

Like Martial, Pliny wrote on minor themes with high polish and an artist's single-minded devotion.[7] To insist upon comparable claims to survival for his own letters would have been ostentatious—but a modest hint was pardonable, and subtly effective.

---

[1] e.g. II. 6 (different food and drink for different categories of guests); II. 14. 2 ff. (bad manners of 'adulescentuli' in the centumviral court); VIII. 23. 3 (conceit and dangerous originality among the young); IX. 12 (an over-austere parent).

[2] I. 5; II. 20; IV. 2 and 7; VI. 2. Regulus is referred to as deceased in the last of these letters. Perhaps already dead when the others were published—hence a clue to the date of publication, cf. App. 21.

[3] VI. 15, cf. p. 91. The letter is addressed to Voconius Romanus, for whom Pliny had solicited an army commander called Priscus (II. 13)—probably in vain. See App. 3.

[4] cf. R. Syme, *JRS* XXVIII (1938), 218, reviewing M. Durry's edition of the *Panegyricus*.

[5] Statius, *Silvae* I. 3 (the Tiburtine villa of Manilius Vopiscus); I. 2 (the *epithalamium* for Stella); III. 3 (Claudius Etruscus); I. 4 (Rutilius Gallicus). Poetical panegyrics of consular worthies are a notable development. Statius also lauds the career of M. Vettius Bolanus (V. 2), legate under Corbulo and governor of Britain. Titinius Capito versified 'clarissimi cuiusque vitam' (*Epp.* I. 17. 3).
[6] III. 21. 6.

[7] cf. A.-M. Guillemin, o.c. 147: 'pour Pline le véritable maître dans la composition est Martial.' Also J. Kruuse, *Classica et Mediaevalia* IV (1941), 248 ff.

It would be of some interest to know at what date the consular orator decided to enhance his fame by putting on the market a selection of his correspondence. The nine books contain letters covering the years 97 to 108. It may have been as late as 105 that Pliny published the first two books, or the first three, the remainder following in quick succession, and dealing with very recent events indeed, so that the latest portion appeared in 109.[1] Some touch of emulation may have prompted him to publish. The year 105 brought rumours, and perhaps more than rumours, of his friend's *Historiae*.[2]

Pliny's essays held up a mirror to contemporary life. There is something more, and highly personal. Cicero's correspondence, though not composed with an eye for publication, does the same, and it unintentionally yields much biographical matter. Pliny, while deprecating the comparison and avowing that his scope is narrower, is not at a loss.[3] He skilfully utilizes his letters to present the closest that was decent or permissible to the autobiography of an orator and a statesman.

Only a few years from his consulship, Pliny lacked the age or the achievement to justify any avowed commemoration of his own life and works. Nor had the genre been widely practised. Princes, it is true, wrote the story of their own lives, just as they had their public monuments. A senator, in the rare event of his being permitted to have any 'res gestae', might properly hesitate to record them. Modesty was better, and it was safer. Few generals had exploits to match those of Domitius Corbulo, and it is not likely that there were many comparable memoirs.[4]

Virtue for its reward in fame had to wait for the funeral laudation, or for the historian of Rome under Trajan. If Pliny thought of his own extinction, he could not have contemplated the occasion with equanimity unless he knew that an admiring colleague such as Cornutus Tertullus would survive to superintend his obsequies. Cornutus, however, was his senior by some twenty years, and the supreme honour of Tacitean eloquence at one's interment might be impaired by various disadvantages. Pliny by publishing his letters stole a march on the funeral oration and captured immediate renown of a personal nature, illuminating his private life as well as his public achievement, such as nobody else could hope for on this side of the grave.

That there might be some place and being after death, at least for souls of superior merit, was maintained by the wise, though not by every sect.[5] The shadowy hope of a shadowy existence did not con-

---

[1] App. 21.   [2] Inferred from the letter to Titinius Capito (v. 8), cf. p. 117.
[3] IX. 2. 3.   [4] For Corbulo's memoirs, p. 297.
[5] *Agr.* 46. 1: 'si quis piorum manibus locus, si, ut sapientibus placet, non cum corpore extinguuntur magnae animae,' &c. Cf. Seneca, *Epp.* 63. 16: 'si modo vera sapientium fama est recipitque nos locus aliquis', &c.

vince the traditional Roman of the governing order. The sole and solid prospect of survival lay in good deeds, with good repute thereafter to posterity. Hence the preoccupation with fame—sharp, insistent, and dominant. Even philosophers, who impugned the validity of opinion, could not deny or repel the temptations of glory.[1] The men of action were sometimes more modest, or at least more reticent. Verginius Rufus, who lived on to see his name in the history books, chose a brief epitaph, but a proud one.[2] Julius Frontinus declined any commemoration: if his merits deserved it, they would survive.[3]

It was evident that fame should be pursued, indefatigably.[4] Were the means adequate? Did the Empire in its mature season offer scope for distinction in the arts of peace or war? Words are a substitute for deeds, and a consolation. But was it not too late, even for oratory? Such were the questions that vexed some of the less enthusiastic among the friends of Pliny.

[1] *Hist.* IV. 6. I (on Helvidius Priscus): 'erant quibus adpetentior famae videretur, quando etiam sapientibus cupido gloriae novissima exuitur.' For the τόπος, P. Wendland, *Hermes* LI (1916), 481.

[2] Cited in VI. 10. 4: 'hic situs est Rufus, pulso qui Vindice quondam | imperium adseruit, non sibi sed patriae.'

[3] IX. 19. 6: 'impensa monumenti supervacua est: memoria nostri durabit si vita meruimus.' The letter has an explicit reference to VI. 10—and it is addressed to Ruso, i.e. P. Calvisius Ruso Tullus (*cos.* 109), son of P. Calvisius Ruso Julius Frontinus (*suff.* 79). Clearly a relative of Frontinus (cf. App. 87).

[4] IX. 14 (to Tacitus): 'posteris an aliqua cura nostri, nescio, nos certe meremur ut sit aliqua, non dico ingenio (id enim superbum), sed studio et labore et reverentia posterorum.'

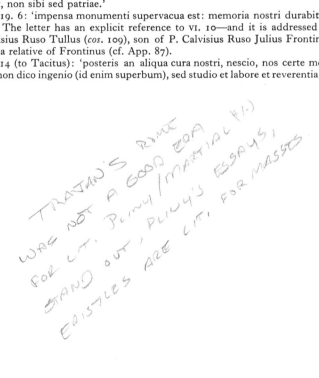

IX. THE *DIALOGUS*

ELOQUENCE like all things was tamed and disciplined by Caesar Augustus.[1] Or so it might seem. The great issues of public policy no longer came for debate before the assemblies of the Roman People, and in the Senate they were more often the theme of exposition than of argument. Diplomacy, management, and intrigue took the place of open competition and free discussion. That was not an unmitigated calamity for the orator. Industry and talent, if diverted from politics, might concentrate the more powerfully upon forensic practice; and, as the Senate's prerogative of taking cognizance of matters that concerned the safety or the dignity of the State was gradually but rapidly extended, a seductive prospect unfolded. Prosecutions for 'maiestas', the curse of the imperial system, came as a blessing for the development of oratory.

A new style arose, pointed and ornate, savage and aggressive. With notable exponents before the death of Augustus, it soon became the dominant fashion, producing its heroes and its martyrs.[2] To win a name and a career by prosecution tempted the ambitious energies of the young, the impoverished, and the obscure. For profit and for protection, the 'delatores' put their eager talents at the service of the government. In the end, wealth, honours, and influence with Caesar involved them in feuds and perils; they suffered in retribution the doom contrived for their victims.[3] Even if a prosecutor survived long enough to mend his ways, bland with success and opulence, and be honoured among the 'principes civitatis', his equivocal beginnings also survived in the ultimate verdict. Domitius Afer was reckoned by an exacting critic as the greatest of all speakers in the times of Claudius and Nero.[4] Yet the obituary notice of Afer does not allow him to stand alone and unrivalled: it pairs him with another man, an orator and historian, who was his equal for genius but superior in reputation.[5]

The next age saw Vibius Crispus and Eprius Marcellus skilfully navigating the surges of civil war, managing the transition from ruler to ruler, and ensconced thereafter in wealth and honours. Next in succession to their bad eminence, for oratorical force and for success at the bar, though not (so it appears) for political influence, came M. Aquillius Regulus. Eprius or Vibius exemplified the contrast

---

[1] *Dial.* 38. 2: 'et maxime principis disciplina ipsam quoque eloquentiam sicut omnia depacaverat.'

[2] Ch. XXV.

[3] *Ann.* I. 74. 2.

[4] Quintilian XII. 11. 3, cf. X. 1. 118.

[5] *Ann.* XIV. 19 (Servilius Nonianus).

between humble antecedents and worldly honours.[1] The extraction of Regulus was aristocratic, perhaps from an ancient house of the nobility.[2] Not but what Regulus, like some aristocrats in the late age of the Republic, was forced to struggle for his 'dignitas' and for that of his family, to thrust his way forward like any *novus homo*. His fortunes had been impaired by the condemnation and exile of his father. To retrieve honour and station the young man went to work, in ruthless energy. The fate of three nobles of consular rank attested his murderous talent, with money and a priesthood for reward.[3] Regulus, like others, should have been vulnerable after Nero's death. Then Eprius had been attacked in the Senate by Helvidius Priscus, hopes ran high, there were violent contentions—and it all came to nothing.[4] If Regulus also was threatened, he incurred no harm. When the next occasion offered, Helvidius again set upon Eprius;[5] and not long afterwards Regulus had to face an attack.[6] Eprius crushed his adversary by skill of argument and imperious force of eloquence.[7] Regulus was rescued by the intervention of his young half-brother, the excellent Vipstanus Messalla.[8]

Eprius and Vibius became a proverbial pair, matched yet contrasted. Vibius enjoyed long life and prosperity, with fame for his wit and humour.[9] Eprius met a paradoxical fate in the last year of Vespasian's reign, being suppressed on an allegation of conspiracy—paradoxical, because the essential virtue of these men was loyalty, or 'pietas'. They were the friends of Caesar, and cherished by him.[10]

Eprius (the story runs) was involved with a certain Caecina Alienus in a plot against the dynasty. Caecina, leaving the Palace one evening after a dinner in all amity with Titus, was set upon by soldiers and killed, documentary evidence of treason being later produced (a speech to the Praetorian Guard in his own handwriting). It is not clear how Eprius comes in. Abnormal imprudence, a mysterious intrigue, or the impulsive violence of Titus Caesar destroyed an eminent servant of the Roman government. Arraigned before the Senate and condemned, Eprius cut his throat with a razor, ending like Tigellinus.[11]

---

[1] *Dial.* 8. 1: 'Capuae aut Vercellis, ubi nati dicuntur.' For Eprius cf. the dedication found near Capua, *ILS* 992.

[2] There would be no reason to deny descent from the Aquillii of the Republic.

[3] *Hist.* IV. 42. 4, cf. Pliny, *Epp.* I. 5. 3.

[4] *Hist.* IV. 6.

[5] IV. 6 ff.; 43 (once again).   [6] IV. 42.   [7] IV. 8.

[8] Regulus' mother had married again, a Vipstanus—perhaps L. Vipstanus Poplicola Messalla (*cos.* 48), whose *cognomina* will permit the conjecture that his parent had married a daughter of the illustrious Valerii Messallae.

[9] His witticisms, Quintilian v. 13. 48; VIII. 5. 15; Suetonius, *Dom.* 3. 1; Dio LXV. 2. 3.

[10] *Dial.* 8. 3: 'ab ipso principe cum quadam reverentia diliguntur.'

[11] Dio LXVI. 16. 3 f.; Suetonius, *Divus Titus* 6. 2. For Tigellinus' exit, *Hist.* I. 72. 3.

A man like Regulus could not have been debarred from honours.[1] That he rendered any especial service to the Flavian dynasty, or even acquired a second consulate, there is no record. Though Regulus did not contribute actively to the ruin of the opposition faction under Domitian, he exulted openly in what had been done, published a pamphlet attacking the memory of Junius Rusticus—and was much disliked.[2] Meanwhile he had been piling up wealth by all methods, from the pursuit of fees to the pursuit of inheritances. Many were the stories related, how he inveigled the rich and the childless of both sexes, and even the widow of an enemy.[3] Avidity and ostentation went hand in hand. Men might have been put in mind of the great Hortensius, who showed pomp and display in his rhetoric as in his style of life. Such were the arts of Hortensius that professional actors did not disdain to take him for a model. If Hortensius gave infinite thought and practice to the sweep of a gesture or the folds of a toga, Regulus went so far as to paint his face.[4]

Despite histrionic affectation and moral obliquity, Regulus had every right to his rank as the leader of the Roman bar. He did not possess the general culture or philosophical education that Roman tradition set up as an ideal, nor had he much in the way of natural gifts. Labouring under many disabilities, such as a weak constitution and a thick utterance, slow faculties and a poor memory, he surmounted them all by his frantic genius.[5] To the deadly force of his attack the supreme testimony is furnished involuntarily by an enemy, citing Regulus' own statement, 'ego iugulum statim video'.[6]

Regulus survived into the reign of Trajan and died about the year 105.[7] Which of his successors was competent to step into his place, or had any already outdistanced him? Hortensius, after the trial of Verres, had to yield the primacy to Cicero. In A.D. 100 the indictment of a proconsul recalled the historic themes of Republican eloquence: a province pillaged and the killing of Roman citizens. Tacitus in his oratory exhibited splendour and majesty.[8] As for the quality of his own performance, Pliny modestly discloses it by stating that one of his speeches at the prosecution lasted for nearly five hours.[9] The

[1] As may be deduced from the invective, *Hist.* IV. 42. 5: 'invenit aemulos etiam infelix nequitia: quid si floreat vigeatque? et quem adhuc quaestorium offendere non audemus, praetorium et consularem ausuri sumus?' Cf. R. Syme, *JRS* XLIII (1953), 161.

[2] *Epp.* I. 5.   [3] I. 20.

[4] VI. 2. 2. For Hortensius cf. Macrobius III. 13. 4. He was called a dancing girl (Gellius I. 5. 3), and professional actors took lessons from him (Val. Max. VIII. 10. 2).

[5] IV. 7. 4.   [6] I. 20. 14.

[7] His decease is first noted in VI. 2.

[8] II. 11. 17: 'respondit Cornelius Tacitus eloquentissime et quod eximium orationi eius inest, σεμνῶς.'

[9] ib. 14.

trial of Marius Priscus was the supremely dramatic opportunity for senatorial eloquence. Such enormities were not likely to recur under the regiment of Trajan. There remained, it is true, the case of another criminal proconsul, Caecilius Classicus. But Classicus had died before the prosecution could get under way. For the rest Pliny now acts as advocate for the defence, and the occasions are not comparable: Julius Bassus was a trivial delinquent, while the charges against Varenus were not easy to verify and may have originated in local intrigues and feuds in the province of Bithynia.

Pliny was not the man to question the value of oratory and undermine the foundations of civilized existence. It was axiomatic that polite studies flourished, and it was manifest. The reception of the *Panegyricus* was proof enough. Audiences were not only keen and indefatigable, they showed a quite extraordinary discrimination.[1] Literary taste and social tact were by no means so strongly in evidence among the lawyers. Pliny is forced to a paradoxical confession. He longs for Regulus. Without Regulus the courts have now become a dreary desolation. Instead of taking pains and rejoicing in their work, barristers are glad to finish as soon as may be. Speeches grow shorter and shorter.[2]

Cornelius Tacitus sought no more laurels after the condemnation of Marius Priscus. There is no trace of any part or intervention in a senatorial debate. Pliny in his reports of the proceedings against three proconsuls in the course of the next half-dozen years names eleven persons of consular station.[3] Cornelius Tacitus is not numbered among them.

How good were those men? Expert testimony offers. Quintilian came out with a firm prediction. Whoever writes next about Roman eloquence (he opines) will discover a happy abundance of talent—we can already see mature speakers, who rival the classic performers, and young men of promise in their train.[4] Quintilian was writing in the last years of Domitian. Conflict and prosecutions sharpened ambition—nor was the teacher averse from complimenting those who had benefited by his instruction. Pliny belonged to that company, and Pliny furnishes laudatory information about sundry consular speakers. One exhibited gravity and pathos, another was prompt and vigorous,

[1] III. 18. 8 f.   [2] VI. 2.

[3] In addition to the six advocates whose style is characterized by Pliny (App. 27), note Libo Frugi (III. 9. 33); Baebius Macer (at this point 'cos. des.') and Caepio Hispo (IV. 9. 16); Cornelius Priscus (V. 20. 7); Acilius Rufus (V. 20. 6 and VI. 13. 5). Tacitus was perhaps away from Rome in 101–4, cf. p. 71.

[4] Quintilian X. 1. 122: 'habebunt, qui post nos de oratoribus scribent, magnam eos, qui nunc vigent, materiam vere laudandi. sunt enim summa hodie, quibus illustratur forum, ingenia. namque et consummati iam patroni veteribus aemulantur et eos iuvenum ad optima tendentium imitatur ac sequitur industria.'

a third clever, biting, and polished, and so on. Six consulars, apart from Cornelius Tacitus, thus acquire their various labels.[1]

Tacitus established his fame by the time he was praetor, many years ago. He now stood not merely in the front rank of contemporary practitioners, but perhaps the foremost of them all—and he makes a pronouncement on the condition of oratory. One of his friends elicited it. Not Pliny, not one of the orators in vogue, but Fabius Justus, who chose the career of provinces and armies. Fabius assumed (and Tacitus concurs) that it was not a time for great orators any more, only for barristers, advocates, and the like. Why had Roman eloquence come to an end?[2]

Tacitus casts the inquiry into the form of a discussion purporting to have taken place in the time of Vespasian when he was quite a young man.[3] The scene of the *Dialogus* is laid at the house of Curiatius Maternus, and the action opens with the visit of Marcus Aper and Julius Secundus, the leading barristers of the day, whose precepts and discourse were eagerly enjoyed by Cornelius Tacitus in the beginnings of his career. Aper was now over fifty, Secundus perhaps about forty. They found Maternus going through the manuscript of his *Cato*. He had recited the drama the day before, not without giving offence to the government, so it was reported, and there was much talk of the matter in the city.[4]

Secundus asks whether Maternus is not at work expurgating his *Cato* so as to produce a safer version. Maternus retorts to the contrary: if the *Cato* has not made his meaning clear enough, there will be no mistake about his next tragedy, a *Thyestes*.[5] At which renewed evidence of the poet's pertinacity, Aper intervenes abruptly. He takes Maternus to task for neglecting forensic practice, for wasting time and talent on mere versification.[6]

A debate engages. Aper urges the primacy of oratory over poetry for utility and advantage, for pleasure and for lasting fame.[7] It equips a man to protect friends and clients, to intimidate his enemies, to abide in security and power. If he is menaced, he will go unscathed. In the courts, in the Senate, and before Caesar, eloquence is a sword

[1] App. 27. So far as known, all consuls of the period 96–102, except Salvius Liberalis, by far the most senior (*suff.* c. 84): his *cursus* is extant, *ILS* 1011.

[2] *Dial.* 1. 1: 'horum autem temporum causidici et advocati et patroni et quidvis potius quam oratores vocantur.'

[3] 1. 2, cf. 17. 3. Presumably in 75, cf. App. 28.

[4] 2. 1: 'cum offendisse potentium animos diceretur, tamquam in eo tragoediae argumento sui oblitus tantum Catonem cogitasset, eaque de re per urbem frequens sermo haberetur.' The prosecution and banishment of the modern Cato, Helvidius Priscus, can (and perhaps should) be dated to 74, cf. p. 212.

[5] 3. 3.   [6] 3. 4.   [7] 5. 3–10. 8.

or a shield. Armed with words only, Eprius Marcellus confronted a hostile assembly and baffled his great adversary.

No less manifest the personal prestige that accrues. Admiring crowds attend upon the performances of the orator, the most eminent in the land must pay him court and solicit his help. Years, opulence, and public station confess their indigence. What they lack may belong to a young man of low estate. It is not conferred by letters of appointment from Caesar, it is not the fruit of intrigue. And, more gratifying than any of the outward signs of success, is the inner satisfaction—the thrill of genius, the consciousness of power, the intoxication of creative energy. The orator's personal talent and efforts bring forth a renown that may echo to the ends of the world. Eprius Marcellus and Vibius Crispus rose from nowhere to occupy the first rank in the friendship of Caesar. They had nothing to thank Vespasian for, it was he who stood in their debt. Wealth and influence, public distinctions and honorific status are only a small part of their glory.

Maternus in reply sketches a brief but telling vindication.[1] The pursuit of poetry is a delight in itself, it harms no man, it promises a greater security of fame. Virgil has fewer detractors than Cicero. The oratory of the prosecutors is a recent development, the evil product of evil times. A valuable weapon, perhaps, but it is better to live without weapons. Virtue may be a safer shield than eloquence. Uncontaminated by the sordid competition of lawyers and intriguers, the poet may take leave of the world, serene and with a good conscience. The lot of the great politicians is not at all to be envied. Deprived of dignity and of liberty, the ministers of the Caesars are caught and held fast in a system of flattery and subservience. They deserve to be rated no higher than imperial freedmen.

A new character now intervenes, the young senator Vipstanus Messalla, who recalled by his *cognomen* the patrician Valerii. Messalla had little liking for present fashions. His strong predilection for the classical orators provokes Aper to violent disagreement, carrying the discussion a long stage further.[2]

In his second speech Aper calls into question the conventional distinction between the old orators and the new. With appeal to chronology, he demonstrates that speakers of the Augustan age such as Messalla Corvinus and Asinius Pollio are in fact comparatively recent. Among the so-called ancients, eloquence was not all of one type. Cicero had critics as well as rivals. And Cicero had to fight the same battle for progress against those who preferred old-fashioned ways. Oratory changes with the times: Cicero's latest speeches marked an improvement on his earlier productions. Those who admire the

[1] 11. 1–13. 6.   [2] 16. 4–23. 6.

classical oratory fasten on Cassius Severus, whom they blame for the change to the worse. They cannot prove him deficient in taste and judgement. Cassius saw what was wanted.

Indeed, the much revered classical orators were marred by signal defects. Cicero was often otiose and redundant; while those who urged against Cicero the claims of a plain and more Attic style of discourse could not always escape the charge of being flat and feeble, prosaic and boring. One way or the other, the ancients did not come up to the requisite standard of vigour and splendour.

Messalla refuses to be intimidated.[1] He maintains against Aper the essential soundness of the classical authors, and, appealing as axiomatic to a general decline in taste and achievement, lays the responsibility on the neglect of the ancient morality, with an especial indictment against parents, teachers, and methods of teaching. Eloquence has become a rhetorical exercise or a venal and sordid trade. Speakers and advocates are ignorant about public law; and they have no philosophical background. Only the ancient days gave a proper training for public life.

So far Messalla. The end of his speech is missing. Julius Secundus may have made some contribution. In the gap, it may be presumed, were his remarks (if any).[2] Curiatius Maternus took up the theme again.[3] He reconciled the disputants by appeal to history, explaining that Republican and modern eloquence are equally inseparable from their time and from the condition of the Commonwealth.[4]

Accepting as now above dispute the greatness of the Republican orators, Maternus shows why they were great—not culture but politics, not education but freedom. Eloquence is like a conflagration, it requires fuel and air, motion and excitement. And eloquence blazed out of the strife and turmoil of the Free State—legislation and elections, indictments of the 'principes', family feuds, and faction everywhere. Reckless competition tore the Commonwealth to pieces. By that process it promoted oratory to power and distinction. The rewards were magnificent—high office, influence with the magnates, authority in the Senate, and, outside the capital, not.towns only but whole nations annexed to the allegiance and *clientela* of the orator.

The persuasion held in that age that no man could get anywhere

---

[1] 25. 1–26. 9; 28. 1–32. 7; 33. 4–35. 5.

[2] Various scholars have argued that a speech by Secundus occurred in the missing portion after 35. 5, e.g. H. Drexler, *Bursians Jahresberichte* CCXXIV (1929), 283 f.; E. Koestermann, ib. CCLXXXII (1943), 87; 91. Against the need for any speech by Secundus, R. Waltz, *Rev. phil.* LXI (1935), 296 ff.; K. Keyssner, *Würzburger Studien* IX (1936), 94 ff.; K. Barwick, *Sächsische S-B, phil.-hist. Kl.* 101, 4 (1954), 4.

[3] 36. 1. Some suppose a second gap, after 40. 1. See, against, K. v. Fritz, *Rh. Mus.* LXXXI (1932), 275 ff.; W. den Boer, *Mnemosyne* 3 VII (1939), 193 ff.

[4] 36. 1–41. 5.

without the aid of public speech. The appetite for renown was sharpened and enhanced by dire necessity: to be mute was to be both
inglorious and helpless. Aristocrats neglected at their peril accomplishments that were not disdained by the men of power and the
leaders of armies, even by Pompeius Magnus and M. Crassus.

Such was the ruinous glory of Rome in the days of Senate and
People. There was not much more for Maternus to say when he drew
the moral. Eloquence is the offspring of that licence which fools call
liberty. It goes hand in hand with civic strife, it plays upon the passions
of the multitude, it knows no discipline or restraint, it is rash, rebellious, and domineering. Well ordered states know it not. Sparta and
Crete had no rhetoric. There the laws were sovereign. At Athens the
mob ruled, and Athens was supreme in the annals of eloquence. Rome
likewise produced her orators in the age of anarchy and tribulation.

When peace, order, and concord came, excellence in public speaking
was cut off from its root and source. A symptom of disease and disintegration, it could not flourish in a healthy community, among a
people salutarily disposed to good conduct and civic obedience. In the
Senate there was no need for long speeches, for men of sense arrive
quickly at the right decision. And there were no more harangues to
the People, for one man had the arbitrament and he the wisest, not
the ignorant multitude.

Republic and Principate, each age had its quality for good or for
evil. You could not have the best of both worlds. If a man accepted
the peace of the Caesars, he must cheerfully forfeit all regret for the
eloquence of the Free State.[1]

The conclusion of the matter, as stated by Maternus, emerges with
inevitable force from a debate in which the opposing arguments are
justly and artistically balanced. No less skilful is the dramatic harmony
between character and discourse. Of Julius Secundus a satisfactory
estimate is perhaps precluded by the gap in the text; it is known that
he was clear and eloquent, but lacking in pugnacity.[2] The speech of
Vipstanus Messalla shows dignity and restraint, style and good sense.[3]
The portrayal of Aper is vivid and masterly. Marcus Aper to make his
way had to contend with notable disadvantages—he was a *novus homo*
from Gaul, and from a community in no great repute, but had reached
the praetorship;[4] he claimed to owe more to native wit and effort than

[1] 41. 5: 'nunc quoniam nemo eodem tempore adsequi potest magnam famam et
magnam quietem, bono saeculi sui quisque citra obtrectationem alterius utatur.'
[2] 2. 2, cf. Quintilian X. 1. 120 f.; 3. 12; XII. 10. 11.
[3] Perhaps recalling also the manner of Messalla Corvinus—'nitidus et candidus'
according to Quintilian (x. 1. 113). Cf. *Dial.* 18. 2. Tacitus' friend may be a descendant
of the orator.   [4] 7. 1, cf. 10. 2. For origin and nomenclature, App. 91.

to education, and he affected to despise literary culture.[1] Aper's character is vigorous and even aggressive, he exults in action and in worldly success.[2] But he revels also in the force of his own oratorical genius.[3] None of the other interlocutors in the *Dialogus* is delineated quite so vividly as Marcus Aper, or quite so fully; and none has a larger share of the discourse.

Whenever forensic eloquence and its greater exponents were discussed, nobody in Trajan's day could omit Marcus Regulus. The *Dialogus* contains neither censure of Regulus, for that would be undignified, nor any praise, for that would be both paradoxical and unduly offensive to contemporary taste. Only a hint, colourless and indeed anonymous. It occurs in the context of Messalla—Regulus was his half-brother.[4] For a theme of coloured contrast, in style of oratory and in the fashion of their lives, nothing could have touched a dramatic portrayal of the two brothers. Such a procedure might not, however, have seemed to Cornelius Tacitus the most delicate form of compliment to the memory of Vipstanus Messalla, the friend of his youth.

Nor was it practicable. More often than not, artistic propriety and convention discountenanced the introduction of the living. When Tacitus composed the *Dialogus*, all the characters in the treatise had been dead for some years, perhaps for many years. Already in the reign of Vespasian both Aper and Curiatius were men of some achievement, well on in middle life: Aper had seen service as an officer when Claudius Caesar invaded the island of Britain.[5] Julius Secundus (so it is recorded) died before he could develop his gifts to their full and predicted flowering.[6] Vipstanus was a good quarter of a century younger than Aper: he had been military tribune in the year 69.[7] No public transaction or official document of the Flavian age attests the name of Vipstanus Messalla. He would be quaestor about 74. Aristocratic birth should have carried him to the consulate a decade later. He may have been cut off before his prime.

Regulus lived on. The great lawyer was hated and traduced in his lifetime; and there was no certainty that posterity would be encouraged

---

[1] 2. 2: 'Aper omni eruditione imbutus contemnebat potius litteras quam nesciebat, tamquam maiorem industriae et laboris gloriam habiturus si ingenium eius nullis alienarum artium adminiculis inniti videretur.'

[2] 5. 3 ff.

[3] 6. 5: 'vulgata dicentium gaudia et imperitorum quoque oculis exposita percenseo: illa secreta et tantum ipsis orantibus nota maiora sunt.'

[4] 15. 1: 'cum oblitus et tuae et fratris tuae eloquentiae neminem hoc tempore oratorem esse contenderes.'

[5] 17. 4, cf. App. 91.

[6] Quintilian x. 1. 120. A friend and coeval (x. 3. 12). Quintilian was born c. 33.

[7] *Hist.* III. 9. 3.

to form a just estimate of his attainments. Accident or design could cover up the memory of a great orator.[1] Tacitus thought that Regulus was a bad man; but Tacitus knew that he was a genius in his way. The *Dialogus* reveals a judicious and equitable inquirer. When Tacitus comes to write history, a passion for justice—and a bitter contempt for conventional opinions—will sometimes induce him to lighten the scales against the wicked. Eprius Marcellus, when his enemy attacks him in the Senate, is firm and unperturbed; he controverts the fanatical, and wins the sympathy of the assembly by a speech of great force and sagacity, conveying the argument for moderation and tolerance.[2]

Nor does Regulus go without recognition. Passing beyond the trivial gossip, the personal dislikes, and the moral preoccupations of contemporaries into the realm of history and of equity, Tacitus pays his tribute. It is unobtrusive and indirect.

Regulus, surviving into the reign of Trajan, survived as the great exemplar of the forensic eloquence of the prosecutors, that eloquence that reeked of blood and smelled of lucre.[3] Regulus, even if deceased, would not have been remote enough for the *Dialogus*, he could not quite have fitted into a polite controversy among friends of Tacitus. Instead, to defend the modern style in oratory, the author introduces, as it were, a purified and sympathetic Regulus, namely Marcus Aper.[4]

Tacitus had to suffer not a little when contemporary mediocrity claimed for feebleness or redundancy the support and precedent of classical models. Tacitus was an innovator himself. Something of his power and intensity, something of his exultant audacity and delight in violence has gone into the portrait of Marcus Aper.[5]

Genius could no longer find scope and exhilaration in the pursuit of forensic or senatorial eloquence. Maternus utters the final verdict of Cornelius Tacitus: he will cast off the yoke.[6] Maternus had already said something else that is highly significant. It is not only that the

---

[1] Quintilian, from anxious loyalty to the dynasty, left out Eprius Marcellus altogether.

[2] *Hist.* IV. 8.

[3] 12. 2: 'lucrosae huius et sanguinantis eloquentiae.'

[4] That Tacitus, knowing well (and wishing to suggest) the Ciceronian dialogues, had in mind the orators M. Antonius and Q. Hortensius, does not weaken this conjecture. The practical and vigorous Antonius despised doctrine and pretended to be ignorant of Greek writers (*De oratore* II. 4, cf. Aper in *Dial.* 2. 2); while the flamboyant and worldly Hortensius scouted philosophy in the lost dialogue that bore his name (*De finibus* I. 2. 2). Those who knew Regulus would not miss the parallel between Regulus and Hortensius.

[5] K. Keyssner, *Würzburger Studien* IX (1936), 113. He argues that Tacitus, portraying Aper and Maternus, equips them with two conflicting portions of his own personality (o.c. 108).

[6] 11. 3: 'iam me deiungere a forensi labore constitui.' The metaphor is vigorous, the word 'deiungo' exceedingly rare.

conditions of the time harm and hamper the orator. Maternus in
scorn and fatigue of an advocate's practice wished to be liberated for
poetry, a superior form of activity.[1]

History in the view of the Romans was a form of literature closely
allied to poetry.[2] They might look back to the beginnings, to the
Bellum Punicum of Naevius and the *Annales* of Q. Ennius.[3] Those
writers had left a deep imprint on the early annalists. Moreover, the
central and eternal subject of Roman history, the 'res publica', might
still be expounded in verse. Annaeus Lucanus chose the epic to narrate the fall of the Republic. 'Libertas', and not any hero or leader,
is Lucan's theme, though Cato naturally emerges in heroic lineaments,
embodying that theme. Curiatius Maternus used tragedy as his
medium. The *Cato* was not his only historical drama. He had also
composed a *Domitius*, honouring an ancestor of Nero in the struggle
against despotism.[4] Perhaps that Ahenobarbus, the adversary of
Caesar, who fell at Pharsalia. Better, his son, the admiral of the
Republic, who deserted Antonius and made his peace with Caesar's
heir a few days before the fate of the world was decided at Actium.
This man was a nephew of Cato. He saw the menace from Egypt's
queen, and vainly tried to keep her out of a Roman war.[5]

The history of Rome was irresistible in its appeal—and it might be
dangerous. Lucan perished for his share in the conspiracy of C. Piso.
Curiatius Maternus was not deficient in courage—he had quelled one
of Nero's favourites, the impudent Vatinius, and his tragedies were
provocative in theme and tone.[6]

Despite his *Cato* and a much more outspoken denunciation of
crime and tyranny (the *Thyestes*),[7] Maternus prayed for a quiet end.
He trusted that virtue would go unharmed, that he would never have
to speak in the Senate in his own dangerous hour, only in another's.[8]
For such confidence there was little support in Rome of the Caesars.
If Maternus in his turn was not destroyed by a despotic government,

---

[1] 4. 2: 'sanctior illa et augustior eloquentia.'

[2] Cicero, *De oratore*. I. 70; Quintilian X. 1. 31.

[3] For the priority of poetry to history writing cf. F. Bömer, *Symbolae Osloenses* XXIX
(1952), 34.

[4] 3. 2: 'Domitium et Catonem, id est nostras quoque historias et Romana nomina.'

[5] Velleius II. 84. 2; Plutarch, *Antonius* 56. Hence relevant to the theme 'Titus and
Berenice'.

[6] 11. 2: 'improbam et studiorum quoque sacra profanantem Vatinii potentiam fregi.'
Cf. J. Stroux, *Philologus* LXXXVI (1931), 338 ff. Vatinius is contemptuously characterized
in *Ann.* XV. 34. 2.

[7] A wonderful theme for anti-dynastic rhetoric and maxims: compare Seneca's *Thyestes*.

[8] 11. 4: 'nam statum cuiusque ac securitatem melius innocentia tuetur quam eloquentia, nec vereor ne mihi umquam verba in senatu nisi pro alterius discrimine facienda
sint.'

it might seem that the author of the *Dialogus* has imported an ironical suggestion deceptively, and without cause.[1]

Whatever happened to Curiatius Maternus, destiny produced a sharper paradox, and quickly—the great Eprius brought to ruin, with no help now from rank and wealth and influence; hitherto Caesar's friend, on the attack and truculent (and it had been easy for him to baffle and crush Helvidius in altercation), but betrayed at the end, and perhaps abandoned in extremity by his own eloquence.[2]

Cornelius Tacitus now turning to history proposes to continue the poets in an exposition of recent and even contemporary transactions. The *Dialogus* advertises and justifies a proud renunciation of oratory. The rewards belonged to the past, like the danger or the splendour, and it was not needed any more.[3]

---

[1] Dio (LXVII. 12. 5, under the year 91) reports that Domitian put to death a sophist called Maternus. See App. 90.

[2] For the oratory of Eprius, *Dial.* 5. 6: 'accinctus ac minax'; *Ann.* XVI. 29. 1: 'torvus ac minax.' Even a ready speaker might fail, cf. *Ann.* III. 67. 2: 'proprio in metu qui exercitam quoque eloquentiam debilitat.'

[3] For the close resemblance between Tacitus and Maternus cf. now K. Barwick, o.c. 101, 4 (1954), 26 ff. For the language of the poet in the *Dialogus*, App. 52. For the dramatic date of the *Dialogus*, and its date of publication, App. 28.

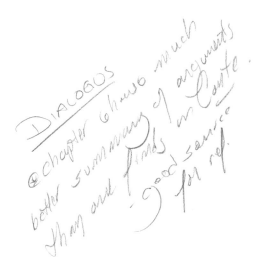

X. FROM ORATORY TO HISTORY

THE *Dialogus* is addressed to L. Fabius Justus, who was consul suffect early in the year 102. The practice of dedicating a composition to a friend or a patron when he entered upon public office was not uncommon. If the *Dialogus* in fact belongs to this year, the date acquires marked and even personal significance—and not merely for Fabius Justus. Coming so soon after the *Panegyricus* and impinging on the recitations of it, a treatise that so authoritatively pronounced the epitaph upon contemporary eloquence cannot have been taken as a compliment to Pliny.

Eleven letters in Pliny's collection bear the address of Cornelius Tacitus.[1] They attest common tastes and the amicable exchange of literary compositions.[2] Each had helped the other in his oratory, and the two went on in amity, candour, and loyalty.[3] Pliny recounts with complacency the fact that their names occur inevitably together in the testament of a friend or in the conversation of a stranger.[4] While conceding the earlier distinction of Tacitus as a speaker, and generously expressing his own admiration, he none the less continues to assert a parity of renown. By thus exalting the accomplishment of his friend, Pliny put forward his own claims, irreproachably.[5]

Pliny means oratory—the passage carries no allusion to the fame accruing from historical writing—but he nowhere indicates that his friend had published any speech, not even an oration against Marius Priscus. Tacitus indeed may have felt discontent with the outcome of that celebrated case. Pliny did not allow himself to be deterred. He consulted one of his friends about the propriety of holding a recitation.[6] It is hardly credible that he would consent to withhold from the world the modern equivalent of the indictment against Verres.

As for Tacitus, there happens to be mentioned twice a book which

---

[1] I. 6 and 20; IV. 13; VI. 9, 16, and 20; VII. 20 and 33; VIII. 7; IX. 10 and 14. Tacitus is mentioned in II. 11. 2 and 17; IV. 15. 1; IX. 23. 2 f. Only two persons are expressly designated as common friends, viz. Asinius Rufus (IV. 15. 1) and Julius Naso (VI. 9. 1), cf. App. 92. Others, however, may be divined, notably Fabius Justus.

[2] VII. 20. 1; VIII. 7. 1.   [3] VII. 20. 2 f.

[4] VII. 20. 6; IX. 23. 3: 'Tacitus es an Plinius?' The testament of L. Dasumius, drawn up in the summer of 108, has the juxtaposed names '] Secundo, Cornelio [' (*CIL* VI, 10229, l. 17).

[5] It is Tacitus the orator, not the historian, who is praised and exalted in VII. 20; and observe IX. 23. 3: 'quod uterque nostrum his etiam ex studiis notus, quibus aliter ignotus.'

[6] II. 19. 8. The speech (no name or title) is called 'pugnax atque contentiosa'. The oration described in I. 2 is presumably the invective against Publicius Certus (cf. IV. 21. 3; VII. 30. 4 f.; IX. 13. 1).

he sent to Pliny for comment or emendation.[1] In a covering missive Tacitus described himself as one orator writing to another, each being at the same time both master and pupil.[2] The volume should therefore be either an oration or a treatise on oratory.

Perhaps the *Dialogus*, now revised for a definitive publication.[3] The letters in question occur at a late point in the collected correspondence (perhaps belonging to 107). It might be doubted whether the historian was bothering about speeches at this season, and there is no need to conjecture that he was refurbishing a funeral oration in decennial commemoration of Verginius Rufus.[4]

Despite the amity between Pliny and Tacitus (and the latter's elegant concession of parity), a suspicion arises—the relationship showed more warmth, and more insistence, on the one side than on the other. It was to Tacitus that Pliny addressed his epistolary essay in deprecation of brevity.[5] Though prepared to defer to the authority of his senior, he would prefer, he says, a reasoned statement from his friend. There is no sign that Pliny received an answer.

Pliny was frank and exorbitant in his demands upon fame. Tacitus, as is elsewhere discoverable, was possessed by an almost morbid fear of self-glorification.[6] Pliny gently reassures him;[7] and Pliny defends himself against the imputation of vanity.[8]

Fame was an eager and jealous pursuit, especially among the orators.[9] Pliny bears witness, extolling as something unusual the concord in which he operated with Lucceius Albinus when they were charged with a prosecution.[10] Apart from Tacitus, Lucceius is the only consular advocate whom Pliny honours with a letter.[11]

Personal rivalry among the masters of eloquence might be sharpened by doctrinal antagonism, and friends of Pliny as well as enemies found his fashion of discourse not at all to their liking. Regulus (it was obvious) would protest, either brutally or with a sly compliment to

---

[1] VII. 20. 1; VIII. 7. 1.

[2] VIII. 7. 1: 'neque ut magistro magister neque ut discipulo discipulus (sic enim scribis), sed ut discipulo magister (nam tu magister, ego contra; atque adeo tu in scholam revocas, ego adhuc Saturnalia extendo) librum misisti.'

[3] cf. App. 28.

[4] Pliny referred to the neglect of Verginius' monument at Alsium 'post decimum mortis annum' (VI. 10. 3).   [5] I. 20.

[6] *Ann.* XI. 11. 1: 'quod non iactantia refero' (his status and functions in the year 88).

[7] IX. 14. 1: 'nec ipse tibi plaudis, et ego nihil magis ex fide quam de te scribo.' Clearly a response to some deprecatory remark in a letter of Tacitus.

[8] IX. 23. 6: 'neque enim vereor ne iactantior videar, cum de me aliorum iudicium, non meum profero, praesertim aput te, qui nec ullius invides laudibus et faves nostris.' The letter is addressed to Maximus, perhaps C. Vibius Maximus, himself a writer (IX. 1. 1 ff., cf. p. 56).

[9] Detraction of Secundus and of Aper is alluded to in *Dial.* 2. 2.

[10] III. 9. 8.   [11] VI. 10.

some other speaker, for example one who did not put himself above the 'eloquentia saeculi nostri'.[1] There were also arbiters of severe taste, men whose preference went to the plain and unadorned. Pliny, when submitting a composition to Minicius Fundanus, is aware that it may be judged pompous and luxuriant.[2] To spare his friend vexation, he will make a sacrifice. He amiably inserts some sober patches (drab and detrimental, he would prefer to call them). Fundanus is clearly an adherent of the Attic school.[3] Not the only one among the Plinian correspondents. Writing to another friend, Pliny sets forth his own doctrine and explains why he cannot wholly approve an unnamed speaker of the time, who is 'rectus et sanus', but not sufficiently 'grandis et ornatus'.[4]

There was splendour and sublimity, if there was nothing else, in the public speeches of Cornelius Tacitus. Pliny affirms that he chose Tacitus as master and model, from the beginning, though there were other orators in high estimation; and, as he reminds Tacitus, not all critics are now prepared to concede the supremacy to Pliny's friend and to Pliny.[5]

The performance of the one has to be divined or deduced. The other is not so fortunate. The *Panegyricus* survives as the solitary specimen of Latin eloquence from the century and a half that had elapsed since the death of Cicero. It has done no good to the reputation of the author or the taste of the age. The speech is a strange and blended product, heavily loaded with poetical ornaments. Though often felicitous, and sometimes forceful, the thing soon palls, through tireless pursuit of the eternal antithesis, through repetitive fervour and exuberant redundance.[6]

Cicero was still the necessary model for students of eloquence. That was the doctrine of Quintilian, leading (but not creating) the literary reaction against the age of Claudius and Nero.[7] Quintilian had a number of pupils, Pliny among them.[8] Tacitus may, or may not, have belonged to the company. The *Dialogus* carries echoes of the *Institutio Oratoria*, and closely similar verdicts about Latin literature. Various strains of dissent can also be detected.[9]

---

[1] I. 5. 11.   [2] VII. 12.

[3] cf. the allusion to 'tenuitas vestra' (VII. 12. 5). For C. Minicius Fundanus (*suff.* 107), about whom a number of details are known, see the alert and sympathetic picture drawn by E. Groag, P-W xv, 1820 ff.

[4] IX. 26. For 'sanitas', cf. *Dial.* 23. 3 ff.; Quintilian XII. 10. 15.

[5] VII. 20. 6: 'nec desunt qui utrique nostrum praeferantur.'

[6] See the full account of M. Durry in his edition (Paris, 1938), 40 ff. For a more favourable view, R. T. Bruère, *Class. Phil.* XLIX (1954), 161 ff. He traces echoes in the writings of Tacitus.

[7] Quintilian X. 1. 112.   [8] *Epp.* II. 14. 9; VI. 3. 3.

[9] R. Dienel, *Wiener Studien* XXXVII (1915), 239 ff.; H. Bardon, *Rev. ét. lat.* XIX (1941),

There was one ground for disagreement deeper than all others. It concerned the general condition of Roman eloquence past and present: decline or recovery, the maladies and the diagnosis. Some critics saw oratory going quickly downhill after the decease of Cicero and denounced the later generations in Augustan Rome, lazy, luxurious, and effeminate.[1] Others put the blame on the schools of rhetoric with their frivolous or empty declamations.[2]

Style (it could be seen) was liable to sundry affectations and aberrations; and types of 'corrupti generis oratio' were analysed by Seneca, ever alert for symptoms of moral distemper.[3] Perhaps the ailments were temporary and corrigible. Quintilian, apart from his major work, had written a tract 'de causis corruptae eloquentiae'.[4] The professor, it may be surmised, discovered the principal causes in education, in morality—and precisely in new fashions such as the style of Seneca. He explains that it was his duty as a teacher to combat the influence and popularity of that style.[5]

Quintilian is complacent about the art he professed, and he proclaims a renascence.[6] The *Dialogus* confutes and supersedes Quintilian. There was no cure or remedy, since eloquence itself was obsolete. Tacitus furnishes a political and historical diagnosis.[7]

Another of Pliny's masters was Nicetes Sacerdos of Smyrna.[8] Nicetes is the sole contemporary Greek to be mentioned in the *Dialogus*, and he is mentioned in sharp dispraise: his kind makes Ephesus or Mytilene reverberate with the noisy chorus of applauding pupils.[9] Further, forensic orations. Pliny drew enormous pride from his speeches concerning the law of property:[10] the *Dialogus* quietly points out that none of the classical orators selected this field for any notable effort.[11] Again, verse writing as a suitable spare-time occupation for eminent orators. Pliny in one of his letters solemnly retails a whole catalogue of precedents.[12] Tacitus quickly disposes of all such by-products and damns them in a biting epigram—Cicero's poems are known about, the others were luckier.[13]

---

113 ff.; R. Güngerich, *Class. Phil.* XLVI (1951), 159 ff. And, characteristically, Tacitus abbreviates Quintilian: for examples, H. Bardon, *Latomus* XII (1953), 488 f.

[1] Seneca, *Controv.* I, *praef.* 6 ff. (very declamatory).   [2] Petronius, *Sat.* I ff.

[3] Seneca, *Epp.* 114.   [4] Quintilian VI, *praef.* 3.   [5] X. I. 125 ff.

[6] ib. 122 (cited on p. 103).   [7] cf. Wilamowitz, *Der Glaube der Hellenen* II (1932), 546.

[8] VI. 6. 3. Note also his enthusiasm for Isaeus, a ready and voluble speaker (II. 3. I ff., cf. Juvenal III. 74).

[9] *Dial.* 15. 3: 'Sacerdos ille Nicetes et si quis alius Ephesum vel Mytilenas concentu scholasticorum et clamoribus quatit.' His style was ὑπόβακχος δὲ καὶ διθυραμβώδης (Philostratus, *Vit. Soph.* I. 19. 1).

[10] IX. 23. I, &c.   [11] *Dial.* 37. 6; 38. 2.   [12] V. 3. 5 ff.

[13] *Dial.* 21. 6: 'non melius quam Cicero sed felicius, quia illos fecisse pauciores sciunt.' It should be noted that Pliny does not seem to have taken seriously to verse much before 104 (IV. 14, cf. V. 10—his hendecasyllables).

Tacitus might have been something of a Ciceronian in his own oratorical practice. Pliny perhaps implies it, by his claim to be a disciple. Nothing in the *Dialogus* lends support. The premium seems to go to innovation and originality.[1] Marcus Aper exposes the faults of Cicero with force and zest—and asserts that the imitators only reproduce those faults.[2] One of them was known and notorious, Q. Haterius, who had exorbitant popularity in the days of Caesar Augustus, and no enduring fame.[3]

Cicero proclaimed that eloquence is the child of peace and concord.[4] Maternus, who demolishes that notion, shows that much of Cicero no longer possessed use and relevance:[5] the public speeches owed their very existence to political liberty and themes of high contention, while the private orations had never added much to his renown.[6]

Tacitus had recourse to the literary treatises of Cicero. He studied them carefully.[7] By composing the *Dialogus* after the manner of Cicero, he demonstrated that Cicero might still be used as a model. For an essay, but not for oratory.

The precise date of the *Dialogus* need not matter. The book may belong a little earlier than the consulate of Fabius Justus—or, first composed in 102, it might have been published later, as much as five years later.[8] The significance remains the same. The *Dialogus* shows a writer who has turned his back on the eloquence of Senate and lawcourts, and is already thinking as an historian.[9]

---

[1] The author nowhere names Seneca. To bring him in would have confused—and weakened—the argument for innovations and newer styles: Seneca was not well thought of.

[2] 22. 3 ff.; 23. 1 f.: 'nam et haec invitus rettuli et plura omisi, quae tamen sola mirantur atque exprimunt ii qui se antiquos oratores vocitant. neminem nominabo, genus hominum significasse contentus.'

[3] Tacitus later condemns this exuberant and Ciceronian orator (Ch. XXV).

[4] *Brutus* 45: 'pacis est comes otiique socia et iam bene constitutae civitatis quasi alumna quaedam eloquentia.' Cf. *De oratore* I. 30; II. 30.

[5] *Dial.* 40. 2: 'sed est magna illa et notabilis eloquentia alumna licentiae, quam stulti libertatem vocitant, comes seditionum, effrenati populi incitamentum, sine obsequio sine severitate, contumax temeraria adrogans, quae in bene constitutis civitatibus non oritur.'

[6] 38. 2.

[7] For a list of Ciceronian motives, A. Gudeman (ed. 2, Berlin, 1914), 83 ff.; for deliberate remodelling of stock Ciceronian phrases, 28. See further F. Leo, *Gött. gel. Anz.* 1898, 169 ff.; R. Helm, *Neue Jahrbücher* XXI (1908), 474 ff.; E. Koestermann, *Hermes* LXV (1930), 396 ff. Tacitus' close study also comes out in small details. Three citations drawn from lost works of Cicero look more accurate than the parallels in Quintilian: *Dial.* 32. 6 = *Inst. Or.* XII. 2. 33; 35. 1 = II. 4. 42; 18. 5 = XII. 10. 2. Cf. R. Güngerich, *Class. Phil.* XLVI (1951), 159 ff.

[8] As has been argued from VII. 20. 1 and from VIII. 7. 1, cf. App. 28.

[9] If a man were writing (or meditating) the reign of Vespasian, he might well be impelled, by the fame and fate of Eprius Marcellus, to consider the use and function of oratory in diverse epochs. Regulus was also a striking figure (*Hist.* IV. 42).

Of the *Historiae* the first hint seems to percolate in the year 105, by a devious channel. Titinius Capito, that zealous patron of letters, advised Pliny to take to history.[1] He was not the only one. To the bland and perhaps insidious solicitation Pliny returns an answer redolent of proud humility. He acknowledges his keen desire for fame, and points to the popularity of history: poetry or oratory need style, but history draws the reader, from curiosity, be it wholly destitute of style.[2] Unfortunately, Pliny's endeavours are monopolized by urgent needs—speeches to go over again and improve with a view to publication. Oratory and history have many things in common, but the differences are greater.[3] Pliny would not wish to mix together and spoil two separate species of literature. Finally, he throws the problem back at his correspondent. What should Pliny take for his subject—an earlier period that others have already dealt with, or recent history, an untouched field?

Pliny admits the drawbacks of both kinds of history—the one type is easy, for it has been written about, but it is a burden to compare and balance the divergent accounts, while the other earns little thanks and may easily get a man into serious trouble.[4]

The consular orator (it appears) was hankering after history.[5] There was one impediment, however, that he does not mention. The best subject, embracing both written and unwritten annals, had already been taken. In the course of the letter to Titinius, Pliny indicates, among the claims that might suitably convert him into one of the Roman historians, a domestic example and precedent, precisely his uncle; and to follow family tradition is counted most creditable by the wise.[6] In fact Pliny had edited his uncle's *Historiae*. The exhortation of Titinius came too late. Pliny's hereditary rights had already been disregarded. The historical work of the uncle not only narrated the reigns of Claudius and Nero, but went on to cover the year after Nero's fall and provide an introduction to the rule of Vespasian.[7] The *Historiae* of Cornelius Tacitus, beginning with the first day of January of the year 69, not only utilized (and thereby superseded) the later

---

[1] v. 8. The relevance to Tacitus was discerned by Mommsen, *Hermes* III (1869), 107 f. = *Ges. Schr.* IV, 441. Sidonius fancied that Tacitus was the author of this letter, first exhorting Pliny, and then himself taking to history (*Epp.* IV. 22. 2).

[2] ib. 4: 'orationi enim et carmini parva gratia, nisi eloquentia est summa: historia quoquo modo scripta delectat.' Cf. Vitruvius V, *praef.* 4: 'historiae per se tenent lectores.'

[3] ib. 9 f. Pliny's notion of the historical style was Ciceronian—'tractu et suavitate atque etiam dulcedine placet.'

[4] ib. 12: 'tu tamen iam nunc cogita quae potissimum tempora adgrediar. vetera et scripta aliis? parata inquisitio, sed onerosa collatio. intacta et nova? graves offensae, levis gratia.'

[5] Observe his dramatic and highly stylized narration about the fate of the Vestal Virgin Cornelia (IV. 11). Cf. H. W. Traub, *TAPA* LXXXVI (1955), 213 ff.

[6] ib. 5. [7] *NH, praef.* 20.

books of the elder Pliny. They furnished the continuation, right through the rule of the Flavian dynasty to the day of September 18, 96.

Obscurely detected for the first time in an informal essay on historiography in 105,[1] the Tacitean masterpiece soon acquires shape and substance. In response to invitation Pliny in 106 supplied Tacitus with historical material. It concerned a natural catastrophe of the year 79.[2] Pliny's uncle perished in the eruption of Vesuvius. The old man deserved to be commemorated, for by a singular bounty of providence he had both made history and written history.

The inference is clear. Of the books of the *Historiae* a portion at least became known in 105, and not perhaps in rumour only, or through manuscript privately circulated. History was like poetry, and history could be recited, although (as Pliny points out) some rigorists might disapprove of the practice.[3]

Posterity knows only four books and the beginning of the fifth. Book I narrates the assassination of Galba, Otho's seizure of power, and the march of the two armies of Vitellius from the Rhine to northern Italy. The second contains the campaign of Bedriacum, the end of Otho, and the proclamation of Vespasian in the East. The third, opening with the invasion of Italy by the Flavian generals, describes the Battle of Cremona, the march on Rome, the abdication and death of Vitellius in December of the year 69. With the fourth, the events on the Rhine in the rebellion of Julius Civilis are fully treated. The fragment of Book V (twenty-six chapters) furnishes the prelude to the siege of Jerusalem by Titus, and goes on to wind up the affair of Civilis. It could be conjectured that the book ended with the triumph of Vespasian and Titus in the summer of 71. Other historians perhaps found that event an attractive—and almost inevitable—termination of their labours. Thus, presumably, Pliny's uncle. Yet Tacitus might have chosen to carry Book V well forward into the years of peace, perhaps as far as 73.[4]

The first two books seem to go together as a natural unit. The conclusion of the second proclaims an emphatic warning against those who wrote under the Flavian dynasty: an episode that was plain treachery they passed off as love of peace and care for the Commonwealth, most dishonestly.[5] Books I and II may have been published

---

[1] A much earlier inception is assumed by those who discover traces of the *Historiae* in Pliny's *Panegyricus* (e.g. in remarks on adoption). According to K. Büchner the *Panegyricus* presupposes Book III (*Rh. Mus.* LXXXVIII (1955), 309). See further p. 207.

[2] VI. 16 and 20.

[3] VII. 17. 3. For a recital by Servilius Nonianus, when Claudius Caesar turned up, I. 13. 3.

[4] For the total of books and the structure, see Ch. XVIII with App. 35.

[5] *Hist.* II. 101. 1: 'curam pacis et amorem rei publicae, corruptas in adulationem causas, tradidere.'

at the same time. Then, after an interval, though perhaps not a long one, came the third book separately, terminating the theme of civil war. Next IV and V together (they are linked), or IV–VI, to form a triad.[1] With the sixth book the author may have reached the death of Vespasian in 79.[2]

How long Tacitus had been at work, it is difficult to say. His reticent and austere character, his loathing for self-advertisement permit a deduction. He would hesitate to challenge publicity unless he had a substantial contribution, both ready and in reserve. That is to say, if he recited or published Books I–II, he was ahead with Books III–VI. Cornelius Tacitus may, or may not, have embarked on his serious researches as early as 98. The subject as a whole demanded careful and detailed study. Especially exacting would be the reign of Domitian, where (it may be presumed) Tacitus had no predecessors. The books on the civil wars, involving comparison and criticism rather than the collection of material, were not so formidable. The style is fluent and confident. If, as might be conjectured but not with safety assumed, Tacitus was absent from Rome on some consular employment in the years 101–4,[3] leisure and a small library may have carried him a long way forward. Whether, on a further hypothesis, the scene of his official occupation lent some geographical knowledge and background to his pursuits, it would be vain to inquire.

The next fact about the *Historiae* is in consonance with the assumption that several books had been completed, if not all published, by 105. A year passes, or not much more, from the faint earliest hint about the *Historiae*, and Cornelius Tacitus is already collecting information about an event at the beginning of the reign of Titus Caesar, a decade from the starting-point of his narrative. Books I–VI may already have been terminated.

The historian would soon be advancing through the fifteen years of Domitian.[4] A letter of Pliny about 107 is instructive. He hastens to augur eternal fame for his friend's work—and make certain that his own virtues found proper commemoration.[5] Not more than the truth, for that would be an offence against the sanctity of history, but also

---

[1] For the publication of the *Historiae* in groups see F. Münzer, *Klio* I (1901), 322 ff. He argues from links, cross-references, and some minor discrepancies. He also suggests (o.c. 329) that Book I appeared before the death of Regulus, Book IV after, because of the ugly allegation about Regulus' behaviour when Piso was killed (IV. 42. 2—in a speech). But it is not likely that Tacitus would in any case have cited such an item in his narration in Book I. For the date of Regulus' decease (?105), p. 97.

[2] Ch. XVIII.   [3] p. 71.

[4] Some discover in the phrase 'cum historicorum more scribas numerum iniri non potuisse' (*Epp.* IX. 16. 1) a hint of Tacitus on the disaster of Cornelius Fuscus in 86 or 87 (cf. Orosius VII. 10. 4, cited below, p. 215).

[5] VII. 33. Compare Cicero to Lucceius (*Ad fam.* V. 12).

not less.[1] The matter referred to was safely consigned to official archives, and so could not fail to be noted by a serious investigator like Tacitus.[2] However, Pliny will expound it, unsolicited. He was anxious that his public conduct in 93, both before and after the prosecution of Baebius Massa, should not be misconstrued. Out of that case, quickly and unpredictably, arose the tragic concatenation of events that brought good men to ruin or exile, destroying the party of Helvidius Priscus.[3]

Pliny's role in the year 93 was accidental, or at least unimportant. Under Nerva he made a deliberate attempt to exact vengeance for the outrages of that year. For that heroic sequel there could be no place in the *Historiae* of Cornelius Tacitus. Pliny was not dismayed. In 108 he composed for the edification of one of his admirers among the senatorial youth a full account of what happened in that famous session of the Senate when he attacked Publicius Certus.[4]

By the end of 109 Tacitus (it may well be) had completed and published the second half of his work.[5] When he dealt with the last years of Domitian, the narrative concerned transactions in which the author and his friends had shared. At recitations the subject or the company sometimes caused awkward moments, when the ministers of a despot were censured, his accomplices arraigned. Then might discreet approach be made to an author, with suggestions to change or omit. An instance is on record, with no names and no clue. The historian agreed to leave out a passage, but refused to expunge it from his text.[6]

Tacitus was a bold writer. The end of his *Historiae* impinged on contemporary events. So did the beginning, when Galba's reign evoked Nerva.

[1] VII. 33. 10: 'nam nec historia debet egredi veritatem, et honeste factis veritas sufficit. vale.'

[2] ib. 3: 'demonstro ergo, quamquam diligentiam tuam fugere non possit, cum sit in publicis actis.' The documents referred to (cf. v. 13. 8; *Ann.* XII. 24. 2) seem to be something different from *acta senatus* or *acta diurna*, cf. F. Leo, *Gött. gel. Nachr.* 1896, 200.

[3] App. 21.

[4] IX. 13 (to the young Ummidius Quadratus).

[5] He might have previously done some work on the Domitianic books.

[6] IX. 27. 1: 'recitaverat quidam verissimum librum', &c.

XI. AN HISTORIAN'S FIRST STEPS

TACITUS had announced that he would write a history. Two monographs came first, the *Agricola* and the *Germania*—but not without some relevance to the project. What quality and promise do these essays show?

Producing an encomium on Verginius Rufus, Tacitus cannot have failed to see that another great and good man might be honoured in like fashion. Verginius survived the emperors whose suspicion and hatred he incurred: Julius Agricola died before the truth could be told. For virtue wronged by a tyrant the delayed and posthumous oration was available, a pious duty. Domitius Corbulo may have been commemorated in this manner; and the deaths of illustrious men as compiled by the devout fervour of Titinius Capito were suitably compared to funeral orations.[1]

To discover the link between Verginius and Agricola requires no insight or perspicacity. Pliny in the letter describing the obsequies of his guardian echoes and adapts the peroration of the *Agricola* on fame and survival.[2]

'Clarorum virorum facta moresque'.[3] The opuscule, opening with a traditional phrase, goes on to defend those who write biographies. It was an ancient and reputable practice, for the ages that produced excellence knew how to honour it, but nowadays calling for excuse— 'tam saeva et infesta virtutibus tempora'.[4]

The subject-matter of the *Agricola*, however, seems to go beyond the theme of a biography. The treatise contains a dissertation on the history and geography of Britain, the narrative of seven campaigns,

---

[1] *Epp.* VIII. 12. 4 f.: 'scribit exitus inlustrium virorum, in his quorundam mihi carissimorum. videor ergo fungi pio munere, quorumque exequias celebrare non licuit, horum quasi funebribus laudationibus, seris quidem, sed tanto magis veris interesse.'

[2] II. I. 10 f.: 'si tamen fas est aut flere aut omnino mortem vocare qua tanti viri mortalitas magis finita quam vita est. vivit enim vivetque semper atque etiam latius in memoria hominum et sermone versabitur postquam ab oculis recessit.' Compare *Agr.* 46. 1 and 4. Another parallel in Pliny is VIII. 14. 9 with *Agr.* 3. 1 f. It has been asserted that there is no trace of Pliny's having read *Agricola* or *Germania* (M. Schuster, *Wiener Studien* XLVI (1928), 234). For echoes in the *Panegyricus*, R. T. Bruère, *Class. Phil.* XLIX (1954), 162 ff.

[3] *Agr.* 1. 1—which adapts the exordium of Cato in his *Origines* (cited in Cicero, *Pro Plancio* 66): 'clarorum virorum atque magnorum.' Or perhaps something else from Cato (*Tusc. Disp.* IV. 3), cf. B. Wijkström, *Apophoreta Gotoburgensia Vilelmo Lundström Oblata* (1936), 158 ff.

[4] I. 4, cf. Cicero, *Orator* 35: 'tempora timens inimica virtuti' (the rule of Caesar the Dictator).

the speeches of generals before battle. Is the expansion excessive?
However bulky, it stands in relation to the central figure, for Britain
is the theatre of 'virtus', and the field of Agricola's exploits as a 'vir
militaris' from first to last—tribune, legionary legate, and conqueror
of the island. Other commanders are scantily treated, and some with
dispraise, especially if they fought no battles, or, coming after the
murderous work of subjugation, showed mildness in their policy and
conciliation towards the natives. Such were the three governors who
fill the interval between Boudicca's rebellion and the resumption of
conquest under the Flavian dynasty.[1] And it is but natural that what
was done by Petillius Cerialis and Julius Frontinus (the Brigantes
broken and Wales subdued) is passed over rapidly and lightly.[2] The
biographies of Cerialis and Frontinus have not survived.[3]

Wilful vagueness enhances the portion of Julius Agricola. Before
that legate arrived, the Roman armies had already advanced a long
way to the north, cutting off the Brigantes from the tribes of Cale-
donia.[4] The first two campaigns covered familiar ground. It was not
till the third that the general penetrated into new territories when his
columns swept onwards as far as the estuary called Tanaus.[5] The
narrative of the northern operations is sparsely equipped with names.
Six in all, a tribe, a harbour, a mountain, and three estuaries. Elsewhere the author likewise avoids detail and precision—no town in
Britain is registered, and none of the legionary stations. Not indeed
that ignorance has to be assigned as the reason for such omissions.[6]
At the same time, however, since Tacitus professed an undertaking to
supply fresh facts now accruing about the geography of the island (to
surpass earlier writers), the performance seems to fall short.[7]

As conquerors in Britain, all must yield to the glory of Agricola,
the eleventh legate since the invasion thirty-five years before.[8] The
other contrast is between the emperor and the senator. Underlying
the whole work, it is brought out and magnified by insinuation and

---

[1] 16. 2 ff. (Petronius Turpilianus, Trebellius Maximus, and Vettius Bolanus).

[2] 17.

[3] The son-in-law of Frontinus, Sosius Senecio, was a man of taste and talent.

[4] cf. E. Birley, *Roman Britain and the Roman Army* (1953), 10 ff.; 31 ff. For the area covered by the Brigantes, I. A. Richmond, *JRS* XLIV (1954), 43 ff.

[5] 22. 1: 'tertius expeditionum annus novas gentes aperuit, vastatis usque ad Tanaum (aestuario nomen est) nationibus.' That Tanaus can be (and should be) the Tay has been too readily ruled out, e.g. by J. G. C. Anderson in his edition (Oxford, 1922). In the next year Agricola consolidated on the isthmus between Clota and Bodotria (23)—not un-naturally some way behind his extreme point of penetration.

[6] Compare the detailed narrations of British campaigns in the *Annales*, which pre-suppose knowledge of where the legions were (p. 395).

[7] 10. 1: 'ita quae priores nondum comperta eloquentia percoluere rerum fide tradentur.' Critics of Tacitus have not always been immune from error, cf. App. 69.

[8] Tacitus furnishes names and sequence (14; 16. 3-17. 3).

rumour. Domitian's morbid jealousy is variously manifested—displeasure at Agricola's great victory, the story of the imperial freedman who was sent out on a secret mission (to promise the province of Syria) but never met Agricola, and at the end the allegation of poisoning.[1]

So flagrant is the distortion when the Emperor is defamed that upon cool reflection doubts might arise about the superior excellence of Julius Agricola, that paragon of civic and military virtue.[2] Tacitus concedes that Agricola was not impressive—one could see that he was a good man, one would gladly believe him a great man.[3] Like Verginius Rufus, he had to be built up. The caution and prudence of the hero fatigues with reiterated documentation. Respect for authority and a conduct that so invariably enlisted the favour of higher officers may be liable to unfriendly imputations. Nor is it at all clear how far Agricola's actions in Britain belong to personal initiative, to normal military routine, or to deliberate imperial policy. Other governors may have been no less prudent in choosing the site of a fort;[4] no less circumspect in the field when they explored estuaries and forests;[5] no less amiable and assiduous when they solicited the natives to build cities, to live in decent comfort, to study literature and eloquence.[6]

The moralist shows through as well as the panegyrist. Agricola's laudable efforts to further the urban way of life in Britain had another side, he must add: ease and refinement become detrimentally seductive.[7] It would be a graver matter if the author's zeal magnified unduly the quality of the general. Some may make play with the names of

---

[1] 39. 1 ff.; 40.2; 43.2. In the last two items the author protects himself with 'credidere plerique' and 'constans rumor'. He knew what such beliefs and rumours were worth in imperial Rome. For the episode of the declined proconsulate (42. 1 ff.) see H. W. Traub, *Class. Phil.* XLIX (1954), 255 f.; K. v. Fritz, ib. LII (1957), 73 ff.

[2] R. G. Collingwood, *Roman Britain and the English Settlements*[2] (1937), 113 f.; G. Walser, *Rom, das Reich und die fremden Völker in der Geschichtsschreibung der frühen Kaiserzeit* (1951), 28 ff.; E. Paratore, *Tacito* (1951), 73 ff.; F. Grosso, *In Memoriam Achillis Beltrami Miscellanea Philologica* (1954), 97 ff. For remarks in protest, A. G. Woodhead, *The Phoenix* II (1948), 45 ff.

[3] 44. 2: 'quod si habitum quoque eius posteri noscere velint, decentior quam sublimior fuit: nihil impetus in vultu: gratia oris supererat. bonum virum facile crederes, magnum libenter.'   [4] 22. 2.

[5] 20. 2: 'loca castris ipse capere, aestuaria ac silvas ipse praetemptare.' Cf. the procedure of Vettius Bolanus (in Armenia, not in Britain), Statius, *Silvae* v. 2. 41 ff.: 'Bolanus iter praenosse timendum | Bolanus tutis iuga quaerere commoda castris | metiri Bolanus agros, aperire malignas|torrentum nemorumque moras.'

[6] 21. 1: 'hortari privatim, adiuvare publice, ut templa fora domos exstruerent,' &c. Note one of the Neronian governors (16. 4): 'Trebellius segnior et nullis castrorum experimentis comitate quadam curandi provinciam tenuit. didicere iam barbari quoque ignoscere vitiis blandientibus.'

[7] Tacitus cannot help moralizing about Agricola's measures (21. 3): 'paulatimque discessum ad delenimenta vitiorum, porticus et balnea et conviviorum elegantiam. idque apud imperitos humanitas vocabatur, cum pars servitutis esset.'

Cerialis and Frontinus, invoking what cannot be ascertained.[1] If Agricola was slow and cautious, it was right to be so. There was no hurry. Nothing invalidates his skill in the design of a campaign or the dispositions for battle.[2]

The war ended with the victory at Mons Graupius. Tacitus claims that Agricola had conquered the whole island of Britain.[3] If that is what the general reported to the Emperor, his sanguine estimate may have influenced the government or caused misconceptions. Other regions of the Empire had their demands. During the sixth campaign Domitian had been able to withdraw detachments from each of the four legions to reinforce his operations in Germany without impeding (so it appears) the process of conquest in Britain.[4] Those troops did not go back at once. More important, the repercussion of the trouble on the Danube. Soon after Agricola's departure (and perhaps very soon) the war against the Dacians caused a whole legion to be removed.[5] What was the subsequent fate of the Roman acquisitions in the land of the Caledonians?

A legionary camp had been established a long way forward in the newly-won territory, facing the mountains. Destined for a permanent occupation, it was held for several years, then evacuated after a methodical demolition.[6] That measure did not entail (and cannot prove) the sudden and complete abandonment of all that Agricola conquered. The time and manner of the Roman retreat remains obscure. One stage (it might be conjectured) had ensued before the end of Domitian's reign, another under Trajan, bringing forts and garrisons back to the vicinity of the line of defence and demarcation chosen by Trajan's successor.[7]

Tacitus does not help—'perdomita Britannia et statim missa'.[8] Such is the verdict pronounced in the prologue of the *Historiae* when

[1] R. G. Collingwood, o.c. 113: 'incapable of inspiring enthusiasm like Cerialis or reverence like Frontinus.'

[2] I. A. Richmond, *JRS* XXXIV (1944), 34 ff.

[3] 10. 1: 'quia tum primum perdomita est.'

[4] *ILS* 1025 shows a tribune in charge of a *vexillatio* of IX Hispana, decorated by the Emperor; but all four (along with the legions of Upper Germany) are represented in the detachments commanded by Velius Rufus (*ILS* 9200). See further *CAH* XI (1936), 163 f.

[5] viz. II Adiutrix. The legion is next heard of on the Danube, by 92 (*ILS* 2719), if not earlier (*ILS* 9193). The latter inscription records a centurion decorated 'ab imp. Caesare Aug. bello Dacico.'

[6] At Inchtuthil, a dozen miles north of Perth. An *as* of Domitian of 87, in mint condition, was found in a demolition layer. See M. V. Taylor, *JRS* XLV (1955), 122 f., summarizing a report of the excavations of I. A. Richmond; also the latter, briefly, in *Proc. Brit. Ac.* XLI (1955), 313.

[7] cf. I. A. Richmond, *JRS* XL (1950), 55.

[8] *Hist.* I. 2. 1. For 'missa' (where many editors since Lipsius have preferred '⟨o⟩missa'), cf. E. Norden, *Altgermanien* (1934), 28; E. Löfstedt, *Vermischte Studien* (1936), 126.

the historian assesses the record of foreign policy, adverse in the West though favourable in the East. Exaggerated if not enigmatic, the phrase has provoked much discussion.[1] The elucidation lies somewhere in the lost books of the *Historiae*.[2]

With the *Agricola*, the laudation has developed into a biography. That genre was described as lying half-way between oratory and history.[3] The style is in accord, in some parts flowing, ornate, and eloquent; in others, and especially where there is narrative, ethnography, or geography, it shows the traditional features of the Roman historical diction in the manner of Sallust and Livy.[4]

When orators turn their talent to the composition of history, they modify their style before they change their habits. The characteristic vices in the annals of the Empire were early diagnosed—praise and defamation.[5] It is easy to indict rhetoric as the origin of certain features in the *Agricola*;[6] and everybody knew that a biographical encomium took liberties not permitted in regular history.[7] The cause lies deeper. The treatise, as has been shown, is concerned with much more than the life and the laudation of Tacitus' father-in-law. It is a document of Roman political literature, a manifesto for the Emperor Trajan and the new imperial aristocracy.[8]

Attempts have been made to specify the place of Tacitus' *Agricola* among the various categories of prose writing. It is best left to be defined in its own terms.[9] At first sight (and on a final judgement), the tract on Germany and its inhabitants is much simpler.

The *Germania* is unique but not original. Latin literature knew precedents in the genre. An historian like Sallust or Livy might have recourse to a copious digression on countries and peoples, welcoming the occasion to illustrate and diversify the bare narrative of events, to exhibit also his own erudition and versatility.[10] The excursus suggested the monograph. Seneca wrote treatises on India and on Egypt.[11]

The themes of ethnographical writing derived from a long tradition.

---

[1] For the last items in a prolonged and not quite conclusive controversy see T. D. Pryce and E. Birley, *JRS* xxviii (1938), 141 ff.; G. Macdonald, ib. xxix (1939), 5 ff.

[2] And, be it added, in archaeological investigation.

[3] Compare Fannius' books on the victims of Nero (*Epp.* v. 5. 3): 'inter sermonem historiamque medios.'   [4] p. 198.

[5] *Hist.* I. 1. 1: 'ita neutris cura posteritatis inter infensos vel obnoxios.'

[6] cf. G. Walser, o.c. 28 ff.

[7] Polybius x. 21. 8, cf. Nepos, *Pelopidas* 1; Plutarch, *Alexander* 1. Compare Cicero's invitation to L. Lucceius (*Ad fam.* v. 12. 3).

[8] Ch. III.

[9] Compare the firm protests of D. R. Stuart, *Epochs of Greek and Roman Biography* (1928), 253; C. Marchesi, *Tacito*[3] (1944), 57 (deprecating 'vaniloquio filologico').

[10] Sallust, *Jug.* 17–19; *Hist.* III, fragments 61–80 ('de situ Ponti'); Livy, *Per.* CIV: 'prima pars libri situm Germaniae moresque continet.'

[11] Servius on *Aen.* VI. 154; IX. 30. Also, for India, Pliny, *NH* VI. 60.

They were a blend of fact and legend, theory and edification. From early times the contrast between the barbarous peoples and the civilized gave rise to wonder and speculation.[1] 'Campestres melius Scythae', that is a constant note. Idealization of the savage (like that of the peasant), nourished on the discontents of the urban existence, lent colour and conviction to fancy pictures of primitive virtue and primitive felicity, with inevitable censure, loud or subtle, directed against luxury, complexity, and corruption. If the topics were conventional, so also was the phraseology. Details and traits originally inherent in one native people were conveyed to another, from Thracians and Scythians to Gauls, and, with enhancement, from Gauls to Germans— the Germans were larger and fiercer, with redder hair.[2]

'Nemo illic vitia ridet.'[3] Beyond the Rhine dwelt sound morality, and custom more potent for good than any legislation.[4] The frivolity of Roman society alarmed the moralist and the statesman, and so did its feebleness, for he was preoccupied with the aristocracy's claim to rule or govern. The Germans were strong and free and numerous, menacing to a political system that rested on servility and corruption, justified riches by refinement, and supplied with culture the lack of vigour and virtue.

Did Tacitus record what he had seen and known, or only what he read in books? Seneca visited the land of Egypt, where his aunt's husband ruled as viceroy for Tiberius Caesar;[5] and Sallust had been governor of a province in Africa, little though the excursus in his *Bellum Jugurthinum* seems to benefit from that fact.[6] Geography was held by Roman writers to be a difficult, abstruse, and rebellious subject.[7] Germany or Britain, Tacitus shows little interest in it.[8] Fresh knowledge accrued mainly from merchants and soldiers.[9] It took a long time to win recognition in literature. A man's own experience might seem less attractive and convincing than what stood in literary tradition, guaranteed by time and famous names. If Cornelius Tacitus was

---

[1] A. Riese, *Die Idealisirung der Naturvölker des Nordens in der gr. u. r. Literatur* (Prog. Frankfurt, 1875).

[2] Strabo VII. 290, &c. See K. Trüdinger, *Studien zur Geschichte der griechisch-römischen Ethnographie* (Diss. Basel, 1918); E. Norden, *Die germanische Urgeschichte in Tacitus Germania* (1920, ed. 3, 1923); G. Wissowa, *Neue Jahrbücher* XLVII (1921), 14 ff.

[3] *Germ.* 19. 3.

[4] 19. 5: 'plusque ibi boni mores valent quam alibi bonae leges.' Cf. Horace, *Odes* III. 24. 35 f.

[5] *Ad Helviam* 19. 4. The wife of C. Galerius, prefect from 16 to 31.

[6] *Jug.* 17–19.

[7] Mela, *praef.*: 'orbis situm dicere aggredior, impeditum opus et facundiae minime capax.'

[8] cf. W. Capelle, *Philologus* LXXXIV (1929), 349 ff.; 464 ff.

[9] Pliny, *NH* VI. 140 f. ('nostri negotiatores' and 'arma Romana'). Cf. E. Norden, o.c. 434 ff.

ever on the Rhine, he discloses no sign of it in the *Germania*.[1] Nor did the senator before taking up the pen make anxious inquiry of eye-witnesses or confront the books with the exact testimony of consular governors, legionary legates, or financial agents.[2]

The *Germania* derives from written information copied very closely, not merely in the general account of country, race, and customs, but also in the explicit catalogue of the tribes. It is a fair surmise that for his main authority Tacitus used and exploited the *Bella Germaniae* of the elder Pliny.[3] That officer had served with the armies of the Rhine;[4] he knew both Upper and Lower Germany from the sources of the Danube to the shore of the Ocean; and he had been on expeditions across the river into the lands of the free Germans.[5] Pliny united relentless energy, encyclopedic tastes, and a keen faculty of observation.

No better source could be imagined. Yet Pliny's researches would require supplementation, for something like forty years had intervened since he wrote. Tacitus was not vigilant enough. In the first sentence of the treatise he takes over phraseology about the boundaries of Germany that seems to have been obsolete even in Pliny's day, being relevant rather to Augustan times.[6] Similarly, he refers in general terms to tribes and kings as having come to Roman knowledge recently: rather something long ago, the result of expeditions in the days of Caesar Augustus that took the Roman arms to the river Elbe or revealed the promontory of the Cimbri.[7]

Elsewhere the *Germania* reflects the conditions that prevailed before the Flavian emperors moved forward the frontiers of Upper Germany and of Raetia beyond the Rhine and beyond the Danube.[8] No less revealing is what Tacitus says about the Danubian Germans, namely

---

[1] The notion that he could have been legate of Gallia Belgica in the period 89–93 must be firmly dismissed (p. 70).

[2] Consular legates of the Germanies still extant in 98 were Vestricius Spurinna, Lappius Maximus, and Javolenus Priscus; and Julius Frontinus might have been on the Rhine with Domitian in 83 (p. 214).

[3] F. Münzer, *Bonner Jahrbücher* CIV (1899), 67 ff.; E. Norden, o.c. 207 ff.

[4] p. 60.

[5] Pliny had been at the source of the Danube (*NH* XXXI. 25); near the mouth of the Rhine, 'extremoque in margine imperii' (XII. 98); at Aquae Mattiacae across the river (XXXI. 20); and also among the degraded Chauci, presumably with Domitius Corbulo in 47 (XVI. 2).

[6] *Germ.* I. 1: 'Germania omnis a Gallis Raetisque et Pannoniis Rheno et Danuvio fluminibus, a Sarmatis Dacisque mutuo metu aut montibus separatur.' Cf. V. Lundström, *Eranos* XXV (1927), 249 ff.

[7] ib.: 'nuper cognitis quibusdam gentibus ac regibus, quos bellum aperuit.' Clearly during the Augustan invasions, not since, cf. the reference to the Elbe (41. 2), and to Oceanus (34. 2 f.).

[8] Thus the Hermunduri, freely crossing the Danube into Raetia: 'passim et sine custode transeunt' (41. 1). Further, as for Lower Germany, the status ascribed to the Batavi (29. 2) is not plausible after 70.

the Marcomanni and the Quadi. For Tacitus they are loyal clients of
the Empire, supported usually by subsidies in money, seldom by
armed intervention of the Romans.[1] Which is peculiar. The defection
of those peoples in the year 89 during Domitian's war against the
Dacians modified the whole frontier policy of the Empire.[2]

Nor, when he is aware of a change, has the author been at sufficient
pains to insert new material. In the catalogue of the nations of Germany there appear to be only three explicit references to recent events.
One of them is of a general nature: it occurs in the historical survey
of Rome's relations with the Germans.[3] The second is the episode of
the Bructeri, exulting in their annihilation.[4] The third is the description of the tract in southern Germany called the 'decumates agri'.[5]
In each there is rhetoric and emotion; and the passage about the
'decumates agri' not only lacks precision—it seems to have been
inserted without due regard to its context.[6]

The author's defects are clear. Faithfully following his source, he
confines his efforts to sharpening and embellishing the style, with a
few epigrams added and a few details to bring the treatise up to date.[7]
To regard the *Germania* as in any sense an introduction to the
Historiae of Tacitus is premature and misleading.[8] Early in that work
came to be recounted the fighting along the Rhine in the rebellion of
Julius Civilis. The *Germania*, which mentions not a single one of the
legionary camps from Vindonissa down to Vetera and Noviomagus,
let alone the odd forts and small tribes, would be of scant service.[9]

Like the first essays of Sallust, the two Tacitean monographs stand
at the threshold of a magnificent achievement. The comparison is not

---

[1] 42. 2: 'vis et potentia regibus ex auctoritate Romana. raro armis nostris, saepius
pecunia iuvantur.' Cf. *Ann.* XII. 30. 2; *Hist.* III. 5. 1.   [2] p. 32.

[3] 37. 6: 'proximis temporibus triumphati magis quam victi sunt.'

[4] 33, cf. p. 46.

[5] 29. 4: 'non numeraverim inter Germaniae populos, quamquam trans Rhenum
Danuviumque consederint, eos qui decumates agros exercent: levissimus quisque Gallorum
et inopia audax dubiae possessionis solum occupavere; mox limite acto promotisque
praesidiis sinus imperii et pars provinciae habentur.'

[6] The Mattiaci precede (29. 3), the Chatti follow, 'ultra hos Chatti' (30. 1). That
definition of the Chatti should place them in relation to the Mattiaci, not to the people
in the 'decumates agri'. The latter passage (29. 4) is therefore an addition, cf. R. Syme,
cited by J. G. C. Anderson in his edition (Oxford, 1938), 151.

[7] That is to say, it was probably written quite rapidly. Some have entertained the notion
that Tacitus had begun the work under Domitian. Thus E. Wolff, *Hermes* LXIX (1934), 155;
E. Kornemann, *Tacitus* (Wiesbaden, 1947), 22. For the epigrammatic and moralizing
character of the monograph cf. A. Gunz, *Die deklamatorische Rhetorik in der Germania des
Tacitus* (Diss. Lausanne, 1934). For its preciosity, J. Perret, *Rev. ét. anc.* LVI (1954), 98 f.

[8] Even if it be regarded as an extended and anticipatory excursus (E. Paratore, o.c.
287 ff.).

[9] Asciburgium happens to be a fort (*Hist.* IV. 33. 1), but it is named in the *Germania*
only for an antiquarian legend (3. 3). The *Historiae* show a remarkable knowledge of
place-names in the Rhineland, cf. p. 174.

wholly apt. Tacitus still had a long way to go. Not in the development of a style only, but in depth and scruple of study. He had to explore documents, question witnesses, sift the written accounts, and establish the truth of long and complicated transactions. The *Agricola*, it is true, discloses something of a Roman historian, for evil as well as for good.[1] None the less, the *Agricola* does not have to be understood as preface and preliminary to a full-length history. Not every author of a biography or an ethnographical pamphlet passed on to the higher historical pursuits—and those who announce projects do not always produce books. A contemporary event, Trajan on the Rhine, with a good army, eager for battle (it should seem) and ready for conquest, helps to explain some features of the *Germania*.[2] Not indeed that Tacitus' keen interest in the peoples of the North should be denied or extenuated.[3]

The political argument of the year 97 is behind the *Agricola*. But the repercussions of that eventful year, manifest in the *Agricola*, do not stop there. The experience goes deeper. It reveals the present and the past in close and startling relationship, it evokes the *Historiae* of Cornelius Tacitus.

Tacitus was suffect consul under Nerva. The fact is decisive for this man's conversion from oratory to the writing of history. One thing only stands on record. It fell to Tacitus to speak the laudation at the obsequies of the eminent Verginius Rufus, who had been *consul ordinarius* of the year as colleague of the Princeps. Which touches another problem. Old Rufus, when rehearsing his 'actio gratiarum' (it may or may not have been designed for delivery on the first day of office), slipped and fell and broke his thigh.[4] A long illness ensued—it did not, however, prevent him from fearing that he might be nominated to serve on an economy commission.[5] The death·of Verginius Rufus may have occurred quite late in the year.

For all that anybody can tell, Tacitus might have been holding the *fasces* in the fateful month of October 97.[6] However it be, whether his consulship belongs to late summer, to autumn, or to winter, he might

---

[1] For the foreshadowing of Tacitus' qualities for good and evil cf. H. Bardon, *Mélanges de la Faculté des Lettres de Poitiers* (1946), 195 ff.; J. Perret, *Rev. ét. anc.* LVI (1954), 90 ff.

[2] The *Germania* should not, however, be regarded as a political pamphlet, designed to recommend any action (or inaction). It is an ethnographical treatise, as Mommsen argued (*Reden u. Aufsätze* (1905), 149), and as Norden and others have proved.

[3] E. Wolff, *Hermes* LXIX (1934), 121 ff.; F. Dirlmeier, *Die alten Sprachen* II (1937), 37 ff.; J. Perret in his edition (Budé, 1949), 41. And it will be pertinent to recall that a Cornelius Tacitus was procurator of Belgica, that the historian himself might have been born in Belgica or on the Rhine (p. 614).

[4] *Epp.* II. I. 5.

[5] App. 2.

[6] For the *suffecti* of 97, App. 10.

have been present, ex-consul, consul, or consul-designate, at the council which decided that Nerva should proclaim a son and successor.[1]

In a laudation upon Verginius Rufus the bare facts were sharp and eloquent—the end of a dynasty, the claimants for power, the temper of the armies. Whichever the month when Tacitus delivered that oration, whether before the adoption—or even after—the character and capacity of the governor of Upper Germany stood out as dominant in Rome's immediate destiny. That general was either the strongest of the candidates, or else already emperor-elect. An orator whose manner combined majesty and subtlety, though constrained perhaps to curb his talent for damaging innuendo, will not have missed the chance to produce a sermon about obedience to the 'res publica', a solemn prophecy on the august theme 'capax imperii'.

Verginius Rufus and his refusal of the power became contemporary with the hopes and fears of 97. Much more so the rapid events of Galba's brief and doomed principate. A new ruler, coming after the sudden fall of a long-established dynasty, loses control and threatens to drag down Rome and the Empire to ruin. The same remedy is essayed. The one adoption fails, the other works. Nobody could ignore or evade the parallel.[2] Less than thirty years had elapsed, with many senators remembering Galba, and consuls still extant from 68 and 69.

Tacitus adverts with disdain or regret upon those who had to write the annals of Rome without knowing about the 'res publica'.[3] What is the 'res publica'? Primarily and precisely the institutions of the Roman State, 'senatus magistratus leges'. The institutions of government, and the rules that guide (or ought to guide) their operation, are only a small part of the political process. The things that matter lie behind or beneath: the sources of power and influence—and the men who manage them. It may be taken that Cornelius Tacitus was adequately informed. Not merely that he had been abroad in the provinces or had heard the Praetorians baying for blood along the Roman streets. Consul under Nerva, Tacitus saw from the inside the disintegration of a government, he may have shared (he will certainly have penetrated) the intrigue, or conspiracy, that created a new emperor and saved the world from war.[4]

The writing of history was commonly the pastime, and the consolation, of politicians whom age or disappointment deprived of action.

---

[1] At Galba's council were Ducenius Geminus (the *praefectus urbi*), T. Vinius, consul, and Marius Celsus, consul designate (*Hist.* I. 14. 1).

[2] Pliny, *Pan.* 8. 5: 'oblitine sumus ut nuper post adoptionem non desierit seditio sed coeperit?'

[3] *Hist.* I. I. I: 'inscitia rei publicae ut alienae.'

[4] Not, therefore, a 'quiet and comparatively sheltered existence' (E. A. Thompson, *The Historical Work of Ammianus Marcellinus* (1947), 125).

The question may now be asked: what was it that induced the eloquent ex-consul to turn to history and emulate the achievement of the senators Sallustius Crispus and Asinius Pollio?[1] There is a ready answer, the compulsion of what he had seen and learned; and, on his own showing and statement in the *Agricola*, not many months subsequent to his consulship, nothing less than those fifteen long years under Domitian, the years dragged out in silence and suffering: 'grande mortalis aevi spatium.'[2] He presents the *Agricola* to the public, but he proposes to embark upon a narration that shall testify to past enslavement and present felicity.[3]

The tyranny of Domitian is not the whole story. Nor was the reign of that emperor unrelieved blackness, or a total silence. Favourable testimony obtains, at least for the first epoch; and, during the worst excesses, which signalized the autumn of 93, shortly after the death of Agricola, Tacitus may still have been absent from Rome.[4] Career and honours, he suffered no retardation under Domitian; and, if he expected that the Senate as a body (or the senator as an individual) would in truth enjoy a more generous margin of freedom in speech or action under the strong rule of a military emperor than in the earlier years of Domitian, Tacitus must have gravely underestimated his own perspicacity. Let it be maintained against Cornelius Tacitus that one year of Nerva was better schooling for an historian than fifteen years of Domitian.

It was a sore temptation to set the matter in writing. Not the governmental version, and not the panegyric, but what really happened in that eventful interlude from the assassination of Domitian to the adoption of Trajan. That would have been premature, not to say impossible. For the subject of his proposed historical work Tacitus in the *Agricola* seems to indicate the reign of Domitian. An interval passed, he showed no haste to set about his task, and in due course he went further back.[5] Not to the fall of Nero. He chose to begin with the first day of the year that saw three emperors perish—'longum et unum annum';[6] and he narrated the whole story of the Flavian dynasty. To the recording of 69 his own experience of affairs in a season of crisis contributed substance, insight, and intensity. Imperial history and a recent theme—but it recalled the last epoch of the Republic and the classic historians of Rome.

---

[1] Some describe him as a late-comer to history, e.g. G. Boissier, *Tacite* (1903), 1; E. Kornemann, *Tacitus* (1947), 16, cf. 45. A modern notion: Tacitus in 98 was about the age at which Sallust and Pollio took to history.

[2] *Agr.* 3. 2. [3] ib. 3 (quoted on p. 19). [4] p. 68.

[5] It would be pointless to speculate whether he had already begun the annals of Domitian's reign.

[6] *Dial.* 17. 4.

PART III

THE *HISTORIAE*

XII. HISTORY AT ROME

HISTORY at Rome took a long time to emerge from humble and documentary origins. The old chroniclers might set down the facts in order, they had no art to exploit and transcend them. Enough for an annalist that he told no untruths, and brevity was the highest praise. Now the fundamental laws of history, as all men know and concede, are veracity and honesty. But history calls for style and composition. It is not enough to record the events, they must be interpreted and judged, with movement and eloquence in keeping. The orator will supply what is needed.

Such were the opinions given utterance by Cicero in the dialogue entitled *De oratore*.[1] Thwarted of scope and action in the field of politics, the saviour of the Republic was looking to letters for compensation; and he brought to perfection themes barely touched, if at all, by the Romans hitherto. The treatise *De re publica* expounds the nature of the ideal state as it is revealed, not by speculation but in the life of man, not among aliens but in the long experience of the Roman People. Rome in the age of the Scipiones consoled him for the failure and vexations of the present. A disappointed politician could also derive comfort from narrating the story of the past. Since the master of civic wisdom was also the master of prose composition, his talents might discover a congenial mission if he elevated history to the dignity of literature, adorning the Commonwealth which he saved and guarded when consul.

The appeal becomes explicit in the prologue of *De legibus*. That dialogue is contemporary, Cicero the main expositor, with subsidiary parts for his brother Quintus and his friend Pomponius Atticus, and the setting is propitious for reflections upon history, for it is near

---

[1] II. 51 ff. Not the whole story. Hellenistic theory, better practice (a large subject), cannot here be discussed. For one of its aspects, B. L. Ullman, *TAPA* LXXIII (1942), 25 ff.; for Cicero's views, M. Rambaud, *Cicéron et l'histoire romaine* (1953).

Arpinum, beside the oak tree which Cicero immortalized in the poem on Marius. Suitably introduced by comments on the licence of poets and the legends of early Rome (literal believers are gently mocked in passing), the discussion centres on the shortcomings of the annalists, scrawny and shaggy in their writing, their productions tedious, incompetent, and unreadable. Even the most recent of the tribe, Cornelius Sisenna, although far ahead of his predecessors, came nowhere near the standard of Ciceronian eloquence or the requisite maturity of judgement.[1]

'Opus . . . unum hoc oratorium maxime.'[2] History must be composed as a speech is composed. Only Cicero is equal to it. Which shall be the period? Quintus is eager for recent events, and Atticus supports him weightily. He will not hear of Romulus and Remus—he demands the exploits of Pompeius and the consulate of Cicero.

Cicero admitted his duty but declined the task: it needed time and leisure, and might perhaps wait for his old age. Years passed, but the proper season never arrived, despite his enforced inactivity under the dictatorship of Caesar. Soon after the assassination of the despot, Atticus exhorted his friend to take up the writing of history; and he reiterated the advice later in the year, in the month of November, when it was much to the point, with private armies levied in Italy, a young adventurer marching on Rome, and a new sequence of civil wars in prospect.[3] The apprehensions of Atticus were quickly justified. The veteran statesman, inveigled into backing the ambitions of Octavianus by the hope and plan of destroying Antonius, came back to save the Commonwealth, and brought it down in ruin.

Roman history still languished, rudimentary and neglected. It was redeemed and exalted by one who wrote about Cicero and Pompeius, but not at all in the right spirit—and Cicero would not have liked the style and manner either.

C. Sallustius Crispus had a brief and variegated career. Tribune of the plebs in the year that witnessed the murder of P. Clodius, the dictatorial consulate of Pompeius Magnus, and the prosecution of Annius Milo, he came into notice and blame through violent harangues against both Milo and his defender Cicero.[4] Two years later Sallust was duly thrown out of the Senate. Caesar brought him back. He commanded armies without conspicuous success, narrowly escaped

---

[1] *De legibus* I. 7: 'is tamen neque orator in numero vestro umquam est habitus et in historia puerile quiddam consectatur.' Cf. *Brutus* 228.

[2] I. 5.

[3] *Ad Att.* XIV. 14. 5; XVI. 13b. 2.

[4] In fact, among the 'abiecti homines ac perditi' who called Cicero a 'latro et sicarius' (*Pro Milone* 47, cf. Asconius 44).

death in a soldiers' mutiny—and his government of a province laid him open to charges of extortion.[1]

If Sallust lost the favour of Caesar, there was no leader or party to tempt him in the contests so rapidly supervening after the Dictator's removal. Next to a share in the making of history the best thing is to write it. Sallust discovered a proper use for his leisure: he would compose some historical monographs. It was too late for ambition, he had freed himself from the errors and the tribulations of his youth, and his judgement would not be distorted by the spirit of party.[2]

After completing the *Bellum Catilinae* and the *Bellum Jugurthinum,* Sallust went no further with separate studies but embarked on a full-length history. The theme was ready to hand, also a clear point of departure. Cornelius Sisenna told the story of the first revolutionary epoch from the secession of the allies in 91 B.C. through the Italian War and, blending with it, the struggle of the Roman factions down to the restoration of the *nobilitas* by Sulla, ending perhaps with Sulla's abdication of the dictatorship, or with his death a little more than a year later. A senator and coeval with the events (he was praetor in 78 B.C.), Sisenna deserves to rank as an historian rather than an annalist, of greater consequence and merit than Cicero seems willing to allow, and he had a splendid subject.[3]

Sallust took up the tale more or less where Sisenna left off, beginning his *Historiae* with the year of the consuls M. Aemilius Lepidus and Q. Lutatius Catulus (78 B.C.). Sisenna was a partisan of Sulla. His continuator was hostile to Sulla and the *nobiles*. He proposed (it may be assumed) to trace the decline and fall of the oligarchy through the thirty years of nominal stability and hollow concord between the two ages of civil war, from the rising of Lepidus down to the contest between Pompeius and Caesar; and it may further be conjectured what place and function he designed for Pompeius Magnus—a Sullan partisan at first, rescuing the government from Lepidus and fighting its wars in Spain, then an enemy of the *Optimates*, with great commands extorted by help of the tribunes, a dynast oppressing the 'res publica' in the compact with Crassus and Caesar, and finally, when he was forced back, jealous for his predominance, to earlier alliances, a false friend of the oligarchy and its partner in catastrophe.

Sallust had covered a dozen years when death overtook him in 35 B.C. Of the five books of the *Historiae* there survive four speeches, two letters, and a number of fragments. Enough, however, when

---

[1] For the governorship in Africa, Dio XLIII. 9. 2. For his political career see now W. Allen, *Studies in Philology* LI (1954), 1 ff. No account is here taken of the *Epistulae ad Caesarem senem*, the authenticity of which is highly dubious.   [2] Sallust, *Cat.* 3. 1 ff.
[3] It also appealed to the senator L. Lucceius, cf. Cicero, *Ad fam.* v. 12. 2.

examined in conjunction with the pair of monographs, to explain an achievement that was recognized, instantly and for ever, as classic and canonical.

Rome could at last take pride in a history that was a work of art. Cicero condemned the annalists and desiderated a style that should be ample, equable, and flowing.[1] Sallust broke away from balance and harmony, and went back to earlier writers for much of his diction. He took over their archaic forms and poetical turns, but added strength and splendour, with many innovations of language. The prose grows tighter and fiercer—short sentences and abrupt endings, speed and variety; and there is a perpetual antithesis of thought, brought out by artful discordance in verbal structure.[2]

To adopt old-fashioned manners of speech was no paradox, for history had commonly been written by retired statesmen or censorious elders, condemning the indiscipline of youth or the corruption of the times in contrast to the grave and worthy standards of the virtuous past. With Sallust archaism is insidious, simplicity a mask, covering subtlety and malice. For all the invocation of ancient morality, Sallust is happiest among those scenes of vice and of violence that he affects so sternly to denounce.[3]

No paradox either that Sallust so deliberately and so savagely wrecked the rhythm, balance, and elaboration of the long and convoluted sentence. The ample oratorical manner which had recently been brought to perfection by Cicero was admirably designed to beguile and persuade an audience: it dealt in generous commonplaces, facile oppositions between right and wrong, and high-minded appeals to vulgar emotion. Roman history originated in the register of bare events before eloquence was known; and, when Roman history came to its maturity in an epoch saturated and nauseated with political oratory, it sought ruthlessly to get at the facts behind the words. Smooth phrases were suspect, their authors in discredit. A plain, hard, and broken style seemed to convey a serious guarantee of incorruptible veracity.

Next to native models among the annalists it was Thucydides who appealed most to Sallust—for style and intensity, for majesty and for disillusionment. The Roman had learned his lesson about men and affairs in the turmoil of the falling Republic, in the wars of Pompeius

---

[1] *De oratore* II. 64: 'genus orationis fusum atque tractum et cum lenitate quadam aequabiliter profluens.' Cf. II. 54.

[2] For the style of Sallust cf. especially E. Norden, *Die antike Kunstprosa* I (1898), 200 ff.; W. Kroll, *Glotta* xv (1927), 280 ff.; E. Löfstedt, *Syntactica* II (1933), 290 ff.; K. Latte, 'Sallust'. *Neue Wege zur Antike* II, 4 (1935); E. Skard, 'Sallust und seine Vorgänger'. *Symbolae Osloenses*, Supp. xv (1956).

[3] K. Latte, o.c. 56 ff.

and Caesar—and in the far worse things that came after Caesar when the tyranny of the Triumvirs re-enacted Sulla, with proscriptions at Rome and massacre throughout Italy. The harsh, angry, and pessimistic fashion of writing history which Sallust evolved was well suited to the age and the theme—and to his own nature.[1]

Sallust came from Amiternum in the Sabine country. Asinius Pollio, who was born only a decade later, was a still newer type of Roman—his grandfather had led the Marrucini when Italy fought for liberty and honour, rebellious against the tyrant city.[2] A Republican at heart, but a Caesarian and an Antonian in his actions, diplomacy kept him from harm and brought him to the consulate in 40 B.C. Not long after, he forswore public life, resisted entanglements, and was the sole neutral in the last contest of all, when Caesar's heir and M. Antonius fought for the mastery.

Not only a spectator but an agent in many momentous transactions, Pollio led armies, governed provinces, and managed negotiations between the dynasts. His courage was resolute, his temper intractable. Experience, insight, and bitterness qualified him to narrate the history of the revolutionary age, and the style he affected was wilfully plain and rugged. The superficial might fancy that the Civil War began when the proconsul of Gaul invaded Italy. Pollio relied on his own judgement—and on the respectable authority of M. Cato, who detested both dynasts. It was not so much their quarrel that broke the peace and ruined the Commonwealth as the original compact many years before, in the consulate of Metellus Celer and L. Afranius (60 B.C.).[3] Pollio chose that date for his exordium, and thereby conferred upon it significance ever after.[4] His historical books dealt with the last decade of the Free State, the war between Pompeius and Caesar, and the subsequent disturbances down to the Battle of Philippi, when 'Libertas' and the faction of the *nobiles* were overwhelmed by the leaders of the Caesarian party, Marcus Antonius and the young Octavianus.[5]

To a general, a diplomat, and a proconsul, no greater contrast than T. Livius. This man had no share in the 'res publica', no office that established his dignity, deepened his understanding, and justified his

Livy

---

[1] R. Syme, *Rom. Rev.* (1939), 248 ff.

[2] Livy, *Per.* LXXIII: 'Herio Asinio praetore Marrucinorum occiso.'

[3] Plutarch, *Caesar* 13; *Pompeius* 47.

[4] Horace, *Odes*, II. 1. 1 ff.: 'motum ex Metello consule civicum | bellique causas et vitia et modos | ludumque Fortunae gravisque | principum amicitias et arma | nondum expiatis uncta cruoribus | periculosae plenum opus aleae | tractas, et incedis per ignis | suppositos cineri doloso.'

[5] For Pollio's *Historiae* and their traces in subsequent writers cf. E. Kornemann, *Jahrbücher für cl. Phil.*, Supp.-Band XXII (1896), 557 ff.; J. André, *La Vie et l'œuvre d'Asinius Pollion* (1949), 41 ff.; E. Gabba, *Appiano e la Storia delle Guerre Civili* (1956).

writing. From the comfortable obscurity of a private station, and from the schools of rhetoric, where he learned the craft of words, and perhaps taught it, Livy came to history and composed the annals of the Roman People from the beginning down to the middle years of the reign of Caesar Augustus. When he began the vast enterprise, about the time of the War of Actium or not much later, he was comparatively young.[1] That Livy had ever been outside Italy there is no sign; and, although the historian was on terms of amity with the reigning house, he was not often at Rome (no anecdotes bring him into touch with other writers or with their patrons), but resided for the most part at his native Patavium.[2]

The allegiances of the North were diverse in origin but not irreconcilable. Acquiring from Caesar the benefit of their full citizen status, the towns of Transpadana were none the less attached to Republican ideals. Patavium had a name for material prosperity and for a tenacious adherence to the ancient ways. Patavine morality was fearsome and proverbial. Nor was it confined to the conduct of private life. The city declared for the Republic against Antonius in 43 B.C., and had to suffer heavy financial exactions when Asinius Pollio held the North for Antonius after the Battle of Philippi.[3]

Yet the North was able to accept with dignity, and embrace with enthusiasm, the new order of Caesar Augustus. To the Roman aristocrat the Republic was a real and palpable thing. Not just a theory or principle, but a cause that was bound up with men and families, rivals or enemies of the Caesars. In the Italian *municipia*, tradition could be honoured without the spirit of discord or any suspicion of disloyalty: Mediolanium retained under Caesar Augustus the statues of Caesar's assassins.[4]

Brutus and Cassius were the leaders of a political party. Cicero had never been that, and Cicero was not worshipped among the martyrs of the Republic. For those whose Republicanism was not political but sentimental and moral the ideals and the eloquence of Cicero might be held exemplary. Admiring the oratory of Cicero, Livy for the writing of history adopted a style that is Ciceronian in many of its features; and, although the early books have an infusion of archaic and poetical elements, as he went on the author reverted to more classical standards.[5]

---

[1] Jerome (p. 154 H) brackets Livy with Messalla Corvinus (*cos.* 31 B.C.) under 59 B.C. Too late for Messalla, as demonstrated by H. Schulz, *De M. Valerii Messallae aetate* (Prog. Stettin, 1886), 6. Rather 64 B.C. The consequence for Livy is drawn by G. M. Hirst, *Collected Classical Papers* (1938), 12 ff.   [2] V. Lundström, *Eranos* XXVII (1929), 1 ff.

[3] Martial XI. 16. 8; Pliny, *Epp.* I. 14. 6; Cicero, *Phil.* XII. 10; Macrobius I. 11. 22.

[4] Plutarch, *Comp. Dionis et Bruti* 5; Suetonius, *De rhet.* 6.

[5] S. G. Stacey, *Archiv für. lat. Lex.* X (1898), 17 ff. See further p. 359.

Livy's design was to supersede the annalists; and he may be regarded not as an imperial author but as the last of the Republican prose writers.[1] The justification for a new historical work, so Livy affirms, is either superior style or superior accuracy.[2] The incentive may be of another kind. Men take up the pen from discontent with the times —and from discontent with history as it is written by other people.

Livy did not like the Sallustian fashion of writing. He spoke with distaste of orators who affect antique and mouldy words, who, striving for gravity, achieve only obscurity; and he criticized Sallust's adaptation of a Greek phrase.[3] Livy must have approved and enjoyed Cicero's censure of those who try to imitate Thucydides.[4]

If Sallust's style was detestable, that was not the worst thing about him. The politician who turned moralist, the Sabine sermonizer of dubious conduct, the comfortable author of a pessimistic history, he was a disquieting figure. Asinius Pollio the consular was little better, a Republican who survived the Republic, enjoying riches and esteem under a régime he professed to disavow, but proud, savage, censorious—and bitterly hostile long years after to the memory of Cicero.

Livy was repelled by those detractors of humanity. Although the present was sombre, the annals of the past showed that no commonwealth had ever equalled Rome for majesty and for morality, none had ever held out longer against the invasion of greed and corruption. History should be instructive and salubrious, showing a patriot what to follow and what to avoid.[5] Livy might have added that no good could come from Sallustian revelations about the hidden springs of action in the conduct of men and states and the inborn ineradicable lust for power.

In narrating the deeds of ancient virtue Livy found solace and respite from the tribulations that the Roman People had for so many years endured.[6] Livy was aware that many of his readers would be impatient to have the story of the revolutionary age.[7] Avowing the

---

[1] E. Norden, o.c. 234; E. Skard, o.c. 8 ff.

[2] Livy, *praef.* 2: 'dum novi semper scriptores aut in rebus certius aliquid allaturos se aut scribendi arte rudem vetustatem superaturos. credunt.'

[3] Seneca, *Controv.* IX. 2. 26; I. 14.

[4] *Orator* 32: 'huius tamen nemo neque verborum neque sententiarum gravitatem imitatur, sed cum mutila quaedam et hiantia locuti sunt, quae vel sine magistro facere potuerunt, germanos se putant esse Thucydidas.'

[5] *praef.* 10: 'hoc illud est praecipue in cognitione rerum salubre ac frugiferum omnis te exempli documenta in inlustri posita monumento intueri; inde tibi tuaeque rei publicae quod imitere capias, inde foedum inceptu foedum exitu quod vites.'

[6] ib. 5: 'ut me a conspectu malorum quae nostra tot per annos vidit aetas tantisper certe, dum prisca illa tota mente repeto, avertam.'

[7] ib. 4: 'festinantibus ad haec nova, quibus iam pridem praevalentis populi vires se ipsae conficiunt.' For oblique criticism of Sallust in the *Praefatio* cf. L. Amundsen, *Symbolae Osloenses* xxv (1947), 31 ff.

superior attractions of early Rome, he implies that the later part of his great enterprise will be distasteful to a Roman and a moralist. He may not have found it so when he came to write it.

Fate has dealt maliciously. Of the whole work in 142 books, a quarter is extant. There survive the first decade, carrying the narrative from the origins down to 293 B.C.; the third, containing the War of Hannibal; and, continuing, Books XXXI–XLV, which go as far as 167 B.C. The selection does not perhaps furnish a fair criterion of Livy's quality as an historian. That he thought the story of the Kings any more authentic than Cicero did, there is no evidence. But he had to narrate it. Leaving legend, he plunges into fictions, without the equipment to disengage the facts. And, although in the later books that survive Livy is on safer ground (and the Hannibalic War proves congenial), he is betrayed by ignorance of politics and warfare, by lack of critical principles—and, above all, by incapacity to dominate the material with design and structure.

Perhaps the best has perished. The two ages of civil disturbance take up the greater part of the second half of Livy's work (Books LXXI–CXLII). There were excellent, though partisan accounts; and full scope offered for the historian to display his narrative and pictorial skill, with the faculty of evoking the emotions of pity and terror. The *Bellum Italicum*, then the affairs of Marius, Cinna, and Sulla, was a magnificent portion of history; and Livy treated Sisenna's theme handsomely, allotting two sections, one of ten books, the other of nine.[1] The story of the Ten Years War contained striking episodes: the solemn oath of the insurgent leaders, the battle among the vineyards in the Marsian country, the extinction of the Italian army trapped in winter in the Appennines, the capture of Rome, the siege of Praeneste, the defeat and massacre of the Samnites, the proscriptions ordained by L. Sulla the Dictator.

As long as Livy had to recount the exploits of the Populus Romanus in its early struggles with the Volscian, the Etruscan, and the Samnite, he was content with the edifying contrast between valour and virtue on the one side, on the other perfidy, cruelty, or cowardice. Knowledge and sympathy are absent. Nor was he disposed to be just to the Carthaginian or the Macedonian in their dealings with the imperial Republic. The *Bellum Italicum* was another matter. It resembled a civil war, and in the time of Caesar Augustus when 'tota Italia' had at last and in reality been achieved, it could hardly fail to be interpreted very much as a civil war. Patavium had never fought against Rome. But Patavium's own recent misfortunes might inspire compassion and understanding for the fate of tribes and towns in that

---

[1] viz. LXXI–LXXX and LXXXI–LXXXIX.

older Italy; and the municipal man knew the pride and the injustice of Roman magistrates.

In the civil strife that ensued before the Italian War was over a large part of the municipal aristocracy took the Marian side. Marius enjoyed and abused the prestige of saving Italy from the northern invaders. The ultimate verdict could only be condemnatory. Livy pronounces it—Marius subverted the Commonwealth, first by craft and then by violence.[1] Sulla fought the wars of the Republic in the East, saved Rome from the Samnites at the Battle of the Colline Gate, and established ordered government. But nobody among the middle class in Italy, devoted though they were to security and stability, could praise the Dictator—and hardly even the *nobiles* whom he gave dignity and power again, with enormous enrichment. Livy adverts upon the cruelty, the like of which was in no man before, that defiled a glorious victory with massacre and spoliation.[2]

More exacting and hazardous as an historian's task was the next sequence of civil wars. The eruption had barely subsided, the fires still glowed beneath the lava crust.[3] In essaying to tell the uncomfortable truth about recent transactions, the consular Pollio relied upon past achievements and rank in society, and he exploited his reputation for obtrusive intractability. Livy, though amicably disposed towards the new order, was saved from some of the excesses of a partisan interpretation by his own good sense—and he could appeal to an orthodox version of the recent disturbances.

Caesar Augustus could not utterly traduce the champions, genuine or ostensible, of what even the victors had to concede was the 'better cause'. Livy exalted Pompeius, and Augustus in no displeasure called the historian a 'Pompeianus'.[4] As Caesar's memory now got less honour from Caesar's heir, Livy was free to debate whether his birth were the greater blessing or the greater curse.[5] And he avowed that Cato's greatness lay beyond the reach of praise or blame.[6] That was not very harmful either. The Princeps himself, when asked his opinion of Cato, replied that anybody who does not wish the existing order to be altered is a good man and a good citizen.[7]

---

[1] *Per.* LXXX: 'vir cuius si examinentur cum virtutibus vitia, haud facile sit dictu utrum bello melior an pace perniciosior fuerit. adeo quam rem p. armatus servavit eam primo togatus omni genere fraudis postremo armis hostiliter evertit.'

[2] ib. LXXXVIII: 'pulcherrimam victoriam crudelitate quanta in nullo hominum fuit inquinavit.'

[3] cf. Horace, *Odes* II. 1. 7 f.

[4] *Ann.* IV. 34. 3: 'Titus Livius, eloquentiae ac fidei praeclarus in primis, Cn. Pompeium tantis laudibus tulit ut Pompeianum eum Augustus appellaret; neque id eorum amicitiae offecit.'

[5] Seneca, *NQ* v. 18. 4.   [6] Cited by Jerome, *In Hoseam* II, *praef.*

[7] Macrobius II. 4. 18.

Cato was out of the way before the young Octavianus started on his career of fraud and violence. Brutus and Cassius were his parent's murderers and his own enemies. None the less, an historian could still write of Philippi without wholly sacrificing liberty and dignity.[1] Cicero, basely proscribed by the youth he had brought forward to save the Commonwealth, was a delicate theme. Livy pronounced a handsome eulogy, but curbed his own enthusiasm: Cicero was not innocent, he suffered at the hands of his enemies precisely the fate he was contriving against them.[2]

For the rest, there were scapegoats to help out the historian, namely Sex. Pompeius, Lepidus, Antonius—and the queen of Egypt. But he had to concentrate more and more upon the virtues and destiny of the victor. The epilogue, the final nine books (CXXXIV–CXLII), dealing with the years of peace and order from 28 B.C. down to 9 B.C., may not have been wholly satisfactory.[3]

Though Livy for the history of the Republic extinguished all predecessors and deterred all competition (save from a stray Sallustian or two), his work was not universally regarded as canonical for the Triumviral period and for the reign of Augustus.[4] A Roman senator, Cremutius Cordus, dealt with those subjects, consigning the authors of the proscriptions to eternal infamy.[5]

As the years passed, other historians arose and wrote about the Caesars. The most notable were Aufidius Bassus and Servilius Nonianus. As they are both commended by Quintilian in the short list of the four historical authors after Sallust and Livy likely to be of service to the student of rhetoric, they cannot have lacked virtues of style and composition.[6] Nor should the influence be omitted of the ingenious and innovatory Seneca on the development of Latin prose during the age intermediate between Livy and Tacitus. Then came the historians who narrated the reigns of Claudius and Nero. Some carried the story further. For Tacitus their importance lay not so much in style as in material—sources for the *Historiae*.[7]

None of the subsequent historians could touch Sallust and Livy— diverse in manner but equal in rank, so Servilius Nonianus observed.[8]

---

[1] *Ann.* IV. 34. 4 (referring to Asinius Pollio and Messalla Corvinus).

[2] Cited by the elder Seneca, *Suas.* VI. 22.   [3] See further Ch. XXVIII.

[4] At least he does not seem to have been followed by Cassius Dio for the period after the Battle of Actium.

[5] Seneca, *Ad Marciam* I. 1 ff.; 26. 1; Tacitus, *Ann.* IV. 34 f. (cf. pp. 337, 517). Possibly the source of Appian, cf. E. Kornemann, *Klio* XVII (1921), 33 ff.

[6] Quintilian X. 1. 102 f. The others are an anonymous historian still living (who must be Fabius Rusticus) and Cremutius Cordus (the name has fallen out, but the person is clearly indicated). See further, Ch. XXI f. Note that the list omits the consulars Asinius Pollio and Cluvius Rufus.

[7] Ch. XVI.   [8] Quintilian X. 1. 102: 'pares eos magis quam similes.'

Though Sallust and Livy will confidently be claimed as the literary models of Cornelius Tacitus, the measure of the debt is not easy to assess. Much will depend on inference and guesswork. No such investigation should omit the *Bellum civile* of Annaeus Lucanus. Pedestrian critics in antiquity asserted that Lucan was not a poet but an historian.[1] A juster appreciation of both poetry and history will vindicate his right to the double title—and reveal his kinship with Cornelius Tacitus.

In his epic poem on the fall of 'Libertas' Lucan went to Livy as the principal and almost the sole source of his information.[2] The outline of events and the main actors were given. With them he would not tamper, but he could select, emphasize, and expand, adding speeches to illuminate character and action. He could likewise invent incidents if they did not conflict with the authentic record, and produce supernumerary characters of minor station—a soldier, a slave, or a foreigner, but not a Roman senator or a Roman knight.

For the causes of the Civil War Lucan took over Pollio's formulation—the original compact of the three dynasts. Historians tended to be much influenced by the shape and structure their predecessors had imposed on the narrative. Livy (it seems) made a break in his work at the point where Cornelius Sisenna ended, where Sallust took up the story with the consulate of Lepidus and Catulus. And, though Livy did not begin a new 'decade' with the year of Metellus and Afranius, he inherited Pollio's conception.[3] Similarly Lucan.[4] A rapid sketch of events in the fifties concentrates on personalities and power, with the clash resulting from Caesar's ambition and Pompeius' jealousy—the one could bear no superior, the other no equal.[5] That probably comes ultimately from Pollio. Further, the general causes of the catastrophe are discovered in the corruption and turbulence of Roman political life.[6]

The characterization of Caesar, in brief phrases, antithetic, abrupt, and varied in structure, recalls the Sallustian manner.[7] Lucan also has resort to speeches with all an historian's licence in their placing and content. When Caesar invades Italy, an anonymous old man, mindful of the past and apprehensive for the future, comes forward and discourses on the previous civil war, the massacres of Marius, and the

---

[1] Servius on *Aen.* I. 382.   [2] R. Pichon, *Les Sources de Lucain* (1912), 51 ff.
[3] Livy, *Per.* CIII; Florus II. 13. 8 ff.; Velleius II. 44. I.
[4] Lucan I. 84 ff.   [5] I. 125 f.   [6] I. 158 ff.
[7] I. 144 ff.: 'sed nescia virtus | stare loco, solusque pudor non vincere bello; | acer et indomitus, quo spes quoque ira vocasset | ferre manum et nunquam temerando parcere ferro | successus urguere suos, instare favori | numinis, impellens quidquid sibi summa petenti | obstaret, gaudensque viam fecisse ruinis.'

proscriptions of Sulla.[1] Cato, when apprised of the death of Pompeius Magnus, produces a short oration comparable to an historian's character sketch.[2] Mercy is suitably tempered with justice. Cato was a Republican, and Cato points out that it is not genuine liberty that ends with Pompeius—it had ended under Marius and under Sulla.[3] Later, in words of encouragement to his companions, Cato explains that a defender of the Republic can now continue the struggle with good hopes and a clear conscience—Magnus removed, only one dynast is left of the three.[4]

That oratory to achieve force and splendour should borrow from the poets, among them precisely Lucan, is an axiom produced by a speaker in the *Dialogus*.[5] The historian Tacitus makes use of poetical language. Much of it comes from his predecessors in prose. For the rest, Lucan is hardly ever the source, but Virgil, whom they both admired.[6]

Lucan here and there in a savage and pessimistic epigram seems to be the model and original of Tacitus—for example, the gods intervening only to punish humanity, never to help.[7] Yet the resemblances may not be close enough to prove a debt. Such 'sententiae' are perfectly in Lucan's manner—and derive almost inevitably from his theme. Thus the speech of the eunuch Pothinus when he advises the King of Egypt to kill Magnus, with numerous maxims of statecraft confirming the incompatibility of virtue and power.[8] These things belong to a common fund of bitter experience, accumulated through civil war, despotism, and disillusion—and refined by generations of speakers and writers. Lucan and Tacitus acknowledge a similar subject and like preoccupations. Lucan, a senator quaestorian in standing and one of the victims of Nero, may be accorded mention, though not rank, beside Cornelius Tacitus; and he shares with Tacitus a sombre, violent, and poetical imagination.

---

[1] II. 45 ff. [2] IX. 190 ff.

[3] IX. 204 ff.: 'olim vera fides Sulla Marioque receptis | libertatis obit: Pompeio rebus adempto | nunc et ficta perit.'

[4] IX. 265 f.: 'unum fortuna reliquit | iam tribus e dominis.'

[5] *Dial.* 20. 5.

[6] cf. H. Schmaus, *Tacitus ein Nachahmer Vergils* (Diss. Erlangen, 1884); L. Robbert, *De Tacito Lucani imitatore* (Diss. Göttingen, 1917).

[7] IV. 808 f.: 'si libertatis superis tam cura placeret | quam vindicta placet.' Cf. *Hist.* I. 3. 2: 'non esse curae deis securitatem nostram, esse ultionem.'

[8] VIII. 489 ff.: 'sceptrorum vis tota perit si pendere iusta | incipit, evertitque arces respectus honesti. | libertas scelerum est, quae regna invisa tuetur | sublatusque modus gladiis. facere omnia saeve | non inpune licet nisi cum facis. exeat aula | qui volt esse pius. virtus et summa potestas | non coeunt: semper metuet quem saeva pudebunt.'

XIII. TACITUS AND HIS MODELS

THE age when the laws were sovereign and the years took their names from consuls, so does the poet Lucan designate the Republic.[1] A free but disciplined people duly elected each year a pair of magistrates to carry the *imperium* and conduct its business at home and abroad. 'Res populi Romani', that is precisely the annalistic register. When the Populus Romanus extended its conquests and won dominion over the nations, when civil disturbances blended with foreign wars, and the monarchic faction-leaders arose, arrogating to themselves the functions of the 'res publica', the magnitude of the events shattered the framework of the traditional record and imposed new devices on the historian.

Sallust, deferring to tradition, began with a consular year, 78 B.C., not with Sulla's abdication or Sulla's death. Although the two consuls, M. Lepidus and Q. Catulus, were at variance from the outset, it was not until the day of Sulla's obsequies that their dissension blazed into open antagonism; and only later did Lepidus come out with the full revolutionary programme and move towards open violence. None the less the historian boldly produces a harangue of the consul Lepidus, denouncing the tyranny of Sulla Felix and summoning the Roman People to liberty under his leadership—while Sulla is still alive.[2] The intention of this peculiar contrivance is artistic. Lepidus tried to overthrow the system of government that Sulla established. The oration of Lepidus attacks Sulla. It thereby makes the situation more dramatic and more personal—and it enables Sallust to describe Sulla's domination with more animus and at greater length than would have been suitable in the historical prologue summarizing events before the year 78.

That prologue opens with consular date and short statement of subject.[3] Certain annalists are touched upon for praise or blame; the author announces that he will write with veracity and with brevity; and he deprecates partisan spirit.[4] He alludes to the early history of Rome, and to the early dissensions, abated by the Hannibalic War;

---

[1] Lucan VII. 440 f.: 'quid tempora legum | egimus aut annos a consule nomen habentis?'

[2] Sallust, *Hist.* I. 55. (The fragments will be cited according to Maurenbrecher's collection.)

[3] I. 1: 'res populi Romani M. Lepido Q. Catulo consulibus ac deinde militiae et domi gestas composui.'

[4] I. 6: 'neque me diversa pars in civilibus armis movit a vero.' Praise of brevity is implied in what he says of Cato, I. 4: 'Romani generis disertissimus paucis absolvit.'

but concord became precarious after the fall of Carthage, greed, ambition, and faction ran riot, powerful individuals sought domination under the fraudulent pretexts of defending People or Senate; the denominations of good citizens and bad bore no relation to any service to the 'res publica', all being equally corrupt, but the men who had wealth and the means to do harm benefited from the better name because they stood for the existing order.[1] Thus might became right.[2] The historian then traces the concatenation of disturbances that led from the Gracchan sedition to the secession of the Italian allies and the civil wars of Marius and Sulla.[3]

Cornelius Tacitus leads off with the first day of a consular year.[4] To explain that, convention might be invoked, the point at which a predecessor terminated, or a Republican's antipathy to the titles of a prince and the era of a dynasty.[5] To no purpose. Where else should the work begin? If at the death of Nero, much that preceded Nero's death would have to go in, namely Vindex, Verginius, and the proclamation of Galba, with a vast military and political imbroglio. On the other hand, the official date of the accession of Vespasian (July 1, 69) was no good at all—it truncated the story of the Rhine and Danubian armies and two invasions of Italy in a single year. No: January 1, 69 is vital and inevitable. That day starts the action on the Rhine. Two legions at Moguntiacum disown the authority of Galba, the news impels him to adopt Piso Licinianus on the tenth of January, and everything follows automatically—the plot and act of Otho at Rome, with Galba and Piso assassinated on the fifteenth day of the month, and in the meantime Vitellius proclaimed in Lower Germany and a new civil war under way, that was begun against Galba but waged against Otho.

As the tradition enjoined, Cornelius Tacitus contributes a prologue expounding his purpose and task. It contains remarks about history at Rome—free, dignified, and eloquent under the Republic, but declining after the War of Actium and the establishment of the monarchy through the political inexperience of writers and their partisan spirit. While adulation can easily be detected and condemned,

---

[1] I. 12.

[2] I. 18: 'et relatus inconditae olim vitae mos, ut omne ius in viribus esset.'

[3] I. 19–53.

[4] *Hist.* I. I. I: 'initium mihi operis Servius Galba iterum Titus Vinius consules erunt.'

[5] Tacitus has been frequently censured for his decision: see, for example, Mommsen, *Hermes* IV (1870), 228 = *Ges. Schr.* VII (1909), 299; O. Hirschfeld, *Hermes* XXV (1890), 363 = *Kl. Schr.* (1913), 855; O. Seeck, *Rh. Mus.* LVI (1901), 227; E. Courbaud, *Les Procédés d'art de Tacite dans les 'Histoires'* (1918), 33 ff. For more reasonable opinions, F. Münzer, *Klio* I (1901), 300 ff. Mommsen assumed that Cluvius Rufus ended with the end of 68. Similarly, but preferring Fabius Rusticus, Seeck.

malice is more attractive and more insidious. As concerns Cornelius Tacitus, the emperors Galba, Otho, and Vitellius meant nothing to him. To the Flavian dynasty he acknowledges promotion and honours, but an historian must tell the truth unimpaired, with favour towards no man, or resentment either. And, if life be vouchsafed, Tacitus will go on and recount in his old age the reigns of Nerva and Trajan.

His present subject he now indicates and describes in the next two chapters—a period rich in catastrophe, with four emperors perishing by the sword, three civil wars, and a variety of foreign wars.[1] The East was not disturbed, but the fortunes of the Empire were imperilled in the West. At Rome oppression reigned, and murder. Birth and wealth were suspect, virtue being the surest guarantee of destruction. Any who lacked enemies were destroyed by their allies. Most odious for their power, influence, and profits were the 'delatores'. Yet the age was not wholly devoid of moral strength. Friends and family kept faith, and senators faced death as bravely as the men of old time. The vicissitudes of human affairs were matched by strange signs and portents in nature. Never was it so powerfully demonstrated that the gods intend, not that men should be happy, but that they should suffer.

The three chapters of Tacitus' prologue—concise, vivid, and intense—disable criticism and baffle eulogy.[2] The form is traditional, and much of what he says, with a manifest debt to Sallust; and, studied in conjunction with the fragments of Sallust, it could embolden conjecture about the kind of preface another historian of civil war must have composed, namely Asinius Pollio.[3]

The strictures which Tacitus passes on the historians who wrote about Augustus do not spare the greatest of them. That he had Livy in mind there can be no doubt. Dignity and discretion forbade him to mention by name either Livy or any other historian; and he says as little as may be about his own person and opinions.

If the prologue is masterly, the eight chapters that follow are unique in their quality.[4] Wherever an historian takes his point of departure, he must allow for the things that went before. Yet he will wish to plunge into the stream of events, stripped for action and unencumbered by the paraphernalia of explanation. Sallust managed it. He employed two devices—a summary in chronological order covering

---

[1] I. 2. 1: 'opus adgredior † opibus casibus, atrox proeliis, discors seditionibus, ipsa etiam pace saevum', &c. Most editors print 'opimum', which is not plausible. Better 'rapidum' (Madvig) or 'varium' (Koestermann).

[2] E. Courbaud, o.c. 26. Ph. Fabia, however, held that an 'esprit sérieux' would not be taken in—'le prestige des mots s'évanouit, découvrant les vices du fond. La page est spécieuse, elle n'est pas bonne' (*Rev. ét. anc.* III (1901), 76).

[3] cf. R. Syme, *Rom. Rev.* (1939), 9. For Lucan's influence on Tacitus' prologue, E. Courbaud, o.c. 39 ff.; E. Paratore, *Tacito* (1951), 352 ff.

[4] E. Courbaud, o.c. 49. For an analysis, E. Koestermann, *Historia* v (1956), 213 ff.

the previous fifty years, and a political oration. However, for all the ruthless brevity of Sallust, the recapitulation may have been a little lengthy, the harangue of Lepidus overbold.

The eight chapters in the form of a digression, with the beginning and the end sharply defined, furnish a kind of second preface.[1] Tacitus proposes to set forth the condition of Rome, the armies and the provinces, the sources of discontent and the elements of power, in order that the reader may understand, not only the course and conclusion of events (often the product of chance) but the causes and the reasons.[2] After describing how government and Princeps were regarded by the different orders in Roman society, with especial emphasis on the Praetorian Guard and the various military detachments now stationed in the capital, the survey ranges round the provinces from west to east. An industrious compiler might have been tempted to furnish an exhaustive enumeration. Tacitus' command of his subject is such that he will deliberately omit facts and names. There is no note about the strength of the armies in Britain and in the Danubian provinces, the identity of their commanders. Important facts—but irrelevant, for they do not explain the origins or influence the course of the immediate crisis. They emerge later, when decisive for plot or action. Alert and unclogged, Tacitus moves from one end of the world to the other and returns quickly to Rome. The survey of provinces and armies is not merely a marvellous device. It appears to lack precedent or parallel in ancient historiography—and, revealing a <u>preoccupation not with events but with the sources of power</u>, it at once stamps Tacitus as a <u>political historian</u>.[3]

Neatly disengaging himself from prolegomena, the historian allows the drama to unfold, promptly. A few days after the first of January, a dispatch from the procurator of Gallia Belgica brings the news of what happened at Moguntiacum.[4] The Emperor's age and waning authority had already given rise to much talk and intrigue; and Galba himself was meditating the choice of a successor. That act now became urgent. The Emperor suddenly calls together a council, reveals his choice, and delivers a set speech in elucidation.[5]

Like Sallust, Tacitus puts a speech on high policy near the beginning of his *Historiae*. His oration is a superior and skilful production—no

---

[1] I. 11. 1 (echoing I. 1. 1): 'hic fuit rerum Romanarum status cum Servius Galba iterum Titus Vinius consules inchoavere annum sibi ultimum, rei publicae prope supremum.'

[2] I. 4. 1: 'ceterum antequam destinata componam repetendum videtur qualis status urbis, quae mens exercituum, quis habitus provinciarum quid in toto terrarum orbe validum, quid aegrum fuerit, ut non modo casus eventusque rerum, qui plerumque fortuiti sunt, sed ratio etiam causaeque noscantur.'

[3] G. Boissier, *Tacite* (1903), 182.

[4] 12. 1: 'paucis post kalendas Ianuarias diebus', &c.

[5] I. 15 f. (summarized on p. 151).

violence to chronology, but dramatic force, insight, irony. Galba's
disquisitions allude to his own elevation, explain his present plight,
and enunciate a central doctrine of political theory under the Empire:
the contrast between tyranny and constitutional government.

Prologue, general survey, and oration—the structure is impeccable.
The prefatory remarks of historians can serve various functions. Livy
in his *Praefatio* discourses at large upon morals and history, upon the
present and the past. He produces an essay, easily separable from the
narrative that follows, and, indeed, not in organic connexion.[1] Livy
says a little too much about his own aspirations. Gracious and engaging though the modesty may be with which he excuses his undertaking,
it is a feeble exordium when an historian in his first sentence conveys
not facts or confidence but a doubt.[2] The senatorial writers do not
allow themselves to be hampered by qualms about the value of their
theme, or the value of success.

Before he embarked upon the 'res populi Romani' from the beginning of Rome, Livy's only compositions had been exercises in the
schools of rhetoric, or at the most some philosophical tracts.[3] Admirable as Livy is in the eloquence of a speech, in descriptive colouring,
and in narrative movement, he shows no comparable skill when events
have to be grouped and interrelated—and no instinct for historical
structure. For disposition as for material he is content on the whole
to follow his sources. Where the subject is straightforward, or a predecessor has knocked the facts into shape, Livy manages well enough.
Thus the 'decade' recounting the Hannibalic War. But the historian's
theme expanded, ever more complicated and menacing. In the preface
of a new section after the War of Hannibal Livy avows perplexity—
a wide ocean confronts him.[4] To set the stage and explain the ensuing
action (Rome's dealings with the kingdoms of the East), the historian
should have furnished a survey of the different powers in the world,
from Macedonia down to Egypt. He was not competent to do it, and
the result is confusion.

Sallust got practice from writing the monographs, and he displayed
in the *Historiae* a notable talent for arrangement.[5] Tacitus also bene-

---

[1] It is therefore given a separate pagination in modern editions.

[2] *praef.* 1: 'facturusne operae pretium sim', &c.

[3] Seneca, *Epp.* 100. 9: 'scripsit dialogos quos non magis philosophiae adnumerare
possis quam historiae, et ex professo philosophiam continentis libros.' These works might
fall later than the inception of the history—as (presumably) the letter to his son extolling
Demosthenes and Cicero (Quintilian x. 1. 39).

[4] XXXI. 1. 5: 'iam provideo animo, velut qui proximis litori vadis inducti mare pedibus
ingrediuntur, quidquid progredior, in vastiorem me altitudinem ac velut profundum invehi.'

[5] K. Bauhofer, *Die Komposition der Historien Sallusts* (Diss. Munich, 1935), 74 ff.
He wrote 'structe' according to Fronto, p. 114 N = Haines II, p. 48.

fited from preliminary essays; and the exordium of his *Historiae* surpasses Sallust. To that great exemplar Tacitus is heavily indebted for structure, episodes, and portraits.[1] By Sallustian language he acknowledges his ancestry, patently and proudly. If that were not enough, there is tone and atmosphere as well.

When civil war came again after thirty years, it took no great effort of the imagination to see the Campus Martius thronged with the ghosts of Sulla's victims, and the terrible Marius emergent from his sepulchre.[2] Not only was the memory of it alive, but also a number of the agents and spectators. The contest between Pompeius and Caesar was comparatively merciful. After Caesar's death the renewed convulsions made the whole Sullan age real and tangible again, with proscriptions and the sacking of cities, the ambition of the dynasts, their alliances, and their rivalries. If Livy felt and reflected it, more violent must have been the impact upon Sallust, who had been involved in the wars and politics of the revolutionary age.

Narrating the 'res populi Romani' from the consulate of Lepidus and Catulus, he found much that bore upon his sympathies, and even his career. Sertorius, brave, energetic, and resourceful, was an enemy of Sulla and the *nobilitas*—but not, assuredly, in thought or act an enemy of Rome. A noble picture and a stirring story. Full credence will be denied. There can be little doubt that the portrayal of Sertorius' dealings has been tinted and arranged.[3] The cause is discovered in sheer partisan bias. It may be deeper and more intimate—Sertorius was, like Sallust, a son of the Sabine country, a *novus homo* eager to find scope for his 'virtus' at Rome, but encountering antagonism and various frustrations.[4]

Sallust brings on a tribune of the plebs with a speech protesting against the tyranny of the *Optimates* and exhorting the People to vindicate its liberties.[5] The tribune was Licinius Macer, also a writer of history, and the speech is splendid and vigorous. Sallust had been a turbulent tribune. The censors of 70 B.C. expelled a batch of undesirables. Sallust will have been equal to the theme—vice and venality, to be sure, and obscure clients whom the *nobiles* were glad to discard, but of some the sole offence was integrity or an allegiance.

To one writing under the Triumvirate the affair of Lepidus was startling and contemporary—word and deed and agents. Lepidus the

---

[1] Ch. XVII.

[2] Lucan I. 580 ff.: 'e medio visi consurgere Campo | tristia Sullani cecinere oracula manes | tollentemque caput gelidas Anienis ad undas | agricolae Marium fracto fugere sepulcro.'

[3] cf. the cogent arguments of H. Berve, *Hermes* LXIV (1929), 199 ff.

[4] See further Ch. XLII.   [5] III. 48.

consul, under pretext of the Commonwealth and invoking humanitarian pleas, makes a bid for personal domination. As proconsul he proceeds to violence. A senior consular, Marcius Philippus, denounces Lepidus in a powerful oration, whips the Senate to action, and carries the ultimate decree in defence of the State.[1] With the holders of legitimate authority is associated the young adventurer Pompeius, who later in the year is sent out to Spain as proconsul, though not yet a senator.

The contest between the Roman government and the military power, great orations to save the 'res publica', the march on Rome, the private armies and the public enemies, all this had been seen in 44 and 43. The facts were enough. Sallust in his *Historiae*, without the need of any especial artifice, could exploit a double privilege, openly attacking Lepidus, the parent of one Triumvir, and covertly alluding to another, to Octavianus, in his portrayal of Pompeius—the young man fair of face but dark within.[2] Their paths lay through treachery and violence, with despotic power as the goal.

Before he died, Sallust had the satisfaction of witnessing the calamitous fall of the one Triumvir, M. Aemilius Lepidus. He could discern the final struggle looming ahead, Caesar's heir against Antonius; for the supreme power, the empire of Rome and the world, permitted no sharing between the monarchic dynasts.

The consular Cornelius Tacitus was no less dominated by recent history and inescapable parallels—the choice of an emperor, the temper of the troops, and the menace of civil war. The whole setting of Galba's reign took on a sharp and contemporary significance. When an audience listened to the recitation of Book I of the *Historiae*, scene, persons, and events leapt into life, startling and terrifying.

The septuagenarian Princeps lacked the decision and energy to direct affairs or even to discipline his own entourage.[3] They intrigued and trafficked, dilapidating the public funds. New sources of revenue were hard to find. An attempt was made to recoup the treasury by penalizing the favourites and beneficiaries of Nero, but little came of it—and the Guard was clamorous for its donative. Once the government got itself disliked, nothing it did could fail to increase its unpopularity. The Emperor's person became an object of derision, detrimentally compared with Nero.

Galba was powerless in the hands of his associates, and careless, so it seemed. They were three in number: Icelus the freedman, T. Vinius

[1] I. 77.
[2] II. 16: 'oris probi animo inverecundo'; 17: 'modestus ad alia omnia nisi ad dominationem.'
[3] I. 12 ff.

(consul of the year), and Cornelius Laco. The early career of Vinius had been diversified by episodes both scandalous and ridiculous. Yet the fellow had once governed a province with some credit.[1] To command the Praetorians, the Emperor chose Cornelius Laco, a person destitute of military experience. Previously a petty law officer, he had only arrogance and obstinacy to supplement his ignorance.[2] The three came to conflict over the choice of an heir and successor for the Princeps, Vinius strongly in favour of Otho, the others without a candidate as yet, but against Otho. Rumour no doubt canvassed various names, with a predilection for the illustrious, who alone might seem worthy to stand in the line of Julii and Claudii. A relative of Galba was available, namely the son of his niece, a certain Cornelius Dolabella, of patrician lineage.[3] There is no sign that any of the army commanders were discussed.

The unhappy Princeps was driven to a hurried decision. Convoking Vinius and Laco and two other persons, he told them that Piso Licinianus was to be the successor, and asked for the young man to be brought in.[4]

In his oration Galba asserts that he has been summoned to power by the will of gods and men: the principate, in the old days an object of armed competition, he will transmit peacefully. There is the precedent of Caesar Augustus. But Augustus looked to his family circle for a successor, not to the 'res publica'. If Galba were choosing Piso to succeed him in a private station, the election would confer lustre on both parties, uniting to the distinction of the Sulpicii and Lutatii the pedigree of Pompeius and Crassus. Piso, however, is singled out by virtue. So far, his birth and merit have known adversity only. Prosperity is a more exacting trial. Piso will have to arm himself against the insidious approaches of flattery, subservience, and false friends. If the huge bulk of the Roman Empire could stand firm and unshaken without need of a ruler to keep it in equilibrium, Galba might have restored the Republic. Now, however, the supreme boon that either Galba or Piso can confer upon the Populus Romanus is the choice of a good Princeps. Under the domination of the Julii and Claudii the Commonwealth was only the appanage of a single family. To introduce the practice of adoption is the nearest equivalent to 'Libertas'. Adoption will discover the best man. To be born in the purple is a

---

[1] I. 48. 4: 'sed Vinius proconsulatu Galliam Narbonensem severe integreque rexit.'

[2] That Laco had been an 'assessor' is recorded by Suetonius, *Galba* 14. 2. Tacitus did not need this item.

[3] Cn. Cornelius Dolabella (*PIR²*, C 1347) was favoured by some (Plutarch, *Galba* 23, cf. Suetonius, *Galba* 12. 2). Tacitus deliberately omits Dolabella (the item would have interfered), reserving for later his vicissitudes and execution (I. 88. 1; II. 63 f.).

[4] I. 14.

fortuitous advantage. The hereditary prestige of the dynasty could not protect Nero from the consequences of his own enormities. Though danger threatens from the armies, the danger is slight and it will be dispelled by the adoption; and that act will abolish Galba's only imperfection as a ruler, his age. Nothing more need be said than a final counsel—Rome is not a despotism, Piso has in his charge a people that cannot be free and will not be enslaved.[1]

So far the Princeps. The revelation of his high fortune evoked from Piso no sign of joy or perturbation. His response was quiet and modest. Then the question arose, where the announcement should be made public—in the Forum, before the Senate, or in the camp of the Praetorian Guard? They decided to tell the Guard first. Galba spoke. He was plain and curt, disdaining any effort to win their sympathies. His address when presenting Piso to the Senate kept to the same austere pattern. Piso, however, showed grace and tact, and his speech was well received.

The Guard remained angry and unappeased, and Otho went to the Guard. On the first news of a proclamation in the camp, Piso made an appeal to the cohort on duty at the Palace.[2] For himself, he said, he could disclaim ambition, or any fears: adversity had taught him better. It would be a grievous thing for Galba, for the Senate, and for Rome if on this day Piso had to kill or be killed. Nero's removal had been achieved without strife or bloodshed in the city, and arrangements had now been made to ensure a peaceful transmission of the power after Galba.

Piso went on to denounce Otho for his vices, to warn the troops against his greed and perfidy. From Otho they could expect no share in the profits, only the ignominy. Nor was it at all in the interests of the Guard if they allowed a handful of treasonable scoundrels to create an emperor. Until now the Guard had been firm in allegiance to the Caesars, even to Nero—it was he who failed them. The evil example would be taken up by the provincial armies, with war ensuing. If the Guard wanted a donative, they did not have to resort to crime and murder: they could earn as much by doing their duty.

The allocution was dignified but unavailing. Reports soon grew precise, the soldiers were approaching. The populace occupied points of vantage. It was like the theatre or the circus. They clamoured against Otho, they would soon clamour for him. Such was their degradation and habit of subservience to the ruler, whoever he might be.[3] Galba was swayed by conflicting currents among his counsellors:

---

[1] 15 f.   [2] 29 f.
[3] 32. 1: 'tradito more quemcumque principem adulandi licentia adclamationum et studiis inanibus.'

to hold and barricade the Palace, or go out and face the insurrection. He had decided on the braver course, when a rumour spread that Otho had been killed, and a glad concourse invaded the Palace—plebs, knights, and senators, protesting loyalty, complaining that vengeance had been snatched from their hands, loud and bold in words, but really a pack of cowards.[1]

Otho in the meantime harangued the Guard. His attitude was base and flattering—'omnia serviliter pro dominatione'—and his appeal combined abuse of Galba with hypocritical protestations.[2] The troops poured out of the camp. Their zeal was such as would befit Roman soldiers bent on dethroning the Parthian monarch. But they entered the Forum to murder their Emperor, an old man and helpless. The Capitol, the temples, and the thought of emperors past and future meant nothing to them.[3]

Such was the behaviour of an emperor and his advisers, of Senate, populace, and troops in January of 69. According to Tacitus, Galba's elevation made public a great 'arcanum imperii'.[4] The attempt of Nymphidius Sabinus had revealed another secret, exploited by Otho— and not forgotten.

The resemblances to the facts or fears of 97 are numerous and striking. And, if more were known of Nerva's principate, sundry details or persons in the Tacitean account might furnish other similarities. Noteworthy is the demeanour of the Senate in political crises, with the varying symptoms of ambition, dishonesty, and dissimulation. Even odd items might be significant—aristocratic candidates for the purple, exiles coming back, the shortage of money amid the prevalence of jobbery and corruption, the choice of provincial governors, the influence of an astrologer, the character of a Praetorian prefect, the removal of suspected officers from the Guard.

Above all, the soldiery in relation to the government. Of the four speeches inserted by Tacitus in Book I of the *Historiae*, three are addresses to the Praetorians.[5] An episode in the brief three months of Otho's reign will repay examination—a mutiny, accorded special prominence by the historian, and enhanced with an oration from the Emperor.

From a trivial cause there flared up a sudden disturbance, all but

---

[1] 35. 1: 'ignavissimus quisque et, ut res docuit, in periculo non ausurus, nimii verbis, linguae feroces.'

[2] 37 f.

[3] 40. 2: 'igitur milites Romani quasi Vologaesum aut Pacorum avito Arsacidarum solio depulsuri ac non imperatorem suum inermem et senem trucidare pergerent, disiecta plebe proculcato senatu, truces armis rapidi equis forum inrumpunt. nec illos Capitolii aspectus et imminentium templorum religio et priores et futuri principes terruere.'

[4] 4. 2.

[5] 29 f.; 37 f.; 83 f. Further, Otho's last oration (II. 47) is also an address to the Guard.

catastrophic to the City.[1] Instructions had been issued to equip one of the urban cohorts for the campaign. The hour—it was nightfall—and the arrangements for secrecy aroused the suspicions of the Praetorian Guard. They scented a plot against Otho—slaves of the senators, so they fancied, were being given weapons. In a moment all was uproar. Some were drunk, others bent on loot, the mass ripe for trouble. They cut down a tribune and some centurions and made for the Palace.

Otho was dispensing hospitality to a large party of senators and their wives. Consternation descended upon the guests. They did not know what was happening—an accidental tumult or a trick of their Princeps—or what to do, stay or depart. Putting on a show of resolution, or betraying their apprehensions, the company fixed their eyes upon Otho, who caused no less terror than he felt. Then the Emperor told them to go away, and there was an undignified dispersal, a few only to their own mansions, the greater part to hide with friends, or better, with their dependants.

The soldiery in a mad surge broke into the Palace, uttering threats against their officers and against the Senate. Otho stood up on a couch, and with tears and entreaty at length induced them to return to their quarters. On the next day the two prefects addressed the Guard, and a huge donative was paid out, five thousand sesterces to each man. Not till then did Otho dare to enter the camp.

The Emperor was influenced by a variety of motives. Anxious for the safety of the City and the Senate, he was none the less aware of the need to indulge and flatter the troops; his Principate had been won by crime, he could hardly strengthen his position by suddenly imposing the rigorous discipline of ancient days. The oration was artfully contrived to play upon their loyalty and solicit their obedience.[2] Otho spoke to the soldiers as friends and comrades, asking only some restraint of their affections—for the disturbance had originated in the very excess of their valour and devotion. Order and subordination, he told them, are the conditions of success in war; and he concluded with a panegyric on Rome, Commonwealth, and Senate.

No more words of menace, he adjures the Guard, against the Senate—the supreme council of the Empire, the select flower of all the provinces. Not even the German allies of Vitellius would be guilty

---

[1] 80. 1: 'parvo interim initio, unde nihil timebatur, orta seditio prope urbi excidio fuit.' Tacitus has clearly built up this incident, cf. M. Treu, *Atti Acc. Peloritana* XLVII (1951), 26 ff. As for the precise origin of the tumult, Tacitus, Plutarch (*Otho* 3), and Suetonius (*Otho* 8) present material discrepancies. For criticism and a reconstruction, cf. E. Hohl, *Klio* XXXII (1939), 307 ff. It appears that *Cohors* XVII was being equipped to embark at Ostia on Otho's naval expedition (cf. 1. 87). Tacitus does not explain why the cohort itself was brought to Rome.   [2] 83 f.

of such criminal audacity. The Guard is the martial youth of Rome, the true sons of Italy. Vitellius is only the master of some native tribes, with the semblance of an army. With Otho stands the Senate of Rome. On the one side is the 'res publica', on the other its enemies. Rome is something more than a construction of walls and buildings. The material fabric of a city can be destroyed or rebuilt, but on the Senate depends the Empire in its 'aeternitas' and the peace of the nations. So was it ordained in the beginning by the Founder of the City, and it has endured from the Kings to the Caesars, perpetual and immortal. Soldiers of the Guard can be senators, and a senator become emperor.[1]

The Guard was placated, but the city remained uneasy. Though the soldiers desisted from rioting, they were still dangerous: they penetrated in disguise into private houses, making sinister and precise inquiries about persons of rank and wealth. When the senators assembled, it was hard for a man to know what demeanour to adopt—silence looked like contumacy, free speech was perilous, and Otho could see through adulation, for he had so recently practised that art. Their perplexity issued in confused and tortuous declarations, noisy invective against Vitellius as a parricide and a public enemy, or common abuse, covered and drowned by the general tumult of voices, or by the speaker's own volubility.[2]

Thus does Tacitus illustrate the temper and conduct of Senate, Emperor, and soldiery. Otho, addressing the Guard, speaks as a military emperor should speak—constrained perhaps to forbear and be indulgent, but firm on the principles of military discipline and magniloquent about Rome, the Empire, and the Senate. Nero, so far as known, made no effort to confront the Praetorians and win them from Nymphidius, even by a histrionic appeal. Galba when he adopted Piso made an allocution to the Guard, resembling that of an 'imperator' only in its brevity. He invoked an ancient institution in the citizen armies of the Republic: one man choosing another for a dangerous task.[3] He added no words of comradely appeal, he gave them no

---

[1] The peroration (1. 84. 4) is notable—'quid? vos pulcherrimam hanc urbem domibus et tectis et congestu lapidum stare creditis? muta ista et inanima intercidere ac reparari promisca sunt: aeternitas rerum et pax gentium et mea cum vestra salus incolumitate senatus firmatur. hunc auspicato a parente et conditore urbis nostrae institutum et a regibus usque ad principes continuum et immortalem, sicut a maioribus accepimus sic posteris tradamus; nam ut ex vobis senatores ita ex senatoribus principes nascuntur.'

[2] 85. 3: 'igitur versare sententias et huc atque illuc torquere, hostem et parricidam Vitellium vocantes, providentissimus quisque vulgaribus conviciis, quidam vera probra iacere, in clamore tamen et ubi plurimae voces, aut tumultu verborum sibi ipsi obstrepentes.'

[3] 18. 2: 'imperatoria brevitate adoptari a se Pisonem exemplo divi Augusti et more militari, quo vir virum legeret, pronuntiat.'

money. The Guard could have been won, with a little money, by that parsimonious emperor.[1] Nor had Piso Licinianus chosen the right tone and language.

When the Praetorians, clamorous for vengeance on the assassins of Domitian, assailed and beleaguered the Princeps in his palace, Nerva lacked the bodily vigour to withstand them, a frail old man. Otho at least, for all his vice and frivolity, was emboldened to put up some show of dignity and courage. Though taken at a loss and helpless when the Praetorians broke up his dinner party, he was able to reinforce bribery with eloquence, restoring discipline in the camp and order at Rome. Otho's speech, one cannot but suspect, ought to have been delivered by M. Cocceius Nerva on a tumultuous day in the autumn of the year 97.[2]

To write about the past in the light of present or recent experience called for judgement and alertness, if an author were not to deceive his readers—and himself. It might seem that the classical historians were not unequivocally to be commended as model and precedent. They exhibit certain dangers.

History with the Romans, never a subject of disinterested inquiry, could not be emancipated from political and moral preoccupations. That was not the only defect. The pride and glory of Rome was military, openly acknowledged by the nations who submitted to her empire, and the greater part of the 'res populi Romani' is the record of wars. Yet those who register and exalt the achievements of the imperial people seem sadly inadequate to the task. Livy as a narrator of battle is beyond reclaim. Sallust, who commanded armies and governed a province in Africa, is convicted of carelessness about time and place. Not only neglect to be precise about chronology and topography, but an indifference verging on distaste, that is the paradox embodied in the Roman historians.

---

[1] So Tacitus affirms, 1. 18. 3: 'constat potuisse conciliari animos quantulacumque parci senis liberalitate.'

[2] Otho and Nerva were products of Nero's court-circle, closely coeval and not dissimilar in some of their tastes (App. 2).

XIV. MILITARY HISTORY I

CORNELIUS TACITUS has been denounced as the most un-military of historians.[1] The charge is powerful, and perhaps misdirected. Accurate intelligence about numbers and regiments, the detail of operations both principal and subsidiary, the times and stages of a march, such were the facts to be registered in the reports of generals or the *commentarii* of military emperors. In short, the materials of history rather than its substance. Even when dignified with such a purity and strength of language as might appear to defy and deter emulation, *commentarii* were not esteemed by the Romans a province of literature. Cicero pays a generous tribute to Caesar,[2] but the dispatches of the proconsul did not represent that ideal of historical composition he was looking for, so far in vain.

The indictment against Tacitus has two counts—he is arbitrary, inadequate, and misleading in the selection of facts, and he fails to discern and expound the strategic purpose behind the events. Military history (it is averred) should record not only what happened but what was intended to happen. Since most of what survives of the *Historiae* is a narrative of warfare, it is necessary to examine the author's performance, establishing how far the accusations are true (and relevant), how far they derive from petulance or pedantry. For convenience and brevity the inquiry will be concentrated upon the chief military transactions of the year 69, the fighting in northern Italy.[3]

Vitellius sent forward two armies to invade Italy by separate routes. The one, starting from Lower Germany under the command of the legionary legate Fabius Valens, had the longer road.[4] Its destination was the pass of the Mont Genèvre, and it proceeded southwards through the interior of Gaul to Lugdunum, thence by Vienna across the territory of the Allobroges and the Vocontii to the foot of the Alps. The historian gives a full account of the march, with names of

---

[1] Mommsen, *Röm. Gesch.* v (1885), 165 = *The Provinces of the Roman Empire* I (1886), 181.

[2] *Brutus* 262: 'nudi enim sunt, recti et venusti, omni ornatu orationis tamquam veste detracta.'

[3] See especially B. W. Henderson, *Civil War and Rebellion in the Roman Empire* (1908); E. G. Hardy, *Journ. Phil.* XXXI (1910), 123 ff.; A. Momigliano, *Stud. it. fil. cl.* IX (1931/2), 117 ff., with appendix on the sources, 171 ff.; A. Passerini, *Studi di antichità classica offerti . . . a Emanuele Ciaceri* (1940), 178 ff. Some points of detail and of controversy are discussed in App. 29 ff.

[4] *Hist.* I. 61 ff.

towns and tribes and a variety of incidents on the way. The crossing
of the Alps, and the first stages of the descent into Italy (Segusio and
Augusta Taurinorum) are omitted. This force is not heard of again
until it arrives at Ticinum, close to the theatre of the hostilities that
have already begun.[1]

The other army, drawn from the troops in Upper Germany, was
led by Caecina Alienus, with the Great St. Bernard for its first
objective. Tacitus allocates most of his narration to a scene of riot and
massacre among the inoffensive but courageous Helvetii.[2] Caecina,
after waiting a few days, learned that a cavalry regiment stationed in
the valley of the Po had declared for Vitellius, thereby securing several
of the most important towns in the region he proposed to invade,
Eporedia, Vercellae, and Mediolanium among them.[3] He therefore sent
ahead some auxiliary troops, himself following with the legions.
Caecina is next discovered in Italy. His manner and conduct are
described, but not the stages of his march (over the pass to Augusta
Praetoria and down the long valley, to emerge at Eporedia, thence
Vercellae). His objective (it is clear) was the Po and two places of
strategic value: Cremona on the northern bank, where the Via
Postumia (coming from Aquileia by Verona) crossed the river, and
Placentia on the southern, where the Postumia joins another great
artery, the Aemilia. Caecina comes into the action not far from
Placentia.[4] That the Vitellian advance guard had captured the city of
Cremona some twenty miles to the east is nowhere expressly stated
by the historian.[5]

The design of warfare being executed by the generals of Vitellius
was simple and straightforward—to occupy as much of northern
Italy as could safely be held, to thrust between Otho's forces from
Rome and the Danubian armies, preventing their junction. Tacitus,
it is true, attributes an idea to Caecina. Before going over the Great
St. Bernard he paused and wondered whether he should not make
a flank movement across Raetia against the procurator of Noricum,
who was believed loyal to Otho.[6] But Caecina dropped the idea—his
advance guard was already over the Alps, there was more glory to be
won by maintaining the parts of Italy already in the hands of the
Vitellians, while Noricum was subsidiary and irrelevant. Whether this
faint and fugitive notion derives from Caecina Alienus, or from
Tacitus, is also irrelevant. As recorded, it can lend no support to the

---

[1] II. 27. I.   [2] I. 67 ff.
[3] I. 70. I, cf. II. 17.   [4] II. 20. 2.
[5] The capture of both Ticinum and Cremona has to be inferred. All that Tacitus says
is 'capta Pannoniorum cohors apud Cremonam, intercepti centum equites ac mille classiarii
inter Placentiam Ticinumque' (II. 17. 2). For these operations see A. Passerini, o.c. 192 f.
[6] I. 70. 2.

theory that Caecina, instead of crossing the St. Bernard and consolidating the position already won, until Fabius Valens should join him, may have thought of striking eastwards so as to descend into Italy by way of the Brenner Pass, and come down on Verona.[1]

Otho's strategy was also very simple. To seize control of the banks of the river Po now that Caecina was already over the Alps, that is the statement of Tacitus.[2] The historian has not added the corollary—to maintain communications with the armies of the Danubian provinces. That was obvious enough.

The West had been lost, for Spain and Gallia Narbonensis transferred their allegiance to Vitellius. Yet Otho held command of the sea. Action by the fleet might have helped, with a prompt attack on the harbour of Forum Julii (a place of great strategic value). Otho in fact planned a diversion. He sent the fleet, reinforced with troops from the garrison of Rome, to attack the coastal zone of the Maritime Alps and the nearer parts of Narbonensis. The commanders were persons of no consequence, the achievement negligible—they did not delay Valens' invasion of Italy or seriously weaken his forces. The Othonians were victorious, it is true, in two small encounters with the auxiliary troops dispatched by Fabius Valens. Then both sides dropped the affair, as though nothing had happened.[3]

For the conduct of the war in northern Italy Otho had selected three generals of senatorial rank: Suetonius Paullinus, Marius Celsus, and Annius Gallus. One of them, Annius Gallus, he sent forward with a force comprising the legion I Adiutrix (which had recently been enrolled from the fleet soldiers), five cohorts of the Guard, and two thousand gladiators.[4]

Annius himself crossed the river, with the larger part of these troops. His was a most important task—clearly, though Tacitus gives no hint of it, to keep open the road north-eastward to Aquileia at the head of the Adriatic and provide a rallying point for the reinforcements expected from the armies of Pannonia, Dalmatia, and Moesia. Nor does Tacitus reveal where Annius Gallus took up his station: presumably beyond Hostilia (the crossing of the Po), towards Mantua and Verona.

Too late or too weak to hold Cremona, Annius Gallus had detached a force under Vestricius Spurinna to make sure of Placentia.[5] Spurinna's first problem was the turbulent Praetorians—they cried out that there was treachery afoot, pointed their weapons at the general, and clamoured to go against the enemy. The sagacious Spurinna

---

[1] B. W. Henderson, o.c. 66 ff. That would involve an intolerable détour. There was no road across the Arlberg to the valley of the Inn.

[2] II. 11. 2: 'ad occupandas Padi ripas.'   [3] On this episode see further App. 30.

[4] II. 11 (also mentioning Otho's own force).   [5] II. 18 f., cf. Plutarch, *Otho* 5 f.

humoured the soldiery, and led them out some distance.[1] When they set about making a camp for the night, the unwonted labour was too much for city troops. They saw reason, and went obediently back to Placentia. Spurinna restored discipline and strengthened the defences of the city. He was then able to beat off Caecina's attack when it came soon afterwards.

Annius Gallus, apprised of the attack on Placentia, was leading the legion to the rescue, but halted at Bedriacum when he heard that Caecina had abandoned the siege of Placentia and was moving eastwards. Bedriacum was a village half-way between Verona and Cremona: at this point the main artery, the Via Postumia, coming from Verona, was joined by a road from Hostilia by way of Mantua.[2] After a time Suetonius Paullinus and Marius Celsus also turned up at Bedriacum.

Meanwhile Caecina had established his base at Cremona. Eager to retrieve his reputation and win some success before the arrival of Valens, he laid an ambush near the place called Ad Castores, on the Via Postumia, twelve miles east of Cremona.[3] The plan was betrayed, and the Othonians set a counter-trap, which succeeded. Though Marius Celsus handled the cavalry with skill,.the Othonians missed a complete victory. Men blamed the excessive caution of that veteran general Suetonius Paullinus. Tacitus' exposition of the fighting is confused—not unnaturally.

Fabius Valens was now reported at Ticinum, and he soon joined Caecina at Cremona. They detested each other, and Caecina was by far the more popular with the troops, but they curbed their feud, waiting patiently for the next move of the enemy—which they were sure would be some act of folly.

There were too many generals on the Othonian side—in addition to the three commanders appointed at the outset they had the Prefect of the Guard, Licinius Proculus, and now the Emperor had appeared on the scene, and the Emperor's brother, Salvius Titianus.

Caecina and Valens did not remain completely idle. They began to build a bridge of boats across the Po a few miles below Cremona. According to Tacitus the construction of the bridge was merely a feint and a means of keeping the troops occupied.[4] He is probably

---

[1] B. W. Henderson (o.c. 82) suggested that the Tacitean account is a travesty of what really happened. For a plausible reconstruction, A. Passerini, o.c. 195.

[2] For the approximate site cf. Mommsen, *Hermes* v (1871), 161 ff. = *Ges. Schr.* IV (1906), 354 ff.; A. Passerini, o.c. 179 ff. (a very full discussion). The Via Postumia ran through Verona (*ILS* 5806), not Mantua, as some have assumed.

[3] II. 24 ff.; Plutarch, *Otho* 7.

[4] 34. 1. Plutarch (*Otho* 10) in a briefer account seems to take the bridging seriously. Cf. also A. Momigliano, o.c. 138; against, A. Passerini, o.c. 217.

right. The operation might, it is true, be serious in design, or have become serious—a general should keep alternate devices in his mind.[1] It is more likely that Caecina intended his bridge as a means to detain a number of the enemy troops on the southern bank of the river, alarm Otho, wear down his patience—and goad him to disadvantageous action.

. Otho, who had chosen Brixellum (some distance away, on the south bank of the river) as his headquarters, came to Bedriacum for the council of war, but returned to Brixellum immediately afterwards. At the debate Suetonius Paullinus counselled delay.[2] The bulk of Vitellius' forces, he said, was already there. Not much could come in the way of reinforcements from the Rhine, or from Britain, or from Spain. Pent up in a corner of Transpadane Italy, the enemy would suffer straits of supply, and their German auxiliaries would not be able to stand the climate if the campaign lasted into the summer months. Otho's cause, however, was supported by the Danube provinces and by the East, by the resources of Italy and the prestige of the imperial city, by the Senate and the People. The Po was a strong barrier, the cities inexpugnable, as Placentia demonstrated. Moreover, only a few days and the famous Fourteenth Legion would be there, along with the forces from Moesia.

Suetonius Paullinus had the backing of Marius Celsus and Annius Gallus. The Emperor was all for a battle, his brother and the Prefect of the Guard concurring. The army was to march out from Bedriacum and force a speedy decision.[3] Thus was ordained the battle that took its name from Bedriacum.

The historian Tacitus supplies in his own version the arguments of Suetonius Paullinus, and not inappropriately allows the general to overstate his case, especially in the remarks about reinforcements soon to arrive. How closely the speech may approximate to what was in fact said, there is no means of knowing, although some of the persons who were there (such as Marius Celsus) may have given a report afterwards.[4] Nor is that question highly relevant.

The principal difficulty in assessing both the general strategical situation and the merits of the decision to do battle is the uncertainty about the strength of the opposing armies. Tacitus is far from helpful. Information about the whereabouts of some troops has to be gleaned from assertions in speeches, optimistic rumours, or subsequent hints. Tacitus does not always distinguish between legionary detachments and whole legions; and, apart from legions, there is a total lack of precision about the numbers of the *auxilia*.

(margin annotation: TACITUS IS VAGUE ON MIL. ESTIMATES?)

---

[1] Caecina was in fact supervising the work on the day of the battle when the news came that the Othonian army was upon him (II. 41. 1).

[2] 32, cf. *Otho* 8.   [3] 33.   [4] For Celsus, App. 32.

First, the Vitellians. According to Tacitus, Valens started out from the Rhine with forty thousand men, Caecina with thirty thousand; and Valens picked up eight cohorts of Batavians in the land of the Lingones, a legion (I Italica) and a cavalry regiment at Lugdunum.[1] It is hard to resist the conclusion that the original figures (based upon four legions in the one army, three in the other) are too large by at least a third. To suppose that the two armies when united near Cremona reached a total of eighty, or even a hundred thousand, puts a strain on belief—and makes the Othonian attack a paradox.[2] Contrariwise, it may be expedient to urge that Otho's muster was somewhat larger than has been fancied.[3]

The various forces which the Emperor sent or conducted from Rome might amount to a handsome total; and he could draw upon the armies of Pannonia, Dalmatia, and Moesia. By good fortune one thing is clear—the detachments of the three legions of Moesia were two if not three hundred miles from the battlefield. They were still the other side of Aquileia.[4] When they heard the outcome of the battle they none the less advanced as far as that city—which debilitates an assertion in the speech of Suetonius Paullinus.

In the provinces of Pannonia and Dalmatia stood four legions, but Tacitus does not specify the strength in each province, or the camps—relevant facts because of the varying distances to be covered. Each of the legions sent forward a *vexillatio* of two thousand men (while the main bulk followed), and there were also auxiliary troops in the vanguard. One whole legion along with a detachment of another is attested at the battle. More should probably be allowed for.[5] If Otho's army be thus augmented (more from Pannonia and Dalmatia, legionaries as well as *auxilia*), his decision is the better to be comprehended, and the armies appear better matched: and the accession of strength to be expected within a few days of the council of war correspondingly less.

Otho wanted a battle. He had to provoke it: the Vitellian forces were encamped beside Cremona, and it was twenty miles (or rather twenty-two) from Bedriacum to Cremona.[6] Otho's army would need

---

[1] I. 61; 64.

[2] About a hundred thousand, G. H. Stevenson in *CAH* x (1934), 819, cf. 823; about seventy thousand against not more than thirty thousand Othonians, A. Momigliano, o.c. 136.   [3] App. 31.

[4] Suetonius, *Divus Vesp.* 6. 2: 'Moesiaci exercitus bina e tribus legionibus milia, missa auxilio Othoni, postquam ingressis iter nuntiatum est victum eum ac vim vitae suae attulisse, nihilo setius Aquileiam usque perseveraverunt, quasi rumori minus crederent.' Cf. also *Hist.* II. 85. 1.

[5] cf. App. 31.

[6] Pompeius Planta (cited by the *scholium* on Juvenal II. 99) has the former figure, the *Tab. Peut.* the latter.

to move forward and take up a new position closer to the enemy, with space for deployment. Hence a march, presumably in two stages: the army could be in posture for battle on the morning of the third day.[1]

The generals set the army in motion. It did not get very far. It advanced four miles along the Via Postumia and encamped for the night.[2] There was some discussion about the plan (and a despatch from Otho insisted that there should be no delay). The march was resumed the next day. Its goal was a point sixteen miles further on, according to Tacitus.[3] Two of the generals, Paullinus and Celsus, became vocal and raised objections.[4] It was a bad thing, they said, to expose tired and encumbered troops to an attack from an enemy who would have only a short distance to traverse, barely four miles; the troops would be taken at a disadvantage, whether marching or making ready their encampment. However, Licinius Proculus and Salvius Titianus overruled those objections (Otho had sent a swift imperious message), and the march proceeded.

The army came within striking distance of the Vitellian camp, sent forward some cavalry, and began to deploy, in haste and confusion.[5] One legion (XIII Gemina) and a detachment of another were on the right flank, the Praetorians occupied the centre astride the Via Postumia, while I Adiutrix on the left had the benefit of open country between the Postumia and the river Po. The Vitellians opened the attack, and after some fierce fighting turned both wings and broke the centre. The final discomfiture of the left wing was due to the Batavian cohorts which had dealt with an Othonian incursion from the other bank of the river.[6] The remnants of the defeated army streamed back in rout towards Bedriacum.

Where the battle occurred is fairly clear. The clash came a few miles short of Cremona. How far did this encounter correspond to Otho's plan, and his generals' execution of that plan? That is the most notorious crux in the whole of Tacitus.[7] He states that the army set out on the second morning with all its baggage, making for the confluence of the Po and the Adua, sixteen miles distant.[8] Something has

---

[1] For the presumed strategy, and for the relation between the accounts of Tacitus (II. 39–44) and Plutarch (*Otho* 11 f.), see App. 30.

[2] II. 39. 2: 'promoveri ad quartum a Bedriaco castra placuit'; Plutarch, *Otho* 11 (fifty stades, i.e. about six miles).

[3] 40. 1. Plutarch (*Otho* 11) indicates not less than a dozen miles—βουλόμενον προάγειν ἐπὶ τοὺς πολεμίους ὁδὸν οὐκ ἐλάττονα σταδίων ἑκατόν. [4] 40. 1, cf. *Otho* 11.

[5] 41. 3: 'apud Othonianos pavidi duces, miles ducibus infensus, mixta vehicula et lixae, et praeruptis utrimque fossis via quieto quoque agmini angusta.'

[6] 43. 2, cf. Plutarch (*Otho* 12), whose account of the contest between I Adiutrix and the Vitellian XXI Rapax and of the Batavians' exploit is more copious.

[7] See further App. 30.

[8] 40. 1: 'non ut ad pugnam sed ad bellandum profecti confluentis Padi et Aduae fluminum, sedecim inde milium spatio distantis, petebant.'

gone wrong. That confluence is six or seven miles up the river, west-wards from Cremona. The two items, confluence and distance, are incompatible. Which is to be preferred? One solution, opting for the former, suggests that the historian erroneously identified the Othon-ians' ultimate goal with their immediate objective—they would first march sixteen miles and get astride the road that leads from Cremona northwards to Brixia, and then, proceeding to the point where the Adua runs into the Po, cut the Vitellian communications with Mediolanium and Ticinum.[1] A refinement upon this theory argues that Otho's army was to march by a flank movement past Cremona, while the envelopment of the whole Vitellian force was to be com-pleted by a fresh army, Danube troops mustering meanwhile at Bedriacum and moving westwards on Cremona.[2]

If the distance to be traversed, namely sixteen miles, is kept, various solutions offer.[3] It has been suggested that the Adua itself may have changed its course.[4] If it could be proved that the Adua in Roman times joined the Po not above Cremona but below Cremona, all would be well. Proof is lacking. As a last resort, the chance might be entertained that the historian himself, being not well informed about the topography of the region, fancied that the confluence was below Cremona, not far from where the battle actually took place.[5]

A grave misconception there has certainly been somewhere, in Tacitus or in his source.[6] The general impression, however, is valid: Otho did not design and order an elaborate strategical movement, he insisted on a pitched battle, in despair more than in hope, certainly with morbid impatience—and perhaps from fear of treachery or desertions.[7] When the gamble failed, he decided to commit suicide. The Praetorians in the Emperor's escort at Brixellum were fierce, loud, and loyal, and there was some talk of the Moesian legions. In Tacitus' view, there is no doubt that Otho might have taken up the struggle again, not without a chance of victory.[8] That is most unlikely.

---

[1] Mommsen, *Hermes* v (1871), 161 ff. = *Ges. Schr.* IV (1906), 354 ff.

[2] B. W. Henderson, o.c. 100 ff.; 340 ff. [3] See App. 30.

[4] G. Niccolini, *Rend. Acc. Lincei* XV (1906), 278 ff.

[5] That, however, might seem a desperate remedy: how and why was the Adua brought in at all by a source of Tacitus? Cf. App. 30.

[6] Perhaps Tacitus conflated two sources unskilfully, perhaps therefore the sixteen miles should be reckoned from Bedriacum, not from the end of the first day's march: see App. 30.

[7] At the council of war he is 'pronus ad decertandum' (II. 33. 1), and on the second morning the generals receive a courier 'cum atrocibus mandatis, quibus Otho increpita ducum segnitia rem in discrimen mitti iubebat, aeger morae et spei impatiens' (II. 40. 2). Compare the diagnosis of Julius Secundus—σπεύδειν ἐγκαλυψάμενος ὥσπερ ἀπὸ κρημνοῦ μεθεῖναι τὰ πράγματα πρὸς τὸ συντυχόν (*Otho* 9).

[8] 46. 3: 'nec praetoriani tantum, proprius Othonis miles, sed praemissi e Moesia eandem obstinationem adventantis exercitus, legiones Aquileiam ingressas nuntiabant,

On the evening after the battle three of the defeated generals, who had reached the camp near Bedriacum, discussed what should be done, and they all resolved to capitulate.[1] They sent envoys to Caecina Alienus the next day.

The Battle of Bedriacum took place on April 14, the suicide of Otho on the morning of the second day thereafter. Six months later, towards the end of October, the Danubian legions had their revenge upon the armies of the Rhine. They invaded Italy again, winning a battle near Bedriacum and capturing Cremona.

Another candidate had emerged. The generals in the East, who had published their allegiance to Galba and to Otho in turn, were not willing for long to acquiesce in the victory of Vitellius. In July the eastern armies proclaimed Flavius Vespasianus as Emperor.

ut nemo dubitet potuisse renovari bellum atrox lugubre, incertum victis et victoribus.' The true position of the Moesian *vexillationes* is shown by Suetonius, *Divus Vesp.* 6. 2, cf. *Hist.* II. 85. 1. Tacitus is here incautious.

[1] 44 f. Plutarch's version (*Otho* 13), with notable prominence for Marius Celsus, is fuller, clearer, and better, cf. App. 32.

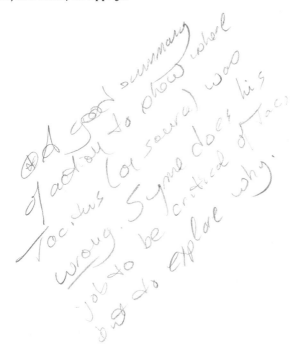

XV. MILITARY HISTORY II

IN the events leading to the seizure of power by Vespasian, Tacitus concentrates his interest on the eastern theatre, and employs a speech of advice from Licinius Mucianus the governor of Syria.[1] Originally at variance, the two generals composed their feud after the fall of Nero, through the good offices of mutual friends and latterly of Titus, and, having sworn allegiance to three emperors, now resolved to intervene against Vitellius with all the resources of the East. They had gone too far in scheming and diplomacy. There was only one way out. As Mucianus observed, 'confugiendum est ad imperium'.[2]

So far the East. For one reason or another, Tacitus does not accord great prominence to the Danubian armies. He states that Vespasian, computing his chances for a civil war, relied upon III Gallica in Moesia because it had belonged to the Syrian garrison, and he hoped that the rest of the legions of Illyricum would follow suit.[3] There was something more—an item that is not revealed until later in the exposition of Tacitus, after Vespasian was proclaimed, and after the Flavian plan of operations was established. The three legions from Moesia (or rather, the *vexillationes*), which had been summoned by Otho, having reached Aquileia, started a riot there, with treasonable demonstrations against Vitellius. Then they went back to their province and stations.[4]

The report of this incident, when it reached Syria, may (or may not) have been a factor of moment. There was also news about the other forces, defeated or cheated at Bedriacum, and very angry.[5] Vespasian and his crafty associate may have negotiated with the governors of the three provinces Moesia, Pannonia, and Dalmatia.[6] Better than those old men (who were timid time-servers) would be legionary legates, or other persons suitably commended by personal ties and a taste for intrigue. The secret history of these transactions could have said something about Aurelius Fulvus, who commanded III Gallica in the days of Domitius Corbulo, and who took it to Moesia.[7]

---

[1] II. 76 f.   [2] 76. 3.   [3] 74. 1.

[4] 85. 1, cf. Suetonius, *Divus Vesp.* 6. 2. Suetonius alleges that, when at Aquileia, these detachments had actually proclaimed Vespasian. This is believed by Ph. Fabia, *Rev. ét. anc.* V (1903), 350, and by W. Weber, *Josephus und Vespasian* (1921), 167; while B. W. Henderson keeps the three Moesian legions, in full strength, at Aquileia, and they are still there when they learn of Vespasian's proclamation in the East (*Civil War and Rebellion in the Roman Empire* (1908), 137).   [5] 74. 1.

[6] For these persons, and their subsequent honours, see p. 593 f.

[7] T. Aurelius Fulvus (*PIR²*, A 1510), commanding III Gallica in Armenia in 64

Tacitus, it appears, has failed to put the incident at Aquileia in proper relation to Vespasian's designs.[1] The reason for the historian's procedure is not far to seek. To mention at an earlier stage what happened at Aquileia would have precluded him from giving a connected and artistic account of the rebellion as it rose and spread among the Danubian camps, the Moesian army taking the lead and quickly dragging in Pannonia. Dalmatia followed.[2]

The adhesion of Illyricum decided the issue of the war but did not at once modify the Flavian strategy, Vespasian proceeding to Egypt thence to organize the blockade of Italy, Mucianus marching with an army to Europe. Tacitus says that Mucianus was in doubts whether he should not make for Dyrrachium when he reached Byzantium.[3] The idea may derive from the historian who recalled the civil wars of the Republic, with Macedonia and the Via Egnatia strategically dominant. The new factor in imperial history is the land route from the Balkans through Moesia and Pannonia to northern Italy.

The war entered Italy sooner than Mucianus expected or liked. That was due to the desperate energy of Antonius Primus, commander of the Seventh Legion in Pannonia—who had been of no service to Otho in the campaign of Bedriacum. Antonius found a congenial ally in the procurator Cornelius Fuscus, a bold impetuous man, rejoicing in risks: Fuscus had come out as a vigorous partisan the year before, causing his colony to declare for Galba.[4] The consular legate carried no weight.

When the leaders met in council at Poetovio, Antonius spoke for action, and prevailed. Taking only the *auxilia*, horse and foot (and Pannonia was strong in cavalry), he swept across the Julian Alps, occupied Aquileia, and advanced as far as Patavium, where he waited for his main force (two legions) to come up. Verona was the next move, to serve as base of operations; and the three legions from Moesia arrived.

Antonius pressed on to Bedriacum, engaged the Vitellian forces in battle outside Cremona, and won a great victory. His daring advance was justified by success. Had he failed, the verdict would be temerity —and Antonius might well have failed but for incompetence and treachery among his adversaries.

The generals of Vitellius had a strategic task comparable to that of Otho six months earlier—to hold the line of the Po and at the same time maintain communications with Gaul and the Rhine. One army

---

(*ILS* 232) and on the Danube in the winter of 68/69 (*Hist.* I. 79. 5). But Dillius Aponianus has the legion at Cremona (III. 10. 1). Fulvus had presumably gone away to join Vespasian.

[1] As is demonstrated at inordinate length in Fabia's paper, *Rev. ét. anc.* v (1903), 329–82.
[2] II. 85 f.   [3] 83. 2.   [4] 86. 3. See further App. 33.

was sent to Cremona, while the larger force, under Caecina Alienus, took up its position a little to the north of the crossing of the Po at Hostilia. Caecina made no move against the Flavians, but allowed them to complete their concentration at Verona. Instead, he slipped away to Ravenna, and, in concert with the commander of the fleet, opened negotiations with the enemy. His treachery, detected, left the legions without a commander. They fell back, crossed the Po, and marched to Cremona, arriving when their comrades had been defeated by Antonius, but renewing at night the battle which ended to their discomfiture with the fall and sack of the city.

Tacitus provides a full account of the fighting, from the Flavian side. In one particular, lack of care or a detail omitted betrays him into obscurity. His description of the Vitellian camp near Hostilia, and the bridge, or bridges, in the vicinity is not clear enough.[1] It has to be inferred that the legions got to Cremona from Hostilia by a march south of the Po.

For the rest, Book III of the *Historiae* may be left to speak for itself. From the outset, from the Flavian council of war at Poetovio in Pannonia to the final dramatic scene, the fate of Vitellius, it is a miracle of speed and splendour.

Wisdom after the event bedevils all historical exposition; and not all critics are willing to concur in the judgement of Julius Caesar—fortune or accident is dominant in military affairs as elsewhere.[2] It is not at all evident that systematic principles of strategy could operate regularly in the campaigns of the year 69. To most of the participants it was in truth a novel and unprecedented form of warfare. Though the army of Upper Germany had fought a pitched battle in the War of Vindex, their opponents were a rabble. Britain and a rebellion of the tribes furnished the latest experience of Suetonius Paullinus—not very useful against disciplined infantry. Other generals had been beyond the Euphrates with Domitius Corbulo in the high plains and mountains of Armenia:[3] that is to say, hard training, long marches, and never a battle. The military reputations complacently reported in the annals of the Empire bore witness to a senator's supervision of operations against natives, his performance of peace-time routine, or

---

[1] III. 9. 1; 14, cf. K. Wellesley, *CQ* XLIX (1956), 207 ff. Mommsen discovered that the Vitellian legions in their retreat must have marched to the south of the Po, *Ges. Schr.* IV, 363. Not, however, in a vast circuit by Parma—rather to Brixellum, where they could cross the Po again, cf. L. Valmaggi, *Klio* IX (1909), 252 f. Dessau takes them north of the Po by Mantua towards Cremona (*Gesch. der. r. Kaiserzeit* II (1926), 358 f.): if so, they would have impinged on the Flavian forces.   [2] *BC* III. 68. 1.

[3] e.g. Marius Celsus (*Ann.* xv. 25. 3). There is no evidence about any previous employments of Ap. Annius Gallus (*suff.* c. 66) or of T. Vestricius Spurinna (still praetorian).

an undeviating loyalty to the government. In the first civil disturbance
for a century Roman generals now faced armies they had trained.

That was not the worst. The legionaries, clients though they were
of the dynasty, acquitted their duty more from the habit of obedience
than from passionate enthusiasm. The fall of Nero, advertising the
purple for competition, fired the spirit of the troops—pride in legion
or army, rancour or contempt for the rest, and a fanatical devotion to
the candidate of their choice. The ranks grew intolerant of orders,
hostile to officers. As in the old wars, there were soldiers' battles now,
tenacious and murderous, mocking the hesitations of their commanders. That was an early stage in civil strife. The time had not yet
come for the comprehensive acts of treason and the mass desertions.

When discipline, inexorable in the years of peace, relaxed utterly,
the soldiery recaptured, as it were, the rights of citizens. They argued
and shouted, chose leaders or did without them. Coercion was impracticable, and persuasion might call for something more than the
tact and patience of Vestricius Spurinna. Caecina ensnared their
affections by youth and vigour, impressive stature, and a clever
address.[1] But the chief exponent of the new eloquence of the camps was
a ruffian and a demagogue, Antonius Primus—energetic and ready of
tongue, a master of calumny, feud, and faction, rapacious and yet
lavish, an evil man in peace and a precious partisan for war.[2]

The turbulence of legionaries and Praetorians, their pride, anger,
and devotion are properly and abundantly illustrated by Cornelius
Tacitus. The marches and manœuvres of troops are not his main preoccupation. To achieve an historian's purpose, he adds or abbreviates,
selects a fact or develops a scene, freely and wilfully. The armies of
Valens and of Caecina, how they marched from the Rhine to the Alps,
furnish an instructive document of his methods.

Tacitus does not allot equal space and detail. Valens' peregrinations
through peaceful territories were longer and slower. That is not the
only factor. The two narratives must be taken in close conjunction
with what precedes—how and why Vitellius was proclaimed on the
Rhine. A brief notice in the second preface of the *Historiae* prepared
the ground.[3] Tacitus now explains the situation fully—commanders
and officers, the temper of the troops, and the condition of Gaul,
largely determined by the disturbances of the previous year.[4] The
legionaries, slow to desert Nero and averse from Galba, were resentful

---

[1] I. 53. 1: 'decorus iuventa, corpore ingens, animi immodicus, scito sermone, erecto
incessu, studia militum inlexerat.'

[2] II. 86. 2: 'strenuus manu, sermone promptus, serendae in alios invidiae artifex, discordiis
et seditionibus potens, raptor, largitor, pace pessimus, bello non spernendus.' For Tacitus'
varying (but not unjust) portrayal see M. Treu, *Würzburger Jahrbücher* III (1948), 241 ff.

[3] I. 7.   [4] 52 ff.

against the partisans of Vindex, exalted by a new confidence in their strength, eager for war and greedy for rapine in Gaul on the way; and the adjacent tribes went with them. The ambitions of Fabius Valens and Caecina Alienus, their detestable characters, and their activity in fomenting trouble are vividly delineated: the one denounced Verginius to Galba, and had been instrumental in contriving the murder of the legate of Lower Germany, the other, after conspicuous services rendered to Galba in Spain, had been found out in peculation.[1]

The sequel discloses generals and soldiers behaving as might be expected. Caecina's enormities are confined to a single but variegated and pathetic scene among the Helvetii.[2] There is much more about Valens, and valuable details—for example, a panic and a massacre among the Mediomatrici, a riot stirred up by the rivalry between the Roman troops and the Batavian auxiliaries.[3] Noteworthy also is the feud between imperial Lugdunum, fanatically loyal to the memory of Nero, and Vienna of the Allobroges (which had supported Vindex), or the threat to set fire to a Vocontian town.[4] Vienna was preserved by its rank and dignity—or rather by a huge bribe to Valens, now flaunting a luxurious old age after a long life of sordid indigence.[5] Among the Vocontii land-owners and municipal magistrates had to pay imposts; and, if cash were not forthcoming, Valens could be assuaged by gratifications of another sort. 'Sic ad Alpes perventum.'[6]

A historian prone to the picturesque might have been tempted or perverted by literary tradition into serving up a description of the hazards and horrors of an Alpine crossing in winter. Tacitus is concerned with the behaviour of men and armies when the restraints of peace are suddenly removed. In comparison, the times and stages of troops on the march do not matter so much. Tacitus could cheerfully have discarded much of that narration without loss to the understanding of the campaign as a whole.

Not that Tacitus should be held lightly—both his accuracy in military matters and his honesty deserve recognition. Errors there may be, as when he presents Syria with one legion too many;[7] he is not always careful to discriminate between legions and *vexillationes*;[8] he

---

[1] I. 52. 3 (Valens); 53. 1 (Caecina).   [2] 67 ff.   [3] 63 f.   [4] 65 f.

[5] 66. 2: 'is diu sordidus repente dives mutationem fortunae male tegebat, accensis egestate longa cupidinibus immoderatus et inopi iuventa senex prodigus.'

[6] 66. 3.

[7] 10. 1; II. 4. 4; 6. 2; 76. 5. There were three legions at this time in Syria (not four), and three in Judaea. Also the 'delecta octo milia' taken by Vitellius from the army of Britain (II. 57. 1) will not be accurate if it represents *vexillationes* from four legions—there were three, XIV Gemina having been removed by Nero (II. 11, &c.). Tacitus does not, however, go wrong about any named legion. Modern scholars are sometimes less careful. Thus Dessau puts XI Claudia in Moesia, *Gesch. der r. Kaiserzeit* II (1926), 338.

[8] e.g. II. 85. 1 (the legions of Moesia).

mentions only one of the camps of the legions in Pannonia, Dalmatia, and Moesia (namely Poetovio); and he fails to reveal whether or no certain portions of those armies arrived in time for the Battle of Bedriacum.[1] But the mistakes are not numerous. In topography, however, the historian betrays negligence or a misconception when defining the goal of the Othonian march towards Cremona: hence an error of the first magnitude.[2] Elsewhere compression leads to obscurity, and he is sometimes reckless in attributing motive.

Much will depend upon the authorities used by Tacitus. Various strands and sources can be traced. Thus the sharp intense portrayal of what happened at Rome in the streets and the Forum goes back to eyewitnesses. Another authority has described the events at headquarters on the Rhine. Behind the itinerary of Fabius Valens there is perhaps an official report, and familiarity with Gaul and with Gallia Narbonensis in particular.[3] The Helvetian episode contains an odd item of some value;[4] and the angry suspicions of the 'municipale vulgus' at Placentia can be hit off in a telling phrase.[5] Persons in the entourage of Otho at Brixellum were able to diagnose the Emperor's frame of mind;[6] yet Tacitus can also chronicle perplexity and discord among the senators left behind at Mutina.[7]

The fighting in northern Italy from Spurinna's defence of Placentia to the Battle of Bedriacum is narrated almost wholly from the Othonian side. The treatment of the various generals is instructive. Spurinna's action, though subsidiary, is copiously narrated, and he shows to advantage, conciliatory yet firm in managing the turbulent soldiery.[8] Then, save for a single non-committal item, he is allowed to fade out, perhaps mercifully: there is no sign of his whereabouts during the

[1] p. 162, with App. 31.

[2] II. 40. 1, cf. pp. 163 f., and App. 30.

[3] cf. F. Köster, *Der Marsch der Invasionsarmee des Fabius Valens vom Niederrhein nach Italien* (Diss. Münster, 1927). Note also the careful detail in the account of the abortive operations on the coastal border of Italy and Narbonensis (II. 12 ff.). Further, and later in the same year, the capture of Fabius Valens by Valerius Paullinus, procurator of Narbonensis and stationed at Forum Julii, his own town of origin (III. 43. 1). The elder Pliny was possibly the next procurator (*NH* XIV. 43), cf. p. 61.

[4] The performance of a Helvetian orator is commended, 'Claudius Cossus, unus ex legatis, notae facundiae sed dicendi artem apta trepidatione occultans atque eo validior' (I. 69).

[5] II. 21. 2: 'municipale vulgus, pronum ad suspiciones, fraude inlata ignis alimenta credidit a quibusdam ex vicinis coloniis invidia et aemulatione, quod nulla in Italia moles tam capax foret.'

[6] Julius Secundus is cited by Plutarch, *Otho* 9. Note also Plutarch's friend and patron, the consular L. Mestrius Florus, in whose company he visited the battlefield (*Otho* 14): nothing emerges about strategy, tactics, or topography.

[7] II. 52 f.

[8] 18 f.; 20 f.; Plutarch, *Otho* 5 f.

battle or at the surrender.[1] Of the principal commanders, Salvius Titianus and Licinius Proculus come off badly. They encourage Otho to do battle, and they refuse to listen to Suetonius Paullinus and Marius Celsus on the morning of the fatal day.[2] Again, although Paullinus is senior in rank and fame, Celsus seems to acquire the greater prominence. Paullinus is censured for an excess of caution,[3] but of Celsus there is only praise (stated or implied) for vigour, sagacity, and honesty.[4]

In their report of the Battle of Bedriacum, those who were there refused to pledge their own accuracy, so it is credibly averred.[5] From the Vitellians there was little to report in this battle, or in the next. Tacitus confesses to uncertainty about their order of battle outside Cremona, which is not surprising.[6] No active partisan of Vitellius is known to have written history or memoirs.

The narration of the Flavian advance into Italy exhibits a proper appreciation of military matters. It registers scrupulously the arrival of reinforcements, the plans and motives of the generals are explained —and authorities are cited by name. Only twice, be it noted. A certain Vipstanus Messalla, tribune in command of a legion, guarantees a striking incident in the night battle;[7] and, for the burning of Cremona, his testimony is balanced against that of the elder Pliny, who put the blame on Antonius Primus.[8]

Finally, in sequel to a Roman civil war, the rebellion on the Rhine that threatened the whole fabric of Empire. Though it started in 69, Tacitus conveniently postpones it to Book IV. Envoys and missives from the Flavian generals were the cause or excuse, trying to prevent the despatch of reinforcements for the armies of Vitellius.[9] Julius Civilis, resentful himself on various counts against the Romans, worked upon the grievances of his own people; the eight Batavian cohorts, proud and truculent, soon took a hand; and tribes of the free Germans from across the river joined with alacrity in attacking the legionary garrisons, a weak and depleted remnant. Sporadic operations ensued, and a counter-move—not from the consular legate (Hordeonius Flaccus), who was tired and incompetent, but from one of the legionary commanders, Dillius Vocula. After the news of

(margin annotation:) GALLIC REVOLT

---

[1] Spurinna is last heard of leaving Placentia and bringing the greater part of his troops to the main theatre of operations (II. 36).

[2] II. 33. 1; 40.   [3] 25. 2.   [4] App. 32.

[5] Plutarch, *Otho* 14: οὕτω μὲν οἱ πλεῖστοι τῶν παραγενομένων ἀπαγγέλλουσι γενέσθαι τὴν μάχην, οὐδ᾽ αὐτοὶ σαφῶς ὁμολογοῦντες εἰδέναι τὰ καθ᾽ ἕκαστα διὰ τὴν ἀταξίαν καὶ τὴν ἀνωμαλίαν. This statement does not prove that Plutarch was using more than one written source.

[6] III. 22. 2: 'ordinem agminis disiecti per iram ac tenebras adseverare non ausim.'

[7] 25. 2.   [8] 28.   [9] IV. 13. 2, cf. V. 26. 3.

Cremona, Civilis could no longer keep up the pretence that he was a partisan of Vespasian in conflict with the Vitellian legions; and a fresh complication supervened when, after the burning of the Capitol, and other signs or reports that the Roman rule was verging upon catastrophe, certain Gallic tribes in the military zone of the Rhine armies, notably the Treveri and the Lingones, who had fought beside the legions against Vindex, now broke into open revolt and attempted to set up an independent 'imperium Galliarum'.

The prime movers were Julius Classicus, of royal stock among the Treveri, and Julius Sabinus the Lingonian, who claimed descent from Caesar the proconsul of Gaul.[1] Roman legionaries made a capitulation, surrendering Dillius Vocula to death, and took an oath of allegiance to the Gallic cause; and, although there was no harmony of act or policy among the insurgents, and the Gallic leaders got little help or encouragement in inner Gaul, Civilis was able in the end to capture the legionary camp at Vetera before the first Roman armies could cross the Alps and begin the reconquest of the Rhineland.

As a specimen of narrative the story of the Batavian war commands assent and admiration, in the face of all the stock charges levelled against a writer who insists upon style and colour.[2] The only military defects that can be discovered are trivial or illusory. Dillius Vocula relieved Vetera, but left that place, taking part of the garrison with him and retreating some distance, so that Civilis was able to invest it once more.[3] The historian has been censured because he did not bother (or did not choose) to adduce the motives influencing a Roman general when he made a decision that turned out to be a mistake;[4] and at a later stage a renewed march on Vetera is reported without explanation.[5] Again, when Petillius Cerialis, after a three days' march from Moguntiacum, meets and defeats the Gallic forces at Rigodulum, not far from the city of the Treveri, the battle is told too briefly for the taste of some critics.[6] Yet the topography and manner of that rapid encounter is clear enough.[7]

Though at times rhetorical (and speeches were needed),[8] the Tacitean

---

[1] IV. 55.

[2] For this type of criticism see, for example, A. Stein, P-W x, 550; E. Swoboda, ib. XIX, 1141; G. Walser, *Rom, das Reich und die fremden Völker in der Geschichtsschreibung der frühen Kaiserzeit* (1951), 86 ff. [3] 35.

[4] B. W. Henderson, o.c. 276: 'the one military puzzle of this war'; G. Walser, o.c. 101.

[5] 57. 1. G. Walser (o.c. 111 f.) enlarges upon Tacitus' omission.

[6] 71. 4 f. E. Sadée (*Bonner Jahrbücher* CXXXII (1927), 165 ff.) discovers abruptness, omissions, and a lack of interest in the general strategic plan.

[7] K. Schumacher, *Mainzer Zeitschr.* VI (1911), 8 ff.

[8] Notable for various reasons are the orations of Dillius Vocula (IV. 58) and Petillius Cerialis (IV. 73 f.)—but even more valuable the exchanges between the Tencteri and the citizens of Colonia Claudia (IV. 64 f.), cf. p. 453.

narrative is very precise. It reveals a number of towns or small tribes in the Rhineland that occur nowhere else in Latin literature, unless it be in the *Naturalis Historia* of Pliny.[1] Further, the Germans are shown in a much less favourable light than in the *Germania* of Cornelius Tacitus. Hypocrisy, cruelty, and torture are disclosed.[2] Their superstitious veneration for priestesses (Veleda in particular) contradicts a statement in the *Germania*;[3] and one learns about images of animals, kept in sacred groves and carried in battle.[4] An expert's eye has picked out the detail of native rites and customs—thus the choice of a war-leader by raising him upon a shield.[5]

Local knowledge or an accurate military report was not enough. The Batavian rebellion was confused and confusing—auxiliary troops against Roman legions, native tribes against the Roman dominion—and, as it spread, it involved a wide region. Civil war or foreign, where ought the emphasis to fall? And there were disturbing factors. Partisans of Vespasian had stirred up trouble on the Rhine. It would be expedient afterwards to find a scapegoat—or otherwise extenuate and disguise the responsibility of the Flavians. The principal source followed by Tacitus was not exempt from these preoccupations.[6]

[1] cf. the prime and indispensable study of F. Münzer, *Bonner Jahrbücher* CIV (1899), 67 ff. The small tribes Baetasii, Cugerni, Marsaci, and Sunuci are mentioned by these two sources only; and the only other writer to distinguish the Canninefates from the Batavi is Velleius (II. 105. 1), who had served on the Rhine. Similarly for place-names. Thus Gelduba (IV. 26. 3, &c.; Pliny, *NH* XIX. 90), while Asciburgium (IV. 33. 1) occurs only in the *Germania* (3. 3). Note also Bingium (IV. 70. 4), Marcodurum (IV. 28. 2), Tolbiacum (IV. 79. 2), and a whole cluster—Arenacum, Batavodurum, Grinnes, and Vada (V. 20. 1). Ptolemy happens to register Batavodurum (II. 9. 8): the other places are attested only on inscriptions, in the *Itineraries* and late authors—or not at all.

[2] Note the hypocrisy of the Tencteri (IV. 64), or Civilis allegedly offering his small son prisoners for archery practice (61. 1); and it is not stated what fate was reserved for the legionary legate 'inter dona missus Veledae' (61. 2).

[3] 61. 2: 'ea virgo nationis Bructerae late imperitabat, vetere apud Germanos more quo plerasque feminarum fatidicas et augescente superstitione arbitrantur deas'; *Germ.* 8. 3: 'vidimus sub divo Vespasiano Veledam diu apud plerosque numinis loco habitam; sed et olim Albrunam et compluris alias venerati sunt, non adulatione nec tamquam facerent deas.'

[4] 22. 2: 'depromptae silvis lucisque ferarum imagines, ut cuique genti inire proelium mos est.'

[5] 15. 2: 'impositusque scuto more gentis et sustinentium umeris vibratus dux deligitur.' Pliny had an eye for native customs, cf. the casual remark about their token of submission, 'quem morem etiam nunc durare apud Germanos scio' (*NH* XXII. 8). It is reasonable to follow Münzer and hold that Tacitus used Pliny for the Batavian War, cf. also E. Norden, *Die germanische Urgeschichte in Tacitus Germania*[3] (1923), 211 ff. Not, however, the *Bella Germaniae*, as some incautiously assume, e.g. G. Walser, o.c. 127; E. Paratore, *Tacito* (1951), 513. There is no evidence that the work went beyond 47. Nor is it likely that Pliny during the period 70–75 was engaged upon two separate accounts of what happened on the Rhine in 69 and 70.

[6] Münzer, o.c. 85 ff. This main source, he argues, was Pliny; and he shows how Tacitus prematurely interpolated into the middle of remarks about the Canninefates a reference to the Batavian regiments—'mox occultis nuntiis pellexit Britannica auxilia,

Some of the blame could be laid on Antonius Primus, because of the missive he sent to Civilis.[1] Another way was to emphasize the tribal insurrections rather than the civil war.[2]

Dillius Vocula is the Roman hero of the Batavian War, perhaps embellished by Tacitus.[3] Petillius Cerialis terminated the rebellion of Gauls and Germans. Tacitus' portrayal of this man is notable for several reasons.[4] Cerialis was bold and dashing, and very careless. At his first introduction in the *Historiae*, when the Flavian forces were marching on Rome, he incurs censure, too slow at the outset but later by rashness responsible for a defeat and a rout.[5] Arriving on the Rhine, Cerialis is buoyant and boastful.[6] Though he wins a victory at Rigodulum, occupying the city of the Treveri the next day, the Romans soon after come close to a disaster when suddenly attacked in the early morning—the general had not been sleeping in camp that night.[7] On a later occasion one of Cerialis' absences is duly certificated by the historian—a lady is named, a certain Claudia Sacrata.[8]

An isolated detail anywhere might yield a clue. The large question remains: which were the author's main sources all through, and how did he employ them? The events narrated in Books I and II will repay a closer investigation, because a parallel narrative has survived.[9]

Batavorum cohortis missas in Germaniam, ut supra rettulimus, ac tum Moguntiaci agentis' (IV. 15. 1, cf. II. 69. 1). An attempt to correct the Plinian version.

[1] 13. 2; v. 26. 3. Cf. Münzer, o.c. 101.

[2] As blatantly in Josephus, *BJ* VII. 75 ff. But Pliny, it appears, was not guiltless, cf. Münzer, o.c. 85 ff. Tacitus is severely (and unjustly) blamed by Walser for having adopted this conception in its entirety (o.c. 127, followed by E. Paratore, o.c. 519).

[3] Ph. Fabia, *Studi Romani* II (1914), 153 ff. Dillius would not be known but for Tacitus and the inscription set up by his wife Helvia Procula (*ILS* 983: Rome).

[4] cf. E. Swoboda, P-W XIX, 1138 ff.

[5] III. 78 f.

[6] IV. 71. 1: 'ipse pugnae avidus et contemnendis quam cavendis hostibus melior.'

[7] 77. 1. He behaved in this battle 'felici temeritate' (ib. 2), and redeemed his carelessness—'ut incuria prope rem adflixit ita constantia restituit' (78. 2). Cf., on a later occasion, 'subitus consiliis et eventu clarus' (v. 21. 3).

[8] v. 22. 3: "Cerialis alibi noctem egerat, ut plerique credidere, ob stuprum Claudiae Sacratae mulieris Ubiae.' Cerialis was a friend and relative of Vespasian (III. 59. 2). Not heard of after his second consulate in 74, but the family stood high for a time. Observe Q. Petillius Rufus, *cos. II ord.* in 83, its last recorded member.

[9] Namely the unknown annalist as reproduced by Plutarch in his *Galba* and *Otho*, cf. Ch. XVI, with App. 29.

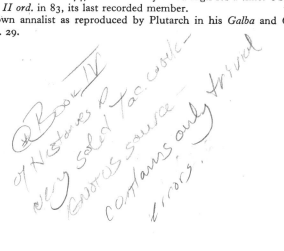

XVI. HISTORICAL SOURCES

TACITUS' own early experiences may have contributed something to his vivid intense picture of what happened before all men's eyes in Rome. When twelve or thirteen years old, Tacitus may have surveyed from a temple or a mansion the tumult in the Forum and the killing of Galba; he may have seen the exits and the entrances of emperors and of armies, the fighting in the streets or the suburbs, the flames of the Capitol. To postulate his presence in Rome, however, would be a cheap device, neglecting the quality of Tacitus' main source for those events—and denying his imaginative powers.

There survived eyewitnesses in abundance. Some had been at the heart of action or behind the scenes, and were ready to tell the truth.[1] Respect for the aged is an amiable feature of aristocratic society; and the elderly senator, if sometimes tedious in his propensity to compare old things and new, might transmit, along with moralizing and anecdote, a copious volume of rare and authentic history. The sagacious Veiento, the Nestor of the age, lived on to adorn Trajan's Senate for a year or two.[2] Silius Italicus also survived, consul of the year 68 and present at secret negotiations between the Emperor Vitellius and Vespasian's brother in the Temple of Apollo.[3] Both Aquillius Regulus and Junius Mauricus were already in the Senate at that time.[4] Above all, three eminent consulars in the circle of Pliny call for a mention— Arrius Antoninus, consul in 69, Julius Frontinus, praetor in 70, and Vestricius Spurinna, who commanded a detachment for Otho in the early stages of the campaign of Bedriacum.

Whether Tacitus ever went on a visit to old Silius in his Campanian retreat, or sojourned with Julius Frontinus on the coast at Tarracina or Formiae, zealous to extract information before it was too late, is a question beyond the asking.[5] He might have applied to Spurinna.

---

[1] cf. *Hist.* IV. 81. 3 (on the miracles of Vespasian at Alexandria): 'utrumque qui interfuere nunc quoque memorant, postquam nullum mendacio pretium.'

[2] Last attested in 98 (*Pan.* 58. 1), but long known to Tacitus as a member of the *XVviri s.f.*

[3] III. 65. 2.

[4] IV. 42. 1 (Regulus); 40. 4 (Mauricus, cf. Plutarch, *Galba* 8, referring to the year 68).

[5] Frontinus at Tarracina (Martial x. 58. 1); at Formiae (Aelian, *Tactica, praef.*, cf. *PIR²*, A 128). Frontinus could have told something about his military operations in Gaul in 70, against the Lingones (*Strat.* IV. 3. 14), to say nothing of later events. Other persons of note who had been active in 68 or 69 were Q. Pomponius Rufus (*suff.* 95) who had a post under Galba (*IRT* 537), and Cn. Pompeius Longinus (*suff.* 90)—if he could be identified with Galba's friend Pompeius Longinus, tribune in the Guard (*Hist.* I. 31. 3).

What he says of Spurinna's operations is not only much more full and explicit than the other account surviving. It looks apologetic.[1]

Verbal instruction, and some of it not less valuable, could have been supplied by men of lower rank—legates and tribunes, equestrian officers or procurators. Antonius Primus, whose desperate energy prevailed over the timidity and sloth of the consular commanders on the Flavian side, winning the war for Vespasian in northern Italy, was cheated of public recognition and consigned to retirement. As late as 95 he was still alive, robust and cheerful in his native Tolosa.[2] But the boastful Antonius might not command full credence as a witness—and his earliest notoriety came from his part in the forging of a will.[3] The dashing Cornelius Fuscus, who by contrast benefits from a favourable presentation by Tacitus, had perished commanding Domitian's army in the invasion of Dacia.[4]

The eloquent and accomplished Julius Secundus, Tacitus' friend, was secretary to Otho and present at the Emperor's end after the defeat at Bedriacum.[5] Secundus, however, had been dead many years before Tacitus thought of writing history. By an odd chance, certain equestrian relatives of Pliny enjoyed a remarkably late survival—one who came to grief under Nero, another who had been an officer in the Flavian army invading Italy.[6]

Whatever the information still to be culled from the living, Tacitus did not have to make anxious search and questionings, at least for events in the year 69. Narratives were to hand, some of great merit, others though respectable yet needing to be cautiously appraised. Pompeius Planta, a knight who rose to high office, wrote about the Battle of Bedriacum.[7] For Cremona there was the memoir of the honest Vipstanus Messalla, Tacitus' friend: he was military tribune and temporarily commanding a legion under Antonius Primus.[8] Certain relevant biographies are also attested.[9] For the events (or

---

[1] p. 171. Not, however, that Tacitus' account need derive anywhere directly from Spurinna, although the old fellow was still alive c. 105 (*Epp.* v. 17).

[2] Martial x. 23.   [3] *Ann.* xiv. 40. 2.   [4] See App. 33.   [5] Plutarch, *Otho* 9.

[6] L. Calpurnius Fabatus (*Ann.* xvi. 8. 3), the grandfather of Pliny's third wife (*Epp.* iv. 1, &c.), and Minicius Justus, *praef. castrorum* of the Seventh Legion (*Hist.* iii. 7. 1), husband of a Corellia (*Epp.* vii. 11. 4), and named in the testament of L. Dasumius in 108 (*CIL* vi, 10229, l. 19).

[7] *Schol.* on Juvenal ii. 99: 'horum bellum scripsit Cornelius, scripsit et Pompeius Planta, qui ait Bebriacum vicum esse a Cremona vicesimo lapide.' Planta died c. 108, cf. Pliny, writing to his enemy Maximus (i.e. C. Vibius Maximus, also an ex-prefect of Egypt), and urging him now to publish his attack on Planta (*Epp.* ix. 1).

[8] iii. 9. 3: 'claris maioribus, egregius ipse et qui solus ad id bellum bonas artes attulisset.' He is cited in iii. 25 and 28. There is no harm in making Messalla the principal and preferred source for the campaign of Cremona, cf. E. Paratore, *Tacito* (1951), 574 ff.

[9] Not merely the famous biography of Helvidius Priscus by Herennius Senecio. A certain

intrigues) before the proclamation of Vespasian in the East, the testimony of Licinius Mucianus could have been highly instructive. The great Mucianus did not need to write an apologia—he was vindicated by success and two more consulates. Instead, he compiled volumes of extracts about natural curiosities and edited ancient documents.[1] Vespasian's own *Commentarii* existed, not perhaps going beyond the military record of his campaigns in Judaea;[2] and one of the procurators had composed a treatise about the Jews.[3]

The inquiry about the sources of Tacitus involves three historical works of some merit and magnitude, and three authors not a little disparate in character, tastes, and accomplishment.[4] Cluvius Rufus the consular was eloquent and wealthy; he had a mild character and conspicuous social attainments.[5] A favoured figure at the court of Nero, he would act as the announcer when the Emperor performed as a singer, both in the capital and on the peregrination of Hellas.[6] Yet Cluvius never used his influence for noxious purposes. Appointed by Galba to govern Hispania Tarraconensis, he duly transferred his allegiance to Otho, and from Otho to Vitellius. In itself a change of side in civil war need not damage the credit of a senatorial historian. Cluvius, it appears, was more indulgent towards Nero than were other writers.[7] Yet it is judgement and equity rather than any Neronian predilections of Cluvius Rufus that can be detected in a famous edificatory anecdote.

Ti. Claudius Pollio (*Epp.* VII. 31, cf. *ILS* 1418) wrote a life of L. Annius Bassus, legate of XI Claudia in 69 (*Hist.* III. 50. 2, where his conduct is praised).

[1] *Dial.* 37. 2: 'haec vetera, quae et in antiquariorum bibliothecis adhuc manent et cum maxime a Muciano contrahuntur, ac iam undecim, ut opinor, *Actorum* libris et tribus *Epistularum* composita et edita sunt.' As for his *mirabilia*, thirty-two items are preserved in Pliny, *NH*: quoted in Peter, *HRR* II (1906), 101 ff.

[2] Josephus, *Vita* 342. They have been discussed at great length by W. Weber, *Josephus und Vespasian* (1920), 106 ff., who, however, insists that Tacitus only knew them through Pliny the Elder (o.c. 148).

[3] That is, if M. Antonius Julianus (Josephus, *BJ* VI. 238) is the same as the Antonius Julianus in Minucius Felix, *Octavius* 33. 4. E. Norden was strongly in favour of their identity, *Neue Jahrbücher* XXXI (1913), 664. Tacitus' source for Jewish antiquities and history has been the subject of much discussion, cf. A. M. A. Hospers-Jansen, *Tacitus over de Joden* (Diss. Utrecht, 1949). A number of scholars claim Pliny as the sole or principal source. One support is invalid, for it is not to be believed that Pliny is the *Ignotus* of the inscription *OGIS* 586 (Aradus), an equestrian officer present at the siege of Jerusalem; cf. the arguments of F. Münzer, *Bonner Jahrbücher* CIV (1899), 103 ff. As evidence of Tacitus' own erudition, note the claim he prefixes to his digression on Serapis—'origo dei nondum nostris auctoribus celebrata' (IV. 83. 1).

[4] Namely Cluvius Rufus, the elder Pliny, and Fabius: all sources for the reign of Nero, cf. Ch. XXIII. The book of Ph. Fabia, *Les Sources de Tacite dans les* Histoires *et les* Annales (1893), is erudite but doctrinaire. A better guide is E. Groag, *Jahrbücher für cl. Phil.*, Supp.-Band XXIII (1897), 711 ff. The opinions of these and of other scholars are briefly discussed in App. 29.

[5] I. 8. 1: 'vir facundus et pacis artibus, belli inexpertus.'

[6] Suetonius, *Nero* 21. 2; Dio LXIII. 14. 3.   [7] Ch. XXIII.

Cluvius, with appeal to the sanctity of history, once asked Verginius Rufus to bear him no ill will if he found in his works some things not wholly to his liking.[1] Verginius gave the answer forthwith: he had done what he did in order that historians might be free to tell the truth. What had Cluvius in mind? The one thing that might need to be palliated or disguised in Verginius' conduct was his fidelity to Nero, when Vindex rose, when Galba was proclaimed, and for some time afterwards. Verginius in his epitaph made a firm assertion of patriotic loyalty to Rome.[2] Perhaps the words conflate the facts. If the defeat of Vindex saved Rome and the Empire, it should also have saved Nero; and Verginius' professed allegiance to the Caesar recognized by Senate and People covered allegiance to Nero until Nero was legally deposed.[3] Galba, the ally of Vindex, was not likely to advertise that awkward truth, and the friends of Verginius did not trumpet it abroad. Instead, the comforting story was put out that Verginius and Vindex at a secret meeting agreed to concert their efforts; their patriotic design was frustrated by Verginius' army, eager to be at the Gallic rebels.[4] Cluvius (one may conjecture) made the attitude of Verginius quite clear.

The histories of Cluvius perhaps began with Caligula, and embraced the reigns of Claudius and Nero, terminating either with Nero's death or with the end of the year 68. It is not likely, however, that he went on into the next year to round off the story with Galba, Otho, and Vitellius.[5]

While Cluvius essayed some defence of Nero, and of his own behaviour, another historian, Fabius Rusticus, was relentless against the tyrant, if only because eulogistic of Seneca, his patron. Fabius came from Spain, and was perhaps not a senator.[6] He certainly wrote of Nero's reign, and he might have dealt with the year 69 as well.[7]

Fabius Rusticus earned the highest of commendations, being reckoned for the splendour of his prose style as equivalent to a new Livy—'Livius veterum, Fabius Rusticus recentium eloquentissimi auctores.'[8] Style of this essence, or the artistic arrangement of a narrative, was beyond the compass of the elder Pliny. Yet he possessed

---

[1] *Epp.* IX. 19. 5.   [2] VI. 10. 4, cited above, p. 99.
[3] cf. R. Syme, *AJP* LVIII (1937), 12 f.
[4] Dio LXIII. 24, cf. Plutarch, *Galba* 6.   [5] See App. 29.
[6] *PIR*², F 62. For Fabii Rustici in Spain, *CIL* II, 1070 (Arva); 2015 = *ILS* 1354 (Singilia Barba): not, however, of any consequence.
[7] The contrary assumption of Fabia (o.c. 211) is too positive—and certain other scholars have simply neglected Fabius Rusticus.
[8] *Agr.* 10. 3. It is generally assumed that Fabius is indicated in Quintilian X. 1. 104: 'superest adhuc et exornat aetatis nostrae gloriam vir saeculorum memoria dignus, qui olim nominabitur nunc intellegitur.' Still alive in 108, if he is the Fabius Rusticus in the testament of L. Dasumius (*CIL* VI, 10229, l. 24).

singular merits of accuracy and diligence. The second of his comprehensive historical works was an annalistic record in thirty-one books,
beginning where an earlier writer, Aufidius Bassus, had left off.[1] For
the end of Pliny's own *Historiae* a convenient point would be the
triumph over the Jews in the summer of 71 and the closing of the
temple of Janus, with an inspiring epilogue on the new Augustus,
the felicity of the times, and the return of order and concord symbolized by monarchy and monarchic succession.

Pliny completed the work some time before the year 77.[2] It was
certainly used by Tacitus, and some claim it as the main source perceptible both in his account of Galba and Otho and elsewhere. Various
reasons tell against that theory.[3]

Loyalty to a patron or a dynasty was more tenacious and more
conspicuous in the knight than in the senator. Pliny was anxious that
his histories should not be published in his lifetime lest he incur a
suspicion of subservience to the Flavian House.[4] Pliny's scruple shows
that he was aware of a prejudice in favour of the Flavians; and it is
clear that he was very bitter against the memory of Nero.[5] Now
Tacitus at the end of the second book of his *Historiae*, expounding the
treachery of Vitellius' general Caecina Alienus, adverts upon the
partiality of writers on the Flavian side—they spoke of patriotism and
the love of peace, in fraudulent palliation.[6] The censure touches Pliny.
Though an honest man and a lover of facts, he was prone to credulity
and enthusiasm. The Roman senator took a more sombre view of men
and motives.

In the *Historiae* of Cornelius Tacitus as extant, Pliny is cited once,
Vipstanus Messalla twice—but only for the second battle.[7] No other
authority is named. The main source remains—or rather the source
also used by the biographer Plutarch in his *Galba* and his *Otho*.
Plutarch shows a remarkable concordance in matter, arrangement,
and even here and there in phraseology.[8] The problem has given rise
to long discussions, often fruitless. A limited approach, without haste
for certitude, may not be wholly unremunerative.

Something can be discovered about the author thus presumed.[9]
His style was eloquent and flowing, sometimes ornate, and not without

---

[1] *Epp.* III. 5. 6, cf. further Ch. XXIII and App. 38.

[2] cf. *NH, praef.* 20.   [3] App. 29.

[4] *NH, praef.* 20: 'ubi sit ea quaeres? iam pridem peracta sancitum et alioqui statutum
erat heredi mandare, ne quid ambitioni dedisse vita iudicaretur.'

[5] p. 292.

[6] II. 101. 1 (p. 118). For these writers see now A. Briessmann, 'Tacitus und das flavische
Geschichtsbild' (*Hermes*, Einzelschriften 10, 1955).

[7] III. 28 (Pliny and Messalla); 25. 2 (Messalla).

[8] See App. 29. Suetonius also used this source.

[9] E. Groag, *Jahrbücher für cl. Phil.*, Supp.-Band XXIII (1897), 771 ff.

delight in point and antithesis. None the less, he was careful in collecting facts, and critical though not penetrating. Anecdotes attracted him, but he was not interested in the transactions of the Roman Senate, and he does not seem to have been a military man. He was present in Rome at the beginning of January 69. He knew more about the entourage of Otho than about that of Galba (though he was not accurate about Otho's marriage),[1] and could reveal the fact that Otho got his governorship in Spain through the influence of Seneca.[2] He was an acquaintance of Julius Secundus,[3] he could cite Cluvius Rufus,[4] and he had questioned eyewitnesses about the Battle of Bedriacum.[5]

Finally, the work of the unknown author was not biographical but annalistic. It dealt with Nero, and it included Vitellius as well as Galba and Otho.[6] It was composed later than 79. That conclusion emerges from the picture of Caecina Alienus as he came over the Alps into Italy, arrogant and offensive in his barbarian trousers.[7] Caecina, prospering from treason, enjoyed the favour and friendship of the new rulers—there is even the story of an amicable gladiatorial bout with Titus Caesar.[8] But Caecina in the year 79 was involved in a mysterious plot, alleged accomplice of Eprius Marcellus. After dining one evening with Titus he was summarily executed at the command of his host.[9]

The identity of the nameless historian defies inquiry.[10] More important is the indirect evidence that accrues, illustrating the methods and merits of Cornelius Tacitus. The Greek biographer was constrained to follow the source fairly closely—though he might abbreviate, he could not transmute, it was beyond his capacity, and it was not his intention. The Roman senator was free to add and subtract, remodel and reinterpret in the light of other sources, his own judgement, and his own artistic sense. Between Plutarch and Tacitus there are a number of discrepancies. What no mere catalogue can provide, a few salient examples will establish.

---

[1] I. 13. 3; Plutarch, *Galba* 19; Suetonius, *Otho* 3. 1. Tacitus was later able to correct this error, silently (*Ann.* XIII. 45. 4).

[2] Plutarch, *Galba* 20.

[3] *Otho* 9: καὶ τοῦτο μὲν διηγεῖτο Σεκοῦνδος ὁ ῥήτωρ.

[4] *Otho* 3: Κλούβιος ὁ 'Ροῦφος εἰς 'Ιβηρίαν φησὶ κομισθέντα διπλώματα . . . τὸ τοῦ Νέρωνος θετὸν ὄνομα προσγεγραμμένον ἔχοντα τῷ τοῦ "Οθωνος. Cf. Suetonius, *Otho* 7. 1. On the interpretation of this passage see App. 29.

[5] *Otho* 14.

[6] That it was used by Plutarch for his *Nero* may be inferred (from *Galba* 2). The continuance of the same source till the end of 69 is proved by concordance between Tacitus, *Hist.* III and Suetonius, *Vitellius*.

[7] II. 20. 1; *Otho* 6.   [8] Dio LXVI. 15. 2.   [9] p. 101.

[10] H. Peter, *HRR* II (1906), clv. Yet there is not a little to be said for Fabius Rusticus, supported by Groag, o.c. 787 ff.

Plutarch relating the adoption of Piso is scrappy and inaccurate.[1] On the news that Vitellius had been proclaimed by the armies of the Rhine, Galba, telling no man of his purpose, sent for Piso, took him to the camp, and there among the Praetorians announced that Piso was to be his son and successor. Tacitus is careful about the chronology —a dispatch had arrived from the procurator of Gallia Belgica reporting treason and riot at Moguntiacum on the first day of January, but about Vitellius as yet no certain report, only rumours.[2] Furthermore, Galba now calls a crown council (four dignitaries are mentioned).[3] He reveals his intention and his choice, and asks for Piso to be brought in.

If Tacitus in this matter deserted the source followed by Plutarch, it is no sign of especial perspicacity. To his own judgement and taste will be credited what follows, an oration by the old Emperor. By making Galba discourse on the theory of the Principate, Tacitus expounds, at the outset, a high political theme.[4] Galba seems to speak, as the 'res publica' should speak, in sober and lapidary language. He presents in the most convincing form the commonplaces of official eloquence and all the special pleadings of politicians.[5] The facts give the lie—the inept choice of Piso Licinianus to be ruler of Rome. And the obituary notice on Galba seals the condemnatory verdict on an Emperor's incapacity.

The unknown annalist pays his farewell tribute to Galba eloquently and admirably. It contains phrases that Tacitus might have taken over, such as the antithesis between fame and power;[6] and there is force and point in the description of Galba, an old-fashioned and feeble ruler, dominated no less than was Nero by his ministers and his freedmen.[7] But there is something conventional in the rhetoric, revealed by the evocation of Scipio, Fabricius, and Camillus.[8] Tacitus goes his own way. A series of inimitable epigrams, not neglecting the fact that Galba had been a governor on the Rhine and a proconsul of Africa, culminates in 'capax imperii nisi imperasset'.[9]

Taking leave of Galba, Tacitus, before passing on to narrate events

---

[1] *Galba* 23. O. Seeck, however, argued that Plutarch is here more credible than Tacitus, *Festschrift für O. Hirschfeld* (1903), 45 ff.

[2] I. 12. 1, cf. 14. 1.

[3] 14. 1 (T. Vinius and Cornelius Laco, also Marius Celsus, consul designate, and Ducenius Geminus, the Prefect of the City).

[4] 15 f. (paraphrased and condensed, above, p. 151 f.).   [5] cf. p. 207.

[6] *Galba* 29: τῇ δόξῃ μᾶλλον ἢ τῇ δυνάμει καθελὼν Νέρωνα.

[7] ib.: ἄκρατος ἦν καὶ ἀρχαῖος αὐτοκράτωρ, Οὐινίῳ δὲ καὶ Λάκωνι καὶ τοῖς ἀπελευθέροις πάντα τὰ πράγματα πωλοῦσι παρέχων ἑαυτόν, οἷον Νέρων παρεῖχε τοῖς ἀπληστοτάτοις.

[8] ib.: ὡς Σκιπίων ἦρχε καὶ Φαβρίκιος καὶ Κάμιλλος. Cf. Pliny, *Pan.* 13. 4; Juvenal II. 153 f. Instead of stock figures Tacitus would have preferred something like 'antiqui duces'.

[9] I. 49. 4.

on the Rhine, inserts, to facilitate the transition, a passage describing the impact made by the proclamation of Vitellius.[1] Civil war was now imminent between Otho and Vitellius. Men openly lamented that fate should have singled out the vilest persons imaginable to be the ruin of Rome. They recalled the Republic and the ominous names of catastrophe—Pharsalia, Philippi, Perusia, and Mutina. Though the contest for primacy shook the world, the victory of Caesar and the victory of Augustus did not break the empire of Rome; and, had Pompeius prevailed, or had Brutus, the 'res publica' would have endured. For which pretender now could men offer up their prayers? Only one thing was certain, 'deteriorem fore qui vicisset'. Some now turned their thoughts towards Vespasian and the armies of the East. But Vespasian's repute was ambiguous as yet.

This is pure Tacitus. He also exploits the mutiny of the Guard. There was probably no speech of the Emperor in Plutarch's source. Tacitus exhibits a deadly technique. Taken in isolation, or taken literally, the oration seems to disclose a new and exemplary Otho— not the corrupt and ambitious wastrel, but a ruler sagacious in discourse on the duties of the military, noble and eloquent when he invokes the majesty of Rome, the destiny of the Empire, the prestige of the Senate.[2]

The facts are enough. Otho was not a 'vir militaris', supporting like Sulpicius Galba the plea for order and discipline in the army. He was a usurper, created by plot and assassination, through favour and act of the Guard, and trembling or suppliant when they broke into the Palace. He then behaved unheroically, 'contra decus imperii'.[3]

Otho refers to the Guard as a source of aspirants to the Senate—his words can apply only to the officers, not to the ranks.[4] In honorific appellation (and not contradicted by the statistics of recruitment), he salutes them as 'Italiae alumni et Romana vere iuventus'.[5] In truth, a pack of ruffians. When the Praetorians were converted to a semblance of good behaviour, it was due not to their Emperor's exhortations but to hard cash, five thousand sesterces each man.

Defying and scouting the pretensions of his rival Vitellius, Otho claims that he has the 'res publica' and the Senate. What do these names avail? The senators dispersed in panic from the imperial banquet; and, when the august assembly is next convened, their behaviour is base, cowardly, and ludicrous.[6]

---

[1] 1. 50.   [2] 83 f. (p. 154).   [3] 82. 1.

[4] Tribunes commanding the Guard cohorts can pass rapidly into the procuratorial career and thus, belonging to the 'equestris nobilitas', are eligible for the Senate. It was not common for a soldier to go so far. Note, however, under Nero, Vettius Valens who rises to the procuratorship of Lusitania (*ILS* 2648: Ariminum).

[5] 84. 3.   [6] 85. 3.

Otho's departure from Rome for the war in the North furnishes another welcome opportunity. Plutarch gives a summary statement of Otho's dispositions, how he chose Vitellius' brother to be of his company on the journey, saw to it that the mother and the wife of Vitellius should come to no harm, and appointed Flavius Sabinus, Vespasian's brother, to be Prefect of the City.[1] Tacitus in this context chooses to mention only the brother of Vitellius.[2] He prefers to describe the setting and the atmosphere, to review the sentiments of the different orders—the chief men of the Senate, enfeebled by age or the long years of peace, the *nobilitas* that had lost the taste and tradition of warfare, and the unmilitary knights. Under a false show of alacrity, they only paraded their fears. Some went out in all the pride of horse and armour, others with the equipment of luxury and vice. The prudent thought of peace and the Commonwealth, while others, frivolous or impoverished, were borne up by vain hopes, seeking salvation or profit from hazard and danger.[3]

Such was the Emperor's retinue. Tacitus appends a digression on the emotions of the mob, now made to feel, for the first time since Augustus established the imperial system, the impact of civil war in its discomforts, its shortages, and its apprehensions.[4] Warfare had been far away, on the frontiers of the Empire. The attempt of Arruntius Camillus, rising against Claudius Caesar, had been crushed as soon as heard of. Rumour, not arms, overthrew Nero. But now a long war was in prospect, with all the resources of West and East. There is nothing of this either in Plutarch.

On the day of his setting forth, the Emperor summoned an assembly and spoke, extolling among other things the majesty of Rome and the unanimous loyalty of Senate and People.[5] The speech was not his own composition, so it was believed—and some could recognize the manner of Galerius Trachalus, ample and sonorous, familiar and long-famed in the courts of law, and well suited to impress the populace.[6] The adverse comment on the style of Galerius is palpably an addition of the historian who was also an orator, able to achieve solemnity without bombast. The next words tell what he thought of the populace. Their applause was loud and dishonest, as usual. They vied in zeal and devotion as though in attendance upon Caesar the Dictator or Caesar Augustus, but it was servility they took pleasure in, like the slaves of a household, each for his own advantage, and with no feeling for the dignity of the Commonwealth.

---

[1] *Otho* 5.   [2] I. 88. I.   [3] 88. 2 f.   [4] 89.

[5] 90. 2: 'maiestatem urbis et consensum populi ac senatus pro se attollens.'

[6] ib.: 'et erant qui genus ipsum orandi noscerent, crebro fori usu celebre et ad implendas populi auris latum et sonans.' Cf. Quintilian x. 1. 119: 'et vocis, quantam in nullo cognovi, felicitas et pronuntiatio vel scaenis suffectura.'

Tacitus' mastery over his materials is further signalized in the prelude to the Battle of Bedriacum. The historical sources reported a strange rumour: the opposing armies might refuse to fight, they might come to an agreement, electing the best candidate among the generals or leaving the choice to the Senate. That was why Otho's generals counselled delay, especially Suetonius Paullinus (according to Tacitus), for he was the senior consular and invested with the honour of warfare in Britain. In Plutarch's view the report about the legionaries seems to carry credence. Their ancestors had fought and suffered in the wars of Marius and Sulla, of Pompeius and Caesar; to endure the same fate on behalf of Otho or Vitellius, to treat the imperial power as a plaything for a wastrel or a glutton, that was abominable. Such beyond doubt were the feelings of those soldiers who had the genuine Roman stamp, disciplined in body and soberly reflective.[1]

The consular historian blights and withers these ingenuous and fanciful speculations.[2] In the silence of their hearts a few men may have prayed for peace and a virtuous emperor. But it was an indecent paradox to credit the criminal soldiery with such innocuous yearnings. Suetonius Paullinus knew better. Moreover, the heterogeneous armies could never have discovered any spring of common action—and most of the officers, needy, avid, and vicious, wanted a prince as depraved as themselves, and docile in return for services rendered.

Tacitus is not content to denounce the troops and their commanders. He fastens on the theme as an excuse for a digression on the love of power; and he evokes the civil wars of the Republic as a device for exposing the gullibility of other historians.[3] Marius, the lowest of the plebs, and Sulla, most savage of the *nobiles*, crushed by force of arms the liberties of the Commonwealth and installed despotism instead. Not so naked the ambitions of Pompeius, but not less evil. The only prize contended for thereafter was the supreme power. At Pharsalia and at Philippi the legions did not lay down their arms. Much less would the troops of Otho and Vitellius have agreed to renounce fighting. The anger of the gods, and human ambitions, rabid and murderous, impelled them to strife, as before.

Speeches and historical comment of this order are convincing examples of Tacitus' independence and power.[4] He also supplements his source or sources with items drawn from official records. By his rank the senator is a part of history, and tradition commands him to

---

[1] *Otho* 9: καὶ οὐκ ἀπεικός ἐστι ... ἐπιπίπτειν τοιούτους διαλογισμοὺς ⟨τοῖς⟩ γνησίοις καὶ διαπόνοις καὶ σωφρονοῦσι τῶν στρατιωτῶν.
[2] II. 37.   [3] 38.
[4] cf. the firm and eloquent vindication of Wölfflin, *Bayerische S–B, phil.-hist. Kl.* 1901, 3 ff.

write history from the point of view of the high assembly. Not the Senate but Caesar now directed policy. Yet the Senate still had its share. If that share might seem small and passive, the Senate was none the less the body that heard and registered the decisions of the government; its debates provided a running commentary on events, instructive though not unfettered, a judicial calendar, and a dated chronicle. The archives of the Senate were properly kept.[1] The *acta* contained the record of proposals that might have been forgotten (especially when no action followed), and significant facts not otherwise to be known.[2]

The study of documentary sources had recently been refined and perfected by men of learning. How it was done for the last age of the Republic could be seen in the recent work of Asconius, the Patavine scholar, familiar no doubt to the highly educated senator. Where the *acta* could help, Tacitus had recourse to them.[3] Indispensable for Domitian's reign, the *acta* might yet be of use for the early books, supplying what the military narrations lacked.

To achieve dignity or intensity the consular historian discards mere facts without compunction. At the same time, by resort to the *acta* he brings in other particulars, and constrains, as far as possible, his narrative to take its direction and its colouring from the Senate. Thus Piso, after being adopted by Galba and presented to the troops, comes before the Senate and delivers a speech: the various sentiments and ambitions of the senators are indicated.[4] Further, the high assembly decides to send an embassy to the German armies, but for one reason or another (and most of them discreditable), no action ensues.[5] Of these transactions Plutarch's account takes no notice.

Subsequently, after Otho's accession, arrangements about the consulates of the year are registered, also priesthoods for elderly senators or young nobles returning from exile. And three senators regain rank. They had been condemned for extortion under Claudius

---

[1] The *acta* were in charge of a senator of quaestorian rank, e.g. *ILS* 1032; 1039; 1040. The earliest attested is the Junius Mauricus 'componendis patrum actis delectus a Caesare' (*Ann.* v. 4. 1).

[2] A senator would normally have access. Pliny looks up the *s.c.* about the freedman Pallas (*Epp.* VIII. 6. 2). For 'publica acta' that recorded a transaction concerning himself (VII. 33. 3) see p. 120.

[3] cf. especially Mommsen's unfinished study, *Ges. Schr.* VII (1909), 253 ff.; E. Groag, o.c. 711 ff.; A. Stein, *Jahresberichte der I. deutschen Staats-Realschule in Prag* XLIII (1904), 5 ff. Fabia suggests that Tacitus hardly needed to consult the *acta senatus* as long as he had the elder Pliny for guide, but concedes his use of them for the history of Domitian (o.c. 262). For the *Annales*, Ch. XXII.

[4] I. 19. 1: 'multi voluntate, effusius qui noluerant, medii ac plurimi obvio obsequio, privatas spes agitantes sine publica cura.'

[5] 19. 2: 'foeda inconstantia nominati excusati substituti, ambitu remanendi aut eundi, ut quemque metus vel spes impulerat.'

and Nero: a clement and dishonest interpretation now made them out to be victims of 'maiestas'.[1] The names clearly derive from the *acta senatus*, being noted and selected for the sake of the historian's satirical comment.

Similarly, in a later place, after Otho has departed for the North, a small detail but significant for the purposes of Tacitus. Vibius Crispus, conspicuous for wealth, influence, and eloquence, arraigned before the Senate a minor informer, and at last secured his conviction, not without discredit to himself—for his own conduct had not been above reproach.[2] Vibius Crispus is scarcely relevant to events in 69, to the fall of Galba, the war of Otho and Vitellius, or the defeat of the Vitellian armies. But Vibius Crispus is close to the central theme of political history—and so is Eprius Marcellus.[3]

That theme emerges powerfully in Book IV of the *Historiae*. Tacitus recounts in some detail the first meeting of the Senate after the fall of Vitellius, towards the end of December 69.[4] Various motions were submitted and approved. First, the Senate confirmed the powers of the new Princeps, it heard dispatches from Vespasian and from Mucianus, and voted a number of victory honours. Then Helvidius Priscus expressed an opinion. Tacitus inserts an estimate of his character, which suitably introduces the next stage in proceedings —a renewed attack on Eprius Marcellus, prompted and excused by a dispute about the method of selecting an embassy to Vespasian. The assault was vigorous, but Eprius made a firm and statesmanlike defence —of himself and of any who had striven to serve the State under bad emperors. Helvidius was frustrated. Nor was he able to carry his point when urging that the Senate should undertake two matters of moment, namely financial economies and the rebuilding of the Capitol, instead of leaving them to the Emperor. Helvidius' conduct was noted and remembered. Finally, Musonius Rufus intervened. His proposal to visit condign punishment upon Egnatius Celer, the philosopher and false friend who had testified against Barea Soranus four years previously, was postponed to the next session, and the debate closed.

After an interval in his narrative Tacitus reverts to the Senate with a report of debates held on January 1, 70, and for several days thereafter.[5] The high assembly transacted various items of business. They condemned Egnatius Celer, defended though he was by Demetrius the Cynic. The motion of Junius Mauricus calling for access to the

---

[1] I. 77. 3: 'placuit ignoscentibus verso nomine, quod avaritia fuerat videri maiestatem, cuius tum odio etiam bonae leges peribant.'

[2] II. 10.

[3] II. 53—another stray incident, a 'notabile iurgium' among the senators at Mutina, involving Eprius Marcellus.

[4] IV. 3–10. [5] 39–45; 47.

private papers of the Caesars was referred to Vespasian. A number of informers came under fire. One of them rounded on his persecutor, the great Vibius Crispus, with a damaging allegation of complicity. The principal episode was the savage oration of a certain Curtius Montanus against Aquillius Regulus. Though unsuccessful, the action excited such warm approbation that Helvidius was emboldened to set upon his enemy once again. Eprius made as though to leave the house, truculently, and Vibius, smooth and smiling, joined him, but their friends induced them to stay. Much wrangling followed, and the day ended.

When the Senate met again, the young Caesar Domitian spoke for an amnesty, and Mucianus supported his plea. The Senate agreed to drop all proceedings against political offenders. To save prestige, however, and dispel any notion of general impunity for crimes committed under Nero, two senators are sternly re-directed to the islands of their penalty; traditionalist sentiments are gratified when a town in Italy is rebuked for gross disrespect towards a member of the Senate; and the conviction of a minor proconsul terminates the session. Then, after a short interlude (trouble with the Praetorians), there is another meeting, with several items, including a proposal for a government loan.[1]

The account of these debates goes back to the official register of the Senate. Tacitus looked for himself. To deny it could only be ignorance or bigotry. The report carries impeccable precision and detail. Thus the debates of January 70 furnish the names of more than thirty persons in half a dozen chapters. Some of them, but only a minority, were to recur in the history of the period. But the historian did not confine himself to reproducing and stylizing the *acta*: the narrative is interwoven with free composition of his own.

Though the speeches of senators may not have been consigned to the official record, but only perhaps a summary along with the 'sententia', some orations had no doubt been published.[2] The historian could not perhaps operate in all liberty: yet it was enough if he kept to the main heads of argument, treating them in his own fashion and in his own order. What Tacitus invents comes from his own experience or insight, namely the various comments on the sentiments of the high assembly, for example how they disapproved the arrogance of Mucianus' dispatch;[3] how in an altercation the majority was

---

[1] 47.

[2] Groag (o.c. 711) argued that there was a verbatim record of senators' speeches, citing Fronto (p. 26 N = Haines I, p. 110): 'ut laudatio mea non in actis senatus abstrusa lateat.' Mommsen, however, refused to go so far, *Ges. Schr.* VII (1909), 254. The orations of notable performers like Vibius and Eprius would tend to get published (or at least circulated).   [3] 4. 1: 'si privatus esset, cur publice loqueretur', &c.

sound, but a powerful minority was pertinacious and resentful.[1]
Again, characteristically Tacitean is the reference to the set speeches
of persons marked by high eminence or long practice in adulation.[2]
And the historian was able to exhibit his talent on the unwonted theme
of praise and sympathy when producing a character sketch of Helvidius Priscus.[3] All in all, the account of these transactions reveals
scruple of investigation and candour of comment.

Finally, with like mastery Tacitus deliberately omits facts. The
unknown annalist had a certain propensity to anecdote. Tacitus
jettisons his story about Galba and the flute-player;[4] and he passes
over the alleged total of Otho's debts.[5] Plutarch's account of the
killing of Galba in the Forum contains the names of four soldiers.
Tacitus has only three. He had deliberately suppressed the fourth,
and with it an ugly detail—the bald head of Sulpicius Galba.[6] The
senator's insistence upon the solemnity of his style and his theme is
manifest. Plutarch's *Vitellius* has not survived, but the Latin biographer can help, furnishing from the same presumed source a precise
and curious report of the Emperor's revolting end.[7] The last to desert
Vitellius were his baker and his cook. Tacitus alludes to them as the
meanest of his establishment.[8] Vitellius stowed himself away in the
porter's lodge, with the dog chained in front, and the bed and mattress
as a barrier. In Tacitus no detail, but only a 'shameful hiding-place'.[9]
The mob cast mud or excrement on their victim, mocked his red face
and great belly, and mangled his body. Tacitus is reticent: they
reviled Vitellius with the same baseness with which they had fawned
upon him when alive.[10]

Tacitus does not merely eschew the squalid and disgusting. Instead,
he emphasizes the feelings of the unfortunate Emperor—his terror at

---

[1] IV. 43. 2: 'cum gliscret certamen, hinc multi bonique, inde pauci et validi pertinacibus
odiis tenderent, consumptus per discordiam dies.'

[2] 4. 3: 'pauci quibus conspicua dignitas aut ingenium adulatione exercitum compositis
orationibus adsentiebantur.'

[3] 4. 5.   [4] Plutarch, *Galba* 16, cf. Suetonius, *Galba* 12. 3.   [5] *Galba* 21.

[6] I. 41. 3. According to Plutarch (27), the soldier Fabius Fabullus cut off Galba's head,
but could not carry it about in his hands, because it had no hair. Similarly Suetonius
(*Galba* 20. 2), who mentions no names. For Galba's baldness and jokes about it, cf. also
Plutarch, *Galba* 13. Tacitus, however, is dignified and reticent, cf. I. 7. 3: 'ipsa aetas
Galbae inrisui ac fastidio erat adsuetis iuventae Neronis et imperatoris forma ac decore
corporis, ut est mos vulgi, comparantibus.' Compare further, on the bald head of Tiberius
Caesar (*Ann.* IV. 57. 2), below, p. 343. That Tacitus, Plutarch, and Suetonius should treat
the data of one and the same source in such different ways is in keeping with their idio-
syncrasies. Momigliano, however, finds it an 'enorme stranezza'. He argues that Plutarch
follows Tacitus here—and supplements him with an added detail from another source
(*Stud. it. fil. cl.* IX (1931/2)), 178.   [7] Suetonius, *Vit.* 16 f.

[8] III. 84. 4: 'dilapsis etiam infimis servitiorum aut occursum eius declinantibus.'

[9] ib.: 'pudenda latebra semet occultans.'

[10] 85: 'et vulgus eadem pravitate insectabatur interfectum qua foverat viventem.'

the silence and solitude of the Palace.[1] And, to terminate the scene, a balanced obituary. Vitellius' rank and prominence was due not to any merits of his own, but to his parentage. His supporters did not know him. Though slothful, he gained the affections of the soldiery. He had certain qualities, such as frankness and generosity. Lacking character, he tried to win friends by paying for them, and failed. That Vitellius should be destroyed was a good thing for Rome, but no credit to his betrayers.[2]

Of Tacitus' bold independence in the selection of material and the construction of a narrative, the proof is overpowering. Plutarch's *Galba* and *Otho* have not infrequently been invoked to support an extreme and dogmatic thesis, that Cornelius Tacitus for the most part was content to follow a single source.[3] The resemblances have been much exaggerated. On the contrary, it appears that he operated with great freedom and discernment, and he could call at will on the supplementary devices of historical exposition—speeches, digressions, and character sketches. The unknown annalist was an important source in the first two books of the *Historiae*, and a good source—clear, accurate, and eloquent, although with limitations: he was perhaps not a senator.[4] Other accounts were available, and Tacitus was well equipped to assess them, even if he had not known most of the authors. Tacitus refers a number of times to a plurality of sources, and he must be believed.[5] He used each according to its value. For information Tacitus had recourse to recent writers.[6] His personal knowledge should be rated very high.[7] His models, however, were the classic historians of Rome who recounted the civil wars of the Republic and the strife for power, the fall of the Free State, the establishment of the monarchy.

[1] 84. 4: 'terret solitudo et tacentes loci; temptat clausa, inhorrescit vacuis.'

[2] 86. 2: 'rei publicae haud dubie intererat Vitellium vinci, sed imputare perfidiam non possunt qui Vitellium Vespasiano prodidere, cum a Galba descivissent.'

[3] App. 29.

[4] Groag, o.c. 772. Nor indeed were the senatorial debates in 69 of much historical significance.

[5] II. 37. 1; 101. 1; III. 29. 2; 51. 1; IV. 83. 1; V. 2. 2 f.; 6. 4.

[6] The account of the death of the elegant and aristocratic Junius Blaesus (III. 38 f.) looks like an insertion from a subsidiary source. More important, the suppression of a proconsul of Africa, L. Piso, coming between the funeral of Vespasian's brother (IV. 47) and the narration of Vespasian's own activities—'at Vespasiano post Cremonensem pugnam', &c. (IV. 51. 1). The episode is fully told. It concerned Baebius Massa, at that time procurator of Africa, 'iam tunc optimo cuique exitiosus et inter causas malorum quae mox tulimus saepe rediturus' (IV. 50. 2). Massa, promoted to the Senate, was prosecuted by Herennius Senecio in 93 (*Agr.* 45. 1, cf. Pliny, *Epp.* VII. 33. 4 ff.).

[7] The mention of Claudia Sacrata, a lady of Colonia Claudia, alleged mistress of Petillius Cerialis (V. 22. 3), might be a useful clue, cf. p. 175. Observe also Tacitus' familiarity with Narbonensis (App. 95).

XVII. THE QUALITIES OF THE
HISTORIAE

ON a superficial view annalistic tradition and the necessity to begin where a year began, tolerable and even helpful for the more rudimentary forms of narration, might appear to hamper and debilitate an historian who expounds the crisis, not of a city but an empire. Tacitus betrays no sign of discomfort. Operating with ease and economy, he throws off a rapid sketch—Rome and the provinces —which enables the drama to unfold without encumbrances, explaining itself. Further particulars about what had happened the year before emerge when required. Book I of the *Historiae* is exemplary for architecture, but it is not an isolated exhibition of virtuosity. Equal all through, the historian, by grouping events, by managing separate narratives, by variety and art of transition, moving at will from the capital to the provinces and back again, demonstrates that he has the subject under perfect control.

When an historian who is also an orator equips his narration with choice specimens of eloquence, and when, moreover, it is more than doubtful whether any such words were ever spoken, a suspicion arises, with the grave charge that he is employing the arts of the rhetorician. Then the precepts of the professors are detected and condemned, the traditional themes of the schools, and all that passes for declamation.[1] Not without show of reason. Tacitus was eager to exhibit a splendid talent, matured and perfected in the courts and in the Senate. There is artifice and ingenuity and soaring eloquence. Perhaps to excess—not for volume of oratory (for he is sparing), but in display of technique, the products being not always congruous with the persons and events. The Emperor Galba delivers a homily, expatiating upon the 'res publica':[2] that is at variance with the situation, and it denies Galba's manner, which was curt and unconciliatory. Piso addresses a cohort of the Guard:[3] small chance that the words were ever consigned to record. Otho's allocution in the Praetorian camp is bold and lavish:[4] another authority affirms that Otho said very little.[5]

[1] Thus E. Courbaud, *Les Procédés d'art de Tacite dans les 'Histoires'* (1918), 82; 217. For a defence against the charge of rhetoric (and moralizing to excess) see R. Pichon, *Journal des Savants* 1919, 183 ff.; E. Paratore, *Tacito* (1951), 421.

[2] I. 15 f.   [3] 29 f.   [4] 37 f.

[5] Suetonius, *Otho* 6. 3: 'ad conciliandos militum animos nihil magis pro contione testatus est quam id demum se habiturum quod sibi illi reliquissent.'

Invention, almost all. To discredit the author it would have to be proved that the speeches are set compositions shoved in for effect, or superfluous. On the contrary, their function is structural, or rather organic. Not all historians went to such pains. The fluent Livy, enormous in output, cannot fail to incur censure, frequently.[1] And it was some time before Sallust won his way to mastery.[2]

A speech may serve various ends. It can portray a character or illustrate a situation; and a pair of speeches usefully expounds two policies in contrast. Thus the historian Sallust produces an oration by Lepidus, to be balanced (and refuted) by Philippus.[3] That device aids clarity and achieves concentration. Not, however, much favoured by Tacitus—perhaps he thought it elementary and schematic. He adopts by predilection a superior procedure that brings out, not the contrast between speech and speech, but the conflict between words and facts.

To render speakers in their diversity Tacitus plays upon the variations of language and movement. Piso is sober, dignified, and melancholy, while Otho's harangue blends flattering appeal with the feverish violence of the temporary desperado.[4] Licinius Mucianus, that guileful diplomat, manages an elaborate orchestration, punctuated by telling epigrams.[5] Antonius Primus is fierce and direct, with a run of rhetorical questions.[6] Eprius Marcellus (it is known) was a truculent speaker: the historian tones down his discourse (for so the occasion demanded), producing the plain man's plea in a sequence of straightforward asseverations.[7]

The orators are often made to betray their predicament or falsity by equivocal argumentation, conventional phraseology—or by simple discordance with the facts. When Otho, addressing the mutinous Guard, ends with a noble peroration,[8] the reader will not be taken in. He knows Otho—and he will soon be told that Otho borrowed his eloquence from that popular practitioner, Galerius Trachalus.[9] He can also assess Mucianus, being warned in advance by the character sketch not far from the exordium of the *Historiae*.[10] And who would not be vigilant when a man like Eprius Marcellus invokes Roman tradition and the 'mos maiorum'?[11]

Tacitus has many resources, veiled or open. An oration can be used to expound some theme that is much in his mind—a theory of Roman political life, the apologia for Roman rule in the provinces, or a

---

[1] W. Soltau, *Neue Jahrbücher* v (1902), 20 ff. Livy as extant has several hundred orations.

[2] H. Schnorr von Carolsfeld, *Über die Reden und Briefe bei Sallust* (1888), 23 ff.

[3] Sallust, *Hist.* I. 55; 77.   [4] I. 37 f.   [5] II. 76 f.   [6] III. 2; 20; 24.

[7] IV. 8.   [8] I. 84. 4 (quoted on p. 155).   [9] 90. 2.

[10] 10. 1 f., cf. also II. 80. 2: 'omniumque quae diceret atque ageret arte quadam ostentator.'

[11] IV. 8. 1: 'nihil evenisse cur antiquitus instituta exolescerent.'

defence of senators compelled to acquiesce under a despotic government.[1] He can even dispense with the known or named spokesman:
the citizens of two communities set forth their contrasting arguments
in the Thucydidean fashion.[2] Tacitus extends his method to reproduce men's reflections in a season of crisis;[3] and he invents soliloquies
for Otho and for Vespasian on the brink of hazardous decisions.[4]

Speech or thought woven into the narrative conduces to variety, and
sometimes permits an easy transition. When Mucianus has declared
himself, summoning Vespasian to take the power, the happy bystanders come out with prophecies and horoscopes. Vespasian was a
believer in astrology—and now Vespasian's mind went back and
dwelt upon the old omens and portents of greatness.[5] After which
interlude, the action goes gaily forward. The device also enables the
historian to keep superstition in a proper and subordinate place.

Oratory itself merges into the story of campaigns and battles. Thus
the three powerful harangues from Antonius Primus—in the council
of war at Poetovio, in front of Cremona, and during the night battle.[6]
Each begins as reported discourse but breaks out before the end in a
direct appeal. The art is consummate, and faithful to the situation, for
it was a civil war, the general a demagogue, and eloquence a part of
the action.

Narrative is the essence of history. To tell a story properly calls for
speed and variety. Those virtues are inherent in the style of Tacitus.
He never allows the action to flag or stagnate. Narrative records and
explains what happened—imagination compels it to be seen and
shared. An artist has free scope with description—he can choose, add,
and invent. Impatient with a lengthy recital of mere events, Tacitus
will omit or condense, or break it up into individual scenes. Thus the
long march of Fabius Valens from the Rhine through the Gallic
territories to the Alps comes out as a run of pictures exhibiting the
behaviour of troops in civil war. But the crossing of the Alps did not
engage his interest, or, for that matter, how Antonius Primus reached
Aquileia when he invaded Italy for Vespasian.

On the other hand, the abdication of a Roman emperor, though
abortive, had dramatic and pictorial value. Vitellius in fact made no
fewer than three attempts to resign.[7] Tacitus compresses them into
a single episode, enhanced with every resource of colour and suggestion.[8] The bystanders are briefly characterized—the crowd loudly
acclaiming their emperor when it was too late, while the soldiers

---

[1] I. 15 f. (Galba); IV. 73 f. (Petillius Cerialis); IV. 8 (Eprius Marcellus).
[2] IV. 64 f. (the Tencteri and the citizens of Colonia Claudia).
[3] I. 50 (p. 183).   [4] I. 21; II. 74 f.
[5] II. 78. 2: 'recursabant animo vetera omina', &c.
[6] III. 2; 20; 24.   [7] Suetonius, *Vitellius* 15.   [8] III. 67 f.

stood silent. Then the historian evokes their sentiments—nobody could help being deeply moved at the sight of a Roman Princeps, until recently master of the whole world, going forth from the residence of his power to abdicate. Next, their reflections, calling up for comparison the history of the past, with the fate of Caesar the Dictator, the assassination of Caligula, the flight of Nero, the killing of Galba and Piso: but there was nothing to equal this spectacle. Finally, the words, demeanour, and gesture of Vitellius, trying to surrender a dagger to the reluctant consul.

The mob would not allow Vitellius to go through with his own deposition, and soon the soldiery intervened. Flavius Sabinus, the brother of Vespasian, was making ready to assume authority, when Vitellius' troops attacked, compelling him to take refuge on the Capitol with a number of friends and partisans. As depicted by Cornelius Tacitus the assault and destruction of the Temple of Juppiter is colourful, packed, and intense.[1] The scene musters the long pageant of the Roman past, from the foundations laid by the king, Tarquinius Priscus, down to the conflagration during another civil war, just before Sulla captured the city, and the rebuilding which the name of Lutatius Catulus commemorated: 'ea tunc aedes cremabatur'.[2]

The multitude soon had another spectacle, when the Flavian forces broke into the city, encountering stubborn resistance and savage battles in the streets—and they revelled in it, cheering and encouraging the combatants.[3] It was the festive season, and the mob was delighted with this additional entertainment—for other pleasures were not interrupted. The city exhibited a hideous carnival, slaughter and rapine amid the taverns and brothels. Armies had fought before now in the streets, among the houses, and before the eyes of the people, when Cinna captured Rome, and Sulla—but with no parallel of horror and degradation.

To the power and splendour of Tacitus as a painter of historical scenes no paraphrase or enumeration does justice. It would be superfluous to insist upon the language and stylistic habits that convey the intensity of his pictorial imagination. Especially urgent and terrifying are the descriptions of masses—and no less impressive when a crowd is tranquil than when it surges with anger and menace or disintegrates in panic. The historian had seen and loathed the populace of Rome, the turbulence of armed men. He was familiar with the behaviour of another crowd, the Senate. Nothing can equal the subtle malice that depicts the comportment of senators—the contrasts between official

[1] 71. The Virgilian quality of this scene was well brought out by J. W. Mackail, *Latin Literature* (1895), 218 f.

[2] 72. 3.   [3] 83. 1.

optimism and private apprehensions, lavish adulation of the ruler and secret detestation, public spirit masking intrigue and ambition, the show of courage and the reality of cowardice, with dignity collapsing ludicrously at the touch of fear.[1]

When an historian's theme is a close-knit drama of war and politics, with a confusing abundance of actors, he has need of skill and variety in their characterization, the more so if impelled to a sombre and almost uniform conception of human nature as necessarily manifested by transactions of violence, craft, and iniquity. Some of the personages are hit off in a brief phrase, like Cornelius Laco (Galba's Prefect of the Guard), of perverse obstinacy.[2] About Piso Licinianus, not much more deserved to be told than his birth, age, and negative virtue.[3] Piso is a lay figure—a victim to his ancestry and station, to the folly of Galba, to the criminal ambitions of Otho. Nor was the character of Vespasian's brother at all conspicuous: unimpeachable in integrity, but he talked too much.[4] Antonius Primus is paraded with a string of vivid and powerful epithets, to be quickly justified by his deeds and also by his words.[5]

The first full-length portrait in the *Historiae* is devoted to Licinius Mucianus.[6] A few details, but relevant, adumbrate the vicissitudes of his earlier life—ambition, an emperor's anger, hence virtual banishment. Then the description: a blend of good and evil—luxury and application to business, social gifts and arrogance. A voluptuary in hours of leisure, Mucianus exhibited great virtues when required. On public actions to be commended, but unsavoury in his private repute; acquiring influence with friends, colleagues, and provincials through varied and diplomatic arts, he found it easier to yield the imperial power to another than take it for himself.

Mucianus stands forth, at the expense of Vespasian. That is artistic, and historically correct. Vespasian is not permitted to come on the scene without further remarks about Mucianus, the capacities of the two generals being evoked for comparison.[7] In January of 69 the governor of Syria seemed the stronger candidate; his attitude decided the proclamation by the eastern legions; and his voice was later dominant in domestic politics. Of the three emperors whose fate is

---

[1] I. 19; 85. 3; II. 90 f.; III. 37.

[2] I. 26. 2: 'ignarus militarium animorum consiliique quamvis egregii, quod non ipse adferret, inimicus et adversus peritos pervicax.'

[3] 14. 2; 48. 1.

[4] III. 75. 1: 'hic exitus viri haud sane spernendi. quinque et triginta stipendia in re publica fecerat, domi militiaeque clarus. innocentiam iustitiamque eius non argueres; sermonis nimius erat: id unum septem annis quibus Moesiam, duodecim quibus praefecturam urbis obtinuit, calumniatus est rumor.'

[5] II. 86. 2 (quoted above, p. 169).   [6] I. 10. 1 f.   [7] II. 5.

told in the first three books of the *Historiae*, each receives his due honour with a separate necrological commemoration.[1] Their characters, however, have been progressively revealed in the narrative and built up by various devices—episode, oration, descriptive comment.[2]

Brief or developed, the character sketch advertises a Sallustian parentage, or at the least an affinity. To portray Mucianus, Tacitus employs juxtaposed nouns, disjointed structure, and an absence of connexions.[3] When historians pass judgement on men and affairs, they are in the habit of enouncing traditional sagacity or the fruit of their own reflections in the form of verdicts or maxims. The Roman annalist might with reason expect that knowledge of the 'res publica' should lend weight and validity to his comments: a veteran statesman wrote not for recreation but to instruct his fellow citizens. Sententiousness was inherent in the genre, but the tone changed in a startling manner under the impact of civil strife, with a more searching inquiry into behaviour and motive. Old men's wisdom and all the improving proverbs about truth, honesty, and loyalty went out of date in the ruthless struggle when might again became right, as in the beginning of time. The meanings of words were now changed and perverted.[4] The historian propagated in his writings what he had learned from experience. It was a harsh and bitter doctrine, using for texts the moral precepts turned upside down and converted into the maxims of statecraft. Life under the despotism of the Caesars and the assiduous competition of refined stylists brought the technique to perfection.

The Licinius Mucianus of the historian Tacitus is not only a Sallustian character suitably depicted in Sallustian language. His speech of counsel to Vespasian is also in the manner.[5] As Mucianus develops his theme—war is safer than peace and empire the only refuge—he confirms the argument with a series of epigrams: subtle and sinister paradox conveyed by a daring and deadly simplicity of words.[6]

Echoes and hints of Sallust will not be interpreted merely as proper homage to the archetypal historian whom Tacitus honoured as 'rerum Romanarum florentissimus auctor'.[7] The resemblances go much

---

[1] I. 49; II. 50; III. 86.

[2] Vitellius, a passive character, is not allowed an oration.

[3] I. 10. 1 f., cf. E. Courbaud, o.c. 173. Likewise in the portraitures of Galba (I. 49); Antonius Primus and Cornelius Fuscus (II. 86); Helvidius Priscus (IV. 5).

[4] Thucydides III. 82. 3: καὶ τὴν εἰωθυῖαν ἀξίωσιν τῶν ὀνομάτων ἐς τὰ ἔργα ἀντήλλαξαν τῇ δικαιώσει. The notion, exploited by Cassius Dio (XLVI. 34. 5, on the politics of 43 B.C.), was familiar to Sallust (cf. *Cat.* 52. 11; *Hist.* I. 12)—and is highly relevant to the phraseology of the revolutionary age, cf. R. Syme, *Rom. Rev.* (1939), 154.

[5] II. 76 f.

[6] e.g. 'confugiendum est ad imperium'; 'satis clarus est apud timentem quisquis timetur'; 'qui deliberant, desciverunt'.

[7] *Ann.* III. 30. 1.

deeper. The Sallustian manner corresponds to an organic necessity in Roman historiography, as Tacitus understood the matter, and not Tacitus only.[1]

Sallust demonstrated, once and for all, that the periodic sentence will not do, either for narration or for picture. It has balance, subordination, amplitude, and a conclusion all too often inevitable; it is persuasive, hence smooth and deceptive. History aims at verisimilitude by stating facts, not in a hierarchy, but one by one, as they present themselves to the observer. The order in which they occur will have the variety and paradox of life itself. The deliberate abruptness of Sallust's style was noted by critics in antiquity. Men spoke of truncated sentences, ending before expected.[2] Tacitus employs a technique of surprise, but often by prolongation, adding by a participle or ablative absolute other facts or comments, so as to develop or modify what went before, not infrequently by innuendo.[3]

The qualities to which Tacitus aspired are evident—brevity, rapidity, splendour, and concentration. Nor will it be expedient to essay any lengthy inquiry or classification.[4] Wherever possible, Tacitus discards verbs of saying or thinking, drops connectives, juxtaposes a series of nouns or adjectives; for vividness, the historic infinitive, and for description, the imperfect tense; while speed and variety come from the broken structure, avoidance of balance, a frequent change of subject. For choice of words the dignity of his theme constrains the historian to eschew banality or tired phraseology. Neologisms are admitted, but he will resort to periphrasis from horror of technical terms. Tacitus' predilection goes to strong and colourful words; he likes metaphors of destruction and conflagration. Poetical language and archaisms had long been favoured by the historical style. The one might lead to florid ornament, the other to pedantry and affectation. Tacitus operates with restraint and vigilance. Some of his finest effects depend upon a naked simplicity of phrase, every word heavy with meaning.[5]

---

[1] cf. E. Wölfflin, *Philologus* XXVI (1867), 122 ff.; G. Schönfeld, *De Taciti studiis Sallustianis* (Diss. Leipzig, 1884); E. Norden, *Die antike Kunstprosa* I (1898), 335 f. Further, Ch. XXVII and App. 53.

[2] Seneca, *Epp.* 114. 17: 'Sallustio vigente amputatae sententiae et verba ante exspectatum cadentia et obscura brevitas fuere pro cultu.' The author artfully brings in a 'Sallustian' expression with the last three words.   [3] E. Courbaud, o.c. 244 ff.

[4] See Ch. XXVI, where the developed Tacitean style is discussed and illustrated. Tacitus moves from eloquence to concentrated vigour—in brief, Livy to Sallust. For Livian style in the *Historiae*, see p. 200 f., with App. 34. As an example of what Tacitus will later avoid, observe IV. 58 (the speech of Dillius Vocula), or, in descriptive writing, III. 83. 2 (the capture of Rome): 'quantum in luxurioso otio libidinum, quidquid in acerbissima captivitate scelerum, prorsus ut eandem civitatem et furere crederes et lascivire.'

[5] e.g. III. 67. 2: 'voces populi blandae et intempestivae, miles minaci silentio'; IV. 42. 6: 'diutius durant exempla quam mores.'

To achieve distinction, a Roman writer did not have to strive after any undue novelty of subject or treatment. He started from conformity not rebellion, and he showed originality by continuing and improving the work of his predecessors, not without acknowledgement, open and honourable, when he adapted a theme or a phrase.[1]

The style was laid down in advance by the literary genre. As the *Agricola* (in one of its aspects) is a funeral discourse, blended, expanded, and strengthened with historical material, it would be expected to show the influence of various manners.[2] In general it lies half-way between history and oratory. Modelled upon Livy and Sallust in the narrative, it draws heavily upon Cicero for the eloquent peroration. Agricola was happy in his end, for the season of his death spared the sight of many calamities.[3] Tacitus develops the parallel with the great orator and statesman, L. Licinius Crassus, who died on the eve of the *Bellum Italicum*;[4] and Ciceronian language is employed to render the necrological commemoration, enhancing the traditional themes of death and bereavement, of fame and immortality.[5]

In the *Germania*, the type and precedent being the historian's excursus on lands and peoples, the Sallustian manner is dominant.[6] The literary essay likewise conforms to a classical model. Tacitus in the *Dialogus* takes to a neo-Ciceronian style, smooth but not diffuse, which Quintilian would no doubt have approved.[7]

In the *Historiae* a Sallustian tone was inevitable. Tacitus conveys it in various ways. A whole passage, like the reflections on the love of power, may be written in Sallust's fashion.[8] The first sentence uttered

---

[1] Seneca, *Suas.* III. 7: 'non subripiendi causa sed palam mutuandi, hoc animo ut vellet agnosci.' Cf. E. Wölfflin, *Archiv für lat. Lex.* XII (1900), 114 ff.; W. Kroll, *Studien zum Verständnis der r. Literatur* (1924), 139 ff.

[2] See the edition of J. G. C. Anderson (Oxford, 1922), LXXX ff. For echoes (not all convincing) of earlier writers see C. W. Mendell, *TAPA* LII (1921), 53 ff.

[3] 45. 3: 'tu vero felix, Agricola, non vitae tantum claritate, sed etiam opportunitate mortis', &c.; 45. 1: 'non vidit Agricola obsessam curiam et clausum armis senatum', &c.

[4] cf. *De oratore* III. 8: 'non vidit flagrantem bello Italiam, non ardentem invidia senatum, non sceleris nefarii principes civitatis reos', &c. Add Cicero's comments on the 'perpetua felicitas' and 'mortis opportunitas' of Q. Hortensius who died shortly before the Civil War (*Brutus* 4 f.).

[5] 46. 1: 'si quis piorum manibus locus', &c.

[6] For vocabulary, syntax, and style see A. Gudeman in his edition (Berlin, 1916), 39 ff. Senecan influences were emphasized by F. Leo, *Gött. gel. Anz.* 1898, 183. Against, E. Wölfflin, *Archiv für lat. Lex.* XII (1900), 114 ff.; R. Reitzenstein, *Gött. gel. Nachr.* 1914, 259 ff. For a balanced view, J. Perret, *Rev. ét. anc.* LVI (1954), 97. It will not be forgotten that the elder Pliny goes in for precious and poetical language: see E. Norden, *Die antike Kunstprosa* I (1898), 314 ff.

[7] cf. App. 28 (the style as irrelevant to the date). For the style in detail, W. A. Peterson in his edition (Oxford, 1893), XLIII ff.; A. Gudeman (ed. 2, Berlin, 1914), 20 ff.; for Tacitean characteristics, A. Gudeman, ib. 25 ff.; H. Bardon, *Latomus* XII (1953), 485 ff. Further, for the stylistic interrelation of the three minor works, J. Perret, *Rev. ét. anc.* LVI (1954), 90 ff.

[8] II. 38 (summarized above, p. 185), cf. Sallust, *Hist.* I. 7; 12 f.

by Mucianus is closely adapted from the exordium of a speech (in letter form) contrived by the earlier historian.[1] Elsewhere a brief phrase may be enough, a characteristic device, or a single word that Sallust favoured, as when the physical deformity of Civilis the Batavian recalls Sertorius.[2] A comment of old-fashioned simplicity will tell its own story.[3] Most instructive perhaps is the epigram not itself borrowed from Sallust but cunningly turned in the traditional mould.

Some of these 'sententiae', sharply formulated and of ultimate perfection, look like Tacitus at his most authentic. Disconcerting facts come to light, and the originals are revealed, for example in the unknown annalist whom Tacitus used and Plutarch copied. He supplies the phrase about Otho at the banquet, 'cum timeret Otho, timebatur'.[4] Likewise Otho and Vitellius in mutual vilification— 'neuter falso'.[5] And Vinius giving counsel to Galba in Spain had already spoken the conclusion to Mucianus' speech—'qui deliberant desciverunt'.[6]

That a reputable author should take over from his source not only material but even his epigrammatical turns is at first sight a cause of disquiet, with ugly imputations: if this is borrowing, what is theft? Reflection elicits a calmer verdict. It is not safe to assume that the unknown annalist, whatever the grade of his accomplishments, was the original inventor of those 'sententiae'. A huge stock was there. Life at Rome reached a high pitch of sophistication, with competition in phrase-making and rhetoric rampant all the way from the schools and salons to the Senate. Point and epigram pervade every province of letters. Enough to refer to Seneca and Lucan: Tacitean maxims about high politics occur in both authors. In Lucan it is only to be

---

[1] II. 76. 1: 'omnes qui magnarum rerum consilia suscipiunt aestimare debent an quod inchoatur rei publicae utile, ipsis gloriosum, promptum effectu aut certe non arduum sit'; Sallust, *Hist.* IV. 69. 1: 'rex Mithridates regi Arsaci salutem. omnes qui secundis rebus suis ad belli societatem orantur considerare debent, liceatne tum pacem agere, dein quod quaesitur, satisne pium tutum, gloriosum an indecorum sit.'

[2] IV. 13. 2: 'Sertorium se aut Annibalem ferens simili oris dehonestamento'; Sallust, *Hist.* I. 88: 'quin ille dehonestamento corporis maxime laetabatur.' This splendid Sallustian word is used with great effect to describe the low company in which Vitellius delighted, II. 87. 2: 'quibus ille amicitiarum dehonestamentis mire gaudebat.' Tacitus has 'mire' (cf. Sallust, *Hist.* I. 55. 24) elsewhere only in *Ann.* VI. 10. 3; XIII. 1. 3.

[3] I. 5. 2: 'nec enim ad hanc formam cetera erant'; II. 10. 1: 'inter claros magis quam inter bonos.'

[4] I. 81. 1; Plutarch, *Otho* 3: φοβούμενος γὰρ ὑπὲρ τῶν ἀνδρῶν αὐτὸς ἦν φοβερὸς ἐκείνοις. Yet the phrase has a long history behind it, cf. Cicero, *De r.p.* II. 45, to which attention was drawn by F. Münzer, *Hermes* XXXIV (1899), 641. See further E. Wölfflin, *Archiv für lat. Lex.* XII (1900), 345 ff.

[5] I. 74. 1; Plutarch, *Otho* 4: οὐ ψευδῶς μέν, ἀνοήτως δὲ καὶ γελοίως.

[6] II. 77. 3; Plutarch, *Galba* 4: τὸ γὰρ ζητεῖν, Νέρωνι εἰ πιστοὶ μενοῦμεν, οὐκ ἤδη μενόντων ἐστίν.

expected, for he was writing an historical poem.[1] Hardly more surprising in Seneca, the statesman and moralist.[2]

Tacitus declares that the victor in civil war is certain to turn out the nastier.[3] If a similar phrase commends itself to Seneca when objurgating Cato for taking sides in a civil war,[4] no need to suppose that Seneca invented the notion. An epigram belongs to the author who puts the final edge. Tacitus must have improved on the 'sententiae' of the unknown annalist, otherwise he would not have bothered to take them over.

Of an enormous literary production, very little has survived, and nothing at all from the Roman historians who wrote in the hundred and thirty years that had elapsed since Livy set about his task. It is not easy to trace that development of the later historical style which culminates in Tacitus. Many features of this highly traditional genre are earlier than Sallust.[5] And, while Sallust was the great original (and also in the long run the strongest influence), Livy should be reckoned with, and the line of historians who followed Livy, some no doubt after his fashion, but not all. The consular L. Arruntius adopted the Sallustian manner, which he carried to ridiculous extremities, in phraseology at least.[6] His subject was the First Punic War. Familiar with Sicily and having commanded ships of war, Arruntius may have found style to be not the only thing that was wrong with Livy.[7]

The *Historiae* of Tacitus are not liable to incrimination for archaistic excesses. Tacitus must have found much to admire in the writing of Livy—poetical and emotional language, orations of noble eloquence, colour, movement, and a strong sense of the dramatic. The extent of the Livian influence on his style is commonly (and not unnaturally) estimated below its due. Both for tone and for details Sallust is more sharply perceptible. Nevertheless, the manner and diction of Livy can often be detected. A few instances will exemplify. The attitude of the soldiery towards Marius Celsus—anger mixed with admiration—has a close parallel in Livy.[8] A remark about Cremona and the Flavian troops recalls Rome and the Gallic invaders.[9] Otho's allocution to the

---

[1] p. 143.

[2] Verse as well as prose. Observe the epigrams about crime and monarchy in the *Thyestes* (e.g. 205 ff.).

[3] I. 50. 3: 'inter duos, quorum bello solum id scires, deteriorem fore qui vicisset.'

[4] Seneca, *Epp.* 14. 13: 'potest melior vincere, non potest non peior esse qui vicerit.'

[5] cf. E. Skard, 'Sallust und seine Vorgänger'. *Symbolae Osloenses*, Supp. xv (1956), 8 ff.

[6] Seneca, *Epp.* 114. 17 ff. (with examples).

[7] Generally recognized as the consul of 22 B.C. (*PIR²*, A 1129). With Sex. Pompeius in Sicily—and later commanding a part of the victorious fleet at Actium.

[8] I. 71. 2: 'eandem virtutem admirantes cui irascebantur'; Livy v. 26. 8: 'eandem virtutem et oderant et mirabantur.'

[9] III. 20. 2: 'noctem et ignotae situm urbis'; Livy v. 39. 3: 'noctemque veriti et ignotae situm urbis.'

Guard commending discipline borrows from the exhortations of Aemilius Paullus.[1] Further, the surrender of a Roman army on the Rhine is portrayed with devices that evoke, by direct reminiscence, the legions at the Caudine Forks;[2] and the Roman general Dillius Vocula duly comes out with a Livian speech.[3]

The portions of Livy that were close and useful for comparison have perished, namely the many books about the various civil commotions in the sequence of sixty years from the outbreak of the *Bellum Italicum* to the conflict between Caesar's heir and Marcus Antonius. The fall and sack of some city of Italy like Perusia may have served as model, in setting and language, for Cremona—'bellis externis intacta, civilibus infelix'.[4] Livy had also described the burning of the Capitol, and savage fighting in the streets of Rome, in the days of Marius, Cinna, and Sulla.

Telling how a soldier killed his brother at the Battle of Cremona, Tacitus registers a like incident from the old wars, with citation of the historian Cornelius Sisenna: on that occasion the soldier committed suicide. Tacitus states that he intends to recall, as is proper, such stories out of the past, for example or for consolation.[5] He did not always need to be specific. Numerous were the parallels, quietly suggested by a choice of language inevitably evoking to his audience the writings of his predecessors.

An estimate of what the *Historiae* of Tacitus signified to men of the time need not be confined to the effusive and necessary testimony of his friend Pliny.[6] Hints and guidance derive from Quintilian, a sagacious literary critic and a mirror of informed opinion. Quintilian compares Livy with Herodotus. He accords signal praise for charm and honesty of narrative, incomparable eloquence in the speeches, language in harmony with character and situation, and an especial gift for rendering the gentler emotions.[7] Sallust, however, he is emboldened to match against Thucydides.[8] He adds no specification in detail. What he has in mind is the brevity, the intensity, and that 'immortalis velocitas'.[9]

---

[1] I. 84. 2: 'parendo potius, commilitones, quam imperia ducum sciscitando res militares continentur', &c.; cf. Livy XLIV. 34. 2 ff.

[2] IV. 62; 72, cf. items from Livy IX. 5. 11 ff.

[3] IV. 58, cf. App. 34.   [4] III. 34. 1.

[5] 51. 2: 'quotiens res locusque exempla recti aut solacia mali poscet.'

[6] *Epp.* VII. 33. 1: 'auguror, nec me fallit augurium, historias tuas immortales futuras.'

[7] Quintilian X. 1. 101: 'neque indignetur sibi Herodotus aequari T. Livium, cum in narrando mirae iucunditatis clarissimique candoris tum in contionibus supra quam enarrari potest eloquentem; ita quae dicuntur omnia cum rebus tum personis accommodata sunt; affectus quidem, praecipueque eos qui sunt dulciores, ut parcissime dicam, nemo historicorum commendavit magis.'

[8] ib.: 'nec opponere Thucydidi Sallustium verear.'   [9] X. 1. 32; 102.

Other remarks from Quintilian supplement and confirm. He can define the Livian style as a 'rich creaminess' that clogs the truth.[1] Further, he states that while Livy is best for boys to begin with in an apprenticeship to rhetorical studies, Sallust is the greater historian.[2]

That Sallust, not Livy, ranked as the foremost of the Roman historians was not (so it appears) the dogma of some clique, a temporary fashion, or a reversion to archaism. For the orator, Quintilian enjoined a Ciceronian style, but he knew (and he proclaimed it) that oratory is a very different thing from history.[3] The persuasion of Quintilian is a firm guarantee; and Sallust's primacy stands axiomatic to the poet Martial.[4] That being so, little search or debate is needed to divine what reception the arbiters of praise or blame ought to have given to the new historian who had all the Sallustian virtues, reinforced and enhanced with the poetry, the pageantry, and the eloquence of Livy.[5]

Tacitus can furnish a generous appraisal of Livy—'eloquentiae ac fidei praeclarus in primis'.[6] Livy was endowed with style and honesty. The style was eloquent, ornate, and flowing, well suited to serve up anew the fairy stories about the Kings of Rome or renovate the edifying narrations that exploited heroes of the early Republic—and veracity was barely relevant there. But was the style tough and tense enough for an authentic record? Honesty was poor protection against the inaccuracy of other historians, whether ingenuous, romantic, or mendacious. Nor did candour, innocence, and ethical aspirations equip a man to unmask the guile of political managers and unravel the complexities of human nature.[7] Modern or recent history required the maturity, the penetration, and the ferocity of Sallust.[8]

---

[1] x. 1. 32: 'neque illa Livii lactea ubertas satis docebit eum qui non speciem expositionis sed fidem quaerit.'

[2] II. 5. 19: 'Livium a pueris magis quam Sallustium; et hic historiae maior est auctor, ad quem tamen intellegendum profectu opus sit.'

[3] x. 1. 31: 'historia quoque alere oratorem quodam uberi iucundoque suco potest; verum et ipsa sic legenda, ut sciamus plerasque eius virtutes oratori vitandas esse.' Cf. Pliny, *Epp.* v. 8. 9 f. (the elucidation of which is helped by Quintilian's remarks in x. 1. 33).

[4] xiv. 191. 2: 'primus Romana Crispus in historia.'

[5] cf. Ph. Fabia, *Rev. phil.* xix (1895), 1 ff. Even, presumably, were he not very original—'en tant qu'historien, l'originalité de Tacite est nulle' (*Journal des Savants* 1922, 56). Many things in the *Historiae* cannot, however, have been at all liked (p. 229).

[6] *Ann.* IV. 34. 3.

[7] The paradoxical notion that Livy is a better historian than Tacitus has been expressed by M. L. W. Laistner, *The Greater Roman Historians* (1947), 139.

[8] That is to say, 'Patavinitas' was not enough. That defect, which Quintilian interpreted as the use of local or dialect words (I. 5. 56; VIII. 1. 3), is perhaps something worse, and deeper, to be divined by what is known about Patavium and about the man who made the remark (Asinius Pollio), cf. R. Syme, *Rom. Rev.* (1939), 485 f.

XVIII. BIAS AND EQUITY

BEING political, it was difficult for Roman historiography not to be partisan. Banished from the conduct of affairs but not remote from the spectacle, the statesman in his retreat, under a fine show of detachment, prosecuted his ideals or his feuds, with a sharp edge against his enemies, a heavy indictment against the younger generation. In the writing of history, Sallust discovered solace for disappointment, Asinius Pollio an apologia for success, not without rancour. Livy was not a senator, and Livy in certain respects is an incongruous figure in the succession of the annalists, Republican and imperial. Yet Livy's work is a panegyric on the Roman People, a defence of its dominion over the nations.

Sallust is peculiarly vulnerable. He had been a partisan of Caesar; and it has been claimed that his first monograph is no better than a political pamphlet, cunningly contrived to disculpate Caesar from suspicion of any share in Catilinarian designs.[1] An extreme opinion. What partiality Sallust's *Bellum Catilinae* shows for Caesar is not outrageous.[2] The balanced confrontation between Caesar and Cato is candid and admirable.[3] Perhaps Cato comes off best; and, although Sallust could not fail to admire Caesar, he could not wholly approve him either.[4]

Sallust's treatment of Cicero is also in question. The Senate had passed the ultimate decree, and the Senate by debate and vote decided the fate of the conspirators. The role and importance of the consul could be variously estimated.[5] Sallust has done him less than justice.[6] Sallust certainly felt a deep antipathy. He declared it best in his own fashion—by the curious and elaborate creation of an anti-Ciceronian prose style.[7]

The *Bellum Jugurthinum* can be impugned for its treatment of persons and parties, its artful subversion of the *nobiles*.[8] And what is known or

---

[1] E. Schwartz, *Hermes* XXXII (1897), 554 ff. = *Ges. Schr.* II (1956), 275 ff.

[2] cf. the arguments of H. M. Last, *Mélanges . . . J. Marouzeau* (1948), 355 ff.

[3] *Cat.* 53. 6 ff.

[4] Some will have it that Cato is the real hero, thus E. Skard, *Symbolae Osloenses* IX (1930), 69 ff.; V. Pöschl, *Grundwerte römischer Staatsgesinnung in den Geschichtswerken des Sallust* (1940), 10 ff.; F. Lämmli, *Mus. Helv.* III (1946), 94 ff.

[5] Brutus' view made Cicero very angry (*Ad Att.* XII. 21. 1).

[6] E. Schwartz, o.c. 576 ff. Some of Sallust's defenders go to the other extreme, e.g. W. A. Baehrens, *Neue Wege zur Antike* IV (1926), 35 ff.

[7] G. Boissier, *Journal des Savants* 1903, 66. But that is not the whole story.

[8] K. v. Fritz, *TAPA* LXXIV (1943), 134 ff.

surmised of the *Historiae* is far from reassuring.[1] Yet Sallust as he went on made progress not only in technique but in insight, revealing the struggle for power behind the words and pretexts and exposing the fraudulent demagogue as well as the fraudulent conservative.

If his standpoint seemed to become moral rather than political, that was not unmixed gain for an historian. He was liable to be influenced by conventional antitheses between virtue and vice, between energy and sloth, by the inevitable contrast between integrity and civic unity in the ancient days and the rapacity, corruption, and violence that marked the Republic in its last and evil epoch. On a severe interpretation, his moralizing is rudimentary, the character-drawing schematic; the prologues of the two monographs are an amalgam of commonplaces, redeemed from tedium and triviality only by a merciful crispness and brevity.[2] It was asserted, indeed, that they had little relation to the subject.[3] A facile dealer in ethical generalizations could supply a prologue for the asking, and even accumulate a stock.[4] Sallust was not a rapid composer. If the products of his long labours exhibit concentrated gravity and stylistic finish, the material is none the less derivative. The fear of the foreign enemy as a factor constraining the Romans to practise virtue, discipline, and concord is present in both monographs and recurs in the *Historiae*.[5]

The Sallustian virtues, essential to any history that deserved the name, might not be wholly conducive to a serene judgement. That he will be strictly impartial every Roman annalist proclaims at the outset (and parody echoes the profession).[6] In the preface of the *Historiae* Tacitus asseverates that he has no personal cause for being unfair to any one of the three rulers Galba, Otho, Vitellius.[7] It does not follow that he must be exempt from strong feelings of one kind or another, devoid of honest prejudice.

Detestation of the soldiery, respect for the 'res publica', and admiration for the ancient names might suggest and condone a sympathetic portrayal of the tragedy of Sulpicius Galba. Tacitus refuses to relent. Galba was an anachronism—'nocuit antiquus rigor et nimia severitas

---

[1] Chs. XII f.; XLII.

[2] E. Howald, *Vom Geist antiker Geschichtsschreibung* (1944), 146. For more friendly opinions, G. Boissier, *Journal des Savants* 1903, 59 ff.; M. Rambaud, *Rev. ét. lat.* XXIV (1947), 115 ff.; A. D. Leeman, *Mnemosyne*⁴ VII (1954), 323 ff.; VIII (1955), 38 ff.

[3] Quintilian III. 8. 9.

[4] Cicero, *Ad Att.* XVI. 6. 4: 'id evenit ob eam rem quod habeo volumen prohoemiorum. ex eo eligere soleo cum aliquod σύγγραμμα institui.'

[5] *Cat.* 10. 1; *Jug.* 41. 2 ff.; *Hist.* I. 12. For this, and other notions, perhaps deriving from Posidonius, cf. F. Klingner, *Hermes* LXIII (1928), 165 ff.

[6] Seneca, *Apocol.* 1. 1: 'nihil nec offensae nec gratiae dabitur.'

[7] I. 1. 3: 'mihi Galba Otho Vitellius nec beneficio nec iniuria cogniti.'

cui iam parès non sumus'.[1] Forbidding but inert, Galba only shows signs of life and interest when money and discipline are concerned. If Tacitus seems over-harsh, there are the anecdotes of Suetonius for corroboration.[2] Galba used to say that a man ought not to be called to account for what he does out of hours.[3] That was not the opinion held at Rome in the days of the Scipiones.[4]

Otho by contrast—affable, pliant, and corrupt—belonged to his own epoch, a choice luxury product of the Neronian court. It is on Otho when he resolves to end his life that the historian lavishes the resources of talent and sympathy, with the setting of a drama, with magnificent eloquence in farewell, with noble words of consolation for friends and family—and no hint that the capitulation of his forces is imminent or already transacted.[5] What draws Tacitus is manifest. Not merely the opportunity to portray a theatrical suicide, such as the taste of the Romans took delight in, but a suicide more truly to be commended than when a good man took his own life in ostentatious rectitude, but with no advantage to the Commonwealth. Otho's resolution averted any further shedding of Roman blood in civil war. Other rulers fail by contrast. Nero could not summon energy for action, or dignity at the end. Vitellius, when his armies were lost, sank into lethargy like a fat animal.[6] He let the futile struggle go on, incompetent even to manage aright his own abdication. The artifice of Tacitus is patent. No deception, no conflict with what the historian has previously revealed about the character, actions, and repute of Otho. Tacitus is quite clear. He sets it on record that Otho had been feared and detested much more than Vitellius.[7]

Civil war was the worst of evils, worse even than submitting to tyranny. That verdict was enunciated, not by some time-server or apologist of the monarchy, but by Favonius, the friend of Cato and of Brutus.[8] Nor did the Romans have any confidence in a happy outcome of the armed strife between citizens. When the last of the faction-leaders prevailed, and, consolidating his power, turned for support

---

[1] I. 18. 3.
[2] *Galba* 2 (snobbery); 9 (cruelty); 12 (avarice); 20 (conceit); 22 (gluttony and homosexuality). Tacitus naturally passed over most of this stuff. Not that he approved of Galba as a man and an emperor, as stated by J. Vogt, *Tacitus als Politiker* (Antrittsrede, Tübingen, 1924), 13. For inconsistencies in his portrayal see now E. Koestermann, *Navicula Chiloniensis* (1956), 191 ff.
[3] ib. 9. 1: 'quod nemo rationem otii sui reddere cogeretur.'
[4] At least by Cato—'clarorum virorum atque magnorum non minus oti quam negoti rationem exstare oportere' (cited by Cicero, *Pro Plancio* 66).
[5] For a defence of Tacitus' portrayal see F. Klingner, *Sächsische S-B, Phil.-hist. Kl.* XCII, 1 (1940), 1 ff.
[6] III. 36. 1: 'ut ignava animalia, quibus si cibum suggeras, iacent torpentque.'
[7] II. 31. 1.
[8] Plutarch, *Brutus* 12: χεῖρον εἶναι μοναρχίας παρανόμου πόλεμον ἐμφύλιον.

to good men, the monarchy was accepted as a necessity, not with enthusiasm. The Roman historians were averse from a mere pragmatic justification of success. Tacitus goes so far as to assert that Vespasian was the only one of all the Caesars who changed for the better;[1] and he condemns any ascription of patriotic motives to the traitors who helped Vespasian to power.[2]

Detesting civil strife and suspicious of power and success, Tacitus achieves a sombre and savage impartiality in the portrayal of the crime and violence of the year 69. Tacitus is harsh and bitter, offering no consolation anywhere. His despair is engendered by the contrasts between word and fact, between ambitions and achievement, by the tragic vicissitudes of men and governments. It has yet to be proved that acerbity or gloom is detrimental in an historian.[3]

Tacitus sometimes resorts to sarcasm or a ferocious humour. When the Flavian army drew near Rome, a senatorial embassy went out but was roughly handled, the praetor Junius Rusticus being wounded. Musonius Rufus, though by rank not a senator, had thrust himself on the mission, and Musonius fell foul of the troops when with 'intempestiva sapientia' he tried to read them a lecture on the blessings of peace: 'id plerisque ludibrio, pluribus taedio.'[4] Vespasian at Alexandria was solicited to try his hand at miraculous healing. The diagnosis of medical men is quoted, in professional language pompously stylized. They pronounce for an experiment, for such may well be the will of Providence—and, if it succeeds, glory for the Princeps; if not, the ridicule will fall on the poor cripples.[5]

Irony is all-pervasive, not only in detail or comment, when a brief phrase quickly discloses some supreme incongruity, but in the setting of whole transactions. Men of taste looked for splendour and majesty in orations composed by Cornelius Tacitus. They came upon other qualities as well—and some very disconcerting.

The Emperor Galba delivers a discourse conveying two main arguments—constitutional government against despotism, adoption in preference to blood and kin.[6] This has a clear bearing upon events

---

[1] I. 50. 4. [2] II. 101. 1, cf. III. 86. 2.

[3] cf. G. Boissier, *Tacite* (1903), 131. By contrast, P. Wuilleumier, *Tacite, l'homme et l'œuvre* (1949), 102: 'le pessimisme ne convient pas à l'historien, qui doit rester impartial, sinon même impassible.' Note an early verdict of Fabia—'pour nous, modernes, l'historien est médiocre: son unique mérite est d'avoir fait un louable effort vers l'impartialité' (*Les Sources de Tacite dans les Histoires et les Annales* (1893), 310). [4] III. 81. 1.

[5] IV. 81. 2: 'medici varie disserere: huic non exesam vim luminis et redituram si pellerentur obstantia; illi elapsos in pravum artus, si salubris vis adhibeatur, posse integrari. id fortasse cordi deis et divino ministerio principem electum; denique patrati remedii gloriam penes Caesarem, inriti ludibrium penes miseros fore.'

[6] I. 15 f. (paraphrased and condensed above, p. 151 f.).

in Tacitus' own time—Nerva's rule with its claim to unite 'libertas' with the 'principatus', and Nerva's choice of the best man as partner and successor.[1] One step more, and it can be held that the historian took the doctrine for valid and was urgent to enjoin it.[2]

The antithesis is obvious between legitimate authority and despotic power. It had been formulated long ago, and published often since—and it was suspect to any man of understanding. The phraseology allotted to Galba is conventional, resembling the legends on coinage, and to be assesssed accordingly. Galba alleges that he has been summoned to rule 'deorum hominumque consensu'.[3] In fact, his elevation was due to force and accident, and his régime was now collapsing.

Interpreted in the light of Galba's predicament, Galba's oration takes on a different colouring. Rising against Nero, Galba asserted the cause of Senate and People against tyranny.[4] A rebel had no choice, or any other plea. Choosing Piso Licinianus to be ruler for Rome, Galba proclaimed that he was following a principle—'optimum quemque adoptio inveniet'.[5] The adoption itself was an act of despair, 'remedium unicum'.[6] Galba having no son (or close kin whom he approved and trusted) could not establish a dynasty of his own blood, but did what was nearest to that.

Even honest Piso in his speech cannot tell the entire truth. He glides over violence at Galba's accession (and bloodshed subsequently), he adjures the Praetorians not to create a pernicious precedent—as though Galba had not been proclaimed emperor by an army in the provinces.[7]

It should seem that the historian Tacitus, so far from ingenuously commending a political doctrine, is employing the same demolitionary

---

[1] Hence parallels in what Pliny says about adoption in the *Panegyricus*. That Pliny drew upon Tacitus has been supposed by E. Wölfflin, *Archiv für lat. Lex.* XII (1900), 350; J. Mesk, *Wiener Studien* XXXIII (1911), 71 ff.; N. Terzaghi, *Maia* II (1949), 121 ff.; E. Paratore, *Tacito* (1951), 454; K. Büchner, *Rh. Mus.* LXXXXVIII (1955), 289 ff.; R. Güngerich, *Festschrift Bruno Snell* (1956), 145 ff. Against, E. Hohl, *Rh. Mus.* LXVIII (1913), 461 ff. The parallels (being indeed obvious commonplaces) do not amount to much, despite R. T. Bruère, *Class. Phil.* XLIX (1954), 161 ff.

[2] It is a natural temptation to regard the *oratio Galbae* as 'il filone aureo' (E. Paratore, *Tacito* (1951), 464) or 'das politische Glaubensbekenntnis' (E. Kornemann, *Tacitus* (Wiesbaden, 1947), 27). On adoption see further below, p. 233 f.

[3] I. 15. 1; also 'consensus generis humani' in Piso's address to the Guard (I. 30. 2). On these phrases, H. U. Instinsky, *Hermes* LXXV (1940), 265 ff. Note also the legend SALVS GEN. HVMANI (*BMC, R. Emp.* I, 314 f.), with Instinsky's comments, *Hamburger Beiträge zur Numismatik* I (1947), 5 ff.

[4] Suetonius, *Galba* 10. 1: 'consalutatusque imperator legatum se senatus ac populi R. professus est.' For the coin-legends, C. M. Kraay, *Num. Chron.*[6] IX (1949), 129 ff.

[5] I. 16. 1.

[6] 14. 1, cf. *Pan.* 8. 3 (on Nerva's action): 'unicum auxilium fessis rebus.'

[7] 29 f. (summarized above, p. 152).

technique that presents Otho with a magnificent peroration on the
Roman Senate and the 'aeternitas' of Rome and the Empire.[1]

The quality of rulers mattered more than any theory or programme.
After the end of Julii and Claudii Galba came to the power, the scion
of the patrician Sulpicii, but failed in the task; and emperors from the
newer stocks, Otho and Vitellius, were found incompetent. Tacitus
put emphasis upon the personality of the successive rulers. The crisis
of the year 69 was wider: it concerned the whole governing class, and
the system of rule. Is Tacitus adequate in his diagnosis of the events
he describes?[2]

The causes were various, and the crisis took many shapes. Tacitus,
it appears, does full justice. So far as known, his *Historiae* demonstrate
for the first time the full impact of provinces and armies on the
Roman government.[3]

The rule of the Caesars had its root and origin in military power.
It was their necessary function to protect the frontiers of empire and
keep the legions under control. The Caesars, while professing a civilian
authority at Rome, had also managed to install a garrison. Hence a
plain duty also to curb the Guard.

Nero's fall gave the impulsion to a sequence of catastrophes. The
purple being in open competition, the armed forces broke loose, and
the resources of the provinces came into play, imperilling the fabric
of empire and the established order of society. Civil war whetted the
appetites of the lower classes—the plebs of Rome and the soldiers.[4]
Then the subject peoples become involved, tribal rebellions ensued,
and danger from the outer nations, as in that earlier age of tribulation,
to abate which the monarchy emerged, rescuing the senatorial order
and slowing down the process of revolution.

The lesson was enforced once again. Stability demanded a strong
monarchy. The steady decline of the Senate would continue. If Galba

---

[1] 84. 4 (quoted above, p. 155). 'Aeternitas' had been quickly enlisted for imperial
publicity. Observe *ILS* 157 (of A.D. 32): 'providentiae Ti. Caesaris Augusti nati ad aeterni-
tatem Romani nominis.' Senatorial coins of Domitian's reign carry the legend AETERNITAS
AVGVSTI (*BMC, R. Emp.* II, 364 f. On the eternity of Rome, and of its rulers, cf. F. Cumont,
Rev. d'hist. et de litt. rel. I (1896), 435 ff.; M. Vogelstein, *Kaiser-Idee, Rom-Idee* (1930), 42;
M. P. Charlesworth, *Harv. Th. Rev.* XXIX (1936), 107 ff.; H. U. Instinsky, *Hermes* LXXVII
(1942), 313 ff.; J. Beaujeu, *La Religion romaine à l'apogée de l'empire* I (1955), 141 ff.
Tacitus did not like the word: elsewhere only *Agr.* 46. 4, and once in the *Annales* (XI.
7. 1—in reported discourse). For Tacitus in relation to coin-legends see further App. 66.

[2] The problem (with the various modern views) is discussed by P. Zancan, *La Crisi del
principato nell' anno 69 d. C.* (Padova, 1939), 121 ff., who states that Tacitus 'ha tradotto
la crisi del 69 in una critica della nobiltà', which is too narrow. Rostovtzeff's account is
marred by a serious error—that the Rhine legions rose in protest against Otho and the
Guard (*Soc. and Ec. Hist. of the R. Empire* (1926), 84 f.).

[3] E. Paratore, o.c. 426.

[4] Not merely the sack of Cremona (III. 33): observe I. 85. 1; II. 56. 1; IV. 1.

conceived any programme of 'constitutional' government, it was never carried out. As the facts duly reported by Tacitus demonstrate, secret politics prevailed, as before, and a camarilla governed.[1] Nothing in Galba's reign implies that the Senate as a body had regained authority.

Nor does Tacitus admit any substance behind the professions of an Otho or a Vitellius.[2] Liberty dawned for a brief moment after the fall of Vitellius. It was slight and fallacious. Quarrels broke out in the Senate, and personal feuds revived, with a chance to discredit or destroy some of the agents of despotism. Tacitus provides a vivid and accurate description of several debates.[3]

A scene and setting such as he knew well from his own experiences. Tacitus brings in Eprius Marcellus, to admonish Helvidius Priscus in tones of quiet reason, and contribute a statesmanlike defence of neutrals and time-servers, using words the like of which Tacitus had heard—or had used himself. There were other resemblances, large and small, to the reign of Nerva. Tacitus does not neglect the opportunity to exhibit a speech in fierce denunciation of a notorious prosecutor.[4]

Nothing came of all the talk and exertions (except that a few minor offenders were condemned). That too was a familiar outcome. The subtle Mucianus brought forward an appeal for amnesty, and the 'patres' went no further in their aspirations to 'libertas'. They were able to satisfy their honour by rebuking an Italian town that had shown disrespect to a Roman senator.

So far the Senate in the first days of Vespasian's reign. The larger actors of future scenes have been clearly delineated. Licinius Mucianus is thrown into prominence by the character-sketch coming so early in Book I;[5] and, soon after the beginning of Book IV, Helvidius Priscus earns a full-length presentation. The clash with Eprius Marcellus is announced in ominous language, momentarily disclosing the theme of 'saeva pax'.[6]

Tacitus reproduced, in a proper and pessimistic vein, the traditional matter of civil war. That was only one part of his *Historiae*. The larger portion, after the establishment of peace and order, dealt with the rule of the Flavian dynasty, bright hopes at first, but turning towards

[1] I. 13. I.

[2] Though such has been asserted, for Otho, by G. Manfrè, *La Crisi politica dell' anno 68–69 d. Chr.* (Padova, 1947), 90, cf. 94; for Vitellius, by A. Momigliano, *Stud. it. fil. cl.* IX (1931/2), 122 f.

[3] IV. 3 ff.; 39 ff. (p. 187 f.).

[4] 42—Curtius Montanus attacking M. Aquillius Regulus. No doubt highly relished by Trajanic readers. Cf. Pliny's 'avenging of Helvidius' (pp. 94, 120).

[5] I. 10 (p. 195).

[6] IV. 4. 3: 'isque praecipuus illi dies magnae offensae initium et magnae gloriae fuit.'

oppression and ending in catastrophe. The later books would bring
both his honesty and his industry to a more exacting trial.

Tacitus owed status and advancement to the Flavian House—and
especially to the Emperor Domitian. He did not allow that to distort
his account of Vespasian and Titus. If there was undue prepossession
in their favour, it was engendered by the historian's views about
Domitian. How far was impartiality possible or even desirable in the
portrayal of a tyrant?

From a persuasion of the complexity of things and a distaste for
conventional and schematic judgements, Tacitus insists that both
sides of a question be given a hearing—and every aspect of a personality be reckoned with. If he lights upon a character perfectly
blended with good and evil components, it is sheer felicity. Elsewhere
an acknowledged villain earns a partial or temporary condonation
because he governed a province with integrity, displayed desperate
energy, or died like a brave man. Tacitus likes to throw in a discordant
detail or a subversive annotation. Not content to redeem the wicked,
his equity or malice operates to undermine the virtuous by exposing
conduct foolish, tiresome, or unprofitable.

It had been easy enough to produce a Domitian, a crafty tyrant as
a foil to the discreet and patriotic virtues of Agricola: an encomium
permitted licence and exaggeration, and some of the devices there
employed by Tacitus were not at all creditable. An historian's task
was different. He had to deal with a long and complicated series of
events, with the interplay of numerous factors—and with the theme
of the imperial power as influenced, not merely by the character of the
ruler but by the secret politics of the governmental oligarchy, by
accident, intrigue, or conspiracy.

There were many features for praise in the general administration of
Domitian, and he enforced exemplary behaviour on provincial
governors.[1] The industry and vigilance of the despot made him the
more formidable and the more detestable. Some of the credit might
go (it is true) to the policy of his predecessors being continued, to
wise counsellors, and to agents who served the Empire rather than
the Emperor; and behind certain measures of penalty or ameliora-
tion might be suspected an envious and cruel nature. Pretence and
guile was the orthodox explanation for the good deeds of a bad ruler,
inevitable to men who knew Domitian—and irresistible to the historian Tacitus. He would trace the whole process, how that prince,
after a fair show of moderation and clemency, gradually, through the
licence and impunity of unlimited power, allowed his ambitions to
develop, his true nature to be revealed (like so many Caesars before

[1] Suetonius, *Dom.* 8. 2.

him), and finally, from pressure of anger and fear, became a monster of iniquity: 'illa immanissima belua.'[1]

Various problems of design and balance confronted an author narrating the whole period from 69 to 96. How and where should he divide the work into its two halves? And how dispose each hexad— three groups of two books or two triads?[2] Furthermore, the annalistic fabric: the end of a book might not always fit the end of a year.[3]

Book V opens with the preliminaries to the Roman siege of Jerusalem. It breaks off with the rebellion on the Rhine already collapsing and Julius Civilis in negotiation for a surrender with Petillius Cerialis.[4] There is no means of ascertaining whether this book ended with the fall of the city (in September of 70), with the joint triumph of Vespasian and Titus in the next summer, or at some later point.[5]

Upon the Jewish triumph of 71 followed another ceremony, announcing that peace prevailed by land and sea throughout the world. The Temple of Janus was closed.[6] Much remained to be done. Though order had been restored in Judaea and on the Rhine, every frontier and every province, damaged in some way or at least neglected since the first disturbances that brought down Nero, called for attention— to say nothing of the capital, the Senate, the whole social and governmental framework.[7] The work of repair was symbolized by the censorship of Vespasian and Titus. There was enough material to carry Book V down to the end of 73—and a dramatic episode was ready to come early in the next book.

The main themes of imperial annals are the wars (foreign and civil) and the relations between Princeps and Senate. The first session of the high assembly after the Flavian forces have captured Rome displays a senator in opposition—Helvidius Priscus. The final clash came some

---

[1] *Pan.* 48. 3, cf. 95. 3: 'ille insidiosissimus princeps.' For the declension in Domitian to cruelty, to greater cruelty, and to rapacity, &c., Suetonius, *Dom.* 10. 1 ff.

[2] *Historiae* and *Annales* comprised thirty books, cf. Jerome, *Comm. ad Zach.* III. 14: 'Cornelius Tacitus, qui post Augustum usque ad mortem Domitiani vitas Caesarum triginta voluminibus exaravit.' It will here be assumed that twelve go to the *Historiae*. See further App. 35.

[3] For the structure and proportions of the lost books there is not much guidance to be got from Suetonius or from Cassius Dio. The biographer's method and choice of materials was sharply (and deliberately) divergent; while Dio (preserved in abbreviations or fragments) appears to have given one book to each of the three Flavians.

[4] v. 26.

[5] The preliminaries, it is true, are narrated at some length; but it would have been a sin against history and proportion to allow Jerusalem and the Jewish triumph to occupy almost a whole book.

[6] Orosius VII. 3. 7; 19. 4, citing Tacitus (= fr. 4 f. in the editions of Fisher and Koestermann).

[7] Suetonius, *Divus Vesp.* 8. 1: 'prope afflictam nutantemque rem p. stabilire primo, deinde et ornare.'

years later, in 74 (so it appears).[1] Vespasian, for all his good sense, became annoyed under criticism; Helvidius was tactless; and Mucianus, the chief minister, never tired of denouncing philosophers as a menace to all ordered government.[2] Helvidius went in for pernicious and subversive doctrines, so it was alleged.[3] He was banished, and later executed against the wish (it was explained) of the Emperor.[4] One of the chief agents in the ruin of Helvidius may be divined—his enemy, Eprius Marcellus, that savage speaker: Eprius was consul for the second time in 74. And one of the historian's devices may also be divined—an oration from Helvidius Priscus asserting a senator's dignity and the right of free speech.[5]

For the rest, there was plenty to make up a record if a man had an eye for selection, variety, and digression. The decease of some notable personage, last link with a past age, would be duly chronicled;[6] and there were odd events at Rome or abroad.[7] Frontier operations, even if inconsiderable in themselves, gained significance from the generals who conducted them—the leading men in the military oligarchy, some consular already under Nero, but others (the majority) active or lucky in the recent civil wars. Thus Petillius Cerialis and Julius Frontinus in Britain, or Ulpius Traianus the governor of Syria, averting by prompt action a threat from the Parthians.[8] Other persons, known to Tacitus, or known as the parents of his coevals, will have taken his fancy for various reasons (and not all for praise).

Some had been quietly noted in the earlier books.[9] Above all, Tacitus would be drawn to the astute survivors, the advocates he had heard, and the great names for senatorial eloquence.[10] As a dramatic and paradoxical finale there offered that conspiracy in the last year of Vespasian (unexplained, and surely never proved) which joined in

---

[1] No source supplies a clear indication of date. In support of 74 note the atmosphere at Rome when Curiatius Maternus recited his *Cato* (*Dial.* 2. 1).

[2] Dio LXVI. 13. 1a. [3] ib. 12. 2 f. [4] Suetonius, *Divus Vesp.* 15.

[5] There had been no speech of Helvidius hitherto, only a brief attack on Eprius Marcellus in reported discourse (IV. 7).

[6] The great jurist C. Cassius Longinus (*suff.* 30) came back from exile and died in Vespasian's reign (*Dig.* 1. 2. 2. 52).

[7] Compare the technique in parts of the *Annales* where Tacitus needs to fill out a book (Ch. XXI).

[8] p. 30. Hence discreet compliment to the Emperor—and (better) the chance to compensate Frontinus (recently deceased) for the brevity of *Agr.* 17. 3: 'subiit sustinuitque molem Iulius Frontinus, vir magnus, quantum licebat.'

[9] Thus, belonging to a certain group, Junius Rusticus (III. 80. 2), his brother Mauricus (IV. 40. 4), Musonius Rufus (III. 81. 1; IV. 10; 40. 3), and the energetic Verulana Gratilla (III. 69. 3), perhaps the wife of Rusticus (Pliny, *Epp.* v. 1. 8); the legionary legates Aurelius Fulvus and Tettius Julianus (I. 79. 5, cf. for the latter II. 85. 2; IV. 39. 1; 40. 2); the infamous Baebius Massa (IV. 50. 2); and, of course, Aquillius Regulus (IV. 42).

[10] Notably Eprius Marcellus, Vibius Crispus, and Fabricius Veiento; also Silius Italicus and Galerius Trachalus. For the orators, App. 26.

calamity Eprius Marcellus, the loyal agent of despotism, and Caecina Alienus, who had betrayed Vitellius.[1]

Vespasian's funeral was remembered for a fine performance by the actor who impersonated the dead man, jokes and all.[2] Though solemn history could not have admitted more than a brief hint of comedy, or a dignified periphrasis, the ceremony, calling up the paradoxical fortunes of a Sabine parvenu, would inspire contrasted verdicts among the spectators, not without malice or sinister forecasts. Not everybody was happy at the prospect of Titus. Men spoke of luxury and cruelty and a second Nero; and the killing of Caecina Alienus was a heavy load for the new ruler.[3]

If the missing portions of Book V along with another book be held adequate to contain the reign of Vespasian down to his death in the summer of 79, a neat solution emerges. The second hexad of the *Historiae* was devoted to the sons of Vespasian, one book for Titus and five for the fifteen years of Domitian.[4]

The *Historiae* are something more than a story of emperors. If there is contrast in the Flavian dynasty, there is also continuity. Titus is not merely the heir of Vespasian—he had been partner in the power almost from the outset. The first period of Domitian's rule (81–85) shows no great change from what had gone before, and the same ministers of state are there.[5] Things began to go wrong with the disasters on the Danube. Two Domitianic books (the one mainly of peace, the other of war) would carry the story to the end of 88. The next year, with Antonius Saturninus proclaimed emperor at Moguntiacum on the first day of January, marked a decisive turn for the worse in Domitian's rule.[6] It gave the historian a year beginning with sharp action, to recall 69. The events concorded miraculously with the demands of structure. Three books thus become available for the tyranny of Domitian.

On this hypothesis the twelve books of the *Historiae* acquire firm proportions. The first hexad splits into two halves, namely, Books I–III with the civil wars (Galba, Otho, and Vitellius), and IV–VI with the reign of Vespasian (foreign war on the Rhine and in Judaea, and war succeeded by ordered government). The second hexad also divides. Its first half recounts inner stability and the dynastic' succession,

---

[1] p. 101. For the incident see also J. A. Crook, *AJP* LXXII (1951), 169.

[2] *Divus Vesp.* 19. 2.   [3] *Divus Titus* 6 f.

[4] Theories that assume six books for Domitian (cf. App. 35) cramp unduly the reigns of Vespasian and Titus.

[5] *Divus Titus* 7. 2. In the first place Vibius Crispus and Fabricius Veiento (the latter's second consulate falls only a few months after the ruin of Eprius). See Juvenal IV. 75 ff. (p. 67). The satirist may have suppressed some (reputable) names.

[6] *Dom.* 10. 5: 'verum aliquanto post civilis belli victoriam saevior.'

passing before the end to the Danubian wars; while the second is devoted to the rest of Domitian's reign, from 89 to 96. Thus the last three books of the *Historiae* form a pendant to the first three, the Domitianic tyranny matching the 'longus et unus annus' in which three emperors met their doom.

A brief summary will illustrate the presumed scope and design of the second hexad. Although Titus, 'amor ac deliciae generis humani', was cut off after two years and two months (79–81), that brief felicity could expand without discomfort to the bulk of a book—the shows and games when the Flavian Amphitheatre was dedicated, the eruption of Vesuvius, the disastrous conflagration at Rome, and a great pestilence; and for further variety would be invoked Julius Agricola advancing far to the north in his third British campaign,[1] or the strange story of a false Nero who appeared in Asia, gathered a company about him, and marched to the river Euphrates.[2]

To Domitian at the outset of his reign the historian might concede moderate and even meritorious actions (not without incrimination of motive). Domitian's first military action was deliberate and felicitous. In 83 he marched against the Chatti. The truth demanded that the war against the Chatti be explained not as a cheap and fraudulent substitute for genuine glory (the device in the *Agricola*), but as a considerable operation, securing the whole frontier of Upper Germany, the credit, however, to belong to the Emperor's military advisers, among them persons like Julius Frontinus.[3] Future developments, however, were quickly foreshadowed in the scandals of the Palace— Domitian first quarrelled with his consort (Domitia Longina, the daughter of Corbulo), and then was reconciled, yet before long he lived openly with his own niece, Julia the daughter of Titus, whose husband Flavius Sabinus he killed. Further, moral legislation and the title of 'censor perpetuus', which he assumed in the year 85, disclosed the rigid authoritarian.

From this point onwards an historian's architecture was firmly and elegantly prescribed by the events—the three crises of the reign, two foreign and one internal. The first began with trouble on the Danube —'nobilitatus cladibus mutuis Dacus'.[4] A Roman army was destroyed in Moesia; and soon after, in the invasion of Dacia, occurred the

---

[1] He would presumably be brief on Agricola. What the epitomator of Dio provides (LXVI. 20) is garbled—and mainly devoted to the episode of the Usipi.

[2] This false Nero was called Terentius Maximus (Dio LXVI. 19. 3 b–c).

[3] Note the references in *Strat.* I. 1. 8; 3. 10; II. 11. 7. Frontinus was praetor in 70; Domitian went to Gaul (*Hist.* IV. 85 f.), and so did Frontinus: the Lingones surrendered to him (*Strat.* IV. 3. 14).

[4] *Hist.* I. 2. 1, cf. pp. 23 f. Though the trouble may have started the year before, Tacitus could have reserved it till the beginning of 86 as an effective début for his second Domitianic book.

disaster of Cornelius Fuscus, the Prefect of the Guard. Tacitus (it happens to be on record) here imitated Sallust and other writers, refusing to reveal the total of the dead in Roman disasters.[1] An excursus on the Dacians was requisite, and not to be compiled without some study—none of his predecessors among the Roman annalists, so far as known, can have furnished it.[2] And, to set off and enhance calamity on the frontiers of empire, there was pageantry at the capital —in 86 the institution of the Capitoline Games, in 88 the *Ludi Saeculares*. Being a member of the sacerdotal college that officiated when the new era was inaugurated, Cornelius Tacitus had scope for knowledge and for irony.[3]

The year 89 opened the next act of the tragedy—a new civil war, but terminated with unexpected rapidity. Then, before the settlement with Dacia (there had been a Roman victory before the end of the previous year), hostilities supervened with Rome's vassals beyond the middle course of the Danube—Marcomanni, Quadi, and Sarmatians. The Emperor's celebrations, in summer or autumn of 89, were exposed to damaging comment: no civil war can provide a Roman victory, Dacia had not been conquered, Domitian was triumphing not over foreign enemies but over the legions he had lost.[4] As a suitable sequel came a disaster in Pannonia in 92. Domitian went to the seat of war. His pomp and indolence (instead of marching he preferred to be transported along the rivers) no doubt was set against the hardships of the troops and the silent anger of the generals on his staff, frustrated of action and glory.[5]

So far the foreign wars. In the next year began the internal crisis, with the eradication of the opposition group and the curbing of the Senate.[6] The tyranny was at its height. Though Domitian reduced the Senate to servitude and complicity, and found (so it seems) the right

---

[1] Orosius VII. 10. 4 = fr. 6: 'nisi Cornelius Tacitus, qui hanc historiam diligentissime retexuit, de reticendo interfectorum numero et Sallustium Crispum et alios auctores quam plurimos sanxisse et se ipsum idem potissimum elegisse dixisset.'

[2] Perhaps dimly to be divined in Orosius VII. 34. 5 = fr. 7. This book would also note the legendary origin of the desert tribe of the Nasamones in Libya (Servius on *Aen.* III. 399 = fr. 8)—and therefore presumably their habits. And, for trouble in Mauretania, cf. *ILS* 9200.

[3] *Ann.* XI. 11. 1, cf. Ch. VI.

[4] Orosius VII. 10. 4: 'Domitianus tamen pravissima elatus iactantia sub nomine superatorum hostium de extinctis legionibus triumphavit'; Dio LXVII. 9. 6: ὁ μὲν οὖν Δομιτιανὸς τοιαῦτα νικητήρια, ἢ ὥς γε ὁ ὅμιλος ἔλεγε, τοιούτους ἐναγισμοὺς ἐπί τε τοῖς ἐν τῇ Δακίᾳ καὶ ἐπὶ τοῖς ἐν τῇ 'Ρώμῃ τεθνηκόσιν ἐποίησε. The coincidence deserves attention—for the preceding sentence of Orosius (= fr. 6) actually cites the authority of Cornelius Tacitus. Hence a further 'fragment'. Note also exact and surprising knowledge about German peoples in scraps from Dio—LXVII. 5. 1 (a king of the Cherusci); 5. 2 (envoys from the Lugii to Domitian); 5. 3 (the king of the Semnones, along with a priestess, on a visit to Domitian).

[5] cf. *Pan.* 82. 4 f.

[6] For the date, App. 19.

men to hold the armies, his alarm and suspicion became morbid and murderous. The Flavian insistence on dynastic succession proved fatal to the family. In 95 Domitian put to death the nearest in kin, his cousin, Flavius Clemens, a person lacking talent or energy, and banished Flavia Domitilla, the wife of Clemens.[1] The catastrophe of the line was not long delayed.

The year 96 was marked by celestial phenomena without precedent, by portents and omens, and by astrological predictions, some delusive and some verified.[2] The scepticism of Tacitus did not debar him from resort to such effects to deepen the atmosphere of gloom and apprehension. Domitian, pacing the halls of the Palatine by night, sleepless and alone, tortured by his crimes and his fears, was a subject worthy of the historian who recounted the last hours and the end of Vitellius; and the *Historiae*, which began with an emperor murdered in the Roman Forum by the Praetorian Guard, terminate with the assassination of a despot in his bedchamber.

---

[1] Suetonius, *Dom.* 15. 1; Dio LXVII. 14. 1 f. Clemens' brother T. Flavius Sabinus (*PIR²*, F 355), *ordinarius* in 82 and husband of Julia, the daughter of Titus, had been destroyed quite early in the reign.

[2] *Dom.* 15 f.; Dio LXVII. 16.

PART IV

TRAJAN AND HADRIAN

XIX. THE REIGN OF TRAJAN

THE dawn of a new era in the Roman Commonwealth was no
longer a novelty. Not only had three emperors, Augustus,
Claudius, and Domitian, celebrated and exploited the *Ludi
Saeculares*, reckoning centuries by the computation that happened to
suit their convenience. Any reign could use the language of the golden
years.[1] With the growth of monarchy each ruler tended to annex the
age and call it his own, from the day of his accession. In the first of
his letters to Trajan, Pliny dutifully acclaims the Emperor's 'saeculum';[2] and Trajan himself, in the conscious pride of integrity and
justice, consigns his strongest reprobation of iniquitous practices with
the phrase 'nec nostri saeculi est'.[3]

Bright hopes had been blasted before, and conventional enthusiasm
discredited, when upon the annunciation of a new era of felicity followed conspiracy or civil war, when the early promise of a principate
faded, disclosing black despotism. This time it all turned out to be
true. The choice of Trajan for emperor showed that human will and
foresight need not be baffled by the hidden malevolent powers.
Fatalism and despair were refuted. Health, vigour, and confidence
came back to Rome.

The Republic in its last age had been afflicted by maladies that only
monarchy could cure or abate. Sulla's remedy was not medicine but
murder.[4] Pompeius in the therapeutic efforts of his third consulate
only aggravated the trouble.[5] Caesar was too sharp and sudden, but

---

[1] Thus, early in Nero's reign, Calpurnius Siculus I. 63 f.; the *s.c.* of 56 (*ILS* 6043,
ll. 41 ff.); and, in a lighter vein, Seneca, *Apocol.* I. 1: 'ante diem III idus Octobris anno
novo, initio saeculi felicissimi.'

[2] *Epp.* X. 1. 2: 'prospera omnia, id est digna saeculo tuo', cf. 3a. 2; 23. 2; 97. 2; *Pan.*
40. 5. And also, naturally enough, 'aeternitate tua' (41. 1). For this notion, pp. 47, 208.

[3] X. 97. 2, cf. 55: 'non est ex iustitia nostrorum temporum.'

[4] Lucan II. 141 f.: 'dumque nimis iam putria membra recidit | excessit medicina
modum.'

[5] *Ann.* III. 28. 1.

Augustus effected a cure, without excessive surgery, so it could be asserted on a favourable estimate.[1] A total collapse had been averted. To maintain health and stability the central control by one man was requisite—the Empire, that vast bulk, was liable to strains and fatigue and crisis.[2] A fresh distemper came to pervade it. The imperial system, as it gradually developed safeguards against change and disturbance (that was necessary under capricious or incompetent emperors), at the same time tended heavily towards routine; and some of the rulers might be blamed, willing prisoners of sloth or timidity. Hence the persuasion that the world was growing old and tired. The elder Pliny has some bitter comments. In earlier days among the warring states and rival kingdoms all manner of discoveries were made. The age of universal peace, with the emperor glad to foster the arts and sciences, failed to show any progress in knowledge. Only greed and luxury prospered.[3]

Men had prayed for order and concord in the world. When that came at last, it brought despotism.[4] Deep calm ensued at Rome—'domi res tranquillae.'[5] There was another side. Peace might be murderous—'saeva pax'. At the best, it was depressing and sterile. Such was the nemesis of the imperial peace. As it endured through the slow years, 'longa pax' issued in neglect and stagnation. Buildings crumbled, and ramparts; the army decayed, and rot was everywhere.[6]

Trajan broke the spell and banished the 'inertia Caesarum'. At his call the ageing Empire awoke from its lethargy. It responded with youthful spirit and vigour. Rome reverted for a season to the old conquering epoch.[7]

Trajan looked like a general of the Republic, and he quickly fulfilled what was expected by Senate and People. When a Roman of the time cast his eyes backwards over the panorama of history, he could

---

[1] *Ann.* I. 9. 5, cf. Dio LVI. 44. 2.

[2] Compare 'fessae res' in Tacitus (*Ann.* XV. 50. 1) and in other authors (*NH* II. 18; *Pan.* 8. 3).

[3] *NH* II. 117 f., cf. XIV. 2 ff. Seneca was more alert and hopeful, *NQ* VII. 30. 5: 'multa venientis aevi populus ignota nobis sciet.' More significant than the aspirations in his *Medea*—'nec sit terris ultima Thule' (379).

[4] Lucan I. 670: 'cum domino pax ista venit.'

[5] *Ann.* I. 3. 7. The word 'tranquillus' occurs nowhere else in Tacitus. Cf. Sallust, *Cat.* 16. 5: 'tutae tranquillaeque res omnes.'

[6] The phrase 'longa pax', alluding detrimentally to the results of the imperial peace, is frequent in Tacitus—*Agr.* 11. 5; *Hist.* I. 67. 2; 88. 2; II. 17. 1; IV. 22. 1; V. 16. 3; *Ann.* XIII. 35. 1. Note also Juvenal VI. 292: 'nunc patimur longae pacis mala.' The phrase 'longa pace cuncta refovente' (Quintus Curtius IV. 4. 21) could help to date its author: certainly not Augustan.

[7] Florus, *praef.* 7: 'a Caesare Augusto in saeculum nostrum haut multo minus anni ducenti quibus inertia Caesarum quasi consenuit atque decoxit, nisi quod sub Traiano principe movit lacertos et praeter spem omnium senectus imperii quasi reddita iuventute reviruit.' Compare Trajan's boast in Julian, *Caesares* 327d.

think of nothing nobler than a war of conquest. Pompeius and Caesar by one count belonged to a baleful past, the age of tribulations. On a better showing those dynasts were builders of empire, and on comparison with most of their successors could be styled 'boni'.[1]

Trajan fought two campaigns against the Dacians (101 and 102). After a brief interval of uneasy peace the war resumed in 105, and in the next year the Emperor subjugated the country, converting it into a Roman province. Meanwhile Cornelius Tacitus had been occupied with the *Historiae*, which he concluded (it may be) about the year 109. In the preface he announced that if life were vouchsafed he would recount the reigns of Nerva and Trajan, a safe and happy period where a man could think and speak as he pleased.[2]

Despite the engaging prospect Tacitus took no action. Advancing years (it could be supposed) darkened his thoughts, and a growing bitterness about men and affairs. It may be so. What survives of Tacitus' works does not permit any such reason to be with safety invoked. Not much light and hope is to be discovered in the *Historiae*. The preface with the words that sum up the horror and iniquities of the Domitianic tyranny goes as far in savage pessimism as anybody could desire.[3] When those events came to be narrated in the later books, atmosphere and detail no doubt answered to the programme: one needs only to look at the *Agricola*, and the recital of all that Rome suffered, all that a man was spared by a providential decease.[4]

It has further been argued that Cornelius Tacitus fell into a disillusionment of a precise and political character. In the *Agricola* he affirmed that Liberty and the Principate were now wedded in harmony.[5] It turned out not to be so, and he changed his opinions in consequence. On an extreme view, Tacitus was deeply disappointed in Trajan.[6] On a milder interpretation, historical studies sharpened his judgement and compelled him to see that the ideal did not correspond with the nature of government and the facts of power.[7]

The persuasion that Tacitus came to alter a fundamental concept of his political thinking appears to derive support from the opening chapters of the *Agricola*, from the end of the *Dialogus*, and from the oration in which Galba is made to expound the argument that a ruler

---

[1] *Hist.* I. 50. 3.

[2] I. I. 4: 'quod si vita suppeditet, principatum divi Nervae et imperium Traiani, uberiorem securioremque materiam, senectuti seposui, rara temporum felicitate ubi sentire quae velis et quae sentias dicere licet.'

[3] I. 2. 3: 'atrocius in urbe saevitum', &c.   [4] 45.   [5] 3. I.

[6] e.g. H. Willrich, *Hermes* LXII (1927), 54 ff.; H. Bardon, *Les Empereurs et les lettres latines* (1940), 388 f.; E. Paratore, *Tacito* (1951), 625 ff.; F. Klingner, *Bayerische S-B, phil.-hist. Kl.* 1953, Heft 7, 26.

[7] R. Reitzenstein, *Gött. gel. Nachr.* 1914, 251. Against, I. Zechner, *Wiener Studien* LIV (1936), 100 ff.; F. Klingner, *Die Antike* VIII (1932), 151 ff. = *R. Geisteswelt* (1943), 310 ff.

selected by adoption will furnish a guarantee of constitutional government. It may be found to depend upon incautious and over-literal interpretations.

What Galba said collapses under scrutiny.[1] As for the *Agricola*, it was expedient for Tacitus, when he composed and published the pamphlet, to take at their face value the professions of the new régime. There was no choice. Nor was it any delusion to speak now of 'felicitas temporum', given what had happened under Domitian. Nothing suggests that the ex-consul was ingenuous or too confident.[2] He knew the perilous equilibrium of the Empire, he had witnessed the crisis under Nerva. He could not discourse about that in the *Agricola*. Again, no choice—and no published revelation of the author's innermost thoughts.[3]

The *Dialogus* is more delicate to assess. The poet Curiatius Maternus in the epilogue states the dilemma—great oratory or good government—and the verdict accepts and defends the existing order, the Emperor being described as 'sapientissimus et unus'.[4] What then emerges? A panegyric of Trajan and the present felicity has been claimed, or the historian's joyful conversion to monarchy.[5] If that were so, Tacitus must indeed have modified his opinions later on. Perhaps it is not so. Since the argument is designed to prove that there can be no great orators any more, because of the monarchy, it follows that the monarchy must be accepted—for nobody could advocate Republic, and chaos. This conclusion reveals not enthusiasm but resignation—and a strain of the historian's irony when he commends civic obedience towards the ruler, or extols the good sense of the Senate, coming quickly and inevitably to the right decisions.[6]

The inquiry is fruitless, irrelevant rather. The facts are plain—the reigns of Nerva and Trajan were wholly impracticable for a writer endowed with insight and veracity. Tacitus' words in the preface of the *Historiae* convey, not a binding pledge, but due homage to the

---

[1] p. 207.

[2] cf. K. Büchner, *Wiener Studien* LXIX (1956), 321 ff. Nor is it safe to hold that Tacitus saw in the reigns of Nerva and Trajan a return to the 'purest Augustan conceptions' (thus E. Paratore, o.c. 507). One would need to know what Tacitus thought about Augustus. On the ambiguity of 'libertas', below, Ch. XLI.

[3] The (opportunistic) acceptance of monarchy presupposed (not to say emphasized) in the account of Agricola's career, should not be left out of account.　　[4] 41. 4.

[5] R. Reitzenstein, *Gött. gel. Nachr.* 1914, 231: 'ein Angriff auf den Prinzipat gilt ihm wirklich als ein Verbrechen', cf. *Neue Wege zur Antike* IV (1926), 8: 'gerade unmittelbar nach der Schreckenszeit Domitians ist er überzeugter Monarchist'; J. Vogt, *Tacitus als Politiker* (1924), 6; E. Koestermann, *Hermes* LXV (1930), 421; C. Marchesi, *Tacito*[3] (1944), 47.

[6] 41. 3 f.: 'minor oratorum honor obscuriorque gloria est inter bonos mores et in obsequium regentis paratos. quid enim opus est longis in senatu sententiis cum optimi cito consentiant?'

régime, necessary but not dishonest. The public record of Nerva's principate, verging on calamity, was refractory enough: the true story of the adoption was a dangerous 'arcanum imperii'. For the rest, the historian was baffled everywhere—things not to be told, or things not worth telling.

Civil peace and wars of conquest abroad: it seemed the time of Caesar Augustus come again. Not wholly a benefit for the writing of history. Livy in his epilogue on the Republic of Augustus encountered (or skirted) a variety of hazards. In those books the best portions were perhaps the safest—the foreign wars, especially the campaigns in Germany and Illyricum.[1]

To a contemporary of Trajan the Dacian Wars must have seemed comparable, a magnificent episode. Tacitus himself confirms with regret how powerfully the reader is drawn to descriptions of foreign countries, of battles lost and won, and the deaths of famous leaders.[2] There were certain impediments, however, to the delineation of the campaigns in Dacia. Too much material, perhaps, and too many experts at hand to help or criticize. The military heroes of Tacitus tend to be energetic generals frustrated of renown by a jealous or timid emperor; but when the head of the government was leading to an inevitable victory the armies of the Roman People, the recording annalist had need of vigilance. There was no place for innuendo or sarcasm.

Tacitus prefers scenes of movement and turbulence—the soldiery in conflict with their officers or with the civilian population, rather than marching in disciplined valour against a foreign enemy. That was not the Emperor's idea. The subjugation of Dacia was slow work and hard work. The pictured scroll on Trajan's Column exhibits Roman warfare as routine and engineering, not battle and splendour and glory.[3]

Gratifying though it was to point the contrast with Domitian, and enhance it, to describe Decebalus broken and vanquished at last, a genuine victory, and a Roman triumph, there was a serious drawback —Dacia was not a fresh field for Cornelius Tacitus. He had already written his *Dacica*, the story of Domitian's wars, during or shortly after the Trajanic conquest. He felt no call to compete with the Column or stylize the *Commentarii* of the Emperor. The Dacian Wars of Trajan could be left to the crowd, to panegyrists, or to the poets. A municipal bard at Comum rose to the task.[4]

---

[1] p. 366 f.

[2] *Ann.* IV. 33. 3: 'nam situs gentium, varietates proeliorum, clari ducum exitus retinent ac redintegrant legentium animum.'

[3] I. A. Richmond, *BSR Papers* XIII (1935), 1 ff.

[4] Pliny, *Epp.* VIII. 4. 1: 'optime facis quod bellum Dacicum scribere paras. nam quae tam recens, tam copiosa, tam lata, quae denique tam poetica et quamquam in verissimis rebus tam fabulosa materia?' For 'lata' it would be preferable (and easy) to propose 'laeta'.

Germany provided the Romans with more triumphs than victories. So Tacitus, in brief dismissal of Domitian's achievement.[1] He could not pursue the topic with the comment that the triumphal *cognomen* of 'Germanicus' had been inherited more often than earned. It was easy to mock and misrepresent Domitian's victorious campaign against the Chatti: Nerva for some trifling operation of a legate (on the Danube, not on the Rhine) took the appellative and transmitted it as part of the imperial titulature to his son and heir. Only a panegyrist could justify and applaud Trajan as 'Germanicus', and he would have to be discreet, saying little, lest he evoke the last legate on the Rhine to become emperor, Vitellius Germanicus. Trajan quickly made it clear that the Roman public must expect no conquests in Germany. A few roads and forts constructed along or near the new frontiers of Upper Germany and Raetia, that is all. The garrison, reduced by Domitian from eight legions to six, soon fell to four, and the two Germanies count as peaceful provinces for the next sixty years.[2]

Nor did the other military zones offer action and movement. In Numidia imperial policy continued the work of the Flavian emperors, constricting ever more narrowly the territories of the nomad Musulamii, reclaiming land for agriculture, and founding cities;[3] the camp of the legion III Augusta had been transferred a long way to the west, and the limits of military control were extended on the southern fringe.[4] Mauretania, however, was a refractory region, and Britain continued to justify the standing garrison of three legions and a large army of *auxilia*; but neither Mauretania nor Britain showed as yet any promise of disturbances on a grand and splendid scale. In the East the Flavian emperors reorganized the frontier, which meant the annexation of several vassal principalities; and in 105 or 106, Trajan's governor of Syria incorporated in the Empire the kingdom of the Nabataean Arabs, no doubt without serious trouble.[5]

---

[1] *Germ.* 37. 6.

[2] cf. R. Syme, *CAH* XI (1936), 182.

[3] ib. 147 f. Note especially the *colonia* of Thamugadi, established in 100 (*ILS* 6841).

[4] Against the late-Trajanic or early-Hadrianic date for the legionary camp at Lambaesis cf. R. Syme, *Rev. ét. anc.* XXXVIII (1936), 182 ff.; *Studies in Roman Economic and Social History in Honour of A. C. Johnson* (1951), 123. Lambaesis was certainly occupied in 81, when L. Tettius Julianus 'muros et castra a solo / fecit' (see the inscription published by L. Leschi in *Libyca* I (1953), 191, whence *AE* 1954, 137). Not perhaps yet, however, the permanent station of III Augusta.

[5] The year is not quite certain. The cities of Petra and Bostra reckoned their era from 105 according to the *Chron. Paschale*, cf. E. Kubitschek in P–W I, 641 f. In favour of 106, however, E. Groag in *PIR²*, C 1412. C. Préaux suggests that the annexation took place in the winter of 105/6 (*Phoibos* V (1950/1), 130, discussing *P. Michigan* 466). There may have been unrest in Palestine. Note that Q. Pompeius Falco passes anomalously to a second praetorian province, Judaea after Lycia–Pamphylia (*ILS* 1035 f.), before his suffect consulate in 108. He knew Judaea, having been military tribune there, and he had had recent experience of warfare in Dacia.

Police work, the extension of the imperial peace, and the conversion of nomads or mountaineers to the orderly existence of citizens and tax-payers, such was the process by which the newer regions were opened to civilization. What went on in the older domains of the Roman State, whether prosperous or decayed, was likewise a dull and restricted theme, even when disorders were provoked by rivalries between cities, intrigue and corruption in the governing oligarchies, and the bitter strife of rich and poor. The provinces, so it might be contended, could not expect to figure in Roman annals unless a governor waged war or committed malpractices; and some senators, not the worst, would deny to provincials any right to express a valid opinion for good or evil about the mandatories of the 'res publica'.[1]

The public provinces and Italy, that was the portion of the Senate for management according to the dispositions of Caesar Augustus and official pronouncements thereafter, especially at the beginning of a new reign.[2] Trajan, crossing the threshold of the House on the first day of January, 100, adjured the senators both singly and collectively to enter again into the possession of 'Libertas' and confidently share with him the common task of governing the Empire.[3] Every ruler had used that language, but none till now could be taken at his word. The senators were eager to follow Trajan's lead, it is affirmed. What had prevented them before was not torpor but fear.[4]

To guide, instruct, or at need chastise, the proconsuls might well appear both the most honourable and the most useful residue of the Senate's prerogative. Various reasons impeded its full and rapid exercise—corporate pride and secret complicity, the influence of groups and coteries, and uncertainty about the true intentions of the ruler. A long interval elapsed before prosecutions against Marius Priscus and Caecilius Classicus (their offences went back to the year 97) could be properly instituted, let alone terminated.[5] A later case, that of Varenus, issued in delays, the need to consult Caesar, and hints of local complications in Bithynia. Trajan, returning after the conquest of Dacia, announced that he would take steps to find out what the Bithynians really wanted.[6] About this time begins the practice of sending imperial legates to investigate and regulate the affairs of the senatorial provinces.[7]

---

[1] *Ann.* xv. 20. 4 (Thrasea Paetus). Note the contrary opinion of Pliny, *Pan.* 70. 9: 'volo ego, qui provinciam rexerit, non tantum codicillos nec urbana coniuratione eblanditas preces, sed decreta coloniarum, decreta civitatum adleget.'

[2] cf. *Ann.* XIII. 4.   [3] *Pan.* 66. 2.

[4] *Pan.* 62. 4·f.   [5] p. 78.

[6] *Epp.* VII. 10. 2.

[7] Maximus to Achaia, *Epp.* VIII. 24 (p. 80), also later the consular C. Avidius Nigrinus (*suff.* 110), cf. *SIG*³ 827 (Delphi); Pliny to Bithynia, followed by Cornutus Tertullus (*ILS* 1024), cf. Ch. VII.

The government had already begun to pay close attention to the needs of Italy. To Nerva belongs a charitable foundation for the benefit of the children of the poor and the recruitment of the army, the 'alimenta'.[1] It was administered by special commissioners, or by the men in charge of the great roads.[2] But the 'alimenta', the construction of roads, bridges, and harbours, or measures designed to relieve landlords, do not exhaust the care of Trajan for 'his Italy'.[3] Agents of the central government might be appointed to supervise municipal finance;[4] and an imperial legate of praetorian rank is found in charge of a whole region of Italy, the Transpadana, as though it were a province.[5]

When Domitian convoked the Senate, it was for purposes baneful or trivial, for mockery when not for mourning.[6] The panegyrist breathes indignation—the august assembly was then consulted about gladiators and fire-brigades.[7] Under Trajan he was to witness high debate, whether a senator be permitted to hold a market on his estate, what should happen to the balance of the salary of a quaestor's secretary deceased.[8] Pliny reports several debates in the Senate, and several prosecutions. The consulars highest in power and influence with Trajan are conspicuous by their absence.[9]

Matters of greater moment were reserved for the Princeps to decide in consultation with his 'consilium', chosen men of repute and sagacity from both orders. Pliny received the imperial summons at least three times. On the one occasion the council had to decide whether athletic contests of the Greek type be permitted at the city of Vienna in Narbonensis. The second case concerned charges brought against a proconsul by one of his 'comites'. The third offered fare of a more varied sort—allegations of demagogic behaviour against the leading man in a Greek city, the misconduct of a military tribune's wife, and a forged will.[10]

---

[1] Victor, *Epit.* 12. 4. J. Asbach argued that Domitian began the system (*R. Kaisertum und Verfassung* (1896), 188 ff.). See now (for Nerva) M. Hammond, *Mem. Am. Ac. Rome* XXI (1953), 147.

[2] p. 71. For details of the system cf. R. P. Longden, *CAH* XI, 210 f.

[3] *ILS* 6106: 'qua aeternitati Italiae suae prospexit.'

[4] At Caere (*ILS* 5918a); Bergomum (6725); the 'civitas Otesinorum' (2722).

[5] C. Julius Proculus, between his legionary command and consulate (autumn 109), was 'leg. Aug. p. p. region. Transpadanae' (*ILS* 1040). That post is the exact equivalent in his *cursus* to the governorship of an imperial province, leading to the consulate. That is not all. Scholars have failed to notice that a commissioner called Priscus, active in the Transpadana c. 106, can be discovered from Pliny, *Epp.* VI. 8; VII. 7 f. Pliny's friend Saturninus was on his staff (VII. 15. 3, cf. 7. 1). This Priscus cannot be identified.

[6] *Epp.* VIII. 14. 8 f.   [7] *Pan.* 54. 4.   [8] *Epp.* V. 4; IV. 12.

[9] There is no sign of the marshals, from Servianus and Sura down to Sosius Senecio, Cornelius Palma, Fabius Justus, and the rest. Nor are the consular jurists named, Javolenus Priscus and Neratius Priscus.   [10] IV. 22; VI. 22 and 31.

The first and last preoccupation of an oligarchy is office, privilege, and preferment. Yet the senatorial corporation seemed hardly competent to administer even those matters with dignity and decency. Attendance at the House being prescribed (and serious business at a discount), energy went into the pursuit and purchase of honours. To stem the abuses of open canvassing for elections, the secret ballot was introduced: many of the tablets were defaced by trivial or obscene annotations.[1] In 105 vigorous but sporadic protests were made against various types of corruption;[2] and in the next year the Senate itself requested the Princeps to help with a bill restraining dinner-parties, gifts, and deposits of money.[3]

Domitian with the title 'censor perpetuus' might supplement the Senate at will. Trajan operated by mere prerogative; he made rapid promotions;[4] he even created new patricians.[5] One man held all the power, yet he allowed to the senators some driblets at least from the beneficent fountain of authority.[6] It was not much. They confessed disquiet at their own inadequacy, they consoled themselves with the thought that the Emperor was there, in his remedial vigilance.[7] If a praetor took it upon himself to correct abuses or assert the traditional rights of the office, his untimely zeal might easily come in for censure from sensible men.[8] On the other hand, absence from the Senate looked bad and was blamed.[9]

Of rebellion or disloyalty, however, no thought or trace. As one of the earliest measures of obeisance to the new ruler, it was decreed that, along with the Emperor's speeches, the loyal acclamations of the Senate should be published in the *acta diurna*: thus would their 'pietas' be proclaimed to all the nations.[10] The relation of clientship could not be more unequivocally documented.

The original and peculiar dependents of the Caesars were the urban populace, to be fed, amused (and if possible disciplined) by their patron

---

[1] III. 20; IV. 25.   [2] V. 9. 3 f.; 13. 6 f.   [3] VI. 19. 3 f.

[4] His Guard Prefect Sex. Attius Suburanus became consul in 101, and again in 104 (as *ordinarius*).

[5] *ILS* 1054 (C. Eggius Ambibulus, *cos.* 126).

[6] *Epp.* III. 20. 12: 'sunt quidem cuncta sub unius arbitrio . . . quidam tamen salubri temperamento ad nos quoque velut rivi ex illo benignissimo fonte decurrunt.'

[7] IV. 25. 5: ἀλλὰ ταῦτα τῷ ὑπὲρ ἡμᾶς μελήσει.

[8] A certain Licinius Nepos, praetor in 105, produced a severe and reforming edict (V. 9. 3 f.), and was otherwise active and vocal (V. 4. 2, cf. 13. 1; VI. 5. 1 ff.). The jurist Juventius Celsus (*pr.* 106) attacked him fiercely, as an 'emendatorem senatus' (VI. 5. 4). Another senator, Nigrinus, incurred no blame for his 'libellus disertus et gravis' when tribune of the plebs in 105 (V. 13. 6). Perhaps, C. Avidius Nigrinus (*suff.* 110), nephew of Avidius Quietus—and enjoying quick promotion (App. 27).

[9] At least among the humbler senators. Pliny gently chides his friend Bruttius Praesens (*Epp.* VII. 3).

[10] *Pan.* 75. 3: 'ut orbis terrarum pietatis nostrae adhiberetur testis.'

and master: 'plebecula', as Vespasian humorously designated them.[1] In the management of the city the Senate had no great share, despite various offices and boards; and, though the *praefectus urbi* was a senator (and a senior consular at that), he owed his appointment to the Princeps. Weight and importance lay with the equestrian officials in charge of the Praetorians, the food-supply, and the police. The reign began well for the 'plebs urbana', with a second imperial bounty coming so soon after Nerva, and Trajan extended the corn doles.[2] His triumphs brought largesse and lavish entertainments. Booty from Dacia and the treasures of Decebalus enabled him after the conquest to pay out an unprecedented sum;[3] and ten thousand gladiators fought and bled for the delectation of the imperial people.[4] Celebrations of one kind or another—gladiators, spectacles, banquets, and distributions—went on, year after year.[5]

Trajan could now set about embellishing the city. A series of monumental constructions for splendour or utility commemorated the Emperor's victories, notably the Forum and Basilica dedicated in 112, the Column in 113.[6] Bounties and buildings might be registered, along with other events deemed publicly valuable, on the *acta diurna* at Rome and copied elsewhere in summary form. They have their place in the *Fasti* of Ostia. But was this the proper matter of history? The dedication of temples or other public buildings, it is true, formed an integral rubric in Republican annals of 'urbs Roma'. But there was a limit to what was worth saying about them. When a diligent compiler filled out the record of a dull year with the dimensions of amphitheatres and the like, the historian was moved to indignant protest.[7] Nor is it likely that Tacitus had any fancy for the contests of gladiators, or other recreations of the 'plebs sordida'.[8] Narrating what happened under bad emperors, he was obsessed and sickened by the monotony of his subject—acts of cruelty at a despot's command and one

---

[1] Suetonius, *Divus Vesp.* 18.

[2] *Pan.* 26, cf. D. van Berchem, *Les Distributions de blé et d'argent à la plèbe romaine sous l'empire* (1939), 33 f.

[3] The *Chronographer of the Year 354* reports a *congiarium* of 650 *denarii*. Even if it represents the total of Trajan's three *congiaria*, it is enormous (Domitian's three add up to 225). Van Berchem finds the sum incredible (o.c. 152). Carcopino invoked the gold of Dacia (Lydus, *De mag.* II. 28, from Trajan's doctor Statilius Crito), cf. his arguments, *Dacia* I (1924), 28 ff. = *Points de vue sur l'impérialisme romain* (1934), 73 ff. For criticism, R. Syme, *JRS* xx (1930), 55 ff.

[4] Dio LXVIII. 15. 1. In fact just short of 5,000 pairs fought in the one year 109 (*FO* XXII).

[5] *FO* xxi f. (down to 113).   [6] *FO* xxii.

[7] *Ann.* XIII. 31. 1: 'cum ex dignitate populi Romani repertum sit res inlustris annalibus, talia diurnis urbis actis mandare.'

[8] Pliny duly commended one of these manly spectacles early in the reign (*Pan.* 33. 1 f.). For modern verbosity in defence of a soldier-emperor's tastes see R. Paribeni, *Optimus Princeps* I (1926), 269 ff.

prosecution after another.[1] The benefactions of 'optimus Princeps' were no less monotonous.

Such was the material which the reign offered, at home and abroad, in the fifteen years that elapsed since the adoption of Trajan and the consulate of Tacitus, an epoch of glory and felicity—and quite impracticable for a historian whose talent had found a congenial subject in the fifteen years of Domitian.

The scope of history was now narrowing—on the one hand local and municipal affairs, on the other the personality and acts of the ruler. It forfeited dignity. The one theme could not be treated by an historian, the other by a senator. And, if the lives of emperors might now attract writers of lesser estate and pretension, a biographer taking relish in the scandals and eccentricities of the Caesars would be baffled and dismayed by a virtuous prince and his chaste consort.

The Emperor now had power no less than Domitian's, but inevitably greater.[2] Senators had fought against tyranny. The struggle had been fierce—and invigorating. Now it was over. Senators could enjoy 'securitas' at last.[3] They had longed for a good ruler, and now he was with them, unremovable. Their 'dignitas' was saved and protected, at the cost of obedience, 'obsequium'.[4] It would not have been strange if the felicity of the times were suffused with melancholy and frustration. The heirs of a great tradition do not always feel happy in repose under a benevolent despotism.[5]

In the *Dialogus* Tacitus perceived the truth and drew the moral. As the years passed, and he brought the *Historiae* to completion, did he feel disappointment in his own aspirations? When a consular looked back to his début in public life, and called to mind the friends and rivals of his youth, he would reflect on human vicissitudes—death or exile, ill health or old age. One of his coevals had opted for ease and retirement, another commanded an army, another stood so well with Caesar that he need not bother himself any more with the routine obligations of the senatorial existence.[6]

Tacitus since his consulate had seen many changes in the front

---

[1] *Ann.* IV. 33. 3: 'nos saeva iussa, continuas accusationes, fallaces amicitias, perniciem innocentium et easdem exitii causas coniungimus, obvia rerum similitudine et satietate.'

[2] R. P. Longden, *CAH* XI, 204; W. H. Gross, *Bildnisse Traians* (1940), 15; E. Paratore, *Tacito* (1951), 637.

[3] For this notion, H. U. Instinsky, *Sicherheit als politisches Problem des r. Kaisertums* (1952), 27 ff.

[4] Tacitus employs this conception in a speech delivered under Tiberius—'tibi summum rerum iudicium di dedere, nobis obsequii gloria relicta est' (*Ann.* VI. 8. 4). For 'obsequium', pp. 28, 58.

[5] cf. Longinus, *De sublimitate* 44. 3, describing the men who were born into the imperial peace— παιδομαθεῖς δουλείας δικαίας.

[6] *Epp.* IV. 24. 3.

ranks of the aristocracy. Nero's reign, it might seem, was not so far away, yet the Neronian consuls were all dead.[1] Men already mature under Nero and consuls in the first years of the Flavian dynasty, but still extant for renewed public recognition under Trajan, had now disappeared.[2] Further, such was the infertility of *novi homines* at Rome, few of them had consular sons. Gaps were also evident among the later Flavian consuls, and several houses old or recent had lapsed without perpetuation.[3] Certain of the 'principes' surviving from that period had faded into retirement;[4] others, however, could show long careers of utility, and some came to distinction late in life.[5]

Of Tacitus' own equals in age, or (not always the same thing) in official rank, he might observe Glitius Agricola governing Pannonia, fighting in the First Dacian War, and consul for the second time thereafter.[6] Then younger men—Sosius Senecio of comparable excellence, Cornelius Palma, the governor of Syria, and Fabius Justus who followed Palma in that command but did not reach a second consulate.[7] Literary tastes in Sosius and Fabius had not prevented them from governing the consular military provinces. As old acquaintances passed away, fresh members entered the sacerdotal college to which Tacitus had belonged these many years;[8] some of the quaestors of 96 or 97 were now consuls;[9] and a senior consular would contemplate (and not always with contentment) the rising tide of claimants to the supreme magistracy as the oligarchy widened, now embracing many provinces, with a notable accession from the eastern lands.[10] Not all of the new-comers had been brought up in the Roman tradition—and there was the general danger that provincial senators might regard Rome and Italy merely as a place of sojourn.[11] Fashions

---

[1] *Epp.* III. 7. 9 ff. (reflections on 'fragilitas humana' evoked by the decease of Silius Italicus, *cos.* 68).

[2] Julius Frontinus died about 103 (*Epp.* IV. 8. 3), and Vestricius Spurinna is last heard of c. 105 (V. 17).

[3] Thus the aristocratic Volusii, with their last consuls in 87 and 92; while Vespasian's allies Licinius Mucianus and Petillius Cerialis were unable to supply consular descendants, likewise Domitian's victorious generals Tettius Julianus and Lappius Maximus.

[4] For T. Pomponius Bassus (*suff.* 94) as a 'pulcherrimae quietis exemplum' a decade later see *Epp.* IV. 23.

[5] p. 477. For some of the consuls of 90–96 surviving see the proconsuls of Asia in App. 23.

[6] *ILS* 1021a.　　　　　　　　　　　　　　　　　　　　　　[7] Ch. V.

[8] App. 22. Among the accessions, M. Pompeius Macrinus (*suff.* 100 or 101), Q. Pompeius Falco (108), and C. Julius Proculus (109).

[9] e.g. A. Larcius Priscus (*ILS* 1055) in 110, C. Julius Proculus (1040) in 109.

[10] Ch. XXXVIII.

[11] Observe Trajan's enactment (c. 106) about candidates for office: 'eosdem patrimonii tertiam partem conferre iussit in ea quae solo continerentur, deforme arbitratus, ut erat, honorem petituros urbem Italiamque non pro patria, sed pro hospitio aut stabulo quasi peregrinantes habere' (*Epp.* VI. 19. 4).

also changed, and tastes emerged that cannot have been wholly to the liking of Cornelius Tacitus.

Transcending by historical composition his own great fame as a speaker, Tacitus inserted specimens of eloquence, demonstrating his characteristic majesty of tone; and he is ever alert and ready to put in a verdict about the capacities of past orators. His own time exhibited rivals—and perhaps imitators.[1] Who were the speakers of repute in the next generation, and what was their style, how far, for example, the younger men conformed to the precepts of a guide and master, there is no means of ascertainment.[2] Valid information about Latin oratory hardly emerges again for some thirty years.[3]

The *Historiae*, when examined in the light of the traditions and categories of the art as practised among the Romans, should stand invulnerable. Yet envy and detraction were abundant everywhere at Rome—and most potent when disguised by care for tradition and the proprieties. To write of the Republic hardly touched anybody's interests or prejudices. Not so the period of the early Caesars and the ancestors, recent enough, of the living—and still less the Flavian annals. When Tacitus narrated the reign of Domitian he no doubt incriminated the Senate as well as the Emperor (the historian's own rank gave licence and excuse for hard words), and he did not spare individuals. There was much that should have been decently covered or devoutly forgotten. To insist upon awkward truths is no way to acquire praise in a society that reinforces the normal hypocrisies with an earnest infusion of political make-believe; while a powerful work of independent genius disturbs and shows up the solemnities or frivolities current in the literary world. The author will have disdained to shield himself anxiously from criticism.

Unobtrusive detail or casual comment touched prominent senators and ancient families. The later books must have included some deadly things, showing up the men who rose and prospered under Domitian. The very beginning of the *Historiae*, with the character sketch of Mucianus, was disquieting enough. Subsequent items dealt with his power and diplomatic arts, his ostentation, and his rapacity. No reader so obtuse that he could miss the other Licinius, also consul three times—the great Licinius Sura—his share in the creation of an emperor, and certain other things.[4]

---

[1] App. 27.

[2] C. Avidius Nigrinus (*suff.* 110) might be a disciple of Tacitus. Prosecuting Varenus Rufus, a certain Nigrinus, spoke 'presse, graviter, ornate' (*Epp.* v. 20. 6). Pliny's comprehensive and exuberant praise of two younger men, Pedanius Fuscus and Ummidius Quadratus (VI. 11, cf. App. 27), leads nowhere.

[3] The next evidence is furnished by the orator M. Cornelius Fronto (*suff.* 143).

[4] Including their vices. Mucianus was 'notae impudicitiae', and Vespasian, discussing

Whatever the reception accorded to the *Historiae* (and there may well have been blame or the wrong kind of praise), Tacitus did not at once go on to any other literary task. He was passing through the middle fifties. The year arrived that made him eligible to govern Asia or Africa. The lot awarded Asia, and he set out for his province in the summer of 112, to hold for a year the twelve *fasces* of a proconsul of consular rank.[1]

More often than not these proconsulates went to birth, wealth, and influence in the fullness of time, without regard for military or civil accomplishments. Tacitus might have coveted or deserved something better. Second consulates were distributed not ungenerously by the Flavian emperors and by Trajan, though each ruler tended after a time to be more selective: Domitian gave only two after 85. Apart from the special honours conferred at the beginning of Trajan's reign (in 98 and 100) upon illustrious survivors from an earlier age, nine senators down to the year 109 were granted an iteration. After Cornelius Palma, previously governor of Syria, the next (and the last) is Publilius Celsus (in 113).[2] Further, and generally coming before or after a second consulate, there was the Prefecture of the City, a rare eminence, but a suitable reward for distinction in the arts of peace. Previous emperors had not denied it to *novi homines* either Italian or provincial.[3]

The government, it appears, had other candidates for the office of *praefectus urbi*;[4] and its second consuls belong to a restricted and definable category. Not pedigree, and not, as often under the Flavian emperors, relatives of the dynasty. Nor did legal studies qualify, that traditional art of the governing class at Rome—Javolenus Priscus for all his excellence was passed over, likewise and more strangely perhaps, the two Neratii, Priscus the jurist and his brother Marcellus, though these men had all governed military provinces.[5] Towards oratory, the military emperor showed no sympathy or encouragement. It was not needed any more. The Flavian emperors employed the best speakers of the day to crush malcontents or expound before the Senate the wishes of the government. Prosecutors or political managers,

him, always ended with the remark 'ego tamen vir sum' (Suetonius, *Divus Vesp.* 13). For Sura, p. 41. It is unfortunate that so little is known about their earlier vicissitudes.

[1] App. 23. [2] App. 12.

[3] e.g. the mysterious Pegasus (App. 68), C. Rutilius Gallicus (from Augusta Taurinorum), and T. Aurelius Fulvus (from Nemausus in Narbonensis).

[4] App. 13. Perhaps Sex. Attius Suburanus (*II ord.* 104) or Ti. Julius Candidus Marius Celsus (*II ord.* 105), certainly Glitius Agricola: the post is registered on one of his many inscriptions (*CIL* v, 6980: Augusta Taurinorum). Q. Baebius Macer (*suff.* 103) held the post in 117 (*HA, Hadr.* 5. 5).

[5] Germania Superior and Syria (Javolenus), Pannonia (Priscus), Britannia (Marcellus), cf. App. 14. Also C. Cilnius Proculus (*suff.* 87), who outlived Trajan, cf. *PIR*[2], C 732.

that class now vanished. For ministers and counsellors, Trajan used his own friends and companions, the chief men in the military oligarchy. The generals in the wars and the governors of the armed provinces have the highest insignia as their preserve.

Licinius Sura took the place of men like Vibius Crispus and Fabricius Veiento. On the surface of things, military renown instead of eloquence or the diplomatic arts. A significant fact emerges—Sura before he became a general earned some note as a speaker; and the report ran that he composed the orations of the Emperor.[1] There may have been no loss of craft and subtlety.

The role of second man to a monarch calls for skill on both sides, and it may depend upon complementary qualities, as Agrippa to Augustus, Mucianus to Vespasian. Mucianus boasted openly that he had made an emperor.[2] Trajan's ally was more modest. Of any disturbance or annoyance in their concord, not a trace. A trivial anecdote attests calumny against Sura, and the unshakeable trust of his friend the Emperor.[3] Such power (and with it great riches) no doubt provoked envy and hostility. Especial friends or enemies among the marshals happen not to be attested. Yet there must have been groups and factions. It was hard for Julius Servianus to be surpassed in rank and honour despite past services and his marriage to the daughter of Trajan's cousin. Other generals may have grown rancorous, imprudent, or unbearable. One of them had to be removed. The unexplained banishment of Laberius Maximus might have something to do with Licinius Sura.[4] Laberius had won great glory in the first war against the Dacians.[5]

Sura, consul for the third time, stands next to Trajan, recalling Marcus Agrippa.[6] Though two widows were available, Marciana the sister of Trajan and Matidia his niece, he was not brought into the family circle of the dynasty.[7] When Sura died, he was accorded the honour of a state funeral. Public baths at Rome preserved his memory (nothing like this had been known since the days of Augustus) and a triumphal arch near Tarraco in Spain.[8]

[1] p. 40.
[2] *Hist.* IV. 4. 1: 'in manu sua fuisse imperium donatumque Vespasiano iactabat.' There may also have been friction with Titus, cf. J. A. Crook, *AJP* LXXII (1951), 162 ff.
[3] Dio LXVIII. 15. 4 ff.
[4] The date cannot be known, the reason is vague or doubtful—'Laberius Maximus qui suspectus imperio in insula exulabat' (*HA, Hadr.* 5. 5).   [5] Dio LXVIII. 8. 3.
[6] The intervening names are instructive: L. Vitellius, Licinius Mucianus, Vibius Crispus, Fabricius Veiento—and, less potent, Verginius Rufus, Julius Frontinus, and Vestricius Spurinna.
[7] For the deceased husbands of these ladies, see below, p. 603. There was also a younger Matidia (*ILS* 327, &c.), sister of Vibia Sabina. A dim, ignored, and perhaps oppressed female: no sign that she ever married.
[8] For the evidence, *PIR*[1], L 174; P-W XIII, 481 f.

Sura's death may have occurred as early as 108.[1] Although Sura carried great weight with Trajan, there is no clear sign that his disappearance explains any change in policy, or brings in new advisers of a different stamp.[2] Little is known, it is true, about the personality and opinions of the other marshals. As for public honours, nobody was allowed to equal the third consulate of Sura, though statues at Rome commemorated the services of Sosius Senecio, of Cornelius Palma who conquered Arabia, of Publilius Celsus.[3] Sosius died before long, and other military men, like Fabius Justus, fade from record. Palma and Celsus would be heard of again—and Julius Servianus lived stubbornly on. In the meantime the body of consuls and governors was replenished by the younger men, notably such as won military repute commanding legions in the Dacian campaigns.[4] Some, but not all, passed quickly to consular provinces.[5]

For equilibrium the system of the Principate depended both on proper relations of confidence between the ruler and the military oligarchy and on a proper control of his domestic entourage. Hitherto the Palace had seldom failed to engender strife and disturbance, from the ambitions and intrigues of empresses, the dominating influence of imperial freedmen, the perpetual traffic in honours. The accession of Trajan promised order, decorum, and sobriety, with family politics now discountenanced, and no undue prominence for the women of the household.[6]

[1] The latest evidence of his survival comes in a suspect statement about Hadrian: 'ob hoc consul est factus, in quo magistratu ut a Sura conperit adoptandum se a Traiano esse, ab amicis Traiani contemni desiit ac neglegi' (*HA, Hadr.* 3. 10). Hadrian's consulate fell in the summer of 108. This evidence for Sura's sentiments towards Hadrian is accepted and developed by R. P. Longden, *CAH* xi, 221. Hadrian's autobiography might be the ultimate (and suspect) source, cf. p. 600.

[2] The conjectures of R. P. Longden (*CAH* xi, 221 f.) depend upon groups or animosities not securely attested before 117 or 118, and even then not clearly to be elucidated, cf. p. 244. Thus Cornelius Palma and Publilius Celsus are invoked—and even Lusius Quietus; also Julius Servianus. Yet it is not quite certain that Servianus was hostile to the prospects of his brother-in-law Hadrian either now or in 117.

[3] Dio LXVIII. 16. 2.   [4] App. 16, registering the younger Trajanic marshals.

[5] C. Julius Quadratus Bassus (*suff.* 105) commanded an army in the conquest of Dacia, passing later to the governorship of Cappadocia, but L. Minicius Natalis (106) and Q. Pompeius Falco (108), despite their decorations (*ILS* 1029; 1035 f.) have to wait a long time for a consular army command (p. 243). On the other hand, men much older seem anomalously to find employment, thus Secundus as legate of Cappadocia in 111 (E. Sydenham, *The Coinage of Caesarea in Cappadocia* (1933), 73), perhaps to be identified as Q. Vibius Secundus (*suff.* 86): he is followed by M. Junius Homullus (*suff.* 102), attested in 113 and 114 (Sydenham, l.c., and Dio LXVIII. 19. 1). Furthermore, Cn. Pedanius Fuscus Salinator (*suff.* c. 84) is attested as governor of an armed province c. 109 (*Epp.* x. 87. 3). Nothing is recorded to explain why Publilius Celsus (*suff.* 102) became consul again in 113, the last man thus to be honoured by Trajan. If the full evidence about governors c. 109 were available, it might well furnish political evidence.

[6] *Pan.* 83 f. Not that Plotina was negligible—'Pompeia Plotina, incredibile dictu est,

In the year 112, however, the dynastic principle seems to acquire a new emphasis. Two imperial ladies, Plotina and Marciana, each bearing the title of 'Augusta' since about 105, now received the right of coinage;[1] when Marciana died in the course of the same year, she was deified, the name 'Augusta' passing to her daughter Matidia.[2] And soon after, the parent of the Emperor, deceased some time before his son's accession, was also consecrated.[3]

Trajan, like so many members of the new imperial aristocracy, had no son, not even a daughter. The next of kin was Vibia Sabina, his niece Matidia's child, who had now been married a dozen years to P. Aelius Hadrianus.[4] The match might have seemed a clear designation to the succession.

Yet the Princeps was scrupulous, or rather rigorous, discouraging any inordinate advancement of his young relative. Quaestor in 101, Hadrian went with the Emperor on the first campaigns against the Dacians.[5] When the war broke out again in 105, he was put in charge of a legion, and after service in Dacia governed for a brief spell the new province of Pannonia Inferior, acceding to the consulship in 108.[6] He was not allowed to be consul eponymous, only suffect; and though he was young, being thirty-two, that was the age at which a *nobilis* became eligible—and the kinsman of the Princeps could surely claim parity without scandal.[7] Even the death of Licinius Sura brought no notable change in his fortunes.[8]

Trajan of set purpose declined to take a step that must have seemed obvious, the adoption, right to the end. Various allegations subsequently gained currency. It was said that he proposed to leave the Empire in the charge of one of the consulars, and Neratius Priscus is

quanto auxerit gloriam Traiani' (Victor, *Epit.* 42. 21). The anecdote (for what it is worth) shows her persuading Trajan to curb the exactions of his fiscal agents.

[1] The title 'Augusta', *ILS* 288; the coins, H. Mattingly, *BMC, R. Emp.* III (1936), lxii.

[2] *FO* XXII. Marciana was 'diva cognominata', before her funeral—apparently a stage short of the full status of consecrated emperors. For the category of 'second-class *divi*' (Trajan's father was one of them), cf. J. H. Oliver, discussing the evidence of the *Feriale Duranum, Harv. Th. Rev.* XLII (1949), 35 ff.

[3] The date is not directly attested. The first coins commemorating 'Divus pater Traianus'—and 'Divus Nerva'—fall about this time, cf. H. Mattingly, *BMC, R. Emp.* III (1936), lxxxi; 100 f. He is not designated 'divus' on an inscription in his honour, of 112 or later (*ILS* 307).

[4] *HA, Hadr.* 2. 10.   [5] ib. 3. 1, cf. *ILS* 308 (Athens).

[6] The *HA* puts his tribunate in 105, his praetorship in 107 (*Hadr.* 3. 4 and 8), which is accepted by Stein in *PIR²*, A 184. But 106 is preferable for the praetorship (P. v. Rohden in P-W I, 498): note the phraseology of *ILS* 308—'praetori eodemque tempore leg. leg. I Minerviae p. f. bello Dacico, item trib. pleb.'

[7] See App. 18—and observe that Nigrinus, *tr. pl.* in 105 (*Epp.* v. 13. 6), perhaps reaches the consulate in 110 (p. 225).

[8] At least so far as can be known. The anecdote in *HA, Hadr.* 3. 10 (quoted above, p. 232) looks suspect. It is possible that Hadrian was pushed rapidly into a suffect consulate because of Sura's illness—or even because of Sura's death.

named.[1] Some fancied that Trajan would emulate Alexander the Macedonian and die without a successor. Others asserted that he intended to send a despatch consigning the choice to the Senate, if anything should happen to him—but with a list of candidates.[2]

Nothing but guesses, defying verification. One thing is clear, and important. Only the Senate could legally confer the supreme power. Trajan therefore respected constitutional principle to the letter. Furthermore, Trajan himself had been selected as emperor. Hence, on the face of things, any senator could be regarded as eligible.[3] And some may have favoured, by an illicit extension, a peculiar theory, that the choice of the ruler ought to be left to the Senate: for collective wisdom and experience would no doubt elect the best man.[4]

Trajan's attitude might seem to confirm some of the theories about the Principate. If so, he displayed a pedantic and dangerous reverence for forms or fancies. Surely it was the duty of a Princeps, not merely to maintain stability while he lived, but to supply, instruct, and designate a successor. Otherwise the Senate, so far from being free to elect, would be compelled to ratify a usurpation, not without the menace or the fact of civil war.

The clue should be sought in human personality. To Trajan in the conscious pride of power and magnificence the thought of his own death was unbearable, not to be imagined. Trajan in 113 was completing his sixtieth year. The sixty-third was the climacteric in a man's life. Trajan might hope to pass it felicitously, like Caesar Augustus, and continue for a long space thereafter.[5] There was work unfinished,

---

[1] HA, Hadr. 4. 8, with an alleged statement of Trajan 'commendo tibi provincias, si quid mihi fatale contigerit'. This is generally taken as weighty and contemporary evidence, e.g. W. Weber, Untersuchungen zur Gesch. des Kaisers Hadrianus (1907), 30; W. Hartke, Römische Kinderkaiser (1951), 115. If Trajan thought so highly of the jurist Neratius Priscus (suff. 97), he might at least have given him a second consulate. According to Weber (o.c. 46), Trajan believed that 'das Wahlkaisertum' was the right and proper solution.

[2] HA, Hadr. 4. 9.   [3] Pan. 7. 6: 'imperaturus omnibus eligi debet ex omnibus.'

[4] The notion seems to have been canvassed after the assassination of Caligula, cf. Josephus, BJ II. 205: κρινεῖν ψήφῳ τὸν ἄξιον τῆς ἡγεμονίας. Otherwise it is not easy to verify outside the pages of the Historia Augusta. Much has been written about the 'ideals of the Stoic opposition' and about adoption as a principle of government in the Antonine period. Cf. e.g. M. Rostovtzeff, Soc. and Ec. Hist. of the R. Empire (1926), 108 ff. For pertinent and sagacious criticism cf. C. Wirszubski, Libertas as a Political Idea at Rome during the Late Republic and Early Principate (1950), 154 ff.; L. Wickert, P–W XXIII, 2157; 2187; 2209. Nerva acted under compulsion—and the first emperor with a son who could succeed him was Marcus Aurelius, a Stoic if ever there was one. On the dynastic character of the imperial succession under the Antonines cf. R. M. Geer, TAPA LXVII (1936), 47 ff.; J. Béranger, Rev. ét. lat. XVII (1939), 171 ff.; J. Carcopino, Rev. ét. anc. LI (1949), 262 ff. For sensible remarks on adoption see now H. Nesselhauf, Hermes LXXXIII (1955), 477 ff.

[5] Compare the cheerful letter to the princes Gaius and Lucius, written by Augustus on his sixty-third birthday (quoted by Gellius xv. 7. 3).

and glorious exploits for his energies, recalling the military origins of the Principate in their better aspect. Caesar the Dictator meditated a double design, conquest in the Balkan lands and war against the Parthian monarchy. Trajan subjugated Dacia as the 'dignitas imperii' and his own ambition demanded.[1] The same causes impelled him against the Arsacid. In the autumn of the year the Imperator went out in majesty, and in anger.

---

[1] Thus Pliny, proleptically, on the Dacian War—'quandocumque te vel inferre vel propulsare bellum coegerit imperii dignitas' (*Pan.* 17. 4).

XX. HADRIANUS AUGUSTUS

CAESAR the Dictator proposed to invade the Parthian dominions. Caesar Augustus used craft and diplomacy. Recovering the standards lost by Crassus and by Antonius, and imposing a Roman vassal to rule Armenia, he confronted, appeased, and defrauded the pride of the Romans in their aspiration for a war of revenge. The expedient of a Roman protectorate over Armenia seemed to issue in a series of frustrations and vexations, distasteful also to the natives and a cause of friction with the Parthians; and it might happen that for long years the land lapsed from Roman control, happily anarchic or plundered by its neighbours. That did not matter very much. Armenia touched no true or vital point of Rome's imperial security and defence.[1]

Armenia, however, could not be frankly neglected or officially renounced. The artifice of Augustus, to magnify his peaceful victories at the expense of Parthia, magnified Parthia also. Prestige was involved. It might be sought by the sending of a crown prince to the eastern lands, it might be required by a new government, eager for cheap success (and Parthian laurels need entail no bloodshed) to contrast with the criminal inertia of the previous ruler.

The Great King, insecure upon his throne and menaced in his own household, could seldom enforce obedience on the vassals throughout the wide regions that intermittently acknowledged his suzerainty. He had no standing army and no artillery. The nomads could make incursions, but not conquests: a single Greek city might defy them for long years.[2] The conduct of the monarch in the face of the Romans was therefore not often provocative: if they but permitted, he inclined to amity and collusive arrangements.

When the young Gaius Caesar went out, the grandson and adopted heir of Augustus, the Arsacid was willing to meet him at the river Euphrates. An agreement was reached. A few years later dissensions among the Parthians reduced them to the expedient of asking Rome for a king; and, though that ruler did not last long (being expelled by his rival Artabanus), the next Roman prince to be sent to the East found nothing hostile from the side of Parthia. Germanicus Caesar made a visit to the Armenian capital and crowned a king there.

After long tranquillity Artabanus at last in the year 35 meddled with Armenia. The Roman government was ready for any challenge.

---

[1] For Roman dealings with Parthia and Armenia from 20 B.C. to A.D. 17 see the brief and masterly review of Tacitus, *Ann.* II. 1–4.

[2] *Ann.* VI. 42 (Seleucia on the Tigris).

Tiberius appointed L. Vitellius to be governor of Syria, with special powers.[1] Vitellius intervened energetically, invading Mesopotamia, and before long a Roman candidate was crowned at Ctesiphon—significant though ephemeral. Artabanus soon recovered his kingdom, but it became clear that he had learned his lesson. There was another meeting at the Euphrates.[2] Artabanus died soon after. Strife and confusion followed for a decade, with appeal to Rome in the end, and Claudius, like Augustus, was able to furnish the Parthians with a king —whose reign was brief.[3]

If such was the proved and recurrent weakness of the Parthian monarchy, Rome could afford to be negligent about Armenia, supporting or abandoning a candidate with equanimity, and discovering an advantage in crime or anarchy. The facts are clear.[4] During the last years of Augustus, Armenia for the greater part of a decade was nobody's possession. No damage ensued (though Rome was embarrassed with the northern wars), and the disgrace was lightly borne. When Tiberius came to the power, he was in no position to condemn the policy of his predecessor, which had also been his own. It was different when Claudius died. The failure and discredit of recent interventions could be profitably advertised, with the promise of vigorous redress.

Nero had clever counsellors. On sudden reports of ostensible alarm—the Parthians were raiding Armenia—they ordered mobilizations and sent out an impressive general. Whereupon the Parthian monarch read the signs and duly surrendered some hostages. Everything now pointed to a discreet accommodation, as previously when L. Vitellius disclosed the strength of Rome. Chance, error, ambition, or prestige interfered. It was not until eight years had been used up in the shifting alternations of action and delay, of policies invented and discarded, of diplomacy and even of warfare, that a compromise emerged: a prince of the Parthian royal family might reign in Armenia, but Rome must decide and confirm the investiture.

The device met mutual interests in stability and a mutual distaste for war. It subsisted under the Flavian emperors. As corollary to the virtual abandonment of Armenia, Vespasian set up a new army command beside that of Syria, two legions in Cappadocia, ready to march eastwards. Not that they were likely to be needed. The Roman government could employ the kingdoms of Iberia and Albania as a control upon Armenia from the rear. Vespasian had a fort built at a strategic

---

[1] *Ann.* VI. 32: 3.
[2] Suetonius, *Vit.* 2. 4, cf. *Cal.* 14. 3, and Dio LIX. 27. 3 (misdated).
[3] *Ann.* XII. 11, cf. 16.
[4] For this estimate of Parthia and of Armenia cf. J. G. C. Anderson, *CAH* x (1934), 254 f.; 773 f.; R. Syme, ib. XI (1936), 137 ff.

point in the land of the Iberians.[1] Domitian, as he showed by his
dealings with certain peoples in inner Germany, knew how to exert
Roman diplomacy far beyond any Roman frontier.[2]

Friction or annoyance could not be wholly precluded. Trouble
threatened under Vespasian, when M. Ulpius Traianus was legate of
Syria, but passed quickly.[3] A better occasion offered for the Parthians
(but still no hostilities) while Domitian was involved in the war with
Dacia.[4]

Dacia and Parthia, the one might save the other. Negotiation between the two kings is attested during Trajan's first war in Dacia.[5]
Further, there is a hint of disturbance or quarrel at the time of the
second war, not alien perhaps to the Roman annexation of Arabia.[6]
Roman pride was now awake and eager to take offence.[7]

Trajan after the conquest of Dacia had legions to spare—he had
withdrawn two from the Rhine, and he had enrolled two more.[8]
Trajan's settlement of the Danubian frontier, though adding a new
consular province across the river, would surely not require a permanent establishment any larger than what he found there on his
accession; and, for one reason or another, he decided against that
further advance which, annexing the lands of the Marcomanni and
Quadi, would have installed the Roman power at a central point of
vantage. Instead, the East. Had not the time come to abolish the
Parthian question by extending Rome's dominion to the Caucasus
and to the mountains that separate Mesopotamia from Persia? Various
reasons spoke for a war of conquest.[9] Trajan was probably preparing
for decisive action.[10]

---

[1] *ILS* 8795 (Harmozica, near Tiflis).

[2] See the inscription discovered near Baku, *AE* 1951, 263: 'Imp. Domitiano / Caesare
Aug. / Germanic. / L. Iulius / Maximus 7 / leg. XII Ful.' Discussed by F. Grosso, *Epi-
graphica* XVI (1954), 117 ff. In Germany Domitian had got into touch with the Semnones
and the Lugii (Dio LXVII. 5. 2 f.), peoples of Saxony and Silesia.   [3] pp. 30 f.

[4] Suetonius *Nero* 57. 2—a false Nero vigorously supported by the Parthians c. 88, but
later surrendered by them, cf. Statius, *Silvae* IV. 3. 110: 'Eoae citius venite laurus.'

[5] Pliny, *Epp.* X. 74. 1.

[6] Suidas, s.v. ἐπίκλημα (= Arrian, *Parthica* fr. 32 Roos), attests a complaint of Pacorus
directed to Τραϊανῷ τῷ βασιλεῖ. Some prefer to assign the reference to Trajan's parent,
c. 75, e.g. R. P. Longden, *JRS* XXI (1931), 12 f., cf. 24.

[7] Note the indignation voiced in *Hist.* I. 40. 2: 'igitur milites Romani, quasi Vologaesum
aut Pacorum avito Arsacidarum solio depulsuri.' By contrast, the low estimate of Parthia
in *Germ.* 37. 3 f.   [8] p. 57.

[9] The commercial motive has been urged (and overestimated) by J. Guey, *Essai sur la
guerre parthique de Trajan (114–117)* (1937).

[10] It would be valuable if the transference of legions could be established by 113, cf.
R. Syme, *Laureae Aquincenses* I (1938), 278 ff.; F. A. Lepper, *Trajan's Parthian War*
(1948), 173 ff. O. Cuntz tried to deduce military designs from Pliny's special appointment
to Bithynia (*Hermes* LXI (1926), 192 ff.). Against, R. P. Longden, *JRS* XXI (1931), 19 ff.

When the chance came, he was ready and truculent. The folly of a Parthian monarch, new to the throne, played into his hands. Chosroes deposed the ruler of Armenia, setting up instead a brother of that prince, Parthamasiris. Then he tried to negotiate. Trajan was obdurate. Entering Armenia with an army, he summoned Parthamasiris to his presence. No plea or excuse availed. The Emperor proclaimed his will—Armenia belonged to the Romans, and Armenia would now have a Roman governor.[1]

Parthamasiris was sent away with an escort of cavalry for his security: he was killed on the journey, not without ugly imputations against the Emperor.[2] Trajan now proceeded to conquer and annex Armenia and north-western Mesopotamia. The work was completed by the end of 115, and here perhaps he might have stopped, with two new provinces to his credit.[3] In 116 he marched out again from Syria, captured Ctesiphon, and assumed at last the title of 'Parthicus'.[4]

The Imperator was dangerously susceptible to the influences of history and legend. A longing now seized him to behold the waters of the Ocean that reaches to India. He went down to the mouth of the Tigris, and, on sight of a merchant ship sailing away, bitterly bewailed his years and spoke with envy of Alexander.[5] In Babylon again, and there rendering homage to the memory of the Macedonian, he learned that rebellion had flared up in the lands of his conquest, among all the various peoples.[6] And the Jews were already in revolt. They quickly filled Egypt, Cyrenaica, and Cyprus with massacre and atrocities.[7]

Trajan set a king over the Parthians, a prince of the royal line called Parthamaspates. The great city of Seleucia had revolted. It was captured and destroyed by two of his legates.[8] Elsewhere the consular Maximus suffered a defeat and fell in battle, but Lusius Quietus took Nisibis and sacked Edessa.[9] Foiled himself before the stronghold of

---

[1] Dio LXVIII. 20. 3.

[2] ib. 20. 4; Arrian, *Parthica*, fr. 39 Roos; Fronto p. 209 N = Haines II, p. p212 f.

[3] cf. the arguments of F. A. Lepper, *Trajan's Parthian War* (1948), 106 ff. Against, M. I. Henderson, *JRS* XXXIX (1949), 121 ff.

[4] Dio LXVIII. 28. 2: καὶ τὴν ἐπίκλησιν τοῦ Παρθικοῦ ἐβεβαιώσατο. For the meaning of the last word (which has been much disputed) cf. Dio XLVI. 47. 5. The Senate had already voted the title, on February 20 of 116 (*FO* XXIII).

[5] Dio LXVIII. 29. 1.

[6] ib. 30. 1.

[7] ib. 32. 1 ff.; *HA*, *Hadr.* 5. 2; Eusebius, *Hist. Eccl.* IV. 2; *Chron.* p. 215 Schöne. The chronology and the course of events present many problems. See E. Groag, P–W XIII, 1881 ff.; F. A. Lepper, o.c. 91 f.; L. Motta, *Aegyptus* XXXII (1952), 474 ff.; A. Fuks, ib. XXXIII (1953), 131 ff. For events at Alexandria, H. A. Musurillo, *The Acts of the Pagan Martyrs* (1954), 181 ff.

[8] Dio LXVIII. 30. 2 (Erucius Clarus and Julius Alexander).

[9] ib. 30. 1 f. For the fate of Maximus cf. Fronto, p. 217 N = Haines II, p. 20; p. 209 N = Haines II, p. 214. The general might be T. Julius Maximus of Nemausus (*ILS* 1016), *cos. suff.* 112 (cf. App. 16).

Hatra in the desert, Trajan led his army back to Syria, not without loss and vexation.[1]

Trajan was preparing (it is said) to march into Mesopotamia again, but his health showed alarming symptoms, and he decided to depart for home, leaving Hadrian in charge of the army in Syria for the conduct of the war.[2] At Selinus, a city on the coast of Cilicia, the Emperor died, suddenly.

On August 9 Hadrian, the governor of Syria, learned that he had been adopted. Two days later, on the report of Trajan's decease, the army proclaimed him Emperor.[3] Thus did Hadrian come to the power. On the better showing there were grounds for perplexity—and some of the things done or published (whether at Selinus or at Rome) seemed to betray embarrassment as well as haste.[4] Allegations gained credence that Trajan died before he could name a successor, that the news was held back until what was necessary had been done; and it was Plotina who signed the despatch from which the Senate learned that Trajan had adopted a son.[5]

The truth cannot be disinterred. The persons present at the Emperor's death-bed at Selinus kept their counsel—Plotina, Matidia, and the Prefect of the Guard, Acilius Attianus.[6]

Speculation leads nowhere.[7] If the transmission of the power was managed by a resolute and sagacious woman, the validity of Hadrian's claim is not impaired—he was the next of kin, it was the will of the army, and the Senate ratified. Whatever Trajan may have thought (or gossip enhanced) about Hadrian's character in certain of its manifestations—and there was no congeniality—whatever verdicts he may have uttered in his cups when names and capacities came under review, Trajan in fact put the army of Syria in Hadrian's hands,

[1] Dio LXVIII. 31; Fronto, p. 204 N = Haines II, p. 202.

[2] Dio LXVIII. 32. 1; 33. 1.

[3] HA, Hadr. 4. 6 f.

[4] The Roman mint put out ADOPTIO on its first emission, but then dropped it, cf. P. L. Strack, Untersuchungen zur r. Reichsprägung des zweiten Jahrhunderts II (1933), 41; H. Mattingly, BMC, R. Emp. III (1936), cxxv ff.; 237. To go on advertising this allegation would have encouraged doubt and gossip. A solitary aureus once existed at Berlin, giving Hadrian the title of 'Caesar' ostensibly before Trajan's death, cf. Strack, o.c. I (1931), 20; Mattingly, o.c. III, 124. The Historia Augusta alleges that he had been designated by Trajan to a second consulate (Hadr. 4. 4): it is not on Hadrian's earliest issues.

[5] Dio LXIX. 1, cf. HA, Hadr. 4. 10. Dio had the information from his father, who was governor of Cilicia (c. 180). The witness of Bruttius Praesens would have been more useful, governor precisely in 117 (AE 1950, 66; IRT 545). He outlived Hadrian.

[6] From Hadrian's own town, and his guardian (PIR², A 451).

[7] Yet the strongest doubt must prevail whether Trajan lived long enough to adopt Hadrian. Dessau went much further, drawing attention to the death of the Emperor's personal servant, M. Ulpius Phaedimus, at Selinus on August 12 (ILS 1792): his remains were only brought to Rome thirteen years later (Festschrift für H. Kiepert (1898), 85 ff. Against, E. Groag, Röm. Mitt. XIV (1899), 269 ff.).

although Hadrian had not commanded troops in the recent war.[1] The absence of a frank or legal recognition of hereditary succession under some of the emperors may lend a specious colour to noble professions or empty theories.[2] In the dynasty that now held the power the hearest in blood would indubitably inherit—or would have to be suppressed.

Hadrian wrote to the Senate requesting honours for his parent (more were granted than he asked) and conferment of the power, with excuse for his precipitance: the 'res publica' could not go on without an 'imperator'.[3] When Hadrian had an unpopular measure to execute, he would allege secret instructions left by Trajan.[4] The first task was to cover a débâcle. Whether or no Hadrian invoked the ready plea, it happens not to be recorded.

Posterity censures Hadrian for abandoning the conquests of Trajan.[5] How much was left to surrender?[6] Trajan had created two provinces, Armenia and Mesopotamia.[7] There may have been some Roman troops in western Mesopotamia when Trajan died, and a part of Armenia could have been held, but the Roman vassal could not maintain himself at Ctesiphon. Hadrian allowed Armenia to revert to the position of a dependent kingdom.[8]

The great design had failed—or at least was for the present postponed. The plea could be urged of disturbances first needing to be quelled, not only in the eastern provinces but on the lower Danube, in Mauretania, and in Britain.[9] However, for the withdrawal of Roman armies, though the renunciation might be explained or palliated, Hadrian had to take the responsibility, with all the risk and damage evoked by the comparison with his glorious predecessor.

Hadrian knew better than to return in haste to the capital: the imperial ladies went home, along with the Prefect of the Guard, conveying the body of Trajan. On arrival Acilius Attianus, it is reported, asked leave to take action against the Prefect of the City, and also against two exiles confined on islands, Laberius Maximus and Calpurnius Crassus.[10] The latter, suspect under Nerva and banished by Trajan, was in fact put to death, though not at once. Hadrian still delayed. He had to make sure of the armies and the marshals.

---

[1] So far as known; and it is too much to designate him 'chief of the general staff' from the outset, as does W. Weber, *CAH* xi (1936), 299.

[2] cf. p. 234.   [3] *HA, Hadr.* 6. 2.   [4] ib. 9. 2.

[5] ib. 5. 3; 9. 1, cf. Fronto, p. 206 N = Haines ii, p. 206; Augustinus, *De civitate Dei* iv. 29—and many modern scholars.

[6] Little or nothing, cf. M. Rostovtzeff, *Klio* xxxi (1938), 285 ff.; M. I. Henderson, *JRS* xxxix (1949), 126 ff.   [7] If not a third, Assyria (cf. Eutropius viii. 3. 2; 6. 2).

[8] *HA, Hadr.* 21. 11, cf. 5. 4.   [9] ib. 5. 2.

[10] ib. 5. 5 f. Nothing is reported about the other Prefect of the Guard at this time, Ser. Sulpicius Similis. The *praefectus urbi* was Q. Baebius Macer (*PIR*², B 20), *suff.* 103, on whom see further App. 25.

During the first decade of Trajan's rule provincial commands and iterated consulates identify the chief personages in the government.[1] For the most part, bare names or public honours. The personalities elude grasp, likewise the groups and parties. After the death of Licinius Sura, the picture grows still more obscure, nor can there be profit in speculating about the advisers who impelled the Imperator (if impulsion was needed) towards war and conquest in the eastern lands.

The campaigns involved personalities in a close nexus with policy in the high command—good counsels or bad, renown or reverses in the field, hence discord, rancour, and feud. Two promotions are significant. A legionary legate, Terentius Gentianus, the son of one of the marshals, passed directly to the consulate in 116: he was not yet thirty.[2] More striking the elevation of Lusius Quietus, whom Trajan created a senator and consul (117). Lusius was a Moorish chieftain, first winning fame as a leader of his own native cavalry.[3] Trajan instructed him to extirpate the Jews of Mesopotamia, after which exploit he seemed the right man to curb and govern their land of origin.[4]

The partisans of Hadrian do not seem to come to the fore until the last years of the war. Some were still praetorian in rank—and not at all conspicuous through birth or rapid advancement. One, Erucius Clarus, had been a very slow beginner.[5] Another, Bruttius Praesens, came to feel distaste for the career of honours and shunned the capital.[6] Bruttius emerges paradoxically to command a legion in 114, earning decorations—and is then sent back to Italy to occupy a post of no consequence, the supervision of a minor road. However, in the month of August 117, he is legate of Cilicia.[7]

[1] Ch. V.

[2] ILS 1046; 1046a. Son of D. Terentius Scaurianus (suff. ? 102 or 104), the first legate of Dacia (CIL XVI, 57; 160; 163; III, 1443; 1081 = ILS 3594).

[3] Dio LXVIII. 32. 4 f., cf. the detailed study of E. Groag, P–W XIII, 1874 ff.

[4] Eusebius, Hist. Eccl. IV. 2. 5; Arrian, Parthica, fr. 79 Roos: ὁ δὲ Τραϊανὸς ἔγνω μάλιστα μέν, εἰ παρείκοι, ἐξελεῖν τὸ ἔθνος, εἰ δὲ μή, ἀλλὰ συντρίψας γε παῦσαι τῆς ἄγαν ἀτασθαλίας. His subsequent governorship in Judaea is attested by Dio LXVIII. 32. 3.

[5] Pliny expressed his disquiet, about the year 101 (Epp. II. 9). Erucius Clarus was a nephew of C. Septicius Clarus. Quaestor presumably in 99, he was still of praetorian rank when he captured Seleucia (Dio LXVIII. 30. 2). Then suffectus, in 117.

[6] Epp. VII. 3. 2: 'quin ergo aliquando in urbem redis? ubi dignitas honor amicitiae tam superiores quam minores.'

[7] For a military exploit in the winter of 114/15, Arrian, Parthica, fr. 85 Roos; for his cursus, AE 1950, 66 (Mactar); IRT 545 (Lepcis), with the remarks of G.-Ch. Picard, Revue africaine XCIV (1950), 25 ff. and, with H. G. Pflaum, Karthago II (1951), 91 ff. Bruttius was born about 70. The road was the Latina, held before a legionary command by Vitorius Marcellus (Statius, Silvae IV. 4. 60) and by M. Pompeius Macrinus Theophanes (IG V, 2, 151). Note, in contrast to Bruttius Praesens, another new man, Platorius Nepos, legate of I Adiutrix in the Parthian War and passing thence to the praetorian province of Thrace before his consulate (ILS 1052). It is, however, conceivable that Bruttius' charge of the Via Latina was nominal.

The consular commands have the arbitrament. Catilius Severus held Cappadocia:[1] he may (or may not) have been in charge ever since Armenia was annexed in 114. It was his first consular post. Avidius Nigrinus was governor of Dacia: how long he had been there cannot be established.[2] Two other names permit something more than a conjecture. Minicius Natalis and Pompeius Falco, legionary legates decorated for service in the first Dacian War, duly became consuls (in 106 and 108), but went without military employment until about 116. The one was then appointed to Pannonia, the other to Moesia Inferior.[3] Falco at least had a strong claim—he was the son-in-law of Sosius Senecio. Natalis had perhaps been an adherent of Licinius Sura.[4] Though many facts are missing,[5] it is clear that Hadrian and his friends were gaining a preponderance with Trajan some time before the conquests collapsed.

When Trajan died, the eastern and Danubian provinces together claimed no fewer than twenty-one of the thirty legions in the imperial army. Hadrian brought Catilius Severus from Cappadocia to take his own place in Syria.[6] Lusius Quietus rose no higher—Hadrian at once removed him from the governorship of Judaea.[7] Dacia before long received a new legate: Avidius Nigrinus, for reasons unknown (perhaps military, not personal), was superseded and went home. A man of more notable achievements took command—Julius Quadratus Bassus, general in the second Dacian War, governor of Cappadocia, governor of Syria.[8]

Hadrian after crossing Asia Minor on his way to the Danubian lands spent the winter of 117/18 on the Marmara. The city elected for his sojourn is not certified—perhaps Byzantium, perhaps Nicomedia.[9]

---

[1] *ILS* 1041; *I. l. d'Afrique* 43. Catilius became consul suffect in 110, after no fewer than six praetorian posts.

[2] Attested by *ILS* 2417 (Sarmizegethusa). His only known other consular post had been civilian, in Achaia (*SIG³* 827).

[3] *ILS* 1029; 1035 f. The beginning of Natalis' command cannot be fixed to a year. The diploma *CIL* xvi, 64 belongs to 116. Observe his son, q. c. 121, serving as tribune in three successive legions, I Adiutrix, XI Claudia, and XIV Gemina, about 115–18 (*ILS* 1029, cf. 1061). Q. Pompeius Falco is first attested in Moesia Inferior in 116, *CIL* iii, 12470; and Trajan is not yet 'Parthicus' on *ILS* 1035. Natalis had previously held the Tiber curatorship, Falco the charge of Trajan's new highway to Brundisium.

[4] They came from the same region of Tarraconensis. Barcino is Natalis' home (*ILS* 1029).

[5] Moesia Superior, Britain, and Germania Superior are void in 115-17: the mysterious 'Ka[nus ? Iunius Niger]' was in Germania Inferior (*CIL* xvi, 62).

[6] *HA, Hadr.* 5. 10, cf. *ILS* 1041; *I. l. d'Afrique* 43.

[7] He also deprived Lusius of his Moorish cavalry (*HA, Hadr.* 5. 8).

[8] For the text of his inscription see A. v. Premerstein, *Bayerische S-B*, 1934, Heft 3, 15 f. That scholar assumes that Hadrian sent Julius Quadratus to Dacia (o.c. 44), replacing C. Avidius Nigrinus: it could, however, have been Trajan, cf. A. Stein, *Die Reichsbeamten von Dazien* (1944), 13 f.

[9] Nicomedia is the only city apart from Alexandria to occur on the 'Nations series' of

He was not thinking merely of comfort and amenities. This was now the central point for the supervision of the Roman armies, and here for a brief spell (not unprophetically) was the residence of power.

From his winter quarters the Emperor directed operations or negotiations on the Danube. He did not reach Rome until the summer, making his entry on July 9.[1] The new ruler came with a heavy reproach already, and his insecurity was unequivocally published by the dispositions he made for the command of the Danubian armies. Julius Quadratus had died in Dacia. To hold that province (and one other at least) Hadrian appointed, not a senatorial legate, but a man of equestrian rank, his friend Marcius Turbo.[2]

In the absence of the Princeps a loyal Senate had sanctioned the execution of four consulars—and contrary to his wishes, so he swore and asserted. The charge was conspiracy against the life of the ruler, the particulars are faintly and vaguely reported.[3] The miscreants were separately apprehended and killed: at Baiae, at Tarracina, at Faventia, and the fourth on a journey. That is the only precision, and it fails to carry conviction of any guilt. Their identity is revealing. By this act perished four marshals of Trajan—Cornelius Palma, Publilius Celsus, Avidius Nigrinus (recently governor of Dacia), and Lusius the Moor.

What joins the four but their fate, no man can tell.[4] Perhaps a common discontent, too openly avowed, with Hadrian's policy of peace in the East: Lusius was a man for vigorous action, and Palma had once been commander of the army in Syria, at a time when war seemed likely to break out. Or was that only their pretext, masking other annoyances, conflicts, and ambitions? Between the three Romans no tie of family is known such as to suggest a political faction. The relationships of the senior marshals, Palma and Celsus, evade inquiry. Avidius Nigrinus, a younger man, belonged to a reputable family of the new nobility, marked by a taste for letters and

---

Hadrian's coinage. P. L. Strack was unable to furnish an adequate reason, *Untersuchungen zur r. Reichsprägung des zweiten Jahrhunderts* II (1933), 165.

[1] *CIL* VI, 32374.

[2] *HA, Hadr.* 6. 7. On Turbo's career, and his position at this time, see E. Groag, P-W XIV, 1596 ff.; A. Stein, *Die Reichsbeamten von Dazien* (1944), 14 ff.; R. Syme, *JRS* XXXVI (1946), 161 f. The inscription from Rapidum (*AE* 1911, 108) and the two fragments from Caesarea (*AE* 1931, 35; 1946, 113) belong to another man of similar nomenclature under Antoninus Pius. See now the inscription at Cyrrhus, published by E. Frézouls, *Syria* XXX (1953), 247, whence *AE* 1955, 225. It certifies his name as '(Q. Marcius) C. f. Tro. Fronto Turbo Publicius Severus', with Epidaurus in Dalmatia as his *origo*, and reveals his career from the second primipilate to the command of the Misenum fleet (in 114, cf. *CIL* XVI, 60).

[3] Dio LXIX. 1. 5; *HA, Hadr.* 7. 1 f. For a detailed inquiry see A. v. Premerstein, *Klio*, Beiheft VIII (1908), with additions in *Bayerische S-B*, 1934, Heft 3, 38 ff.

[4] The *HA* grotesquely alleges that two of them were suspect before Trajan's death— 'in adoptionis sponsionem venit Palma et Celso, inimicis semper suis et quos postea ipse insecutus est, in suspicionem tyrannidis lapsis' (*Hadr.* 4. 3, cf. 5. 8 on Lusius).

learning.[1] And he was a close friend of Hadrian.[2] A brave orator, Avidius may have been a rash talker.[3]

A new reign began, as often, in crime. Calpurnius Crassus merely paid the penalty of a dynastic name, an anachronistic survival. The execution of the four consulars, however, empoisoned the relations between the Princeps and the whole upper order in society. Hadrian consoled the Senate with words, affirming upon oath that none of its members should be put to death without their sanction. To the urban populace, duly remunerated already on his accession, he gave a double *congiarium*; and to publish a vast remission of debts to the Treasury, the account books were burned in the Forum.[4]

Hadrian soon had the armed provinces in firm control. He abolished the anomalous Danubian command of Marcius Turbo. Not that Dacia reverted to consular governors: the garrison was reduced to one legion, under a praetorian legate.[5] Other provinces were in the custody of Hadrian's friends among the marshals.[6] Not all of the recent consuls resplendent with glory for exploits in the field could safely be employed.[7] Hadrian promoted certain new men who went out quickly to command the armies.[8] The earliest consulates of the reign also disclose a whole group of significant names—the near associates and the political allies.[9]

The Senate had every reason to dislike the Princeps—things known long since or suspected, and recent actions. Men of sombre thoughts who reflected upon the past might discern a new Domitian or fear the unfolding of a Tiberius.

Hadrian experienced discomfort in his family and entourage, and there might be rancour and sharp discord. To his sister Domitia

[1] Nephew of T. Avidius Quietus (*suff.* 93).

[2] To be deduced from *HA, Hadr.* 7. 1—Hadrian would have made Avidius his own successor (presumably from the autobiography).

[3] Pliny, *Epp.* v. 13. 6 f.; 20. 6; VII. 6. 2 ff. (App. 27).

[4] Dio LXIX. 8. 12; *HA, Hadr.* 7. 3 ff.; *ILS* 309. Cf. now M. Hammond, *Mem. Am. Ac. Rome* XXI (1953), 127 ff.

[5] *ILS* 1056, cf. *CIL* XVI, 68 (Sex. Julius Severus). At the same time the province was divided, with Dacia Inferior under an equestrian governor.

[6] Catilius Severus was in Syria (*ILS* 1041; *I. l. d'Afrique* 43). Pompeius Falco went from Moesia Inferior to Britain (*ILS* 1035 f., cf. *CIL* XVI, 69). Minicius Natalis, holding Pannonia at Trajan's death (*ILS* 1029), was not given a second command. Who succeeded Catilius in Syria in 119 is not known.

[7] Terentius Gentianus got no armed province, cf. *ILS* 1046 (he was appointed, anomalously, to Macedonia, cf. Groag in P–W v A, 660); perhaps Erucius Clarus and Julius Alexander (Dio LXVIII. 30. 2) did not either.

[8] A. Platorius Nepos (*suff.* 119) to Germania Inferior (*ILS* 1052), L. Coelius Rufus (*suff.* 119) to Moesia Superior (cf. *PIR*[2], C 1246); and the legate of Moesia Inferior in 120, '[Se]rtorius' or '[A]rtorius' (*CIL* III, 7539) is presumably a recent consul. Bruttius Praesens must have become consul early in the reign. He went on to govern Cappadocia and Moesia Inferior (*AE* 1950, 66; *IRT* 545).

[9] Ch. XLIV, with App. 87.

Paullina he denied the title of 'Augusta'—she had a husband, the senior consular Julius Servianus. He could never agree with his wife, Vibia Sabina—had he been a private person he would have divorced the tiresome creature.[1] Yet he behaved with exemplary respect to her mother, Matidia, with consecration on her decease (in 119), aromatics for the plebs and gladiatorial contests, furthermore a funeral eulogy of his own composition and delivery.[2] Hadrian owed much more to Plotina. When she died three years later, she was commemorated by a temple and by poems.[3] Yet in some respects Matidia seemed to have the advantage. No issue of coins proclaimed the deification of Plotina.[4] Had their relations cooled—or was Hadrian anxious to avoid any more talk and publicity about the adoption?

Ingratitude or worse towards friends and relatives was prompted by Hadrian's devious nature: it is reported that he went in for espionage, intercepting the correspondence of senators.[5] Knights should have been trustworthy—and several of the high officials had not been born in that order but rose from very low, from the centurionate.[6] Yet Hadrian speedily conceived a dislike for his ally and helper, Acilius Attianus. In 119 Acilius was dismissed from the command of the Guard along with his colleague Sulpicius Similis.[7] Next to Acilius, Hadrian owed most to Marcius Turbo. He became the next Prefect, paired with a man of minor consequence, Septicius Clarus. The latter kept his master's approbation for three years only.[8] If Turbo lasted longer than Septicius Clarus, he too in the end fell from favour.[9]

Of Hadrian's senatorial allies some forfeited his friendship for reasons various or trivial.[10] Nor was he generous with honours. The distinction of a second consulate became rarer—only one of the military men prominent in the critical early years, Catilius Severus, achieved it (in 120). Others who might have properly aspired thereto he passed over.[11] Few earned the honour, and late in life.[12]

[1] *HA, Hadr.* 11. 3.

[2] ib. 9. 9; 19. 5 (cf. *CIL* VI, 2080); *CIL* XIV, 3579. She became a full 'diva'; and Hadrian also promoted the deceased Marciana to that rank, cf. J. H. Oliver, *Harv. Th. Rev.* XLII (1949), 37.

[3] Dio LXIX. 10. 3[1]. Also a basilica at Nemausus (*HA, Hadr.* 12. 2). Her death probably occurred in 122.

[4] Because Hadrian was too busy, according to H. Mattingly, *BMC, R. Emp.* III (1936), cxxxiii.

[5] *HA, Hadr.* 11. 4 ff.   [6] e.g. Sulpicius Similis (Dio LXIX. 19. 1).

[7] *HA, Hadr.* 9. 3 ff. In August of this year Q. Rammius Martialis was removed from Egypt (*P.Oxy.* 2205), making way for T. Haterius Nepos (*ILS* 1338). Rammius did not go on to the Guard.   [8] ib. 11. 2.   [9] ib. 15. 7.

[10] ib. 15. 2 ff.; 23. 4 f. Among them was Platorius Nepos. For discord (and deaths) late in the reign, see p. 600.

[11] Thus Neratius Priscus, Minicius Natalis, and Pompeius Falco.

[12] The statement in *HA, Hadr.* 8. 4 is false. Six men received iterations (most of them very elderly), two a third consulate (Annius Verus and Julius Servianus). Cf. App. 12.

Ancestry, merit, or popularity incurred suspicion—and the link of blood or propinquity might be more damaging. Hadrian's first years of rule were precarious. Next in the dynastic succession (if it could be maintained) stood Pedanius Fuscus, who had married Hadrian's niece, Julia, the daughter of Julius Servianus.[1] Pedanius, sharing the *fasces* with Hadrian in 118, was a dozen years older than Hadrian was when Trajan came to the power. Yet Pedanius fades out without further commemoration for good or ill, only a name on the consular *Fasti* and a link in genealogy.[2]

If an emperor encountered discomforts at Rome or suspected danger, he could escape to the provinces. The Senate had to endure Hadrian's presence for nearly three years until he set out on a tour of the western lands, which he had not seen since his military tribunate in Upper Germany over twenty years before. It was his purpose to inspect and organize the resources of the Empire, survey the frontiers, and discover the most economical means for their defence. In 121 the Emperor was in Gaul and on the Rhine.[3] The next year saw him in Britain, where he brought Platorius Nepos from Lower Germany to supersede Pompeius Falco.[4] There had been trouble in the north, with a whole legion recently destroyed.[5]

After debate and decision about the construction of the wall that was to form a continuous barrier from sea to sea, the Emperor returned to Gaul, passed onward into Spain, and wintered at Tarraco; his own townsfolk, the men of Italica, did not see their emperor—he bore them some kind of grudge.[6]

In the course of the year 123 the routine of Hadrian's journeyings was disturbed by a threat of trouble from the side of Parthia. He ordered troop movements, came himself to the eastern frontier, and met the monarch in conference.[7] Whatever the claims in dispute, or the concessions they mutually admitted, the result turned out well enough. The doubts and hopes that still lingered at Rome were abolished. Hadrian put stability before glory. Policy and aims might be conveyed and advertised by appeal to the precedent of Augustus:

---

[1] Pliny, *Epp.* VI. 26. 1.

[2] Pedanius Fuscus is absent from Dio, the *HA*—and from most modern histories.

[3] Some put his departure from Rome in 120. Not plausible.

[4] *CIL* XVI, 69 (of July 17, 122).

[5] viz. IX Hispana. Vexillations were brought from the Continent (*ILS* 2726); also (probably a little later) a legion, VI Victrix (*ILS* 1100), perhaps conducted by its legate P. Tullius Varro (*suff.* 127) in 121 or 122 (*ILS* 1047), and first attested under the governorship of Platorius Nepos (*AE* 1938, 116). Some have argued for a longer survival of IX Hispana, thus E. Ritterling, P–W XII, 1668 f.; E. Birley, *Roman Britain and the Roman Army* (1953), 20 ff. For the disaster (or disasters) see further p. 490.

[6] Dio LXIX. 10. 1. Cf. probably the corrupt passage *HA, Hadr.* 12. 4 (a scene at Tarraco).

[7] *HA, Hadr.* 13. 8.

in this year, or very soon after, the ruler adopted for imperial titulature on his coins the simplified and powerful legend 'Hadrianus Augustus'.[1]

The titulature heralds a notable anniversary—one hundred and fifty years from the Senate's vote conferring the name 'Augustus' upon the saviour of Rome and second founder of the city. It signifies much more than the stated recurrence of any numerical cycle. Chronology accorded miraculously with a new 'Pax Augusta'.

Trajan when he came to the power was aged forty-four. Like Trajan, Hadrian succeeded young to the purple, younger even than his predecessor—he was only forty-one. Trajan reached and passed the climacteric, but did not survive to complete another year, while Hadrian was cut short during the ominous sixty-third. For both princes a long tenure might confidently have been predicted. Fate robbed Trajan of his Parthian triumph, also of his 'vicennalia'.[2] Hadrian celebrated that anniversary, but without pomp or emphasis,[2] and died soon after in his twenty-first regnal year.

The parallel is close, but fortuitous, and such coincidences are more for the vulgar than for men of understanding. In all things else, so it should seem, the divergence is sharp, the contrast antithetic between reigns and rulers: war and peace, a soldier and a scholar.[3] Trajan seized the imperial power, Hadrian succeeded to it on a claim that was not the less dynastic because not properly announced and prepared. Each, it is true, had passed through the sequence of offices and commands to the consulate, each assumed authority only after long subordination. But the experience was not comparable. While the one had merely to play the sturdy and stylized role of loyal servant to an autocrat, the other, something more than a senator, something less than a crown prince, endured under the eye of his formidable kinsman an apprenticeship from which he might be emancipated too late, if at all. Trajan, by virtue of his accession, rescuing order, peace, and the 'res publica', found it easy to enact the show of an Augustan principate, and not least through his own training and personal tastes. Trajan, like Augustus, wanted power, and regarded theory with indifference. Hadrian was hampered by a tortuous character, a keen intellect, and an intensive education.

It is not easy for a ruler to be wholly equitable towards the man marked out to take his place. Trajan could spare himself the effort.

[1] P. L. Strack, *Untersuchungen zur r. Reichsprägung des zweiten Jahrhunderts* II (1933), 12 ff.; 105; H. Mattingly, *BMC, R. Emp.* III (1936), cxxxiv; clxvii; M. Grant, *Roman Anniversary Issues* (1950), 101.

[2] P. L. Strack, o.c. 184 ff.; H. Mattingly, *Proc. Brit. Ac.* XXXVI (1950), 159; 184.

[3] Thus, for example, E. Kornemann, *Weltgesch. des Mittelmeerraums* II (1949), 125 ff.; H. Kähler, *Kaiser Hadrian u. seine Villa bei Tivoli* (1950), 143 ff.

The tastes and pursuits of his young kinsman were not at all to his liking—but an added irritant, if they engaged the sympathetic interest of Plotina, who was a subtle and cultivated woman. There was much to draw them together, and perhaps their age as well.[1] Hence, at the least, an amiable propensity in Plotina. Scandal added something more.[2] The Imperator, from uncongenial, may have become crudely oppressive to his wife. Some of his habits are known. And, where Trajan paraded rank and authority, the younger man was prone to see pomposity and inhumanity. Never reluctant to encounter his inferiors, Hadrian comported himself with ease as any man's equal.[3]

Moreover, Trajan could invoke an excuse, the 'res publica' (specious and not quite honest), for deferring the claims of Hadrian; and, if the Imperator gave a thought to the reigns of Caesar Augustus and Tiberius Caesar, he might discover a reason for quiet confidence, hoping to outlive an heir who was only twenty-three years his junior. All of which Hadrian saw. He was constrained to dissemble—and his personality hardened and sharpened under the pressure of an unavowed animosity.

Hadrian's character was various and peculiar.[4] Of a wondrous native aptitude, he grasped with ease and avidity all arts, all sciences. He wrote abundantly, prose and verse (the poems were marred by preciosity and obscurity), he excelled in painting, music, and sculpture. With a phenomenal memory, decided tastes in literature (he turned with aversion from the Latin classics to the early writers), and no reluctance to talk and argue, Hadrian was a blessing to artists and professors—and a peril, because of the polymath's pride and jealousy, for he would always mock, contemn, and crush them. When the Emperor tried to force his own plans on the great architect Apollodorus, an angry retort ensued, a quarrel—and Apollodorus was put to death, so it was alleged. The sophist Favorinus, an ostentatious celebrity, took refuge for once in discretion: who can argue with the master of thirty legions?

So far the contrast. Beneath the surface the two reigns are linked

---

[1] Plotina might have been nearly twenty years younger than Trajan; and no certainty that she was his first wife. For the coins, *BMC, R. Emp.* III (1936), 106 f.; 124; 229 f.; 245 f.; her iconography, R. West, *R. Porträtplastik* II (1941), 75 ff., who emphasizes the Capitoline and Vatican heads (pl. XIX, 70 and 73). She looks a little weary, but amused around the eyes.

[2] The motive of 'favor Plotinae' recurs in *HA, Hadr.* 2. 10; 4. 1; 4. 4. Also 'factio Plotinae', 4. 10. Dio speaks of ἐρωτικὴ φιλία (LXIX. 1. 2, cf. 10. 3). Who can tell?

[3] *HA, Hadr.* 20. 1: 'in conloquiis etiam humillimorum civilissimus fuit, detestans eos qui sibi hanc voluptatem humanitatis quasi servantes fastigium principis inviderent'; 17. 6: 'fuit et plebis iactatissimus amator'; 17. 5 f. (bathing publicly in anybody's company); 16. 10 (a friend of Epictetus).

[4] For the details, *HA, Hadr.* 14. 8 ff.; 15. 10 ff.; 20; Dio LXIX. 3 ff.

and blended in an essential unity.[1] The Empire had come to adult stature. That was evident when the ruler advertised the titulature of 'Hadrianus Augustus', evident already when Trajan had been reigning for a decade.

The Principate, arising out of civil convulsions, was accepted from necessity, to control the armies and maintain the stability of the Empire. The Principate had done much more than that. It established a whole system of government, by annexing the attributes of the 'res publica' and by creating new organs. A century and a half having passed since the Battle of Actium, the perspective of the long process could be discerned, and the steady aggrandisement of the imperial power. In conflicts open or secret the old aristocracy, the peers of Julii and Claudii, had been reduced and almost annihilated, all opposition had been tamed, and educated opinion was reconciled to the government.

'Libertas' had regularly been invoked by a new ruler, and then dropped, quickly and quietly: it vanished from Vespasian's coinage in the third year of his reign.[2] Trajan, in conspicuous revulsion from Nerva, would have nothing to do with the notion—until, suddenly, 'Libertas' emerges some ten years after his accession.[3] About the same time, when obsolete currency had been withdrawn and melted down, the mint isued a large batch of commemorative coins, reproducing the names and types of Republican moneyers along with such emperors as had not incurred obloquy.[4] The design is manifest—to recall and solemnize the ancient glory of the Free State, to assert and demonstrate the continuity between past and present. It proved the contrast. The demise of Republic and Republicanism could not have been more clearly ratified.

The 'imperatores' installed at Rome an autocratic power which they had wielded abroad in command of armies and provinces. Caesar Augustus, after three long absences in the first epoch of his rule, hardly stirred from Italy again. For his successor, Rome was 'caput rerum', not wisely or safely to be neglected.[5] Despite promises or projects Tiberius never went to the provinces. Yet the great 'arcanum

---

[1] The contrary view has been proclaimed, namely that the year 117 is the most important date in the development of the Roman Empire down to Diocletian: see E. Kornemann, *Kaiser Hadrian und der letzte grosse Historiker von Rom* (1905), 1. Nobody, to be sure, would wish to deny that Hadrian was a conscious and notable reformer. See, for example, F. Pringsheim, *JRS* XXIV (1934), 141 ff.

[2] P. L. Strack, o.c. II (1933), 178.

[3] P. L. Strack, o.c. II (1933), 177; H. Mattingly, *BMC, R. Emp.* III (1936), lxix; xcii.

[4] Dio LXVIII. 15. 31, cf. H. Mattingly, *Num. Chron.*[5] VI (1926), 232 ff.; *BMC, R. Emp.* III (1936), lxxxvi ff. Further, for vexed problems about Trajan's 'decennalia', *Proc. Brit. Ac.* XXXVI (1950), 183.

[5] *Ann.* I. 47. 1, cf. III. 47. 2.

imperii' could never be wholly suppressed. It emerged alive and menacing when Nero fell.

Both Trajan and Hadrian were proclaimed abroad. Neither showed any haste to come back to Rome. Hadrian had been away for several years, and he was soon at his travels again (121–5). The second long absence lasted for six years (128–34).

Hadrian was devoured by an insatiable curiosity for strange lands and alien habits. To serve as a museum of all his experiences, he constructed an enormous palace on the slopes below Tibur.[1] If travel gave refreshment to a restless soul, it was now a necessity for a conscientious ruler. Vigorous in body and addicted to hunting, like so many of the provincial aristocracy, Hadrian showed tenacity and endurance, marching bare-headed in sun or snow when he visited the armies for encouragement or rebuke.[2] Parades and exercises attested his care for discipline, not unaccompanied by allocutions and critical comment;[3] and an expert's eye inspected or modified the design of frontier works, not always perhaps to advantage.[4]

Hadrian's long peregrinations (perhaps excessive, and sometimes petulant)[5] capture attention and seem to manifest the great change. Yet Trajan in the first decade of his rule was absent as often as present, and the Senate never saw him again after the year 113.

Hadrian, as his acts and journeys appear to show, had for his task to assess, codify, and regulate the world-empire. The facts and habits and procedure were valid before his accession. Names abide—the Roman Senate and the consecrated order of the city magistracies. In reality, the Emperor, the cabinet, and the provincial governorships; and beside the personages of senatorial rank are the equestrian bureaucratic officials, at Rome or in the provinces.[6] Trajan's reign had shown a steady development. Everything converged. More and more fiscal posts were created, giving employment to knights.[7] Senators in the service of Caesar now saw the total of praetorian provinces rise from eight to twelve,[8] hence better prospects of a consulship. Trajan's favour brought rapid promotions—and some scandalous. The true

[1] H. Kähler, *Kaiser Hadrian u. seine Villa bei Tivoli* (1950).

[2] Dio LXIX. 9. 3 f.; *HA, Hadr.* 23. 1.

[3] ib. 9. 1 ff.; *HA, Hadr.* 10. Cf. the address at Lambaesis to the army of Numidia (*ILS* 2487).

[4] Some of the changes in Britain may have been due to the Emperor's personal intervention. For the Wall and its problems, I. A. Richmond, *JRS* XL (1950), 43 ff.

[5] Criticism of Hadrian's instability is implied when Marcus praises Pius for τὸ μὴ εὐμετακίνητον καὶ ῥιπταστικόν, ἀλλὰ καὶ τόποις καὶ πράγμασι τοῖς αὐτοῖς ἐνδιατριπτικόν (*Ad se ipsum* I. 16).

[6] cf. H. M. Last, *CAH* XI, 426 ff.

[7] The total of equestrian procuratorships, sixty-two under Domitian, is brought to over eighty by Trajan, cf. H. G. Pflaum, *Les Procurateurs équestres sous le Haut-Empire romain* (1950), 54 ff.; P–W XXIII, 1249 ff.   [8] App. 15, cf. 18.

function of the supreme magistracy had long been clear: the office could now be held away from Rome.[1] The Emperor encroaches everywhere on the Senate—not only special commissioners in the towns of Italy, but for a time the Transpadana under a legate, and interventions in certain of the public provinces.[2] While Caesar's friends stand high in privilege, the Senate is abased and transformed. Regions or cities so far unsuspected contribute their consuls, and the august assembly broadens, taking on a cosmopolitan aspect.

Before Trajan, however, can be discerned the Flavian system of imperial government, of which Trajan himself is the product and exponent; and, further back, Claudius and Nero, whose palace and dynasty could not mask or disguise, but even advertised, the passage of power from Rome and Italy to the provinces. Men now cast their eyes backwards and contemplated the history of the Caesars as it unfolded from the beginning. Was that process no less ordained by destiny than the rise of Rome to primacy in Italy and dominion over the nations?

The Principate started on an auspicious course (and distance made the first epoch seem fairer), but it encountered hazards, deviating into tyranny and dishonour. At some point or other a turn for the worse intervened—a ruler's personality, immutable fate, or the 'deum ira in rem Romanam'.[3]

A man might now recount the whole story with an understanding made sharper by present transactions. Even without the incentive of Trajan's conquests or the accession of Hadrian the theme called imperiously for an historian. The only question was: ought he to lead off with Caesar Augustus or with Tiberius Caesar?

---

[1] It cannot be believed that Terentius Gentianus and Lusius Quietus (above, p. 242) went back to Rome to hold the office (in 116 and in 117). The same phenomenon might have occurred in 97 or 98; and Petillius Cerialis (on the Rhine before he could have held the *fasces*) may not have been the only instance of an absent consul in 70.

[2] p. 224. [3] *Ann.* IV. 1. 2, cf. XVI. 16. 2.

PART V

THE *ANNALES*

XXI. THE STRUCTURE OF THE *ANNALES*

CORNELIUS TACITUS decided to begin with the death of Augustus. What survives of his annals of the Caesars from Tiberius to Nero (in bulk not much more than the half) indicates a structure of three groups, each containing six books.[1] The first hexad embraces the principate of Tiberius, in two equal portions, sharply and explicitly divided.[2] That the reign of a Caesar fell into two parts, the earlier marked by the hope and profession of good government (and often the performance also), the later declining or corrupted and verging to inevitable discord and calamity, was not merely a persuasion of the vulgar or a convenient literary schema, as exhibited at the crudest in the operations of a biographer: it corresponded not seldom with the facts of autocratic rule, and, even if not wholly valid, might well be confirmed beyond dispute by an assassination, by a revolution, or by the Senate's refusal to consecrate the deceased emperor.

The reign of Tiberius Caesar began well, the power being safely transmitted; a just and sagacious administration went on for a long time; and, if Roman tradition had not become increasingly preoccupied with the congenial task of converting Augustus into an ideal figure, it could have proclaimed this epoch not merely comparable

---

[1] App. 35. The plan can stand, even if the author did not survive to complete the Neronian hexad. The title (or perhaps subtitle) of the work was 'ab excessu divi Augusti', as the *Codex Mediceus* shows: cf. R. P. Oliver, *TAPA* LXXXII (1951), 235. It has been asserted that Tacitus himself used the title 'annales' (F. Jacoby, *Atthis* (1949), 111). That rests upon a misconception. In Tacitus, 'annales' is the normal, as it is the traditional and Latin, term for 'history', e.g. *Ann.* III. 65. 1: 'quod praecipuum munus annalium reor', &c.; IV. 34. 1 (the books of Cremutius Cordus). When he says 'annalis nostros' (IV. 32. 1), he means 'the history I am writing'. Compare Livy XLIII. 13. 2: 'ea pro dignis habere quae in meos annales referam.' There is a negative test: Tacitus never employs 'historia' (singular or plural) with the meaning of 'history'.

[2] IV. 1. 1: 'C. Asinio C. Antistio consulibus nonus Tiberio annus erat compositae rei publicae', &c.

with the later Augustan years, but far surpassing them for liberty and for felicity. Yet in the end, after plots and counterplots and the long sequel of judicial murders, the experiment of a constitutional principate ignominiously collapsing and naked despotism revealed, a morose septuagenarian perished amid the execration of Senate and People.

It remained to speculate about the causes of the change and to register the year or the event that signalized a turn for the worse. The causes were sought for the most part in the personality of the ruler, either as influenced by the impact of events or else gradually disclosing its hidden nature. Various themes offered, such as the suspicions and rancour of Tiberius, evoked by (or expressed in) the fear of rivals, and the growth of prosecutions for high treason; and various cardinal dates could be used—the death of Germanicus, the death of Drusus, the retirement of Tiberius from Rome, or even the decease of his mother Livia. Which was the historian to choose?

Germanicus was inescapable. Tacitus exploits him in every way. Not only the radiant figure compounded of all virtues and excellence (and popular in proportion) to set against the dark soul of Tiberius Caesar—the historian needs Germanicus for variety, for movement, and for continuous narration. The young prince takes up wide tracts in the first three books of the *Annales*: the mutiny of the legions on the Rhine, the elaborate expeditions into Germany, the travels in the eastern lands, the quarrel with Cn. Piso the legate of Syria, the melancholy end at Antioch, and, not least in importance, the official inquiry, with Piso prosecuted before the Senate for high treason. None the less, the death of Germanicus was hardly suitable for the turning-point.[1] To choose the year 19 would curtail unduly the prosperity in government that even the most hostile could never deny to Tiberius Caesar; the reign was still only in its fifth year; and, with Drusus the son of Tiberius alive, both ruler and dynasty seemed secure.

When Drusus died four years later, the succession beckoned to the sons of Germanicus, and the entourage of the Princeps became a ferment of hopes and fears and intrigues. Germanicus left three sons, and the widow was a proud intractable woman, conscious of all she claimed as the granddaughter of Caesar Augustus, and ready to take a second husband. Tiberius was impatient to escape from that noxious environment. He was now in his sixty-fourth year, and he came to depend more and more upon his favourite and counsellor, L. Aelius Seianus, Prefect of the Guard. Three years elapsed, and he left the capital, never to return. Most historians (so Tacitus affirms) gave a

---

[1] Dio emphasized it, LVII. 7. 1 f.; 13. 6; 19. 1; 19. 8. Cf. Suetonius, *Cal.* 6. 2.

reason—the wiles of Seianus. The minister would have in his control the Emperor and access to the Emperor—who in the course of time (old age and the lure of leisure) might be persuaded to hand over the reins of government.[1]

What guides Tacitus is clear. Grouping the second half of the reign around the figure of Seianus, significant as is Germanicus for the first half, the historian makes a new start with 23, announced at the opening of Book IV by a full-length presentation of Seianus, and emphasized a little further on by a general survey of Tiberius' acts and policy down to that year.

Book IV exemplifies in various ways the ambition of Seianus and his influence as it steadily mounted, with Tiberius going away to Campania in 26 and ensconced already on the island of Capreae in 27—and disposed, it would seem, to resign more and more of the imperial authority to his indispensable minister. Book V ushers in the year 29. After chronicling the death of Livia, the Augusta (a character sketch is added), it proceeds immediately to relate how a missive arrived at Rome from Princeps to Senate, with grave incriminations against Agrippina, the widow of Germanicus, and against the eldest son. Then the narration breaks off,[2] and with it goes most of the history of the years 29–31.

The gap robs posterity of a drama unsurpassed in plot and catastrophe. The final act is known—it was played out in open day, before the high assembly, and in the streets of the capital. Tiberius Caesar had raised up Seianus, and now he resolved to destroy him. A lengthy despatch came from Capreae, 'verbosa et grandis epistula'.[3] The consul, privy to the Emperor's design, proceeded to read it out, while Seianus, without suspicion, expected to hear further honours and a full partnership with Tiberius in the imperial power. The artful convolutions ended in a sharp and sudden denunciation. Seianus, deceived and dazed, could offer no resistance. As they dragged him away to death, he saw his statues already being cast down: trusty agents had secured all the city troops, and a new prefect now commanded the Guard.

What led up to the plot devised by Caesar against his minister is another matter. There are many obscurities.[4] Too much to hope that all would be dispelled by the Tacitean narrative. But it would supply

---

[1] IV. 57. I, cf. 41.

[2] At v. 5. The manuscript exhibits an interval of only three or four letters. The narration then passes to an event late in the year 31 (numbered v. 6 in modern editions): the first sentence is an isolated fragment, but without any mark of hiatus before or after.

[3] Juvenal x. 71.

[4] Despite Dio's full account of the year 31 (LVIII. 7. 2–16. 7, beginning with an extract from Xiphilinus but passing quickly to the original). That there was a 'conspiracy of Seianus' remains to be proved. See App. 65.

at the least some valuable information about the political manœuvres
of the years 29–31, revealing the allies of Seianus (those who survived as well as those who perished), and the especial enemies of the
ambitious parvenu; and not least, perhaps, the aristocrats who were
disposed to stand loyally by Tiberius Caesar, whatever might be their
personal likings, their ties of kinship, or their dynastic claims.[1]

The concluding book of the hexad carries a dreary epilogue down
to the extinction of the old emperor, with many prosecutions and
deaths, with little extraneous or antiquarian matter for variegation.
A powerful summary at the end diagnoses the life and character of
Tiberius, stage by stage.[2]

Such is the first hexad of the *Annales*, covering twenty-three years.
The second, containing the reigns of Caligula (37–41) and Claudius
(41–54), is marred by the loss of its first four books and a part of its
fifth. The truncated fragment begins some way through Book XI, in
the year 47, and, with a single episode engrossing much space, comes
almost to the end of 48. Book XII takes the narrative to the death of
Claudius.

The historian split his first hexad into two halves. He could hardly
do that with the second, making Caligula equal with Claudius, four
years with nearly fourteen; and, as will be seen, there is no trace of
any such division in the third. Two books for Caligula and four for
Claudius should satisfy the demands of chronology and equity.[3]
Those two Caligulan books will have exhibited a sharp and dramatic
contrast as the young prince disclosed his tyrant's nature (sagacious
observers had predicted it), and men's hopes turned to fear and
detestation.

Rome after the death of Tiberius was like a city liberated. To the
joy of loyal subjects the prince responded with largesse and pageantry,
with exemplary conduct and noble professions: 'pietas' displayed to
the memory of Germanicus his father, extravagant honours for his
sisters, and such reverence for the 'res publica' that the ruler gave
back the elections to the arbitrament of the Roman People.

Concord and felicity persisted for a season, before the perils and the
temptations of the supreme power were revealed, and with them the
true character of the Emperor. It was not until the year 39 that
Caligula grew suspicious about the aristocracy, the generals, and his
own relatives. In the autumn he went off in some precipitation to

---

[1] p. 384 f.   [2] VI. 51.
[3] Dio, after two books for Tiberius, allots one to Caligula (LIX); and the next book
probably takes Claudius down to the end of 46, cf. Boissevain in his edition (Berlin, 1898)
II, xxii.

Gaul, ostensibly to conduct armies of invasion into Britain or across the Rhine. The upshot was a plot discovered and suppressed. Young Aemilius Lepidus now perished, who had been for a short time the husband of Drusilla, one of Caligula's sisters, and who was designated for the succession.[1] What happened was more than a mere murder in the family. Lentulus Gaetulicus was also executed, who had been commander of the army of Upper Germany for the last ten years.[2]

That no doubt marked the turning-point in the reign. Henceforth cruelty, arrogance, and megalomania—and not confined in repercussion to the capital of the Empire. Yet the tyrant was not dethroned by a provincial rising or some general's proclamation. The conspiracy formed at Rome, officers of the Guard plotting with senators, and Caligula was assassinated on January 24, A.D. 41.[3]

The Senate was convoked. One of the consuls delivered an oration on liberty and spoke of restoring the Republic—from sincere belief, from homage to convention, or in order to gain time; and certain men of birth and consequence were already putting up a claim to the Principate when soldiers of the Guard discovered a forgotten Caesar whom joyously they acclaimed, and, after prolonged and delicate negotiations between the camp and the Senate, the power was duly conferred upon Claudius, the brother of Germanicus.

Claudius never forgot that perilous and awkward interregnum. He soon had other grounds for rancour and suspicion. In the second year of the reign Arruntius Camillus, the legate of Dalmatia, cast off his allegiance.[4] The proclamation was abortive but alarming, not least because of the ancestry of the pretender, the character and quality of certain senators among his adherents.[5]

The principal subjects around which the historian would concentrate his narrative derived from the previous reign, notably palace politics, the influence of the imperial freedmen, and strained relations between Princeps and Senate; and the same persons stood in prominence, the friends of the dynasty and ministers of state. As for foreign affairs, the revolt in Mauretania arose out of the annexation by Caligula and took several years for its suppression; while the Emperor in person superintended the invasion of Britain. Diverse though the two rulers might be in character and in policy, it was not beyond the skill of the historian to exploit the elements of continuity and impart a certain unity to the second hexad. Down to 48 inclusive his treatment

---

[1] *PIR²*, A 371.
[2] *PIR²*, C 1390.
[3] The full story is given by Josephus, *AJ* XIX. 17–273 (reproducing a good Latin source).
[4] *PIR²*, A 1140 (L. Arruntius Camillus Scribonianus, *cos.* 32).
[5] For the pedigree of Arruntius, below, p. 382; his supporters (among them the consular Caecina Paetus), p. 559.

is very generous. While Mauretania and Britain offered scope (and welcome it was) for details of warfare and geography, Tacitus would need much domestic material to fill up these three books (IX–XI). He could find it easily. The social life of the capital was gay and glittering, with wits and orators—and decorative celebrities of both sexes. Display and competition, intrigue, corruption, and crime— nothing was lacking.

Tiberius Caesar had avoided the company of women, and he disliked any ceremonial or fashion. A court was waiting to revive, with a whole cluster of princesses who transmitted the blood of Julii, Claudii, Antonii—and all the discords of the dynasty. In the forefront the three daughters of Germanicus, the daughter of Drusus, the two sisters of Domitius Ahenobarbus.[1] Drusilla died in the second year of Caligula and was emphatically consecrated, but Julia Agrippina and Julia Livilla went on in splendour and scandal. Early in the reign of Claudius allegations of adultery consigned Livilla to exile, where she was promptly killed.[2] Agrippina, left a widow by the decease of Domitius Ahenobarbus, cast about for a new alliance and took the husband of his sister, namely Passienus Crispus, wealthy, witty, and eloquent. The extinction of Passienus not long after is put down to her contriving.[3]

Powerful females of dynastic pedigree and behaviour waged feud with Agrippina or went in for other dangerous practices (incest and magic did not fail to be alleged). Many of the great ladies were avid and ruthless, but nothing is certified to the discredit of Julia, the daughter of Drusus, who, once betrothed to Aelius Seianus, was found a safe and steady husband;[4] and the graceful Junia Calvina wins the tribute of an expert appraiser—'festivissima omnium puellarum'.[5]

Valeria Messallina, the consort of Claudius Caesar, gives her name to the epoch, at least in the more lurid of its manifestations; and political murders tend to be laid to her account. The catalogue includes two princesses, Julia and Julia Livilla.[6] Nor were men of birth and rank immune. Messallina brought about the murder of her mother's third husband, one of the Junii Silani.[7] In the year 46 died M. Vinicius (who had been married to Julia Livilla), with

[1] Observe also Junia Calvina and Junia Lepida, whose maternal grandparents were L. Aemilius Paullus (*cos.* A.D. 1) and the younger Julia.

[2] *PIR*[1], J 444.

[3] Suetonius (ed. Roth, 1898), p. 290. His previous wife was Domitia, *PIR*[2], D 171.

[4] viz. C. Rubellius Blandus (p. 576).

[5] Seneca, *Apocol.* 8. 2. Cf. *Ann.* XII. 4. 1: 'sane decora et procax'.

[6] Dio LX. 18. 4; 8. 5.

[7] ib. 14. 3 f. He was C. Appius Junius Silanus (*cos.* 28), husband of Domitia Lepida (*PIR*[2], D 180).

a public funeral for commemoration: poisoned, they said, by the Empress.[1]

It was a season of sharp enmities, and also of conspiracies, real or fabricated. Two aristocrats who fell under suspicion escaped by reason of their patent futility.[2] But an historic name, aggravated by perilous alliance with the line of Pompeius Magnus, brought destruction on Crassus Frugi. His wife and son shared his fate.[3]

Messallina happens not to be blamed for this transaction. In the next year, however, she went on to compass the ruin of the illustrious consular Valerius Asiaticus. She worked upon the fears of Claudius, her instruments being his chief minister L. Vitellius and the freedmen of the household.

What survives of Book XI opens with that act. Miscellaneous items follow, notably the measures enacted by Claudius when holding the office of censor; and the book is soon engrossed with the scandalous behaviour which the Empress carried to a reckless extremity, provoking her fall and death.

The selection of a new wife for Claudius Caesar suitably introduces Book XII. The freedmen passed three candidates in review. With Pallas on her side and L. Vitellius adding support, Agrippina won the competition, Germanicus' daughter and niece of the imperial bridegroom; her arts and influence invade the government of Rome, she persuades Claudius to adopt her son, his claim to the succession is gradually enforced. The historian in the meantime, for relief and variety from palace politics, has recourse to a pair of digressions on affairs beyond the eastern frontier under the years 49 and 51 (not of any great moment or relevance);[4] and a resumptive section registers a long period in the Roman subjugation of Britain (since 47), with dramatic interest, not to say pageantry, concentrated upon the insurgent leader Caratacus.[5] Finally, Claudius being disposed of by the poisoned mushroom, Nero is presented to the Guard as emperor, and the 'auctoritas' of the Senate ratifies the choice of the soldiery.

Claudius Caesar, as depicted by Tacitus, is little better than a puppet figure, except for what he did during his censorship. Much of value has perished along with the annals of the first six years. How far the historian conceded merit in this unexpected and paradoxical Caesar, and allowed for deterioration, at what point he put the change, these questions evade certitude. The tradition, as preserved by other writers, shows the Emperor almost from the outset a prisoner of his

---

[1] Dio LX. 27. 4.

[2] Suetonius, *Divus Claudius* 13. 2, cf. Dio LX. 27. 5. Statilius Corvinus is named (*cos.* 45), and an Asinius Gallus.

[3] M. Licinius Crassus Frugi (*cos.* 27), his wife Scribonia, their son Cn. Pompeius Magnus: see below, p. 385 f.   [4] XII. 10–21; 44–51.   [5] 31–40.

entourage, helpless in the hands of wife and ministers.[1] Nor is the structure of the missing books at once discernible. Where did Book IX end, and where Book X? And how closely did the author still adhere to the annalistic schema?

The invasion of Britain lent itself for a climax or turning-point in the narration—and perhaps in the reign. Following upon the drama of the accession (no doubt copiously expounded) and the proclamation of Arruntius Camillus, Britain could round off a substantial book, bound together and unified by a powerful motive—the insecurity of the new emperor and his need for military prestige. Although the next three years (44–46) contained no episodes of comparable magnitude, miscellaneous matters—foreign and domestic—could fill up a book, especially the latter, to be exploited in contrast to the previous emphasis of the reign and to foreshadow Book XI by crime, conspiracy, and sudden death.[2]

Book XI, it might be conjectured, began with the year 47: the eighth centenary of the city of Rome, which Claudius Caesar took as an excuse for his *Ludi Saeculares*.[3] Beside Claudius stood L. Vitellius, holding the consulate for the third time. That honour was without parallel since the earliest epoch of the Principate;[4] and so was the ovation celebrated in this year by A. Plautius, the legate of Britain.[5] Here an historian might recapitulate the British campaigns subsequent to 43 (the Roman armies had been advancing a long way to the west and north). If that was Tacitus' procedure, Book XI showed careful balance and variety of composition: Britain, the censorship of Claudius, the folly and fate of Valeria Messallina.

Book XII by its compression exhibits a sharp contrast. On any account, when the hexad is examined as a whole, the disparities are significant—something like twelve years spread over Books VII–XI, but, on the other hand, six years crammed into the last book of the hexad, as though the historian, having exhausted his Claudian topics, was impatient to move forward. Much detail had been devoted to Caligula, and much to Claudius, as far as the end of 48. There was very little to be said about the last years.[6]

---

[1] Suetonius, *Divus Claudius* 25. 5, cf. 29. 1; Dio LX. 2. 4; 14. 1 ff.

[2] There were operations in Thrace, in the Black Sea regions—and in Cilicia Aspera (conducted by Q. Veranius, cf. *AE* 1953, 251).

[3] cf. Dio LX. 29. 1—where Boissevain puts the beginning of LXI.

[4] i.e. since M. Agrippa, *cos. III* in 27 B.C.

[5] Dio LX. 30. 2. No senator had been allowed to celebrate a triumph after 19 B.C.

[6] Compare the distribution in Dio: one book for Caligula, one for Claudius down to the end of 46, but the next book, condensing the later years of Claudius, runs into Nero's reign, so it appears, terminating at the end of 58, cf. Boissevain II, xii f. In Tacitus the brief record of 49–57 inclusive (XII. 5–XIII. 33) covers one-sixth of his period (nine years out of fifty four). Note also how much of Book XII is devoted to foreign affairs, not all important.

Nero takes for himself the third portion of the *Annales*, and that portion by its exordium is powerfully stamped as a fresh beginning. The first crime of the new principate, thus did Tacitus define the killing of Agrippa Postumus, the grandson and adopted son of Augustus, at the outset of the reign of Tiberius.[1] A parallel in deed and phrase ushers in Book XIII with the murder of M. Junius Silanus, the proconsul of Asia.[2]

That is not the only device. The author insists that his narrative shall at once be self-explicatory, without too much knowledge pre-supposed, or the need for many references backwards.[3] To that end he attaches brief and vivid annotation to persons already familiar from the previous reign, and brings them into a close nexus with one another and with events—a nexus perhaps more close than the facts warranted. The principal Neronian themes can quickly take shape and carry the story unimpeded onwards. Not many historians have been to such pains for the benefit of their readers.

The murder of Silanus is put down to the contriving of Agrippina. Innocuous and unharmed by other rulers (Caligula used to call him 'the golden sheep'), Silanus was yet suspected by Agrippina—she had killed his brother—and she was eager to remove any rival of dynastic blood and claims. It was widely held (so the author alleges) that a man of mature years was surely preferable to a mere boy like Nero, and Silanus' lineage was not inferior in the descent from Augustus.[4] Agrippina also drove Narcissus to his death, the freedman of Claudius Caesar, and loyal to his master. There would have been other murders, but Annaeus Seneca and Afranius Burrus intervened (their functions and characters are rapidly conveyed). They had to contend against the violent and domineering nature of the Emperor's mother—and against the influence of Pallas, here recalled as her principal ally in gaining Claudius for husband and inducing him to adopt her son.

The funeral oration keeps Seneca in prominence (he composed it), and furnishes a brief glance back to the reign and character of Claudius Caesar.[5] Subsequent comment on the oratorical attainments of the Roman Caesars sets Nero at the end of a long perspective of history. Further, what Tacitus says about his education and artistic tastes foreshadows later developments. The tone of Tacitus is deceptively amicable. In a similar fashion, the summary of the first speech from

---

[1] I. 6. I: 'primum facinus novi principatus fuit Postumi Agrippae caedes.'

[2] XIII. I. I: 'prima novo principatu mors Iunii Silani proconsulis Asiae.'

[3] C. Bretschneider, *Quo ordine ediderit Tacitus singulas Annalium partes* (Diss. Strassburg, 1905), 11 ff.

[4] XIII. I. I: 'quippe et Silanus divi Augusti abnepos erat.' See the stemma in *PIR¹*, J 550. It runs through Julia, the granddaughter of Augustus.

[5] 3.

the throne, with its promise of a government after the model of Augustus, introduces the theme of Princeps and 'res publica'[1]— ironically, if the reader reflected on how it was to end, but fitting the context which goes on to chronicle some acceptable or salutary acts, passing neatly from domestic to foreign policy. Rumours of renewed disturbance in the eastern lands cause much talk at Rome, so Tacitus avers: how will a young prince and a new government comport themselves at this critical juncture? A wise decision is made. They dispatch an excellent general, Domitius Corbulo, the national honour will be vindicated, and everybody is content.[2]

The author at the same time both demonstrates a new start and introduces the leading persons and subjects. For Seneca the prime task and effort was to thrust Agrippina aside from the power. That ambitious woman, with the example of the Augusta Livia before her, intended to take a large share in the government. Seneca succeeded. Out of Agrippina's discontent and her wild threats arises the next important episode: Nero, becoming suspicious, was incited to contrive the poisoning of Britannicus, Claudius' son, whom he had supplanted.[3] Then the record glides rapidly through the uneventful annals of good government (56 and 57 demand very little space),[4] and foreign affairs fill out most of the rest of Book XIII (recounted under 58).[5]

Soon or late came the inevitable declension towards tyranny. How was an historian to divide and apportion his Neronian books? Down to 59 a tolerable 'quinquennium' offered, if he wished.[6] Book XIV ushered in that year with the murder of Agrippina, related in full detail.[7] Some writers might there discover a significant turn.[8] Yet it was not wholly suitable—Seneca and Burrus were important political factors, and their influence still dominated (so far as known) in the entourage of the prince. Burrus died in 62. That event, according to

---

[1] XIII. 4.   [2] 6 ff.

[3] 15 ff. Tacitus, to avoid clogging the narrative with names, and dispersing the interest, had carefully kept the name of Britannicus out of the opening chapters of the book. Similarly, Octavia, the wife of Nero, is first mentioned in c. 12.

[4] 25–30; 31–33.

[5] 34–41 (Armenia); 53–57 (Germany).

[6] That can hold, whatever view be taken of the peculiar passage in Victor, *De Caes.* 5. 2: 'quinquennium tamen tantus fuit, augenda urbe maxime, uti merito Traianus saepius testaretur procul differre cunctos principes Neronis quinquennio.' J. G. C. Anderson, emphasizing the buildings, argued that the 'quinquennium' which Trajan had in mind was the last period of Nero's reign, *JRS* I (1911), 173 ff. Compare also F. Haverfield's comment—'perhaps 60–65, if any definite period was meant' (ib. 178 f.). Victor a little later says 'eo dedecore reliquum vitae egit', &c. (5. 4, and cf. the *Epitome* 5. 2 ff.): therefore Victor took the good part of Nero's reign to be at the beginning (cf. Anderson, o.c. 176).

[7] xiv. 1–13.

[8] Dio probably made his book LXI begin with 59.

Tacitus, was decisive. Seneca's power snapped.[1] Forestalling super-session or disgrace, he approached Nero with the plea of years and infirmities, and the pretext that the Emperor was now mature enough to be his own master. An old friend, 'nos seniores amici', asked to be released.[2] The request was granted, and the man of many millions devoted himself to the exquisite refinements of the plain life.

Tacitus nowhere makes so sharp a cut as in the first hexad. Develop-ment is more gradual, narration more fluid.[3] He employs, it is true, the removal of Agrippina as a motive: it enabled Nero to indulge without restraint his passion for driving chariots and singing to the harp.[4] And, as Tacitus constructs the story, the retirement of Seneca evokes the sudden emergence of Ofonius Tigellinus to play an evil role as a second Seianus:[5] in quick succession follow the execution of two eminent nobles and the murder of Octavia, the wife of Nero, con-cluding Book XIV.[6] The climax was yet to come.

Three more years pass. Operations in the East and the great fire at Rome go to fill up most of the first half of Book XV, while the second expounds a large subject in lavish detail, the conspiracy of the year 65, designed to substitute C. Piso for Nero.

That affair showed Nero the hatred he had incurred, the danger from officers in complicity with senators, recalling the fate of Caligula. The feud between Caesar and the 'res publica' now became open and savage. Seneca on false incrimination had been driven to suicide; in the aftermath of the conspiracy various other persons were destroyed. Book XVI, opening with an extraneous interlude, carries on that story of murders. Nero soon resolved (in 66) to crush the Senate by an attack upon its most eminent members, two men of austere con-duct and high principle, Thrasea Paetus and Barea Soranus. Able and unscrupulous prosecutors were at Nero's call, and the Senate (not far from the sight and sound of armed men) voted the condemnation of the two consulars.

Book XVI breaks off towards the middle, with an unfinished sen-tence, the scene being the suicide of Thrasea Paetus.[7] The total of Tacitus' historical works stands on record as thirty books. That demands twelve for the *Historiae*, eighteen for the *Annales*.[8] The notion that into the second half of Book XVI Tacitus crammed the

---

[1] XIV. 52. 1: 'mors Burri infregit Senecae potentiam.'   [2] 53 f.

[3] It could be argued that Tacitus had not yet made up his mind about certain parts of the third hexad. Cf. p. 361 f., and App. 60.

[4] 14. 1: 'vetus illi cupido erat', &c.

[5] 57. 1. He had already been casually mentioned in 48. 1.

[6] 57–64. The actual end of the book is a brief note (65), containing a forward reference to the conspiracy of Piso.

[7] XVI. 35. 2: 'post lentitudine exitus gravis cruciatus adferente, obversis in Deme-trium . . . .'   [8] cf. App. 35.

remaining events of the year 66, and everything that happened down
to the death of Nero (perhaps with an epilogue beyond it), runs
counter to good sense.

The matter was rich and remunerative, the main themes being the
Hellenic tour, the Jewish insurrection, and the risings in the West.[1]
Of those themes, the first two were strikingly relevant to Tacitus' own
time—and to the prejudices of the narrator. Jewish troubles had already
in the *Annales* been adumbrated with Caligula—conflicts with the
Greeks at Alexandria and the menace of revolt in Judaea when the
tyrant tried to set up his image in the Temple at Jerusalem. The freaks
and follies of Caligula were an ominous foreshadowing of Nero. It
would involve no undue strain on the imagination to speculate about
the structure and arrangement these books received from Tacitus, the
balance, the emphasis, and the colouring.[2]

In 66, following close upon the prosecutions against Barea Soranus
and Thrasea Paetus, came other victims—exiles, deaths, and the
exploits of various 'delatores' who were to turn up again in later
reigns.[3] Next, as pendant to spectacles of tyranny and degradation,
the extravagant pageantry when the Arsacid Tiridates, the ruler of
Armenia, made obeisance to the Emperor at Rome.[4] Nero conceived,
advertised, and even prepared grandiose designs of eastern conquest
that ranged to the Caucasus and to Ethiopia. All he achieved was a
parade of his histrionic accomplishments, earning easy adulation from
the Greeks for his generosity towards the home of arts and letters,
detestation for his rapacity. He set out from Rome towards the end of
the year.[5]

Meanwhile, as a result of Jewish recalcitrance and Roman oppression or reprisals, a great revolt broke out in Judaea, culminating in
a serious defeat inflicted on the governor of Syria (late autumn, 66).[6]
Nero dispatched one of the consulars from his company in Greece,
Flavius Vespasianus, under a special commission to wage war in
Palestine, while Licinius Mucianus took up the Syrian command. In
the course of 67 Vespasian reduced Galilee, and by the summer
of 68, the open country being under control, he might have launched
his assault upon Jerusalem. But Vespasian was waiting upon events in
the West, and so was Mucianus. Vespasian in Galilee had received
a firm prediction that he would be raised up to rule the world.[7]

---

[1] For a convenient summary see Furneaux' edition of the *Annales* (Oxford, 1907) II[2],
473 ff.

[2] On the hypothesis (be it understood) that he survived to complete the *Annales*.

[3] Notably M. Aquillius Regulus (cf. *Hist.* IV. 42).

[4] Suetonius, *Nero* 13; Dio LXIII. 1 ff.   [5] *CIL* VI, 2044.

[6] These events could have been narrated at the beginning of Book XVII.

[7] *Hist.* V. 13. 2; Josephus, *BJ* VI. 312 f., &c.

Nero's sojourn among the Greeks was signalized by two acts above all, and savage in their contrast—Corbulo was done to death, and Hellas was proclaimed free. Before a great concourse at the Isthmus he announced it (November 28, 67).[1]

But the news from Rome was bad, and he had to return quickly. Nero had crushed conspiracy, he had silenced the Senate. At the same time he neglected the legions and alienated the sympathies of the upper classes in the western lands. Armies and provinces might overthrow him. Not long back in Italy, the Emperor heard about Julius Vindex and the rebellion in Gaul (spring, 68). Then Spain proclaimed Galba. Though Vindex was defeated by a loyal commander, the uncertainty grew, and, on reports of armies or generals revolting, Nymphidius Sabinus induced the Guard to declare for Galba. Nero committed suicide in a back room of his freedman's house in the suburban vicinity of Rome (June 9).

Such is the compass of the last two and a half books of the *Annales*. Nero's death looks like the dramatic finale, managed by fate for the historian and challenging the talent that described how Vitellius ended, and how Domitian. Inevitably, it might seem.[2] Yet there is no certainty that Book XVIII was to conclude precisely at this point. Annalistic practice (so some contend) prescribed that the historian should go on to the end of the year; and he might well wish to bind the last book of the *Annales* tightly to his earlier work.[3] The argument by itself lacks cogency. It derives support (though not complete) from a passage in Book XV, after the Pisonian conspiracy. Among the loyal friends of Nero then honoured is introduced Nymphidius Sabinus, as a name prophetic of calamity. Tacitus appears to convey a strong hint that he will tell the whole story about Nymphidius.[4] Further, as though to enhance this character, he states without trying to discredit it the claim of Nymphidius to be an illegitimate son of Caligula.

It need not be fancied that Tacitus, with merciless detail (and re-peating or expanding much of what he had previously brought into the early part of the *Historiae*), insisted upon carrying the record of Galba's reign down to the last day of December 68. He could stop

---

[1] *SIG*³ 814 = *ILS* 8794, cf. p. 517. Suetonius (*Nero* 24. 2) explicitly puts the pro-clamation at the end of the Hellenic tour. On the other side, Dio, in a rhetorical antithesis (LXIII. 11. 1).

[2] That was the opinion of Justus Lipsius. Cf., at great length, Ph. Fabia, *Journal des Savants* 1901, 423 ff.; 563 ff.

[3] Schanz–Hosius, *Gesch. der r. Literatur* II⁴ (1935), 624.

[4] xv. 72. 2: 'consularia insignia Nymphidio * * * quia nunc primum oblatus est pauca repetam: nam et ipse pars Romanarum cladium erit. igitur', &c. The sentence is inter-rupted by a lacuna. The word 'erit' deserves emphasis, and Tacitus would not have reckoned Nymphidius' desertion of Nero among 'Romanae clades', cf. C. Bretschneider, *Quo ordine ediderit Tacitus singulas Annalium partes* (Diss. Strassburg, 1905), 73.

well before that. A brief survey would suffice, damagingly selective, and for main episode Nymphidius, the bastard of Julian descent who had dethroned Nero, now making his own bid for power with help of the Praetorians—an ironical epilogue to the annals of the dynasty, and ominous for the future.

In large things and small the *Annales* reflect wide divergences of selection, proportion, and emphasis. Hexad against hexad, the first and the third permit a confrontation and exhibit a contrast. It is very striking.

In content and in articulation Books I–VI conform with close fidelity to the annalistic prescription. Each book begins with a fresh year, superscribed with the actual names of the consuls—except for the third where the date is given a little later in parenthesis.[1] A closed compartment segregates the events of each year, without overlapping; certain subjects thus have to be apportioned over a series of years; and, so strict is the regard for sequence and chronology that within the same year different stages in a single transaction may be separately registered. Moreover, each book is imperiously conducted to a sharp and dramatic termination: the concluding item, not perhaps in itself noteworthy, generally carries words of point and weight and power, evocative of the past or quietly foreboding.

Book I ends with the first consular elections of the new reign and the public professions of Tiberius Caesar touching procedure and candidatures: though Caesar's phraseology was noble, the thing was a hollow mockery, and, the fairer the homage paid to Republican forms, the darker the enslavement destined to ensue.[2] As an effective epilogue to Book II, Tacitus evokes the campaigns of Germanicus (whose sad end he had just depicted) by bringing in the death of his adversary Arminius—a bold anticipation upon chronology. Arminius he styles the liberator of the Germans; and he adds a comment on fame and history.[3] The end of the next book recalls the Roman liberators. Sixty-four years after the Battle of Philippi the city witnessed the obsequies of Junia, Cassius' widow and sister of Brutus, the emblems of twenty-four noble families being exhibited in procession—but the images of Cassius and Brutus were conspicuously absent.[4]

---

[1] III. 2. 3.

[2] I. 81. 2: 'speciosa verbis, re inania aut subdola, quantoque maiore libertatis specie tegerentur, tanto eruptura ad infensius servitium.'

[3] II. 88. 3: 'caniturque adhuc apud barbaras gentis, Graecorum annalibus ignotus, qui sua tantum mirantur, Romanis haud perinde celebris, dum vetera extollimus recentium incuriosi.'

[4] III. 76. 2: 'sed praefulgebant Cassius atque Brutus eo ipso quod effigies eorum non visebantur.'

The last item in Book IV is not dramatic in its formulation but sober and ostensibly innocuous—a wedding ordained by Tiberius Caesar. Julia Agrippina, the daughter of Germanicus, was consigned in matrimony to Cn. Domitius Ahenobarbus, not only of illustrious lineage himself, but close kin to the dynasty, and in fact a grand-nephew of Augustus.[1] The names were enough. Tacitus forbore to add what all men knew, the fruit of that marriage. As for Book V, it is generally assumed that it terminated with the fall of Seianus.[2] Otherwise the last event of 31 could serve, a dispute between two consuls, ferocious and not to be allayed by the public intervention of many senators.[3] The choice of episode is neither fortuitous nor inartistic. The two names together recapitulate the signal catastrophe of the year: the one consul had been an adherent of Seianus, the other was among the principal agents in his downfall.[4] Further, consuls discordant in their last days of office served as a lively reminder of Rome's history under the Republic. The hexad concludes with the verdict upon Tiberius Caesar.[5]

The era of the 'res publica' was no more. An historian could not now recount how the Senate held debate, the People voted (laws and elections, war or peace), the magistrates acted. The People had been thrust aside, and fresh elements of power and authority superadded, namely Princeps and soldiers. Hence new formulations and new interrelations. It was the task of Tacitus, employing the old annalistic pattern, to interweave the chronicle of the Caesars with what survived of the 'res publica'. That survival consisted in official transactions of the high assembly—debates, prosecutions, and the management of the public provinces.

Other writers, engrossed with the story of the Caesars, might have passed almost without a break from the death of Germanicus to the death of Drusus. Tacitus had a different plan. He can abridge and condense when he likes, as in the last years of Claudius and the first of Nero: for his arrangement of the reign of Tiberius, however, he had decided to put the beginning of the second half of the hexad at the

---

[1] IV. 75: 'in Domitio super vetustatem generis propinquum Caesaribus sanguinem delegerat; nam is aviam Octaviam et per eam Augustum avunculum praeferebat.'

[2] Lipsius opted for the end of 31. But the *Codex*, which registers the conclusions of Books I–IV, gives no similar sign at this point (i.e., after V. 11 in the standard numbering of chapters). H. Haase insisted on the value of this clue (*Philologus* III (1848), 152 f.), since when all modern editors have assumed that v. 1–11 belongs to Book VI. Without those chapters (and some more), it is argued, that book (VI. 1–51) would be disproportionately brief.

[3] V. 11. 2: 'multisque patrum orantibus ponerent odia in perniciem itura, mansere infensi ac minitantes donec magistratu abirent.'

[4] L. Fulcinius Trio and P. Memmius Regulus: each a character of some interest to Tacitus. For Trio, p. 327; for Regulus, XIV. 47 and App. 79.   [5] VI. 51.

year 23. For structure and balance he therefore needed to give space
and meaning to the interval after Germanicus' death and the ensuing
inquiry: how was he to fill out the rest of Book III? Senatorial
business was the solution—and not at all a makeshift. It demonstrated
that there now subsisted 'quaedam imago rei publicae';[1] and the
senatorial transactions that later came to be reported in the last
book of the hexad (mainly the prosecutions of senators and their
deaths) would be seen to stand in sharp and melancholy contrast to
the early years of a reign that in its course had destroyed that 'res
publica'.

The years in question (20, 21, and 22) were barren of momentous
events, except for the rebellion in Gaul of the chieftains Julius Florus
and Julius Sacrovir, which is fully narrated.[2] For the rest, Cornelius
Tacitus is not dismayed. Africa and Asia stood out among the provinces left to the management of the Senate, with governors consular
in rank. The proconsul of Africa could still regard himself as an
armed mandatory of the Republic, and he might even earn distinction
in the field. In Book III Tacitus can relate the campaigns of two proconsuls against the Numidian insurgent Tacfarinas;[3] and the choice
of a competent proconsul, involving negotiation between Senate and
Princeps, supplies valuable detail about governmental technique, the
capacities of certain aristocrats, and the scrupulous respect of Tiberius
Caesar for constitutional proprieties.[4]

Asia was a richer source of business as of history. When the claims
of the cities to exercise the right of asylum came up for scrutiny, it
was a great day.[5] The Senate held free debate, pronouncing upon
privileges conferred by the Roman People in the ancient time, treaties
with allied peoples, even the decrees of kings and the cult of the gods.
Further, an indictment enables the author to supply (for the first time
in the *Annales*) a full-length exposition of the procedure adopted
when a proconsul was put on trial—and when the Princeps felt bound
to intervene decisively.[6]

More significant, however, are a number of accessory matters or
abortive senatorial discussions. The tradition that a certain priesthood
debarred its holder from a province was called into question—but
maintained.[7] The *Lex Papia Poppaea* was discussed and modified—
but not in essentials.[8] Nothing came of proposals that proconsuls
should be forbidden the company of their wives, or that senators of

[1] The phrase itself belongs to a later reign (XIII. 28. 1).
[2] III. 40–46.   [3] 20 f.; 73 f.   [4] 32; 35.
[5] 60. 3: 'magnaque eius diei species fuit', &c.
[6] 66–68 (C. Silanus, proconsul of Asia).
[7] 58 f.; 71.
[8] 25, cf. 28.

notorious immorality should be excluded from proconsulates;[1] and Tiberius Caesar skilfully parried a demand that he should undertake governmental action to curb luxury and extravagance.[2]

These items give the historian an excuse for a variety of speeches from prominent senators, and notably from the Princeps;[3] they enable him to introduce digressions on sacerdotal law, the history of legislation, or the changes in Roman morality.[4]

The annalistic structure is thus dominant throughout the first hexad, and strikingly exemplified by the contents of Book III. The third hexad stands in marked contrast. Only Book XIII ends at a year's end, and the item lacks significance or emphasis.[5] Moreover, the whole treatment is more free and flowing, with events concentrated around personalities or themes, not merely consecutive or segmentated.

The changed exposition is already perceptible in the remnant of the second hexad. Book XI ends with Messallina, and Book XII deliberately introduces Agrippina before the year 48 is brought to its conclusion. Further, the grouping of foreign affairs. In the first hexad the vicissitudes of the rebellion of Tacfarinas in Africa, being related year by year as they occur, figure in three books;[6] and Book II has the provinces and princes of the East in four separate sections.[7] But in Book XII a continuous narrative carries seven years of the Roman conquest of Britain;[8] and the treatment of eastern affairs foreshadows the way Corbulo's campaigns will be recounted in the Neronian books.[9]

Where is the reason to be sought? Not merely in any difference between the written sources employed by Tacitus, and not in any improvement of his literary skill. The history itself had changed its shape and substance, and the historian's choice was conscious, or rather enforced. When Tiberius Caesar presided over the Roman State, it could still be regarded as a continuation of the Republic, its annual chronicle to be narrated in the traditional manner. With Nero Rome became dynastic and regal—or rather, already with Caligula, where the second hexad of the *Annales* began. Caligula was a prince, of the royal blood of Divus Augustus, whereas Tiberius, a Roman

[1] 33 f.; 69.   [2] 52 ff.
[3] 33 f. (Caecina Severus and Valerius Messallinus); 53 f.; 69 (Tiberius Caesar). Note also the noble speech of M. Lepidus (50) in abatement of a penalty.
[4] 58 (in the disguise of reported speech); 26 f.; 55.
[5] XIII. 58 (a prodigy that seems to portend nothing).
[6] II. 52; III. 20 f. and 73 f.; IV. 23–26.
[7] II. 1–4; 42; 56–62; 68 ff.
[8] XII. 31–40.
[9] 10–21 (taking up from XI. 8–10); 44–51.

aristocrat among the 'principes civitatis', was consul and commander of armies before he succeeded, an old man already, to the Principate. With Caligula emerge again the monarchic tendencies which, manifest under Augustus, had been deprecated or resisted by Tiberius Caesar, suppressed or at least disguised in his vain attempt to preserve and perpetuate the forms and spirit of the Commonwealth.

XXII. THE SOURCES I

SINCE Roman history from Tiberius to Nero underwent a change in texture and colour, becoming less Republican and more dynastic, a change faithfully reflected in the historian's portrayal, it will be expedient (and perhaps remunerative) to discuss the sources of the *Annales*, not as a single problem admitting a single answer of universal validity, but consecutively, hexad by hexad.

In the books about Tiberius Caesar the author appeals to the historians of the period, but only in general terms, alluding to their character and credit, their concordance or discrepancies. No names, however; and, if he twice specifies a source, each time it is only for a minor detail guaranteed by a subsidiary authority.[1] The annalistic predecessors of Tacitus having perished, the inquiry must take an indirect path, through comparison and inference. Two authors offer, diverse in epoch, attainments, and purpose—Suetonius Tranquillus, the biographer of the Caesars, and a Greek from Nicaea in Bithynia called Cassius Dio, who held the consulship not much more than a century after Cornelius Tacitus. Dio's earliest productions were a pair of pamphlets—a treatise on the dreams and omens that heralded the destiny of Septimius Severus and an account of the Emperor's seizure of the power. He later composed a history of Rome from the origins down to his own time. Ten years were devoted to research, twelve more to the writing of it, so he avers.[2]

In their general presentation of Tiberius as man and emperor, Suetonius and Dio go in harmony with Tacitus. Detail and selection, emphasis and structure are notably divergent.[3] The biographer has his own method—a loose and often disjointed succession of topics, with material highly variegated in provenance and quality. He is therefore less amenable to treatment than the historian. Dio furnishes a narrative with the latter portion of his concluding book on Augustus and with the next two books (not, however, entire), which embrace the reign of Tiberius. Certain resemblances can be discerned between Dio and Tacitus (in the opening chapters of the *Annales*). Yet Dio, it is clear, is not here reproducing Tacitus.[4] The question of a common source at once arises.

---

[1] I. 69. 2 (the elder Pliny); IV. 53. 2 (the younger Agrippina).
[2] Dio LXXII. 23. 1 ff. (the seventy-eight books down to the death of Septimius Severus: he later added two).
[3] App. 36.
[4] He will have read Tacitus, but the traces are slight at the best, cf. App. 36.

Tacitus after a short preface recapitulates in order the dynastic plans devised by Augustus, passes rapidly to the illness and death of the Princeps, inserts in immediate sequence the execution of Agrippa Postumus, and, along with other particulars (and comments) attendant upon the accession of Tiberius, relates what happened when the Senate met for the first time (the testament was read out, a variety of honours advocated, accepted, or rejected, the procedure for the funeral arranged), and goes on briefly to report the solemn obsequies in the Campus Martius. The next public business is a second session of the high assembly, at which the consecration of Augustus was authorized—and the position of his successor discussed.

Augustus left three state papers.[1] One was the record of his actions in relation to Rome and the 'res publica', which (so he enjoined) was to be inscribed on pillars of bronze in front of the Mausoleum. The historian says nothing about this curious document. Not ignorance but art—he can echo or controvert its affirmations, he can parody the themes and phraseology.[2] After the funeral, and before the consecration, Tacitus interpolates his own summing up. He sets forth what men of judgement had to say about the whole life and career of Caesar Augustus.[3] The necrological commentary falls sharply into two parts, for and against. Eulogy is the shorter portion.

The device looks like a typical manifestation of the Tacitean manner. Yet it is not wholly his own invention. Cassius Dio shows a parallel. Not content with serving up at inordinate length a funeral oration delivered by Tiberius Caesar, Dio subjoins the popular verdict of the Romans upon their dead ruler—but only, and that might be expected, the favourable half.[4]

Dio and Tacitus go back to a common origin. Of what type and epoch? It has been argued that, immediately after the death of Tiberius Caesar, a writer of genius went to work, setting his stamp indelible for ever after upon all the written history. He it was who invented the two-faced and contrasted necrology.[5] Tacitus took it over entire, the praise and the blame, but Dio (a fervent advocate of monarchical rule) selected only the praise. Not only that. This unknown author constructed (and imposed upon later writers) the remarkably consistent characterization of Tiberius. Tacitus accepts and reflects it, as may be seen in isolated passages all through the hexad. Dio, however, reproduces it with exact fidelity in the elaborate character sketch which he prefixes to his narration of the new reign.[6]

The theory is seductive, but not convincing. It explains too much. The historical tradition about a ruler at Rome was not formed and

---

[1] Suetonius, *Divus Aug.* 101. 4.   [2] F. Haverfield, *JRS* II (1912), 198.
[3] I. 9 f.   [4] LVI. 43 f.   [5] E. Schwartz, P-W III, 1716 f.   [6] LVII. 1.

transmitted, during the first and second generations at least, by writers only, still less by a single man. It arose from experience and recollection, it was created by the talk and opinions of a large group—the upper classes. An historian writing soon after the decease of Tiberius could hope to achieve success, and exert influence subsequently, only if he departed not too widely from what men of the time said and thought about that emperor. The assumed dominance of the unknown annalist becomes difficult to credit.

Nor will every reader consent to father upon a Roman historian of the early Empire (and one, so the hypothesis demands, esteemed and exploited by Cornelius Tacitus) the prefatory disquisition of Dio upon the character of Tiberius. It lacks bite, intensity, and colour; it is antithetic but not epigrammatical, tortuous without profundity, and portentously abstract.

There are, to be sure, the similarities of phrase between Tacitus and Dio. They attest a common stock ultimately. How closely does Tacitus adhere to that predecessor? Three sentences employed by Dio in his panegyrical necrology of Augustus also turn up in the *Annales*.[1] Their distribution must be noted: one of them only in the parallel Tacitean verdict, the other two elsewhere and separately, in preceding chapters. Tacitus, it is clear, operates with complete freedom when he selects and arranges this inherited material. Tacitus was also inventive and constructive. No need to postulate that he discovered in an earlier writer the blame of Augustus as well as the praise. Surely it was his own congenial device—insisting upon the unfavourable side of things, demolishing, as it were, the conventional façade of a funeral laudation.

Other points of contact with Dio in the early chapters of the *Annales* may be registered, down to and including the second session of the Senate. Then the similarities become fewer; and Dio's account of the years 15 and 16 is not at all like anything in Tacitus. Moreover, comparison soon becomes impracticable. The text of Dio breaks off in 17, to resume again only in 31, just before the catastrophe of Seianus; and, although epitomators of Dio supply a narrative to cover the gap, it forms no secure basis for argument. Nor is Tacitus entire. Book V is lost except for the small remnant at the beginning, but Book VI runs parallel with the rest of Cassius Dio to the end of the reign.[2]

Critics tend to single out the items of resemblance. They thus become enhanced out of all proportion: their value dwindles when the divergences are examined. The problem is very complex. Though passages in Dio (and also in Suetonius) derive from the ultimate

[1] LVI. 44. 2 ff., cf. *Ann.* I. 9. 5; 2. 1; and 3. 7 (cited in App. 36).
[2] On Dio LVIII. 17 ff. see App. 36.

source, or rather sources, of Tacitus, too many unknown factors are involved. If one written source can be detected in the opening chapters of the *Annales*, it need not be the only one: another may be employed for the campaigns of Germanicus, yet another for the rest of the hexad.

Two writers of mark and consequence dealt with the principate of Tiberius Caesar, namely Aufidius Bassus and Servilius Nonianus. Neither is cited in the *Annales*, nothing survives anywhere of their writings save one stray quotation from Servilius, two from Aufidius.[1] The hunt for historical sources, often a pretext for frail hypothesis or tenuous argumentation, must here avow its affinity to guess and fancy.

Aufidius, the elder of the two annalists, died in the middle period of Nero's reign.[2] An old man, and never strong in body, he faced the sudden onslaught of utter decrepitude and waited for the end, cheerful and unperturbed, being of the Epicurean persuasion. Seneca, who expatiates upon the calm resolution of Aufidius, says nothing about any products of his pen—and there is no sign or hint that he was still writing in the last years of his life. Quintilian, however, gives him high praise for style, with an especial note of commendation for the books of the *Bellum Germanicum*.[3]

The scope and content of that work is uncertain. Presumably not the earlier campaigns, but the sequence of warfare that started in A.D. 4.[4] In that year Tiberius came back to the armies. This was the proper exordium for a *Bellum Germanicum*. It was safe, and it was splendid. How the tale might be told, with what colour, emphasis, and design, does not lie wholly beyond conjecture.[5] Tiberius was the indispensable marshal, 'vindex custosque imperii'; joy and confidence awoke in the legions at the sight of their old commander; two campaigns brought them in conquest to the river Elbe, and the Germans, broken in spirit, revered the majesty of Rome in the person of Tiberius; in the third year he launched the double invasion of Bohemia to destroy the great empire of Maroboduus, the king of the Marcomanni.

[1] viz. Servilius' verdict on Sallust and Livy (Quintilian x. 1. 102), and two pieces of Aufidius on the death of Cicero, preserved by the elder Seneca (*Suas.* vi. 18 and 23). Pliny cites the dimensions of Armenia according to Aufidius (*NH* vi. 27); and he was used by Cassiodorus (*Chron.* pp. 630 and 659). See H. Peter, *HRR* ii (1906), cxxv ff.

[2] Seneca, *Epp.* 30 (a disguised obituary: the fact of the man's decease is not stated). He might be the L. Aufidius Bassus who made a dedication to Aesculapius and Valetudo (*ILS* 3832: Athens), cf. *PIR*², A 1381.

[3] Quintilian x. 1. 102 f.: 'qui (*sc.* Servilius) et ipse a nobis auditus est, clari vir ingenii et sententiis creber, sed minus pressus quam historiae auctoritas postulat. quam paulum aetate praecedens eum Bassus Aufidius egregie, utique in libris belli Germanici, praestitit, genere ipso probabilis in omnibus sed in quibusdam suis ipse viribus minor.'

[4] App. 38.

[5] The loyal Velleius Paterculus can give an idea.

Only the accident of the rebellion in Illyricum saved Maroboduus; and, although the historian soon had a calamity to relate (three legions lost in Germany), the government took no blame since Quinctilius Varus was the scapegoat, enhancing Tiberius by contrast. Tiberius repaired the damage, courageous as ever, vigilant, insistent upon military discipline. In conclusion, the heroic enterprises of the young Germanicus. Panegyric, however exuberant, could appear innocuous. Did not Tiberius Caesar in his mature wisdom stand arbiter of the issue?

More important than the monograph of Aufidius is the full-length history. It covered a long period, beginning perhaps with the assassination of Caesar the Dictator—the two fragments derive from an obituary on Cicero—and some part of it had been written before the end of Tiberius' reign.[1] The assumption that the *Bellum Germanicum* was prior in time permits a conjecture: namely, that Aufidius, when he came to write his history, curtailed the account of the German wars in proportion to other events. A trace of such curtailment can be detected in Cassius Dio, who followed Aufidius, it may be supposed, for a part at least of the reign of Augustus. Dio is brief and meagre for the German campaigns of Tiberius in A.D. 4–6—no mention of even the name of Maroboduus[2]—but he furnishes a copious narrative of the insurrection in Illyricum (A.D. 6–9).

While the *Bellum Germanicum* (if correctly identified as the campaigns of the period from A.D. 4 to 16) was not an encroachment upon Livy, but an epilogue, Aufidius in his full-dress history, before breaking new ground, recounted afresh the matter of three Livian 'decades' (44 to 9 B.C.). For the estimate of both writers it would be worth knowing the strength of the challenge. Likewise the quality of the sequel from 9 B.C. onwards. Another problem concerns the terminal date, and belongs in another place.[3]

Aufidius did not stand alone or unrivalled. He was matched by Servilius Nonianus. Such was the verdict of Quintilian, and the author of the *Dialogus* concurs.[4] They were concerned with style, and Quintilian rated Aufidius above Servilius, who was diffuse—'minus pressus quam historiae auctoritas postulat'. But style is not the chief requisite in an historical source. Knowledge, accuracy, and insight count for more. Aufidius, for one reason or another, may have commended himself to Cassius Dio as a canonical authority. Nothing follows for Cornelius Tacitus.

---

[1] This is clear, since the elder Seneca could cite Aufidius (*Suas.* VI. 18 and 23). There is a faint chance, however, that the citations come from a monograph on the last epoch of Cicero's life (as suggested in App. 38).

[2] LV. 28. 5 f.; 29. 1, cf. 30. 2—that is all.   [3] p. 288, with App. 38.

[4] *Dial.* 23. 4, cf. Quintilian X. 1. 102.

It would be another matter if Aufidius could be proved a senator. Evidence is lacking of military or political pursuits: his health and his brand of philosophy are consonant with the quiet existence of a literary man, in the succession of Livy. Servilius, however, by rank and attainments was among the foremost in state and society—a *nobilis*, an orator, a consul, a proconsul of Africa.[1]

Junior by some years to Aufidius,[2] he entered the Senate under Tiberius and rose to the consulate in the year 35. Servilius enjoyed long years of success at the bar, and his proconsulate (about A.D. 47) marked the apex of a senator's career. History claimed him. His recitations were loudly applauded—Claudius Caesar turned up one day, uninvited and unexpected.[3] Dying in 59, Servilius has a resplendent commemoration in the *Annales*.[4] If Tacitus gave marked or exclusive preference to any single source for the first hexad (and that is a large question), his choice went to the eloquent ex-consul who reported what a senator saw and experienced in the days of Tiberius Caesar.[5]

Aufidius cannot compete. The use and value of his history for Tacitus remains problematical. If there are traces of Aufidius in the early chapters of Book I (as the parallels in Cassius Dio might be taken to convey), they are scanty enough, and do not carry the inquiry very far. That Aufidius was the principal written authority for the Tiberian hexad is not at all probable.[6] At the most, conjecture can fasten upon a single theme. The highly rhetorical treatment that Tacitus accorded to the campaigns of Germanicus might suggest a debt of colour, structure, and incident to some published narration, not implausibly to be identified with the monograph of Aufidius. Tacitus there cites another source (Pliny's *Bella Germaniae*) for a supplementary detail—Agrippina at the bridge on the Rhine, welcoming her husband and the army, believed lost, but returning from a perilous expedition.[7]

Nothing more need here be said about Aufidius or Servilius. There were other writers—and Tacitus claims that he consulted the full

---

[1] *PIR*[1], S 420. Add his proconsulate, *CIL* VIII, 24585a and *AE* 1932, 24. His father was M. Servilius (*cos.* A.D. 3), mentioned in II. 48. 1 and III. 22. 2. The latter passage shows him a friend of P. Sulpicius Quirinius (*cos.* 12 B.C.).

[2] Quintilian X. 1. 102. Servilius will have been a close coeval of Ser. Sulpicius Galba (*cos.* 33), who was born probably in 3 B.C. (cf. *PIR*[1], S 723).

[3] Pliny, *Epp.* I. 13. 3. His uncle knew Servilius, cf. *NH* XXIV. 43; XXVIII. 29; XXXVII. 81.

[4] XIV. 19 (p. 338).

[5] Not only in the Senate: he might have been able to report the thoughts of Cocceius Nerva (VI. 26), or the last words of L. Arruntius (VI. 48. 1 f.). And he may have visited Capreae, cf. Suetonius, *Tib.* 61. 6.

[6] It was confidently assumed by Fabia, *Les Sources de Tacite dans les Histoires et les Annales* (1893), 392 ff.

[7] I. 69. 2.

body of information.[1] Of some the name is known, of some not. Suetonius refers to the testimony of a 'vir consularis' who wrote 'annales'—presumably Servilius Nonianus.[2] A certain Velleius Paterculus, who entered the Senate after serving as an equestrian officer in diverse lands, announced the intention of composing a full-length historical work.[3] All that he lived to produce was a summary. The elder Seneca, prodigious in memory and vitality, was not content to chronicle the performance of all the orators and declaimers he had heard: he left the record of his own times, to be published by his son.[4] Poems and pamphlets were also available, speeches and memoirs. The exploits of Germanicus evoked epic verse;[5] biographies of the prince have been surmised;[6] and posterity held in esteem an oration from one of his friends and avengers.[7]

Tiberius Caesar consigned to writing a short account of his own life. He did well to be brief when he essayed an apologia about Seianus—he punished his minister (such was the explanation) on learning of his murderous feud against the sons of Germanicus.[8] There was more to be got from the memoirs of an outspoken woman. The younger Agrippina, angry with her son, exclaims that she does not at all mind having the most recent crimes and scandals of the dynasty brought out and shown up.[9] Perhaps a gentle hint of the family chronicle she went on to compose. Tacitus cites Agrippina for a curious particular about her mother, not noticed by any of the Roman

[1] IV. 11. 2: 'neque quisquam scriptor tam infensus extitit'; 53. 3: 'id a scriptoribus annalium non traditum'.

[2] *Tib.* 61. 6 (an incident on Capreae).

[3] Velleius II. 96. 3, &c.

[4] Seneca, *De vita patris* (fr. xv Haase): 'ab initio bellorum civilium, unde primum veritas retro abiit, paene usque ad mortis suae diem.' The work has left no trace. Suetonius reports a detail about the death of the Emperor—'Seneca eum scribit, intellecta defectione, exemptum anulum quasi alicui traditurum parumper tenuisse', &c. (*Tib.* 73. 2). There was only one Seneca that Suetonius could have meant, or his readers understood, 'sic nude'. Similarly Lactantius, *Div. Inst.* VII. 15. 14: 'non inscite Seneca urbis tempora distribuit in aetates', &c. One must allow for works of Seneca that have not survived. For the contrary and common view see Schanz–Hosius, *Gesch. der r. Literatur* II[4] (1935), 341, with much literature there cited.

[5] Albinovanus Pedo, quoted in Seneca, *Suas.* I. 15.

[6] G. Kessler, *Die Tradition über Germanicus* (Diss. Berlin, 1905), 89 ff.: criticized by F. B. Marsh, *The Reign of Tiberius* (1931), 267 ff.

[7] Pliny, *NH* XI. 187 (the speech of P. Vitellius against Cn. Piso, cf. *Ann.* III. 13. 2). The story of how Titius Sabinus, the friend of Germanicus, was betrayed and denounced by four senators (IV. 68–70) probably comes from a subsidiary source: the contradiction about the *gentilicium* of one of them, here (twice) 'Latinius', but 'Lucanius' later in VI. 4. 1 ('Lucanius' is probably correct, cf. R. Syme, *JRS* XXXIX (1949), 13) might be an indication. The later passage may derive from the *acta*.

[8] Suetonius, *Tib.* 61. 1: 'ausus est scribere *Seianum se punisse quod comperisset furere adversus liberos Germanici filii sui*: quorum ipse alterum suspecto iam, alterum oppresso demum Seiano interemit.'

[9] XIII. 14. 3.

annalists: in the year 26 she requested Tiberius to find her a husband.[1] It was not a trivial matter. An historian could be pardoned if he grew curious about the prospect of a fresh marriage for the widow of Germanicus—and the political implications. Moreover, since Tacitus had been according preponderance to public and senatorial transactions, he became aware of gaps and might be forced to look for certain things that no document disclosed. It would be worth knowing where he came upon Seianus' petition for the hand of a princess, recorded (and elaborated) in the previous year.[2]

No solution or clue can be discerned in this obscure and miscellaneous aggregate. There need be no regrets. The straight path of inquiry leads to the archives of the Senate. That is the only 'single source'. The first hexad of the *Annales* contains an abundance of information patently deriving from the official protocol, and only there to be discovered. Convincing and conclusive are the strings of personal names, the odd authentic details, the debates that led to no sort of action or legislation.

When the Senate discussed the order of ceremonies appropriate to the funeral of Augustus, sundry proposals were put forward. Tacitus cites two—and a third that lapsed, but is registered by him for the sake of a damaging comment on adulation. If the scene and the details excited the interest of the senatorial historian, more so the men: three personages of note, whom he intended to bring in later, more than once.[3]

Again, after the debate about the position of the new ruler ended, the Senate passed on to various items of routine business, among them the election of praetors for the following year.[4] A new system being now introduced, Tacitus subjoins remarks of his own in explanation. He then winds up, reverting to senatorial business: details about the provision of games to be celebrated each year in memory of Divus Augustus, and the funds to pay for them. The thing is almost an anticlimax. It could have been omitted without loss. It reflects the *acta senatus* and the documentary scruple of a Roman annalist.

At the end of 15 the domestic transactions of the year are detailed, a dozen heterogeneous items.[5] The chronicle concludes with the

---

[1] IV. 53. 2.

[2] 39 f. A plethora of scandal and malice from the Tiberian books (but not this item) has been put to the credit of Agrippina by B. R. Motzo, *Studi Cagliaritani* I (1927), 19 ff. By contrast Fabia only admits IV. 53 (o.c. 333)—because one ought not to concede that Tacitus deserts 'sa source ordinaire' unless he says so. Both are extreme hypotheses.

[3] I. 8. 3 f. (Asinius Gallus, L. Arruntius, and Valerius Messallinus).

[4] 14 f., cf. App. 67.

[5] 72–81. The items are filled out or enlivened by Tacitus in various ways. For the parallel, but discrepant, account of Dio (LVII. 14) see App. 36. Dio follows an annalist who had made a different selection.

consular elections, the first to be held under the new ordinances. What method was used to approve candidates and present them to the Senate? The inquirer must confess his perplexity. He cannot tell, for all that he had consulted the relevant pronouncements of Tiberius Caesar.[1]

In the course of the next year, when a prosecution for high treason is duly terminated (Scribonius Libo the accused in the meantime having committed suicide), the Senate voted lavish decrees of official thanksgiving. The sponsors are named and certified, seven men of rank. The historian announces the reason for this precision of documentation—he will demonstrate that subservience and falsity began to flourish very soon.[2] He did not need to specify the source.

To commemorate Germanicus Caesar a long sequence of honours was devised and enacted.[3] In the body of the account comes the proposal for a large medallion bust of the prince, all of gold, to signalize him in the company of the great orators. The Emperor objected: the normal size and material would do, for a man's eloquence does not depend upon his station, and it was a sufficient distinction for Germanicus to be reckoned among writers of classical rank. The observation is beyond doubt authentic. It derives from the record. Tacitus not only provides details. In epilogue he affirms that most of the ceremonies are still in force, whereas some were soon dropped or with the passage of time discontinued.[4]

Here and there the annalistic structure faithfully preserves the actual order of senatorial business by reporting at intervals the different stages of a single transaction. Two examples from Book III are instructive, both arising out of the allocation of the consular provinces. Early in the year 21, Africa being again disturbed, Tiberius by letter advised the Senate to suspend the normal procedure and select a proconsul of military competence.[5] After some talk the Senate carried out the balloting for the one province, Asia, but referred Africa back to the Princeps; it discussed at length another matter and then adjourned. At the ensuing session the senators heard the answer of Tiberius. He now put before them two names, those of M. Lepidus and Junius

---

[1] 81. 1: 'de comitiis consularibus, quae tum primum illo principe ac deinceps fuere, vix quicquam firmare ausim: adeo diversa non modo apud auctores sed in ipsius orationibus reperiuntur.'

[2] II. 32. 2: 'quorum auctoritates adulationesque rettuli ut sciretur vetus id in re publica malum.'

[3] 83. 1 ff.

[4] ib. 4: 'pleraque manent: quaedam statim omissa sunt aut vetustas oblitteravit.' An item that the historian omitted has been revealed by the *Tabula Hebana* (App. 67). It will have recurred among the 'honores' when Drusus died (IV. 9. 2), cf. *AE* 1952, 80 (Ilici in Tarraconensis).

[5] III. 32. 1.

Blaesus. The latter was likely to have their suffrages (he was the uncle of Seianus), and the former drew back.[1]

Next year the Senate prorogued Blaesus' tenure of Africa. For Asia one of the senior consulars, the patrician Lentulus Maluginensis, asserted eligibility. It was false, he said, that his priesthood (he was *flamen Dialis*) debarred its holder from leaving Italy. Dissent arose among the senators, with appeal to Tiberius as head and supervisor of the state religion.[2] Tiberius took his time. Various items then came up and were debated at leisure (among them the asylum rights of the cities of Asia and the trial of a proconsul), until finally the Princeps, with full sacerdotal documentation, pronounced against the plea of Maluginensis.[3]

That Tacitus consulted the Senate's archives is proved by the character of the material, by its distribution—and often by its amplitude. To that repository went the reports of proconsuls. Hence Tacitus can furnish particulars of campaigns conducted by no fewer than four governors of Africa.[4] But there is something more. Tiberius in scrupulous deference to the Senate would often consult it upon military matters, and he even affirmed that proconsuls had the full right to confer decorations.[5] Tacitus records the Emperor's statement to the Senate about the armed forces, including what he thought about the value of volunteer recruits.[6] Nor was that ruler reticent of information about the actions of his own legates. In the year 21 the chieftains Julius Florus and Julius Sacrovir raised an insurrection in Gaul. Not until it was suppressed did Tiberius make a statement to the Senate: it was full and honest, not adding to the truth or taking from it.[7] Five years later the legate Poppaeus Sabinus crushed a rebellion of the Thracians, for which exploit the Senate on the motion of the Princeps voted the *ornamenta triumphalia*.[8] Both transactions are related in the *Annales* with a noteworthy abundance of detail. Like the Numidian War they have left but scanty or fortuitous traces elsewhere in the record of imperial history.[9]

Next to warfare, the religious institutions of the Roman State. The selection of a new virgin of Vesta will not be omitted.[10] Tiberius

---

[1] III. 35.   [2] 58.   [3] 71.
[4] II. 52; III. 20 f. and 73 f.; IV. 23–26.   [5] Suetonius, *Tib.* 30.
[6] IV. 4. 2.
[7] III. 47. 1: 'neque dempsit aut addidit vero.' This verdict shows that the historian knew what he was talking about. Compare another incident, where the official statement was misleading—'clarum inde inter Germanos Frisium nomen, dissimulante Tiberio damnum' (IV. 74. 1).   [8] IV. 46–51.
[9] Velleius has brief references to Gaul and Africa (II. 130. 5), but not to Thrace. Nothing in Suetonius or Dio; and the name of Tacfarinas occurs elsewhere only in Victor, *De Caes.* 2. 3.
[10] II. 86.

Caesar was erudite and vigilant, as befitted a patrician. Not only did he weigh carefully the petition of Lentulus Maluginensis. When Lentulus died, the Princeps suggested that certain of the ritual interdictions adhering from ancient custom to his priesthood might now be modified and mitigated, by law or by the Senate's decree.[1] And he would intervene at any time to rebuke ignorance or impropriety. When Livia fell ill and the Senate voted ceremonies of intercession to be superintended by the major colleges, a senator of consular rank came out with the notion that the *fetiales* should also participate. Tiberius checked him at once, citing tradition and the precedents.[2]

Religion could be invoked to embarrass the government. When Asinius Gallus proposed a consultation of the Sibylline books, no doubt knowing what things would emerge, the Princeps refused.[3] Even on the island he was alert. One of the *quindecimviri* tried to get a volume of prophecies incorporated in the official collection. Tiberius sent a sharp admonition: a priest of rank and experience must know that any such documents are subject to rigorous control, as Augustus prescribed. The historian adds annotation (and who was better qualified?) about the Sibylline oracles.[4]

The *acta*, it appears, have been put to close and continuous use. Who did the work, Tacitus or a predecessor? Cornelius Tacitus was no stranger to industrious investigation. Passages in Book IV of the *Historiae* carry clear testimony.[5] As that enterprise went forward, the author required constant access to the register of the Senate. No proof, perhaps, for the *Annales*—if a number of historians had written about these transactions, he might claim exemption from the duty of independent research. On the contrary. Tacitus knew the nature of imperial history, vilification when it was not flattery. The *acta* enabled him, not merely to test, correct, or supplement those writers, but to build up much of the history afresh, in his own fashion.

Tacitus implies as much. He claims command of information and liberty of choice: he will only register such proposals in the Senate as are noteworthy examples of good or evil.[6] How select, save by recourse to the *acta*? If Tacitus from time to time appears to violate his own principle, it is through the very wealth of his documentation, conspicuously attested in that part of the first hexad where the historian's design tempted or compelled him to expound in full the annals

---

[1] IV. 16.   [2] III. 64.

[3] I. 76. I. Gallus was one of the *quindecimviri sacris faciundis* these many years (cf. *ILS* 5050, of 17 B.C.).

[4] VI. 12.   [5] Ch. XVI.

[6] III. 65. I: 'exequi sententias haud institui nisi insignis per honestum aut notabili dedecore.' Cf. XIV. 64. 3: 'neque tamen silebimus si quod senatus consultum adulatione novum aut patientia postremum fuit.'

of the 'res publica', during the interval between the prosecution of Cn. Piso and the death of Drusus, the son of Tiberius.[1]

There is no express citation of the *acta* in those pages. Nor was any needed. Fabric and material suffice. The *acta* of the Senate, so it happens, are quoted only once in all the *Annales* as extant—and not until the end of Book XV.[2] However, an isolated reference to some other official records proves that his diligence was exemplary. Tacitus can report, on the basis of the *acta diurna*, which members of the imperial family (including the easily omitted Claudius) were present at funeral ceremonies in honour of Germanicus Caesar—Antonia his mother made no appearance in public.[3]

Some would deny that Tacitus consulted the archives of the Senate either constantly or at all.[4] They have failed to win full assent.[5] A single passage absorbs much of the argument impugning the historian. In comment upon a prosecution of the year 32 Tacitus adds the names of two men who became involved. The one was Julius Africanus, belonging to the Santoni in Gaul, but he cannot discover where the other, a certain Seius Quadratus, came from—'originem non repperi'.[6] But, it is alleged, Tacitus had only to look, in the *acta*: his admission proves that he did not look.[7]

One stage further, and the argument kills itself. What in fact stood on the protocol? A man's name, and a man's tribe—but not his 'civitas'. Tacitus could supply the origin of Julius Africanus—his son was an orator of note, and Tacitus must have known his descendants.[8] But Tacitus could not thus annotate the name of the obscure Seius Quadratus. To explain why, he employs the language of documentary inquiry, and he deserves to be taken at his word.[9]

Items from the abundant stock of the trials for treason, so Tacitus proceeds, have been frequently omitted by other writers, through

---

[1] p. 268 f.   [2] xv. 74. 3: 'reperio in commentariis senatus', &c.

[3] III. 3. 2: 'matrem Antoniam non apud auctores rerum, non diurna actorum scripta reperio ullo insigni officio functam.'

[4] Notably Nipperdey (ed. 11, revised by G. Andresen, 1915), 28 f.; O. Clason, *Tacitus und Sueton* (Breslau, 1870), 105 ff.; Ph. Fabia, o.c. 312 ff. Fabia reiterated his view in *Journal des Savants* 1903, 458. Even the sagacious Boissier assumed that the *acta* would generally have been repulsive to Tacitus (*Tacite* (1903), 72 f.).

[5] See A. Stein, *Jahresberichte der I. deutschen Staats-Realschule in Prag* XLIII (1904), 5 ff.; Th. Mommsen, *Ges. Schr.* VII (1909), 253 ff.; F. A. Marx, *Hermes* LX (1925), 74 ff.; F. B. Marsh, o.c. 259 ff.

[6] VI. 7. 4.

[7] Fabia (o.c. 314), and others in the sequel, e.g. E. Ciaceri, *Tiberio*[2] (1944), 69 f.: 'è chiaro che Tacito non aveva direttamente esaminati gli Atti del senato.' Ciaceri's verdict is quoted by M. L. W. Laistner, *The Greater Roman Historians* (1947), 178.

[8] App. 91.

[9] For the researchers' language cf. Asconius 9: 'socrus Pisonis quae fuerit invenire non potui'; Suetonius, *Divus Aug.* 2. 3: 'nec quicquam ultra . . . repperi'; *Divus Vesp.* 1. 4: 'ipse ne vestigium quidem de hoc, quamvis satis curiose inquirerem, inveni.'

fatigue or distaste; whereas Tacitus has been able to adduce many important particulars not noticed by his predecessors.[1]

The entry hardly seems to deserve the emphatic comment. Did not the archives hold material incomparably more precious? The orations or missives of the Caesars revealed much more than facts or decisions —they might contain a ruler's principles of government, convey his manner, or provide a clue to his secret nature. Tacitus even quotes verbally the exordium of a strange unhappy letter from Capreae.[2]

Tacitus began by exploiting the *acta* in the main as a source for items of public business. He soon grew bolder;[3] but it was not until he reached the end of the year 16 that he decided to reproduce an imperial oration. There are five such renderings in direct discourse. Rebutting a decayed nobleman's request for financial help from the State, Tiberius begins abruptly and harshly, proceeds without mercy or amenity, and in termination delivers a powerful homily on the evils of subsidized idleness.[4] When the trial of Cn. Piso comes on, the Princeps admonishes the Senate in a firm allocution: he draws the line between personal quarrels and offences against the State, deprecates certain manœuvres of the friends of Germanicus, and insists upon a proper and undisturbed inquiry.[5] The longest of the orations is devoted to proposals for abating luxury and immorality. It is closely reasoned and impressive. Legislation, so Tiberius argues, did not help in the past, or recently. It is impracticable, and can easily become pernicious. Remedy must be left to the individual: official intervention would be invidious, and an intolerable burden upon the Princeps.[6]

A short speech in plain and moving language commends to the protection and guidance of the Senate the sons of Germanicus, now heirs to the supreme power for good or for evil;[7] and when deputies from one of the provinces ask permission to set up a temple to Tiberius and to Livia, the Princeps expounds his aristocratic conception of duty to the 'res publica', and of the proper reward, in posthumous fame.[8]

[1] VI. 7. 5: 'neque sum ignarus a plerisque scriptoribus omissa multorum pericula et poenas, dum copia fatiscunt aut quae ipsis nimia et maesta fuerant ne pari taedio lecturos adficerent verentur: nobis pleraque digna cognitu obvenere, quamquam ab aliis incelebrata.' The last sentence is solemn and Sallustian, even did it not contain the word 'incelebratus'. Nowhere else in all Latin, save in Sallust's remarks on the historical tradition about Sertorius—'multaque tum ductu eius peracta primo per ignobilitatem, deinde per invidiam scriptorum incelebrata sunt' (*Hist.* I: 88).

[2] VI. 6. 1: 'quid scribam vobis, patres conscripti, aut quo modo scribam aut quid omnino non scribam hoc tempore, di me deaeque peius perdant quam perire me cotidie sentio, si scio.' Cf. Suetonius, *Tib.* 67. 1.

[3] Note the gist of 'crebrae epistulae' to Germanicus (II. 26. 2), perhaps based on a speech or speeches.

[4] II. 38. [5] III. 12.

[6] 53 f. (actually a dispatch to the Senate). [7] IV. 8. 4 f. [8] 37 f.

Apart from set speeches the historian includes many reports and summaries. Thus a firm answer from Tiberius when it was suggested that private morality be made the test for a proconsulate.[1] The abbreviation of an edict conveys what notion he held about the majesty of an imperial people, or a dynastic family.[2] Pride in his own achievements is forcibly expressed in the oration about the power of Maroboduus, no less formidable to Rome than the monarchs whom the Republic baffled or subjugated.[3] Ferocious irony demolishes through feigned gravity a silly proposal that the Princeps should be attended by a bodyguard of senators: who, he inquired, ought to be selected? always the same persons, or in rotation? ancient dignitaries or younger men? and how would it look when senators girded on swords at the door of the House?[4]

Tacitus had recourse to these documents. His versions, summaries, or extracts convey authentic utterances of the prince, barely modified.[5] Tiberius' proclamation to the Senate affirming his distaste for divine honours contains two instances of archaic diction.[6] The inventive verisimilitude of the historian may be responsible—or it may not. Elsewhere a single word stands out. Thus 'peregrinatio', which is somewhat alien to the Tacitean style: three instances only in his works, all in the first hexad, and two of the three embedded in reported language of Tiberius Caesar.[7]

Commenting upon the return after long absence of a certain nobleman, D. Silanus, and acknowledging the thanks of his brother, the Emperor announced that he too was gratified that Silanus had come back from a 'peregrinatio' in far lands.[8] The word is pompously ironical—and the Emperor himself had known just such a sojourn abroad, in self-imposed banishment for reasons of high politics. There is no humour but only anger in the second instance. An obsequious consular of noble birth suggested that Tiberius on his return from a visit to Campania should be permitted to hold an ovation when he entered the city. The reply was a missive of castigation: was the Emperor, who in his youth had conquered so many of the most warlike nations, with all the triumphs earned or rejected, now to petition in his old age for an empty recompense for a peregrination in the suburban vicinity of Rome?[9]

---

[1] III. 69.   [2] III. 6.   [3] II. 63.   [4] VI. 2. 4.   [5] App. 39.

[6] IV. 38. 1: 'mortalem esse et hominum officia fungi'; 3: 'duint' (in a prayer to the gods). Tacitus has 'fungi' with the accusative only in one other place (III. 2. 1).

[7] The other is in VI. 14. 2, 'nullas probabilis causas longinquae peregrinationis adferebat' (the man arrested at the Sicilian Strait, apparently in flight to Parthia).

[8] III. 24. 4: 'respondit se quoque laetari quod frater eius e peregrinatione longinqua revertisset.'

[9] 47. 4: 'igitur secutae Caesaris litterae quibus se non tam vacuum gloria praedicabat

One question only remains. Tacitus cites or reproduces speeches of Tiberius: did he have to go to the *acta* to find them? A collection might have existed.[1] If so, who made it, and for what purposes? The one valid surmise would point to the Emperor Domitian, who, in spite of earlier devotion to literature, read nothing at all (so it is alleged) when emperor, except the state papers of Tiberius Caesar.[2]

Imperial orations would forfeit almost all their value for a senatorial historian if divorced from the transactions that evoked them—and from their consequences. Other items, manifold and heterogeneous, point to the archives of the Roman Senate—and to an alert investigator. It would be fanciful to suppose that one of the annalists among the predecessors of Cornelius Tacitus made that kind of choice and apportionment.

Had the writings of those authors survived, they would probably reveal striking divergences of theme, proportion, and treatment.[3] It is not illicit to look in the first hexad for clear signs of the idiosyncrasy and preoccupations of Cornelius Tacitus, emerging in the selection of items from the *acta*—for example, sacerdotal technicalities, the allocation of consular provinces, and the affairs of the province Asia.[4]

A negative indication could perhaps help. If Tacitus in certain sections kept close to the *acta*, he might miss some fact that found no place among the transactions of the Roman Senate. The year 15 has a detailed chronicle—but nothing about Seius Strabo, whose promotion to the prefecture of Egypt left his son in sole command of the Praetorian Guard.[5] Not irrelevant to the rise of Aelius Seianus. Again, odd particulars concerning the tastes and habits of the ruler, which the historian later saw to be significant: Tiberius' addiction to astrology is not disclosed anywhere in the first four books.

Employment of the *acta*, such as is here proved (or postulated), called for industry and judgement. About the methods of Tacitus opinion has been very far from unanimous. It has sometimes been maintained that his operations were summary or mechanical, that he went on without looking far ahead.[6] That is not likely. Instances may, it is true, be discovered or surmised of a later insertion or revision.[7]

ut post ferocissimas gentis perdomitas, tot receptos in iuventa aut spretos triumphos, iam senior peregrinationis suburbanae inane praemium peteret.'

[1] Fabia affirmed it as beyond doubt (o.c. 326 f.).

[2] Suetonius, *Dom.* 20.

[3] Dio (though not a mere copyist) furnishes useful guidance.

[4] For Asia, Ch. XXXV. What earlier writer would have reported at such length on the asylum-rights of the cities (III. 60–63)? Commenting on the Senate's role, Tacitus reflects the nostalgia of his own time (III. 60. 3).

[5] The date is deduced from the tenure of his successor, C. Galerius (*PIR*[2], G 25).

[6] F. B. Marsh, o.c. 284.

[7] App. 37.

They are few, in proportion to the bulk and complexity of the narration. Yet they can furnish valuable clues. Thus two references to Tiberius' sojourn at Rhodes, which look like later annotation by the author.[1]

On the other hand, abundant proof of thought and design. Not only does Tacitus furnish here and there an unobtrusive sign and warning of future events: he will frequently remove from the annalistic record a fact or a name, saving it up for later and better use.[2] Registering the provinces allocated to Poppaeus Sabinus in 15, he jumps with no transition to sundry comments on Tiberius' practice of leaving governors in office to the end of their days. Abrupt and enigmatic, were it not clear what is in the author's mind— the decease of Poppaeus Sabinus twenty years later.[3]

While composing the first hexad, Tacitus appears familiar already with an oration of Claudius Caesar, taking from it material for a digression in Book IV;[4] the digressions are not afterthoughts but structural devices; and some of the cardinal episodes have been prepared a long way in advance.[5] It is not rash to conclude that Tacitus, after reading and excerpting the historians of the period (and some he quickly rejected), decided to build up much of the first hexad on a steady and conscientious employment of the primary material.

[1] I. 4. 4 and IV. 57. 2 (discussed in App. 37).

[2] The concentration of the Praetorian Guard in one camp probably occurred in 20 (Dio LVII. 19. 6): Tacitus reserves it for his account of Seianus' rise to power (IV. 2. 1).

[3] I. 80. 1; VI. 39. 3.

[4] The resemblance between *ILS* 212, col. ii, ll. 21 f., where Claudius discourses on the Etruscan Caeles Vibenna, and the excursus on the Mons Caelius (IV. 65. 1) is clear: each has the rare word 'appellitatus', cf. H. Furneaux' note on the passage. See further App. 41 for a hint of Claudian material in the digressions on legislation (III. 26 ff.) and on the *praefectura urbis* (VI. 11).

[5] cf. Ch. XXXIV (Tacitus on Gaul).

XXIII. THE SOURCES II

OF the second hexad more than two thirds has perished, and in what survives the historian adduces no authority by name. Hazardous for Claudius, discussion should be hopeless for Caligula. Chance intervenes and offers a temptation. The Jewish apologist Flavius Josephus decided to relate in disproportionate amplitude (his reasons are not clear) how the plot was hatched against Caligula, the deed executed, and Claudius Caesar installed in the power.[1] With Josephus may be compared Suetonius, also Cassius Dio in the mutilated conclusion of his Caligulan book.[2] That is not the main advantage. Josephus reproduces a Latin original, the style of which shows through—vivid, eloquent, and delighting in metaphor; and opinions there emerge about state and society not inappropriate in one of the annalistic predecessors of Cornelius Tacitus. Thus the lethargy of the aristocracy is blamed for the despotism of the Caesars, while soldiers and people accept the new dispensation because the Senate's rule had been unjust and oppressive.[3]

Who was the unknown historian? A clue is detected in the narration of the conspiracy. A senator sitting beside the consular Cluvius in the theatre put him an indiscreet question and then went on to startling revelations: that day would see enacted the slaying of a tyrant. Cluvius with an apt quotation from Homer told him to keep quiet.[4]

It has been argued (and most believe without question) that Cluvius the consular is none other than Cluvius Rufus the historian: an anecdote of this kind can derive only from Cluvius Rufus himself, and not verbally, but precisely from his writings.[5] None the less, some cause for hesitation will subsist, and other authors will be canvassed before there can be any certainty about the Roman historian whom that learned Jew (or his team of literary collaborators) with such fidelity transcribed. The consular Servilius Nonianus ought to have been among the spectators, not the least in prominence; and nothing

---

[1] *AJ* XIX. 17–200; 212–73.

[2] Book LIX breaks off in 40: the end of the reign is represented by extracts and summaries.

[3] *AJ* XIX. 180 f.; 224; 228. Cf. M. P. Charlesworth, *Camb. Hist. Journ.* IV (1933), 117.

[4] *AJ* XIX. 91 f. See further p. 294.

[5] Mommsen, *Hermes* IV (1870), 320 = *Ges. Schr.* VII (1909), 248. It has been argued by Momigliano that Cluvius is the main and common source of Josephus, Suetonius, and Dio for this reign, *Rendiconti della R. Accademia dei Lincei*[6] VIII (1932), 305. Against, J. P. V. D. Balsdon, *The Emperor Gaius (Caligula)* (1934), 227 f.; W. Steidle, *Sueton und die antike Biographie* (1951), 77 ff.

forbids the assumption that Servilius wrote about Caligula as well as about Tiberius.[1] And there is always Aufidius Bassus.

That author (one suspects) is generally overvalued at the expense of Servilius. Quality apart, a vexatious problem keeps Aufidius in the flow of discussion. It concerns the main historical sources for the reign of Claudius. After the *Bellum Germanicum* Aufidius began his annalistic history, still under Tiberius, it is presumed.[2] As Aufidius went on, how far did he choose to conduct his narrative? Speculation makes play with a variety of dates: the fall of Seianus, the death of Tiberius, the assassination of Caligula, several places in the period 47–51, even the death of Claudius Caesar.[3] And speculation is baffled. This much can be said: the lower dates become less and less plausible. The season at which he wrote the latest books must be taken into account. If the elderly Aufidius was still at his task under Nero (which no evidence attests), the reign of Claudius had not yet become a safe and easy subject, even in its earlier half—and quite impracticable for the later years, unless a man were extremely bold or extremely mendacious. If he went beyond Caligula (and that is a question) Aufidius might discover a happy conclusion with Claudius' invasion of Britain, or with the eighth centenary of Rome. He could hardly risk himself as far as the fall of Messallina. Still less the sequel. He could not touch Agrippina, her marriage to her uncle, and her predominance. That epoch ran continuous into the first years of Nero.

The other side of the problem concerns Pliny the Elder. Aufidius by his *Bellum Germanicum* achieved success but did not deter emulation. Pliny resolved to do better, with the advantage of personal experience—less attention to style and more to facts. When on service with the armies of the Rhine he began to compile an account of all the wars that Rome had ever waged against the Germans.[4] It was a substantial work, in twenty books. Pliny adduced a fair pretext— Drusus appeared before him in a dream, begging to be rescued from oblivion—and there may be a motive in addition. If Aufidius, writing under Tiberius, had been duly (or unduly) compliant towards the restrictions imposed upon a contemporary historian, Pliny was in a position to redress the balance and at the same time advertise loyalty to the dynasty, honourably soliciting the approval of Claudius Caesar (Drusus was his father), and, more potent, the favour of Agrippina, the daughter of Germanicus.[5]

The *Bella Germaniae* of Pliny may have gone down to the year 47,

---

[1] There is no evidence or guidance to show where Servilius began and where he left off.
[2] p. 275.　　　　　　　　　　　　　　　　　　　　　　　　[3] App. 38.
[4] As his nephew testifies, *Epp.* III. 5. 3 f.
[5] F. Münzer, *Bonner Jahrbücher* CIV (1899), 67 ff.

when Domitius Corbulo, active beyond the lower Rhine and eager for conquest, was recalled by a jealous emperor.[1] When in due course a more ambitious design captured the fancy of Pliny, he began his imperial annals where the other historian left off, 'a fine Aufidii Bassi'. A compliment to that now classic (and deceased) author, continuing Aufidius as Aufidius continued Livy—and an assertion of rank in the world of letters. Perhaps also a matter of chronological convenience. If Pliny's own *Bella Germaniae* had terminated with the year 47, to make an exordium so soon afterwards would be attractive, with Agrippina and the new turn in the reign of Claudius Caesar.

None the less, it would not be expedient to assume without careful scrutiny so late an inception. Pliny described his major work as a 'history of his own times, from the end of Aufidius Bassus'.[2] Though the first stage of Pliny's service as an equestrian officer belongs to 46 or 47, he had seen things deserving commemoration in the days of Caligula, when he was at Rome. As a youth Pliny was present at state banquets, he beheld Lollia Paullina in all her pearls and splendour, he was much in the company of an eminent personage (and highly scholarly), Pomponius Secundus, the half-brother of the woman who was Caligula's last consort.[3]

The second hexad, however, cannot yield very much. For Nero three authorities are certified. Tacitus, as has been demonstrated, takes especial care that Book XIII shall lead off as the exordium of a new section of the *Annales*. Before long he names his sources. To Nero in the course of the year 55 came the report of an obscure conspiracy, implicating Burrus, the Prefect of the Guard. According to Fabius Rusticus, the Emperor decided to dismiss Burrus, and had already issued letters of appointment to another man, but Seneca intervened, and Burrus kept his charge. However (so Tacitus proceeds), Pliny and Cluvius state that the loyalty of Burrus was not in doubt—and Fabius (he adds) is prone to glorify Seneca, who was his friend and patron.[4]

The names as cited by Tacitus permit a conjecture. When he brings in a new character, it is the habit of Tacitus to describe him by two names, not by one only.[5] On this occasion he has 'Plinius' and

---

[1] F. Münzer, o.c. 77.

[2] *NH, praef.* 20: 'opere iusto, temporum nostrorum historiam orsi a fine Aufidii Bassi.' The nephew names the title, and the total of thirty-one books (*Epp.* III. 5. 6).

[3] *NH* IX. 117 (Lollia Paullina); XIV. 56 (the banquet offered by Pomponius to Caligula, with fabulous wine); XII. 10 (Caligula's picnic near Velitrae). Pomponius and Milonia Caesonia were among the children issuing from the six marriages contracted by a lady called Vistilia, *NH* VII. 39, cf. C. Cichorius, *Römische Studien* (1922), 429 ff.

[4] XIII. 20. 2.

[5] cf. C. Bretschneider, *Quo ordine ediderit Tacitus singulas Annalium partes* (Diss. Strassburg, 1905), 32.

'Cluvius', but by contrast 'Fabius Rusticus', with annotation about that person. It might follow that the histories of C. Plinius and Cluvius Rufus had been quoted at an earlier point (somewhere in the second hexad), but that Fabius Rusticus (whether or no he began with the accession of Nero) had not been utilized hitherto.

More important the remarks in sequence. Tacitus makes a pledge: he will abide by these authorities when they are in agreement, noting divergences by name.[1] How far does he honour that pledge? The next confrontation occurs near the beginning of Book XIV. Touching the charge of incestuous overtures between Nero and his mother, Cluvius put the blame on Agrippina, Fabius on Nero; but the other historians had the same version as Cluvius, and it is the more plausible.[2]

For the rest, the *Annales* show one citation of Pliny, one of Fabius, both in the narration of the Pisonian conspiracy. Pliny had vouched for a peculiar story: Antonia, the daughter of Claudius Caesar, agreed to go with Piso to the camp of the Praetorian Guard. Tacitus avers that it is his duty not to suppress anything that stood on record, even if (for the reasons which he gives) it seemed 'absurdum'.[3] As for Fabius, he is quoted for the movements of the officer who conveyed to Seneca the Emperor's command that he must die.[4]

That is all. Despite the general (and remarkable) consensus of the historical tradition about Nero, it is hard to believe that the authorities exhibited no variants other than those Tacitus mentions as worthy to be registered. One, indeed, is notorious. Tacitus in the *Historiae* stated that Nero, having fallen violently in love with Poppaea Sabina, found for her a compliant husband in the person of his friend Salvius Otho, and deposited her in a temporary matrimony until he should have got rid of Octavia.[5] Such is the version also transmitted by Suetonius, by Plutarch, and by Cassius Dio.[6] In the *Annales* Tacitus discards the story—no argument, no hint of any variant: Nero took away a friend's wife.[7] Yet the odds are that one or other of the three main authorities for the reign of Nero was responsible for the vulgate version which Tacitus adopted in the *Historiae* but on better knowledge rejected—hardly Cluvius Rufus the consular (he was intimate with the Court), but Pliny and Fabius (either or both) might have been misled, innocent or avid for scandal.

Again, about other items, Tacitus refuses to specify.[8] He leaves it open whether the great fire at Rome was accidental or started by

---

[1] XIII. 20. 2: 'nos consensum auctorum secuturi, quae diversa prodiderint sub nominibus ipsorum trademus.'

[2] XIV. 2. 2.   [3] XV. 53. 4.   [4] XV. 61. 3.   [5] *Hist.* I. 13. 3.

[6] Suetonius, *Otho* 3. 1; Plutarch, *Galba* 19 f.; Dio LXI. 11. 2.   [7] XIII. 45 f.

[8] For the full list see H. Peter, *HRR* II (1906), clxvi f.; F. B. Marsh, *The Reign of Tiberius* (1931), 250 f.

Nero.[1] Pliny (it happens to be known) rendered Nero responsible.[2] Nor does Tacitus care to name the writers, but only refutes them, who alleged that Nero poisoned Poppaea.[3]

The sum and result is disappointing. Whatever the reason or excuse (and excessive annotation was distasteful), Tacitus did not carry out his promise.[4] It remains now to estimate the quality and the utility of the three named sources.

Rigid dogma has not infrequently been invoked to arraign and condemn the historians of classical antiquity. For all that they appeal to a plurality of authorities and adduce names or facts, they shall not be taken at their word. It is only convention, and it may be deception: the historian generally selects a single source and adheres to it closely; he abbreviates rather than supplements; and, if he alters, it is style not substance that is modified.[5]

In this dogma there are manifold attractions: the scope of historical inquiry can be narrowed on the plea of precision, the idiosyncrasy of a writer dismissed as irrelevant or barely existent.[6] The *Annales* are put to the question and severely censured. The theory of the single source, pursued with pertinacity, and often with great confidence, leads to strange conclusions. For the earlier part of the *Annales* the predilection tends to fall upon Aufidius.[7] Then Pliny emerges as a strong favourite.[8] So signal, it has been claimed, were the merits of that writer, so complete the dependence of Tacitus, that Tacitus hardly consulted the other authorities at all: what he reports about Cluvius and Fabius he got from Pliny.[9]

The other historians, of necessity, elude inquiry, but Pliny is not wholly out of reach. His encyclopedia is extant. The *Naturalis Historia* in its vast compass contains several references to the historical work, various items of value for Caligula, Claudius, and Nero, and notable information about Germany.[10] Conjectures about the *Bella*

---

[1] xv. 38. 1.   [2] *NH* xvii. 5.   [3] xvi. 6. 1.

[4] It turned out impracticable—and in any case it was inartistic. Tacitus never cites the principal historians in the first hexad—and, had he revised (? or completed) the third, there might have been no such entries.

[5] H. Nissen here set the fashion, but should not be blamed for all the extravagances of the *epigoni*.   [6] cf. p. 190, with App. 29 (on the *Historiae*).

[7] See especially the frank avowal of Ph. Fabia, *Les Sources de Tacite dans les* Histoires *et les* Annales (1893), 397.

[8] H. Nissen, *Rh. Mus.* xxvi (1871), 497 ff.; A. Gercke, *Jahrbücher für cl. Phil.*, Supp.-Band xxii (1896), 230 ff.; A. Momigliano, *Rendiconti della R. Accademia dei Lincei*[6] viii (1932), 310; 323; 327. In the view of those writers Pliny is also the 'sole source' for 69 as well. Cf. App. 29.

[9] A. Momigliano, o.c. 328 ff.; *CAH* x (1934), 702 (with reference to Cluvius Rufus and Fabius Rusticus): 'Tacitus ordinarily only knows of them what Pliny passes on.'

[10] For the historical items, A. Gercke, o.c. 165 ff; H. Peter, *HRR* ii (1906), clx ff.; for the material about Germany, F. Münzer, *Bonner Jahrbücher* civ (1899), 73 ff.—to which add *NH* ix. 45 (a monstrous fish in the river Main).

Germaniae thus become valid;[1] and a casual particular here and there may illustrate the sources of Tacitus in the *Annales*—for example Agrippina presiding at a pageant (Pliny saw her) in a cloak of woven gold.[2] The work also reflects the author in method and opinions.[3] He is hostile to Nero, and also to Agrippina, as might be expected, for all his earlier devotion to the line of Germanicus; he is comparatively indulgent towards Claudius Caesar, as befits a writer himself addicted to erudition and the collection of oddities; and some have argued (with no warrant at all) that he was bitter against Seneca.[4]

What matters most is the intrinsic quality of Pliny as an historian of imperial Rome. Three questions should be asked: how far did Pliny possess the requisite capacity and insight? what means of information were at his disposal? and when did he write the work?

Insatiable as was the curiosity of Pliny and tireless his industry, he suffered from certain shortcomings: he was credulous and superstitious, enamoured of petty detail, and prone to prejudice.[5] Pliny cannot be dissociated from the Flavian writers against whom Tacitus issues a general and anonymous warning in the *Historiae*.[6] In the *Annales* Pliny incurs blame for sponsoring a silly story about the daughter of Claudius;[7] writers who fill out their pages with the dimensions of public buildings (material only suitable for the *acta diurna*) commit an offence against the dignity of history;[8] and Pliny may also be alluded to in other derogatory hints, or disdainfully masked by the plural 'quidam auctores'.[9]

To understand what was going on, a man had to be in the city, if not in the Senate. Now Pliny for a considerable portion of the years 46–58, perhaps for nine years in all, was out of Italy on military service, though not continuously.[10] All wasted, it appears. Loyalty to the house of Germanicus earned no recompense; his patrons offered no public employment.[11] The rest of Nero's reign he passed in retirement, occupied with literary studies: no indication that he had already begun his *Historiae*, and no anecdotal trace in the *Naturalis*

---

[1] F. Münzer, o.c. 73 ff.; E. Norden, *Die germanische Urgeschichte in Tacitus Germania*[3] (1922), 207 ff.

[2] *NH* XXXIII. 63, cf. *Ann.* XII. 56. 3 (at the Fucine Lake).

[3] E. Ciaceri, *Processi politici e Relazioni internazionali* (1918), 387 ff.

[4] Id. (o.c. 429 f.), deriving thence any unfriendly traits in Tacitus' portrayal; F. A. Marx (*Klio* XXIX (1936), 101), arguing from Dio, with the further refinement that Pliny drew upon Cluvius Rufus.

[5] Cf. A. Gercke, o.c. 165 ff., arguing from parallels in the *NH* to passages in Suetonius and Dio.

[6] *Hist.* II. 101. 1.   [7] XV. 53. 3 f.   [8] XIII. 31. 1, cf. *NH* XVI. 200.

[9] e.g. XV. 6. 1 (the poisoning of Poppaea), or the 'plures' of XIV. 51. 1 (the poisoning of Burrus).

[10] F. Münzer, o.c. 122 ff. Cf. p. 60. The interval is probably 52–55.

[11] The catastrophe of Agrippina in 59 may have ruined his hopes of a procuratorship.

Historia of friends in high places at Rome or of social diversions as in the days of his youth under Caligula.

The preface to the encyclopedia, published in 77, contains a reference to the *Historiae* as a completed work.[1] It must therefore have been composed in the period 70 to 76—when Pliny was again absent from Rome, traversing the intensive career of a procurator with posts held in rapid succession.[2] Further, the *Historiae* were only given to the world at some date subsequent to the author's decease (August 24, 79). These facts are not always taken into account. They have a double significance. First, writing when he did, Pliny may not have been able to use Cluvius and Fabius. Secondly, since the work cannot have been published until a dozen years after the death of Nero, it could not exercise much influence upon other writers or upon the opinion of the time. The tradition about Nero had already taken shape.

So much for the elder Pliny, in rebuttal of large claims and unguarded assumptions. How soon or how late Fabius Rusticus was writing (and how far he carried his history) is not a question that admits precision of answer. Fabius somewhere described the geography of Britain. Eloquent rather than accurate, he assigned to the island a shape which the voyage of Agricola's fleet in 84 disproved:[3] hence the inference (by no means secure) that his account must have been composed before that year.[4] However, Fabius had achieved great distinction as an historian by the last years of Domitian.[5] Finally, a Fabius Rusticus by name figures as legatee, along with Tacitus, Pliny, and other persons, in a will drawn up in the summer of 108.[6] It may have been quite a young man who came to enjoy the friendship of Seneca, recently arriving from one of the Spanish municipalities—and not prominent enough to incur danger or exile.

Nor is Cluvius Rufus exempt from questionings. The initial and the terminal points of his history both remain unverifiable: some would even take the work backwards to the death of Augustus, and forward beyond Nero to include the civil war of the year 69.[7] And his age is uncertain. Flavius Josephus, narrating the conspiracy against Caligula,

[1] *NH, praef.* 20.   [2] p. 61.

[3] *Agr.* 10. 3: 'formam totius Britanniae Livius veterum, Fabius Rusticus recentium eloquentissimi auctores oblongae scutulae vel bipenni adsimulavere', &c.

[4] E. Groag, *Jahrbücher für cl. Philologie*, Supp.-Band XXXII (1897), 789.

[5] Cf. the reference (without the name) in Quintilian's list of historians (x. 1. 104).

[6] *CIL* VI, 10229, l. 24 (the testament of L. Dasumius). Generally identified as the historian—who, however, might have been dead when the *Agricola* was published. On Fabius Rusticus as a possible source for the *Historiae*, Ch. XVI.

[7] e.g. M. P. Charlesworth in *CAH* x (1934), 867. E. Norden argued that Cluvius is Josephus' source for the Jewish scandals of 19 at Rome (*Neue Jahrbücher* XXXI (1913), 641). For the controversy about the terminal point see App. 29.

mentions 'Cluvius the consular'.[1] If Josephus is correct and valid, Cluvius must have held the *fasces* in 39 or 40 (for the consuls of the previous years are known), and he was therefore well on in life when he acted as herald and announcer for Nero during the Hellenic tour and when he was appointed by Galba to govern the province of Hispania Citerior—in fact, coeval with Galba, which would not in itself be improbable.[2] Yet the former occupation is perhaps less compatible with advanced age than the latter. Josephus might have erred, attaching the label of rank anachronistically.[3]

While Pliny during the last years of Nero's reign lived apart from the main stream of events, Fabius Rusticus was also debarred from useful information, first by his patron's fall from favour in 62, and then by his death. Pliny was a knight, and it is not likely that Fabius was a senator. When authorities are discussed in the *Annales*, Cluvius is never criticized or rejected; and in the *Historiae* Tacitus confers a testimonial of esteem upon the eloquent statesman who acquired great influence but harmed no man, who by diplomatic arts won the confidence of several rulers in succession, coming through the wars without discredit.[4]

Many historians, says Flavius Josephus, wrote about Nero, some excessive in praise, the others in detestation.[5] The former category Tacitus disdains to cite: of the latter, Cluvius may be the most sane and temperate. Tacitus also employs Pliny and Fabius. The reasons of his choice are not far to seek. Diverse in age, origin, and station, in taste and in experience, the three historians furnished testimony that was often complementary, and when concordant reassuring, especially if they wrote in independence the one of the other, precluded from mutual borrowings. At least Pliny can hardly have had access both to Cluvius and to Fabius—Fabius was himself the primary authority for much that concerned Seneca—and Cluvius Rufus the consular possessed resources superior to either.[6]

Personal acquaintance or recollection enabled Tacitus to assess the quality of these writers and allow for their defects or omissions. There was less need for documentary research than in the first decade—and

---

[1] *AJ* XIX. 91: Οὐατίνιός τις τῶν συγκλητικῶν, ἀνὴρ ἐστρατηγηκώς, ἤρετο Κλούιον παρακαθεζόμενον αὐτῷ, καὶ τοῦτον ὑπατικόν.

[2] Cluvius, not of consular parentage, is unlikely to have become consul before forty.

[3] If so, Cluvius is a Claudian, or early Neronian, consul. Further, for doubts about his identity with the man in Josephus (and the MSS. have κλούιτον), cf. E. Groag, *PIR*², c 1202; 1206.   [4] *Hist.* IV. 43. 1, cf. p. 178.

[5] *AJ* XX. 154: πολλοὶ γὰρ τὴν περὶ Νέρωνα συντετάχασιν ἱστορίαν, ὧν οἱ μὲν διὰ χάριν, εὖ πεπονθότες ὑπ' αὐτοῦ, οἱ δὲ διὰ μῖσος καὶ τὴν πρὸς αὐτὸν ἀπέχθειαν, οὕτως ἀναιδῶς ἐνεπαρῴνησαν τοῖς ψεύσμασιν ὡς ἀξίους εἶναι αὐτοὺς καταγνώσεως.

[6] Compare the case for Servilius Nonianus against Aufidius Bassus (p. 276). Like Aufidius, Pliny tends to be overvalued, grossly.

it had much less to offer. As monarchy and bureaucracy by a steady and parallel process invaded the domain of the 'res publica', the importance of senatorial debates waned, and with it the value of the acta. None the less, Tacitus did not neglect them.[1] For Claudius his use of the archives is reflected in two ways.

First, the speeches of the Emperor. One is a direct rendering, the discourse about the admission to senatorial rank of notables from Tres Galliae.[2] Three speeches are given in the form of summaries;[3] and there are brief excerpts.[4] That does not exhaust the count. Tacitus appends antiquarian digressions to certain measures of Claudius or events in the reign.[5] Their origin is patent and palpable.[6] With this guidance some short pieces of Tacitean annotation can also be assigned to Claudius.[7] Further, proper scrutiny permits one to detect several more Claudian disquisitions.[8]

For Tacitus the oration about the Gallic *principes* had supreme value and appeal. The others could be used to fill out and variegate the narration. Above all, to exhibit unobtrusively (and not without malice) the manner of Claudius Caesar—pedantic and paternal, complacent (not to say boastful), and prone to incongruities. Governmental statements were not always truthful. Tacitus is careful to point out that Claudius omitted relevant facts.[9]

Next, various items of senatorial business.[10] Combined or alternated with the digressions and with other material adapted from the imperial orations, they supply several continuous stretches of narrative. Thus, in Book XI, the concluding acts of Claudius' censorship,[11] after which the historian turns to a new and contrasted theme, the fall of Valeria Messallina. In Book XII the metropolitan chronicle of five unpromising years (49 to 53 inclusive) is largely built up in this way, eked out by the three long surveys of what happened in Britain and in the East.[12] Tacitus has assiduously exploited Claudius Caesar and the acta. Not much is left for the portion of Pliny and the others.[13]

[1] cf. Th. Grigull, *De auctoribus a Tacito in enarranda Divi Claudii vita adhibitis* (Diss. Münster, 1907), 21 ff. His results are here used and amplified. See, in detail, App. 40.

[2] XI. 24, cf. *ILS* 212 (Lugdunum).

[3] XI. 15 (the *haruspices*); XII. 11 (Parthia); 61 (Cos).

[4] Thus XI. 25. 3 and XII. 52. 3 (unsatisfactory senators); XII. 22. 2 (Lollia Paullina); 52. 1 f. (the son of Arruntius Camillus); 53. 3 (Pallas).

[5] XI. 14 (the alphabet); 22 (the quaestorship); XII. 23. 2–24 (the *pomerium*); 60 (the *equester ordo*). [6] App. 40. [7] e.g., XI. 25. 2 (the patriciate).

[8] On Mithridates of Bosporus (XII. 20); on adopting Nero (25, from the speech of Pallas)—and perhaps on the corn supply (43. 2).

[9] XII. 11. 1: 'omissa Tiberii memoria, quamquam is quoque miserat'; 22. 2 (on Lollia Paullina): 'nam de C. Caesaris nuptiis consulto reticebat.'

[10] e.g. XII. 22 f.; 52 f.   [11] XI. 22–25.   [12] XII. 10–21; 31–40; 44–51.

[13] It follows that much of the 'Quellenforschung' brought to bear on the Claudian books was on the wrong track.

Even under Nero the *acta* can be traced, as when a dozen heterogeneous items supply the full record of the uneventful year 57.[1] The *acta* were still useful, if only for the sake of an entry to terminate each year in the traditional fashion.[2] They would also furnish an odd particular or significant name that other authorities had missed—the casual intervention of some historical character, the sponsor of some notable resolution, a series of honorific enactments.[3] In epilogue on the murder of Octavia the historian announces that he will not pass over any decree of the Senate that registered the refinement of adulation or the depths of abasement.[4]

In the second and third hexads a number of subsidiary sources might be surmised. An historian who had consulted the memoirs of Agrippina surely did not miss the instruction or entertainment to be derived from the autobiography of Claudius Caesar.[5] He may have looked at other productions of this erudite and prolific author, such as the treatise on the alphabet;[6] and he had certainly inspected poems of Nero.[7] He will have known various speeches and pamphlets such as the *De clementia* of Seneca—or the scandalous productions of Fabricius Veiento, eagerly sought after at first because banned but quickly forfeiting their appeal.[8] Further, he can refer to inscriptions in public places.[9]

For the foreign wars, writings of no small competence were available. First of all, the *Bella Germaniae* of Pliny, probably as far as the year 47. Subsequent transactions on the Rhine, chronicled in some detail in the *Annales*, especially at the end of Book XIII, will owe something to Pliny's later work.[10] Next, the dispatches of three

---

[1] XIII. 31–33.

[2] Each Neronian year ends thus (three of them with obituary notices, two with 'prodigia'). But they are not always well managed, cf. App. 60.

[3] XIII. 33. 3 (Eprius Marcellus prosecuted); 49 (Thrasea Paetus); XIV. 19 (deaths of Domitius Afer and Servilius Nonianus); XV. 74 (thanksgivings after the Pisonian conspiracy, with the name of one sponsor, Anicius Cerialis)—to say nothing of XV. 71 with its list of twenty-four names.   [4] XIV. 64. 3.

[5] Suetonius, *Divus Claudius* 41. 3: 'composuit et *De vita sua* octo volumina, magis inepte quam ineleganter.' For Claudius as an author cf. A. Momigliano, *Claudius: the Emperor and his Achievement* (1934), 6 ff.

[6] ib. Some would take this (and not the *acta senatus*) to be the source of *Ann.* XI. 14— where, however, the next item is the summary of a speech delivered in the Senate (on the *haruspices*).

[7] XIV. 16. 1: 'quod species ipsa carminum docet, non impetu et instinctu nec uno ore fluens.'

[8] XIV. 50. 2. Also perhaps the pair of speeches which the poet Lucan composed about the crime of Octavius Sagitta (Suetonius, ed. Reifferscheid (1860), 78 f.). Tacitus has a full account of this *cause célèbre* (XIII. 44). For various reasons the *Laus Pisonis* and the *Octavia* need not be held to matter.

[9] XI. 14. 3 (the Claudian letters of the alphabet); XII. 24. 2 (boundary stones of the *pomerium*).

[10] XIII. 53–57. Yet even here the use and function of the *acta* should not be neglected:

generals. Suetonius Paullinus recorded his campaign in Mauretania, the first crossing of Mount Atlas and a long march to the south;[1] he might also have transmitted information about Britain.[2] Domitius Corbulo was a recent source for Armenian geography, exploited by Pliny in his encyclopedia.[3] He is expressly cited by Tacitus for one of the campaigns.[4] Corbulo's work, so it appears, was not confined to official dispatches but took the more elaborate form of memoirs.[5] The role and the treatment of Corbulo in the *Annales* differentiate him from other generals (e.g. Ostorius Scapula and Suetonius Paullinus), whose actions do not transcend an ordinary military narrative, deriving from a report through the channel of the *acta senatus*. Direct use of Corbulo ought not to be denied.[6] There may also have been a posthumous laudation or an encomiastic biography.[7] Furthermore, some of Corbulo's legates took up the pen—not only Licinius Mucianus (who wrote about curiosities of nature),[8] but Marius Celsus.[9] Finally, the *commentarii* of Vespasian on the Jewish War.[10]

Biographies or family papers augment the catalogue of sources for the second and third hexads. Pliny on Pomponius Secundus no doubt disclosed curious sidelights upon literary and social life at Rome under Caligula.[11] Above all, the memorials of the opposition to the Caesars.

observe that 53. 1 follows a prosecution in the Senate, and is linked to senatorial business by a reference to the *ornamenta triumphalia*.

[1] Pliny, *NH* v. 14.

[2] For the account of Boudicca's rebellion see p. 395 and App. 69.

[3] *NH* II. 180; v. 83; vi. 23, cf. 40.

[4] xv. 16. 1.   [5] H. Peter, *HRR* II (1906), cxxxii ff.

[6] It is argued by Momigliano that Tacitus got his Corbulonian material through the medium of Pliny's *Historiae* (*Rendiconti della R. Accademia dei Lincei*⁶ viii (1932), 334). Dio derives from the same source (ultimately) as Tacitus, cf. his account of the operations of 61 (LXII. 21). That does not, however, disprove Tacitus' use of Corbulo's narrative, or, for that matter, of the *acta*. Tacitus not only cites Corbulo but criticizes him (xv. 16. 1). Observe, furthermore, that one campaign in Tacitus, that of 58, terminates with the vote of victory celebrations by the Senate, registering the comments thereon of C. Cassius (xiii. 41), after which comes other senatorial business.

[7] D. T. Schoonover, *A Study of Cn. Domitius Corbulo as found in the 'Annals' of Tacitus* (Diss. Chicago, 1909), 52.

[8] Pliny cites Mucianus for the source of the Euphrates (*NH* v. 83), and he may be among those in error about the Caspian Gates, 'etiam qui in Armenia res proxume cum Corbulone gessere' (vi. 40).

[9] A late authority cites Κέλσος ὁ Ῥωμαῖος τακτικός on the Parthians, with mention of Corbulo (Lydus, *De mag.* iii. 33). On Marius Celsus, legate of XV Apollinaris under Corbulo in 63 (*Ann.* xv. 25. 3) and suffect consul in 69, see App. 32. This man might have written an historical narrative.

[10] p. 178.

[11] cf. *NH* xiv. 56, referring to the biography, which the nephew duly catalogues (*Epp.* III. 5. 3). Pomponius' campaign against the Chatti in 50 is narrated by Tacitus (xii. 27 f.). Pliny, there can be no doubt, served under him. Note also that Tacitus can report an excuse put forward by the deleterious brother of Pomponius (vi. 18. 1); and he presumably knew about the poet's mother, Vistilia (*NH* vii. 39). On Pomponius see further C. Cichorius, *Römische Studien* (1922), 423 ff.; W. Otto, *Philologus* xc (1935), 483 ff.

Thrasea Paetus, who wrote a life of Cato,[1] might have discovered a congenial topic in the traditions of his own family circle—Caecina Paetus, his wife's father, implicated in the treason of Arruntius Camillus and committing suicide on the exhortation and example of the heroic Arria.[2] Thrasea in his turn received commemoration. The *Annales* convey a full account of the discussion between Thrasea and his intimates: should he go to the Senate House and confront the prosecutors or should he stay at home? The company included young Junius Rusticus: he was tribune of the plebs, and he boldly offered to interpose his veto, but Thrasea restrained him, pointing out that the act would be futile.[3] The notice is probably Tacitus' way of hinting at his source, for Rusticus later composed a biography of Thrasea, duly fatal to its author.[4]

The recourse to similar material might be looked for elsewhere in the third hexad.[5] Tacitus has a full account of the killing of Rubellius Plautus (exiled in Asia), where the gist of a letter from his wife's father L. Antistius Vetus is given.[6] He can also report a divergent view about the tenor of that missive.[7] Again, the death of Vetus himself.[8] Further, a different source may sometimes betray a faint clue, by an item of nomenclature. The destruction of Ostorius Scapula was brought about by a certain Antistius Sosianus.[9] In earlier passages the historian styled him 'Antistius', repeatedly.[10]

The genre became popular. Not all aspirants were close in time to the events. Roman knights compiled the deaths of illustrious men:[11] what opinion the consular had of their credentials might deserve the hazard of a guess. Apart from any written sources, Tacitus' own personal knowledge about the late Neronian years must be admitted and evaluated.

There is nothing in the notion that Cornelius Tacitus merely selected a single author whom he proceeded to transcribe and stylize, with little care for variants and none at all for documentation. The whole work is infused with majesty and power. A scholar who has dwelt long with his subject cannot always suppress the assurance that

---

[1] Plutarch, *Cato minor* 25; 36.   [2] Pliny, *Epp.* III. 16. 6 ff.   [3] XVI. 25 f.
[4] *Agr.* 2. 1. Rusticus may have had access to memoranda by Thrasea justifying his policy, cf. the statement Tacitus puts into Thrasea's mouth 'rationem poscentibus amicis' (XIII. 49. 4). Indeed, Herennius Senecio used *commentarii* for his biography of Helvidius Priscus, supplied by the widow (Pliny, *Epp.* VII. 19. 5).
[5] cf. F. A. Marx, *Philologus* XCII (1937), 83 ff., esp. 89 ff.
[6] XIV. 58. 4.   [7] 59. 1.
[8] XVI. 10 f.   [9] 14. 1.
[10] XIII. 28. 1 (twice); XIV. 48 f. (four times).
[11] C. Fannius and Titinius Capito (p. 92). The latter had a statue set up in memory of L. Silanus (Pliny, *Epp.* I. 17. 1), one of Nero's victims (XVI. 9).

derives from honesty and industry.[1] Something much stronger is conveyed by Tacitus—that authority of rank, weight, and maturity which pronounces a consular verdict upon men and affairs, peremptory and incorruptible.

For information, and much more for guidance, Tacitus could draw upon rich resources, nothing less than the whole tradition of the governing class, arising immediately out of the events he proposed to narrate, or with the interval of a single generation. Born at the beginning of Nero's reign and occupied under Vespasian with the apprenticeship to public life, Tacitus had access to men (a handful but enough) who had sat in the high assembly since the days of Tiberius Caesar; and the student of eloquence could not fail to learn all that mattered about the great speakers of that earlier age, not memorials and models of discourse only, but the actions that first brought an advocate into notoriety, the surge or ebb in the tide of his public performance, the trenchant or humorous 'dicta' that adhered to an historic name.

Aged senators told him something about the prosecution of Cn. Piso. They had seen Piso with a document in his hands more than once, a document which, dared he divulge it, would dispel all guilt in the matter of Germanicus Caesar (and incriminate the Emperor).[2] And he can report a curious particular going back ultimately to persons who sojourned on Capreae with Tiberius Caesar. The consular Cocceius Nerva, foremost for knowledge of the law in all its provinces and an intimate friend of the Emperor, resolved to make an end of his life. His decision stood, immovable against entreaty. What was the motive? Tacitus can supply it. He appeals to the authority of those familiar with what was in Nerva's thoughts at the time: indignation and melancholy forebodings.[3]

Every age of the Roman aristocracy honoured its portents of longevity, active or at least vocal to the end of their days. Old men extend across wide tracts of time. L. Piso the *pontifex*, who came into the world when Caesar and Pompeius fought for the power, prolonged his life into the late years of Tiberius' principate.[4] That ruler himself is closely comparable as a relic (Philippi marked the year of his birth); while L. Volusius, only four years junior to Tiberius Caesar, lived to

---

[1] VI. 7. 5 (quoted above, p. 283). The Sallustian language carries emphasis and solemnity. Compare the rare verb 'antehabeo' used in an affirmation about his historical method (IV. 11. 3). Apart from I. 58. 3, nowhere else in Latin (cf. *TLL*).

[2] III. 16. 1. These were men 'qui nostram ad iuventam duraverunt'.

[3] VI. 26. 2: 'ferebant gnari cognitionum eius, quanto propius mala rei publicae viserat, ira et metu, dum integer, dum intemptatus, honestum finem voluisse.' It will be recalled, however, that one of the historians had been on Capreae at least once (Suetonius, *Tib.* 61. 6), surely Servilius Nonianus (p. 277).

[4] VI. 10. 3.

see Nero as emperor, dying at ninety-three in the year when the son of his old age held the *fasces*.[1] One of the Tiberian consuls survived into the reign of Vespasian, no less a person than the jurist Cassius Longinus.[2] Another lasted even longer, L. Piso, the son of Germanicus' enemy.[3] Tacitus could have heard the laudations over these men—and Tacitus in his own tenure of the consulate presided at the obsequies of Verginius Rufus, a senator born in the last year of Caesar Augustus.[4]

Women also qualify. The sister of Marcus Brutus protracted her life until the year 22.[5] The widow of A. Plautius was still alive, devout and dignified, forty years after her husband conducted the invasion of Britain.[6] Half-way through the reign of Trajan Roman society noted the decease of a powerful matron who retained and avowed her delight in the equivocal pastimes of an earlier age: she was devoted to dicing and to pantomimes, but kept her grandson safe from any contagion.[7] This was Ummidia Quadratilla: her father had entered the Senate in A.D. 14.[8] And Domitia Longina, Corbulo's daughter and an emperor's widow, was still extant in the reign of Hadrian, elderly but undeterred by modesty or reticence.[9]

When Tacitus was composing the *Annales*, it was not too late to question witnesses surviving from the last years of Nero. He could also employ the narrative of Fabius Rusticus, himself in the near vicinity of peril when so many were killed or relegated—and supping, it may well be, with his patron Seneca when the officer came with the fatal mandate.[10] And he could supplement Fabius. He appeals to the testimony of some of those exiled for complicity in the conspiracy of C. Piso, the phraseology implying that they were still alive.[11]

Nor were the dead forgotten by friends or family. Tacitus has good information about the officers of the city garrison, and notably about a tribune of the Guard called Subrius Flavus, one of the prime movers. Part of what he tells is cautiously conveyed as report only—that Subrius in the previous year thought of assassinating Nero, either while he

---

[1] XIII. 30. 2, cf. Pliny, *NH* VII. 62; XI. 223. Consul suffect in A.D. 3, his son *ordinarius* in 56.

[2] *Dig.* I. 2. 52. He had been *cos. suff.* in 30. Tacitus shows no little interest in him.

[3] Pliny, *Epp.* III. 7. 12, cf. *PIR*², C 293. He was consul in 27.

[4] *Epp.* II. 1.   [5] III. 76.

[6] XIII. 32. 3 (Pomponia Graecina, 'superstitionis externae rea' in 57).

[7] *Epp.* VII. 24. 1 ff. The grandson, C. Ummidius Quadratus, was *suffectus* in 118.

[8] *ILS* 972 (C. Ummidius Quadratus, *cos. suff.* c. 40, legate of Syria from 51 to 60).

[9] Her survival is attested by tile-stamps, *CIL* XV, 553, &c. (123); 554 (126); 552 (c. 129, 'Severo et Arrian. cos.'). For her character, Suetonius, *Divus Titus* 10 (discussed in App. 76).

[10] XV. 60. 4 (Seneca with his wife and two friends); 61. 3 (Fabius Rusticus cited for a detail about the officer's movements).

[11] 73. 2.

performed on the stage or during the confusion of the great conflagration;[1] that Subrius plotted to kill not Nero only, but Piso too, for both were stage-players.[2] However, when the tribune, arrested and examined, boldly avowed his guilt, casting detestation of Nero in the tyrant's face, Tacitus quotes the actual phrase, as not likely to be well known;[3] and he does not omit to describe the execution of Subrius, with further words from that brave man.[4]

Given the time of his birth, the author of the *Annales* could recapture without undue exertion the atmosphere of Neronian Rome; and the recollection of what he had heard in his youth would carry him a long way further back, towards Tiberius. Not that it is at all easy to discover how much may derive from reminiscence and verbal transmission. Nor have many attempts been made. In Tacitus' treatment of the alleged conspiracy of Scribonius Libo may be seen (so it is argued) the family version, at variance, and deliberately, with the official account.[5] That is not at all plausible.[6] But a certain atrocious fable about the poisoning of Drusus Caesar, current in the historian's own day, might be the property of some aristocratic group.[7]

A way of tentative approach lies open. Tacitus introduces certain characters not so much for any word or deed as for their prominence in subsequent history. Thus Antonius Primus among those who forged a will, and Fabricius Veiento as the author of scandalous pamphlets.[8] A rapid glimpse discloses A. Vitellius in a senatorial debate, noisy, exultant, and aggressive on the side of the majority, but terrified when anybody answers back;[9] Vespasian falls asleep during a Neronian entertainment;[10] a bare phrase without comment registers the military decorations conferred upon Cocceius Nerva, praetor designate in 65.[11]

By the same token personal choice or knowledge can be surmised. Governors of Britain appeal to Tacitus.[12] Likewise the relatives of a friend or coeval. In the year 66 three men found themselves caught up in a political case that had incest and magic among the indictments.[13]

---

[1] 50. 4.

[2] 65 (with a statement of Subrius, not guaranteed by Tacitus). Note by contrast 58. 4, where Subrius' readiness to draw his sword and cut down Nero is reported as a fact.

[3] 67. 3: 'ipsa rettuli verba quia non, ut Senecae, vulgata erant, nec minus nosci decebat militaris viri sensus incomptos et validos.'

[4] ib. 4.   [5] F. B. Marsh, *Class. Phil.* XXI (1926), 291 ff.   [6] p. 400.

[7] IV. 10. 1. The Asinii might have perpetuated this story, for the sons of Asinius Gallus (who married Vipsania when Tiberius divorced her) were half-brothers of Drusus.

[8] XIV. 40. 2; 50.   [9] 49. 1.   [10] XVI. 5. 3.   [11] XV. 72. 1.

[12] This interest naturally embraces members of their families: thus the wife of A. Plautius (XIII. 32. 2), the son of Ostorius Scapula (XII. 31. 4; XIV. 48. 1; XVI. 14 f.), the parent of Q. Veranius (II. 56. 4, &c.).

[13] XVI. 8. 3 (the prosecution of L. Silanus, accused of incest with his aunt, the wife of C. Cassius Longinus).

They appealed to Caesar, evaded immediate condemnation—or any subsequent molestation, for they were not persons of consequence. One of them happens to be the grandfather of the younger Pliny's wife, still among the living when forty years had elapsed.[1]

Other minor characters, isolated and undefined, may carry a clue by their bare names, unmistakable to any contemporary. For, if some entries are due to simple scruple of documentation, others look deliberate, revealing the forebears of senators known to Tacitus. Thus an earlier Junius Rusticus is guilty of evil or foolish conduct;[2] Caepio Crispinus heralds the whole class of 'delatores';[3] an adherent of Seianus comes to a deserved end, the knight Julius Marinus who had lived at Rhodes and at Capreae in the company of Tiberius Caesar;[4] and Q. Servaeus (also a friend of Seianus, though not so culpable) turns informer when put on trial and condemned.[5] Especially significant should be ancestors of Tacitus' coevals among the consulars, named perhaps for praise and from amity, but more often without commendation, like Asinius Marcellus, the aristocrat who operated with the band of forgers—a respectable man, but holding poverty the prime calamity.[6]

None of the Asinii, descendants of the great Asinius Pollio, would escape his notice.[7] He also shows some interest in the Volusii, recondite facts as well as obvious singularities. That family, consular for the first time under Augustus, was not remarkable for longevity only. They accumulated wealth without disrepute and prospered in the friendship of the Caesars.[8] When Tacitus, inventing a speech of

---

[1] viz. the knight L. Calpurnius Fabatus (*PIR*[2], C 263).

[2] v. 4. 1: 'is fatali quodam motu (neque enim ante specimen constantiae dederat) seu prava sollertia', &c.

[3] I. 74. 1, cf. his descendants (p. 326).

[4] vi. 10. 2: 'quo laetius acceptum sua exempla in consultores recidisse.' Perhaps an ancestor of L. Julius Marinus (*ILS* 1026), *pr.* c. 87, *cos. suff.* with L. Arruntius Stella (*ILS* 6106), probably in 101, cf. App. 18.

[5] vi. 7. 2. Observe Q. Servaeus Innocens (*suff.* 101).

[6] xiv. 40. 2: 'Marcellus Asinio Pollione proavo clarus neque morum spernendus habebatur nisi quod paupertatem praecipuum malorum credebat.'

[7] Thus he registers the decease of Saloninus (an otherwise unattested son of Asinius Gallus), affianced to one of the daughters of Germanicus—and himself a half-brother of Tiberius' son (III. 75. 1). Also that of (M.) Asinius Agrippa, mentioned with praise (IV. 61), though otherwise only known as and because *ordinarius* in 25. For the stemma of the family cf. J. H. Oliver, *AJP* LXVIII (1947), 147 ff. Of consular Asinii in the historian's own time note especially Q. Asinius Marcellus (his year is uncertain, cf. App. 10) and M. Asinius Marcellus (*cos.* 104).

[8] Tacitus has obituaries of L. Volusius Saturninus (*suff.* 12 B.C.) and his homonymous son (*suff.* A.D. 3). The former was 'opumque quis domus illa immensum viguit primus adcumulator' (III. 30. 1). Of the latter he says 'L. Volusius egregia fama concessit, cui tres et nonaginta anni spatium vivendi praecipuaeque opes bonis artibus, inoffensa tot imperatorum amicitia fuit' (XIII. 30. 1). He was *praefectus urbi* when he died (Pliny, *NH* VII. 62), an office presumably registered along with other particulars in the lost books.

response for the Emperor Nero in a private disquisition with Seneca, adduces an example of opulence, the name that occurs spontaneously is a Volusius.[1] In Tacitus' own time and generation were two Volusii (*consules ordinarii* in 87 and 92), quiet men, it may be presumed, and no more molested by a despot than had been their nonagenarian grandfather.

The historian is well informed about a certain Ostorius Scapula, the son of the second legate to govern Britain and decorated for conspicuous courage in the campaigns of his father. Scapula on various incriminations (including a horoscope) received, or rather anticipated, the command to end his life. Tacitus recounts his suicide with knowledge, with sympathy, and with indignation.[2] The son of Nero's victim held the consulate, it appears, in the same year as Cornelius Tacitus.[3]

Friends of Tacitus or at least in the circle of his acquaintance (and obliquely to be touched in comment upon their ancestors), a Volusius or an Ostorius may, like other personages of the time, have supplied the historian with special information—not always, perhaps, aware of what they were doing.[4] What emerges, however, is the knowledge Tacitus can bring to the subject, and the independent judgement, whatever be the extent and value of the writings he consults.

[1] XIV. 56. 1: 'quantum Volusio longa parsimonia quaesivit.'
[2] XVI. 14 ff. (M. Ostorius Scapula, *suff*. 59).
[3] Deduced from the fact that a M. Scapula was proconsul of Asia in 114/15, cf. App. 10 and R. Syme, *JRS* XLIII (1953), 153 f.
[4] For Tacitus' coevals see further Chs. VI and XXXV; App. 24.

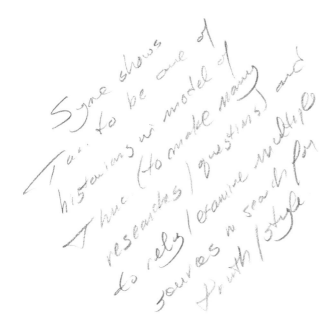

THE matter was heterogeneous—both literary and documentary, stylized with elegance or baldly prosaic, removed by three generations or recent and personal. How was Cornelius Tacitus to evince his mastery, blending and transmuting? His principal devices are structure, digression, comment, and speeches. And not least, omission—which more recent exponents of imperial Rome have seldom skill or courage to emulate.

The exordium of the *Historiae* exhibited a technique firm, confident, and mature. The *Annales* from the opening words go to the limit of brevity and intensity. The prologue falls into two parts, first the vicissitudes of governmental power at Rome, in summary from the Kings to Caesar Augustus, next the character of history-writing and the author's design.[1] In the *Historiae* Tacitus was impelled to say something about his own career in the State, and his relation towards the rulers of Rome, nor could he avoid a senator's tactful homage to Nerva and Trajan, whose happy epoch an historian might be happy to commemorate one day. The remarks in the *Annales* are ruthlessly depersonalized, and the odious pronoun is restricted to the writer's enunciation of the subject: 'I propose to say but little about Augustus, only the very end, thence to narrate the Principate of Tiberius and what came after Tiberius, having no personal reason to be for or against any of the rulers.'[2]

So far the prologue. Next the introduction, with Augustus' rise to power.[3] Then, after an analysis of his contrivances for the dynastic succession (rumour and insinuation are generously interspersed), the Princeps breathes his last, and (due provision having been made) the reign of Tiberius Caesar begins, suitably inaugurated by a violent death.[4] The oath of allegiance follows, a session of the Senate, the funeral, and a second session;[5] after which, the narration is firmly under way, and the scene changes to Pannonia and the Rhine.[6]

It is a delicate decision for an historian how much prefatory matter he needs in order that the story shall run clean and free, explaining itself. Cassius Dio was clumsy: not only the funeral oration but a lengthy account of all the pageantry. Tardy and prolix in his farewell to

---

[1] Editors would have done well to print the first chapter in the form of two paragraphs, the second beginning with an appropriate and Sallustian 'sed'.

[2] I. I. 3: 'inde consilium mihi pauca de Augusto et extrema tradere, mox Tiberii principatum et cetera, sine ira et studio, quorum causas procul habeo.'

[3] 2.   [4] 3–6.   [5] 7–15.   [6] 16 ff.

Augustus, he ushers in the new reign with an elaborate character-sketch of Tiberius, to be followed before long (but still under the year 14) by a digression on his methods of government.[1]

Tacitus is economical with the preliminaries, barely answering even to his own programme, which is 'pauca de Augusto et extrema'. From the dead ruler he wished to break free, quickly. Information about Augustus could be worked in subsequently. Various procedures offered. Formal eulogy Tacitus disdained—and he could do much more with the reflections of the 'prudentes', for and against, at the funeral.[2] Anything else might encumber and retard the exposition.[3] A catalogue of the armed forces of the Empire is boldly transferred to Book IV.[4] A similar mastery of structural problems will be shown at the opening of Nero's reign; and, on the analogy of the virtuosity exemplified in the early chapters of the *Historiae*, a guess may be hazarded about the concluding book of the *Annales*: the rising in the West against Nero would lead off with a survey of provinces, armies, and generals.

The annalistic framework, it might seem, is a primary obstacle: it breaks and disperses a genuine theme or sequence, it juxtaposes unrelated items in mere enumeration. Examples abound, some very striking.[5] Tacitus himself deplores the restriction;[6] and he can adduce reasons (some sentimental, others practical) for overstepping the annual limits.[7]

A doubt arises. The traditional schema is a blessing to compilers—it spares the effort of thought and design. On the better showing, it is congenial to years that offer no single or guiding theme. Nor could it hamper a bold and resourceful artist.[8] In the second and third hexads at least Tacitus won emancipation, grouping events much as he pleased. And how far did it ever harm him? Some will contend (and it is no paradox) that the rigid articulation of the first hexad contributes not a little to its artistic superiority.[9]

---

[1] LVII. 1 (Tiberius); 7–13 (his government).   [2] I. 9 f.

[3] As it is, the digression on Augustus' plans for the succession (I. 3), with so many names and facts, gives him trouble. That was perhaps unavoidable. But when he insists on inserting the rumour about the journey to Planasia (5) and the anecdote about the 'capaces imperii' (13. 2 f.) he overloads the structure, cf. App. 37.

[4] Some argue that this should have been put at the beginning of Tiberius' principate, e.g. P. Wuilleumier, *Tacite, l'homme et l'œuvre* (1949), 142.

[5] e.g. XIII. 31–33 (the events of 57).

[6] IV. 71. 1: 'ni mihi destinatum foret suum quaeque in annum referre, avebat animus antire.'

[7] VI. 38. 1: 'quae duabus aestatibus gesta coniunxi quo requiesceret animus a domesticis malis'; XII. 40. 5: 'haec, quamquam a duobus pro praetoribus pluris per annos gesta, coniunxi ne divisa haud perinde ad memoriam sui valerent.'

[8] For Tacitus' management of the annalistic schema cf. W. Kroll, *Studien zum Verständnis der r. Literatur* (1924), 369 ff.; W. Graf, *Untersuchungen über die Komposition der Annalen des Tacitus* (Diss. Bern, 1931).

[9] W. Graf, o.c. 94.

For the arrangement of facts and the build of a plot Cornelius
Tacitus has no equal. Much has been written about his technique,
with less praise for the historian than for the dramatist.[1] At the outset
the portrayal of Livia and the whole episode of Agrippa Postumus is
instructive, and disquieting.

In the summary of Augustus' dynastic plans Livia first appears in
a parenthetical innuendo—she might have been responsible for the
deaths of Gaius Caesar and of Lucius Caesar[2]—and then, securing
adoption and designation for her own son, Tiberius,[3] she induces
Augustus to send away his sole remaining grandson, Agrippa Postumus, to banishment on the island of Planasia:[4] Agrippa is briefly
characterized.[5] When the Princeps' health begins to fail and the end
is near, men conjecture variously and darkly about their new rulers,
and some affect to regard Agrippa as still a potential candidate for the
succession, while denying his capacity.[6] An exaggeration, to use no
other word. It is succeeded by fiction. The historian reports a rumour,
knowing it to be such:[7] some months before his death Augustus went
on a secret visit to the island (Livia was not to know, and the aged
Princeps had only one companion with him), and there, after an affect-
ing scene, he was reconciled to his grandson.

What all this leads up to soon becomes clear—the execution of
Agrippa, standing out as the first crime of Tiberius' reign, 'primum
facinus novi principatus'.[8] Tiberius made no report of the matter to
the Senate—it was his excuse and defence that the dead Princeps had
left precise instructions for the deed. The historian, however, allows
himself to be sceptical about those instructions—he invokes kinship
and humanity, and prefers to incriminate Tiberius and Livia.[9] The
whole business was managed for them by Sallustius Crispus, who
controlled all the secrets of the palace, and who warned Livia that no
public statement must be made.[10]

The theme of Agrippa Postumus was by no means exhausted.

---

[1] e.g. P. S. Everts, *De Tacitea historiae conscribendae ratione* (Diss. Utrecht, 1926);
C. W. Mendell, *Yale Classical Studies* v (1935), 1 ff.; B. Walker, *The* Annals *of Tacitus*
(1952), 35 ff.

[2] 1. 3. 3: 'mors fato propera vel novercae Liviae dolus.' Imputations of this type were
not invented by Tacitus. Cf. Dio LIII. 33. 4, on the death of Marcellus.

[3] ib.: 'non obscuris, ut antea, matris artibus, sed palam hortatu.'

[4] ib. 4: 'nam senem Augustum devinxerat,' &c.

[5] ib.: 'rudem sane bonarum artium et robore corporis stolide ferocem, nullius tamen
flagitii compertum.'

[6] 4. 3.   [7] 5. 1 f., cf. App. 36.

[8] 6. 1, cf. Suetonius, *Tib.* 22; Dio, however, postpones the item (LVII. 3. 5 f.).

[9] ib. 2: 'propius vero Tiberium ac Liviam, illum metu, hanc novercalibus odiis,
suspecti et invisi iuvenis caedem festinavisse.'

[10] ib. 3: 'quod postquam Sallustius Crispus particeps secretorum (is ad tribunum
miserat codicillos) comperit', &c.

Later in the year, when Tacitus registers the decease of Julia, another exile, the name of her son naturally recurs.[1] In 16 a false Agrippa appeared. To Sallustius Crispus was given the mandate for arrest, and the impostor, after being questioned by Tiberius, was suppressed in all discretion.[2] When the great minister of state came to die, and his services to the dynasty are recapitulated, the obituary notice will not omit Agrippa Postumus.[3]

Act and situation were to recur. Tacitus did not have to wait for the murder of Britannicus by Nero. At the exordium of Book XIII when a new reign begins, a descendant of Caesar Augustus must be put to death. 'Prima novo principatu mors'—the phrase suffices, with Nero's mother as instigator, recalling the role of Livia at the accession of Tiberius Caesar.[4]

The device of Tacitus is patent. Insisting so heavily upon Agrippa Postumus, prolonging and recalling the episode, he intends to evoke, as dominant notes in the Principate, dynastic crime and secret politics.

Livia is tied up with the affair of Agrippa Postumus in a closely woven nexus of insinuations. Some suspected that she accelerated the end of Augustus—for she found out about the journey to Planasia.[5] That was only rumour. But the historian takes much more licence. He expresses a doubt whether Tiberius, called back in all haste, found the Princeps still living when he arrived;[6] and he adds a detail—Livia picketed the roads and put out optimistic bulletins about the health of Augustus in order to gain time and provide all that was requisite for the transmission of the power.[7]

Compared with this confident allegation, subsidiary hints seem trifling. When men made ominous forecasts about the coming reign, they feared the domineering nature of Livia;[8] she is duly chronicled among the detrimental phenomena of Augustus' rule;[9] Tiberius at the outset was anxious to advertise constitutional proprieties and avoid imputations about his mother's role in the adoption;[10] and he was disposed to regard public honouring of the Augusta as prejudicial to himself.[11]

The influence of Livia, with various items to illustrate her 'potentia'

---

[1] 53. 2. [2] II. 39 f. [3] III. 30. 3. [4] XIII. I. I.
[5] I. 5. 1 f., cf. Dio LVI. 30. 1 f. (the poisoned figs).
[6] ib. 3, cf. Dio LVI. 31. 1 (given as the version of most, and the best, authorities). Suetonius (*Tib.* 21. 1) expresses no doubt.
[7] ib. 4. This detail is not in Dio. For the parallels between the deaths of Augustus and of Claudius see H. Willrich, *Hermes* XLII (1927), 76 f.; R. H. Martin, *CQ* XLVIII (1955), 123 ff.
[8] 4. 5: 'accedere matrem muliebri impotentia.'
[9] 10. 5: 'postremo Livia, gravis in rem publicam mater, gravis domui Caesarum noverca'.
[10] 7. 7, cf. App. 37.
[11] 14. 2: 'muliebre fastigium in deminutionem sui accipiens.'

(and also some insinuations of discord), will recur in the *Annales* down to her death.[1] How it affected her son in his behaviour and government was a legitimate theme for conjecture, and even for emphasis. What emerges, however, in the course of those fifteen years hardly corresponds with the sinister intimations; and the obituary notice is mild by contrast.[2]

For the second half of the reign Tacitus proposes to concentrate interest upon the figure of Aelius Seianus. He is introduced twice in Book I, as though in passing, with suitable hints.[3] After that, the author manages to withhold him for several years, and maintain suspense.[4] In the third hexad Agrippina after initial prominence quickly fades out—from three years of annalistic history (56–58) her name is excluded. She comes in again only to be murdered, and the manner of bringing her back into the narrative betrays a questionable artifice.[5] Thrasea Paetus is not noticed until 58. That is the first of five incidents, spaced at intervals,[6] but the catastrophe does not come till 66.[7]

How soon a character shall enter the action or how long he can with advantage be kept off the stage is an important problem of dramatic design. Premature entry or repetitive foreshadowings of futurity can be tedious and harmful. Among the historical personages of Neronian Rome, no fewer than four were destined to wear the purple very soon after Nero—and two others might have had the power. Salvius Otho belongs to the central narrative because of Poppaea Sabina, and his exit also must be chronicled—Nero sent him away in 58 to be governor of Lusitania.[8] Two years later Sulpicius Galba went to Spain.[9] The fact is suppressed, for Galba will be kept out of the hexad almost until the end, to shoot up in Book XVIII, suddenly, as the old man forgotten for many years, or believed innocuous, despite the prediction uttered long ago by Tiberius Caesar.[10] In the extant books Verginius Rufus is only a consular date, whereas Licinius Mucianus does not occur at all, although he had been in

---

[1] For the emergence of discord as a motive see App. 37.

[2] v. 1. 3: 'sanctitate domus priscum ad morem, comis ultra quam antiquis feminis probatum, mater impotens, uxor facilis et cum artibus mariti, simulatione filii bene composita.' The theme of discord between mother and son appears to derive largely from second thoughts of the historian, cf. App. 37. Note also (and more serious) that Livia had been protecting Agrippina (v. 3. 1). This undermines much that Tacitus had previously alleged.

[3] I. 24. 2: 'magna apud Tiberium auctoritate, rector iuveni et ceteris periculorum praemiorumque ostentator'; 69. 5: 'accendebat haec onerabatque Seianus, peritia morum Tiberii odia in longum iaciens, quae reconderet auctaque promeret.'

[4] He next occurs in III. 16. 1 (a report that Tacitus cannot guarantee).

[5] xiv. 1 f. (the role of Poppaea and the incest story).

[6] XIII. 49; XIV. 12. 1; 48 f.; xv. 20 f.; 23. 4. Cf. p. 556.

[7] XVI. 21 ff.   [8] XIII. 46. 3.   [9] Suetonius, *Galba* 9. 1.   [10] VI. 20. 2.

Armenia with Corbulo.[1] Yet, for all necessary and artistic restraint, the historian cannot help disclosing Vespasian once, in a humorous incident, and Vitellius, maliciously.[2]

To effective grouping, as to easy flow of narration, much of the annalistic matter was highly refractory. An alert and careful writer had to forge his links of sequel and relation. Sometimes connexion is of the loosest, as when a vague indication of time suffices—'per idem tempus'. Elsewhere, being tight, explicit, and confident, it often betrays strain and artifice. Tiberius Caesar frequents assiduously the Senate and listens for many days to the embassies from Asia—because he wished to divert attention from an awkward incident in the palace.[3] Following upon a catalogue of deaths comes the marriage of a princess to a commoner—for that, too, in public opinion, was reckoned a calamity.[4] Nero, liberated by his mother's removal, plunges into every kind of vicious indulgence—at once.[5]

Not that Tacitus is deficient in subtle inventions for smooth transition. On a surface view the purpose of an excursus seems obvious —necessary annotation of a text, welcome variety and relief (distant lands or the remote past), or perhaps an excuse for specialized erudition.[6] By paradox, its value is often structural. In the design of such architectonics no historian can come near Cornelius Tacitus.[7] Tiberius, when explaining to the Senate problems touching the recruitment of the legions, cursorily noted their strength and stations. With this guidance the historian himself passes in review the whole armed force of the empire (auxiliary troops and royal levies added), and cleverly subjoins a survey of the general policy and administration of Tiberius.[8] Again, after registering a series of trials for high treason, the historian complains about the subject-matter of these imperial annals and slips into an excursus on the writing of history,[9] which heralds and brings in the next year with the next episode—precisely the prosecution of a Roman historian, Cremutius Cordus.[10]

These digressions, and many others, avow their nature openly by label or by content.[11] Tacitus also has recourse to concealed digressions

---

[1] Pliny, *NH* v. 83.   [2] XVI. 5. 3; XIV. 49. 1.   [3] IV. 55. 1.   [4] VI. 27. 1.

[5] XIV. 13. 2: 'seque in omnes libidines effudit quas male coercitas qualiscumque matris reverentia tardaverat.' There follows a description of his charioteering and harp playing— 'vetus illi cupido erat', &c. (14. 1).

[6] cf. W. Theissen, *De Sallustii Livii Taciti digressionibus* (Diss. Berlin, 1912); E. Hahn, *Die Excurse in den Annalen des Tacitus* (Diss. Munich, 1933).

[7] Digressions in Livy are often afterthoughts and not closely linked to the context, cf. W. Soltau, *Hermes* XXIX (1894), 611 ff.

[8] IV. 5 f.   [9] 32 f.   [10] 34 f.

[11] It is not easy to draw the line. E. Hahn (o.c. 4) confines the total in the *Annales* to thirteen, viz. seven on 'Staatsrecht' and six on 'Kulturgeschichte'. The digression on Byzantium (XII. 63) is not included; and other items were perhaps worth noting, such as the monuments of Egypt (II. 60 f.), Capreae (IV. 67. 2), or the Sibylline Books (VI. 12. 3).

—episodes not requiring to be narrated so lavishly, or even at all, for historical value, but exploited for variety, for contrast, or to facilitate a transition. The last item of the year 25 tells how a Roman governor in Spain was assassinated by a native, though not through private vendetta: his official conduct, it is suggested, had been harsh.[1] The next year opens with an insurrection of the Thracians which is reported in a dramatic narration of unusual (and perhaps inordinate) length.[2] In 58 an episode of crime and sex (Octavius Sagitta, a tribune of the plebs, murdered his mistress) serves as explicit introduction to Poppaea Sabina.[3] Contrast can be no less effective. Tigellinus organizes a water festival for Nero, with all the apparatus of luxury and debauch: another spectacle follows abruptly, the conflagration of the city.[4] For the beginning of Book XVI Tacitus chooses the peculiar story of an official hunt for fabulous treasure in Africa:[5] a light interlude after the Pisonian conspiracy, before the next murders begin.

The *Historiae*, with a unitary theme and rapid events, did not often require the help of supplementary devices. Nor did Tacitus allot any undue space to the early history of Cremona, to the Roman Capitol, to the tribe of the Batavi—or to his own reflections on civil war and the lust for power.[6] There are, however, three digressions of some magnitude, exhibiting certain peculiarities.

When Titus on his way back to Syria came to the island of Cyprus (some put his return down to love of the Queen Berenice), he was seized by a desire to visit the temple of Venus.[7] Tacitus goes into the history and particulars of the Paphian cult and, linking the end of the episode, like the beginning, to his main narrative, produces a sacerdotal consultation, so that Titus can rejoin his father and the army, bringing the confidence of success and glory. Similarly, when Vespasian at Alexandria, after initial scorn and incredulity, was induced to perform miracles, the event emboldened him to apply for guidance to Serapis. Tacitus subjoins an erudite disquisition on the enigmatic deity: no Roman writer, he affirms, had yet dealt with Serapis.[8]

Paphos and Serapis are frankly exotic, almost extraneous. Not so the third digression. Though lengthy, and crammed with odd and often inaccurate pieces of miscellaneous erudition, the account of the geography of Palestine, the religion and the history of the Jews, can be justified as a Sallustian excursus, not only a necessary prelude (in

---

[1] IV. 45. 3.   [2] 46–51.

[3] XIII. 44 (Octavius Sagitta); 45. 1: 'non minus insignis eo anno impudicitia magnorum rei publicae malorum initium fecit.'

[4] XV. 38 ff.   [5] XVI. 1 ff.

[6] *Hist.* III. 34 (Cremona); 72 (the Capitol); IV. 12. 2 f. (the Batavi); II. 38 (civil war).

[7] II. 2. 2: 'atque illum cupido incessit', &c.

[8] IV. 83. 1: 'origo dei nondum nostris auctoribus celebrata.'

some at least of its particulars) to the siege and destruction of Jerusalem, but a proper emulation of the great forerunner.[1] Later on the historian must have had something to say about the Dacians.[2]

The *Annales* exhibit a contrast. Of exotic interest, nothing but the brief elucidation of the monuments which Germanicus Caesar inspected in Egypt, and the disquisition on the phoenix.[3] Nor are geography and ethnography elsewhere much in the thoughts of Tacitus (though some allowance will be made for Mauretania in the missing books, and it is a question how the author of the *Agricola* would manage his Britain). On the other hand, a new type of excursus makes its appearance: Roman antiquities.

Such items cannot fail to excite curiosity. Whence do they derive? Perhaps from a single antiquarian handbook, with a guess about the authorship.[4] That can hardly be.[5] More to the point, the historian's mind and intention. Tacitus, not far on with the *Annales*, announced that, if he lived long enough, he would turn back and narrate the times of Augustus.[6] Hence (it has been suggested) a preoccupation with public law—for the central theme of the future Tacitean history (it is obvious) would be the legal and constitutional position of Caesar Augustus in the Roman State.[7]

The notion betrays several misconceptions, artistic as well as historical. An antiquarian excursus, even when related to the institutions of the Principate, has a different and a deeper justification. In the *Historiae* Tacitus generally recalls the Republic by evoking the sentiments of Romans in the vicissitudes of civil war (and he once adds his own meditations upon the strife for power in its roots and in its development).[8] The digressions in the *Annales*, so it might properly be contended, are a conscious artifice to keep alive the memory of the 'res publica'—and to advertise the author's own design, his conformity with the tradition and technique of the old annalists. Despite the monarchy—and because of the monarchy. Furthermore, given the season of the Empire at which Tacitus wrote, with grievous ignorance no doubt now prevalent among the younger generation of senators (and many were extraneous in origin, even alien), the consular would

---

[1] V. 2–10.   [2] p. 215.   [3] II. 61; VI. 28.

[4] F. Leo, *Gött. gel. Nachr.* 1896, 191 ff., followed by many, e.g. W. Theissen, o.c. 90. Leo argued that the author was somebody in the line and tradition of Ateius Capito. Against, E. Hahn, o.c. 17 ff.; 90 ff.

[5] Indeed the erudite material in XI and XII derives patently from Claudius Caesar himself, by way of the *acta*, cf. App. 40.

[6] III. 24. 3.

[7] E. Hahn, o.c. 104. Cf. the doubly peculiar notion of another writer, namely that Tacitus puts into these digressions material that would belong to the central theme of a modern historian (E. Howald, *Vom Geist antiker Geschichtsschreibung* (1944), 210 f.).

[8] II. 38.

tell them their duty, expounding without reluctance a traditional and indispensable science.[1]

The Roman year still began with consuls, but many staple items of the annalist had lapsed or had lost all virtue: no elections, no triumphs conducted by the mandatories of the Roman People, no public buildings dedicated by them or constructed. An historian might be driven back upon signs and omens. Such are in fact registered by Tacitus. Only once, however, as bare record.[2] Elsewhere the 'prodigia' stand related to the nexus of events. Thus a comet, portending evil to the rulers of mankind and adduced by Nero as grounds for dispatching to distant exile a nobleman of dynastic blood.[3] Or again, at the end of the year 64, various omens and oddities, among them the birth of a calf malformed. The *haruspices* interpreted the matter—a new head growing for the rule of the world, but abortive.[4] The narration at once plunges into the conspiracy of C. Piso. Also, and characteristic for Cornelius Tacitus, the portents after the murder of Agrippina: they were terrifying, but void of any meaning, the gods cared not, and Nero went on for many a year in all iniquity.[5]

It was late in the *Annales*, and not until the year 51 that Tacitus took to reporting signs and wonders.[6] Various reasons might be canvassed.[7] Another traditional practice was more congenial, the decease of illustrious men. The earliest instance (under the year 20) was surely not the earliest accruing since the accession of Tiberius Caesar.[8] And the choice is significant. Along with L. Volusius, a senator of consular rank, he names a Roman knight, none other than Sallustius Crispus.[9] Originally the formal vote of a public funeral put such entries on the record, whence they passed to the annalists, and the summary catalogue of a man's life and career became a regular feature. Sallust used it in moderation, while Livy was more generous, subsequent historians being quite lavish.[10]

The commemoration of deaths gives the historian scope for epi-

---

[1] cf. the indignation expressed by Vipstanus Messalla in *Dial.* 32. 3.

[2] XIII. 58 (the 'ficus Ruminalis').

[3] XIV. 22. 1 (Rubellius Plautus). It is significant that he does not bother about the famous comet in the year of Claudius' death (Dio LX. 35. 1; Pliny, *NH* II. 92). He did not need it.

[4] XV. 47. 2.   [5] XIV. 12. 2.

[6] XII. 43. 1, linked to a severe famine and the mobbing of Claudius in the Roman Forum.

[7] Some have conjectured (vainly) that Tacitus had now adopted a new written source, perhaps Pliny.

[8] Certain 'viri triumphales' such as M. Vinicius (*suff.* 19 B.C.) and M. Plautius Silvanus (*cos.* 2 B.C.) may have outlived Augustus.

[9] III. 30 (cf. p. 372).

[10] Seneca, *Suas.* VI. 21: 'hoc semel aut iterum a Thucydide factum, item in paucissimis personis usurpatum a Sallustio, T. Livius benignius omnibus magnis viris praestitit: sequentes historici multo id effusius fecerunt.'

gram, for praise or blame without subsequent appeal. Twelve necrological notices are presented in the *Annales*, devoted to twenty men.[1] Most of them belong to the first hexad (as is not inappropriate).[2] They are chronicled at the year's end, or close to it;[3] and most of the persons are grouped in pairs.[4]

Tacitus extends the range of the obituary, not stopping with the public funerals, and he brings in persons not of senatorial station: Sallustius Crispus and the last of the Antonii (the son of Iullus Antonius), who died in reclusion at the university city of Massilia.[5] The coupled names exhibit sharp contrasts of birth, talent, and character—for example, an orator and an historian, a venerable old man and a lawyer of evil life.[6]

With full freedom to choose and arrange, the author unobtrusively suggests lessons of conduct, paradoxes of survival, the gap between past and present. Like the digression, the obituary can be a marvellous device for transition. The decease of an imperial jurist evokes his rival, who was Republican by family and allegiance.[7] The next item is the funeral of Junia, the sister of Marcus Brutus.[8]

That is not all. Tacitus assigns a place of predilection to ancestors of aristocratic families still extant in his own time, like the Asinii and the Volusii, even though their attainments might not demand it.[9] His selection is always instructive. And not less his omissions. The latter are sometimes due to inadvertence, notable persons slipping away unperceived.[10] But not often. Structural or literary reasons may operate. When Pomponius Secundus, legate of Upper Germany, is awarded military distinctions (an author and an excellent man), Tacitus alludes to his other claims, leaving nothing more to be said when Pomponius came to die.[11] Of L. Vitellius he had already supplied a highly finished characterization on his first appearance in the sixth book.[12] The second hexad bore the main testimony to the performance of Vitellius as a courtier and a political manager, culminating in the speech before the Senate to advocate the marriage of Claudius and

[1] Not reckoning Tiberius, or Livia (and three other ladies)—or Arminius (II. 88. 2 f.).

[2] With three exceptions (XIII. 30. 2; XIV. 19; 47).

[3] Except for Lucilius Longus (IV. 15. 1) and L. Piso (VI. 10. 3).

[4] All the persons except six. In IV. 44 three men are grouped together—Lentulus the *augur*, L. Domitius Ahenobarbus, and L. Antonius.

[5] III. 30; IV. 44. 3.

[6] XIV. 19 (Domitius Afer and Servilius Nonianus); XIII. 30. 2 (L. Volusius and Caninius Rebilus). For Rebilus (not elsewhere attested as a lawyer) see App. 68.

[7] III. 75 (Ateius Capito, with a reference to Antistius Labeo). Cf. App. 68.

[8] III. 76.   [9] p. 302 f.

[10] No obituary in Hexad III after 61. The last is that of Memmius Regulus (XIV. 47), which presents certain peculiarities, cf. App. 60.

[11] XII. 28. 2. Tacitus therefore does not register his death—which occurred not long after, cf. W. Otto, *Philologus* XC (1935), 483 ff.   [12] VI. 32. 4.

Agrippina, after which a casual item illustrates his 'potentia' still effective in 51,[1] and he fades out quickly, no attestation of his end.

A man's character might either be depicted once and for all in a single portrait or allowed to grow out of his actions, gradually. The former procedure is the more common in the *Historiae*, and it is still used in the *Annales*. Seianus is accorded a full-length portrait, establishing him at once as the dominant character in the second half of the first hexad.[2] Poppaea Sabina makes a comparable and stylized entrance.[3] Also the conspirator C. Piso, and ironically, for he did nothing at all.[4]

Indirect characterization, however, prevails. The agents are more closely interwoven with the narrative than in the *Historiae*, more insidiously revealed by epithet, comment, or oration. Tiberius progressively discloses himself throughout the first six books.[5] Similarly both the elder and the younger Agrippina. No portrait of either, though Poppaea has one: Poppaea is not so dynamic a character. Pride, anger, energy, ferocity, and ambition are manifested in all these women say and all they do. A powerful epithet renders them, or a sharp phrase for comment in passing.[6]

Negative portrayal is no less significant. Claudius Caesar lacks shape and colour, decision and movement.[7] Afranius Burrus the Prefect of the Guard is also static, but all for the best. Military experience is the kernel of his first presentation, sound morality of the second.[8] A few scattered touches, a passive role when accused of conspiracy, inevitable condonation of dynastic murders, and inevitable presence at Neronian entertainments, and honest Burrus passes away (some spoke of poison), perishing with a soldierly reticence that echoes an aristocratic general in a lost cause.[9]

Labelling and describing his characters at entrance or exit, an historian, however impersonal his manner, could not fail to leave the imprint of his own judgement. To render the action coherent, intelligible, and dramatic, he had to intervene all the time, unobtrusive and covering up his operations variously. The technique of comment,

---

[1] XII. 42. 3.   [2] IV. 1 (cf. p. 353).

[3] XIII. 45. 1: 'erat in civitate Sabina Poppaea',. &c.   [4] XV. 48. 2 f.

[5] The annalistic record of 15 (I. 72–81) is cleverly exploited for this purpose.

[6] Thus the younger Agrippina, XII. 22. 1: 'atrox odii'; 64. 3: 'truci contra ac minaci Agrippina'; 66. 1: 'sceleris olim certa et oblatae occasionis propera'; XIII. 14. 2: 'praeceps posthac Agrippina ruere ad terrorem et minas.' On Tacitus' portrayal cf. E. Paratore, *Maia* v (1952), 32 ff.

[7] Tacitus' devices are well summarized by I. S. Ryberg, *TAPA* LXXIII (1942), 404.

[8] XII. 42. 1: 'Burrum Afranium, egregiae militaris famae, gnarum tamen cuius sponte praeficeretur'; XIII. 2. 1: 'Burrus militaribus curis et severitate morum.'

[9] XIV. 51. 1: 'Burrum intellecto scelere, cum ad visendum eum princeps venisset, aspectum eius aversatum sciscitanti hactenus respondisse: *ego me bene habeo.*' Cf. Livy, *Per.* CXIV (Metellus Scipio).

appraisement, and motivation is simple or elaborate, evasive, but sometimes unashamed.[1]

As a vehicle of comment the ideal spectator is available, with pertinent or insidious reflections. He comes in very useful at public spectacles. Soldiers to keep order while the obsequies of Augustus are being conducted, that was enough to excite general mockery, for the pretext only underlined the contrast between a monarch's orderly passing and that other scene which men knew by recollection or hearsay—Caesar the Dictator tumultuously cremated in the Roman Forum, and the loud acclamation of liberty.[2] Derision again when Claudius Caesar superintends a ceremonial expiation according to the ancient rites prescribed by one of the Kings of Rome, the sin of incest being alleged between a nobleman and his sister (they were in fact victims of a dynastic plot),[3] whereas Claudius had just been united by a newly legalized form of wedlock to his own niece. Laughter is also heard at the funeral of Claudius.[4]

Reflections of no small variety or amplitude can be interpolated in this manner. The 'prudentes' expatiate upon the whole career of Caesar Augustus. Since Germanicus was so generously depicted in his exploits, a funeral laudation would be tedious and intolerable. Tacitus neatly discharges the burden of eulogy upon anonymous well-wishers at Antioch.[5] When the Emperor Tiberius in a firm and noble discourse deprecates inordinate honouring of himself, the comment is threefold —some put his attitude down to modesty, others to distrust, others again to meanness of spirit. The last and malignant interpretation is enlarged upon.[6] Shortly after the accession of Nero, on news from the East, the duties and aptitudes of the new government are discussed in the guise of public talk at Rome.[7]

To argue that the comments and rumours with which the Tacitean exposition is so lavishly interlaced might be genuine is vain and superfluous. Some of them came from earlier writers, themselves not immune from inventiveness; whereas Tacitus' own contributions are not

---

[1] cf. I. S. Ryberg, o.c. 383 ff.; B. Walker, o.c. 33 ff. (on 'non-factual material').

[2] I. 8. 6. Note that Dio also has this item, expressed more mildly, and without the derisive comments of spectators (LVII. 2. 2).

[3] XII. 8. 1 (L. Silanus and Junia Calvina).   [4] XIII. 3. 1.   [5] II. 73.

[6] IV. 38. 5: 'optumos quippe mortalium altissima cupere: sic Herculem et Liberum apud Graecos, Quirinum apud nos deorum numero additos. melius Augustum, qui speraverit. cetera principibus statim adesse: unum insatiabiliter parari, prosperam sui memoriam; nam contemptu famae contemni virtutes.' It is premature to adduce this passage merely as evidence of Tacitean malice towards Tiberius. He is mocking conventional opinions— hence allusion to Greek deifications and stock Augustan themes (cf. Horace, Odes III. 3. 9 ff., with Hercules, Bacchus, and Quirinus). Tacitus was glad to be able to demonstrate that the language of adulation might also be used for disparagement. For 'insatiabiliter' see App. 52.

[7] XIII. 6. 2 ff.

always empty of substance. A curious item reveals how he might operate. Claudius, when about to adopt Nero although he already had a son, proclaimed more than once that nobody hitherto had secured admission to the house of the patrician Claudii in this manner.[1] On the lips of Claudius the remark was damaging and inept. Tacitus takes it from the Emperor and serves the dignity of history by assigning it to well-informed contemporaries—'adnotabant periti'.[2]

On the whole, the device is legitimate. Narrating the past, the historian puts himself in close proximity to the events, not content with the bare recital, but evoking the men of the time, whether their sentiments happen to stand on record or have to be surmised.[3] A senator knew how happy senators feel when retribution overtakes one of their number;[4] or, for that matter, it was clear that Seianus grew more arrogant when all that he saw was abasement before him.[5] And it may be, so the historian confesses, that surmise is as convincing as it is unavoidable: human nature and political situations did not wholly change.[6] A different question arises, not literary technique but historical equity—has not Cornelius Tacitus gone to unauthorized extremities of malicious insinuation, guarded but none the less culpable?

Tacitus goes still further, suppressing entirely the anonymous guarantors of popular talk or enlightened criticism. He vouchsafes direct characterization of persons and events. Sometimes by a single and deadly word. Thus Tiberius Caesar declining a proposal at his first meeting with the Roman Senate—'adroganti moderatione'.[7] Elsewhere a phrase or a sentence carries the historian's comment and betrays his contriving. Of two interlocutors Tiberius makes answer to the one, not to the other—because of deeper resentment. How did Tacitus know?[8]

These are small matters, for Tacitus will produce without any qualm a whole sequence of motives or train of argument that no witness could sponsor. Court and boudoir have no secrets for him. A minister and his sovereign stand revealed in petition and elaborate written reply, or in confrontation, each with a cordially evasive oration: thus Seianus and Tiberius, Seneca and Nero.[9] Agrippina cascades her anger on Nero in a bitter flow of words.[10] Poppaea Sabina reproaches

---

[1] Suetonius, *Divus Claudius* 39. 2 (among the instances of his 'oblivio et inconsiderantia').

[2] XII. 25. 2.

[3] cf. L. Ferrero, *Riv. di fil.* LXXIV (1946), 50 ff.   [4] VI. 10. 2; XIV. 46. 1.

[5] IV. 74. 4: 'satis constabat auctam ei adrogantiam foedum illud in propatulo servitium spectanti.'

[6] III. 29. 2: 'sed neque tum fuisse dubito qui eius modi preces occulti inluderent.'

[7] I. 8. 5.

[8] 13. 4: 'in Haterium statim invectus est; Scaurum, cui implacabilius irascebatur, silentio tramisit.' Yet he is probably right. Scaurus did not reach the consulate till 21.

[9] IV. 39 f.; XIV. 53–56.   [10] XIII. 14.

the imperial lover, with detrimental comparison of Otho.[1] Then she insists on marriage, querulous, repetitive, and sometimes using witticism: her importunacies are summarized in a single and reported discourse.[2] In fact the speech is the principal contrivance that enables the historian, cutting loose from the trammels of fact and chronology, to assert full independence, with a full commentary upon men and events.[3] Combined with his other devices, it takes Tacitus a long way in the direction of drama or prose fiction—as is manifest in his portrayal of Seneca.

The speech may be direct, indirect, or mixed. Notably effective is the exordium in reported discourse, breaking by intensity of the emotion into appeal and argumentation.[4] In the *Annales* the orations tend to be much shorter than in the *Historiae*, and the antithetic procedure of speeches in pairs is generally eschewed because it looks artificial. Relevance commands a high premium, and temptations to conventional eloquence are resisted—sometimes the more easily because of earlier indulgence. In the *Agricola* the Caledonian chieftain was allowed the decorative luxury of a long tirade before battle, with response from the Roman general. Boudicca, however, is brief and concentrated, and so is Suetonius Paullinus.[5]

Exhortation in the field or argument in secret conclave, Tacitus was free to invent. Verisimilitude is easier than veracity: how was he to deal with a speech that had been delivered before the Senate, consigned to the official archives, and perhaps published elsewhere? Accident for once permits historian and document to be confronted.

Claudius Caesar in the course of his censorship decided to admit certain of the notables of Tres Galliae to senatorial rank. Advisers in the privy council sought to restrain the Emperor. In vain.[6] He proceeded to the Curia and spoke his mind to the senators, with an oration most peculiar: it combined erudition and irrelevance, condescension and malice, good sense and outrageous fraud. The greater part of the *Oratio Claudi Caesaris* happens to be preserved, in authentic record on a bronze tablet at Lugdunum.[7]

Tacitus' operation is twofold. First, he imagines the scene in the privy council and invents the objections, indignant and highly rhetorical.[8] Next, the speech. The subject is the growth of the Roman

[1] 46.   [2] XIV. 1. Cf. further her denunciation of Octavia (XIV. 61. 2 ff.).

[3] Whole groups of people can be reported at some length, e.g. XI. 7 (barristers); 23 (the counsellors of Claudius); XIII. 26 f. (senators on *liberti*); XIV. 20 f. (a discussion about public spectacles).

[4] IV. 40. 4: 'falleris enim, Seiane.'

[5] XIV. 35 (Boudicca); 36. 1 f. (Paullinus).

[6] XI. 24. 1: 'his atque talibus haud permotus princeps.'

[7] *ILS* 212. For the modern literature, App. 40.   [8] XI. 23.

Commonwealth throughout the ages, the ever widening recruitment of the governing class. Delving deep into the past and remorseless with erudite controversy about regal Rome and monarchs of Etruscan origin,[1] the orator takes a long circuit before he comes to the point. Tacitus condenses, with little more than a generalized aphorism to recall the whole antiquarian disquisition.[2] The style of Claudius is lumbering and involved (some honour it by calling it periodic). Tacitus employs a sequence of sharp, alert phrases, and a different vocabulary.[3]

Tacitus does not confine himself to abbreviating and stylizing. He omits, transposes, and adds. Claudius obtruded his personality, showing himself petty, dishonest, and rancorous. Claudius interpellates himself, with the injunction to reveal at last his design to his senators;[4] he refers to the place of his birth;[5] he names a friend and helper from Narbonensis, but only one, of equestrian rank;[6] he alludes odiously to one of the political victims of his reign;[7] and he invokes a Gallic *cognomen* borne in the past by one of the patrician Fabii.[8]

Worst of all, the line of argument was defective or fallacious whereby Claudius sought to justify the creation of Gallic senators.[9] Tacitus strengthens and supplements it. He adds Spain as a source of provincial senators (which Claudius omitted);[10] he notes the admixture of Roman and native in the colonial foundations;[11] and he emphasizes intermarriage, the common way of life, and the provincial contribution thereto.[12] Finally, while Claudius Caesar terminated feebly with a reference to the fatigues of holding a census, Cornelius Tacitus

[1] *ILS* 212, col. i, ll. 8–26: 'quondam reges hanc tenuere urbem', &c.

[2] XI. 24. 4: 'advenae in nos regnaverunt.'

[3] cf. Ph. Fabia, *La Table claudienne de Lyon* (1929), 135 ff. But he will artfully employ a Claudian word here and there, as in other adaptations of Claudian material, cf. App. 41.

[4] *ILS* 212, col. ii, ll. 20 f.: 'tempus est iam, Ti. Caesar Germanice, detegere te patribus conscriptis, quo tendat oratio tua.'

[5] ib. 28 f., cf. p. 460 (on Lugdunum).

[6] ib. 10 ff.: 'ex qua colonia (*sc.* Vienna) inter paucos equestris ordinis ornamentum L. Vestinum familiarissime diligo et hodieque in rebus meis detineo.'

[7] ib. 14 ff.: 'ut dirum nomen latronis taceam, et odi illud palaestricum prodigium, quod ante in domum consulatum intulit, quam colonia sua solidum civitatis Romanae beneficium consecuta est.' This is Valerius Asiaticus (*suff.* 35, *II ord.* 46), from Vienna in Narbonensis.

[8] ib. 25 ('Allobrogicus').   [9] See further, p. 460.

[10] XI. 24. 3: 'num paenitet Balbos ex Hispania nec minus insignis viros e Gallia Narbonensi transivisse?' Claudius may, however, have mentioned the Balbi in the missing portion: Gades, their city, was no longer the farthest point in the western world now that Claudius had carried Rome's arms across Oceanus and conquered Britain. The boast would be characteristic—but he had already made it in the speech (col. ii, ll. 39 f.). For arguments against a mention of the Balbi, cf. K. Wellesley, *Greece and Rome*[2] 1 (1954), 28 f.

[11] XI. 24. 3: 'cum specie deductarum per orbem terrae legionum additis provincialium validissimis fesso imperio subventum est.'

[12] ib. 6: 'iam moribus artibus adfinitatibus nostris mixti.'

winds up the oration and reinforces it with a telling phrase: the measure that is now defended by appeal to the past will one day itself become a precedent.[1]

Such is the version of Cornelius Tacitus. A speech ought to dramatize a situation or depict a personality. Impeccable as he is when summarizing the stages in the progressive enlargement of the Roman State, Tacitus is ruthless towards Claudius Caesar. Next to nothing is left of the imperial orator. The reason is not far to seek. The theme was solemn and majestic, nothing less than eight centuries of Roman history—and not to be spoiled and degraded by the Claudius whom men knew (and the document revealed), trivial, inept, and wantonly impairing the validity of his own argumentation. Instead of Claudius a depersonalized imperator must speak for Rome.[2]

The Claudian fashion of discourse was highly repulsive.[3] And the Emperor's character had forfeited by now whatever interest it may have had for Cornelius Tacitus: never perhaps an enigma to be scrutinized and penetrated. Mere oddities palled, and the lack of dignity became an offence.[4]

Very different was Tiberius Caesar. To his oratorical talent, an impressive tribute from the historian—Tiberius weighed well his words, they were full of meaning or deliberately ambiguous.[5] That is to say, a style of discourse congenial as none other to Cornelius Tacitus.[6] When he operated upon a Claudian speech he found little worth preserving: language and argument had to be drastically re-modelled. Tiberius (it will seem plausible) gave much less trouble.[7] From Tiberius, as has been demonstrated, the historian twice adopts a typical and ironical word; and (in a single speech) a pair of archaisms stand out.[8] A further step may now be taken. The speeches as reproduced by Tacitus reveal and exemplify certain qualities— dignity, concentration, and irony. Some credit will go to the Emperor himself—perhaps even the authorship of certain powerful aphorisms barely needing to be stylized by Cornelius Tacitus. Thus 'offences against the gods are no concern of men', or 'princes come and go, but the Commonwealth is perpetual'.[9]

---

[1] ib. 7: 'inveterascet hoc quoque, et quod hodie exemplis tuemur inter exempla erit.'

[2] cf. Otho's peroration on the grandeur of Rome (*Hist.* I. 84. 4).

[3] For a more friendly estimate of the speech cf. now K. Wellesley o.c. 13 ff.; F. Vittinghoff, *Hermes* LXXXII (1954), 362 ff.

[4] Not but what Tacitus makes frequent use of other Claudian orations, for various purposes, notably to suggest the Emperor's peculiarities. See App. 40 f.

[5] XIII. 3. 2: 'Tiberius artem quoque callebat qua verba expenderet, tum validus sensibus aut consulto ambiguus.'   [6] p. 429.   [7] App. 39.

[8] III. 24. 4; 47. 4 ('peregrinatio'); the archaisms, IV. 38 (p. 284).

[9] I. 73. 4: 'deorum iniurias dis curae'; III. 6. 3: 'principes mortalis, rem publicam aeternam esse.'

The first hexad of the *Annales* discloses an inquirer diligent in consultation of the *acta senatus*. If the present argument carries weight, the Tiberian speeches acquire an enormous significance, not merely for the study of historical sources or literary technique, but for penetrating the psychology of the Emperor—and perhaps that of the historian. Apart from brief remarks or summaries there are five regular discourses;[1] and further, one that has not survived, namely, the despatch from Capreae that conveyed the doom of Aelius Seianus.[2]

Worthily to render that masterpiece of hidden meanings and convoluted deception was the supreme challenge—and no doubt taken up with alacrity. Tacitus was waiting for it. In Book IV occurs a petition from the minister to his sovereign (Seianus was hoping for marriage with a princess), and the Emperor's elaborate reply.[3] Seianus began with gratitude and past favours, enlarged upon a soldier's sense of duty, a friend's honest zeal to help his emperor; and he ended on a note of modest devotion—to have lived under such a prince was enough and more than enough.[4] Tiberius for his part praised the 'pietas' of his friend and asked for time, but none the less went through a whole series of arguments earnestly, asseverating his sincerity more than once. He let slip a hint of plans not yet ripe for disclosure, and he concluded with phrases of firm reassurance: no elevation was too high for the merit and loyalty of Seianus, and that in due time would be announced at Rome to Senate or People.[5]

Historians are prone to complain about their subject-matter, alleging that it is arid, refractory, or hideous, rather than frankly to avow delight in their workmanship. Tacitus in a strain of melancholy calls up for witness the annals of Republican Rome, with themes of splendour and a wide horizon.[6] A writer's genuine predilections cannot always be disguised. Tacitus revels in the speeches. Whether he adapts or has recourse to free composition, he displays vigour, confidence, even gaiety. He might elect for an oration any subject that captured his fancy; and the speeches, like the digressions, are often a clue to the writer's closest preoccupations.

In the course of the *Annales* the Tacitean idiosyncrasy or a strong personal interest comes out in many particulars—sacerdotal procedure,

---

[1] p. 283.   [2] Dio LVIII. 10. 1 ff.; Juvenal x. 71 f.   [3] IV. 39 f.

[4] 39. 4: 'nam sibi multum superque vitae fore quod tali cum principe explevisset.'

[5] 40. 7: 'ipse quid intra animum volutaverim, quibus adhuc necessitudinibus immiscere te mihi parem, omittam ad praesens referre, id tantum aperiam, nihil esse tam excelsum quod non virtutes istae tuusque in me animus mereantur, datoque tempore vel in senatu vel in contione non reticebo.'

[6] 32. 1: 'pleraque eorum quae rettuli quaeque referam parva forsitan et levia memoratu videri non nescius sum. sed nemo annalis nostros cum scriptura eorum contenderit qui veteres populi Romani res composuere. ingentia illi bella', &c.

the allocation of consular provinces, the antiquities of the Roman State, moral legislation, or the history of Gaul; and much in Tacitus' selection and presentation of material is influenced by the events of his own day, by his origin, career, and rank in society. Of these things more can be said later. For the present, one only among the preoccupations of Cornelius Tacitus needs to be singled out, as proving deliberate and personal choice: precisely the Roman orators.

XXV. ROMAN ORATORY IN THE
ANNALES

THE *Annales* embody an outline history of eloquence under the Caesars of the Julian and Claudian line, built up in diverse ways, through persons or incidents artfully introduced, through literary criticism, necrological notices, or renderings of orations. Any detail may be highly significant, or any hint.

Under Augustus the prime orators were Messalla Corvinus and Asinius Pollio, sharply in contrast for character and for style. Each carried something of the Republic into the Principate. With Messalla it was aristocratic elegance—and aristocratic opportunism. The scion of the patrician and primeval Valerii stood out among the most loyal adherents of the monarchy, not disdaining to propose in the Senate the title of 'pater patriae' for Caesar Augustus. But Asinius Pollio, the Italian *novus homo*, asserted the Republican prerogative of a free spirit and unbridled words.

Pollio and Messalla enjoyed length of days, surviving into the last decade of Augustus' reign. Chronology debarred them from the pages of the *Annales*, but only chronology. The features of those classic orators might be recalled and evoked in the words and actions of their sons or descendants. The direct line of Messalla did not outlive the last descendant of Caesar Augustus, but there were still consular Asinii among the coevals of Cornelius Tacitus.[1]

When the Senate was convoked for the first time after the death of Augustus, it discussed the ordering of the funeral. The historian selects and cites the more noteworthy proposals, naming three orators of consular station. First Asinius Gallus, then L. Arruntius, after whom Valerius Messallinus came forward with a wholly extraneous supplement: the oath of allegiance to the new ruler should be renewed year by year. The notion, he explained, was all his own—and a mark of independence and of public spirit.[2]

Messallinus was the elder son of Messalla Corvinus. He claims no great political consequence in the reign of Tiberius, and he probably died not long after the year 21.[3] None the less, the author of the

[1] p. 302.
[2] I. 8. 4. As Tacitus observes, 'ea sola species adulandi supererat'. Note also his proposal after the death of Cn. Piso (III. 18. 2).
[3] He was consul in 3 B.C., and is last mentioned in III. 34. 1. No obituary.

Annales gives him early (and emphatic) entrance, and later endows him with an oration in the Senate.[1] The matter was not of prime moment (should proconsuls be permitted to take their wives with them to the provinces?), the discussion abortive. Messallinus led off with a dignified plea in favour of that humane spirit which had already done so much to abate the harshness of ancestral usages among the Romans. Now Tacitus designates Messallinus as one who in eloquence reflected his father.[2] The speech is no doubt intended to convey and reinforce that pleasing persuasion: nobility, candour, and grace were held characteristic of Messalla Corvinus.[3] No evidence, however, that the son came up to the parent in performance or reputation.

His brother Cotta Messallinus was probably a greater orator by far, and he was still alive late in the reign of Tiberius;[4] but Tacitus required Cotta Messallinus for another role, that of the degenerate *nobilis* subservient to power.[5] The last of this illustrious line took financial subsidy from Nero. Introducing the year 58 with a Messalla as consul along with the Emperor, Tacitus adds a comment to put the reader in mind of historical perspective and of certain other things: a few old men could still remember that his great-grandfather the orator had held the consulate with Augustus for colleague.[6]

Such were Messalla Corvinus and his posterity. Asinius Gallus, however, inherited in ample measure the 'ferocia' of the intractable Pollio. Gallus intervened in the senatorial debate after the consecration of Augustus, abrupt and embarrassing, with an awkward interrogation levelled at Tiberius Caesar.[7] Along with Gallus are named three other orators of the first rank: each, in one way or another, said the wrong thing, and some by inadvertence. L. Arruntius and Aemilius Scaurus also deserve prominence for political and family reasons; the author reverts to them, as to Gallus, again and again.[8] The third, Q. Haterius, was a *novus homo*. He carried no weight in matters of state, and even his exuberant oratory was now a spent force. Not that his introduction at this point is adventitious[9]—and he will figure later

---

[1] III. 34.

[2] ib. 1: 'ineratque imago paternae facundiae.' Cf., in similar language, Ovid, *Tristia* IV. 4. 3 ff.

[3] *Dial.* 18. 2; Quintilian X. 1. 113.

[4] VI. 5. 1. By his full name, M. Aurelius Cotta Maximus Messallinus: identical with the consul of 20 (M. Aurelius Cotta), despite the doubt of Groag in *PIR*[1], A 1488. Cf. App. 63.

[5] p. 574.

[6] XIII. 34. 1. Tacitus extenuates, referring to 'paupertas innoxia'.

[7] I. 12. 2.

[8] See further, p. 381. Scaurus (*PIR*[2], A 404) was 'oratorum ea aetate uberrimus' (III. 31. 4) —but lazy, cf. Seneca, *Controv.* x, *praef.* 2 f. Seneca does not mention L. Arruntius (*PIR*[2], A 1130).

[9] He grovelled before Tiberius, and was protected by Livia (I. 13. 6).

as an example of loathsome subservience.[1] Nor will his descendants be omitted.[2] What is most significant is the obituary notice, linking Haterius to a man named for praise, a son of Asinius Gallus.[3] Tacitus, whose own manner insisted upon weight and depth and concentration, passes judgement, severely, on one whose popularity was enormous and ephemeral: Haterius was all fervour and fluency, but he would not give time and labour to style, and only style abides.[4] It was right to condemn Haterius.[5]

Haterius was a very old man, one of the few who had 'seen the Republic';[6] and it was his habit to declaim about Cicero and liberty.[7] Tacitus eschews those facts, for they were irrelevant and would have marred the unity of his pronouncement. The Republic and its orators could be illustrated, if he wished, in some more telling fashion— a notable name, the style of discourse, or some theme that recalled a classical debate.

In the year 55 B.C., when the consuls tried to promote a law against extravagance, Hortensius, the adept of luxury and splendour, took up the challenge. He orated upon the greatness of an imperial city, extolling the value of display and magnificence.[8] The arguments of Hortensius recur in the *Annales*, on the lips of Asinius Gallus.[9] Like Hortensius, Gallus prevailed—and not least through the friendly complicity of a pleasure-loving audience.[10]

---

[1] III. 57. 2.

[2] viz. Q. Haterius Agrippa (*cos.* 22), Q. Haterius Antoninus (*cos.* 53). For the former, I. 77. 3; II. 51. 1; III. 49. 2, cf. 51. 1; VI. 4. 4; the latter, XIII. 34. 1.

[3] IV. 61: 'Asinius Agrippa, claris maioribus quam vetustis, vitaque non degener.' No word or act of his had been registered by Tacitus.

[4] ib.: 'monimenta ingeni eius haud perinde retinentur. scilicet impetu magis quam cura vigebat, utque aliorum meditatio et labor in posterum valescit, sic Haterii canorum illud et profluens cum ipso simul exstinctum est.' For the last phrase cf. Cicero, *De oratore* III. 28: 'profluens quiddam habuit Carbo et canorum.' Tacitus uses the adjective 'canorus' nowhere else.

[5] For his volubility cf. Seneca, *Controv.* IV, *praef.* 7 ff., with Augustus' comment 'sufflaminandus est'. Tacitus' verdict is confirmed (if need be) by the total silence of Quintilian.

[6] Haterius (*suff.* 5 B.C.) was coeval with Messalla Corvinus, having been born c. 63 B.C.: nearly ninety when he died (Jerome, *Chron.*, p. 172 H, under the year 24), which was in 26 (IV. 61). Haterius had a link by marriage with the dynasty, as Tacitus knew, cf. the remark about his son (II. 51. 1).

[7] Seneca, *Suas.* VI. 1 f.; VII. 1.

[8] Dio XXXIX. 37. 3: ὁ γὰρ Ὀρτήσιος φιλαναλωτὴς ἐν τοῖς μάλιστα ὢν ἔπεισεν αὐτούς, τό τε μέγεθος τῆς πόλεως ἐπεξιών, καὶ ⟨αὐτοὺς⟩ ἐπί τε τῇ οἴκοι πολυτελείᾳ καὶ ἐπὶ τῇ μεγαλοφροσύνῃ ἐπαινῶν, καταβαλεῖν τὴν γνώμην, ἅτε καὶ συναγωνιστῇ τῶν λόγων τῷ βίῳ σφῶν χρώμενος.

[9] II. 33. 2: 'auctu imperii adolevisse etiam privatas opes, idque non novum, sed e vetustissimis moribus: aliam apud Fabricios, aliam apud Scipiones pecuniam; et cuncta ad rem publicam referri, qua tenui angustas civium domos, postquam eo magnificentiae venerit, gliscere singulos.'

[10] ib. 4: 'facilem adsensum Gallo sub nominibus honestis confessio vitiorum et similitudo audientium dedit.'

Close upon this incident Hortensius' own grandson comes on the scene, but not in pomp and splendour.[1] An oration brings his claims and his misfortunes to the notice of Princeps and Senate. Political vicissitudes had prevented him from inheriting or acquiring wealth, popularity, or the eloquence that should go with his name and descent; Augustus stepped in with a subsidy, and Hortensius reared four sons, but now he needed more money. Such was the plea, expressed with some dignity. It did not move Tiberius Caesar. His response was abrupt and unfriendly, and the line of the great Hortensius lapsed into a shameful destitution.

A different artifice enables Tacitus to set on record the names of the most important 'patroni' early in the reign of Tiberius. When Cn. Piso, the legate of Syria, was indicted, three advocates agreed to undertake his defence. But Piso had approached five others. Tacitus furnishes all the names.[2] Consulars, with one exception—an orator of great promise who was a grandson of Asinius Pollio on the maternal side.[3]

The prosecution did not stand in need of weighty names. Three friends of Germanicus Caesar, who had served on his staff in the eastern lands, took the leading role under the claim of 'pietas', and eager for vengeance—P. Vitellius, Q. Servaeus, and Q. Veranius. The speech of Vitellius was a notable performance, and all three received priesthoods for reward.[4] Vitellius later came to grief as a partisan of Seianus.[5] Servaeus likewise had transferred his allegiance. Though not deeply implicated with Seianus, he was put on trial, the angry Emperor insisting, and turned informer.[6] Veranius, who in the meantime had gone on to signalize himself by launching an indictment for *maiestas* against the brother of Cn. Piso, may (or may not) have evaded the fate that overtook his erstwhile associates, the 'comites' of Germanicus.[7]

The record of prosecutions allows the historian to satisfy a personal interest by introducing characters of no great political consequence— and some remembered for their talents and devices in the schools of rhetoric at Rome. In the late years of Augustus a new style came into

---

[1] II. 37 f. (M. Hortensius Hortalus). [2] III. 11. 2.

[3] M. Claudius Marcellus Aeserninus (*PIR*[2], C 928). Praetor in 19, not attested as consul, presumably dying before that predictable honour.

[4] III. 19. 1. For the speech of Vitellius (13. 2) cf. Pliny, *NH* XI. 187.

[5] V. 8.

[6] VI. 7. 2 ff. The remarkable *cognomen* which the family later advertises looks like a protest: observe [Servaeus In]noc(ens) and Q. Servaeus Innocens (*suffecti* 82 and 101).

[7] In IV. 21. 2, where the *Codex Mediceus* has 'pisonemque gravius', one could read 'Pisonemque Veranius', cf. R. Syme, *JRS* XLVI (1956), 20. The standard texts carry Lipsius' emendation 'Pisonem Q. Granius'. Veranius' son, quaestor in 37, *cos.* 49, has some place in history (p. 386).

fashion, which was largely associated with Cassius Severus, an aggressive and objectionable person of humble antecedents—and a great orator.[1] He got into trouble with the government. The Senate decreed his banishment at the urgent insistence of the Princeps: the first time that 'maiestas' was used to incriminate the written or spoken word.[2] Tacitus very pertinently records it, and he can mention Cassius Severus once again.[3]

This man had many successors during the Principate of Tiberius, ill-famed informers or prosecutors—and now for the most part on the side of the government. At the outset, under the year 15, the historian deliberately inserts a highly stylized picture of a 'delator', archetypal and prophetic.[4] A certain Caepio Crispinus adopted the profession. Lacking birth, wealth, or character, he insinuated himself into the confidence of a cruel emperor by secret denunciations, and duly went on to attack persons of the highest distinction. Thus he won power and influence with one man, and general detestation. And with this guide to show the way, men rose from poverty to riches; instead of being despised, they were now feared; they contrived destruction against others, and in the end brought it upon themselves.[5]

Junius Otho and Bruttedius Niger soon turn up, active and successful in prosecuting a proconsul of Asia. The former, who had kept a school of rhetoric for a long time, came into the Senate through the patronage of Seianus. Base though that beginning was, his cynical audacity was baser still. Bruttedius, however, was endowed with fine talents. Had he embraced honourable pursuits, he might have achieved the highest distinction. But Bruttedius was impatient. He incited himself to outstrip equals, and then superiors, to overleap even his own ambitions. That has also been the ruin of many men of merit (the historian adds), risking all in the appetite for success and scorning to wait for what comes safely in due season.[6]

---

[1] In Quintilian's catalogue (x. 1. 116, cf. xii. 10. 11) he is the only Augustan orator named after Messalla and Pollio.

[2] I. 72. 3, cf. Dio lvi. 27. 1 (a.d. 12).

[3] iv. 21. 3: 'sordidae originis, maleficae vitae, sed orandi validus.'

[4] I. 74. 1 f.: 'nec multo post Granium Marcellum praetorem Bithyniae quaestor ipsius Caepio Crispinus maiestatis postulavit, subscribente Roman⟨i⟩o Hispone, qui formam vitae iniit, quam postea celebrem miseriae temporum et audaciae hominum fecerunt. nam egens ignotus inquies, dum occultis libellis saevitiae principis adrepit, mox clarissimo cuique periculum facessit, potentiam apud unum, odium apud omnes adeptus dedit exemplum quod secuti ex pauperibus divites ex contemptis metuendi perniciem aliis ac postremum sibi invenere.'

[5] The archetypal prosecutor characterized in I. 74. 1 f. appears to be Caepio Crispinus, not Romanius Hispo; cf. App. 37. The historian was not oblivious of the contemporary consulars A. Caepio Crispinus and Ti. Caepio Hispo (*PIR*², C 150; E 83). For the *nomen* and *cognomen* of Romanius Hispo, *JRS* xxxix (1949), 14 f. 'Hispo' is very rare: observe Hispulla, wife of Corellius Rufus (Pliny, *Epp.* iii. 3), and Calpurnia Hispulla (iv. 19; viii. 11). Ti. Caepio Hispo (*suff.* c. 101) was perhaps an orator (App. 25, cf. 27).   [6] iii. 66.

The names are not fortuitous. Speakers of vigour, point, and ingenuity, Bruttedius and Otho are frequently cited (and sometimes praised) by a critic who knew the schools and canons of rhetoric, namely the elder Seneca.[1] The language and comment of Tacitus is ominous, foretelling the evil destiny of ambitious talents. The catastrophe of Seianus was waiting for them.[2]

Fulcinius Trio went further. Notorious already before his first presentation (so it is said), he lays the indictment against Scribonius Libo, a case which Tacitus sets in sharp prominence.[3] Profits and advancement ensued.[4] Trio was also first in the field against Cn. Piso.[5] And, although friends of Germanicus at once took a hand, thrusting him into a minor role, Trio did not go empty away. Tiberius Caesar promised support in the career of honours, but spoke an admonition: Trio must be careful not to ruin his gifts by haste and violence.[6] Trio took heed—and was not forgotten. He next emerges in possession of the consulate, colleague of Memmius Regulus when Seianus was destroyed.[7] Though Trio had been a partisan of Seianus, he passed that ordeal, and weathered the quarrel with Regulus.[8] Both, however, were in peril early in the next year, being accused of mutual connivance by the detestable Haterius Agrippa, the son of the old orator.[9] Trio could never feel secure. In the fourth year from the fall of Seianus, faced by a prosecution, he took his own life.[10]

'Delator' and consul, Fulcinius Trio earns a place in history, conspicuous among those whom Tiberius favoured and promoted, but succumbing to retribution ultimately.[11] Fortunate was Domitius Afer that he came to no such end. Avid for distinction at any cost, he undertook to prosecute a great lady in the year 26—no less than Claudia Pulchra, daughter of a niece of Augustus.[12] Afer succeeded, and the next year he set upon her son. The historian's comment is savage. Nobody, he says, was surprised that Afer after long years of

---

[1] Bruttedius four times, Otho more than a dozen times.

[2] The fate of Bruttedius happens to be certified (Juvenal x. 83). Otho (and Caepio Crispinus) may have recurred in Book V.

[3] II. 28. 3: 'celebre inter accusatores Trionis ingenium erat, avidumque famae malae.'

[4] 32. I.   [5] III. 10. I.   [6] 19. I: 'ne facundiam violentia praecipitaret.'

[7] He came to his suffect consulate (July 1, 31) from the governorship of Lusitania, where he is attested on January 22 (*AE* 1953, 88).

[8] V. 11. Dio alludes to him, but does not name him, in his narrative of Seianus' destruction (LVIII. 9. 3).   [9] VI. 4. 2.

[10] 38. 2; Dio LVIII. 25. 2 ff. (with no awareness that he was the consul of 31).

[11] Trio is not named by the elder Seneca: various reasons might be canvassed. But for Tacitus (and the two notices in Dio), he would be only a name, not a person. Tacitus might well have introduced Trio, not Caepio, as the master 'delator' (cf. II. 28. 3), if he had not decided to put the type earlier, in 15 (I. 74. 1), for reasons of his own, though the 'maiestas' items in that prosecution were dropped.

[12] IV. 52. 1: 'is recens praetura, modicus dignationis et quoquo facinore properus clarescere.'

impoverishment and an ill use of his recent gains was ready for further acts of infamy.[1] However, the condemnation of Claudia Pulchra elevated Afer among the foremost for eloquence. The Emperor's verdict ratified popular fame: Domitius Afer, so said Tiberius Caesar, was an orator in his own right.[2] Tacitus himself passes judgement upon Afer's career as an advocate (renown rather than good repute), and tells how he persisted in old age, his talent in a decline, but unwilling to give up and be silent.[3] An anticipation of the obituary notice, which only comes later, when more than thirty years have elapsed.[4]

Further mention of Domitius Afer must have occurred, not once but several times, in the lost books of the *Annales*. Menaced by Caligula, he escaped harm by an exhibition of nauseating flattery and won the consulate.[5] But he could apparently be courageous. He held his ground against Claudius Caesar in the Senate, he even defied the imperial freedmen.[6] Afer was incomparably the most impressive of all orators in that age, and worthy to rank with the ancients.[7] Not only forensic success and vigour of eloquence. Afer was a great wit. His 'dicta' circulated in book form.[8]

Coeval with Domitius Afer, but not (like Afer) surviving long enough to attest his own decrepitude, was the orator Passienus, who inherited the name, the wealth, and the influence of Sallustius Crispus.[9] Subtle and elegant, he adorned the life of court and capital, signalized by a second consulate and by marriage with two princesses.[10] Equal in guile to the great Vitellius, Passienus could captivate or elude Caligula.[11] The second of his marriages proved fatal: he was poisoned, they said, by Julia Agrippina.[12] But of all this nothing is preserved in Tacitus, only a witticism about Caligula.[13]

---

[1] IV. 66. 1: 'nullo mirante quod diu egens et parto nuper praemio male usus plura ad flagitia accingeretur.'   [2] 52. 4: 'suo iure disertum.'

[3] ib. 4: 'mox capessendis accusationibus aut reos tutando prosperiore eloquentiae quam morum fama fuit, nisi quod aetas extrema multum etiam eloquentiae dempsit, dum fessa mente retinet silentii impatientiam.' Cf. Quintilian on the decline of Afer, with somebody's witticism, 'malle eum deficere quam desinere' (XII. 11. 3).

[4] XIV. 19.   [5] Dio LIX. 19. 1 ff.   [6] Jerome, *Epp.* LII. 7. 3; Quintilian VI. 3. 81.

[7] Quintilian XII. 11. 3; X. 1. 118: 'quem in numero veterum habere non timeas.'

[8] id. VI. 3. 42.

[9] *PIR*[1], P 109. His full nomenclature, 'C. Sallustius Crispus Passienus' (*AE* 1924, 72); originally son of L. Passienus Rufus (*cos.* 4 B.C.), not (as erroneously in *Rom. Rev.* (1939), 384) of Sallustius Crispus. He was *suff.* 27, *II ord.* 44.

[10] viz. Nero's aunt, Domitia (*PIR*[2], D 171) and Nero's mother.

[11] *Schol.* on Juvenal IV. 81 = Suetonius, ed. Roth (1898), p. 290: 'interrogatus haberetne sicut ipse cum sorore consuetudinem, *nondum* inquit, quantumvis decenter et caute.'

[12] ib. His death would surely have been registered by Tacitus. Therefore early in 47, at the latest. It cannot fall in 48, as R. Hanslik, P–W XVIII, 2097 f. (the article contains other defects and errors).

[13] VI. 20. 1: 'unde mox scitum Passieni oratoris dictum percrebuit neque meliorem

Consular grandees might be a reminder of the old days of the Republic when eloquence was exhibited for renown, in the defence of clients, in open competition for the honours awarded by the sovereign people—and not, so it was averred, for any profit in money: the Empire converted oratory into a sordid profession. In the year 47 the iniquities of rapacious and dishonest advocates, causing public scandal, led to a debate in the Senate, with a clamour to revive an exceedingly ancient law that prohibited fees.

The consul designate spoke for the law.[1] He made solemn appeal to antiquity; he recalled the Augustan prime with Messalla Corvinus and Asinius Pollio, and examples yet more recent. But there was opposition—from Suillius Rufus, Cossutianus Capito, and others, precisely those whose malpractices were under attack. The historian takes it upon himself to equip them with an apologia.[2] To aspire to fame as one's sole reward, they said, was presumptuous. A barrister had to expend time, effort, and money—and nobody went in for any activity without some prospect of personal advantage. They were quiet decent men pursuing a respectable profession—and that profession would be ruined if rewards and incentives were abolished. All very well for Pollio and Messalla—the magnates could afford to look down on forensic remuneration, secure in the profits they amassed during the Civil Wars, from the bounty of Antonius, and from the generosity of Augustus. And other orators named for virtue were sons of the amply endowed. If the Republic were invoked, everybody knew how much certain political orators were paid for their harangues.

Tacitus expounds with a barrister's skill, with sympathy even, arguments which he feels bound to describe as 'minus decora'. Those arguments prevailed with Claudius Caesar, and a modest scale of fees was duly established.

Tacitus has evoked the shining names and examples on the roll of public eloquence. Lesser lights are not omitted. Bare mention or concise annotation will specify some consular whose talent is not elsewhere attested, a prosecutor remembered for a single speech of classic excellence, or a barrister with whose theoretical treatise the historian was no doubt familiar.[3]

umquam servum neque deteriorem dominum fuisse.' Other sayings: Seneca, *De ben.* I. 15. 5; Pliny, *Epp.* VII. 6. 11. Seneca, his friend, and a good judge, says: 'Crispus Passienus quo ego nil novi subtilius in omnibus rebus, maxime in distinguendis et curandis vitiis' (*NQ* IV, *praef.* 6).   [1] XI. 6.   [2] 7.

[3] Thus C. Vibius Marsus (*suff.* 17), 'inlustris studiis' (VI. 47. 2); M. Vinicius (*cos.* 30, II ord. 45), 'comptae facundiae' (VI. 15. 1); D. Laelius Balbus (*PIR*[1], L 28), 'truci eloquentia' (VI. 48. 4). There was a famous speech of Laelius Balbus (Quintilian X. 1. 24). For a full list of the prosecutors in *Ann.* I–VI see R. S. Rogers, *Criminal Trials and Criminal Legislation under Tiberius* (1935), 212 ff. Further, observe Votienus Montanus of Narbo

His virtuosity manipulates the types and specimens of oratory. As the importance of senatorial business declined, Tacitus discovered a duty and a melancholy satisfaction—he would illustrate by example what language and style of debate was requisite in the high assembly, and he duly singles out two men of character and integrity, Cassius Longinus and Thrasea Paetus, whose manner and sentiments recalled the ancient days.[1]

These two consulars may, or may not, have enjoyed rank and celebrity among the orators of the day. Perhaps not: their arguments made appeal to the past, and Tacitus deliberately suggests an old-fashioned note in their discourses.[2] Cassius and Thrasea speak with logic, restraint, and dignity—virtues more and more rare in the Senate of imperial Rome.

For the ceremonial exuberance of official spokesmen the author of the *Annales* will not spare more than a brief and blighting comment in transit.[3] He disdains a full exposure. Panegyrists might be turned to ridicule had there not been the superior material of anger and irony. A senatorial historian could not fail to argue that the rule of the Caesars degraded 'bonae artes' by encouraging the men of smooth persuasion or truculent invective.

Both types are portrayed, the diplomat and the 'delator', through their oratorical performances. The behaviour that in the patrician Valerii of the early Principate might be excused and palliated as a graceful concession to changed times soon degenerated into the base arts of a courtier or the guileful operations of a political manager.

Entering the Senate House one day, L. Vitellius craved permission to speak on a matter of serious public import.[4] The Princeps, he said, who laboured under the heavy burden of governing the whole world, would not be free to devote an undivided attention to the general welfare unless he were relieved from anxiety in his home and family. For a censor, what more appropriate support and solace than wedlock? A wife is a man's partner in happy or adverse seasons, the repository of his confidences, the custodian of his infant children. Claudius Caesar deserved to be married. He had been noted for the uniform regularity of his conduct from youth upwards: pleasure and vice had no place among his habits.

(*PIR*[1], V 674), described as 'celebris ingenii vir' (IV. 42. 1): he wrote on rhetoric (Seneca, *Controv.* IX. 6. 18—not noticed in *PIR*). Also the *rhetor* Volcacius Moschus (*PIR*[1], V 621), who had died in exile at Massilia (IV. 43. 5).

[1] XIV. 43 f.; XV. 20 f. Cf. previously the short speech of M. Lepidus (III. 50).
[2] p. 355.
[3] XVI. 2. 2: 'nova ubertate provenire terram et obvias opes deferre deos, quaeque alia summa facundia nec minore adulatione servilia fingebant, securi de facilitate credentis.'
[4] XII. 5. 3: 'ipse curiam ingreditur, summamque rem publicam agi obtestans', &c.

After which preamble, and a pause for the joyous approbation of senators, the orator went on.[1] He spoke the name of Agrippina, catalogued her virtues, rendered thanks to divine providence that she was available, being a widow, and welcomed the opportunity to establish, once and for all, a model for matrimony among the Caesars. To marry one's niece (it might be objected) was something new at Rome. But not at all anomalous: customs change with time and circumstance, and this innovation will in due course become a regular usage.

Such was the line of argumentation devised for L. Vitellius by Cornelius Tacitus.[2] The oration does not merely reproduce the smooth Vitellian artifices, with many a touch of irony and various felicities of verbal malice.[3] It recalls something that Valerius Messallinus had said about the comforts of matrimony;[4] and it terminates in parody of Claudius Caesar, echoing the final phrase from the historian's version of the speech about the Gallic notables.[5] Caesar's minister or a governor abroad, expounding his mandate, might slip into the manner as well, through inadvertence or design.[6] Vitellius was an old familiar friend of Claudius and very artful.[7] Did he not deserve, like another of that company, to be designated as 'homo Claudiana lingua disertus'?[8]

Skill and subtlety will also be evident when Tacitus renders a cruder style, that of the 'delatores'. The venal but persuasive advocates introduced in the year 47, namely, Suillius Rufus and Cossutianus Capito, were to be heard of again. Suillius, indeed, had already

---

[1] 6. 1.

[2] How much belongs to Tacitus and how much to Vitellius? Speeches of senators would not normally be reproduced in full in the *acta*, one would think (cf. p. 188). But this was a special (and state) occasion: some of the speaker's language might pass into the *senatus consultum* (cf. App. 40). Note also how a consul designate proposes the betrothal of Nero to Octavia 'haud disparibus verbis ac nuper Vitellius' (XII. 9. 2).

[3] Thus 'gravissimos principis labores, quis orbem terrae capessat', for which compare Seneca, *Ad Polybium* 7. 2: 'ex quo se Caesar orbi terrarum dedicavit'; the phrase 'maritandum principem' (the verb is unique in Tacitus) is wilfully prosaic and suggests the Augustan law 'de maritandis ordinibus'; the orator speaks of Agrippina's 'sanctimonia', a word used by Tacitus only of elderly Vestal Virgins (II. 86. 1; III. 69. 6); and 'provisu deum' is very choice, occurring in no other author. (Agrippina was providentially a widow —if, as alleged, she had got rid of Passienus Crispus.)

[4] XII. 5. 3: 'quod porro honestius censoriae mentis levamentum, quam adsumere coniugem?' Cf. III. 34. 2: 'quod honestius quam uxorium levamentum?'

[5] XII. 6. 3: 'morem accommodari prout conducat, et fore hoc quoque in iis quae mox usurpentur.' Cf. XI. 24. 7: 'inveterascet hoc quoque', &c.

[6] Compare the edict of Fabius Persicus the proconsul of Asia, describing the Emperor's sense of justice and his universal benevolence (*SEG* IV, 516 A). For Claudian language embodied in a *senatus consultum* (*ILS* 6043) see App. 40.

[7] Seneca, discussing 'adulatio', alludes to Munatius Plancus and calls him 'artifex ante Vitellium maximus' (*NQ* IV, *praef.* 5). Congratulating Claudius on the *Ludi Saeculares*, Vitellius exclaimed 'saepe facias' (Suetonius, *Vit.* 2. 5).

[8] Seneca, *Apocol.* 14. 2, alluding to P. Petronius (*suff.* 19), a 'vetus convictor' of Claudius.

reached the consulate.[1] Not for long was he to enjoy the prestige and comforts of success. In the early years of Nero, forfeiting influence but not abating his ferocity, Suillius became vulnerable. Seneca was one of his enemies, Seneca was still at the height of his power— and Suillius provoked him, it was alleged, by the things he kept on saying.

Suillius, the notorious accuser now forced to speak in his own defence, could not fail to be a fine and dramatic subject. Tacitus might have allotted him a full-length speech at the trial. Instead, he anticipates: he takes the objectionable remarks formerly uttered by Suillius and casts them into the form of an invective against Seneca.[2]

That man, said Suillius, had a feud against the friends of Claudius, the prince who had consigned him to exile (and very rightly). He envied anybody whose eloquence was vigorous and active, not (like his own) academic and nourished upon the callow admiration of the young. Suillius had been the quaestor of Germanicus Caesar, whereas Seneca committed adultery with one of his daughters: the seduction of a princess is a graver offence than taking honest fees from willing clients. And how did the precepts of philosophy help a man to a royal fortune? At Rome Seneca angled for legacies; Italy and the provinces he sucked dry through extortionate usury. But Suillius' fortune was of his own gaining, and moderate. Sooner would he incur prosecution or condemnation than capitulate before the prosperous upstart.

The invective allows Tacitus free scope and intense concentration. He can present the reader with a living specimen of the eloquence of the prosecutors—strong, savage, and unbridled.[3] And he does it again, with even more gusto. Nero in the year after the Pisonian conspiracy resolved to destroy Thrasea Paetus and Barea Soranus. Not that the tyrant required much encouragement, but Tacitus supplies an instigator. He ushers Cossutianus Capito into the presence of Caesar, with a chronicle of the misdemeanours of Thrasea.[4]

Cossutianus quickly passes on to a diatribe against enemies of the monarchy, appealing in direct speech to Nero—Thrasea has acquired the stature of a Republican party leader, a new Cato for obstinacy and contumacy, and the sectaries who imitate Thrasea in their bearing, grim and austere, are a visible reproach to the gay demeanour of the prince. The attack proceeds with short stabbing phrases, violent antithesis, and wild exaggeration. Not to hold Poppaea a goddess (he exclaims) shows the same spirit that refuses to swear allegiance to

---

[1] cf. *PIR*[1], S 700, with *AE* 1949, 250. Tacitus had already brought him in a long way in advance (IV. 31. 3).

[2] XIII. 42.

[3] Observe, for example, the violent metaphor 'corrumpere cubicula principum feminarum' (ib. 3).

[4] XVI. 22.

the *acta* of Divus Julius and Divus Augustus—contempt for religion and contempt for the laws.[1] Cossutianus goes on to invoke the lessons of conventional or tainted history, alludes to the harm that Republicans had inflicted upon the Republic, and, after an epigram—'they use the cry of freedom as a pretext to destroy government, and if they succeed, they will attack freedom itself'—[2] he concludes by asking one thing only of Nero, that the Senate be left to decide.

When the high assembly met to witness the trial of Thrasea and ratify his condemnation, Cossutianus opened the indictment, followed and surpassed by Eprius Marcellus. Eprius began by solemnly affirming that the highest interests of the Commonwealth were at stake: 'summam rem publicam agi'.[3] He continued with other hypocritical arguments, asserting that Thrasea was a traitor to Roman tradition and religion—'contra instituta et caerimonias maiorum'.[4] The speech was savage, and so was the orator, 'torvus ac minax'.[5]

The name of Eprius and the scene brought Tacitus back to the familiar atmosphere of the *Historiae*. The bland and elegant Vibius Crispus will also emerge, the vigorous M. Regulus with the destruction of three consulars for his début in public life, the booming and theatrical Galerius Trachalus.[6] It is the period of orators known to Tacitus—and some his admired instructors. The cycle of eloquence from the great Augustans to the author's own time seems complete— and the *Dialogus* had pronounced the epitaph upon Roman oratory.

One name, however, remains, that of the dominant literary figure in the age of Caligula, Claudius, and Nero. The author of the *Annales* would be primarily concerned with the character, policy, and actions of Annaeus Seneca as a minister of state; but he could not fail to essay somewhere or other an appreciation of his style and talent. Seneca wrote the laudation for Nero to deliver at the obsequies of Claudius. Tacitus is equal to the scene.[7] A characteristic device evokes the emotions of the audience, from earnest attention during the recital of the ancient renown of the *gens Claudia* to open mockery

---

[1] ib. 3: 'eiusdem animi est Poppaeam divam non credere cuius in acta divi Augusti et divi Iuli non iurare. spernit religiones, abrogat leges.'

[2] ib. 4: 'ut imperium evertant, libertatem praeferunt: si perverterint, libertatem ipsam adgredientur.'

[3] 28. 1, the phrase used by L. Vitellius (XII. 5. 3).

[4] Compare Eprius defending the 'antiquitus instituta' against Helvidius Priscus (*Hist.* IV. 8. 1).

[5] 29. 1.

[6] Also Silius Italicus (*cos.* 68), Paccius Africanus (*suff.* c. 66)—and Cingonius Varro (*des.* 68) who wrote the oration for Nymphidius (Plutarch, *Galba* 14), and was killed by Galba. Cf. further, p. 101 f. and App. 26.

[7] XIII. 3.

when they heard the deceased emperor commended for sagacity and forethought. And the old men present had something to say—no ruler before Nero had to depend upon borrowed eloquence. The fiction is barely disguised. It permits Tacitus to pass in review the salient features in the attainments of all the Caesars. The Dictator was peer and rival of the foremost orators. Augustus' style of eloquence was ready and flowing, befitting a 'princeps'. Tiberius was a master in the art of weighing well his words, they were full of meaning, and he could be ambiguous at will. Even the mental derangement of Caligula could not impair his force; and when Claudius delivered a set speech, you would not look in vain for elegance.

The brief powerful sentences convey an expert's summing up. And it is an expert who comments at this juncture upon the oration composed by Seneca: it showed much polish, for Seneca had an elegant talent, and well suited to the taste of that age.[1]

Nero's address to the Senate, announcing the programme of a constitutional monarchy, is sketched in a brief sequence of contrasting phrases.[2] A little later comes a reference to frequent orations from the Emperor emphasizing 'clementia'—Seneca (says Tacitus) wanted to demonstrate the excellence of his instruction, or indeed advertise his own talent.[3] Tacitus does not choose to reproduce an official speech. For various reasons—and perhaps such conventional and inevitable themes as the authority of the Senate, the precedents of the Augustan Principate, and a monarch's profession of mercy had been adequately expounded when Caligula came to power, and when Claudius.[4]

There was a better way to convey the style and character of Seneca, subtle and unimpeded. The Emperor at last became tired of tutelage, and lent a ready ear to detraction: Seneca (so his enemies alleged) went on piling up riches, putting even the Emperor in the shade by the splendour of his mansions and gardens; he affected a monopoly of eloquence, he had now taken to writing verse with assiduity, to outdo Nero; the other pastimes of the prince he would deprecate or deride; but Nero was old enough to do without a tutor, while tradition and pedigree would teach him all he needed.[5]

[1] ib. 1: 'quamquam oratio a Seneca composita multum cultus praeferret, ut fuit illi viro ingenium amoenum et temporis eius auribus accommodatum.' The remark befits one who presumably shared some of Quintilian's opinions (x. 1. 125 ff.).

[2] 4.

[3] 11. 2: 'clementiam suam obstringens crebris orationibus quas Seneca testificando quam honesta praeciperet, vel iactandi ingenii, voce principis vulgabat.'

[4] cf. the professions of Caligula (Dio LIX. 6. 1), and his successor's oath 'per Augustum' (Suetonius, *Divus Claudius* 11. 2). Claudius in his message from the Praetorian camp announced (how could he not?) that he would be a προστάτης, not a τύραννος (Josephus, *BJ* II. 208).

[5] XIV. 52. 2 f.

Seneca sought audience with Nero. His discourse was elegant (and not less the response, for both speakers had to be diplomatic and evasive: the pupil even surpassed the master).[1] A prince, Seneca suggested, might graciously permit a minister to retire when his work was done. There were valid and Augustan precedents. His modest privilege it had been to instruct Nero in the art of speech. In return he had acquired high rank, with opulence beyond his needs, and at variance with his professions. The recompense was both embarrassing and invidious. He now asked to be relieved of the burden, and gladly would he surrender his great wealth.

The sentiments are highly appropriate to an author of ethical treatises who in fact insisted that mere deprivation of riches does not spell impoverishment to a wise man.[2] More than this, hints or echoes can be caught of an authentic Seneca. He duly cites 'exempla' from history.[3] One platitude is unashamed, nothing less than the 'journey of life'.[4] Another familiar image is accompanied by a deprecatory phrase, as is the fashion of preachers and sermonizers.[5] He can also coin an epigram.[6] And he does not disdain the crude and vigorous.[7]

The language is vivid and rhetorical, with personification of abstractions and metaphors of pomp and splendour. Thus wealth is presented as a thing that dazzles and blinds.[8] Seneca calls up a picture of his own 'novitas' all radiant on parade among the ancient emblems of the *nobiles*.[9] And the philosopher takes his soul to task, reproaching it for proud and ostentatious behaviour.[10]

---

[1] 53–56.

[2] Seneca, *De vita beata* 26. 4: 'sapienti quisquis abstulerit divitias omnia illi sua relinquet.' The whole chapter is instructive.

[3] XIII. 53. 3: 'utar magnis exemplis nec meae fortunae sed tuae. abavus tuus Marco Agrippae Mytilenense secretum, C. Maecenati urbe in ipsa velut peregrinum otium permisit.' The former example is bad history.

[4] 54. 2: 'in hoc itinere vitae.' Cf. *De brevitate vitae* 9. 5: 'hoc iter vitae adsiduum et citatissimum.'

[5] 53. 4: 'studia, ut sic dixerim, in umbra educata.'

[6] Maecenas' 'peregrinum otium' in the heart of Rome (53. 3).

[7] 'nec me in paupertatem ipse detrudam' (54. 3).

[8] 54. 3: 'traditis quorum fulgore praestringor.' For the collocation of the two words cf. *Ad Polybium* 12. 3 (on Claudius): 'fulgor eius illos, ut nihil aliud possint adspicere, praestringet.' There is only one other instance of 'fulgor' in all Tacitus, in the letter of Seianus (IV. 39. 2); also 'praestringo' used metaphorically (*Hist.* I. 84. 3, in the speech of Otho).

[9] 53. 5: 'inter nobilis et longa decora praeferentis novitas mea enituit?' For the expression cf. *De clementia* I. 9. 10: 'tantumque agmen nobilium non inania nomina praeferentium, sed eorum qui imaginibus suis decori sunt.' For 'novitas mea', Sallust, *Jug.* 85. 14 (Marius); Cicero, *Ad fam.* I. 7. 8.

[10] ib.: 'ubi est animus ille modicis contentus? talis hortos extruxit et per haec suburbana incedit et tantis agrorum spatiis, tam lato faenore exuberat?' The reference to 'suburbana' is not general (as Furneaux ad loc.), but precise, to Seneca's Nomentanum (*Epp.* 104. 1; 110. 1; Pliny, *NH* XIV. 51). And, as for 'tam lato faenore', the historian knew the story about Seneca's loans in Britain, cf. App. 69.

Of Seneca's sermons the most eloquent and most notorious necessarily defied the historian. Seneca when life ebbed called for his
secretaries and dictated a philosopher's last message to the world. It
was published. Tacitus therefore eschewed a rendering.[1] He cites,
however, Seneca's words of consolation to the wife who wished to
share his end—highly antithetical and characterized by close ob-
servance of prose rhythm.[2]

Seneca was the greatest figure in Latin literature since the days of
Augustus, the creator of a fashion, the embodiment of an epoch. The
next generation canvassed his qualities. Educators were disposed to
be especially critical. The judicious Quintilian, in his catalogue of
orators, reserves Seneca for separate treatment, and explains what
was wrong.[3] Seneca's style, he held, was seductive and corrupting;
Seneca was too clever—he lacked discrimination; by his 'dulcia vitia'
he was a bad influence on the young.

The genius of Seneca was copious and versatile, manifold his productions. Tacitus could allude to some of them. Thus an indirect
reference to the treatise *De clementia* dedicated to Nero, and the
faintest of hints about the tragedies.[4] But he could not mention
Seneca's pasquinade on Divus Claudius. That was alien to the
dignity of history.[5]

Literature had no place by its own right alone in the chronicle of
the Roman State. In the third year of Tiberius Caesar died the poet
Ovid, far from Italy, with no necrological entry from the author of the
Annales.[6] Ovid could perhaps have stood in historical record as a
victim of the 'auctoritas' of Caesar Augustus, among those men who,
without sentence by court of law or the Senate's decree, understood
that they had to go.[7]

The aristocratic Aemilius Scaurus was in the front rank of speakers:
that he also wrote tragedies, however, would scarcely be registered,

---

[1] xv. 63. 3: 'quae in vulgus edita eius verbis invertere supersedeo'.

[2] ib.: 'vitae, inquit, delenimenta monstraveram tibi, tu mortis decus mavis: non
invidebo exemplo. sit huius tam fortis exitus constantia penes utrosque par, claritudinis
plus in tuo fine.' Norden suggested that these are the actual words of Seneca, his αὐτοφωνία
(*Die Antike Kunstprosa* I (1898), 332).   [3] Quintilian x. 1. 125 ff.

[4] XIII. 11. 2 ('clementia' in official orations); 52. 3 (Seneca's 'carmina').

[5] Likewise the *Satiricon*, which, however, might be implied in Tacitus' tribute to
Petronius, XVI. 18. 1: 'ac dicta factaque eius quanto solutiora et quandam sui neglegentiam
praeferentia, tanto gratius in speciem simplicitatis accipiebantur.' Cf. H. Bogner, *Hermes*
LXXVI (1941), 223 ff., citing 'novae simplicitatis opus' from the poem in *Sat.* 132.

[6] Jerome (*Chron.* p. 171 H.) has 17, perhaps a year too early.

[7] cf. III. 24. 3: 'exilium sibi demonstrari intellexit.' This was D. Silanus, one of the lovers
of the younger Julia (banished in A.D. 8). Ovid's disaster, about the same time, was not
wholly unrelated to that scandal. Ovid's relegation, however, was enjoined (or confirmed)
by an *edictum* of Augustus (*Tristia* II. 135 f.).

had not a 'delator' exploited his allusions to a legendary tyrant.[1] When Tacitus inserts a reference to the works of another consular dramatist, Pomponius Secundus, it is justified by what precedes, namely the military distinction earned by Pomponius.[2] In the story of the Pisonian conspiracy the poetry of Lucan was doubly relevant—the initial grievance when Nero from envy prevented him from displaying his talent, and the act of suicide which Lucan performed with recital of his own lines about the dying soldier.[3]

Oratory and legal eminence ('illustres domi artes') were the civilian qualification for public honours. Two juristic luminaries adorned the age of Augustus, diverse in character, teaching, and political success. The one, Ateius Capito, astute and subservient to power, got the consulate. Recording his decease, Tacitus is able to circumvent obstacles and commemorate the better man—whom Caesar Augustus deliberately passed over.[4] Even a great orator may have to be omitted from the *Annales* if he is not involved with politics;[5] and even history is irrelevant unless composed by a man of senatorial station. The octogenarian Livy passed away in the same year as Ovid, unnoticed;[6] and it is no concern of Tacitus that an historical author of some fame and consequence died about the middle of Nero's reign, namely Aufidius Bassus.[7]

Not that Cornelius Tacitus could be debarred from alluding to the art and practice of history, with suitable tribute to predecessors, if he so desired. The death of the imperial minister Sallustius Crispus evokes the name of his great-uncle.[8] Digression or oration would permit much more. An excursus in Book IV sets out the superior merits of the Republic as against the Empire.[9] It forms a skilful transition to the case of Cremutius Cordus, prosecuted by two clients of Seianus: he had written in praise of Marcus Brutus, he styled Cassius the last of the Romans. Cremutius in his own defence speaks with dignity, vindicating the freedom of speech and opinion.[10] He cites examples of candour, licence, or governmental toleration from the recent past—which enables Tacitus to pay a handsome compliment to Livy, to allude to the histories of Asinius Pollio and the

---

[1] VI. 29. 3.   [2] XII. 28. 2.

[3] XV. 49. 3; 70. 1.   [4] III. 75, cf. App. 68.

[5] viz. Julius Africanus, cf. *Dial.* 15. 3: 'Afer aut Africanus'; Quintilian X. 1. 118; XII. 10. 11.

[6] Jerome, *Chron.* p. 171 H.   [7] Seneca, *Epp.* 30.

[8] III. 30. 2: 'C. Sallustius, rerum Romanarum florentissimus auctor.'

[9] IV. 32. 1 (cited above, p. 320).

[10] 34 f. The speech is all Tacitus. Cremutius' writings were not the sole, or even the main, charge against him: the testimony of Seneca is here valuable (*Ad Marciam* 1. 2 ff.; 22. 4). Cf. G. Columba, *Atene e Roma* IV (1901), 361 ff.; R. S. Rogers, *Criminal Trials and Criminal Legislation under Tiberius* (1935), 86 f.

memoirs of Messalla Corvinus; and certain poets can be noticed who impinged upon political struggles in the closing epoch of the Free State.

The oration of Cremutius ends with a firm appeal to the verdict of posterity.[1] When a maker of verses asserted that he would conquer time and oblivion, nobody minded. Historians (for such was the custom) generally affected more modesty, with dignified emphasis upon the importance or the utility of their task. If an historian's preface announced no overt and personal claim to immortality, some hint or hope might be inserted elsewhere, unobtrusively, in the guise of generous testimony to the virtues of another writer, or by the visible and avowed emulation of illustrious predecessors.

Mere contemporary applause did not mean that an orator would be remembered. Such is Tacitus' dismissal of Q. Haterius.[2] Incomparably superior to Haterius was Domitius Afer. When Afer died in 59 he was long past his prime; the record of the last dozen years had not admitted his name; and, like L. Vitellius, he might have slipped away without commemoration at the end, for his character had been delineated long since. But Tacitus can use this bad man. He can match him with a poet or an historian.

According to a speaker in the *Dialogus*, Afer could have no advantage in personal repute or in enduring fame over the dramatist, Pomponius Secundus.[3] In the *Annales* Servilius Nonianus is available for contrast by the peculiar coincidence of his death in the same year as Afer. Orator against historian: their talents were equal, but as men they were poles apart.[4]

Tacitus admires Servilius for his 'elegantia vitae'. The identical quality, 'elegantia morum', is discovered in Pomponius Secundus at his first introduction in the pages of the *Annales*.[5] These labels carry a strong note of social and moral approval. More remarkable, however, than anything else in all the works of Tacitus is the summing-up of Pomponius (in a disguised obituary).

When legate of Germania Superior, Pomponius earned the *ornamenta triumphalia*: no great accession, says Tacitus, to the glory of one whom posterity holds in such honour for his poetical works.[6] The remark quietly subverts traditional values and the supreme good of

---

[1] 35. 3: 'nec deerunt, si damnatio ingruit, qui non modo Cassii et Bruti set etiam mei meminerint.'

[2] 61 (p. 324).   [3] *Dial.* 13. 3.

[4] XIV. 19: 'ille orando causas, Servilius diu foro, mox tradendis rebus Romanis celebris et elegantia vitae, quam clariorem effecit, ut par ingenio ita morum diversus.'

[5] v. 8. 2. It is also used of Junius Blaesus (*Hist.* III. 39. 2). Compare further the whole portrayal of the 'elegantiae arbiter', Petronius (XVI. 18. 2).

[6] XII. 28. 2: 'decretusque Pomponio triumphalis honos, modica pars famae eius apud posteros in quis carminum gloria praecellit.'

the Romans. Not warfare, the service of the State, or the governing of the nations. The consular historian awards the palm to literature.[1]

The performance of men like Pomponius and Afer might well evoke comparison with classical models. Reflecting upon the history of morality at Rome, Tacitus affirms that not all things were better in previous generations. The present epoch, he continues, has an achievement in polite arts that will deserve to be imitated by posterity.[2]

[1] This praise for poetry is more striking than Cicero's exaltation of the 'magnus orator' over the 'minuti imperatores' (*Brutus* 256).

[2] III. 55. 5: 'nec omnia apud priores meliora; sed nostra quoque aetas multa laudis et artium imitanda posteris tulit. verum haec nobis ⟨in⟩ maiores certamina ex honesto maneant.' A Virgilian echo should be noted here, cf. *Georgics* II. 174: 'res antiquae laudis et artis.' Observe also the historian's (ostensible) depreciation of his own theme—'nobis in arto et inglorius labor' (IV. 32. 2). What he wished to suggest, but could not claim, was 'in tenui labor: at tenuis non gloria' (*Georgics* IV. 6).

XXVI. THE STYLE OF THE *ANNALES*

THE supreme master of the spoken word gave up oratory and turned to another occupation, discovering there what others might in poetry, a 'sanctior et augustior eloquentia'.[1] The art of history had reached the term of a long development, and it recalled its origins by numerous conventions of style and structure. Tacitus proposed to honour those conventions, and to put a renewed emphasis on what was old and traditional.

On first comparison with the *Historiae*, the *Annales* are less eloquent and fluent, much more condensed, austere, and enigmatic. In short, Sallust rather than Livy.

The Tacitean idiosyncrasy can be clearly traced from its inception to maturity. The *Dialogus* with its Ciceronian style (the result of choice and propriety) stands apart from the reckoning, for it belongs to a distinct form of literature. The *Agricola* and *Germania* provide the starting-point. In each may be recognized the typical manifestations of Latin imperial prose—pointed, rhetorical, and ornate. While the *Agricola* embodies a blend of styles (yet not a farrago), the *Germania* is more uniform (as the subject demanded) and hence more Sallustian, with some influences from Seneca.[2] Both monographs betray the author in search of a style. The *Germania* can often be obscure and precious, while the *Agricola* exhibits from time to time the contrasted defects of harshness and redundance.[3]

The language of the *Historiae*, for all its eloquence, splendour, and force, does not represent the ultimate Tacitus. There is a clear line of advance. It attests an increasing divergence from the normal and the conventional, an insistent predilection for unusual grammatical forms or constructions, for a vocabulary vivid, powerful, solemn, and archaic.[4]

The choice and changing frequency of a few words will suffice for testimony.[5] 'Glisco' makes its first appearance in the *Historiae*: in the

---

[1] *Dial.* 4. 2.

[2] p. 198. For the excess of preciosity and rhetorical devices see J. Perret in his edition (Budé, 1949), 33 ff.; *Rev. ét. anc.* LVI (1954), 98 f. For poetical words, App. 42.

[3] cf. J. G. C. Anderson in his edition of the *Agricola* (Oxford, 1922), lxxxv ff. Note 'quies et otium' used twice (*Agr.* 6. 3; 21. 1). For synonyms and hendiadys (later diminishing steadily) cf. K. Jax, *Studi in Onore di U.E. Paoli* (1956), 423 ff.

[4] As demonstrated by the pioneer studies of E. Wölfflin, *Philologus* xxv (1867), 92 ff.; xxvi (1867), 92 ff.; xxvii (1868), 113 ff. (reprinted in *Ausgewählte Schr.* (1933), 22 ff.). See also E. Löfstedt, *Syntactica* II (1933), 276 ff.; *JRS* xxxviii (1948), 1 ff. For the vocabulary of the *Hist.*, App. 46, cf. 51.

[5] cf. the table in App. 47. Also the negative evidence of words discarded after the earlier works (App. 44 ff.).

Annales it suppresses 'cresco'. A heavy preference goes to frequentative verbs, and to the simple verb against the compound.[1] The historian now takes up the archaic 'apiscor'. Further, he conceives an affection for 'patro' and 'reor', he almost abandons 'invenio' for 'reperio'. As is fitting, both 'priscus' and 'vetustus' rise sharply; 'senecta' prevails against 'senectus', while 'cupiditas' is driven out by 'cupido'.

Not only the colour and atmosphere of words, but their shape and sound. The verbal substantive of action ('turbator', 'cupitor') appeals by reason of its concentrated energy.[2] Certain terminations conveyed power and majesty. A Roman could not fail to respond to the forms in '-tudo', which evoked the solemn splendour of the ancient tragedians.[3] Running level with 'claritas' in the *Historiae*, 'claritudo' wins dominance in the finished Tacitean style.

Another weighty ending ('-mentum') had been favoured by vigorous orators of the old Republic.[4] Sallust knew its value. He produced 'dehonestamentum'. Who could resist among the Roman historians? The word enjoyed a fortune.[5] And the form encouraged new coinages, or a fashion.[6] The dignified 'cognomentum' occurs once only in the *Historiae*, but seventeen times in the *Annales*.[7]

A negative test avails. It is doubly valid. Tacitus is careful to avoid excess: the *Annales* eschew some of those impressive words which he had admitted for adornment in the *Historiae*.[8] At the same time the author keeps away from some that had been domiciled long since in standard prose.[9]

The effects to which the Tacitean idiom aspires are no mystery—the writer will be swift and splendid, intense and majestic. All manner

---

[1] Thus 'dictito', 'imperito', 'certo'. And, for simple verbs, observe 'ago', 'teneo', 'trado', 'traho', 'turbo' in the *Lexicon Taciteum* of Gerber–Greef.

[2] For specimens first attested in Tacitus, among them three that are apparently not even to be found in late, scholiastic, and ecclesiastical authors, see App. 51.

[3] These words have 'dignitas', says Gellius (XVII. 2. 19), discussing 'sanctitudo': for a list, G. Schönfeld, *De Taciti studiis Sallustianis* (Diss. Leipzig, 1884), 4 ff.; W. Kroll, *Glotta* XXII (1934), 5. The pompous Trajan actually used 'animi mei integritudo' (*Dig.* XXIX. 9. 1). The word is unique in Latin.

[4] C. Gracchus used 'inhonestamentum' and 'dedecoramentum' (Isidorus, *Orig.* II. 21. 4).

[5] Sallust, *Hist.* I. 55. 22; I. 88. Cf. Tacitus, *Hist.* II. 87. 2; IV. 13. 2; *Ann.* XII. 14. 3; XIV. 21. 4. Note also Ammianus XXVI. 6. 16, and see further *TLL*.

[6] For examples in Sallust, Livy, and Tacitus cf. G. Schönfeld, o.c. 8 f. Add 'imitamentum', first attested in the *Annales* (III. 5. 2; XIII. 4. 1; XIV. 57. 3).

[7] Messalla Corvinus liked it (Seneca, *Suas.* II. 17).

[8] Thus 'hortamentum' (Sallust and Livy) and 'turbamentum' (Sallust), each once in the *Hist.* (IV. 18. 2; I. 23. 1): dropped from *Ann.*

[9] Thus 'firmamentum' (only *Hist.* V. 8. 3): the word is frequent in Cicero. And no example of 'incrementum'. Similarly for words in '-tudo': the *Annales* forgo 'amplitudo', and Tacitus nowhere allows 'turpitudo' (both Ciceronian).

of devices contribute.[1] Tacitus likes his words to be hard and fierce, heavy and ominous. The selection develops almost predictably— poetic, archaic, and elevated. Despite marked preferences, he is abundant and varied, avoiding monotony (Sallust was not always successful), and risking innovations. Many Tacitean words are portentously rare;[2] and the choice vocabulary is supported by free extensions of meaning.[3]

The theme demanded many synonyms for death, and Tacitus responds. Tiberius Caesar, though he dissembled to the end, was not able to deceive the court doctor, who ascertained that the Emperor was nearing the ultimate term—'eum adpropinquare supremis'.[4] And, when death was beyond doubt (having been accelerated), the extinction of Tiberius is registered in a phrase which, plain and majestic, stands unique in the literature of the Latins—'sic Tiberius finivit'.[5]

Even a slight modification in the form of a familiar term may lack parallel. Nobody else thought of varying 'bella civilia' with 'bella civium'.[6] That being so, it may not be fanciful to suppose that some of the unusual expressions that emerge for the first time in Tacitus, and seldom or never again, might be of his own creation.[7] He conjures up these striking locutions when an especial emphasis is required: for example, Nero is labelled as 'incredibilium cupitor'.[8] When such turns occur (especially in character sketches or obituary notices) they suggest Sallust, himself the great 'novator verborum'.[9] L. Volusius is designated 'primus adcumulator' of the huge family fortune;[10] as L. Vitellius was the archetype of all flatterers, so he is stamped for ever as the 'exemplar adulatorii dedecoris';[11] and the angry Agrippina mocks the 'professoria lingua' of Annaeus Seneca.[12]

What Tacitus avoids can be no less instructive. The grand manner is hostile to the anecdote, it deprecates sordid or humorous items, and refuses the precise detail of scandalous revelations. Tiberius Caesar was notoriously addicted to strong drink.[13] That failing elicits no

---

[1] For a catalogue see H. Furneaux 1 (ed. 2, 1896), 42 ff., based mainly on A. Draeger, *Über Syntax und Stil des Tacitus*[3] (1882).

[2] App. 51.

[3] Note especially the verb 'traho': nearly five columns in the *Lexicon Taciteum* of Gerber–Greef.

[4] VI. 50. 2. The only instance of this verb in the *Ann.*   [5] ib. 5.

[6] I. 3. 7, and thrice in the *Hist.*, cf. E. Löfstedt, *Syntactica* I[2] (1942), 123.

[7] Caution is requisite, cf. App. 51.

[8] XV. 42. 2. The word had been employed effectively in XII. 7. 2: 'repertus est unus talis matrimonii cupitor.'

[9] Gellius I. 15. 18: 'novatori verborum Sallustio' (referring to a critic's contention that Sallust wrote 'loquentia', not 'eloquentia' in *Cat.* 5. 4).

[10] III. 30. 1.   [11] VI. 32. 4.   [12] XIII. 14. 3.

[13] Suetonius, *Tib.* 42; Pliny, *NH* XIV. 144 f.

comment from Tacitus.[1] And, if the consequences of wine have to be alluded to, all that is trivial or vulgar will be shunned.[2]

Bodily appearance is evoked only in the most general fashion, like the beauty of Poppaea Sabina or the impressive build of Domitius Corbulo.[3] Tiberius, however, tempts the historian to go further. Not merely 'grim-visaged and smiling his perfidiousness':[4] Tacitus risks a startling picture (the diction is very choice) of the recluse in his repellent old age—tall but emaciated and bent, his face scarred and blotched, and he had no hair left.[5]

Bald men were common enough at Rome. Only one of them will be admitted to the dignified pages of the senatorial annalist, and the word 'calvus' is eschewed: instead, a poetical periphrasis alludes to the denuded summit of a Roman emperor—'nudus capillo vertex'.[6] Another exception speaks for itself. It is Agrippina, truculent and merciless, who derides Afranius Burrus for his deformity—'trunca scilicet manu'.[7] When Tacitus makes comment upon a repulsive and maleficent cripple called Vatinius, he declines to say more than 'detorto corpore'.[8]

Vatinius the ex-cobbler is honoured with the elevated designation of 'sutrinae tabernae alumnus'; and a pompous circumlocution commonly skirts the procedure and equipment of manual occupations. Technical phrases are barred, especially foreign words. The poison which the Athenians used may not be named.[9] Nor can 'philosophus' and 'tyrannus' secure more than one entry.[10]

The terminology of the Roman administration was awkward or monotonous. Tacitus varies or evades it.[11] For 'proconsul' he can revive the archaic 'praetor';[12] he will go to any lengths or contortions

---

[1] Unless it was in Book V (banquets at Capreae).

[2] No 'ebrii', 'vinosi', or 'vinolenti' in the *Ann.* The superior word 'temulentus' occurs four times; also 'vino incalescere' and 'per vinum et epulas incalescere' (XI. 37. 2; XIV. 2. 1).

[3] XIII. 45. 3 (Poppaea); 8. 3 (Corbulo).

[4] IV. 60. 2: 'torvus aut falsum renidens vultu.' Cf. Silius, *Punica* XIII. 375: 'obtutu torvum contra et furiale renidens'; Ammianus XIV. 9. 6: 'torvum renidens.'

[5] IV. 57. 2: 'quippe illi praegracilis et incurva proceritas, nudus capillo vertex, ulcerosa facies ac plerumque medicaminibus interstincta.' The word 'praegracilis' is exceedingly rare.

[6] ib. The baldness of Valerius Asiaticus (Dio LX. 29. 5) is naturally eschewed, like that of the Emperor Galba in the *Hist.* (p. 189).   [7] XIII. 14. 3.   [8] XV. 34. 2.

[9] XV. 64. 3: 'venenum quo damnati publico Atheniensium iudicio exstinguerentur.' Similarly 'Mesopotamia' has to be explained (as though the word had not already occurred in the previous chapter)—'campis qui Euphrate et Tigre inclutis amnibus circumflui Mesopotamiae nomen acceperunt' (VI. 37. 3).

[10] XIII. 42. 4; VI. 6. 2.

[11] As Sallust had done, cf. W. Kroll, *Glotta* XV (1927), 299. Also Livy, e.g. 'comitia consulum' (four times in Book IV—but never again).

[12] I. 74. 1: 'Granium Marcellum praetorem Bithyniae.' But it is almost too much thus to style the imperial legate governing Hispania Citerior—'praetorem provinciae L. Pisonem' (IV. 45. 1). An admiral even becomes 'praefectus remigum' (XIII. 30. 1).

rather than denominate the governor of an imperial province by the
exact title; and the convenient but prosaic neologism 'praeses' slips in
only twice.[1] Again, 'praefectus praetorio' is successfully avoided.

A number of time-honoured appellations belonging to the structure
of the Roman Commonwealth might have seemed unobjectionable.
Yet Tacitus insists on paraphrasing 'leges annales' and modifying
'virgo Vestalis', or 'sella curulis'.[2] Deliberate avoidance of technical
precision may sometimes be a cause of perplexity, for example 'ius
adipiscendorum in urbe honorum'.[3]

Since the historical prose of the Latins owes so much in language,
structure, and sentiment to a revulsion from political oratory, it will
be no surprise that Tacitus tries to avoid the words that inevitably
recall Cicero, like 'infinitus'.[4] For the same reason he will be sparing
with superlatives and with certain types of abstract nouns. Ever on the
alert for fraud, he shuns the noble and ethical terms that had much
too often been employed by the politicians: he seldom needs them save
for calculated derision.[5]

Next to the tired and tarnished words, the feeble, trivial, or
patently colloquial. The preposition 'propter', so Tacitus decided,
was not good enough for serious prose: he insists upon 'ob' without
exception in the *Annales*.[6] Again, never 'subito', always 'repente'.[7]
He saw that there was something wrong with 'culpo';[8] he gave up
'nequaquam';[9] and he conceived a strong distaste for 'parvus'—
except when applied to infants, it occurs only twice in the *Annales*.[10]
Likewise various ugly words, never allowed unless to damn some
odious character. The adjectives ending in '-osus' demand attention,
most of them pejorative.[11] Sallust (it appears) had coined the repulsive
'discordiosus'.[12] Tacitus is sparing and rigorously selective.[13]

Tacitus had no good opinion of the exuberant orator Haterius. The

---

[1] VI. 41. 1; XII. 45. 4. Pliny used it (*Pan.* 70. 4), and Trajan (*Epp.* X. 44).

[2] II. 36. 3: 'leges quae sua spatia exercendae candidatorum industriae quaerendisque
aut potiundis honoribus statuerint'; I. 8. 1: 'virgines Vestae'; II. 83. 1: 'sedes curules.'

[3] XI. 23. 1. It clearly ought to mean the *latus clavus*, cf. XIV. 50. 1: 'venditata ab eo
munera principis et adipiscendorum honorum ius.' For his deliberate imprecisions (especially in military matters) cf. L. Valmaggi, *Riv. fil.* XXXVI (1908), 372 ff.

[4] Twice in the *Ann.*, viz. III. 25. 2 and 53. 4 (a dispatch of Tiberius). Similarly 'in-
credibilis' only three times there, but 'singularis' in none of his works.

[5] pp. 412 ff. with App. 66.

[6] E. Löfstedt, *Philologischer Kommentar zur Peregrinatio Aetheriae* (1911), 219 ff.

[7] ib. 169.

[8] Four times in *Hist.*, never in *Ann.*

[9] Only in I. 12. 2—after ten cases in the *Hist.*

[10] III. 31. 2; IV. 32. 1. He prefers 'modicus' (forty times in *Ann.*); and 'exiguus' is not in
Ann.

[11] But not all, cf. Gellius IV. 9. 1 ff., rebutting the opinion of Nigidius Figulus.

[12] *Jug.* 66. 2.

[13] For some avoidances and rejects see the lists in App. 42 ff.

son of Haterius is thrown into sharp relief—'libidinosus' juxtaposed with the rare and poetical 'marcidus'.[1] Tacitus was distrustful of ethical pretensions. In a society seamed with falsity it is only a philosopher, Egnatius Celer, who carries the label 'perfidiosus'.[2]

The style has many facets: vivid or unusual words for dramatic effect in the narration, but a much quieter vocabulary in the speeches.[3] Tacitus has an acute sense for shades and atmosphere. Not merely in what he admits or discards. It is his habit to operate by echo and allusion, most insidiously, evoking resemblances of scene or person. Sometimes it is the daring expression, the shock of which compels belief.[4] Elsewhere by contrast the word may be ordinary or conventional, but of rare occurrence in the *Annales*: repeated, it conveys a parallel, not always benevolent.

The portrayal of Tiberius runs through the whole gamut. That emperor's demeanour is 'inclementia'—which suits inexorable forces of nature, or the angry gods.[5] At the other extreme of style, 'crudelis'.[6] Neither word occurs elsewhere in all the writings of Tacitus. Nor is any other person in the *Annales* described as 'cunctabundus' or saddled with 'tristitia'.[7]

Normal words acquire a strange emphasis. The 'taciturnitas' of the secretive ruler can be matched only by the 'taciturnitas' of those who kept silent a great conspiracy.[8] In the *Annales* 'comparatio' is used only of the comparison between Tiberius and his predecessor;[9] only Tiberius betrays 'haesitatio';[10] and 'dubitatio' in three instances out of four is attached to the ruler—twice of his attitude, once in his epistle to Seianus.[11]

Tiberius (so the historian proclaims) cherished dissimulation as his prime virtue.[12] He also cherished Aelius Seianus.[13] The verb ('diligo') occurs only once again in the *Annales*, denoting a man's affection for his wife.[14] Seianus in petition to his master and friend affirmed that he had been thought worthy of a 'coniunctio' with the house of the

---

[1] VI. 4. 4: 'somno aut libidinosis vigiliis marcidus.'

[2] XVI. 32. 3: 'animo perfidiosus subdolus.'

[3] For words admitted only in the speeches see App. 50.

[4] cf. B. Walker, *The* Annals *of Tacitus* (1952), 57 ff.

[5] IV. 42. 3. Cf. *Aen.* II. 602 f.: 'divum inclementia, divum | has evertit opes.' Apart from Tacitus, first applied to persons by Fronto, p. 53 N = Haines I, p. 102.

[6] VI. 4. 4 (in the passage about Haterius Agrippa).

[7] I. 7. 5; 76. 4. Also 'suspicax' (13. 4), elsewhere once only in Tacitus (III. 11. 2).

[8] I. 74. 4; XV. 54. 1. Similarly 'recondo'—only of Tiberius (I. 7. 7; IV. 57. 2) and of Seianus (I. 69. 5).

[9] I. 10. 7; 76. 4.

[10] I. 80. 3.

[11] I. 7. 7; III. 41. 3; IV. 40. 6.

[12] IV. 71. 3.

[13] VI. 51. 3: 'dum Seianum dilexit timuitve.'

[14] XV. 63. 2 (Seneca and Paullina).

Caesars.[1] Tiberius in his equivocal answer takes up 'coniunctio'. But also, reassuring his minister, he uses 'excelsus'—as previously in an oration.[2]

It is no surprise that the loyal and subservient L. Vitellius should echo Claudius Caesar and parody his manner.[3] Verbal devices and felicities link together several friends and ministers of the Caesars. Vitellius told the Senate that Claudius needed 'adminicula' to help him bear the grievous burden of empire; and Seneca in his address to Nero craves an 'adminiculum', like an old soldier or a weary traveller.[4] The modest Seianus conventionally deprecates any desire for the 'fulgor honorum', and Seneca avows his eagerness to be protected from the 'fulgor' of resplendent fortune.[5] Suillius Rufus in peril and adversity casts in the face of Seneca his 'subita felicitas'—and Seneca, asking to be superseded, admits to 'felicitas mea'.[6] Suillius had been 'praepotens', and so was Seneca.[7] The same context also designates Seneca as 'praedives'—which is singularly appropriate, uncommon, but not remote and poetical.[8]

So far the selection of words, the common as well as the rare. In his ambition to be strong, subtle, and dignified, the historian is helped not only by single words, but by choice of grammatical forms, and even by orthography.[9] And he invokes a wide range of devices to ensure variety.[10]

Like Virgil, Tacitus has a propensity towards anything that obviates the need for prepositions. He exploits the dative case to a notable degree—deliberately running counter to a strong tendency in contemporary speech;[11] and some of his ablatives are extremely audacious.[12] Hence welcome aids to a tightly packed or rapid phrase.

All for brevity, Tacitus is alert for any chance to discard the

---

[1] IV. 39. 3: 'ut coniunctione Caesaris dignus crederetur.'

[2] IV. 40. 7, cf. III. 53. 3 (on the rank and duties of the Princeps). No other instances in the *Ann.*

[3] p. 331.

[4] XII. 5. 3; XIV. 54. 2. Ciceronian: elsewhere only in *Dial.* 2. 2.

[5] IV. 39. 2; XIV. 54. 3. Like 'splendor' (only in *Dial.* 37. 4; 38. 2; *Hist.* I. 84. 3—an oration) the word had probably been tarnished through conventional usages.

[6] XIII. 42. 4; XIV. 53. 2.   [7] IV. 31. 3; XV. 64. 4.

[8] Juvenal x. 16: 'Senecae praedivitis hortos.' The satirist also applies the word to the proverbial wealth of Licinus (XIV. 305)—and Suetonius (*Tib.* 49. 1) uses it for the wealthy and unamiable Sulpicius Quirinius: cf. *Ann.* III. 48. 2: 'sordidamque et praepotentem senectam.' For further echoes and repetitions see App. 52.

[9] e.g. the perfect in '–ere', or the unassimilated compound forms (hence 'a⟨d⟩fluentia', not 'a⟨f⟩fluentia', should be read in III. 30. 2).

[10] See the thorough analysis of G. Sörbom, *Variatio sermonis Tacitei aliaeque apud eum quaestiones selectae* (Uppsala, 1935).

[11] E. Löfstedt, *Syntactica* I² (1942), 185; 190; 197; 212.

[12] ib. 293 f.; 301. Note especially the impersonal ablative absolute (A. Draeger, o.c. 87; E. Löfstedt, *Syntactica* II (1933), 281).

auxiliary verb. The imperfect tense is heavy with meaning, the participle becomes omnicompetent, and he likes to extend the function of the historic infinitive from vivid acts to the portrayal of states of mind.[1] The omission of words and connectives goes to ruthless extremes for the sake of speed, concentration, and antithesis; and stages in a sequence of thought or action are suppressed, baffling translation (but not hard to understand).[2]

The rounded oratorical period with balanced members and a foreseen conclusion was totally unsuited to historical exposition.[3] Tacitus if he wishes can compose a long development, as when, after a prologue cut up into short sentences, he carries the origins of the monarchy at Rome from the Battle of Philippi in a vast sweep to the established and accepted power of Caesar Augustus.[4] Or again, an elaborate structure, as at the outset of Book XIII when the murder of M. Silanus is explained.[5]

Tacitus seldom bothers to write a genuinely periodic sentence. Whereas Sallust was abrupt and truncated, stopping before the reader expected,[6] Tacitus goes ahead with preternatural prolongations, piling on new items, often loosely co-ordinated, eked out with a participle or ablative absolute, on which may depend another construction, until the sentence when it ends has generally carried the story several steps forward, perhaps modifying or subverting the initial statement. Not incompetence but artifice—and highly appropriate, for it is better that the historian should set down the facts first, with interpretation or comment in the sequel.

Deliberate again, the harsh juxtapositions. Balanced antithesis belonged to the habits of conventional rhetoric—too smooth to be authentic. Tacitus learned from Sallust the art of 'inconcinnitas', most effective and deadly when he wished to insinuate a variety of motives, with the ostensible equity of suspended judgement, but implying the worst. One of his chosen adverbs is 'varie'.[7] Verbal disharmonies reflect the complexities of history and all that is ambiguous in the behaviour of men.

The insight of the historian is matched by a vivid and vigorous

---

[1] cf. J. J. Schlicher, *Class. Phil.* IX (1914), 386 ff.

[2] Thus victims of the plague, XVI. 13. 2: 'servitia perinde et ingenua plebes raptim exstingui, inter coniugum et liberorum lamenta, qui dum adsident, dum deflent, saepe eodem rogo cremabantur.'

[3] p. 197.

[4] I. 2. 1: 'postquam Bruto et Cassio caesis . . . tuta et praesentia quam vetera et periculosa mallent.'

[5] XIII. 1. On which cf. F. Klingner, *Hermes* LXXXIII (1955), 187 ff.

[6] Seneca, *Epp.* 114. 17 (quoted above, p. 197).

[7] At least in Book I, where it occurs five times (admitting Acidalius' emendation from 'variae' in 80. 1).

imagination. His theme was savage and sinister, with no place for hope or ease or happiness.[1] Instead, 'potentia', 'saevitia', 'dominatio', 'servitium'; and it might be guessed that among other words of his predilection are 'acer' and 'atrox', and the verbs 'ingruo', 'rapio', 'traho', 'turbo'. The style abounds in violent metaphors, drawing imagery from light and dark, rapid movement, growth and decay, destruction and conflagration.[2] Men rush headlong towards enslavement, Seianus tries to snatch the power, Agrippina prostrates herself before the will and wishes of the freedman Pallas;[3] Messallina is open-mouthed with greed for the gardens once owned by Lucullus, Claudius grows all aflame for incestuous matrimony, and the orator Eprius Marcellus blazes with his eyes, countenance, and voice.[4]

In like fashion, a bold use of personification. The face of the heavens is sullen and savage;[5] the price of food becomes merciless;[6] the Palace shudders with horror or rocks to its foundations;[7] the imperial power casts a heavy shadow, and the Augustan peace is sanguinary.[8]

Potent or subtle contrivances compel the sound to convey the sense—alliteration, assonance, light or ponderous words, short phrases in sequence or a long development. Thus the quick rout of Numidian insurgents—'trahi, occidi, capi'[9]—or the accelerated suicide of the consul Julius Vestinus.[10] Again, after splendour and pathos, simplicity is concentrated at the end.[11] The harsh lot of a Roman soldier is translated into a remorseless catalogue—summer, winter, war or peace, always the same without end ever.[12] Light tripping words call up a gay dance at the garden party of Valeria Messallina.[13] When Roman knights are crushed by the crowd during Neronian entertainments, the phraseology is suitably oppressive.[14]

The Tacitean style plays upon many variants of tone and colour

---

[1] For the avoidance of hopeful and friendly words see p. 545.

[2] H. Furneaux, o.c. 50; B. Walker, o.c. 66 ff.

[3] I. 7. 1; IV. 1. 2; XIV. 2. 2.   [4] XI. 1. 1; 25. 5; XVI. 29. 1.

[5] II. 24. 1: 'truculentia caeli.' The word is otherwise absent.

[6] II. 87.   [7] XI. 28. 1; XII. 1.1.

[8] XIV. 47. 1; I. 10. 4. The verb 'praeumbro' is rare if not unique. The ugly word 'cruentus' is applied to 'epistulae' of Tiberius in III. 44. 3.

[9] IV. 25. 2. Cf. Sallust, *Jug.* 101. 11: 'sequi fugere, occidi capi.'

[10] XV. 69. 2: 'clauditur cubiculo, praesto est medicus, abscinduntur venae, vigens adhuc balneo infertur, calida aqua mersatur.'

[11] XV. 16. 4: 'decesserat certamen virtutis et ambitio gloriae, felicium hominum adfectus: sola misericordia valebat, et apud minores magis.'

[12] I. 17. 4: 'verbera et vulnera, duram hiemem exercitas aestates, bellum atrox aut sterilem pacem, sempiterna.'

[13] XI. 31. 2: 'ipsa crine fluxo thyrsum quatiens iuxtaque Silius hedera vinctus gerere cothurnos iacere caput, strepente circum procaci choro.'

[14] XVI. 5. 2: 'constitit plerosque equitum dum per angustias aditus et ingruentem multitudinem enituntur obtritos.' For rhythm and musical effects in Tacitus see A. Salvatore, *Stile e ritmo in Tacito* (1950), 182 ff.

between the plain and the ornate. Action can be rendered simply and directly after the fashion of the old writers;[1] a monotonous structure will register a traditional annalistic entry;[2] and the careful choice of bare words lends an inevitable solemnity to the verdict upon some man of note.[3] At the other extreme, picturesque or elaborate language when the historian turns his talents to portray the fabulous Arabian bird or the monuments of Egypt, the festival organized by Tigellinus, or the great storm that overwhelmed the fleet of Germanicus on the northern ocean.[4]

Diction most delicate conveys the tranquillity of the island which Tiberius Caesar elected for his retreat, the gentle air and the lovely prospect—to imply a savage contrast.[5]

Elevation is one of Tacitus' favourite devices for irony and for mockery. The obsequies of Claudius Caesar are shown up for what they were—'peractis tristitiae imitamentis';[6] and the poetical operations of Nero, 'pangendis carminibus', excite the distrust of the reader.[7] Otherwise a deadly simplicity or a brief collocation of the incongruous. Men of rank and station are 'falsi ac festinantes' when a new ruler comes to the power;[8] and the Prefect of the Guard stands in compulsory attendance, 'maerens Burrus ac laudans', while Nero plays and postures.[9] Sometimes a single word will do. It may be choice and pompous, like 'alumnus';[10] or it may be charged with all the bitterness that 'clementia' or 'pietas' held for men of understanding in Rome of the Caesars.[11]

Similarly, the employment of bathos. Credulity and legend produced the marvel of guardian serpents at the cradle of an infant prince—whereas, on the testimony of Nero (here honoured with the stylish designation of 'haudquaquam sui detractor'), one snake and nothing more had been observed in the bedroom.[12] When Poppaea Sabina was

---

[1] II. 80. 4: 'vertunt terga Cilices seque castello claudunt.'

[2] VI. 10. 3 (L. Piso): 'patrem ei censorium fuisse memoravi; aetas ad octogesimum annum processit; decus triumphale in Thracia meruerat.'

[3] 27. 4 (M. Lepidus, cited below, p. 354).

[4] VI. 28 (below, p. 472); II. 61; XV. 37; II. 23.

[5] IV. 67. 2: 'importuosum circa mare et vix modicis navigiis pauca subsidia, neque adpulerit quisquam nisi gnaro custode. caeli temperies hieme mitis obiectu montis quo saeva ventorum arcentur; aestas in favonium obversa et aperto circum pelago peramoena.'

[6] XIII. 4. 1.

[7] 3. 3. The verb 'pango' for poetry-making is used elsewhere only of Nero's assistants (XIV. 16. 1).

[8] I. 7. 1.

[9] XIV. 15. 4. Rendered by Gibbon as 'mournful and applauding.'

[10] Applied to Caligula (I. 44. 1), to the sons of Hortensius (II. 37. 4), to a Parthian prince (XII. 11. 3), and to the ex-cobbler Vatinius (XV. 34. 2).

[11] p. 414 f.

[12] XI. 11. 3. Tacitus was aware that Cato the Censor had been called 'haud sane detrectator laudum suarum' (Livy XXXIV. 15. 9).

delivered of a daughter, the Roman Senate in devout alacrity ordained a plethora of thanksgivings and commemorations, which came to nothing —'quae fluxa fuere, quartum intra mensem defuncta infante'.[1]

The most direct and easy form of the Tacitean discourse is found in the speeches. Well aware that the abrupt, enigmatic, and complicated manner would be out of place, the author allows the argument to develop harmoniously, without surprises or treachery. The verb is not omitted, grammar reverts to more normal habits, and the language abates something of its aspiration towards the rare and the startling.[2]

Diverse types and colours of oratory are skilfully conveyed, from the bland polish of L. Vitellius to the savage invective of Suillius and Cossutianus; while Cassius Longinus and Thrasea Paetus, firm, dignified, and a little old-fashioned, speak for Roman tradition and defend the privileges of the governing order.[3] Nor is the peculiar majesty of Tacitus' own manner and performance beyond recovery. It is manifest in the *Historiae* when an emperor makes appeal to the long centuries of antiquity, to 'aeternitas rerum et pax gentium';[4] when a general asseverates Rome's dominion over the nations, ordained by destiny and immense power, with no sequel, if it were ever subverted, but ruin and universal confusion.[5]

There is even an intensification of that Tacitean grandeur.[6] Although splendid and impressive, the speeches in the *Historiae* are in the line of Livy—eloquent, redundant, patriotic, and perhaps a little conventional.[7] The *Annales* exhibit a more concentrated genius, as when Tiberius Caesar speaks, or, notably and by paradox, when an oration of Claudius on the progressive enlargement of the Roman Commonwealth is transmuted into the language of Cornelius Tacitus.[8]

That theme carried a strong appeal for the historian: innovation justified by tradition. His own style blends the old and the new. A composite product (the archaic along with the modern, and poetical embellishments woven into the fabric of prose) might easily turn out

---

[1] xv. 23. 3. The prosaic detail follows on a stylish expression ('fluxus' is Sallustian).

[2] For 'Ciceronian' vocabulary, App. 42. Compare Cicero's view of the style appropriate for speeches in works of history—'tracta quaedam et fluens expetitur, non haec contorta et acris oratio' (*Orator* 66). As for vocabulary, the Tiberian speeches in Tacitus (with their archaisms) stand in contrast to his normal procedure (App. 39).

[3] p. 355.   [4] *Hist.* I. 84. 4 (quoted above, p. 155).   [5] IV. 74. 3.

[6] R. Reitzenstein said that he was not able to discover it (*Gött. gel. Nachr.* 1914, 205). For the σεμνότης of Tacitus, E. Norden, *Die antike Kunstprosa* I (1898), 330 ff.; J. Perret, *Rev. ét. anc.* LVI (1954), 107 ff. The Latin equivalent of σεμνός is 'sanctus' (Quintilian VIII. 3. 6; 24).

[7] Notably the oration of Dillius Vocula (IV. 58, cf. App. 34).

[8] p. 318.

grotesque and pretentious, a mere congeries of affectations.[1] What is the source and validity of the various elements that make up the style of Tacitus?

Latin historical writing avows a strong tendency to the archaic and to the poetical (which are sometimes the same). In the language of poets resided a double hazard. Not only the over-ornamental, but the conventional and cheapened. For example, 'aerumna', which had passed into imperial prose. Quintilian lays his interdict on the word.[2] Tacitus was vigilant. He rejects outright certain words that had been admitted by historians.[3] A dozen or so preciosities of the *Germania* are banned in the sequel;[4] and he came to repent of some that he had admitted in the *Historiae*.[5] Comparison can be instructive with ambitiously ornate writers of inferior talent before and after.[6]

In most forms of stylized discourse emulation of the ancients held out constant temptations to the Romans. Who could resist the venerable word 'priscus', and all that it stands for?[7] Quintilian duly warns the young aspirant. Old-fashioned words (he says) convey dignity, and the plain style of the ancients is strong and virile. But maturity and discrimination are requisite. Otherwise the results may be ludicrous and incongruous.[8] Quintilian further commends the exemplary taste of Virgil; and Virgil, as may be ascertained, is temperate and careful, eschewing oddities and standing by the poetic usage of recent predecessors.[9]

The archaic colouring of Tacitus is deep and pervasive—forms and spellings, words, meanings, and constructions.[10] Whence does it derive? Not from study of the earliest writers, despite certain rare or obsolete words.[11] Rome had known (and ridiculed) the pedantic zeal that impelled men to compile Catonian glossaries or ransack the archives to enrich a vocabulary;[12] and the next generation after Tacitus

[1] Quintilian VIII. 3. 60: 'si quis sublimia humilibus, vetera novis, poetica vulgaribus misceat.'
[2] ib. 2. 6. Virgil had shunned the word. Sallust has it twice (in speeches), Livy once, but Ammianus no fewer than forty-three times (cf. *TLL*).
[3] Thus 'defloresco' and 'marcesco' (Livy), 'musso' (Sallust and Livy), &c. See App. 54.
[4] App. 42.
[5] Thus 'crudesco', 'grandaevus', 'indigus', 'sopor', 'temno'. Cf. App. 52; 54.
[6] For the preciosity of the elder Pliny, E. Norden, o.c. 315 ff. But the best evidence comes from the historian who emulated Tacitus. See especially H. Hagendahl, *Studia Ammianea* (Diss. Uppsala, 1921), 21.
[7] For 'priscus' and 'vetustus', App. 47. Cicero confessed that he would not feel hostility towards archaic and poetical words like 'proles' and 'suboles' (*De oratore* III. 153).
[8] Quintilian I. 6. 39 ff.; II. 5. 21 ff.; VIII. 3. 24 ff.
[9] VIII. 3. 24. Cf. E. Norden in his commentary on *Aen.* VI (Ed. 2, 1916), 365 ff.
[10] F. Degel, *Archaistische Bestandteile der Sprache des Tacitus* (Diss. Erlangen, 1907).
[11] cf., against F. Degel's view (o.c. 45), W. Kroll, *Studien zum Verständnis der r. Literatur* (1924), 256.
[12] Suetonius, *De gram.* 10; Seneca, *Epp.* 114. 13.

was to see those aberrations emerge again to honour and reward.[1] Tacitus is discreet—and highly discriminatory.

He experiments, and rejects. An archaism that was risked in the *Historiae* may be avoided in the *Annales*: Tacitus decided that 'torpedo' was a mistake.[2] With the *Annales* the old-fashioned words rise sharply.[3] And some come in not used before.[4] They do not all stay. Several of the novelties of the first hexad will be subsequently discarded.[5] Second thoughts, a finer taste—and the correct judgement. An archaic infusion that suited Tiberius Caesar and the annalistic record of the 'res publica' was not appropriate to the story of other reigns.

For antique language Tacitus does not go back beyond Sallust, and he puts that author to double employ. He borrows from his model—but, more often and more significant, he resorts to free composition in the Sallustian manner.

[1] Fronto criticizes Cicero because he has no 'insperata atque inopinata verba' (p. 152 N = Haines I, p. 6); and Gellius derides Seneca (hostile to archaism) as 'ineptus et insubidus homo' (XII. 2. 11).

[2] *Hist.* III. 63. 2. In Cato (quoted by Gellius XI. 2. 6), and in Sallust, *Hist.* I. 77. 19; III. 48. 20; 26. Similarly 'ducto' (only once, *Hist.* II. 100. 2): typical of Sallust (five times), cf. Quintilian VIII. 3. 4. Nor does the Sallustian 'abunde' recur after *Hist.* II. 95. 3.

[3] See App. 47: 'patro', 'proles', 'reor', 'suboles' are archaic. The archaic and the poetical sometimes coincide, but not always. See B. Axelson, *Unpoetische Wörter* (Lund, 1945), 27 f., discussing 'apiscor', 'coepto', 'imperito', 'patro', 'rogito', &c.

[4] App. 53. For example 'vecordia' (six times), or 'apiscor' (twelve)—the latter (strangely) not in Sallust.

[5] App. 48. For example, 'belligero' (II. 5. 2; III. 73. 3; IV. 46. 1); 'pessum' (I. 9. 4; 79, 2; III. 66. 4).

XXVII. TYPES AND CHANGES OF STYLE

'URBEM Romam a principio reges habuere.' At the outset, monumental simplicity of language—and a reminiscence of Sallust, improving upon that author.[1] Again, the exordium of Book IV. The first sentence announces a new phase in the reign of Tiberius, with an ominous expression modelled on Sallust;[2] and Aelius Seianus is promptly brought on the scene—origin, family, career, and historical magnitude. The characterization follows—a quick tight sequence of nouns and adjectives, juxtaposed, antithetic, and lacking verbs.[3]

Open and avowedly, Tacitus brings Seianus on parade as a second Catilina. A female counterpart had been put on exhibit by the narrator of the conspiracy, namely the notorious Sempronia.[4] Tacitus duly conforms. Poppaea Sabina is ushered in as a seductive and potent influence for evil, enhanced by the distinction (rare in the third hexad) of a full and stylized portraiture.[5] Verbal details proclaim the literary parentage.[6] More striking, however, a whole sentence that owes nothing to Sallust's Sempronia but renders to perfection the studied bareness of his manner—'huic mulieri cuncta alia fuere praeter honestum animum'.

Other parallels offered, of scene or character.[7] Tacfarinas was an obvious pendant to Jugurtha; and the Numidian War (welcome relief from the annals of Rome under Tiberius Caesar) showed speed and movement in the empty lands of the nomads.[8] Sallust's *Historiae* were incomparably richer than the monographs: Spain or Cilicia, Lucullus in conquest beyond the Tigris, the portrayal of the regions along the Pontic shore or beneath the mountain of Caucasus. Long narrations in several books of the *Annales*, escaping from crime or futility at Rome, carried the reader to Nineveh or Adiabene, to realms of legend and the story of the Argonauts.[9]

Sallustian style even crops up among senatorial business or in the

---

[1] Sallust, *Cat.* 6. 1: 'urbem Romam, sicuti ego accepi, condidere atque habuere initio Troiani.'

[2] IV. 1. 1: 'cum repente turbare fortuna coepit, saevire ipse aut saevientibus vires praebere.' Cf. *Cat.* 10. 1: 'saevire fortuna ac miscere omnia coepit.'

[3] ib. 3: 'corpus illi laborum tolerans, animus audax; sui obtegens, in alios criminator; iuxta adulatio et superbia; palam compositus pudor, intus summa apiscendi libido,' &c. Cf. *Cat.* 5. 3 ff.   [4] *Cat.* 25.   [5] XIII. 45. 1 ff.

[6] e.g. *Cat.* 25. 5: 'verum ingenium eius haud absurdum.' Cf. *Ann.* XIII. 45. 3: 'sermo comis nec absurdum ingenium.'

[7] See App. 53, where six of the passages here to be noted or cited are treated more fully.

[8] It is superfluous to exemplify the Sallustian colouring of the chapters about Tacfarinas.   [9] VI. 31–37; 41–44; XI. 8–10; XII. 10–20; 44–51.

summary version of an imperial oration. Discussion and perplexity about a recusant vassal, Mithridates the prince of Bosporus, brings in for argument the iron coast and the pathless wastes that had been depicted by the author of the classic excursus *De situ Ponti*;[1] and, when Byzantium sends an embassy, a digression expatiates upon the past renown of that city, its site of advantage for the transit of armies, and great profit accruing from the waters.[2]

Whole episodes (it appears) have been selected and worked up in the precise design of evoking the great precursor. Sallust furnished a copious narrative of operations conducted by a Roman proconsul against the mountain tribes of the Taurus.[3] It was present to the mind of Tacitus when he resolved to write about Poppaeus Sabinus in Thrace—and write at some length.[4]

More familiar was a certain digression in the *Bellum Catilinae*, how a governor of Hispania Citerior, Cn. Piso, came to a violent end.[5] When therefore the record of the year 25 disclosed a member of that aristocratic family (L. Piso) also assassinated by a native in that country, Tacitus saw his chance and knew his duty. He relates the detail of the affair, terminating with phraseology that quietly and firmly establishes the parallel.[6]

Tacitus is not concerned merely with odd resemblances in history and curious repetitions. He aims at a general and pervasive adaptation of Sallust. A single word or short phrase will often furnish the clue, the rest being free composition in the unmistakable vein. It is most easily detected in the portraiture of individuals.

If it happens that a nobleman exhibited accomplishments worthy of his ancestry, Tacitus will honour the man and recall Republican history by a borrowed expression. Thus Marcus Lepidus, whom the historian 'ascertains to be a wise and weighty man'.[7] The phrase comes from the *Bellum Jugurthinum*.[8] An oration of Lepidus has the appropriate colouring.[9] Likewise the notice of his death.[10]

Tacitus introduces Cassius Longinus with a sober and impressive commendation, rendering Roman tradition in traditional language.

---

[1] XII. 20.   [2] 62 f.   [3] Sallust, *Hist.* II. 87.

[4] IV. 46–51.   [5] *Cat.* 19.

[6] IV. 45. 3: 'sed Piso Termestinorum dolo caesus habetur.' Cf. App. 53.

[7] 20. 2: 'hunc ego Lepidum temporibus illis gravem et sapientem virum fuisse comperior.'

[8] *Jug.* 45. 1: 'Metellum . . . magnum et sapientem virum fuisse comperior.' Tacitus nowhere else has the verb in the deponent form. Observe also a little further down 'pergere iter' (cf. *Jug.* 79. 5).

[9] III. 50, showing reminiscences of *Cat.* 15. 4 and 51. 8. Further, Lepidus refers to the person concerned (the poet Clutorius Priscus) in pure Sallustian language—'studia illi ut plena vecordiae, ita inania et fluxa sunt'.

[10] VI. 27. 4: 'quippe Aemilium genus fecundum bonorum civium, et qui eadem familia corruptis moribus, inlustri tamen fortuna egere.'

Cassius, who excelled all men in science of the law, had command of the army in Syria.[1] It was a season of peace, discouraging effort. But Cassius enforced the 'priscus mos' of stern military discipline, as befitted a name and family not unknown in those parts. When Cassius a dozen years later delivers a speech in the Senate (it concerns another 'vetus mos'), the exordium contains a clear echo of Sallust.[2] So does the peroration.[3] Thrasea Paetus will also recall ancient dignity in an oration defending the honour of the senatorial order.[4]

Bad men by their number and diversity are more promising, or evil and turbulent times. From first to last a digression on legislation turns out to be an essay in the manner.[5] Not only does Tacitus evoke the period about which Sallust wrote in his *Historiae*. Coming to the third consulate of Pompeius Magnus, he duly pronounces a strong condemnation on the dynast whom Sallust disliked.[6] The next sentence passes at once to the twenty years of tribulation that ensued before the monarchy was founded.[7]

Elsewhere Sallustian language contemptuously alludes to the decline and fall of the Triumvirs Lepidus and Antonius;[8] it brings into sharp relief the crafty contrivings of Tiberius Caesar;[9] it characterizes the class of senators that praise an emperor's every utterance uniformly;[10] and, as is proper, it also advertises the first manifestation of the 'delator' in Book I.[11] Again, in Book III, when a second specimen of the loathsome tribe is delineated: Tacitus devises an elaborate structure of tortuously disjointed antithesis, outdoing Sallust in the evocation of Thucydidean pregnancy.[12]

---

[1] XII. 12. 1: 'ea tempestate Cassius ceteros praeminebat peritia legum: nam militares artes per otium ignotae, industriosque aut ignavos pax in aequo tenet. ac tamen quantum sine bello dabatur, revocare priscum morem,' &c.

[2] XIV. 43. 1: 'ne nimio amore antiqui moris studium meum extollere viderer.' Cf. *Jug.* 4. 2. Like Cato (*Cat.* 52. 7) he uses 'saepe numero', old-fashioned by the time of Tacitus and nowhere else admitted by him.

[3] XIV. 44. 4: 'nam et ex fuso exercitu cum decimus quisque fusti feritur.' For the military allusion so fitting on the lips of Cassius compare III. 21. 1 (a scene in Africa): 'sorte ductos fusti necat', which is taken from Sallust, *Hist.* IV. 22.

[4] XV. 20 f. Note 'aequabilius atque constantius' (21. 4), from *Cat.* 2. 3.

[5] III. 26 ff. See further App. 53.

[6] 28. 1: 'suarumque legum auctor idem ac subversor, quae armis tuebatur armis amisit.'

[7] ib.: 'exim continua per viginti annos discordia, non mos non ius; deterrima quaeque impune ac multa honesta exitio fuere.'

[8] I. 9. 4: 'postquam hic socordia senuerit, ille per libidines pessum datus sit.' Cf. *Jug.* I. 4: 'ad inertiam et voluptates corporis pessum datus est.'

[9] II. 30. 3: 'callidus et novi iuris repertor.' Cf. Sallust, *Hist.* IV. 69. 7: 'callidi et reportóres perfidiae' (Mithridates on the Romans).

[10] II. 38. 4: 'ab iis quibus omnia principum, honesta atque inhonesta, laudare mos est.' Cf. *Jug.* 80. 5: 'quis omnia honesta atque inhonesta vendere mos erat.'

[11] I. 74. 1 f. (p. 326). For 'ex contemptis metuendi' cf. Sallust, *Hist.* I. 77. 3: 'se ⟨e⟩ contempto metuendum effecit.'

[12] III. 66. 4: 'quod multos etiam bonos pessum dedit, qui spretis quae tarda cum securitate

Even if there be extant no phrase of Sallust for attestation, the colouring alone will often suffice. Thus the portrait of a variegated and dubious character, L. Vitellius—'of that man I do not lack knowledge that many loathsome things stand on report, and an evil repute at Rome: yet Vitellius was of ancient virtue in the governance of provinces', and so on.[1]

Possessing the repertory and freely developing the idiom, Tacitus in the course of his work goes on to produce new Sallustian types. Thus the sinister court-buffoon or the treacherous philosopher.[2] And sometimes, to understand a passage properly, it is expedient to have in mind the deceptive bareness of the archaic manner. At the beginning of the year 37 a man of mark and consequence, L. Arruntius, resolved to die. What was the gain, he asked, if one waited for the extinction of Tiberius? A worse tyranny was on the way. Death would liberate a man from past and future tribulation equally. Speaking thus, with a prophet's solemnity and passion, Arruntius made an end to his life; and, the historian adds, 'what followed will stand as proof that Arruntius put death to good employ'.[3] In that comment some detect bathos or an interpolation.[4] On the contrary, supreme artistry: the wilful descent from the fervid eloquence of a vaticination to plainest prose.

When Tacitus asserts the diligence of his inquiries he uses a rare Sallustian word.[5] The historical prose of the Latins avows itself the product of labour and much contriving. To build up his style, Sallust looted Cato.[6] Nobody was deceived, and not everybody blamed him. Sallust was a slow composer, they said—and you could see the effort in his writing.[7] Such is the verdict of Quintilian, and investigation confirms, showing words deliberately taken up or dropped, sudden changes of linguistic habit, and a notable development after the pioneer monograph.[8]

Prose of the imperial age had been drawing more and more of its ornaments and devices from the poets. A speaker in the *Dialogus*

---

praematura vel cum exitio properant.' For 'pessum' cf. I. 9. 4; 79. 2. The preceding sentence has the Sallustian 'si rectum iter pergeret', for which phrase cf. IV. 20. 3 and *Jug.* 79. 5.

[1] VI. 32.·4: 'eo de homine haud sum ignarus sinistram in urbe famam, pleraque foeda memorari; ceterum regendis provinciis prisca virtute egit', &c.

[2] XV. 34. 2 (Vatinius); XVI. 32. 3 (Egnatius Celer).

[3] VI. 48. 3: 'documento sequentia erunt bene Arruntium morte usum.' The expression 'bene uti' is presumably archaic, cf. Plautus, *Cist.* 23: 'beneque amicitia utier.'

[4] The text of H. Fuchs (*Ed. Helv.*, 1946) encloses the sentence in brackets.

[5] VI. 7. 5: 'ab aliis incelebrata,' cf. Sallust, *Hist.* I. 88 (above, p. 283).

[6] Suetonius, *Divus Aug.* 86. 3; *De gram.* 15; Quintilian VIII. 3. 29.

[7] Quintilian X. 3. 8: 'et sane manifestus est etiam ex opere ipso labor.'

[8] cf. A. Kunze, *Sallustiana* III (Leipzig, 1897), 49 ff.; E. Löfstedt, *Syntactica* II (1933), 290 ff.

advises orators to exploit Horace, Virgil, and Lucan.[1] The historian
Tacitus is not notably in the debt of Horace.[2] Lucan might seem more
useful, as well as more congenial by topic and sentiments.[3] It is Virgil
who dominates.

Virgilian words and expressions are frequent, showing how well
Tacitus knew the text of the classical epic.[4] Not that any catalogue will
explain how Tacitus proceeds. As with his use of Sallust, it is rather a
matter of sympathetic assimilation.

Virgil had an especial value for Tacitus. Colouring, atmosphere,
and emotion, the poet furnished everything that Livy had, and more.
A Livian phrase or motive was welcome, it is true, when the historian
wished to depict scenes of riot and rhetoric in a Roman camp, or the
dramatic vicissitudes of warfare and adventure beyond the Rhine; and
heroic figures dominated the action, recalling more spacious days—
Rome's conquering general, or Rome's resourceful adversary. When
Germanicus Caesar confronts the mutinous legionaries, his appeal
carries a reminiscence of Scipio Africanus in a like emergency. The
oration also confesses a Virgilian debt.[5]

Describing the storm on the ocean, Tacitus not only echoes Virgil
in language, but suggests his pictorial and musical effects. At first
the quiet level sea, 'placidum aequor', with no sound or motion save
the oars and sails of a thousand ships. Then the dark mass of clouds,
and sudden fall of hail—'mox atro nubium globo effusa grando'—and
finally, all sea and sky surrenders to the might of the south wind—
'omne dehinc caelum et mare omne in austrum cessit'.[6]

More than that, the historian can conjure up the Virgilian strain of
mystery, majesty, and compassion. When the Romans approach the
place where Varus and the legions lay unburied, the whole army is
affected. Not with the thought of friends and relatives only. They are
moved to meditate upon vicissitudes of war and the general lot of
mankind—'casus bellorum et sortem hominum'. And the ground
they tread is mournful—'incedunt maestos locos'.[7]

Writing with a poet's language and imagery, the historian ran the
risk of lapsing into metre. Tacitean hexameters have been detected,
but they are not wholly genuine specimens, and were certainly not
deliberate.[8] The author would also avoid certain collocations of

---

[1] *Dial.* 20. 5.

[2] The closest echo is II. 14. 4: 'taedio viarum ac maris', cf. *Epp.* I. 11. 6.

[3] p. 142 f. Yet not extensively drawn upon, as L. Robbert confesses, *De Tacito Lucani imitatore* (Diss. Göttingen, 1917), 94 f.

[4] cf. H. Schmaus, *Tacitus ein Nachahmer Vergils* (Diss. Erlangen, 1884). For a short list, A. Draeger, *Über Syntax und Stil des Tacitus*[3] (1882), 126 f.; H. Furneaux, I (ed. 2, 1896), 74.

[5] I. 42. For this, and other Livian passages, App. 54.   [6] II. 23.   [7] I. 61. 1.

[8] A. Draeger, o.c. 121. V. Lundström even claimed the first sentence of the *Annales* as a hexameter from Ennius (*Eranos* XV (1915), 1 ff.).

poetical words that might evoke a verse ending. One example is instructive. Tiberius Caesar brought the unfortunate Julia to a lingering death in exile and neglect—'omnis spei egenam inopia ac tabe longa peremit'.[1] Tacitus by a subtle and ironical reminiscence alludes to the forlorn victims of unhappy love—'quos durus amor crudeli tabe peredit'.[2] He ventures as far as prose permits: 'longa tabe peremit' would be detrimental.

The components, derivation, and devices of the Tacitean style have now been touched upon in brief survey. The Roman historians subsequent to Livy have perished utterly, and not all the innovations first attested in Tacitus proceed from his own invention. From first to last his performance reveals an unerring taste in selecting words by their strength and colour, and his original genius is confirmed by the verifiable enhancement between *Historiae* and *Annales*. No great regret need be felt for the disappearance of an Aufidius or a Servilius. They were eclipsed by Cornelius Tacitus, who passed beyond Sallust and beyond Livy, more resourceful and ornate than the one, stronger, prouder, and fiercer than the other. Tacitus took possession of the Latin language, bent it to his will, and pushed to the utter limits all that it knew or promised of energy, gravity, and magnificence.[3] If the qualities of Tacitus need a commendation from antiquity, it may be discovered in a Greek writer's verdict upon Thucydides.[4]

Splendour, intensity, and structural coherence, the *Annales* are the typical Tacitus—and the first hexad exhibits the manner in mature perfection. Book I has virtuosity and variety on show, with notable ventures in syntax and construction; technical phraseology is defied or skilfully sublimated; and vivid or unusual words occur in conspicuous frequency.[5] All of which might have been expected—and no need for the hypothesis that Book I represents a second edition.[6]

The *Annales* on analysis turn out by no means uniform. In composition and technique the third hexad goes a different way from the first.

---

[1] I. 53. 2.

[2] *Aen.* VI. 442. The parallel seems to have been missed by commentators and collectors.

[3] The style is patently a creation, a 'Kunstsprache', cf. R. Reitzenstein, *Gött. gel. Nachr.* 1914, 268 f. Hence 'lingua morte, con una luminosità opaca e una sonorità senza più eco nelle nostre orecchie' (C. Marchesi, *Tacito*[3] (1944), 289). E. Fraenkel describes it as relentless and fatiguing (*Neue Jahrbücher* VIII (1932), 232 f.). For a more sympathetic verdict, E. Norden, *Die antike Kunstprosa* I (1898), 342 f.

[4] Dionysius, *De Thuc.* 24: τὸ ποιητικὸν τῶν ὀνομάτων, τὸ πολυειδὲς τῶν σχημάτων, τὸ τραχὺ τῆς ἁρμονίας, τὸ τάχος τῶν σημασιῶν. Tacitus' qualities conform to the critic's estimate—but do not derive from Thucydides himself. Cf. J. Perret, *Rev. ét. anc.* LVI (1954), 111.

[5] e.g. 'morti deposcit' (23. 5), 'incessitque itineri et proelio' (51. 2), 'in prominenti litoris' (53. 5), 'umido paludum' (61. 1); 'virgines Vestae' (8. 1), 'campus Martis' (8. 5); 'in cassum' (4. 2), 'in domo regnatrice' (4. 4), 'pessum datus' (9. 4).

[6] For possible traces of revision or insertion, App. 37.

Tacitus deviates from the sharp articulation of the annalistic structure and tends to group his material in single episodes. Reported speech becomes more common, there are fewer set orations. Personality tends to express itself in acts and words, largely dispensing with the formal character sketch.

Some of these changes correspond to the changed fabric and content of the history itself. With Nero instead of Tiberius, the author was no longer able to portray the Princeps and the yearly chronicle of the 'res publica' bound together and closely interdependent. The Roman Senate hardly ever witnessed a debate of any consequence—and Tacitus inserts only two senatorial orations in direct discourse.[1]

Other phenomena may be noted. What survives of the Claudian section shows no fewer than five digressions (and they were appropriate to that reign).[2] Only two occur in Books XIII–XVI.[3] Fewer digressions, portraits, and obituary notices—therefore less Sallust;[4] and even where a Sallustian colouring might seem highly suitable (Corbulo in Armenia recalling Lucullus) Tacitus makes no great use of it.

A writer might discard some items of his verbal experimentation, use up the stock of traditional themes, or lose sight of an attractive locution through sheer inadvertence. Coming from the *Historiae* to the *Annales*, Tacitus, by departure from his normal tendency, forswears one or two poetical or archaic expressions; and words may occur in the first book, or in the first six books, but never again.[5] What emerges in the third hexad, however, is more serious—not sporadic but variously pervasive. In some ways it resembles the changes perceptible in Livy after the first decade, some (but not all) to be explained by the passage from legend to history. Not only do Livy's colouring and vocabulary become less poetical. Various forms and words diminish their frequency or disappear outright: especially remarkable is the author's growing aversion from the frequentative verbs so common in the early books.[6]

Livy moves in a steady line. Tacitus after achieving his developed manner in the first hexad of the *Annales*, does not sustain it after Book XII. He can still venture a new and notable device of syntax, or a bold and decorative word.[7] But he seems to modify his style in verifiable particulars, reverting to more conventional usages.[8]

---

[1] XIV. 43 f. (Cassius Longinus); XV. 20 f. (Thrasea Paetus).

[2] And there is other antiquarian material, probably from Claudius (App. 40).

[3] XIII. 29 (the *aerarium Saturni*); XIV. 20 f. (theatrical history).

[4] App. 53, with remarks on the style.   [5] p. 352, cf. App. 49.

[6] S. G. Stacey, *Archiv für lat. Lex.* x (1898), 17 ff.; E. Löfstedt, *Syntactica* II (1933), 294 ff. For criticism, which does not invalidate Stacey's thesis at all points, see K. Gries, *Constancy in Livy's Latinity* (Diss. Columbia, 1949).   [7] App. 58.

[8] As argued by E. Löfstedt, o.c. 282 ff.; N. Eriksson, *Studien zu den Annalen des Tacitus* (Lund, 1934). See further App. 55 ff.

Certain changes are striking. The form 'forem' won predominance over 'essem' in the *Historiae* and kept it in the *Annales*—until the third hexad, which offers a solitary example. Nor does Tacitus insist any more on 'quis' for 'quibus': it nearly fades out. As for conjunctions, the relation between 'quamquam' and 'quamvis' undergoes a complete reversal; and 'ni' instead of 'nisi', to which the historian took such a fancy, occurs once in Book XIII and never again. The verb 'coepto' is dropped. The adjective 'grandis' had been banished utterly from the *Annales*: it now returns, and so does 'amplus'. Conversely, 'necessitudo' disappears, expelled by 'necessitas', and 'claritudo' occurs only once.[1]

The phenomena are not fortuitous or isolated. Notable elements in the vocabulary seem to be going a different way. Words absent before turn up, some that had occurred sporadically in the earlier works, some nowhere, not even in the *Dialogus*. A number can be brought under one category: standard and inconspicuous words (often Ciceronian), in sharp contrast to the author's predilections hitherto.[2] The style is copious, vivid, and elevated; not so tight and ferocious; and not so malignant.[3] The author writes swiftly and confidently, for he is sure of the facts. He does not have to bother, as in the first hexad, about documents, the enigma of a ruler's character—and about style all the time. The new manner is patent in the narration of the great conspiracy against Nero.

The facts are not in dispute. They have even been taken to show a certain lapse in time during the composition of the whole work, between the first hexad and the third—or further, an appreciable interval after the second.[4] The third hexad, it will be recalled, proclaims emphatically a fresh beginning.

It may be so, and it may not. How explain the alteration in style? It could fit the theory of a late date of composition, well into the reign of Hadrian.[5] Language and sentiment, much in Tacitus is a product of opposition, sometimes unconscious, often deliberate. The poetical and archaic manner set his writing at a distance from the ordinary and the conventional. If the historian found that fashion now overtook him, carrying those qualities to an excess of preciosity and antiquarianism, he might have been impelled to revert towards classical usage in grammar and in language.

A firmer explanation offers—the history itself was no more the same. Tiberius, who came to the power as an old man, a century before Tacitus began to write the *Annales*, was ancient history in his

[1] App. 58.   [2] App. 42.
[3] Much less malicious comment, cf. I. S. Ryberg, *TAPA* LXXIII (1942), 383 ff.
[4] E. Löfstedt, o.c. 289; N. Eriksson, o.c. 108.   [5] Ch. XXXV.

own person. Nero was close to the author's time—and in many ways contemporary, for men saw much of Nero return with Hadrian.[1] Antique grandeur was out of place.

Not everything is admirable in the third hexad. No decline anywhere, it is true, in power of narration, of grouping events, of depicting character, or inventing an oration. But a decline might be suggested by sundry phenomena of language in Books XV and XVI. The writer is in a hurry, he seems to become negligent.[2]

Perhaps the *Annales* lacked the final revision.[3] It does not have to be assumed that the last section ended, as it now ends, with a broken sentence in Book XVI—the recorded total of thirty books for *Historiae* and *Annales* together speaks for completion.[4] Yet the author, terminating the third hexad, may not have lived long enough to impress upon his text a Tacitean perfection comparable to the earlier books.

Omissions, impediments, or incoherence in the narrative will help that hypothesis—could they be certified. The search is not at first sight remunerative. The extant books have nothing, it is true, about the situation on and beyond the river Danube since the reign of Claudius. Transactions of some note had occurred.[5] Yet they hardly touched the central theme of the historian, and could be kept for a recapitulatory chapter or two.[6] Again, the conspiracy of Piso carries a full catalogue of names and persons, more than thirty of them packed into a single chapter.[7] Excessive perhaps, and fatiguing. None the less, it would argue a failure to understand what Roman and senatorial history is like if anybody fancied that remorseless documentation about persons is a sign of incompetent or unfinished workmanship.

A more searching inquiry into the third hexad might lay bare a number of compositional stop-gaps, residues of annotation, misleading clues, or imperfectly managed transitions. Though no single item could be convincing, the cumulation of heterogeneous symptoms may tilt the balance. All sections in the Neronian annals did not inspire the historian equally, and it was a temptation to press forward to the climax with its liberating prospect of swift narration in a large field: he could return later to tighten, emend, elucidate, or omit. If such was the procedure of Tacitus, it might leave some traces—episodes fully worked up (such as the campaigns in Armenia and Britain), but not always clearly related in chronology to the annalistic sequence,

[1] Ch. xxxviii. [2] For instances, App. 59.

[3] E. Koestermann, *Gnomon* xi (1935), 322. That scholar also suggests that Tacitus may have been interrupted by death.

[4] App. 35.

[5] cf. the *elogium* of Ti. Plautius Silvanus Aelianus, governor of Moesia (*ILS* 986).

[6] cf. Ph. Fabia, *Rev. ét. anc.* xxxiv (1932), 139 ff.

[7] xv. 71.

speeches completed and stylized, but sometimes lacking proper explanation of their historical context, and miscellaneous items that he might ultimately discard for artistic reasons.[1]

The Tiberian books of the *Annales* show the historian in his developed idiom, in full mastery of structure and coherence. The style there stands at its uniform perfection—most Tacitean, with demonstrable efforts and devices. It is not easy to divine why Tacitus should deliberately choose to become less like himself, abating his intensity.[2]

Of what manner shall be the final verdict on Tacitus? His literary genius being incontestable, but not his merit as an historian (for the canons are subject to variation, not to say aberration), a formula has been devised that shall pacify or flatter the professional conscience of scholars: he was not an historian but a poet.[3] Some think by this axiom to dispose of Tacitus, others (and the better) to redeem him. If they mean well by literature, and contribute sensibly to its understanding, they do not render a service to history.[4] The like defence avails for Livy, and there is much truth and persuasiveness in the notion that Livy is a kind of prose Virgil. Since, however, the notion is not fully valid for Livy save where he deals in the mythical or the unverifiable, it must fall a long way short of the truth about Tacitus.

An orator or stylist might turn for solace to dramatic poetry, transferring to an earlier scene the discontents and conflicts of the present. In the estimation of Quintilian, the prime orator among those he had known was Domitius Afer, the prime tragedian Pomponius Secundus;[5] and it might be represented that the latter did not yield to the former in his claim to enduring renown.[6] Legendary subjects now seemed remote or incapable of renovation (Seneca's productions bore witness), even though some *Atreus* or *Thyestes* might come in useful for invective against palace and dynasty, for maxims of subversive statecraft.[7]

---

[1] For signs of incompleteness, App. 60.

[2] The difference of subject is perhaps the best answer to that question. It does not, however, cover all the phenomena perceptible towards the end of the *Annales* as extant. The various deficiencies cannot prove, but might·make it plausible, that the author did not live to achieve his plan. And, if it were further to be argued that he wrote no more than what now exists of Book XVI, the theory that the *Historiae* account for twelve books (not fourteen) in the total of thirty (Ch. xvii, cf. App. 35) becomes vulnerable.

[3] F. Leo, *Tacitus* (Kaisergeburtstagsrede, Göttingen, 1896). And dramatic Hellenistic history-writing can be adduced in comparison, cf. E. Norden, *Die r. Literatur*[5] (1955), 93.

[4] The greatness of his work is not impaired by his understanding even less of politics than of warfare, according to E. Bickel, *Bonner Jahrbücher* cxxxiii (1928), 27. And, to E. Fraenkel, Tacitus is an historian without a subject (*Neue Jahrbücher* viii (1932), 231).

[5] Quintilian xii. 11. 3; x. 1. 98.   [6] *Dial.* 13. 3.

[7] Thus Seneca's *Thyestes*, that of Curiatius Maternus (*Dial.* 3. 3), or the *Atreus* of the consular orator Aemilius Scaurus (Dio lviii. 24. 3 f., cf. *Ann.* vi. 27. 3). The *Atreus* of Accius had produced the classic 'oderint dum metuant' (Cicero, *De off.* i. 97).

Roman history gave scope for poetry and for high politics, notably the catastrophe of the Republic. Hence the *Cato* composed by Curiatius Maternus (senator, orator, and poet) whom the young Tacitus knew and admired. And, if Cato or Brutus were exhausted, did not the tragedy of the Caesars embody a sequence of dramatic themes, with ambition, power, and crime recalling the House of Atreus? The aptitude disclosed in the *Annales* might have found expression and renown with a *Sejanus* or an *Agrippina*.

There was also the epic, itself closely germane to history. Lucan showed the way, but Lucan had taken the best theme, Cato and the fall of 'Libertas'; and the latest heroic poem at Rome, the *Punica* of Silius Italicus, attested only a praiseworthy intention, a noble nostalgia, a tedious anachronism. The thing had been achieved long ago by Livy. Epic and drama were finished, and so was political eloquence. They could be perpetuated only if transfused into another medium. If history was that medium, it demanded the talents of orator, dramatist, and poet. It would have to be narrated with splendour and dignity and power.

The style of Tacitus exploits to the utmost the native resources of the Latin language; and he writes with that imagination which is the soul of history as it is the soul of poetry.[1] The historian of imperial Rome is the crown and summit of imperial literature. History, however, must also stand the question for accuracy and integrity, for range and depth.

---

[1] Cf. H. Taine, *Essai sur Tite-Live* (1860), 332: 'si le but de l'histoire est de ressusciter le passé, nul historien n'égale Tacite.' To Mommsen, historians belong rather with the 'Künstler' than with 'die Gelehrten' (*Reden u. Aufsätze* (1905), 11).

PART VI

THE *ANNALES* AS HISTORY

XXVIII. THE SUBJECT OF THE *ANNALES*

THE victory of Caesar Augustus signified that a cycle ended in the long annals of Rome. In the beginning the Kings, and then the Free State, which yielded to the age of the dynasts; and the last of the dynasts brought in the monarchy again. The formulation was easy and inescapable.[1] Tacitus adopts it in the exordium of the *Annales*, setting down in brief phrases the vicissitudes of power from the Kings to the Principate.[2]

The words convey the impression of a narrative to start from civil peace and the new order. It is abruptly dispelled. Tacitus chooses to begin with the death of Augustus and the accession of Tiberius Caesar. For various reasons (and some of them may be divined), but he acknowledges only one.

Excellent historians, 'decora ingenia', had not been lacking to narrate the reign of Augustus—at least until subservience became prevalent.[3] What had been written about the successors, however, was false all through, the living adulated, the dead defamed.[4] Tacitus will revise that story, in a spirit of severe impartiality.

The excuse for omitting Augustus is literary rather than historical, and, on the author's own showing, not wholly valid. The growth of subservience, to which Tacitus alludes, was not the chief impediment. From its inception the Principate hampered inquiry—and by its very nature, long before it began to reward flattery and penalize freedom.

---

[1] Dio LII. 1. 1; Appian, *BC* I. 6.

[2] The Republic ends in the strife for power and a rapid sequence of dominations down to Caesar's heir, 'qui cuncta discordiis civilibus fessa nomine principis sub imperium accepit.' For the line of the dynasts see *Hist.* II. 38, and, omitting certain names to emphasize a murderous continuity, Lucan IV. 822 f.: 'Sulla potens Mariusque ferox et Cinna cruentus | Caesareaeque domus series.'

[3] I. 1. 2: 'temporibusque Augusti dicendis non defuere decora ingenia donec gliscente adulatione deterrerentur.'

[4] ib.: 'Tiberii Gaique et Claudii ac Neronis res florentibus ipsis ob metum falsae, postquam occiderant, recentibus odiis compositae sunt.'

Tacitus knew. In the preface to the *Historiae* he puts the blame on the monarchy itself. The 'magna ingenia' lapsed after Actium, and truth was perverted, first of all because men now lacked political knowledge and insight.[1] A later writer, Cassius Dio, states the problem firmly.[2]

Under the dispensation of Senate and People (he explains) matters of moment were openly debated and generally known; though some writers might be influenced by fear or favour, the truth could more or less be ascertained from others; and there were public records. Under the reign of the Caesars the principal decisions were taken in secret. What was made public evaded verification and tended to be discredited, for men suspect that all transactions of word or deed proceed by will of the rulers and their allies in the power. Wherefore rumour descants upon many things that never happened, authentic events do not even become known, and almost everything is wrongly interpreted.

Moreover, he continues, the size of the Empire and the complexity of its affairs put accurate knowledge out of reach. Such is the warning with which Cassius Dio ushers in the epoch of the Caesars—and his own narrative attests the correctness of his diagnosis.

Deceit and distortion set in at once. In 29 B.C. the victor of Actium celebrated his triumph, terminating the twenty years of anarchy. Normal government appeared to return, by a visible sign: the next year saw the consular *fasces* passing between the ruler and his colleague by the proper and Republican alternation.[3] Other measures followed;[4] and, in January, 27 B.C., the master of the Roman world duly announced that the 'res publica' had been given back to the charge of Senate and People. Each year from 31 onwards he had been consul, and that was his sole basis of legal authority in the State. A further definition was now required.

Caesar Augustus consented to assume through delegated powers a special mandate, taking as his portion the provinces of prime military strength for a term of ten years. There were pretexts, and a reason: he feared proconsuls with armies. The ruler's decision was in some way influenced, it may be, by a vexatious incident. It concerned an ambitious nobleman, the proconsul of Macedonia, who infringed the

---

[1] *Hist.* I. I. I: 'simul veritas pluribus modis infracta, primum inscitia rei publicae ut alienae, mox libidine adsentandi aut rursus odio adversus dominantis.' For the elder Seneca, 'veritas' declined from the outset of the Civil Wars (quoted on p. 277).

[2] LIII. 19.

[3] Dio LIII. I. I (presumably on February I). This passage has seldom been either correctly interpreted or properly exploited. Some have taken it to imply the previous bearing of twenty-four *fasces*: wrongly, as the language of Dio proves.

[4] cf. esp. *Ann.* III. 28. 2: 'sexto demum consulatu Caesar Augustus, potentiae securus, quae triumviratu iusserat abolevit deditque iura quis pace et principe uteremur.' In most modern accounts the transactions of January 27 tend to obscure everything else.

martial monopoly of the new Romulus. The written record assigns it no relevance.[1]

Next, the year 23, when the prosecution of a proconsul raised embarrassing questions about the prerogative of Caesar Augustus. It also produced a conspiracy—one of his principal adherents was involved, the consul Varro Murena, brother-in-law of Maecenas. Augustus himself fell grievously ill. When he recovered, the legal basis of his predominance was again modified. The account of Cassius Dio disturbs the sequence, transferring prosecution and conspiracy to the next year.[2] Given a distortion of this magnitude, there is less cause for surprise that another aspect of the situation should be obscured, namely the struggle for power in the entourage of a ruler believed near to death. Marcus Agrippa came out of it with a clear accession of authority.[3]

It was the strength of Sallust and Pollio that they wrote about high politics from personal knowledge, with nobody to stop them. Even under the rule of Caesar Augustus a man might recount the recent disturbances without undue subservience towards the victor.[4] Various reasons contributed. They soon ceased to operate. Livy might have terminated his history of Rome with the end of the wars and the triumph of Caesar's heir, but, emboldened to go on, he produced another 'decade' by way of crown or epilogue, carrying the tale down to 9 B.C. in nine books (CXXXIV–CXLII). With how much ease or success, it might well be asked.

The fabric and institutions of the Republic being restored, with annual consuls duly elected by the People, Livy could revert to the annalistic grouping of events, as in the old and happy days. For his material he had the public transactions of the Roman State. That is, elections, the passing of laws, and debates in the Senate; and, abroad, the wars of the generals. Valuable items were the ceremonies and pageantry enacted or revived by the Princeps.

The epilogue involved much hard work (Livy can have had few predecessors here), and it was beset by many traps and perplexities. How could a contemporary of Augustus, writing in the last years of that ruler (or at least completing the work soon after his decease), deal with such episodes as the conspiracy of the consul Varro Murena and the tremendous crisis of 23 B.C.? It was easier to decide where to end.

---

[1] For M. Licinius Crassus (*cos.* 30 B.C.) cf. Dio LI. 24. 4 (first exploited by E. Groag, P–W XIII, 283 ff.).

[2] LIV. 3. It is no accident that the name of A. Terentius Varro Murena, *ordinarius* for 23, fails to appear on all the calendars—except for the *Fasti Capitolini* (*Inscr. It.* XIII, 1, p. 58).

[3] viz. a share in the provincial *imperium* of Caesar Augustus. Not stated by Dio, or by any other authority. It has to be deduced from Dio LIII. 32. 1; LIV. 11. 6. Cf. R. Syme, *Rom. Rev.* (1939) 337; 340 ff.   [4] IV. 34 (the oration of Cremutius Cordus).

Stopping at 9 B.C., when Drusus died on campaign beyond the Rhine, Livy was able to commemorate the imperial victories of the re-invigorated Republic under the guidance of Caesar Augustus, with proud melancholy for the end of Drusus, and warm appreciation for the 'pietas' of his brother.[1] Not long after that date the voluntary exile of Tiberius, succeeded by the scandals and calamities of the dynasty, made it quite impossible to go any further.[2]

Livy's nine books on the Republic of Caesar Augustus cannot have been wholly satisfactory. They will have shown up some of his characteristic failings—he was docile, he lacked political understanding, he refused to take historical problems by the throat.[3]

Some of Livy's troubles may be surmised. Nothing could stop Velleius Paterculus. His loyal fervour insists everywhere on rendering praise where praise is safe and profitable, with manifold convolutions of deceit and flattery. The whole world, so Velleius exclaims, felt the shock of Tiberius' departure to Rhodes;[4] but, when Tiberius was adopted by Augustus, men could at last feel confidence in home and wife and property, and count on all felicity.[5] When Augustus yielded up to Heaven his heavenly soul, Rome and all people trembled on the verge of ruin: Velleius affirms with pious horror how narrowly was calamity then averted, and modestly declines to go into detail.[6] The assertion is negligible, no more meriting credence than what the same person has to relate about the phenomenal virtues of the Tiberian régime, instantaneously apparent in total contrast to all that went before.[7]

Velleius is voluble and unscrupulous. Velleius can forge a date;[8] and, when registering the relegation of Agrippa Postumus, he clearly implies that the youth died some time before the end of Augustus' reign.[9]

Velleius concludes with a prayer to the gods of Rome: when

---

[1] Livy, *Per.* CXLII, cf. Val. Max. v. 5. 3, &c.

[2] The accepted notion is that the historian died pen in hand, cf. A. Klotz, P–W XIII, 818; and Schanz–Hosius, *Gesch. der r. Lit.* II⁴ (1935), 300, can essay no other explanation for his ending with 9 B.C. Less than justice has been done to Livy's sense of propriety, both artistic and historical, and to his prudence. It is also a question how far Cremutius Cordus felt able to proceed with the reign of Augustus: he is cited for an event of 18 B.C. (Suetonius, *Divus Aug.* 35. 2).

[3] There is no trace of Dio's having used him subsequent to 30 B.C.; cf. E. Schwartz, P–W III, 1698.

[4] Velleius II. 100. 1.   [5] 103. 5.   [6] 124. 1.

[7] 126. 2: 'revocata in forum fides, summota e foro seditio, ambitio campo, discordia curia, sepultaeque ac situ obsitae iustitia aequitas industria civitati redditae; accessit magistratibus auctoritas, senatui maiestas, iudiciis gravitas.'

[8] Caesar's heir marched on Rome and seized the consulate (August 19, 43). Velleius suppresses a damaging fact, changes the date to September 22, and further puts the consulship subsequent to the formation of the Triumvirate (II. 65. 2).

[9] 112. 7 (under A.D. 6), ending with the words 'moxque crescentibus in dies vitiis dignum

Tiberius Caesar has fulfilled the duty of his station on earth, may he transmit the power to one whose shoulders are strong enough to carry it.[1] Velleius was writing in 29 or 30. He duly inserted a panegyric of Seianus. Starting from precedents in Roman history for the 'magni adiutores' who share the burden of rule, he terminates with the virtues of the indispensable minister, not omitting that modesty which asked for nothing and was awarded everything.[2] In 31 Seianus became consul, as colleague of the Emperor. When Seianus fell, his ruin involved a numerous company of clients, intriguers, and careerists. Among them one historian at least.[3]

Such was history under the Caesars. Velleius, though early in date, exemplifies the mature imperial age in its abasement before power. Cornelius Tacitus, narrating that epoch and theme, set his exordium at the year 14. Perhaps the true date lay further back.

If an historian were anxious to escape complete entanglement in the reign of Caesar Augustus, he might begin half-way, where Livy ended, where chance had ordained the perfect dichotomy in the forty four years since the Battle of Actium. Livy left off with Ti. Claudius Nero patently the first man in the State next to Caesar Augustus. Discord soon intervened, and Tiberius went away in sullen anger. There ensued a concatenation of intrigues and catastrophes eminently congenial to the talent of Cornelius Tacitus.

The career and prospects of Tiberius, it seemed plain, were terminated. His peers and rivals emerge to command the great armies on the Rhine and in Illyricum. Augustus, anxious to ensure the succession for the princes Gaius and Lucius (the sons of Agrippa and Julia), was forced to lean heavily for support on various groups and families in the *nobilitas*. Monarchy and aristocracy became closely entwined.[4] The government survived the shock of a dynastic intrigue (Julia was sent away to an island, and several of her paramours were executed, among them the son of Marcus Antonius), and the Princeps passed safely the sixty-third year of his age. Soon his dearest hopes were shattered. The princes perished in turn. In the summer of A.D. 4

furore suo habuit exitum'. It becomes difficult to accept (or understand) the amicable opinion expressed in *CAH* x (1934), 871: 'an honest man, such as Velleius was.'

[1] 131. 1 f.: 'custodite servate protegite hunc statum hanc pacem ⟨hunc principem⟩, eique functo longissima statione mortali destinate successores quam serissimos, sed eos quorum cervices tam fortiter sustinendo terrarum orbis imperio sufficiant quam huius suffecisse sensimus, consiliaque omnium civium aut pia ⟨iuvate aut impia confringite⟩.'

[2] 127. 4: 'virum severitatis laetissimae, hilaritatis priscae, actu otiosio simillimum, nihil sibi vindicantem eoque adsequentem omnia, semperque infra aliorum aestimationes se metientem, vultu vitaque tranquillum, animo exsomnem.' For the language used after his destruction see Valerius Maximus IX. 11, *ext.* 4.

[3] Bruttedius Niger (Juvenal x. 103), compare the prophetic allusion in *Ann.* III. 66. 4 (p. 326).

[4] cf. *Rom. Rev.* (1939), 419 ff.

Tiberius Claudius Nero (who had been permitted to return to Rome two years previously) became Ti. Caesar.

That year designated the ruler of Rome, though Rome saw but little of him in the next decade. Two campaigns in Germany brought the Roman armies to the Elbe. The next task was to break the empire of Maroboduus. It was interrupted by the great insurrection in Illyricum. Barely were the Pannonians and Dalmatians reduced when calamity supervened in Germany. Tiberius hastened to the Rhine, and he had to defer for three years his Pannonian triumph.

If Cornelius Tacitus disdained to compose annalistic books 'a fine Titi Livi' (and he aspired to be something more than a continuator), he had a subject and a date. Not the accession of Ti. Caesar, but the decisive turn of events ten years earlier and the genuine inception of a new period. Various administrative and fiscal changes had then been introduced.[1] More important, a new governmental party emerges in the aristocracy. The rivals of Tiberius recede, and the consular list advertises his adherents—noble houses of Republican or Pompeian allegiance, and by contrast yet not anomalous, a notable accession of new men.[2]

To begin at A.D. 4 might seem over-bold. Authoritative reasons spoke for 14, at least on the face of things. Cornelius Tacitus, whom some have censured for his fidelity to the annalistic schema at the opening of the *Historiae*, ought perhaps to acquire merit for choosing a ruler's accession. It marked a firm date. Being transmitted, the imperial authority acquired definition. The Principate was now recognized as a permanent form of government, with prerogatives not granted separately (and some ostensibly for a period of years), but confirmed in one act, and for the lifetime of the ruler.[3] Not only that: the Republic ended, openly and legally. That the Roman People chose the men to lead in peace and war was the palladium of the Commonwealth—at the same time aristocratic and democratic.[4] Caesar Augustus, who restored the 'res publica', honoured the form however much he impaired the substance: arrogating to himself the functions of Senate, laws, and magistrates, the Princeps was yet constrained to keep until the end some semblance at least of popular election. When he died the final blow could be dealt with the utmost propriety. One of the earliest acts of Tiberius Caesar was to take the elections from the People and transfer them to the Senate.[5]

---

[1] In 6 the *aerarium militare* was established, and the city police was organized under an equestrian prefect; and a *praefectus annonae* was created soon after. Note also the *Lex Valeria Cornelia* of 5, modifying the electoral procedure (revealed by the *Tabula Hebana*, cf. App. 67).   [2] *Rom. Rev.* (1939), 434 f.   [3] p. 411.

[4] I. I. I: 'libertatem et consulatum L. Brutus instituit.'

[5] 15. I: 'tum primum e campo comitia ad patres translata sunt: nam ad eum diem, etsi

So far the law and the constitution. On sharper scrutiny the year 14 must forfeit much of its importance. It is not the vital date. How grave in fact was the crisis provoked by the decease of Augustus, how delicate the transmission of the supreme power? It was tempting to exaggerate. Tacitus cannot be acquitted of the charge.[1]

Tiberius Caesar already held the essential powers of the Principate.[2] It was clear that he had exercised them. Allegiance was promptly rendered by oath, the city of Rome remained tranquil; while loyal adherents from among the consulars commanded the provincial armies. If the legions on the Rhine and in Pannonia raised mutiny, they did not protest against system or succession. The troops merely seized the chance to voice their legitimate grievances long postponed or cheated.

Intent as he is upon the realities of power (to the scorn of forms and names and all pretence), Tacitus ought to have gone back to A.D. 4. He would gain a clearer vision of the character of Ti. Caesar, of policy foreign and domestic, of the imperial authority in its steady development. Prosecutions for treason, the condition of the armies, the German wars and the disputes about Armenia—none of these were new phenomena. Historical proportion would benefit, and artistic balance.[3]

For, indeed, his choice entailed a variety of discomforts. Ever and again the author must pause and reflect: which persons and incidents could be taken as known, which of them required elucidation? Tacitus was attentive and scrupulous, adding prefatory material, digressions, and footnotes. Though annotation affords relief in the Tiberian books, it often impedes the flow of narration.

Before Tacitus had gone very far with the *Annales* he became conscious of his predicament—if not of his mistake. One thing was patent: the new ruler professed all the time that he was acting in the spirit and policy of his predecessor.[4] Not the whole truth, but many of the facts lent support. In foreign affairs as in domestic, the main themes lead back to the days of Augustus, namely the German wars and affairs in the East: the former explain themselves, supplemented with a number of references to the disaster of Quinctilius Varus, while the latter require a digression of some length at the beginning of Book II. Both

potissima arbitrio principis, quaedam tamen studiis tribuum fiebant.' Cf. I. 81 (the consular elections in 15). See further App. 67.

[1] At least in what he says when the decease of Augustus seemed imminent—'pauci bona libertatis in cassum disserere, plures bellum pavescere, alii cupere' (I. 4. 2).

[2] p. 410.

[3] Maroboduus and the Varian disaster having been narrated, the subsequent operations would be seen in their true light—and it would scarcely have been possible to give Germanicus so much space.

[4] IV. 37. 3: 'qui omnia facta dictaque eius vice legis observem.' Cf. Strabo VI. 288.

subjects are in a sense epilogues. Even a minor matter like the rising of Tacfarinas is only a resurgence of the troubles in Numidia temporarily suppressed by the Gaetulian War a decade earlier.[1]

It was too late for the historian to modify his present design, but he might make amends later. A cluster of passages in Book III would be significant even if it did not contain an avowal and a pledge.

Under the year 20, after winding up the inquiry into the death of Germanicus Caesar, Tacitus inserts two chapters continuing the story of Tacfarinas, and reverts to domestic history with the prosecution of Aemilia Lepida.[2] That lady, formerly the wife of an elderly consular, the unamiable Sulpicius Quirinius, had once been betrothed to the prince Lucius Caesar. Both names echo back to the Principate of Caesar Augustus, to the central subject of dynastic politics (and to the earlier vicissitudes of Tiberius himself). Further, the author was soon going to tell something more about Quirinius, when that person died.[3] The next episode is explicit. There returned to Rome from distant and voluntary exile a certain nobleman, D. Junius Silanus, who had been implicated in the scandal of the younger Julia, the grand-daughter of the Princeps, twelve years before.[4]

After brief annotation explaining how Augustus, by treating adultery as an offence against the State, broke with the ancestral tradition of clemency (and went beyond the letter of his own legislation), Tacitus affirms that he will relate the affair along with the other history of that age if life be vouchsafed after the termination of the *Annales* for more tasks than one.[5] The phrase carries a hint of an old project, now perhaps ostensibly practicable, if Trajan was dead. But only a hint. The thoughts of the author had come to dwell much more upon Caesar Augustus—he goes on to discuss moral legislation and concludes the year 20 with remarks about the ministers of Augustus.

The Senate discussed a proposal for mitigating the penalties of the *Lex Papia Poppaea*, designed to deter celibacy (and enrich the public finances).[6] Therefore a long excursus on the origin and development of legislation, with the emphasis on force or turbulence.[7] Coming closer to the present, Tacitus rebukes Pompeius Magnus, the legislator who

---

[1] Dio LV. 28. 3 f. The war was won by Cossus Cornelius Lentulus, consul in 1 B.C. (*AE* 1940, 68 = *IRT* 301).   [2] III. 22 f.

[3] 48—the vote of a public funeral, which drew from Tiberius remarks about his own sojourn at Rhodes, about Gaius Caesar, and about the long-deceased consular M. Lollius.

[4] 24.3. That mysterious affair occurred in A.D. 8. It appears to have involved the death of Julia's husband, L. Aemilius Paullus (*cos.* A.D. 1), for conspiracy (Suetonius, *Divus Aug.* 19. 1).

[5] 24. 3: 'sed aliorum exitus simul cetera illius aetatis memorabo, si effectis in quae tetendi plures ad curas vitam produxero.'   [6] 25.

[7] 26 f. For the source of this excursus, patently Sallustian in language but perhaps owing something to an oration of Claudius Caesar, see App. 41.

violated his own enactments, and, across the twenty years of anarchy, terminates with Augustus' measures of 28 B.C., repealing all the acts of the Triumvirate—and ordaining how Rome was to continue under the régime of 'pax et princeps'. That meant control and repression henceforth: 'acriora ex eo vincula, inditi custodes'.[1] The *Papia Poppaea* (though passed much later, in A.D. 9) was an example, and the historian enlarges upon its detrimental consequences.[2]

The next entry also concerns the founder of the Principate. Tiberius, begging the Senate to consent to an exemption for one of the sons of Germanicus, urged a precedent—himself and his brother, on the petition of Augustus. The historian cannot stifle a personal comment: even then, he says, there must have been men who secretly mocked at such entreaties.[3] Two or three items of dynastic interest follow, and with the year's end Tacitus chronicles the demise of two illustrious survivors—the first occurrence of such obituary notices in the *Annales*.

L. Volusius and Sallustius Crispus passed away. In the former, an opulent consular of good repute, not much that compelled commemoration.[4] Very different the latter. Crispus, the grand-nephew of the historian, stood next to the great Maecenas and took his place as minister of state.[5] Mere knights by rank, Maecenas and Crispus far surpassed in power any of the senators decorated with the emblems of consulate or triumph. Both were proverbial for luxury in the manner of their life, for alertness and capacity beneath the mask of indolence. Both rendered notable and often clandestine service to the government—and neither kept the friendship of his master till the end. Tacitus is moved to meditate upon the favourites of princes, and the transience of their 'potentia'.

The historian thus betrays, repeatedly, a preoccupation with Augustus. In the preface he spoke well of Augustan historians. No names, but he meant Livy in the first instance, a contrast in tone to the general allusion in the exordium of the *Historiae*. It now suited his purpose to be complimentary. Tacitus need not have revised his estimate of Livy. The phrase 'decora ingenia' does not carry one very far. He knew that style and honesty are not enough. It demanded

---

[1] III. 28. 3.

[2] 25. 1; 28. 3. Compare the sane and humane observations of F. Schulz on marriage and matrimonial legislation (*Classical Roman Law* (1951), 107 f.).

[3] 29. 2 (cited in App. 54).

[4] 30. 1: 'Volusio vetus familia neque tamen praeturam egressa: ipse consulatum intulit, censoria etiam potestate legendis equitum decuriis functus, opumque quis domus illa immensum viguit primus adcumulator.' On the family, p. 302 f.

[5] Tacitus may have known that Maecenas, like Crispus, was responsible for a 'primum facinus'—the execution of young Lepidus, a nephew of Brutus (*PIR*[2], A 368), in the year after Actium.

great efforts to disinter the whole truth about the first epoch of the Principate—and courage to publish it.

While working on the early books of the *Annales*, Tacitus might discover soon and easily how inadequate was Augustan history when written by the contemporaries of Augustus—or of Tiberius. The second half of Augustus' long reign was peculiarly liable to be mis-construed—for many reasons. The decade when Tiberius was absent from affairs produced embarrassment and concealments; while for the next ten years the large theme of the foreign wars tended to cover up domestic politics or scandal in the dynasty.[1]

It was a dark and enigmatic period that now began to excite the curiosity of Cornelius Tacitus.[2] Inspection would perhaps show the last years of the Augustan Principate not so different from the familiar quality and texture of imperial history. And the whole reign needed revision: it might disclose the great secret, how and why the Principate took an evil course. Although not a little was remembered to the discredit of the Princeps and his friends, the happy era of peace and order after the Civil Wars became the dominant theme, which was re-inforced by the prestige of Augustan literature (the great names belonged to the early years), and by subsequent tribulations under the tyranny of the Caesars.

Tradition had been over-indulgent. Inquiry brought up startling facts. Not even the Augustan programme of moral and social reform was immune from doubt and ambiguity: a public statement from Tiberius Caesar avowed the defects or failures of his predecessor's legislation.[3] Thus encouraged, Tacitus comes out with his own verdict on the much advertised frugality of the Augustan age. Nothing had stemmed the tide of extravagance: luxury rolled on exuberantly all the time, from the aftermath of Actium to the fall of the dynasty.[4] In like fashion, the commerce of the sexes evaded regimentation. Tacitus might start with a quiet assumption about licence or hypocrisy among the holders of power or leaders in society. Nothing emerged to contradict. Malicious talk or some truthful biography passed on revelations about the conduct of Roman matrons, and his own research disinterred ancient scandal without effort.[5]

---

[1] And still tends: Julia and L. Paullus have no place in *CAH* x (1934).

[2] More obscure, in truth, than the twenty years of Trajan's reign, over which Gibbon sighed—'the glimmerings of an abridgement, or the doubtful light of a panegyric.' For the time of Trajan the Plinian letters bear witness—and all Tacitus. There is hardly any contemporary testimony for 6 B.C.–A.D. 14.

[3] III. 54. 2: 'tot a maioribus repertae leges, tot quas divus Augustus tulit, illae oblivione, hae, quod flagitiosius est, contemptu abolitae securiorem luxum fecere.' As for the marriage laws cf. Tiberius' steps to mitigate the *Papia Poppaea* (III. 28. 4).   [4] 55.

[5] Tacitus might know about Vistilia, the lady of the six husbands (Pliny, *NH* VII. 39). Among her children were Pomponius Secundus, Domitius Corbulo, Suillius Rufus, and

*Tac. as
a skeptic*

Too much, the historian perceived, had commonly been taken for granted about the rule and epoch of Caesar Augustus. Hence an impulsion to show up credulity, error, or deceit. That may not be the only reason behind Tacitus' decision to revert one day to Augustus. Perhaps also the suspicion, nascent or by now corroborated, that he had made a bad start with Tiberius Caesar.

So far the choice of subject—and its discomforts, both historical and artistic. In execution, the work lies open to various animadversions, some valid, but many premature or perverse. First, the selection of material. Too much, surely, about Rome, the Senate, and the dynasty. The author is aware of the objection. Many things, he concedes, in his Tiberian narrative must appear trivial and unimportant.[1] He has a retort. In all ages there are different forms of government: to wit, the rule of one man, of the few, of the many (for the mixed constitution, including all three elements, is more easily praised than produced— and it cannot last). At Rome under the Republic it was expedient to know how to manage the mob; and men who studied with especial care the character of the Senate and of its leaders earned a reputation for political sagacity. By the same token, now that one man in effect held the power, matters such as Tacitus registers will furnish instruction and guidance.[2]

Tacitus might have added (but it was superfluous) that, since he wrote as far as he could in consonance with the tradition and canons of the 'res publica', it was an historian's duty to insert a full measure of senatorial transactions, however unexhilarating or even repellent, if his *Annales* were not to degenerate into a dynastic chronicle and end as a sequence of imperial biographies.

If the defence is valid, it does not wholly cover the historian. A grave charge subsists: scenes and characters, especially dynastic, deliberately enhanced for colour and effect, while historical proportion suffers. Thus Germanicus Caesar in the long narrations that relate the mutiny on the Rhine, the campaigns in Germany, the mission to the eastern lands, the death of the prince and the subsequent inquiry at Rome. Again, the wives of Claudius engross too much space; while Corbulo, Seneca, and Thrasea seem isolated and magnified in order to contrast,

Milonia Caesonia the consort of Caligula: cf. C. Cichorius, *Römische Studien* (1922), 429 ff., who, however, took Suillius to be Vistilia's husband. Another Vistilia sought official sanction for an irregular life—'licentiam stupri apud aediles vulgaverat more inter veteres recepto' (*Ann.* II. 85. 3). Perhaps a paradoxical protest against the matrimonial adventures of her aunt (rather than, as *PIR*[1], V 491 suggests, her sister). For the family and origin cf. R. Syme *JRS* xxxix (1949), 16 f.

[1] IV. 32. I.

[2] 33. 2: 'sic converso statu neque alia re Romana quam si unus imperitet, haec conquiri tradique in rem fuerit.'

by virtue and achievement, with the Emperor Nero—who was a tyrant, a murderer, and a fool.[1]

Much of the criticism abates on a proper understanding of the author's design, of the structural necessities of his work. History cannot afford to eschew narration. Much of the material was cumbrous and refractory. Tacitus imparted life and movement by what means he could.[2] Nor is drama and artistry the whole story. Tacitus' personal opinions intervene in a way not always suspected, likewise the influences of his own time.

The mutinies in A.D. 14 are told abundantly and vividly—as befits a writer who is preoccupied (as before in the *Historiae*) with the behaviour of soldiers.[3] Moreover, the scene is well placed at the outset of a narrative which carries as one of its themes (always present but not always explicit) the relation between the government and the army—and which is designed to terminate with a series of military insurrections. Further, the palace being the centre of influence and power, the entourage of the ruler—empress, favourites, and freedmen—claims predominant interest, patently with Claudius, and no less with Nero, when the personalities change, and the public professions, but not all the channels of patronage and devices of government.

Yet it is not clear that the historian can everywhere earn a plenary exculpation. He luxuriates in the follies of Valeria Messallina, the marriage festival she celebrated with C. Silius—and all the details of her destruction.[4] After Messallina, another woman, and another tragedy. The younger Agrippina is the central figure in the story of Claudius' last years. Rightly. Her arts secured matrimony with her uncle, and his compliance; she directed policy, corrupt but vigorous; ensconcing her adherents at the points of vantage and control, she prepared the succession of her son and managed the business through crime—and with no civil or military disturbance. Agrippina retains due prominence in the narrative for a time—it was the most urgent task of Nero's ministers to block, circumvent, and subvert the authority of the Augusta. Tacitus traces the stages and devices in her demolition with skill and subtlety, as is proper—for power is the essential subject of political history. Agrippina was quickly reduced to impotence. Was it necessary, however, to recount at such length the epilogue, delayed for several years?

---

[1] For their importance to Tacitus, and to history, below, Ch. XLI f.

[2] Modern writers have not achieved conspicuous success in narrating the early Empire.

[3] Not all is turbulence and drama. Observe valuable items such as the grievances of the soldiers expounded in the speech of Percennius (I. 17), or the picture of the oppressive subaltern officer Aufidienus Rufus (I. 20. 2).

[4] XI. 26–38. The brevity of Suetonius might here seem to deserve commendation (*Divus Claudius* 26. 2; 29. 3; 36).

The murder of Agrippina, like the catastrophe of Valeria Messallina, seems to show a wilful neglect of historical proportion. Agrippina as a central theme crowds out information (surely relevant and valuable) about her political adherents in the senatorial order, about the changes in the army commanders both when she was winning control of the government and when she lost it, betrayed by Annaeus Seneca and Afranius Burrus.

The dramatic concentration of interest upon a few figures in the Neronian books (the Emperor and his successive victims, Agrippina, Seneca, Thrasea, and Corbulo) entails grievous disadvantages. Policy suffers, events remain unelucidated or are forced into an unconvincing sequence of cause and result. Though Book XIII opens in clarity and power, the historian seems to have missed an opportunity. He does not explain how the government was carried on during that felicitous but impermanent partnership between the monarchical power and the Roman Senate.[1] He moves away with alacrity to Corbulo and the East. Not that foreign policy will be made wholly intelligible. After waiting for several years the great general invades Armenia in 58: whose the decision, and for what reason?

Armenian affairs in the subsequent narration betray several changes of plan—effective suzerainty, conquest, and finally compromise. Tacitus nowhere expounds the problem as a whole. Hence easy censure upon the historian, and an occasion for lengthy argumentations.[2] It should, however, be noted that much of what is dignified by the name of imperial policy appears to derive less from design than from accident or improvisation. Tacitus confines his account to what happened. Though the story is obscure in patches and sometimes incoherent, the situation and outcome are in no way mysterious.[3]

Elsewhere the motivation is abundant but misleading. The murder of Agrippina supplies the opening scene of Book XIV. Why did Nero decide to kill his mother precisely now—not sooner and not later? Poppaea Sabina incites him. She insists upon marriage—yet the marriage will not be solemnized until nearly three years have elapsed.[4]

---

[1] The reason may be obvious—that, despite public professions, most depended on diplomatic arts and secret management. Some modern accounts exaggerate ingenuously the role and liberty of the Senate as a body.

[2] Henderson assigns the main credit to the Emperor (*The Life and Principate of the Emperor Nero* (1903), 153 ff.), Schur to his counsellors ('Die Orientpolitik des Kaisers Nero', *Klio*, Beiheft xv (1923), 37 f.). For Momigliano it is the Senate that directs policy (*Atti del II Congresso nazionale di Studi Romani* I (1931), 368 ff.), while Hammond lays stress upon the character of Corbulo (*Harvard Studies* XLV (1934), 81 ff.).

[3] Since Tacitus had a firm grip on what went before and came after.

[4] XIV. 60. 1—after the divorce of Octavia, which had been delayed by Nero (the author alleges) because of his apprehensions touching Rubellius Plautus (59. 3). Proper emphasis (and the dynastic reasons) should have been assigned to the long delay in divorcing an

Moreover, the allegation of an incestuous offer is imported to incriminate Agrippina and enhance her son's aversion and suspicions. That is rather late in the day: anecdote and motive ought to belong to the early months of the reign.[1]

The imperfections of the Neronian books are various in nature and origin—and the author, it may be, had not worked upon all parts with equal care and finish.[2] Tacitus' own predilection for climax and catastrophe is not always to blame. Sometimes he went astray because he put too much faith in his authorities (they seemed reputable), as in the incest story.[3] Elsewhere critical faculties would not avail. Many of the facts, the opinions, and the personalities that operated behind the scenes to influence governmental decisions lay out of reach, not recorded in any document, and not verifiable. Reconstruction was hazardous. A man might well turn to the known and public figures of the Palace, in their undisguised behaviour or credible ambitions.

The story of the Caesars, from Tiberius to Nero, forms a linked sequel of dramatic actions. The facts were there.[4] Tacitus does not invent. But he takes considerable liberties.[5] His boldness in composition and portrayal may be excused or extenuated.[6] Not perhaps the best way (or even necessary) to redeem his credit as an historian. Tacitus deserves something better than a pedestrian justification.

unloved wife. It might appear that the influence of Poppaea has been much exaggerated. A modern scholar goes so far as to suggest that 'diese exzentrische Frau' may have turned Nero into a singer and player (R. Hanslik, P–W xxii, 86).

[1] The detail that the freedwoman Acte was persuaded by Seneca to intervene is suspicious: did she still matter?

[2] p. 361 f. and App. 60.

[3] Notably the consular Cluvius. Still, Tacitus does not quite affirm the fact—'sed quae Cluvius eadem ceteri quoque auctores prodidere, et fama huc inclinat' (xiv. 2. 2).

[4] Not everybody is willing to accept them. Thus M. L. W. Laistner, to support his theory that the imperial portraits are distorted, says of Messallina and Agrippina: 'there is no parallel in all history . . . unless it be Fredegund and Brunhild in the lurid pages of Gregory of Tours' (*The Greater Roman Historians* (1947), 132). For Agrippina see, however, Ph. Fabia, *Rev. phil.* xxxv (1911), 144 ff.; E. Paratore, *Maia* v (1952), 32 ff.

[5] As in composing letters between Tiberius and Seianus (iv. 39 f.) or the antiphonal speeches of Seneca and Nero (xiv. 53 ff.).

[6] Dessau states that Tacitus never overstepped the limits between history and poetry—'er arbeitet nur mit erlaubten Mitteln' (*Gesch. der r. Kaiserzeit* ii (1926), 100).

XXIX. THE ACCURACY OF TACITUS

ORNELIUS TACITUS does not need to be vindicated for accuracy. He consulted a variety of sources, and he was at pains to establish the truth. Not pedantically, however—he eschews elaborate refutation, with names and dates and all the paraphernalia, of other men's mistakes. Tacitus is content with a hint, or a typical example. Similarly, for errors committed in his own earlier works— silent correction. Thus, having made a mistake about Poppaea Sabina, as did others (and it was venial, irrelevant perhaps, whether the lady had in fact been the lawful wedded wife of M. Salvius Otho when she was taken over by his friend the Emperor Nero), Tacitus prefers not to delay the reader and pester him with an elaborate rectification.[1] On the other hand, odd particulars everywhere guarantee him alert and diligent.

Mistakes could not fail to occur—especially if the historian went his own way, scorning to transcribe a corpus of received truth, but independently using research, memory, and judgement (all fallible, in scholars as in senators). Divergences from standard tradition about early Rome will be variously interpreted, and not always to his discredit;[2] but he was imperfectly informed about the last century of the Roman Republic. In a digression he states (part ignorance, part abbreviation) that the dispute about the jury courts was perhaps the main issue in the war between Marius and Sulla.[3] Further, he has one or two peculiar statements about later events, such as the incorporation of Italy in the Roman State;[4] he attributes to Augustus an extension of the sacred circuit of the city;[5] and statements about the *tribunicia potestas* of Tiberius neglect exact chronology.[6] Not having investigated properly the annals of Augustan Rome, Tacitus could sometimes be taken in by a conventional opinion.[7]

The early Principate had now receded a long way into the past, and

[1] p. 290.   [2] p. 397.

[3] XII. 60. 3—in a digression, presumably from Claudius Caesar (App. 40).

[4] XI. 24. 3 (in his version of the *Oratio Claudi Caesaris*, cf. App. 93).

[5] XII. 23. 2 (clearly from Claudius).

[6] I. 3. 3, cf. App. 61. More serious is the misleading way in which the adoption of Germanicus (A.D. 4) is introduced, I. 3. 5: 'at hercule Germanicum Druso ortum octo apud Rhenum legionibus imposuit adscirique per adoptionem a Tiberio iussit.' Germanicus' Rhine command began early in 13.

[7] At least he allows Seneca to say 'abavus tuus Augustus Marco Agrippae Mytilenense secretum . . . permisit' (XIV. 53. 3). The reference is to Agrippa's retirement in 23 B.C., reported by a number of sources. A legend—and a total misconception, cf. *Rom. Rev.* (1939), 342.

the stream of genuine tradition (that is to say, persons and families above all) began to peter out. For the wife of Nero's grandfather, Tacitus gives the younger daughter of Marcus Antonius, not the elder.[1] Referring in Book I to Caligula, then an infant in his parents' company on the Rhine, Tacitus labels him as a child of the camp, with allusion to the nickname.[2] The actual place of birth set the learned at variance. Suetonius established the facts by appeal to the 'acta publica': nowhere near the Rhine, but at Antium.[3] Suetonius was arguing against weighty authorities—a consular legate, and (more formidable) an erudite procurator who had noticed an inscription.[4] For history it hardly matters. Less pardonable would be mistakes (they can be suspected but not proved) about families whose descendants belonged to Tacitus' own time and rank.[5]

So many names and agents, such is the nature of senatorial annals; and, if an error here and there, a lack of clarity or an omission is proved against the historian, it does not wreck his credit for diligence. Of positive errors, surely not very many.[6] The author, however, ought sometimes to have been more explicit about a man's origin, family, or connexions when relevant (as so often) to his career and activities. Several noblemen in the time of Tiberius are inadequately documented.[7] Some were very important.

Though defeated when the Free State fell, the *nobilitas* survived the wars of the dynasts and emerged from tribulation to renewed splendour, allies or rivals of the victor, to share the power of the Caesars, or subvert it. The successor of Augustus was a Claudius: it might have been some other aristocrat.[8]

In the competition for monarchic power at Rome, two Triumvirs were discarded. Their descendants did not forfeit very much. The daughters of Marcus Antonius were nieces of Caesar Augustus; and Iullus Antonius was not left out of the family circle.[9] The nephew of Lepidus had been quick to see the better way, and safe honours: his elder son was chosen to marry Julia, the grand-daughter of the Princeps.[10]

The Domitii continued and prospered. The son of Caesar's enemy had been admiral of the Republic and a partisan of Antonius.

---

[1] IV. 44. 2: Likewise in XII. 64. 2. The error would arise from an unconscious assumption that the elder Antonia went to Drusus, the stepson of the Princeps, not to L. Domitius Ahenobarbus (*PIR²*, D 128). However, the latter (*cos.* 16 B.C.) was about ten years older than Drusus.　　　　　　　　[2] I. 41. 2.　　　　　　　　[3] *Cal.* 8. 1.

[4] viz. Lentulus Gaetulicus and the elder Pliny.

[5] See App. 62 on the parentage of Lollia Paullina (XII. 1. 2) and the descendants of Pompeius Theophanes (VI. 18. 2).

[6] App. 61.　　　　　　　　[7] App. 63.　　　　　　　　[8] cf. *Rom. Rev.* (1939), 419 ff.

[9] Consul in 10 B.C., proconsul of Asia, and husband of the elder Marcella (*PIR²*, A 800).

[10] L. Aemilius Paullus, *cos.* A.D. 1 (*PIR²*, A 391).

He left a son, who married a daughter of Antonius.[1] Time would show many a paradox of blood or destiny among the successors of Caesar Augustus.

Other houses of the *nobilitas* soon acquired a connexion with the reigning family, such as the Fabii and Valerii; while some, notably the Cornelii Lentuli, avoided entanglement, or were not solicited. At the same time a rival group formed, linking the descendánts of Sulla, of Crassus, of Pompeius. Hence rivalry, rancour, and peril.

Tiberius Caesar in due and prescribed modesty assured the Senate that only Augustus had been capable of bearing the whole burden of rule. Having shared it himself, he could testify to the trials and the hazards. In a commonwealth that abounded in talents, the Senate ought not to consign all the power to one man: a syndicate was preferable to a monarchy.[2] In the further course of the debate Tiberius let drop an incautious suggestion—not the undivided authority but whatsoever portion the Senate might allot to his custody.[3] Whereupon Asinius Gallus broke in with a pointed question—which portion?

Gallus tried to gloss over the interjection—he meant to show that the power was one and indivisible—and he wound up with praise of Tiberius. Tiberius was not mollified. He had good reason already for disliking Asinius Gallus, the husband of his former wife Vipsania (whom he had divorced by order of Augustus), and a bold ambitious man. The next speaker, L. Arruntius, also gave offence. Not that Tiberius bore any ancient grudge—only suspicions.[4] Of what nature, the historian now specifies, inserting a very peculiar story.

It runs as follows. Augustus when his end was near discussed what might be the capacity for empire of certain senators. He mentioned three names. Marcus Lepidus, he said, had the parts but not the ambition; Gallus was eager but not equal to it; Arruntius, however, was not unworthy of the supreme power—and might be disposed to take a chance.[5]

Other versions (so Tacitus remarks) knew a variant name, Cn. Piso instead of L. Arruntius.[6] Even were there good reasons for believing

---

[1] p. 379.

[2] I. II. I: 'solam divi Augusti mentem tantae molis capacem; se in partem curarum ab illo vocatum experiendo didicisse quam arduum, quam subiectum fortunae regendi cuncta onus. proinde in civitate tot inlustribus viris subnixa non ad unum omnia deferrent: plures facilius munia reipublicae sociatis laboribus exsecuturos.'

[3] 12. I, cf. Dio LVII. 2. 4 f. See App. 36.

[4] 13. I: 'quamquam Tiberio nulla vetus in Arruntium ira, sed divitem promptum, artibus egregiis et pari fama publice, suspectabat.'

[5] 13. 2: 'M. Lepidum dixerat capacem sed aspernantem, Gallum Asinium avidum et minorem, L. Arruntium non indignum et si casus daretur ausurum.'

[6] 13. 3: 'de prioribus consentitur, pro Arruntio quidam Cn. Pisonem tradidere.' Why

the anecdote to be authentic, the speculation was idle, for the matter had been settled ten years earlier when Augustus adopted Tiberius as his son and successor. The true relevance of the story is rather to the technique of the historian Cornelius Tacitus.[1] He adds that these men (with the exception of M. Lepidus) subsequently fell victims to the machinations of Tiberius.[2] The malice of Tacitus is patent—for, if Tiberius nourished rancour against Asinius Gallus, it was not until 30 that he was put under arrest. As for Arruntius, the fact that Tiberius, after appointing him governor of Tarraconensis, kept him at Rome for long years, created inevitably the belief and tradition that Tiberius must have feared him.[3] Yet Arruntius was loyal, it appears, to Tiberius. He ended his life by suicide a few weeks before the Emperor's own decease.

The function which the three 'principes' assume in Tacitus' account of the reign of Tiberius repays investigation, but would involve a long disquisition. Their names, which recur again and again, show that senators of birth and rank still counted—and prevent the narrative from taking on a colouration too dynastic. A question arises: do the three consulars deserve that prominence?[4]

Gallus stands for oratory and great ambitions, with a truculence recalling his parent, Asinius Pollio. If Gallus was rash and provocative in debate, he could also be insidious, coming out with proposals that seemed frank and innocuous. The intent was to annoy Tiberius. So far Gallus typifies a petulant or sterile opposition. After the deaths of Germanicus and of Drusus he began to acquire some political consequence. Was the widow of Germanicus to be found a husband? She was still young, so she pointedly reminded Tiberius.[5] There is no hint of Asinius Gallus in this context, or of anybody else; but Gallus was not far distant. His sons by Vipsania were cousins of the children of Germanicus. Gallus, despite his years (coeval with Tiberius Caesar), may have conceived a desire to become consort of Agrippina, thus stepfather and guardian of princes to whom the succession beckoned. There was no lack of a precedent, in hope or in fear. Men

Piso's name was brought into the story is clear—his subsequent conduct as legate of Syria, and his ruin.

[1] Precisely so, if it turns out to be a later addition by the historian. Cf. App. 37, where it is suggested that the insertion begins with the comments on Arruntius, 'sed . . . suspectabat', and ends before the next speakers in the debate are named, 'etiam Q. Haterius et Mamercus Scaurus', &c.

[2] ib.: 'omnesque praeter Lepidum variis mox criminibus struente Tiberio circumventi sunt.'

[3] *Hist.* II. 65. 2 (cf. further, p. 443).

[4] It is, however, a misconception to claim that 'historically none of these men are of first rate importance with the exception of Cn. Piso' (C. W. Mendell, *Yale Classical Studies* v (1935), 13). Piso is adventitious.

[5] IV. 53. 1 (p. 277 f.).

could have in mind the presumed aspirations of Iullus Antonius, the paramour of Julia.[1]

L. Arruntius was endowed with wealth, energy, and eloquence. Though his father (an admiral and an historian) was the first consul in the family, Arruntius probably depends on aristocratic connexions as well as personal resources. Descendants of Sulla and of Pompeius, kept out of prominence and honours during the greater part of Augustus' reign, emerge in the last decade, not without help and favour from Tiberius, who was responsive to Republican and Pompeian allegiances.[2] Some were dull and inert, corrupt or futile.[3] With those noblemen the son of the *novus homo* had a double link.[4] On the talent and energy of Arruntius converged the claim of Sullan and Pompeian blood to stand in competition for the Principate with Julii or Claudii.

Marcus Lepidus is a scion of the patrician Aemilii. As the *Annales* of Tacitus unfold, Lepidus begins to acquire the lineaments of greatness, not least in the historian's impressive testimony to that wisdom whereby, avoiding the extremes of truculence and servility, he saved his dignity and won the esteem of Tiberius Caesar.[5] The main credentials of Lepidus are not registered in the *Annales* as extant—Scipionic ancestry and a military reputation.

His lineage was resplendent. Paullus Aemilius Lepidus (the nephew of the Triumvir) married a Cornelia, in the descent of the Scipiones.[6] That Cornelia, being the daughter of Scribonia, was a half-sister to Julia, the daughter of Caesar Augustus. The match produced two sons. The elder married a princess and succumbed in a mysterious catastrophe, designated as conspiracy against the ruler.[7] The younger, Marcus, became consul in 6. Soon after, he held a command in the field as legate under Tiberius, in the reconquest of Illyricum, and earned the *ornamenta triumphalia*.[8] In the year of Augustus' death, Lepidus was in charge of Tarraconensis, with three legions.[9]

---

[1] *Rom. Rev.* (1939), 427. [2] ib. 434 f., cf. 424 f.

[3] Thus M'. Aemilius Lepidus (*cos.* 11), who had that double descent (cf. III. 22. 1): no good, III. 32. 2. There is no sign that Cn. Cinna Magnus (*cos.* 5) had any capacity. The reign of Tiberius brings consulates to a Scribonius Libo (descended from Magnus) and to two Cornelii Sullae. For the descendants of Magnus see *Rom. Rev.*, Table V.

[4] He was related to L. Sulla Felix, the consul of 33 (III. 31. 3). That would give him a Pompeian connexion, cf. *PIR*², C 1463. Perhaps also some other link, earlier than that attested by the nomenclature of his son by adoption, L. Arruntius Camillus Scribonianus, the consul of 32 (*PIR*², A 1140).

[5] IV. 20. 2.

[6] Propertius V. 11. 63. For the problem of her precise extraction see E. Groag, *PIR*², C 1395; R. Syme, *Rom. Rev.* (1939), 229 f.

[7] Suetonius, *Divus Aug.* 19. 1. Cf. p. 404.

[8] Velleius II. 114. 5; 115. 2 f.; Dio LVI. 12. 2.

[9] ib. 125. 5. Cf. *CIL* II, 2820 (Uxama).

Marcus Lepidus stood close indeed to the name and fortune of the Caesars.[1] He had several children. A daughter was given in matrimony to Drusus, the son of Germanicus.[2] She turned out badly. A son was the friend and favourite of Caligula, married to Drusilla, and promised the succession. He was put to death for high treason.[3] That was the end of the family. The *gens Aemilia* had produced many 'boni cives' through the ages, and even the wicked Aemilii were illustrious.[4]

The historian's predilection goes to a safe and prudent Lepidus. So much so that he magnifies the importance of Lepidus' activities under Tiberius.[5] The historian was aware of the parentage of Marcus Lepidus.[6] None the less, to estimate and bring out the full significance of Lepidus, and of other aristocrats, it was expedient to have studied the family politics of the preceding age.

The deaths of illustrious men furnished an incentive, though Tacitus was slow to see it.[7] Consulars coeval with Tiberius Caesar (or even older) threw shafts of light far back into the past. Some were related to the dynasty. L. Domitius Ahenobarbus, the husband of an Antonia, had crossed the river Elbe with a Roman army; dying in 25, he earns an obituary, although absent hitherto from the annalistic record.[8] L. Piso, however, remained in prominence as Prefect of the City down to his death in 32, when his family and services are registered, including the war in Thrace long ago.[9] Of certain younger men in the *nobilitas*, especially those who became consuls in the last decade of Augustus' reign, the historian has less to report; and there is no mention of honours won in the epoch of the great wars in Germany and Illyricum from 4 to 9.[10] The exposition suffers.

The 'magna nomina' served to illustrate the aristocratic complexion

[1] ib. 114. 5: 'vir nomini ac fortunae Caesarum proximus.' Clearly, therefore, the 'capax imperii'.

[2] VI. 40. 3. The match had been registered in Book V—a suitable occasion to note the ancestry of her father.

[3] *PIR*², A 371.

[4] VI. 27. 4 (the obituary of M. Lepidus).

[5] Nothing that he did came to much. That may also be the lesson.

[6] III. 72. 1 (the repair of the Basilica Aemilia). For the problem of distinguishing Marcus (*cos.* 6) from Manius (*cos.* 11) see App. 64, and, in detail, *JRS* XLV (1955), 22 ff. On that reconstruction (which involves one alteration in the *Codex Mediceus* instead of eight), M'. Lepidus (an inferior character) is named twice in the *Annales*, viz. III. 22. 1; 32. 2.

[7] p. 372.

[8] IV. 44. 2. The 'pontes longi' which he constructed in Germany had been carefully noted in I. 63. 4.

[9] VI. 10. 3. Being the son of the consul of 58 B.C., Piso was the little brother of Caesar's Calpurnia. He was not, however, brought into any of Augustus' dynastic marriage alliances.

[10] For example by M. Aemilius Lepidus (*cos.* 6) or by M. Valerius Messalla Messallinus (*cos.* 3 B.C.), though the former is accorded a (brief) obituary notice (VI. 27. 4).

of Tiberius' principate, and to evoke the old Republic. Tacitus employs various contrivances. Brief touches hit off an individual; the consular orators are put under contribution; significant names are made to recur at intervals in the narration; and contrasts in demeanour prevent homonyms from being confused.[1] None the less, many characters could only be names. For all his alertness, Tacitus was often baffled. Senators keep turning up (old families or new) whose importance depends upon their previous rank, alliances, or actions. Not all were common property to the contemporaries of Tacitus, for many families had lapsed and perished in the course of the century.

Aelius Seianus also called for proper annotation. In the stylized portraiture the historian duly notes his town of origin and equestrian parentage, quickly going on to denounce the 'municipalis adulter' who seduced a princess of the blood of Caesar Augustus.[2] Now Aelius Seianus was not merely son of Seius Strabo, Prefect of the Guard when Tiberius came to power. The maternal line counts. Seius married a wife of patrician stock, from the house of the Cornelii Lentuli.[3] And something more, surpassing any aristocratic pedigree: the mother of Seius Strabo was a Terentia, sister of Maecenas' wife and of an ambitious ill-starred consul, Varro Murena. The 'potentia' of Aelius Seianus is entwined about the very roots of the dynasty.[4]

Neither the allies nor the enemies of Seianus are clearly defined in the *Annales* so far as extant. Some of the missing names were probably supplied in Tacitus' account of the intrigues and struggles of the year that saw his apparent supremacy and sudden catastrophe. It was all very complicated. At that juncture L. Arruntius and one at least of the Cornelii Lentuli came to matter very much. An attempt was made to prosecute Arruntius (described as an enemy of Seianus), but it was a Lentulus who intervened to enforce a stay of proceedings.[5] Probably old Cossus, not a rash man, and deep in the confidence of Tiberius.[6] At the same time the son of Cossus, namely Gaetulicus, commanding in Upper Germany, was linked to Seianus by the betrothal of their children.[7] Family ties apart, Seianus claims other allies in the high aristocracy.[8]

---

[1] e.g. to distinguish the two L. Pisones (App. 63).   [2] IV. 3. 4.

[3] *ILS* 8996 (Volsinii): ignored in *OCD* (1949), 822.

[4] The relationships of Aelius Seianus were first investigated by C. Cichorius, *Hermes* XXXIX (1904), 461 ff. For the connexion with the Cornelii Lentuli see Groag's stemma (*PIR²*, C, facing p. 328), which is adopted in *Rom. Rev.*, Table VI. For his 'consulares fratres' (Velleius II. 127. 3) see now F. Adams (*AJP* LXXVI (1955), 70 ff.), who suggests Q. Aelius Tubero (*cos.* 11 B.C.) and Sex. Aelius Catus (A.D. 4).

[5] Dio LVIII. 8. 3 (without the name of Arruntius): cf. the interpretation of R. S. Rogers, *Class. Phil.* XXVI (1931), 40.

[6] *PIR²*, C 1380 (*cos.* 1 B.C.).   [7] ib. 1390 (*cos.* A.D. 26).

[8] Note the consuls of 30, L. Cassius Longinus and M. Vinicius, both easy-going men

If Seianus had acquired a formidable following, many of his adherents accrued through the manifest favour of the Emperor.[1] Those allies could not all be counted upon in an extremity. And, so it happened, birth and wealth came off unscathed, while the small senators and lesser men perished along with their patron. The Emperor was able to destroy his minister without imperilling the fabric of government. Tiberius, though in his nature grim and distrustful, numbered personal friends of long date among the aristocratic consulars still extant from the reign of Augustus, notably L. Piso and Cossus Lentulus.[2]

The lost Caligulan books and the first six years of Claudius Caesar must also be allowed for. The assassination of Caligula brought noble pedigrees into sudden debate and notoriety.[3] And, before long, the whole nexus of family interests represented by L. Arruntius was revealed, and sharply—Arruntius Camillus, the legate of Dalmatia, made an unsuccessful proclamation in the second year of Claudius.[4]

Arruntius was not the only consular confronting Claudius with dynastic claims of ancient prestige. The line of the great Crassus, which had coalesced with one branch of the Pisones, acquired the Pompeian connexion when M. Licinius Crassus Frugi (consul in 27) married Scribonia, a descendant of Magnus on the female side.[5] Claudius in the first months of his reign, to consolidate his position, devised a double counterstroke. He had two daughters. The one, Octavia, he betrothed to L. Silanus, who carried the blood of Augustus (transmitted through the Aemilii Lepidi).[6] The other, Antonia, was at once consigned in matrimony to Cn. Pompeius Magnus, the eldest son of Crassus Frugi.[7] The device of annexing and neutralizing the descendants of Magnus proved a failure. Crassus Frugi was stupid, and perhaps pretentious.[8] An alleged conspiracy destroyed him, along

---

(VI. 15. 1). The former at the instigation of Seianus spoke in the Senate in 30 against Drusus the son of Germanicus (Dio LVIII. 3. 8). The latter was the patron of Velleius Paterculus. For a list of 'Seianiani', Z. Stewart, *AJP* LXXIV (1953), 70 ff.

[1] cf. the defence made by the knight M. Terentius (VI. 8).

[2] His boon-companions, and deep drinkers (Seneca, *Epp.* 83. 14 f.). Cossus became *praefectus urbi* in 33, after the brief tenure of Aelius Lamia (cf. *PIR²*, C 1380). Another Lentulus, the *augur* (*cos.* 14 B.C.), a close friend of Tiberius, had died in 25 (IV. 44. 1): on him, App. 63.

[3] Not, however, the oldest. M. Vinicius (*cos.* 30) is named (Josephus, *AJ* XIX. 251), husband of Julia Livilla, the daughter of Germanicus. [4] *PIR²*, A 1140.

[5] See the stemma in *PIR²*, vol. II, facing p. 54. The line previous to the consul of 27 must now be modified. A new fact, showing that M. Licinius Crassus (*cos.* 14 B.C.) had the *cognomen* 'Frugi' (*IRT* 319), overturns the previous assumption that these people descend from L. Piso the *pontifex* (*cos.* 15 B.C.).

[6] M. Junius Silanus (*cos.* 19) married Aemilia Lepida (*PIR²*, A 419), daughter of L. Aemilius Paullus and Julia. [7] *PIR²*, A 886.

[8] Seneca, *Apocol.* 11. 2: 'Crassum vero tam fatuum ut etiam regnare posset'; 5: 'hominem tam similem sui quam ovo ovum.'

with his wife and son.[1] The line, however, was prolific. It furnished a sequence of suspects, pretenders, and victims. No historian would be able to neglect their vicissitudes.[2]

Other individuals and factions may also have emerged in clearer outline. Tacitus is ever lavish of information about the freedmen ministers of state. He will also have indicated the consulars who provide the continuity in imperial administration, linking the reigns of Tiberius, Caligula, and Claudius. The most notable in a notable group (and many of them were allied by blood or marriage) was L. Vitellius, commended for the capacity he showed as legate of Syria in the last years of Tiberius—and damned for his subservience later at Court.[3] Vitellius supervised the capital (and the government) when Claudius went to Britain with a large company of the illustrious, some for the honour, others perhaps not safely to be left behind.[4]

In the ambit of his allies Vitellius embraced the Plautii (high in favour with the dynasty since the days of Augustus), and the Petronii, a new family comparable to his own.[5] Meritorious in the provinces (P. Petronius followed Vitellius in Syria, while A. Plautius conducted the invasion of Britain), the consulars might well possess the arts for influence at home on policy and patronage. Others earned recompense for long attachment to the house of Germanicus. For example, Q. Veranius.[6] Tacitus would not fail to register the first campaigns of Veranius, obviating detail subsequently when his name recurred in high command.[7] Nor would Domitius Corbulo be at all enigmatic—some mention at least under Caligula.[8] Tacitus had already given space to Corbulo's father.[9] A telling fact—the great general, half-brother to the Emperor's wife—was no doubt accessible.[10] Moreover, the operations in Mauretania and the invasion of Britain brought to the fore certain men of merit, with rapid promotion to the consulate and

---

[1] *PIR*[1], L 130; P 477; S 221.

[2] Notably Piso Licinianus (whom Galba adopted), and the perpetual conspirator Calpurnius Crassus.

[3] VI. 32. 4.

[4] For the list see R. Syme, *C Q* XXVII (1933), 143. Among them were Ser. Sulpicius Galba and M. Vinicius. Add perhaps A. Didius Gallus (*suff.* 36), cf. *AE* 1947, 76, supplemented in *AE* 1949, 11.

[5] The wife of P. Petronius (*suff.* 19) was the daughter of a Vitellia (III. 49. 1): clearly the 'Plautia P. Petroni' of *CIL* VI, 6866. This lady has no entry in *PIR*[1] or in P–W; nor is she noted under P–W XIX, 1199 ff. A new inscription from Caunus, published by G. E. Bean (*JHS* LXXIV (1954), 91 f., whence *SEG* XIV, 646), styles her Πλαυτίαν Αὔλου θυγατέρα: presumably daughter of A. Plautius, *suffectus* in 1 B.C. A Petronia married the elder son of L. Vitellius (*Hist.* II. 64. 1), presumably the daughter of this match.

[6] Q. Veranius (*cos.* 49), the son of the 'comes' of Germanicus (p. 325).

[7] As the first legate of the new province Lycia-Pamphylia he operated against sundry mountain tribes (*AE* 1953, 251).

[8] For the problem of his consulate, App. 83.   [9] III. 31. 3 ff.

[10] Pliny, *NH* VII. 39 (the marriages and children of Vistilia, cf. p. 373).

prospects of a command later on.[1] To this class belongs Suetonius Paullinus, the rival in renown to Domitius Corbulo. They had both been kept waiting for many years.[2]

Corbulo and Paullinus were extracted from retirement by the counsellors of Nero. Seneca in those years captures the public eye and earns the historian's benevolent attention. Yet the prince was not wholly destitute of friends among the consulars, discreet or clever survivors from earlier reigns. A casual anecdote attests the esteem Nero professed for the sagacity of Memmius Regulus, the consul who helped to suppress Seianus.[3]

Nor is Seneca intelligible in isolation. He owed everything to diplomatic talent and palace influences. For the maintenance of his position, however, he had need of allies and agents. A little more information would have been useful. Some names occur incidentally, others may be surmised, but the weight and force of Seneca's party as a whole is hard to estimate.[4] Again, his rivals, and his successors in the favour of the prince and the direction of policy. Ofonius Tigellinus is the open, disgraceful, and dramatic supplanter of Seneca.[5] The quiet operations of persons superior in birth, rank, and talent might also be surmised.[6]

Error or omission will not be taken lightly where influential figures in the governmental oligarchy are concerned. For the rest, Tacitus deliberately passed over many acts or proclamations as petty, conventional, or irrelevant to his design. Nothing, for example, about a commemoration of Tiberius Caesar's 'clementia' and 'moderatio' by a loyal and grateful Senate,[7] about Chaeremon the learned Alexandrian in his role of educator of the boy Nero,[8] about Nero's magnanimous refusal of the title 'pater patriae'.[9] If any deplore such omissions, they have no right to complain.

---

[1] In Mauretania Suetonius Paullinus (*NH* v. 14, &c.), in Britain T. Flavius Sabinus (*suff.* ? 45) and his less successful brother Vespasianus (*suff.* 51), cf. Dio LX. 20. 3 f.; Suetonius, *Divus Vesp.* 4. 1. P. Ostorius Scapula may also have earned in Britain his consulship (? c. 44), and his governorship there (from 47).

[2] For Paullinus no consular command is known after his consulship (c. 43) until Britain (58 or 59). Corbulo had Germania Inferior but was recalled in 47 (*Ann.* XI. 20).

[3] XIV. 47 (on the occasion of his death in 61). Not that this proves much, cf. App. 60.

[4] See further, p. 591 (the consulars Pompeius Paullinus and Duvius Avitus).

[5] XIV. 51. 2 (under 62).

[6] Among them perhaps the bland and eloquent Vibius Crispus (*suff.* c. 62), and the subtle Petronius (who may be T. Petronius Niger, *suff.* c. 62). Eprius Marcellus was *suffectus* in 62.

[7] Only coins attest it, cf. C. H. V. Sutherland, *JRS* XXVIII (1938), 129 ff.; R. S. Rogers, *Studies in the Reign of Tiberius* (1943), 60 ff.

[8] *PIR*², C 706. He is said to have been a Stoic. For Tacitus it was Seneca that mattered.

[9] Suetonius, *Nero* 8.

For comparison of accuracy and relevance, Suetonius and Cassius Dio are to hand. Their treatment of Tiberius is instructive.[1] The biographer falls into frequent errors of fact, and many of his generalizations are unwarranted—defects largely due to the method of compilation, which absolved him from the necessity of presenting either a coherent narrative or a consistent picture. He lacks insight and political grasp.[2] Sadly ignorant about foreign affairs, he is content for the most part to retail vague rumours: he asserts that Tiberius in the last years, sunk in torpor, neglected the defence of the frontiers.[3] As for Dio, he differs frequently from Tacitus (and not to his own advantage), for instance about the accession of Tiberius.[4] He is at the mercy of his sources, and is liable to commit mistakes of identity;[5] he misses persons of moment in the politics, open or secret, of Senate and dynasty.[6]

Dio was too remote in time to recapture the colour and texture of Roman society under the early Caesars. Instead, he has got hold of some queer material, often anecdotal in character.[7] Thus the consul who, aspiring to eloquence, acquired for wife a lady once married to Cicero;[8] the praetor who organized troupes of men with shaven heads to parade at the Floralia in mockery of Tiberius;[9] and, touching a certain Sex. Marius, a story to illustrate his opulence and an allegation in his defence that he kept his daughter in seclusion to protect her from the lusts of the Emperor.[10] Now Tacitus is always discriminatory and valuable in his comments on the Roman orators; he alludes only with dignity and discretion to the bald head of a Roman Emperor;[11] and he sticks to the essential facts about Sex. Marius—the wealthiest man in all Spain, a mine-owner, condemned on a charge of incest with his daughter.[12]

---

[1] cf. F. B. Marsh, *The Reign of Tiberius* (1931), 272 ff.

[2] By exception he is firm and sagacious about Augustus' reasons for choosing Tiberius as successor (*Tib.* 21. 3), cf. App. 36.

[3] *Tib.* 41: Armeniam a Parthis occupari, Moesiam a Dacis Sarmatisque, Gallias a Germanis vastari neglexerit'. That is ludicrous. Tacitus records the vigorous measures taken in the East (VI. 32 ff., cf. p. 237).

[4] App. 36.

[5] For Dio (or for his source) M. Silanus, the 'golden sheep', is the *suffectus* of 15, not the *ordinarius* of 46. And Dio may have made a mistake about the Domitius Corbulo consul suffect in 39 (see App. 83).

[6] Like Suetonius, he nowhere names Sallustius Crispus; and he fails to see that L. Arruntius was worth mentioning in 31 (LVIII. 8. 3).

[7] Hence indirect evidence about the quality of certain historians whom Tacitus decided not to follow.

[8] LVII. 15. 6 (C. Vibius Rufus, *suff.* 16, husband of Publilia).

[9] LVIII. 19. 1 f. (L. Apronius Caesianus, *pr.* 32, *cos.* 39).

[10] 22. 2.

[11] IV. 57. 2: 'nudus capillo vertex', cf. p. 343.

[12] VI. 19. 1, cf. IV. 36. 1.

Small things, but significant. Yet, by invoking Dio or Suetonius, attempts have been made to impugn the reliability of Tacitus in transactions of some moment. One example will suffice—the accession of Tiberius. Tacitus knows of two meetings of the Senate after the death of Augustus. At the first, arrangements for the funeral, and nothing else; at the second, the consecration, and thereafter the discussion about the imperial power. Was there in fact only one debate, and not rather a series, and has not Tacitus compressed several sessions into one?[1] Such a procedure, if proved, could perhaps be defended by the artistic and dramatic canons of Roman historiography. But it is not proved, or even likely. The position of Tiberius Caesar in relation to the Roman State was discussed and defined (in so far as it needed to be defined) in a single session of the Senate: that which voted the deification of Augustus (September 17, A.D. 14).[2]

Nor does any new evidence accruing impair confidence in the accuracy and judgement of Tacitus, though inscriptions from Laconia may attest the zeal of provincials, the Emperor's distaste for the extravagances of conventional homage;[3] though a papyrus yields two edicts issued by Germanicus Caesar in Egypt, the one in restraint of improper commandeering of transport, the other deprecating divine honours, such as belong only 'to the Emperor, who is veritably the saviour and benefactor of the whole human race, and to the Emperor's mother'.[4]

More serious at first view is the bronze tablet that reveals the method first enjoined by a law of A.D. 5 for the 'destinatio' of consuls and praetors—ten *centuriae* specially constituted from senators and knights, and bearing the names of the Caesars Gaius and Lucius; they were supplemented by five more in honour of Germanicus after the death of that prince.[5] None the less, the document does not in fact invalidate the historian's affirmation that in 14 the *Comitia* were transferred from the assembly of the People to the Senate.[6] Tacitus, it is true, is vague about the electoral procedure hitherto obtaining in the last years of Augustus. Deliberately—he did not wish to be

---

[1] As argued by A. Lang, *Beiträge zur Geschichte des Kaisers Tiberius* (Diss. Jena, 1911), 11 ff. Many scholars concur, e.g. M. Gelzer, P–W x, 496; D. M. Pippidi, *Autour de Tibère* (1944), 129; J. Béranger, *Recherches sur l'aspect idéologique du Principat* (1953), 24; F. Klingner, *Bayerische S–B, phil.-hist. Kl.* 1953, Heft 7, 33.

[2] *CIL* I², p. 244 (*Fasti Amiternini*), cf. E. Hohl, *Hermes* LXVIII (1933), 106 ff. See further, p. 411 and App. 36.

[3] *AE* 1929, 99 f. (Gytheum) = *SEG* XI, 922 f.

[4] Hunt and Edgar, *Select Papyri* II (Loeb, 1935), 211.

[5] The *Tabula Hebana* (cf. App. 67).

[6] I. 15. 1. The transference is not recorded by Suetonius or by Dio, though the latter writer might be said to imply it by his comments about elections later on, under the year 32 (LVIII. 20). See further App. 67.

involved in complicated annotation. And, a little later, coming to the first consular elections to be made in the Senate, in 15, he confesses to perplexity about what happened then, and subsequently, in the presentation of candidatures: neither historians nor imperial speeches gave clear guidance.[1]

There was some excuse for a refusal to go deeper into the detail of those formalities—for formalities they were—and the practice varied widely. Other things matter for history: who controlled the choice of magistrates ultimately, which men were elected, and with what support of birth and wealth, of personality, and of patronage. Where there is lack of precision in Tacitus, it derives from various preoccupations, notably stylistic, as when he goes out of his way to avoid technical terms. Similarly, he eschews full details of time and place. The behaviour of this historian not seldom arouses distress and even anger in those who look to his writings for complete and accurate information about warfare and geography.

How, indeed, could one register time, dates, and intervals in an historical exposition? Tacitus had to work with the annalistic framework. Various tricks and devices helped, and he operated with great freedom in grouping his material, notably in the later books of the *Annales*. None the less, pairs of consuls were cumbrous for use as signposts, and the Roman senator could not bear to use the regnal years of emperors.[2]

Exact chronology was often impracticable—and often superfluous. No need, surely, for dates when the historian, turning for the first time to the East, explained about Parthia and traced in brief summary the vicissitudes of Armenia ever since the days of Marcus Antonius: the summary is good.[3] Nor was precision indispensable when he recounted what happened in those regions during the reign of Claudius—little of it touched or influenced the policy of the Roman government.[4] It is another matter when large Roman armies take the field. The campaigns of Germanicus are exempt from problems of time and date. Not, however, the other operations of warfare most fully described in the *Annales*, namely the subjugation of Britain and the war in the East.

British affairs had been narrated in the missing portion down to the year 47 when A. Plautius, who conducted the invasion, returned to

---

[1] I. 81. 1.

[2] Only 'nonus Tiberio annus' (IV. 1. 1), for abnormal emphasis.

[3] II. 1–4. He omits an ephemeral Tigranes (c. A.D. 6), but knows about him (VI. 40. 2); and he is careful to register the Artavasdes (*PIR*², A 1163), whose name, linked with Roman failure and defeat, was suppressed by the author of the *Res Gestae*.

[4] The 'sub idem tempus' of XI. 8. 1 (under 47) may refer to events as early as 43.

Rome.[1] The sequel is divided into two segments, under the years 50 and 61. The first conveys its date by implication at the outset, for it begins with the arrival of the new legate, Ostorius Scapula.[2] The story goes on with Ostorius in various operations, one point of time only being marked, the capture of the native prince Caratacus in the ninth year from the invasion;[3] it notes the death of Ostorius;[4] and, after some remarks about the uneventful governorship of his successor, old Didius Gallus, the digression terminates without chronological guidance.[5] The reader, still within the framework of the year 50, is left to guess that he has been carried forward to the last year of Claudius Caesar (54).[6]

Thus a seven-year period compresses into a single episode. The author resumes in Book XIV, continuing with Didius Gallus, the brief tenure of Q. Veranius (he died within a year), and the momentous governorship of Suetonius Paullinus, to describe at once the attack on the island of Mona and the rebellion of Boudicca.[7] Not only are the events narrated under 61, the consulate of Petronius Turpilianus and Caesennius Paetus; Tacitus expressly assigns the catastrophe in Britain to that year; and, expressly again, Petronius, the legate appointed to replace Suetonius, arrives in the course of the year, straight from his consulate.[8] A serious difficulty arises: the events as recounted seem to exceed the compass of a single year. The revolt must have broken out in 60, not 61.[9]

Next, Armenian affairs under Nero. Tacitus apportions the material in five groups. The first, under the year 54, includes the sending of Corbulo and the preliminary diplomatic interchanges;[10] the next two (58 and 60) relate the invasion and conquest of Armenia.[11]

As Tacitus clearly states, warfare began in 58.[12] After a winter passed in the high country within the borders of Armenia, Corbulo set forth, and, with some fighting on the way, marched to Artaxata, the capital city, which he captured and destroyed. After these transactions, narrated under the year 58, Tacitus records the victory celebrations at Rome and passes to other matters.[13] Armenia and Corbulo next recur

---

[1] There will have been a resumptive section under that year early in Book XI (cf. p. 260).

[2] XII. 31. 1. It follows events on Rhine and Danube (27–30).

[3] 36. 1. That is, 51, as generally held (e.g. *PIR*[2], C 418), possibly even 52. This incident, with its pageantry at Rome (36–38), is the climax of the British digression. Why, then, under 50? Perhaps because the author needed 51 for a long excursus on eastern affairs (XII. 44–51).

[4] 39. 3. [5] 40.

[6] Similarly for eastern affairs, where XII. 50 f. (the end of the excursus under 51) is the direct preliminary to XIII. 6.

[7] XIV. 29–39. [8] 39. 3: 'qui iam consulatu abierat.'

[9] See App. 69. [10] XIII. 6–9. [11] 34–41 and XIV. 23–26.

[12] XIII. 34. 2: 'eius anni principio.' [13] 41.

under 60. The general, so it is affirmed, was eager to exploit the terror ensuing from the destruction of Artaxata.[1] He now marched on Tigranocerta and received the surrender of that city. Then, after other and minor operations, a prince, Tigranes, is sent out from Rome; some troops are left in Armenia to support him; and Corbulo goes away to take up the command in Syria.[2] Next, under 62, the various events of 61 and 62, culminating in the campaign and capitulation of Caesennius Paetus;[3] and lastly, under 63, Corbulo again, and the end of active hostilities.[4]

The Tacitean account has given rise to discussion, much of it vain and inconclusive, about Roman policy and changes of policy.[5] The main point of uncertainty has a bearing upon chronology and strategy. It is this—were Artaxata and Tigranocerta captured in the same year? Some contend that they were, with no little force and assurance.[6] That assumption runs counter to any rational interpretation of annalistic technique. Tacitus breaks the narrative after the fall of Artaxata, indicating the end of a campaigning year. Of winter quarters, no word—why should there be? It was left to the understanding—and the historian had already described in suitable detail one winter in Armenia, at the outset.[7] Hence Tigranocerta should belong to the next year after Artaxata, namely 59, the advent of Tigranes to 60.[8]

So far chronology. From errors of geography the Roman historian was preserved not a little by reluctance to clog the narrative and annoy the reader with a superfetation of details. The procedure was both artistic and rational, at least when applied to the foreign and frontier wars. Not merely because many of the terms were unfamiliar, uncouth, and repulsive—there were few if any cities, and cities by their identity, history, and situation are fixed points and known magnitudes. He had to deal mainly in rivers, mountains, and tribal territories—all unsatisfactory.

Censure fastens with ease and ferocity upon the campaigns of Germanicus Caesar: so much space for the telling, and so little precision about the movements of armies. Tacitus produces a wealth of colour, emotion, and scenic incident, enhanced by eloquence and

---

[1] XIV. 23. 1.

[2] 26—the events of two years (i.e. 59 and 60), though no break between the two is here indicated (but note the hint in xv. 6. 2 of winter quarters at Tigranocerta).

[3] XV. 1–17. Caesennius clearly arrived in 62, not, as argued by E. Groag (*PIR²*, C 173) in 61. Cf. xv. 6. 2 f.

[4] 24–31.   [5] p. 376.

[6] In 59, B. W. Henderson, *The Life and Principate of the Emperor Nero* (1903), 170 ff.; in 58, W. Schur, *Klio* XIX (1925), 87 ff.

[7] XIII. 35.

[8] Thus H. Dessau, *Gesch. der r. Kaiserzeit* II (1926), 194 ff.; J. G. C. Anderson, *CAH* x (1934), 760 ff.; M. Hammond, *Harvard Studies* XLV (1934), 90.

invention—Arminius and his renegade brother exchange boasts and insults across the breadth of a considerable river; Germanicus on the eve of battle roams in disguise among the tents, drinking in the conversation of his devoted soldiery; and a poetical set-piece depicts a fearful storm on the ocean.[1]

The serious inquirer (intent as he often is upon geography, strategy, or antiquarian detail) objects and rebels. For various reasons (honourable or parochial) he would wish to establish the locality in which Quinctilius Varus and three Roman legions perished. It is not defined adequately.[2] And, when the army of Germanicus approaches the melancholy spot, the historian, loading the pathos and majestically vague, leaves in doubt the precise spectacle that met their gaze—two Roman camps in succession or only one?[3] On the way back the legate Caecina Severus in his perilous crossing of the marshlands is visited by a terrifying dream—Varus with voice and gesture beckoning him to destruction.[4] It would be more useful to have the direction and duration of Caecina's march along the causeway of the 'pontes longi'.[5]

In the ambitious campaign of the next year, when Germanicus brought a large force in ships to the estuary of the Amisia, he landed the troops (so it seems) on the western bank.[6] After the crossing of that river, without any march being recorded, the army suddenly appears encamped on the Visurgis.[7] Other perplexities occur, likewise instances of vagueness and wilful abbreviations—yet, on the final estimate, no serious errors. And the general situation of the plain called Idistaviso where the Romans, having crossed the Visurgis, fought a pitched battle with the Germans is hardly in doubt.[8]

Examined as a whole, Tacitus' account of Germanicus beyond the Rhine, shaped and coloured as it is by a number of preoccupations (not all of them obvious), is vulnerable to criticism. But criticism often goes astray. It neglects two things—the author's purpose (he

(margin annotation, handwritten:) VARUS

---

[1] II. 9; 13; 23.

[2] I. 60. 3: 'ductum inde agmen ad ultimos Bructerorum, quantumque Amisiam et Lupiam amnis inter vastatum, haud procul Teutoburgiensi saltu.' Was it possible to be much more precise—or necessary?

[3] 61. 2: 'prima Vari castra lato ambitu et dimensis principiis trium legionum manus ostentabant; dein semiruto vallo humili fossa accisae iam reliquiae consedisse intellegebantur: medio campi albentia ossa', &c. For a novel and not unattractive explanation (a reduced entrenchment within the ambit of the three-legion camp) see W. John, *Die Örtlichkeit der Varusschlacht bei Tacitus* (Göttingen, 1950).

[4] 65. 4.

[5] 63. 4.

[6] II. 8. 2. For the interpretation of this vexed passage see now K. Meister, *Hermes* LXXXIII (1955), 92 ff.

[7] 9. I. Nothing in comparison with Caesar, who omits the duration and details of the march (about twelve days) that took him from Firmum in Picenum to the bridge on a river (not named) near Corfinium (*BC* I. 16. 1 f.).

[8] cf. F. Miltner, *Rh. Mus.* XCV (1952), 343 ff.

was not compiling a technical manual of warfare) and the lack of comprehensible landmarks in western Germany. Such existed in the Rhineland, and they were utilized in the *Historiae*; and adequate detail informs the isolated annalistic notices of events on or near the frontier.[1]

To pursue the theme in other regions. The raids of Tacfarinas naturally baffle localization. Tacitus furnishes hardly a place-name. As he observes (though not in defence of his own exposition), there were no cities even then in that part of Numidia.[2] The same holds for Thrace. Reporting at some length how Poppaeus Sabinus crushed a rebellion and beleaguered a hill fort, Tacitus dispenses with all particularization ('mons Haemus', and nothing more).[3]

The treatment of Britain is instructive on several counts. The second legate, Ostorius Scapula, among his earliest measures decided to extend the zone of direct military control. To define the area thus annexed the historian could have recourse only to natural features (in a region singularly devoid of them). He gives as limits two rivers, Sabrina and Trisantona: which is satisfactory.[4] The next sentence shows the author familiar with the geography, and with the military implications. Ostorius' action provoked the Iceni to rebel. Tacitus does not need to give the reason, namely, that the move outflanked the Iceni on the north-west and cut them off from the Brigantes.[5] Similarly, a brief and almost enigmatic statement a little later, that a military colony was founded at Camulodunum so as to facilitate the transference of a legion to a camp where it could deal with the Silures:[6] at first sight the Silures, far to the west, would seem wholly out of relation to anything that might happen at Camulodunum. As for

[1] IV. 72 f.; XI. 18–20; XII. 27 f.; XIII. 53–57.

[2] II. 52. 2: 'nullo etiam tum urbium cultu.' It can be presumed that he would know the difference between Tupusuctu, a Roman *colonia* near the coast, and Thubursicu Numidarum: the latter lurks in the 'Thubuscum oppidum' of IV. 24. 1, cf. R. Syme, *Studies in Roman Economic and Social History in Honour of A. C. Johnson* (1951), 113 ff.

[3] IV. 46–51.

[4] That is, with a satisfactory text. The *Mediceus posterior* has 'cunctaque castris Antonam et Sabrinam cohibere parat' (XII. 31. 2). The first river might be 'Trisantonam' (i.e. the Trent), whence 'cis Trisantonam' (Heraeus and H. Bradley), for 'castris Antonam'. The idea was developed by other scholars, thus 'castris ⟨ad Tris⟩antonam' (F. Haverfield, and, without comment, H. Fuchs in his edition); or, better, 'castris ⟨cis Tris⟩antonam' ('alii' according to H. Koestermann in his apparatus: that editor, like C. D. Fisher, prints the older conjecture 'Avonam ⟨inter⟩' for 'Antonam'). The 'Sabrina' being the Severn, '⟨Tris⟩antona' as the Trent fits the military and geographical postulates admirably.

[5] The Brigantes had been mentioned previously (as is deduced from XII. 40. 2), at least once. The Romans had entered into relations with that people not long after the invasion, cf. I. A. Richmond, *JRS* XLIV (1954), 47. In view of what is missing (of *Historiae* as well as *Annales*) it is not certain that Tacitus (as Richmond suggests, o.c. 43 and 52) failed to grasp the political role of the Brigantian principality and the Queen Cartimandua.

[6] XII. 32. 2.

Ostorius' operations against the elusive Caratacus, the country was wholly refractory to geographical terminology. No name could be given to the river and the fortress in the land of the Ordovices where he encountered and defeated the native leader.[1]

The prime document is Tacitus' story of the great insurrection, more often incriminated than praised.[2] Omissions have been blamed. Yet omissions were intentional, for the sake of brevity, speed, and concentration. They attest knowledge, not ignorance. Tacitus knew much more about Britain than when he wrote the *Agricola*.

On receipt of the news, Suetonius Paullinus left Mona and marched to Londinium.[3] Tacitus leaves out his motives. They were not obscure—to hold the town if possible, to keep open communications with western England and the Continent, to gain time for the legions to come together. He was compelled to modify the plan (the Ninth Legion met with a reverse, the Second never moved), and so went back again the way he had come, not giving battle until joined by a sufficient number of the troops available. While the character of the engagement could be described, the actual site was not named (for adequate reasons). The whole account presupposes an author familiar with military movements and properly informed about the distribution of the four legions of Britain. Small details confirm. He does not neglect the disaster that befell the Ninth Legion under Petillius Cerialis;[4] he can supply the name of the officer whose caution or timidity defrauded the Second Legion of a share in battle and victory.[5]

Britain and Armenia engross the military laurels of Nero's generals, with Suetonius Paullinus spurred to active emulation by the fame of Domitius Corbulo.[6] Armenia, though remote, was historic ground to the Romans, recalling Lucullus, Pompeius, and Antonius—and all the glorious past now revived and transcended by the conquests of Trajan. Every motive should have incited the historian to adorn his pages with the names that marked the passage of the legions, Republican or imperial.

Yet he registers very few. Of the military stations along the river Euphrates, only Melitene.[7] Nothing about Elegeia, at the western entrance to Armenia, on the way that leads thence to Artaxata;[8] no

[1] XII. 33.
[2] See further App. 69, where an attempt is made to indicate the merits of *Ann.* XIV. 29–39.
[3] XIV. 33. 1: 'at Suetonius mira constantia medios inter hostes Londinium perrexit.'
[4] 32. 3.   [5] 37. 3, cf. App. 69.
[6] At least 'rumore vulgi' (XIV. 29. 2).
[7] XV. 26. 2. Here Corbulo crossed the river in 63 (as Caesennius Paetus must have the year before, cf. XV. 7. 1 f.).
[8] Trajan, entering Armenia in 114, convoked the vassal princes at Elegeia (Dio LXVIII. 19. 2 f.).

designation for the site or region of Corbulo's first winter quarters;[1] and only one name to illustrate the moves that ended in the capitulation of Caesennius Paetus.[2]

Everybody, it is true, would know the route of invasion taking Corbulo to Artaxata;[3] and the march from Artaxata to Tigranocerta carries indications that help to localize the latter city.[4] But in another place Tacitus furnishes a detail that cannot harmonize—Tigranocerta is put thirty-seven miles distant from Nisibis.[5] No fault of his own, perhaps, but from a source;[6] and, as Tigranocerta was probably deserted in the time of Trajan, the historian saw nothing wrong.

For one reason or another (and reticence is generally more plausible than ignorance), Tacitus on Armenian geography falls short of the precision that might have been expected—especially since he had access to dispatches or memoirs of Domitius Corbulo. Was he perhaps reluctant to compete with Trajan's bulletins of victory that astonished the Senate[7]—especially when so rapidly blasted by failure and renunciation?

Be that as it may, enough has been said to defend Tacitus from the cruder forms of misapprehension. Granted that he is in general both diligent and accurate. Much more is required of a political historian. Has he the acumen to cut through document, authority, or tradition, and penetrate to the truth, has he the vigour to emerge victorious from the secret warfare which the holders of power in every age conduct against contemporaries and against posterity?

---

[1] XIII. 35. Presumably near the modern Erzerum, in the region Caranitis. Pliny for the source of the Euphrates gives Caranitis, citing Corbulo and Mucianus 'ex iis qui proxime viderant' (*NH* v. 83).

[2] XV. 15. 1—Caesennius' camp beside the river Arsanias. Dio supplies the name, Rhandeia (LXII. 21. 1).

[3] Pompeius went that way in 66 B.C. Also Trajan.

[4] The mention of the Mardi attacking his flank (XIV. 23. 3), and his passage through the 'regio Tauraunitium' (24. 3). But the author ought to have indicated that there was a high range of mountains to cross (the Armenian Taurus) before Corbulo reached Tigranocerta. As the campaign of Lucullus shows, Tigranocerta, even if not identical with the later Martyropolis (the choice of C. F. Lehmann-Haupt, argued at great length in P–W VI A, 981 ff.), must lie somewhere in the upper valley of the Tigris (between Taurus and Masius), north of that river.

[5] XV. 5. 2.   [6] cf. App. 61.   [7] Dio LXVIII. 29. 2.

XXX. THE SCEPTICAL HISTORIAN

IT was a task to overpower any novice, and not to be managed by rhetoric or mere erudition. Tacitus came to the *Annales* with a proper equipment, mature in experience, and well trained through having written about contemporary events. He is alert and vigilant, if ever historian was. But he came against barriers and limits, those of his time and epoch in the development of human thought. Not to Tacitus was it permitted, or to anybody else, to defy, confute, and explode a century-old tradition supported by the consensus of reputable authorities. The method had not yet been invented.

Still less for the remote past. It might seem wholly beyond the reach of criticism, because consecrated by time and custom, or not conceivably verifiable. A Roman lacked the will for disbelief as well as the tools and the technique.[1]

It suited the design of Tacitus to insert at intervals a number of antiquarian notices concerning institutions and topography. No words need be wasted on the fig tree of Romulus or the altar and shrine dedicated by the Arcadian Evander when he received a visit from Hercules.[2] Such things had a place, like the report of 'prodigia', in Roman annals, and an author's belief or disbelief does not come into the question. More vulnerable is Tacitus' excursus upon the origins of law.[3] The picture of primeval men, living in concord and equality, with no need of reward, or punishment, or legislation, will be allowed to pass as harmless homage to literary or sociological convention; but Tacitus goes on to express anomalous views about Servius Tullius and the code of the Decemvirs.[4] And some may feel disquiet because elsewhere he departs from standard tradition on two points of detail, how the quaestorship arose in the beginning, and when the 'gentes minores' were admitted to the patriciate.[5]

About early law and institutions at Rome his studies may have been imperfect or superficial. It is not proved.[6] A small phrase slipping out discloses the scepticism of a powerful intelligence. The sacred and patriotic story told how an Etruscan king, baffled by the heroism

---

[1] At Rome history began in tradition and remained patriotic: among the Greeks history was critical and could transcend state and nation.

[2] XIII. 58; XV. 41. 1. [3] III. 26 f.

[4] Servius Tullius as a legislator (III. 26. 4), the 'duodecim tabulae' as 'finis aequi iuris' (27. 1).

[5] XI. 22. 4; 25. 2.

[6] Rather should he be convicted of perverse erudition derived from speeches of Claudius Caesar, cf. App. 40.

of the Romans and disarmed in admiration, offered honourable terms of peace and went away. Tacitus affirms that Rome capitulated.[1]

'Porsenna dedita urbe.' Three words demolish several pages of Livy. Not that it is legitimate to blame Livy for his treatment of the legends or the early history: he was aware of the real character of much that he recounted. The later period demonstrates credulity and lack of political insight. The attack upon the Scipiones was an imbroglio (too late to unravel it), and Livy honestly avows that he is in trouble.[2] Many other things eluded him among the tangled feuds and alliances of those years: the operations of the Roman aristocracy were by no means as honourable as Livy fancied. He cannot resist or criticize the carefully staged reconciliation of two political enemies, heralded and enjoined by a moving address on 'concordia' from the venerable lips of an elder statesman.[3] When the narrative came closer to his own age, he was not proof against elementary misconceptions.[4] And benevolence became a danger. It impelled him to extenuate acts of violence or treachery in the early career of Pompeius Magnus.[5] Nor would Livy wish, for any reason, to undermine the assertions of a leader who took up arms in a just cause, rescued Rome (more than once), and restored the authority of Senate and People.

The prime quality of Cornelius Tacitus is distrust. It was needed, if a man were to write about the Caesars. Eloquence and anger denounce that period as no better than the fraudulent or fragmentary annals of the early Republic.[6] The protest is petulant but instructive.

The Republic in its closing age exhibited history in the full light of day. With the Empire a veil descends, and the truth about many matters of high policy, more or less disguised at the time, became impenetrable to posterity. The sharpest insight might have to confess itself baffled.[7]

---

[1] *Hist.* III. 72. I. In all the writings of the Romans the only other trace is in Pliny, who states that a treaty with Porsenna forbade the use of iron weapons (*NH* XXXIV. 139). Similarly, against the patriotic consensus of the annalists, there may have been a tradition that the Gauls captured the citadel of Rome, cf. O. Skutsch, *JRS* XLIII (1953), 77 f.

[2] Livy XXXVIII. 56.

[3] XL. 45 f. For a reconstruction of the manœuvres, F. Münzer, *Römische Adelsparteien und Adelsfamilien* (1920), 200 ff.

[4] Livy, if the epitomator of Book LX be trusted, reported a proposal of C. Gracchus to add six hundred members to the Roman Senate and thus treble its size. Which is incredible.

[5] The Livian version of the death of Cn. Domitius Ahenobarbus in Africa (in Orosius V. 21. 13) is contradicted by Valerius Maximus (VI. 2. 8); as for the killing of M. Brutus after his capitulation at Mutina, Pompeius had sent contradictory reports to the Senate (Plutarch, *Pompeius* 16), and there was sore need for apologia (cf. Orosius V. 22. 17). See Münzer, P–W V, 1328; X, 973.

[6] Mommsen exclaims that 'the tales told of Fabricius and of the emperor Gaius are almost equally insipid and equally mendacious' (*The Provinces of the Roman Empire* I (1886), 4).　　　　　　　　　[7] Dio LIII. 19 (paraphrased above, p. 365).

About the killing of Agrippa Postumus no official statement was ever published. Sallustius Crispus issued the order to a military tribune, and a centurion carried out the deed.[1] That is certain. The ultimate source and validity of that order remained an enigma, with wide scope for conjecture ever after, as the written sources all attest.[2]

So much for the last grandson of Caesar Augustus. Two years later a false Agrippa turned up, and was quietly put out of the way. Tacitus relates the story with names and details. It was believed that the impostor had friends and partisans. No investigation took place, and Tacitus says nothing more.[3]

The operations of an historian on the borderland of fact and fraud are the most exacting test of his powers. Several episodes establish the superior strategy of Cornelius Tacitus. First, the affair of M. Scribonius Libo. Tacitus affirms that he must expound it in careful detail, as of prime significance in the baneful record of the reign.[4]

This young nobleman had fallen into the snares of the astrologers, the magicians, and the interpreters of dreams. And what might he not hope from his pedigree, being a descendant of Pompeius Magnus? A friend of Libo conceived it his duty to put the Princeps on his guard. Tiberius, however, exhibited no change in his demeanour towards Libo, and allocated him a praetorship for the year 16. Then, in the autumn of that year, a practitioner in magic gave information to a prosecutor of great talent, Fulcinius Trio, who went to the consuls with the demand that the Senate investigate the case.

The trial began. The attitude of Tiberius was neutral and exemplary. The evidence was produced. Another prosecutor added to it. One piece was poor stuff, and childish, revealing only Libo's craving for fabulous wealth. Another document looked more serious—it contained the names of the imperial family and of senators, with enigmatic or sinister marks appended. Libo denied that it was his handwriting. Whereupon Tiberius gave instructions that his slaves be put to the torture (an innovation in procedure, according to the historian).[5] That caused Libo to ask for an adjournment. He went away to his

---

[1] This is clear from Tacitus. Suetonius (*Tib.* 22), and Dio (LVII. 3. 5 f.) are confused about the agent; and neither names Sallustius Crispus. Velleius Paterculus did his best to dissociate the incident from the accession of Tiberius (II. 112. 7), and recent inquirers have recourse to ingenious apologia. Perhaps Agrippa died a natural death, W. Allen, *TAPA* LXXVIII (1947), 131 ff.; perhaps there was a plot, justifying his execution, A. E. Pappano, *Class. Phil.* XXXVI (1941), 30 ff.

[2] In Suetonius and Dio, as in Tacitus. For the view that Augustus before his decease had decided the matter (Tacitus chose to regard the responsibility of Tiberius and Livia as 'propius vero'), cf. E. Hohl, *Hermes* LXX (1935), 350, followed in *Rom. Rev.* (1939), 439.

[3] II. 40. 3. For a sober but acute analysis, J. Mogenet, *L'Antiquité classique* XXIII (1954), 321 ff.

[4] II. 27. 1: 'eius negotii initium ordinem finem curatius disseram, quia tum primum reperta sunt quae per tot annos rem publicam exedere.'   [5] 30. 3.

house, and, when an attempt at private intercession with Tiberius had failed, he dined in despair and alarm, and committed suicide that evening. The indictment, however, was not dropped. When the case terminated, the estate of the condemned man was divided among the prosecutors; and seven persons of rank moved their various proposals for public thanksgiving. The Senate ordered all astrologers and magicians to depart from Italy. Two of them were arrested and executed by the consuls.

Attempts have been made to impugn the validity of the Tacitean account. Perhaps Libo was an authentic and formidable conspirator;[1] perhaps Tacitus has been taken in by some family tradition in the aristocracy, which extenuated his guilt.[2] The testimony of Suetonius or Velleius can be played against Tacitus. And there is confirmation unimpeachable: an entry in the state calendar attests the 'nefaria consilia' of Libo.[3]

The reconstruction is open to an attack more damaging than any Tacitean narration deserves. Governmental truth under the Principate, with whatever solemnity of word or pageantry proclaimed, will carry its own corrective. Velleius duly reflects it,[4] and enough is known about Velleius. As for Suetonius, he is both trivial and imprudent. He adduces the danger from Scribonius Libo (and from the false Agrippa) among the reasons that made Tiberius hesitate to accept the Principate.[5] So far what passes for evidence. No accomplices in conspiracy can be detected anywhere, save among the adepts of forbidden arts. Nor can a supposed tradition help—as though a noble family even in decay would disown among its ancestors a genuine conspirator against the Caesars and prefer a fool or a coward. That Libo was a fool is abundantly clear. Seneca disposed of him effectively—'tam stolidus quam nobilis'.[6] The account of Tacitus will stand.[7]

---

[1] A. Lang, *Beiträge zur Geschichte des Kaisers Tiberius* (Diss. Jena, 1911), 26 ff.; E. Ciaceri, *Processi politici e relazioni internazionali* (1918), 290 ff. and *Tiberio*[2] (1944), 266 ff.; R. S. Rogers, *Criminal Trials and Criminal Legislation under Tiberius* (1935), 12 ff. and *Studies in the Reign of Tiberius* (1943), 115 ff.

[2] F. B. Marsh, *Class. Phil.* xxi (1926), 291 ff.; *The Reign of Tiberius* (1931), 59 f.

[3] *CIL* I[2], p. 244 (*Fasti Amiternini*).

[4] Velleius II. 129. 2: 'quam celeriter ingratum et nova molientem oppressit'; 130. 3: 'quid hic meruit, primum ut scelerata Drusus Libo iniret consilia?'

[5] *Tib.* 25. 1. Dio (LVII. 15. 4 f.), inaccurate, like Suetonius, about the man's *praenomen*, is brief and adds nothing.

[6] *Epp.* 70. 10. For the stemma, *PIR*[1], S 214. Not only Pompeian blood and a link with the dynasty (because of Scribonia, once married to Augustus, and mother of Julia), but (presumably) a second link, with relatives of Livia: note M. Livius Drusus Libo (*cos.* 15 B.C.), about whom nothing is known. But for Tacitus (II. 29. 2), the conspirator's brother likewise would be only a date on the *Fasti* (*cos.* A.D. 16). The strength of the Pompeian faction now resided with L. Arruntius, a man of personal distinction (p. 382).

[7] As demonstrated by A. Passerini, *Studi giuridici in memoria di P. Ciapessoni* (Pavia,

The Emperor was involved much more deeply when the quarrel between Germanicus Caesar and Cn. Piso became the subject of public inquiry, with all manner of allegations and surmise. Tiberius had little sympathy for Germanicus, and some cause for disapproving his conduct in the eastern lands. Piso had been chosen not only to guide the prince, but to curb him. The whole truth could not be let out. Rumour spoke of 'secreta mandata' from the Princeps to the governor of Syria.[1] The inference was natural enough.[2] Tiberius had been confronted with an awkward problem. Anybody could see that the relation between a prince of the dynasty, invested with proconsular *imperium*, and Caesar's legate in Syria was a tricky matter; and Tiberius remembered the clash between the young Gaius Caesar and M. Lollius twenty years before.

Tacitus, recounting the trial of Piso, alludes to a curious piece of evidence (perhaps such a document) on the verbal authority of old men he had known. They had seen the paper in Piso's hands; and Piso (his friends affirmed) would have disclosed it to the Senate had he not been tricked by Seianus. Tacitus refuses to sponsor the story.[3] And, winding up that affair, he utters a general warning. There is no certitude to be had about the most important transactions. Some men take any casual rumour for ascertained fact, others convert truth into falsehood, and the passage of time only augments the damage.[4]

The decease of Drusus was an added reason for an historian to be cautious. After describing the funeral ceremony Tacitus inserts a digression.[5] He had adopted the report of the best authorities— poison, administered by the contriving of Seianus and with the complicity of Drusus' wife, Livia Julia, whom he seduced. Tacitus now intervenes to register and refute a version current even to his own time: Tiberius, having been secretly warned against Drusus by an emissary of Seianus, himself presented the poisoned cup to his son.

The story was wholly unsupported. Capable though they were of anything, the writers hostile to Tiberius never went so far. The thing was incredible, given the sagacity of the Emperor, his slow, deliberate, and suspicious nature. Yet it won belief, so Tacitus proceeds, because

---

1947), 219 ff. That scholar demolishes completely the notions of Lang, Ciaceri, Marsh, and Rogers. All that can be held against Tacitus is his allegation that the Emperor at first dissembled his resentment against Libo—'adeo iram condiderat' (II. 28. 2). Not much— and it might be a justifiable inference.

[1] II. 43. 4.

[2] L. Piso the *pontifex* (*cos.* 15 B.C.) was given 'secreta mandata' by Augustus for his Thracian War, also by Tiberius when he was *praefectus urbi* (Seneca, *Epp.* 83. 14).

[3] III. 16. 1. A document may well have existed.

[4] 19. 2: 'adeo maxima quaeque ambigua sunt, dum alii quoquo modo audita pro compertis habent, alii vera in contrarium vertunt, et gliscit utrumque posteritate.'

[5] IV. 10 f.

Seianus was held the author of each and every crime, and Tiberius
was infatuated with his minister; both were objects of detestation—
and rumour is relentless when there is death in the dynasty.[1]

With this text and example Tacitus exhorted his readers, solemnly
and indeed passionately, to keep to authentic history, like his own
Annales, abjuring rumour and sensation. About the death of Drusus
the truth only came out eight years later, after the fall of Seianus (as
Tacitus reveals and concedes). The woman Apicata was the source,
his divorced wife. Before committing suicide she wrote it all down and
sent it to Tiberius: a court doctor and a eunuch confirmed her avowals,
when put to torture.[2] Nobody seems to have felt disquiet about the
validity of those revelations.

The atrocious and childish rumour which Tacitus is at such pains to
refute shows the historian acutely aware of a disturbing factor—
namely that the craft and the criminal designs of Seianus might be
falsely enhanced. Perhaps only intermittently aware, to judge by
what he had already said or hinted.[3]

Accuracy and a sharp critical sense were not enough to establish
the truth. Tacitus soon had to confess his own dubitations in another
matter that concerned Seianus. It was Seianus who persuaded the
Emperor to leave Rome—that was the version transmitted by most of
the authorities.[4] Accepting it, Tacitus cannot withhold a certain disquiet, for Tiberius remained on Capreae after the fall of Seianus to
the end of his days. Perhaps, therefore, other reasons had to be
looked for—in Tiberius' own nature. The historian adduces some of
them. Tiberius (he suggests) wanted to cover up the traces of his
cruelty and his vices; he had become sensitive about his age, and also
about his physical appearance; and he could no longer stand the dis-
agreements with his mother.[5]

Seianus, if rescued from melodrama and the trappings of a second
Catilina, would exemplify more subtly, and in the end more forcibly,
the predicaments of minister and monarch. The relationship was
nothing new at Rome. On a proper scrutiny Aelius Seianus and Vip-
sanius Agrippa were closely comparable and mutually illuminative.
A contemporary could see it: he was happy to develop the parallel for

---

[1] 11. 2: 'sed quia Seianus facinorum omnium repertor habebatur, ex nimia caritate in
eum Caesaris et ceterorum in utrumque odio quamvis fabulosa et immania credebantur,
atrociore semper fama erga dominantium exitus.'

[2] Highly suspect, cf. H. Dessau, *Gesch. der r. Kaiserzeit* II (1926), 32; E. Paratore,
Maia II (1949), 113 f.

[3] e.g. IV. I. I: 'quo facinore dominationem raptum ierit.'

[4] 57. I.

[5] The digression in IV. 57 extends from 'causam abscessus' to the end of the chapter. The
notion of discord between mother and son is a late motive in the first hexad—and the
reference to Rhodes is a patent (and unskilful) insertion in the digression itself. See App. 37.

praise.[1] That contemporary had also heard vague echoes of friction between Augustus and Agrippa.[2] Later writers could enjoy an advantage. If they meditated upon Agrippa (history or legend), they might ask how that man managed to enforce his claims on the ruler—and avoid a fate like that of Aelius Seianus.

Caesar Augustus needed Agrippa; he was compelled to grant him a share in the power, and Julia for wife; had it not been for fate and savage accident, 'atrox fortuna', as Augustus confessed,[3] the succession would have gone to the sons of Agrippa and Julia. The other *novus homo* stood close to the power when chance or his own contriving began to remove the sons of Germanicus and Agrippina, the princes who were grandsons of Agrippa and Julia.

Conspiracy alleged or detected, proved or punished, is an elusive theme. The Emperor Domitian once observed that the lot of a ruler is far from happy—he will never be believed unless and until he is assassinated.[4] The perils that beset the Caesars will be invoked to explain or condone some of their actions. But the reputation of an emperor is not the principal cause of sorrow or perplexity. What is conspiracy? When an individual or a group is incriminated for nefarious designs against the person of Caesar or the security of the State, the count can subsume anything from treasonable talk to daggers and poison. Verification is generally precluded, documents are forged or fallacious, and the inquirer must use his own judgement: did a plot exist, who formed it, and with what precise purpose? Not all historians ask these questions when discussing the consul Varro Murena, or his grand-nephew Aelius Seianus.[5]

The comforting assurance that a conspiracy has been unmasked and disarmed with opportune promptness cannot fail to excite a legitimate suspicion in any age; and the surmise will often be valid that some court intrigue or a clash of ambitions has disturbed the inner economy of the governmental oligarchy. Varro Murena was condemned in absence, and executed. Cassius Dio at the interval of more than two centuries felt bold enough to admit a doubt about his guilt.[6] Dio was a senator who had lived under despotism, and he enounces principles about the credibility of conspiracies.[7] But Dio was not always on the alert. It is not clear that he interpreted with sufficient perspicacity the kind of situation that compelled Augustus to banish his daughter—and again, nine years later, his grand-daughter. Moral

---

[1] Velleius II. 127. 1.

[2] 93. 2. [3] Suetonius, *Tib.* 23 (from the will of Augustus).

[4] *Dom.* 21: 'condicionem principum miserrimam aiebat, quibus de coniuratione comperta non crederetur nisi occisis.' [5] For the 'conspiracy' of Seianus, see App. 65.

[6] Dio LIV. 3. 4. He doubts the complicity of Murena—but not the fact of the conspiracy engineered by Fannius Caepio. [7] 15. 1 ff.

delinquency was alleged, or a harsh penalty to prove it. Men of the time would discern conflict in the Palace, and dangerous ambitions brought to a fall.[1]

An historian might be confronted with fiction as well as deceit. Dio fancied that he had discovered both genuine history and a laudable excuse for prolix moralization when he came across Cinna Magnus, the nobleman who plotted to take the life of the Princeps—and who was brought to his senses by a sermon from Caesar more than two hours long.[2]

Descendants of Pompeius Magnus such as Cinna or Scribonius Libo engrossed more attention than they deserved. It was in the family circle of Augustus that danger was discovered and something closer to treason—Iullus Antonius perishing on that count, the husband of his niece and alleged paramour of his daughter, then Aemilius Paullus who had for wife the younger Julia. If the Roman knight Aelius Seianus became a menace, it was Tiberius Caesar who made him so.

Seianus rose to such a pinnacle that one of two things must ensue—supremacy or catastrophe. The outcome cast its shadow backwards over all that had gone before; and the story of criminal ambition could not but appear coherent and convincing. Thus adultery and poison in 23. And two years later the historian can report without misgivings a secret petition from Seianus to the Emperor: he asked for the hand of Drusus' widow.[3] Tacitus might have felt prompted to inquire whether such high aspirations are likely to have taken firm shape so early.

The growing discord between Tiberius and Agrippina showed Seianus how to proceed. He played upon the fears and resentments of the Emperor, and through prosecutions discredited and undermined the party of Agrippina. Yet it was not until the year 29 that the chance offered—not to seize the power but to glide into it gently under the grateful conduct of Tiberius Caesar.

The Senate passed sentence of banishment against Agrippina and her eldest son, Nero. Tacitus relates the affair in immediate sequence to the death of Livia, with an explanation—they had been more or less

---

[1] Dio expatiates on the immoralities of Julia (LV. 10. 12 ff., cf. Seneca, *De ben.* VI. 32. 1). For the political significance of this obscure transaction, *Rom. Rev.* (1939), 427. Dio's account of the younger Julia (A.D. 8) is lost through a gap in the manuscript. Her husband, L. Aemilius Paullus (*cos.* A.D. 1), was executed for conspiracy, cf. Suetonius, *Divus Aug.* 19. 1—the sole clear record of his fate. The younger Julia was brought to the notice of Tacitus by the return to Rome of D. Junius Silanus (III. 24. 1 ff.), cf. p. 371.

[2] Dio LV. 14 ff. (under A.D. 4), cf. Seneca, *De clem.* I. 9 (apparently indicating the period 16–13 B.C.). It hardly matters. The episode is edifying fiction, cf. *Rom. Rev.* (1939), 414.

[3] IV. 39 f. One might wonder where the historian discovered this item, which he exploits to its full irony.

safe so long as the Augusta lived. Tacitus states that no charge of conspiracy was brought up.[1] His account is full and explicit—the scene in the senate when Tiberius' missive arrived, the motion of an eminent consular (Cotta Messallinus). The magistrates hesitated, the senator whose duty it was to draw up the official records made a rash intervention, and there came a second letter from the angry Emperor.[2]

Two years later Seianus was consul, as colleague of the Emperor. He received proconsular *imperium*;[3] and he was betrothed to a princess, Julia, the daughter of Drusus Caesar and Livia Julia.[4] The example of M. Agrippa was before his eyes. Aelius Seianus had everything to gain by time and caution. Why plot to remove Caesar his benefactor, the source of his power? Dynastic loyalty had struck deep roots by now. Seianus could scarcely hope to seize and hold the supreme authority after an assassination.

The Emperor had encouraged his minister long since to extend his patronage through the disposal of honours and provinces.[5] No danger or rival seemed to threaten from the army commanders. Syria and Spain were vacant, without their consular legates these many years.[6] Closest to Italy lay Germany and Pannonia. Lentulus Gaetulicus held Upper Germany, with his father-in-law, L. Apronius, in the other command:[7] it is not known who was the legate of Pannonia.[8]

At Rome and in the camps of the legions, men saw the statues of Tiberius and Seianus side by side; and their names were conjoined by a loyal Senate's devotion, commemorating their virtues by altars to clemency and friendship.[9] Nor did Seianus neglect the effort to attach the urban populace, the peculiar clients of the Caesars. When he was elected consul, some form of pageantry was staged on the

---

[1] v. 3. 2: 'verba erant quaesita asperitate: sed non arma, non rerum novarum studium, amores iuvenum et impudicitiam nepoti obiectabat.'

[2] It has been argued that Tacitus distorted the order of events, that the attack on Agrippina occurred earlier, in 27. See M. P. Charlesworth, *Class. Phil.* XVII (1922), 260 f., followed by D. M. Pippidi, *Ephemeris Dacoromana* VIII (1938), 45 = *Autour de Tibère* (1944), 61, and by R. S. Rogers, *Studies in the Reign of Tiberius* (1943), 57 ff. Meanwhile, the author of that suggestion had unobtrusively retreated, but still asserted (against the plain statement of Tacitus) that conspiracy must have been alleged (*CAH* x (1934), 635). That theme had been developed at some length by R. S. Rogers, *TAPA* LXII (1931), 141 ff. Apologists of Tiberius can be ingenuous and insatiable.

[3] Dio LVIII. 7. 4.

[4] Zonaras XI. 2, cf. *Ann.* v. 6. 2; VI. 8. 3; Dio LVIII. 7. 5. She is *PIR*[1], J 422, her mother L 211. Suetonius and Dio call her mother Livilla.

[5] IV. 2. 3.   [6] VI. 27. 2 f. (cf. p. 442).

[7] 30. 2 ff. Cf. *PIR*[2], C 1390; A 971.

[8] The governor of Dalmatia was perhaps the aged L. Volusius Saturninus (*suff.* 3), cf. *ILS* 923, &c. The *novus homo* C. Poppaeus Sabinus (*cos.* 9) was in Moesia (VI. 39. 3): like Volusius, surely a safe support of the dynasty—yet his son-in-law T. Ollius was an adherent of Seianus and perished in 31 (XIII. 45. 1).   [9] IV. 2. 3; 74. 2.

Aventine, the historic plebeian hill.[1] He also took the image of Fortuna from the shrine built by Servius Tullius to be his protecting and domestic deity.[2] Servius was the archetypal *novus homo*, just, benevolent, and a friend of the Roman plebs. Astute careerists read the signs, eagerly extolling merit against the claims of birth, and entreating the gods to guide Tiberius aright in the transmission of the power.[3]

The succession was passing from the line of Caesar Augustus. Of the sons of Germanicus, Nero was executed this year on his island of banishment; Drusus had been taken into custody the year before; only Caligula remained.

Something went wrong. Tiberius began to waver.[4] He saw that he had committed himself too deeply to his minister. Seianus was hoping for the *tribunicia potestas*.[5] The messages from the island were vague and ambiguous. Obstacles arose.[6] Several months passed.[7]

A letter from Capreae demolished Aelius Seianus (October 18, 31).[8] Had there been a conspiracy? Seianus numbered personages of mark among his friends and relatives. Yet no man of consular rank (so far as is known) shared his fate except his uncle, Junius Blaesus.[9] Nor were any governors of the armed provinces brought back to Rome in disgrace. The victims were numerous. But victims and an informer do not prove treason. When a man spoke in defence of the innocent adherents of Seianus, it was expedient for him to admit the official or current version of an abominable plot in which they had no share.[10]

Seianus towards the end took (it may be) some imprudent or desperate step, as he felt the toils closing around him. Tacitus adduces the name of an informer—of what credit, it is not at all clear.[11] The alert historian might have seen the need to correct exaggerations of disbelief. However it be, the only plot that can safely be assumed and narrated is the plot devised and executed by Tiberius Caesar.[12] Seianus was deep and crafty. He met his master.[13]

[1] *ILS* 6044: 'improbae comitiae / [q]uae fuerunt in Aventino ubi / [Sei]anus cos. factus est.' Cf. R. Syme, *Hermes* LXXXIV (1956), 257 ff.

[2] Dio LVIII. 7. 2. Cf. Pliny on the vestments of the statue, which endured intact for five hundred and sixty years 'ad Seiani exitum' (*NH* VIII. 197).

[3] Velleius II. 127 f.; 131.

[4] He received a warning from Antonia (Josephus, *AJ* XVIII. 181 f.). Perhaps, as many assume, about a threat to Caligula: cf. *Ann.* VI. 3. 4.

[5] Suetonius, *Tib.* 65. 1, cf. Dio LVIII. 9. 4.

[6] Thus he was thwarted in an attempt to have L. Arruntius prosecuted (Dio LVIII. 8. 3), cf. p. 384.

[7] The indications in Dio are very useful, cf. App. 65.

[8] *ILS* 158 (Gortyna in Crete), cf. 157 (Interamna Nahars): 'sublato perniciosissimo hoste p(opuli) R(omani).' [9] V. 7. 2.

[10] VI. 8 (the speech of the knight M. Terentius).

[11] viz. Satrius Secundus (VI. 47. 2, cf. 8. 5). It appears that he did not succeed in saving his skin, cf. App. 65.

[12] p. 255. See further App. 65. [13] IV. 1. 2: 'quippe isdem artibus victus est.'

Posterity might well refuse to credit many things that happened at Rome. The consort of Claudius Caesar went through a ceremony of marriage with C. Silius in the open light of day. Tacitus affirms the fact, invoking an unimpeachable tradition, the oral and the written.[1] Similarly, the great conspiracy against Nero. Popular talk at the time suggested that there was nothing in it—only a pretext for Nero to destroy those whom he feared or hated. Tacitus goes out of his way to vouch for authenticity. He appeals to the testimony of conspirators who survived.[2]

It was necessary to be cautious about many of the particulars. An informer denounced Seneca. Nero fixed on the charge with alacrity. Yet, as Tacitus points out, Nero had no valid evidence.[3] It is only as a rumour that Tacitus notices a project emanating from some of the officers (and not unknown to Seneca himself), to kill Piso as well as Nero and install Seneca in the power.[4] The caution of Tacitus is exemplary.[5] It has been left to later writers to pronounce with airs of certitude on the complicity of Annaeus Seneca.[6]

Ignorance or deception tended to multiply the victims of tyranny. In the year after the conspiracy a certain Anicius Cerialis, being denounced to Nero, promptly put an end to his life. Some historians extenuated the earlier career of this man.[7] Tacitus, who had reported his extravagant proposal of a temple for 'Divus Nero',[8] exempts the fate of Anicius from any commiseration—men remembered that he had given evidence to Caligula about a conspiracy.[9]

Such is the distrustfulness of Tacitus that even eyewitnesses, reputable old men, may be doubted, or the great Corbulo refused credence—Corbulo made false allegations to enhance the discredit of another general.[10] Most of the historian's critical work is lost to view, the polemics being veiled, and he seldom cares to specify the grounds for choice or rejection. From time to time a fact, a name, or a comment, while unobtrusively revealing his methods, will show him vigilant all through.

---

[1] XI. 27: 'sed nihil compositum miraculi causa, verum audita scriptaque senioribus tradam.'

[2] XV. 73. 2: 'ceterum coeptam adultamque et revictam coniurationem neque tunc dubitavere quibus verum noscendi cura erat, et fatentur qui post interitum Neronis in urbem regressi sunt.' Observe the proud and plain solemnity of language—'verum noscendi cura.' The historian himself had just been demonstrating diligence by a catalogue of twenty-four names (XV. 71).

[3] 60. 2: 'non quia coniurationis manifestum compererat.'   [4] 65.

[5] It is not likely that Seneca, a 'sagacissimus senex', wanted the power—or fancied that he could hold it.

[6] E. Ciaceri, *Processi politici e relazioni internazionali* (1918), 370; A. Momigliano, *CAH* x (1934), 728. They can appeal to Dio (LXII. 24. 1)—not at all good evidence for anything concerning Seneca. Moreover, his account (fragmentary) does not happen to name Piso.   [7] Dio LIX. 25. 5.

[8] XV. 74. 3.   [9] XVI. 17. 6. .   [10] XV. 16. 3: 'augendae infamiae composita.'

XXXI. THE PRINCIPATE

THE large and primary matter that detained and engaged the
sceptical attention of Cornelius Tacitus was the Principate itself.
That the supreme authority in the Commonwealth had to be concentrated in the hands of one man was inevitable, if Rome was to
regain peace and stability. The axiom is approved alike by the men of
understanding at the funeral of Augustus and by the author of the
Historiae in his prologue. Inevitable also that the authority be legally
defined, as delegation from Senate and People. Two reasons contributed. The first was heavily advertised—Roman tradition and respect
for the proprieties. Yet not devoid of force, since to a people that has
known for centuries the rule of aristocracy within the framework of a
republic, mere despotism is a crude, ugly, and precarious form of
government. Less was said about the second, namely the convenience
of the ruler. Authority gains when it can apply compulsion through
legal form, and governments are never at a loss for lawyers on their
side. Law and the Commonwealth enabled Caesar Augustus to evade
criticism and check rivalry, to control or modify the organs of government, to canalize patronage, to ensure a smooth transmission of the
power.

Between the formula and the realities a wide gap yawned. The main
elements in the supremacy of Augustus derive from sources outside
the Roman constitution. Tacitus insists ever and again upon the
contrast between words and substance. The sentiments of the writer
conspired most happily with the demands of style and technique—
brevity, speed, and ruthless omission.

The preface defines 'princeps' as the name, 'imperium' the fact.[1]
The second chapter reveals Caesar's heir as the last of the dynasts and
carries a summary sketch of his predominance as it developed after
the Battle of Actium. It eschews constitutional terminology almost
entirely, and slides over the stages perceptible between the aftermath
of Actium and the year 23 B.C.

The stages, put briefly, are as follows. Openly monarchic at first,
Imperator Caesar as consul lacked nothing the Triumvir had. Next,
early in 28, the ruler's consulate appeared to become normal, with
alternation in the twelve *fasces* between colleague and colleague.[2] Then,
in January, 27, Senate and People having been declared sovereign,

---

[1] I. I. I: 'nomine principis sub imperium accepit'; 9. 5: 'non regno tamen neque dicta-
tura sed principis nomine constitutam rem publicam.'   [2] Dio LIII. I. I (p. 365).

Caesar Augustus was voted a vast *provincia* as his charge for ten years. He still kept the consulate, year after year. But, in 23, abdicating the consulship yet retaining the provincial *imperium* (which he was permitted to hold even if resident in Rome, and which was now defined as superior to that of any proconsul), Augustus also took the *tribunicia potestas*.[1] The twin pillars of predominance stand out clearly.[2] The one power avowed its origin by a direct continuity—it was the absolute *imperium* which the proconsuls of the imperial Republic held abroad in the provinces, and which the last of the dynasts duly installed in the city.[3] The other was vague, portentous, unprecedented —and valued the more highly for those reasons, although the ruler could have exercised the supreme authority without it.[4]

Instead, Tacitus has a continuous description. It passes through the feigned moderation of the despot (he no longer owned to the title of Triumvir, claiming only to be consul, and his tribunician privilege was assumed only to protect the plebs) to stealthy aggrandizement as he usurped the functions of Senate, magistrates, and laws.[5] Some will put heavy blame on Tacitus, deploring vagueness or a wilful neglect of constitutional law. Not without reason.[6] Yet it remains a question whether Tacitus' version is not the true reflection of the historical process as an historian must see it: namely, the consolidation of power, whatever be the names and forms thereto subservient.[7]

[1] ib. 32. 5.

[2] In 19 B.C. Augustus was granted consular authority (Dio LIV. 10. 5). Accepted and exploited by A. H. M. Jones, *JRS* XLI (1951), 117: against, L. Wickert (P-W XXII, 2282), who points out that the ὥστε defining the ἐξουσία τῶν ὑπάτων could be taken in a restrictive sense. It is hardly correct to say that Augustus henceforth held and exercised *imperium consulare*. What he could be deemed to have received is the right to bear the *insignia* of that provincial *imperium* which he retained (even in Rome) since 23. There would now be two sets of twelve *fasces* at Rome—inconceivable in a Republic, cf. Cicero, *De re publica* II. 55.

[3] There is no evidence that the power of the Caesars in Rome was conceived and defined as *imperium consulare*. In 51 the boy Nero was granted 'proconsulare imperium extra urbem' (XII. 41. 1). Now proconsular *imperium* by its very nature ought to be valid only 'extra urbem'. The addition of the phrase in this passage implies that the central imperial power was normally conceived as a proconsular *imperium* which had been domiciled at Rome and legitimized there.

[4] III. 56. 2: 'id summi fastigii vocabulum Augustus repperit ne regis aut dictatoris nomen adsumeret ac tamen appellatione aliqua cetera imperia praemineret.'

[5] I. 2. 1: 'posito triumviri nomine consulem se ferens et ad tuendam plebem tribunicio iure contentum, ubi militem donis populum annona cunctos dulcedine otii pellexit, insurgere paullatim, munia senatus magistratuum legum in se trahere.'

[6] At first sight the simultaneity of consulate and tribunes' powers appears both misleading and erroneous. Augustus took the full *tribunicia potestas* in 23, dating it thence year by year—as Tacitus knows (I. 9. 2). The grant of *ius auxilii* late in 30 (Dio LI. 19. 6) ought not to be neglected: it is presumably alluded to in the 'tribunicio iure contentum' of Tacitus.

[7] Likewise continuity. Tacitus deliberately refuses in this passage to mention the much vaunted 'Restoration of the Republic' in 28 and 27. Deliberately again, he draws no distinction between the ruler's consulates before and after 28. Elsewhere he dates the legal establishment of the Principate precisely to 28 (III. 28. 2).

Similarly, the accession of Tiberius. Tacitus sets forth in careful detail the oath of allegiance and shows the new ruler in actual and open exercise of the essential powers of the Principate: by the *imperium* he issues orders to the troops and dispatches to the armies, and in virtue of *tribunicia potestas* he convokes the Senate to arrange the funeral.[1] It was not until four weeks had elapsed from the demise of Augustus that the constitutional position came to be discussed in the Senate: the first item after the vote that consecrated Augustus as a god. The situation was a political one, and is expounded as such by the historian, with none the less relish for its being fundamentally unreal. The succession had already been determined, one way through the adoption, the other through powers conferred the year before.[2] Moreover, the oath of allegiance had been sworn at once to the successor of Augustus.[3] If he did not intend to continue in the power, he would have to abdicate.

The stage was set for a solemn comedy, the attitudes and language pre-ordained. Tiberius wished to extort a frank admission that his own primacy in the Commonwealth was indispensable. He therefore had to offer a show of reluctance.[4] Lacking the talent of his great predecessor, he was ill at ease in a false but necessary role. Not content to have spoken about partnership in the supreme authority, he went on to asseverate (with detail and document) the magnitude of Empire, and professed himself willing to take only a portion for his rule.[5] That drew an awkward question from one of the senior statesmen. Others voiced impatience.[6] The assembly grew tumultuous.

The debate had been introduced by a motion of the consuls, the tenor of which is nowhere specified by Tacitus.[7] The upshot, as he reports it, was vague and inconclusive.[8] Argument led to misunderstandings and fatigue; and, although Tiberius ceased persisting in his negative, he did not unequivocally avow that he was accepting the

---

[1] I. 7. 3 ff.

[2] viz. *imperium* over provinces and armies equal to that of Augustus (Velleius II. 121. 1; Suetonius, *Tib.* 21. 1).

[3] 7. 1 f.

[4] Suetonius calls it an 'impudentissimus mimus' (*Tib.* 24. 1). For the prescribed 'refus du pouvoir', see J. Béranger, *Recherches sur l'aspect idéologique du Principat* (1953), 137 ff.

[5] 12. 1, cf. Dio LVII. 2. 4 f. According to Dio, Tiberius actually named τρία μέρη, viz. Rome and Italy, the armies, the rest of the provinces. That can hardly be right, cf. E. Hohl, *Hermes* LXVIII (1933), 114.

[6] Q. Haterius and Mam. Scaurus (p. 323), following Asinius Gallus and L. Arruntius in the debate.

[7] Indicated at the outset by the words 'versae inde ad Tiberium preces' (I. 11. 1), and mentioned later by Scaurus—'spem esse ex eo non inritas fore senatus preces quod relationi consulum iure tribuniciae potestatis non intercessisset' (13. 4).

[8] cf. the comment of Ph. Fabia, 'la conclusion sans netteté qui convenait mieux à ce débat sans loyauté' (*Rev. phil.* XXXIII (1909), 58).

Principate.[1] That an ostensibly important debate can flag and peter out (with the main point tacitly conceded) is not alien to the ascertained and sometimes predictable behaviour of political assemblies; and it might be contended that Tiberius in truth already possessed the powers and therefore needed no ratification.[2] However, one thing is clear. The debate on that topic found an end. The Senate went on to other matters. One of the items should prove that the position of Tiberius Caesar was now regarded as settled—*imperium proconsulare* was conferred on Germanicus.[3]

It can hardly be believed, however, that the session closed without any decree concerning the powers and authority of the ruler himself. The clue lies in the missing 'relatio consulum'.[4] Tacitus is guilty of a gratuitous omission.

No light is thrown upon this obscure transaction by any subsequent word or deed.[5] If Tacitus can go to such an extremity of imprecision by reason of his preoccupation with ruler and Senate in their conduct and motives, no surprise will ensue when he leaves out minor offices or titles held by the Caesars. Tiberius duly became *princeps senatus*;[6] and he was installed as *pontifex maximus* some six months after his accession.[7] Facts, but irrelevant to Tacitus, and firmly discarded, like the empty formality of the decennial anniversary.[8]

Nor do the multiple ceremonies which loyalty or adulation so ingeniously devised for the Caesars and their family, for their virtues and their victories, hold appeal or value for Tacitus, except in depreciation. It was a fraud from the beginning.[9] The homage paid to appearances was a cynical defiance of what all men knew to be the truth.[10] Tacitus does not need to insist, but he is ready with brief

[1] I. 13. 5: 'fessusque clamore omnium, expostulatione singulorum flexit paullatim, non ut fateretur suscipi a se imperium, sed ut negare et rogari desineret.'

[2] H. Dessau, *Gesch. der r. Kaiserzeit* II (1926), 6.   [3] I. 14. 3.

[4] Presumably a confirmation of the powers without limit of time. Dio, noticing the *decennalia* of 24 and 34, states that no formal renewal of the power was necessary (LVII. 24. 1; LVIII. 24. 1). That some measure was passed is indicated by Suetonius (*Tib.* 24. 2). Compare also Tiberius' words, 'dixi et nunc et saepe alias, p.c., bonum et salutarem principem, quem vos tanta et tam libera potestate instruxistis, senatui servire debere', &c. (ib. 29).

[5] It has been argued that what Tiberius lacked to make him Princeps was the *imperium consulare*, cf. A. H. M. Jones, *JRS* XLI (1951), 119. But it is not at all clear that he exercised it as ruler, cf. A. Passerini, *Studi giuridici in memoria di P. Ciapessoni* (Pavia, 1947), 208. Against the whole notion of an *imperium consulare* cf. above, p. 409.

[6] When, there is no sign. The conjecture that it was included in the 'relatio consulum' (M. P. Charlesworth, *CAH* x (1934), 612) does not help to elucidate the accession of Tiberius.

[7] *CIL* I², p. 233 (*Fasti Praenestini*): on March 10.

[8] Dio LVII. 24. 1; LVIII. 24. 1.

[9] Lucan v. 385 f.: 'omnes voces per quas iam tempore tanto | mentimur dominis.'

[10] xv. 18. 1: 'dum adspectui consulitur spreta conscientia'; xiv. 59. 4: 'gravioribus iam ludibriis quam malis.'

comments, bitter or ironical, upon the gala performances of official orators.[1] Even the account of the posthumous honours for Germanicus is prefaced with a faint sneer from the historian—and interrupted by a sarcastic aside from Tiberius Caesar.[2] When Drusus died, similar but more elaborate manifestations elicit their due dispraisal.[3]

For Cornelius Tacitus the essential falsity of the Principate lay in the fiction that the supreme authority in the Roman State was voluntarily offered and legally conveyed, or at least ratified. The opening chapters of the *Annales* deny the Republic of Augustus, reveal the working of dynastic politics, and demonstrate that Tiberius was already in possession of authority before the Senate was invited to express an opinion.

By contrast, real power in its origins and its acts. The normal phraseology of Tacitus concedes no palliation. To denominate the regiment of the Caesars he singles out a term than which the Latin language knows none stronger, 'rerum potiri'.[4] It occurs no fewer than eleven times in the *Annales*. Again, Tacitus modifies and subverts the traditional formula of 'Senate and People'. He interpolates (and very properly) the new source of power that grew up, with the Principate itself, out of the wars: hence 'senatus milesque et populus'.[5]

The sacred name of 'res publica' will not be spared. The interests of the Commonwealth are invoked to cover up intrigue, deceit, or violence—by a politician for Claudius' marriage with his brother's daughter, by an imperial freedman for the adoption of the boy Nero, and by a prosecutor for the destruction of Thrasea Paetus.[6] Agrippina, when turning Claudius away from Britannicus, lays emphasis on the legality of Nero's adoptive status, with fervent appeal to the enactments of Senate and People.[7] Nero in his turn, after murdering Britannicus, publishes grief in an edict: deprived of a brother's support, he must concentrate his hopes upon the 'res publica', while Senate and People for their part will cherish their Princeps with an affection all the warmer now that he alone survives of a family ordained for empire.[8]

Nor can the historian countenance benevolent notions about the the 'auctoritas' of the emperors. Caesar Augustus asserted that after he had consigned the 'res publica' to the charge of Senate and People he

---

[1] XVI. 2. 2: 'summa facundia nec minore adulatione' (panegyrists of Nero).
[2] II. 83. 1: 'ut quis amore in Germanicum aut ingenio validus.' Cf. p. 279.
[3] IV. 9. 2: 'plerisque additis, ut ferme amat posterior adulatio.'
[4] cf. Lucretius II. 13: 'ad summas emergere opes rerumque potiri'; Caelius in *Ad fam.* VIII. 14. 2: 'qui rerum potiuntur' (the dynasts Pompeius and Caesar).
[5] I. 7. 2; XI. 30. 2. Cf. XIV. 11. 1: 'militi patribusque et plebi.' Also, omitting 'populus', XII. 69. 2; XIII. 4. 1.
[6] XII. 5. 2 (L. Vitellius); 25. 1 (Pallas); XVI. 28. 1 (Eprius Marcellus).
[7] XII. 41. 3: 'quaeque censuerint patres iusserit populus, intra penatis abrogari.'
[8] XIII. 17. 3: 'reliquas spes in re publica sitas.'

excelled all men in 'auctoritas'.[1] The word, on the shortest definition, means power and influence, but not such as derives from the tenure of magistracy or can be defined by legal enactment. Of this nature was the authority belonging to the Senate of the Republic as a body, or to the senator individually, if he had station, age, and reputation.[2]

'Auctoritas' conveys a strong prepossession. To discredit the term Tacitus will resort to various devices, learned from Sallust if he needed to learn. First, omission.[3] He employs 'auctoritas' but seldom in the *Annales*, least of all for an emperor's authority.[4] Secondly, he applies it outside the official and constitutional sphere, with deliberate malice and irony, to emphasize personal or illicit influence exercised by a knight or a freedman. The first introduction of Aelius Seianus extols his 'auctoritas' with Tiberius Caesar;[5] Pallas by virtue of his 'auctoritas' accelerates the adoption of Nero;[6] and Nero as emperor, dispatching another freedman, Polyclitus, to Britain, has every confidence that the 'auctoritas' of that agent will be doubly effective, with Roman officials (the legate and procurator), and with the natives.[7]

The third device is more insidious. As the historian Sallust pointed out in a diagnosis of political terminology, what some call 'amicitia' others will call 'factio': interpretation is variable and partisan.[8] By the same token the pejorative synonym of 'auctoritas' cannot escape. It is 'potentia'. How strongly Tacitus is drawn to the word needs little documentation.[9] Caesar's heir, when restoring the Republic, stood supreme and invulnerable. No fear, constraint, or rival—he was 'potentiae securus'.[10] Official terminology preferred 'auctoritas'. It could never admit to 'potentia'. The knights C. Maecenas and Sallustius Crispus transcended by their 'potentia' many senators who boasted consulates and triumphs.[11] A friend, in sincere devotion, or an apologist daring a little, might have attributed 'auctoritas' to those imperial ministers.[12]

[1] *Res Gestae* 34.

[2] The notion, which is not mysterious in its origin and applications, has evoked an enormous amount of writing. See, for example, A. Magdelain, *Auctoritas Principis* (1947). That author (like A. v. Premerstein) tries to give a juridical force and content to the 'auctoritas' of Augustus. In fact, all his main tenets seem vulnerable, cf. H. M. Last, *JRS* XL (1950), 119 ff.; G. E. F. Chilver, *Historia* I (1950), 420 ff. Perhaps it is time for the lengthy argumentations about this word to abate.

[3] One sees why Sallust refused to use the term 'optimates'.

[4] In fact, never. He was less rigorous in the *Historiae* (e.g. I. 29. I).

[5] I. 24. 2.   [6] XII. 25. I.   [7] XIV. 39. I.

[8] *Jug.* 31. 15: 'sed haec inter bonos amicitia, inter malos factio est.'

[9] Almost three columns in the *Lexicon Taciteum* of Gerber–Greef. For 'potentia' as the other face of 'auctoritas' compare Cicero, *De re publica* I. 68: 'ex nimia potentia principum'; *Brutus* 166: 'C. Claudius, etsi propter summam nobilitatem et singularem potentiam magnus erat.'   [10] III. 28. 2.   [11] 30. 2.

[12] And indeed in the *Historiae* Tacitus allowed himself to attribute 'auctoritas' to Roman knights, quite neutrally (III. 4. I; IV. 53. I).

Power or adulation duly annexed various ethical qualities to the glorification of the Caesars or the strengthening of their rule.[1] In gratitude for the Republic restored, Senate and People, having conferred the *cognomen* of 'Augustus', ordained that a golden shield be set up, inscribed with the virtues of Caesar Augustus.[2] The list was short and impressive. First 'virtus' itself, that Roman quality, the proud and powerful word that inspired the cause of the Republic in the struggle against Caesarism. Next, 'clementia', 'iustitia', and 'pietas'. On a cool scrutiny neither 'clementia' nor 'pietas' was unimpeachable when attached to Augustus. Both terms had a dubious and variegated history behind them. Seized and exploited by leaders or parties in the Civil Wars, they passed into the monopoly of the victor. When Caesar the Dictator paraded a merciful and forgiving spirit (certainly from calculation, and perhaps from generosity), he did not endear himself to all men in his own class and order.[3] Clemency depends not on duty but on choice or whim, it is the will of a master not an aristocrat's virtue.[4] To acquiesce in the 'clementia Caesaris' implied a recognition of despotism. The son of one of Caesar's adversaries refused the victor's pardon, young Cn. Domitius Ahenobarbus.[5] And, when the exercise of 'clementia' is commended by Seneca to the great-grandson of that Domitius, the argument is frankly monarchical.[6] It is evident that Tacitus will tend either to avoid this governmental term, or to apply it ironically.

In the year 28 the Senate, so Tacitus affirms, resorted to subservience as a palliative for their own disquiet and alarm. They voted an altar to clemency and an altar to friendship, not omitting statues of Tiberius and of Seianus, and urgently implored that those personages should honour Rome with their presence.[7] When Valerius Asiaticus stood on trial before Claudius Caesar in the palace, his eloquent defence moved Messallina to pity: leaving the chamber to wipe away her tears, the Empress adjured the faithful Vitellius not to let this victim escape. And Vitellius, in tears himself, spoke of old friendship and the virtues of Asiaticus, with other reasons for lenience and mercy

---

[1] See now J. Béranger, *Recherches sur l'aspect idéologique du Principat* (1953): a lucid, discerning, and sceptical study. For 'imperial virtues' see also App. 66.

[2] *Res Gestae* 34. Cf. the copies, *ILS* 82 (Potentia in Picenum); *AE* 1952, 165 (Arelate, dated 'cos. VIII', i.e. 26 B.C.). On the latter, W. Seston, *CRAI* 1954, 286 ff.

[3] For 'clementia Caesaris' see M. Treu, *Mus. Helv.* v (1948), 197 ff.

[4] Cicero, speaking about the Catilinarian business, extols his own 'lenitas' and 'misericordia' (*Pro Sulla* 1, cf. 87; 92). Sallust is careful not to use the word 'clementia' in relation to Caesar—or to contemporary politics at all. His sole instance is Lepidus' appeal to the 'clementia' of the Roman People (*Hist.* I. 55. 1).

[5] Cicero, *Phil.* II. 27.

[6] *De clem.* I. 3. 3: 'nullum tamen clementia ex omnibus magis quam regem aut principem decet.'

[7] IV. 74. 2.

—and ended with the plea that Asiaticus be permitted to choose freely the manner of his own death. Claudius Caesar added his contribution, couched in a strain of like clemency.[1]

Wholly different in nature from 'clementia' and comparable to 'auctoritas' in dignity, the quality of 'pietas', which derives from devotion to family and religion, was the more thoroughly debased by partisan and official exploitation. When Caesar's heir took up illicit arms, it was in obedience to a sacred duty, the avenging of his parent.[2] The plea of 'pietas' is duly urged by one set of 'prudentes' at the funeral, to be scouted by the others as a hollow pretext.[3] Shortly before the death of Augustus there was a proposal to confer the *cognomen* of 'pius' upon the son whom he had adopted.[4] No doubt most distasteful to that son; and Tiberius Caesar in the *Annales*, when paying homage to his predecessor, eschews the word 'pietas'. Indeed, it is used to describe the conduct of only one ruler in the line of Augustus. Ostensible 'pietas' helped Nero to thwart his mother's ambition;[5] and the freedman, running through with Nero the arrangements for the murder, points out that when the artificial shipwreck has done its work the Princeps can make his filial contribution—a temple and altars, 'et cetera ostentandae pietati'.[6]

'Pietas', in the terminology of the Empire, denotes more commonly a subject's virtue—loyal homage (with an emotional tinge) rendered by Senate or senator, by soldier or citizen;[7] and, by corollary, high treason becomes 'impietas'.[8] Now 'pietas', in the sense of political loyalty, was flaunted and degraded everywhere—most shamefully on the monuments that commemorated for devotion to their Emperor such persons as L. Vitellius and the freedman Pallas.[9]

Along with 'clementia' and 'pietas' the shield of Caesar Augustus advertised the virtue of 'iustitia'. It might have seemed harmless. Tacitus refuses to relent when language forfeits honour through service to the government. 'Virtus' and 'libertas' were too strong to be discredited or submerged by 'Virtus Augusti' or 'Libertas Augusta';

---

[1] XI. 3. 1. Not but what the word can sometimes be used without malice or irony, e.g. III. 22. 2: 'adeo vertit ac miscuit irae et clementiae signa' (of Tiberius); 68. 2: 'multum de clementia principis praefatus' (the excellent L. Piso).

[2] *Res Gestae* I.   [3] I. 9. 3; 10. 1.

[4] Suetonius, *Tib.* 17. 2.

[5] XIII. 5. 2: 'ita specie pietatis obviam itum dedecori.'

[6] XIV. 3. 3.

[7] Thus Cn. Piso about his devotion to the Emperor's mother (III. 16. 3), Tiberius to Seianus (IV. 40. 1), Tiberius about the loyalty of the Senate (III. 51. 1): the sole instances of this sense in the *Annales*. 'Obsequium' was a less obtrusive and emotional term.

[8] Only once in all the works of Tacitus (VI. 47. 2).

[9] Suetonius, *Vitellius* 3. 1; Pliny, *Epp.* VII. 29. 2 and VIII. 6. 1 (the funeral monument of Pallas). Pliny goes on to quote extensively from the *senatus consultum*.

but 'iustitia' and several other words had succumbed. They are banished almost completely from the pages of the *Annales*.[1]

A few escape his disapproval. Tacitus does not regard 'constantia' as compromised through association with the Caesars.[2] Further, and much more significant, 'moderatio'. It was consistently emphasized by Tiberius as the demeanour proper for the First Citizen in his relation to the 'res publica', deprecating any undue honour for his own person and avoiding encroachments upon the sphere of the Senate. That appealed to Tacitus. 'Moderatio' occurs four times in a Tiberian context, and only once is its authenticity impugned.[3]

'Providentia', the care of a prince for the prosperity and well-being of his people (though approaching the monarchic in its implication), might also seem not wholly objectionable. Not, however, when the ruler's foresight and vigilance is extolled because he provides for the security of state and dynasty by suppressing conspiracies. That was what happened during the reign of Tiberius, notably after the destruction of Seianus.[4] In the *Annales* there is a solitary instance of this imperial virtue: when it was commemorated at the funeral of Claudius, the audience could not help laughing.[5]

The master of the world was not only wise and modest. He could be noble and generous. The splendid claim of 'magnitudo animi' had been affected by men of spirit and honour in the last age of the Republic. And Nero liked it, as Tacitus notes and neatly exemplifies, in a very peculiar episode. At a senatorial debate on customs and excise Nero intervened with a liberal suggestion: such taxes were vexatious, what nobler boon to the human race than their universal abolition? Senators in alarm checked this impetuous and catastrophic proposal. They prefaced their objections, however, by copiously lauding the prince for his 'magnitudo animi'.[6]

The incident has been variously interpreted. Not perhaps a prince's whim but the enlightened advocacy of free trade throughout the Empire —hence evidence unimpeachable that Nero was a great statesman.[7]

---

[1] See further App. 66. [2] For 'constantia', below, p. 544.

[3] I. 8. 5: 'adroganti moderatione.' The other instances are II. 36. 2; III. 50. 2; 56. 1.

[4] Valerius Maximus IX. 11, *ext*. 4. Compare the dedications, *ILS* 157 (Interamna Nahars); 158 (Gortyna in Crete, set up by a proconsul). For the coins with PROVIDENT. (not closely datable) see M. Grant, *Roman Anniversary Issues* (1950), 62 f.; C. H. V. Sutherland, *Coinage in Roman Imperial Policy 31 B.C.–A.D. 68* (1951), 99.

[5] XIII. 3. 1: 'postquam ad providentiam sapientiamque flexit, nemo risui temperare.' The 'providentia optumi principis' naturally stands at the head of a *senatus consultum* (*ILS* 6043). There was also the 'principis benignitas' (in the decree for Pallas, Pliny, *Epp.* VIII. 6. 13). In Tacitus 'benignitas' is confined to fortune or the gods, with one exception (*Hist.* II. 30. 2). [6] XIII. 50. 2.

[7] B. W. Henderson, *The Life and Principate of the Emperor Nero* (1903), 82 f.; M. A. Levi, *Nerone e i suoi tempi* (1949), 142 ff. In the view of the latter writer, Nero's vexation at being thwarted led to a serious breach between ruler and Senate.

Or further, so sagacious was the proposal that it surely originated not with Nero but with Seneca, for Seneca was a good man of business.[1]

Neither of these attempts to evade or invalidate the plain testimony of Tacitus deserves countenance. Seneca showed great skill in managing the relations between the prince and the Senate—not least by diverting Nero from too pronounced an interest in public affairs. When a ruler forgets his tuition or gaily expounds ideas of his own in public, the consequence may be a comical or deplorable revelation. Such was this incident. It will also serve to illustrate the discernment of Tacitus, down to the choice of a telling word.[2]

Sceptical about the Principate and derisive about so many of its outward manifestations, Tacitus turns to the study of power in its effects upon those who pursue and wield it. Ever and again the pitiless diagnosis of a senatorial historian condenses into an aphorism, acrid, intense, and unanswerable. Tiberius and Livia disliked the wife of Germanicus—the more keenly because unreasonably.[3] Emperors may affect to be friendly and civil: they never forget a jest at their expense.[4] It is the common fate of a minister's 'potentia' not to last—and minister and sovereign tire of each other, for the one has nothing more to ask, the other nothing to give.[5] In truth, eminent service to the ruler earns the reverse of gratitude.[6] As for power, Seianus knew that it would grow and spread if he disdained the show and trappings;[7] while, as Nero's mother after her fall soon learned, nothing in human affairs is more flimsy and transitory than that which has no solid base of power.[8] That Antonia the daughter of Claudius was ready to associate in a conspiracy, that C. Piso to marry her would cast off the wife he adored was an absurd notion—unless it be that the lust for power quenches all other passions.[9]

To penetration and judgement Tacitus unites a poet's imagination,

[1] Or at least Seneca and Burrus, according to Momigliano, *CAH* x (1934), 712 f.

[2] There is no other example of the expression 'magnitudo animi' in Tacitus, but observe Seneca to Nero, 'infra tuam magnitudinem iacet' (XIV. 54. 1). Nero himself when liberating Hellas extolled ἡ ἐμὴ μεγαλοφροσύνη (*SIG*³ 814). Tacitus and the inscription were alike ignored by U. Knoche in his study, 'Magnitudo Animi', *Philologus*, Supp. XXVII (1935), Heft 3. He cited (o.c. 82 f.) 'magnus animus' and 'magnanimitas', applied to Nero in the *De clementia* (I. 5. 3 ff.).

[3] I. 33. 1: 'causae acriores quia iniquae.'   [4] v. 2. 2; XV. 68. 3.

[5] III. 30. 4: 'idque et Maecenati acciderat, fato potentiae raro sempiternae, an satias cepit', &c.

[6] IV. 18. 3: 'nam beneficia eo usque laeta sunt dum videntur exolvi posse: ubi multum antevenere pro gratia odium redditur.'

[7] 41. 3: 'et minui sibi invidiam adempta salutantum turba sublatisque inanibus veram potentiam augeri.'

[8] XIII. 19. 1: 'nihil rerum mortalium tam instabile ac fluxum est quam fama potentiae non sua vi nixae.'

[9] XV. 53. 4: 'nisi si cupido dominandi cunctis adfectibus flagrantior est.'

strong inner conviction, and a fine sense of structure and drama. Style, thought, and design blend to perfection. The combination is impressive, and not without its dangers.[1]

Tacitus operates with the utmost licence. If his interpretations are usually better than those of other writers (because he had more knowledge and a keener understanding), his statements may be reckless and misleading. Tacitus is frequently moved to suspend judgement (authorities varied or were inadequate, and there was no certitude to be had), yet his hesitations, and their general propensity to the worse, carry him beyond mere scepticism along the path of innuendo and malice.[2] What first crops up as a hint or allegation may quietly usurp the status of a fact. Labelling as a rumour the visit of Augustus to Agrippa Postumus on the island, Tacitus is not deterred from narrating it most circumstantially, with the name of the Princeps' sole companion: it supports an imputation against Livia which he surely knew to be false.[3] And he seems to have felt no qualms about the story of the three 'principes' whose capacity Augustus debated when near his end: here was the place for gentle scepticism.[4] An alert historian might also have gone further in his dubitations about the guile and the deep designs of Aelius Seianus.[5]

From first to last, Germanicus Caesar is adorned and enhanced, although there were grounds for construing not at all favourably his conduct, whether during the mutiny, as a general in Germany, or as deputy for the Emperor in the eastern lands.[6] The historian, had he so chosen, might have questioned the tradition.[7] Nor are the imputations against Tiberius borne out by what was revealed at the prosecution of Cn. Piso. Above all, Tacitus insists upon rendering Tiberius

---

[1] At the lowest estimate, a style so vivid and powerful, with a Roman distaste for the hypocrisies of understatement, would lead a man to verbal exaggeration (neither reluctant nor unconscious).

[2] By contrast, Livy: 'frequentissime dubitat', as Quintilian observed (II. 4. 19). Livy's doubts were about facts or dates, not motives.

[3] p. 307. The Princeps' alleged companion was Paullus Fabius Maximus (*cos.* 11 B.C.). Some have innocently believed in the visit to Planasia, e.g. V. Gardthausen, *Augustus und seine Zeit* 1 (1904), 1252 f.

[4] The story appears to be accepted by writers as diverse as E. Hohl, *Hermes* LXVIII (1933), 111, and W. Weber, *Princeps* 1 (1936), 70.

[5] He had begun to wonder about what he found in the written record (cf. IV. 57. 1—the reasons for the departure of Tiberius). There is no means of knowing how far he conceived or admitted doubts in the narration of climax and catastrophe.

[6] M. Gelzer, P–W x, 456 f.; M. P. Charlesworth, *CAH* x (1934), 622.

[7] The encomiastic nature of the tradition is patent in Suetonius, *Cal.* 1–6. It owed much to historians writing under the son and the brother of Germanicus, but had begun early. Note also Dio's enhancement of the exploits of Germanicus in Illyricum in A.D. 7–9: for which see now E. Koestermann, *Hermes* LXXXI (1953), 345 ff. The devices employed by Tacitus to heighten the contrast between Germanicus and Tiberius were analysed by F. Krohn, *Personendarstellungen bei Tacitus* (Diss. Leipzig, 1934), 74 ff.

responsible for the development of treason trials, although he had before him the authentic record of the earliest cases, how they arose and ended, and what the Emperor said or did. The first, trivial charges against two men of no consequence, evoked a firm and sarcastic missive from Tiberius to the consuls.[1] The second, brought up in the prosecution of a proconsul, made him very angry.[2] Not, however, that the ruler should be held blameless for much of what happened in the sequel.[3]

And finally, a more dangerous factor in general than mere prejudice or any wilful violence of statement: the author of the *Annales* presents characters and arranges events in undue coherence. That is the manner of historians in every age.

---

[1] 1. 73. 3: 'non ideo decretum patri suo caelum ut in perniciem civium is honor verteretur', &c.

[2] 74. 4: 'ad quod exarsit adeo ut rupta taciturnitate proclamaret se quoque in ea causa laturum sententiam palam et iuratum.'

[3] Much (and perhaps too much) has been written on the whole subject of 'maiestas' under Tiberius. See, for example, the works of Ciaceri and Rogers cited above, p. 400. Distrust of Tacitus has sometimes been pushed to extreme lengths. Thus he is taxed with ignorance of the law by Rogers, *TAPA* LXIV (1933), 18 ff. Against such opinions note the protest of the jurist B. Kübler, *Phil. Woch.* 1937, 380 ff., especially 386. Rogers (in various papers, e.g. *TAPA* LXXXIII (1952), 279 ff.) asserts that there is a common (hence suspect and rhetorical) 'pattern' in the treason trials as reported by Tacitus, both under Tiberius and under Nero. The critics of Tacitus deserve censure for many of their assumptions and fancies. See now C. W. Chilton, *JRS* XLV (1955), 73 ff.; E. Koestermann, *Historia* IV (1955), 72 ff.

XXXII. TACITUS AND TIBERIUS

'SINE ira et studio.' Tacitus professes to relate the truth about the Caesars, with no personal feeling for or against any one of them.[1] Towards the Principate he is harsh and malicious. How will he deal with the Caesars as men, and with what verdict upon the acts and quality of their rule?

It is mainly for his treatment of Tiberius that Tacitus comes under censure. The inquiry starts with a double and varied charge of inconsistency. First, the different stages in the reign. It was clear that the ruler underwent a change.[2] For Tacitus the economy of his first hexad demanded that the change for the worse should begin with the year 23. To omit minor discrepancies, that division is at variance with the stages of decline and deterioration in the character of Tiberius, as enumerated in the epilogue at the end of Book VI. Public report (says the historian) had nothing but praise for the years before Tiberius came to the power; while the princes Germanicus and Drusus yet lived, craft and dissembling were a shield; until his mother died, a mixture of good and evil; under the influence of Seianus (affection but also fear) he was cruel, but lust was kept out of sight; and finally abominable when, with nothing and nobody to fear or respect, he came out as his true self.[3]

Next, while the words and conduct of Tiberius Caesar are registered by the historian with a fidelity that shows the use of documents, the comments which he subjoins often clash and jar. Tacitus himself seems to become vaguely aware of discrepancies.[4]

The portrait is variously vulnerable. The first problem that arises is literary: is the Tacitean Tiberius largely and mainly the creation of the author? That thesis has been argued with eloquence and ingenuity, and sometimes with obstinacy.[5] Certain reasons tell powerfully

---

[1] On this famous phrase see J. Vogt, *Würzburger Studien* IX (1936), 1 ff. It is necessary, however, to keep carefully in mind what follows—'quorum causas procul habeo'. How Tacitus' 'professio' should be interpreted is shown by *Hist.* I. 1. 3: 'mihi Galba Otho Vitellius nec beneficio nec iniuria cogniti.'

[2] The dichotomy which the tradition asserts in the reign of each Caesar may appear suspect and artificial. Yet it reflects facts. Furthermore, Tacitus had experience of Domitian, and he would soon discover that the reign of Augustus fell easily into contrasted halves.   [3] VI. 51. 3.

[4] cf. IV. 31. 2: 'quo magis mirum habebatur gnarum meliorum et quae fama clementiam sequeretur tristiora malle.'

[5] cf. especially D. M. Pippidi, *Ephemeris Dacoromana* VIII (1938), 233 ff. = *Autour de Tibère* (1944), 11 ff.: against, J. P. V. D. Balsdon, *JRS* XXXVI (1946), 168 ff.

against it. Suetonius and Dio are in general concord with Tacitus. They can rank as independent authorities. There is no clear sign that Suetonius used Tacitus.[1] Yet the biographer, though casual and incoherent, reflects the same diagnosis of Tiberius—duplicity, with hidden vices (especially cruelty) gradually breaking out.[2] As for Dio, while it is rash to deny that he cannot anywhere have been influenced by Tacitus, it is also superfluous. The account of Tiberius' accession makes it clear that Dio went back to sources nearer the events—as, on the face of things, an historian's duty prescribes.[3]

The memory of Tiberius was not officially condemned at Rome.[4] He had held the supreme power for long years, and faint or scattered hints survive of a tradition less hostile than that which confronted Tacitus, Suetonius, and Dio. It may be that the picture darkened somewhat in the course of the first two generations after his decease— and some will invoke the effects of Domitian's reign.[5] One fact counsels caution. The written authorities that Tacitus cites (but never names) were uniformly unfavourable to the Emperor. When the historian corrects them, it is to propose a milder version.[6]

About the figure of Tiberius Caesar, as known to the contemporaries of Trajan and Hadrian, a modest and plausible conclusion emerges. Their Tiberius belonged to the consensus of educated opinion. Tacitus took that picture. He cleansed it of trivial accretions, heightened the colours, sharpened the outline, and converted it into a work of art.[7] Literary technique and historical research conspired to the same end. Since Tacitus for his Tiberius drew so much upon documentary sources, distrusting the historians, he could not help adding his own comments and reconstructions in generous measure.

The manner and tone of the Tacitean interpretation acknowledged various influences or constraints, variously to be appraised. The way of thought of the ancients was prone to conceive a man's inner nature as something definable and immutable. A change in observed behaviour was therefore not a change in essence, but only a manifestation of what was there all the time;[8] and, if Tiberius at the end stood revealed as a bad man and a tyrant, it was legitimate to ask how and when the faults of his character, which previously had been curbed by discipline or disguised by craft, at last came to the surface. There

---

[1] App. 36.   [2] *Tib.* 42. 1; 57. 1; 61 f.; *Cal.* 6. 2.   [3] p. 273.

[4] F. Vittinghoff, *Der Staatsfeind in der r. Kaiserzeit* (1936), 85 ff.; M. Grant, *Roman Anniversary Issues* (1950), 48; 85; 97.

[5] e.g. F. B. Marsh, *The Reign of Tiberius* (1931), 222.

[6] Ph. Fabia, *Les Sources de Tacite dans les* Histoires *et les* Annales (1893), 371. Tacitus neglected those who had written under Tiberius, naturally.

[7] M. Gelzer, P–W x, 535; G. A. Harrer, *AJP* XLI (1920), 57 ff.

[8] Compare Plutarch's diagnosis of Philip V (*Aratus* 49): not the conception of Polybius.

were doubts and hazards in the inquiry—and Tacitus is both over-rigid and inconsistent. He can report a verdict not wholly in harmony with his own schema: for example, it was the tenure of imperial power (said L. Arruntius) that perverted and destroyed Tiberius Caesar.[1]

In the historian's own experiences there was nothing to predispose him in favour of Tiberius. He knew a reign that went to the bad after it began well on a safe dynastic succession with the promise of equity and moderation. A satirist called Domitian 'the bald Nero'.[2] The superior insight of an historian might have discerned a juvenile Tiberius. There was deep resentment in Tiberius—and Domitian had been set back by his father and by his brother.

Domitian made a habit of studying the state papers of Tiberius Caesar.[3] Both rulers were noted for a careful management of the Empire, choosing their governors well, repressing abuses, and protecting the subject population. And both reigns were indelibly stamped with the reproach of indictments for high treason. Whatever the causes and the allocation of blame, the reign of Tiberius plunged into a welter of 'maiestas'.[4] Eager ambition saw its chance, and the warfare of factions in the Senate used the weapon, as is abundantly revealed. The Emperor came to feel insecure; and the Emperor himself seemed amicably disposed towards some of the prosecutors.[5] It therefore became difficult for Tacitus not to regard 'maiestas' as a device and instrument of the government. He was impelled to incriminate Tiberius.[6]

None the less it is too simple a view that Tacitus was merely, or largely, rewriting another tyrant, that he could not shake off the memory of the last years under Domitian. It is open to anyone to argue that his Tiberius would be much what it is if Domitian had never been. The weight and consensus of tradition was too much for the historian. That tradition had not been constructed by a single writer shortly after the death of Tiberius, still less could it be over-turned by a single writer nearly three generations later.

The principal charges are craft, rancour, and cruelty— for the allegations of secret vice to which Tiberius' seclusion on the island gave rise may be treated as subsidiary.[7] The dissimulation of Tiberius

---

[1] VI. 48. 2: 'cum Tiberius post tantam rerum experientiam vi dominationis convulsus et mutatus sit.'

[2] Juvenal IV. 38.   [3] Suetonius, *Dom.* 20.

[4] Seneca, *De beni* III. 26. 1: 'sub Tiberio Caesare fuit accusandi frequens et paene publica rabies.'

[5] III. 19. 1 (Fulcinius Trio); IV. 52. 4 (Domitius Afer).

[6] Similarly Domitian. If more were known about his reign, private ambitions and feuds would presumably be discovered behind many of the treason trials.

[7] But instructive. The abominations on Capreae are a late motive in Tacitus (VI. 1). He transfers the theme of secret vice to Rhodes, cf. the (presumed) insertions at I. 4. 4 and

is an integral part of the tradition.[1] It is also confirmed by facts. Slow, cautious, and secretive, he had learned to cloak his thoughts and repress his feelings. Private affections had been overruled for reasons of high politics, and the 'dignitas' of a proud aristocrat suffered outrage more than once from Caesar Augustus; and yet, after multiple humiliations, he must behave as though nothing had occurred, resuming on command from his taskmaster the servitude of office and the mask of cheerful subordination.

The scene and ceremony of the accession prescribed a false attitude, with much official and inevitable hypocrisy in the sequel. On state occasions, and especially when the Senate sat in justice, it was expedient for the holder of the ultimate authority to conceal his true purpose.[2] His own statements might easily reinforce the impression of dishonesty. Tiberius said repeatedly that he would have to go to the provinces and visit the armies: he never went.[3] As late as 23 he still spoke of resigning the power—the consuls or somebody else might have it.[4] All this was nothing to the drama of deceit which the Emperor staged when discarding and destroying his minister. After the letter from Capreae no man could doubt that Tiberius was a master of guile and dissimulation.[5]

Evidence also showed that Tiberius was vindictive. It was alleged that in the first months of the reign he hastened the end of his former wife, the exiled Julia. That cannot be substantiated; but he ordered the execution of her lover, Sempronius Gracchus, an ancient enemy.[6] Tiberius disliked Asinius Gallus.[7] He arranged that the missive denouncing the septuagenarian consular should reach the Senate while he was being entertained at Capreae.[8]

The behaviour of Tiberius after the catastrophe of Seianus and the ensuing revelations confirmed the worst that was believed about his character. Tiberius wrote an autobiography. He there asserted that he punished Seianus because of Seianus' intrigues against the family

IV. 57. 2 (App. 37). If there were serious contemporary allegations, it is strange that they did not appeal to Seneca, who had probably been on the island (cf. Suetonius, *Tib.* 73. 2). The source of some stories may be in covert defamations of Domitian: thus aquatic diversions (not quite of the same nature) of each emperor, cf. *Tib.* 44; *Dom.* 22.

[1] Suetonius, *Tib.* 24 f.

[2] III. 22. 2 (the prosecution of Aemilia Lepida): 'haud facile quis dispexerit illa in cognitione mentem principis.'

[3] IV. 4. 2: 'exim vetus et saepe simulatum proficiscendi in provincias consilium refertur.'

[4] IV. 9. 1: 'ad vana et totiens inrisa revolutus, de reddenda re publica utque consules seu quis alius regimen susciperent, vero quoque et honesto fidem dempsit.'

[5] p. 406. Cf. Suetonius' account of his 'dolus et astus' (*Tib.* 65).

[6] I. 53.

[7] I. 12. 4: 'nec ideo iram eius lenivit, pridem invisus.'

[8] Dio LVIII. 3. 3 f. It is strange that Marsh should claim that Tiberius was neither suspicious nor vindictive (*The Reign of Tiberius* (1931), 190; 223).

of Germanicus.[1] Yet the fall of Seianus brought no release or alleviation for Agrippina or for Drusus, her second son. They were still kept in close confinement, and when they perished two years later Tiberius did not relent. He was exultant. He recited a documentary and savage indictment against the young prince, with the record of all his days and hours in prison. The decease of Agrippina fell upon the anniversary of Seianus' destruction. She was lucky, said Tiberius, that she too was not strangled by the executioner, and her body exposed on the Scalae Gemoniae—but, he added, the coincidence deserved to have public thanksgiving and a permanent commemoration in the calendar of the Roman State.[2]

Tiberius on his accession had made a firm statement to the Senate about his own nature: it would never change so long as he remained in control of his intelligence.[3] Later, in an oration that repulsed excessive forms of homage, he uttered a solemn prayer that the gods might vouchsafe repose of mind and a judgement unimpaired to the end.[4] The outcome showed all the malice of fate. The Tiberius of the last years was a warped and unbalanced character.

To understand what had happened, an historian would have to go back, not only to the first period of Tiberius' government, but even further, and investigate the original predicament of the man in relation to his surroundings, family, and career. Tiberius was in his fifty-fifth year when he came to the power.

On no estimate was the *gens* of the patrician Claudii a normal or predictable portion of the Roman *nobilitas*. Tradition made them out to be tyrannical, contemning, and oppressing the common folk. That was the fabricated version of their enemies—not the plebs but the aristocracy.[5] Alert, unscrupulous, and arrogant towards their rivals, the Claudii in the competition for power and honour at Rome exploited demagogic politics, extraneous alliances, and the promotion of *novi homines*. They did not forget their own origin out of the Sabine country long ago.

Tiberius Claudius Nero united a double Claudian strain, the Pulchri as well as the Nerones.[6] Yet Tiberius was a most anomalous

---

[1] Suetonius, *Tib.* 61. 1. The biographer becomes indignant.

[2] VI. 25. 3. By contrast, E. Ciaceri, *Tiberio*[2] (1944), 309: 'la leggenda dell' odio di Tiberio contro la famiglia di Germanico è in pieno contrasto coi fatti.'

[3] Suetonius, *Tib.* 67. 3: 'similem se semper sui futurum nec umquam mutaturum mores suos, quam diu sanae mentis fuisset.'

[4] IV. 38. 3: 'ut mihi ad finem usque vitae quietam et intellegentem humani divinique iuris mentem duint.' The archaic form 'duint' is notable and appropriate.

[5] Th. Mommsen, *Römische Forschungen* I[2] (1864), 285 ff.; G. C. Fiske, *Harvard Studies* XIII (1902), 1 ff.

[6] The father of Livia Drusilla, M. Livius Drusus Claudianus, was probably a Pulcher, perhaps son of C. Claudius Pulcher (*cos.* 92 B.C.).

Claudian: not a politician but a general, not an innovator but a conservative. Even his literary tastes were archaic.[1] He liked old-fashioned words; and he was a purist. His preference in poetry went to certain Greek writers whom the previous generation held in esteem; and he showed no interest in the writers of that Augustan prime in which he grew to manhood.

The resentments of Tiberius, personal and political, have an early origin in his life. His father fought against Caesar's heir in the War of Perusia, and he fled for refuge (taking his wife and son) to Sextus Pompeius in Sicily. Not long after his return to Rome he was forced to surrender Livia Drusilla to the importunate matrimony of his erstwhile opponent.

The mother of Tiberius married the Triumvir, who was the declared enemy of the aristocracy, the destroyer of the Republic. That the victor in civil war should in due course become a legitimate ruler did not improve matters. Tiberius developed his nature and formed his habits in revulsion from his environment.[2] Promoted by his stepfather (but not grateful), aloof and austere amid the grace and ease and smooth perfidy of fashionable society, Tiberius stood in visible and wilful protest against both renegade Republicans and fraudulent Pompeiani.[3]

The greater favour and liking seemed to go to his brother Drusus, whom some alleged to be in truth the son of the Princeps.[4] There were rivals in the family group all the time, and dynastic arrangements that led to friction and culminated in a clash when the supreme design of Augustus became patent and flagrant—rapid exaltation of the princes of his blood, the young Caesars Gaius and Lucius. Augustus intended that his stepson should serve and further that design.

Tiberius rebelled and went away to Rhodes. That episode gave clues to his character that no historian should have missed.[5] Nor did Augustus forget. When, with no choice left, he decided to adopt Tiberius, he made sure that posterity would learn his reasons.[6] The Princeps continued to advertise his disappointment at the loss of his

---

[1] Suetonius, *Tib.* 70 f.

[2] See the searching psychological study of J. H. Thiel, *Mnemosyne*[3] II (1935), 245 ff.; III (1935/6), 177 ff.; IV (1936/7), 7 ff. Thiel regards Tiberius as 'Vertreter eines oppositionellen Typs'. Also the medical man G. Marañon, *Tiberio. Historia di un resentimiento* (Buenos Aires, 1939; translated: Paris, 1941; Munich, 1952; London, 1956).

[3] For his Pompeian loyalties, *Rom. Rev.* (1939), 424. It was surely Tiberius rather than Augustus who made Cinna Magnus (the grandson of Pompeius) consul in A.D. 5.

[4] Suetonius, *Divus Claudius* 1. 1, &c.

[5] Rhodes helps to explain Capreae; but the notion only occurred to Tacitus at a late stage, cf. App. 37. Suetonius (*Tib.* 10) adduces a variety of motives, quite in the Tacitean manner—as indeed the theme demanded.

[6] Suetonius (*Tib.* 23) quotes the exordium of his will—'quoniam atrox fortuna Gaium et Lucium filios mihi eripuit', &c. Cf. *Res Gestae* 14: 'eripuit for[tuna]'.

sons, the Caesars Gaius and Lucius.[1] He had also adopted Agrippa Postumus; and he compelled Tiberius to take Germanicus into his family, though he had a son of his own. The inheritance of Caesar Augustus carried a heavy burden of memories, and a sure promise of discord.[2]

Tiberius was grim and inclement.[3] His deliberate ferocity, or 'diritas', incurred the disapprobation of Augustus.[4] It grew with the years. His manner and habit is revealed by anecdote or aphorism, showing arrogance, anger, and rancour, things said without tact and things said to wound and annoy. Claudian pride combined with conscious rectitude and a hatred of shams.[5] Not sparing himself, Tiberius would not spare others; and a man who is 'severus' can easily pass for 'tristior'.[6] Some of the admonitions he visited on senators were extremely harsh.[7] Though he was circumspect, and slow to anger, the outburst might be formidable.[8] The Emperor's resentment lost nothing by being retarded, or conveyed in writing. Through long years the Senate had to listen to a sequence of missives from Capreae, carping or ferocious, ambiguous or deceitful.[9]

Of the Princeps' deportment in public, Tacitus furnishes some remarkable renderings deriving from an eyewitness, from the documentary record, or from bold divination. After denouncing Hortensius, who made an importunate request for financial subsidy, Tiberius saw that he had gone too far for a Princeps, paused for a time, and resumed in a strain of conciliation.[10] Or again, bitter resentment, as when Tiberius recapitulated the career of Sulpicius Quirinius. It brought back the history of twenty years before and the humiliations endured at Rhodes. The Emperor could not repress a savage reference

---

[1] The coin series C. L. CAESARES continued for a number of years after A.D. 4; and it was not till A.D. 10 that Tiberius was allowed to have his name and portrait on the currency. Cf. C. H. V. Sutherland, *Coinage in Roman Imperial Policy 31 B.C.–A.D. 68* (1951), 73 ff. Nor was Tiberius allowed to equal M. Agrippa with a third consulate.

[2] There lies the clue to all the discords of the next reign, cf. E. Paratore, *Maia* II (1949), 108.

[3] Pliny, *NH* XXVIII. 23: 'tristissimus, ut constat, hominum.

[4] Suetonius, *Tib*. 21. 2; cf. the 'acerbitas et intolerantia morum' about which Augustus complained in 'codicilli' sent to Livia (ib. 51. 1). For 'diritas', K. Scott, *AJP* LIII (1932), 139 ff.

[5] Suetonius, *Tib*. 59. 2: 'oderint dum probent.'

[6] *Hist*. I. 14. 2 (Piso Licinianus). Tiberius is the only person in the *Annales* about whom the word 'tristitia' is used (I. 76. 4), cf. p. 345.

[7] Seneca, *Epp*. 122. 10; *De ben*. II. 7. 2 (a 'contumeliosa admonitio').

[8] III. 69. 5: 'prudens moderandi, si propria ira non impelleretur'; IV. 71. 3: 'lentum in meditando, ubi prorupisset, tristibus dictis atrocia facta coniungere.'

[9] Observe the personal attack on Junius Gallio, 'violenter increpuit velut coram rogitans' (VI. 3. 1), or the despair of Galba's brother who committed suicide, 'tristibus Caesaris litteris provinciam sortiri prohibitus' (VI. 40. 2). The rhetorical reference to 'cruentae epistulae' in III. 44. 3, however, is anachronistic.

[10] II. 38. 4.

to a hated name, that of Marcus Lollius, the author of discord and iniquity.[1]

Tacitus, however, had debarred himself from full insight. He ought to have made the *Annales* begin at an earlier point. As has been shown, the year 4 would have been highly suitable for narrative and for the grouping of material. Most of the main themes, domestic and foreign, run continuous into the Principate of Tiberius.[2]

There is something else: not continuity but a contrast, authentic, powerful, and illuminating. The period of Tiberius' absence from Rome had witnessed a strong trend towards the monarchical; and it is not likely that the Princeps encouraged the Senate to hold frequent or public debate during the crisis of the northern wars. Moreover, various signs indicate that the government was not altogether skilful in managing opinion—prosecutions for libel and the burning of books.[3] Friction at Rome, disasters abroad, and scandal in the dynasty—that was the last decade of Caesar Augustus.[4]

The accession of Tiberius marked a restoration of the Republic more genuine in many respects than that proclaimed and enacted by his predecessor—if behaviour be valued higher than legal formula. Tiberius professed an intention of governing like a true 'princeps', according to the will and sentiments of the Senate. The profession (though not to be pushed to an extremity of literalistic interpretation) was not all hypocrisy, neither was the intention wholly impracticable. Tiberius was a Roman aristocrat, one of the 'principes', not an adventurer who rose out of civil strife to become lord of the world and saviour of the nations. Forty years of internal stability might augur well for a liberal régime under the presidency of a ruler who for the greater part of the previous decade had been fighting the wars of the Republic in the northern lands.

It turned out otherwise. Absence told against him. The new ruler was out of touch—not ten years but thirty, for he had seldom seen the Senate since his praetorship in 16 B.C. Tiberius forgot (or tried to forget) how far that body had been corrupted and debased by Caesar Augustus. At his accession he was confronted by a Senate both suspicious and unduly subservient.[5] Compelled to honour the precedents set by Augustus everywhere, Tiberius was hampered in thought

---

[1] III. 48. 1 f.: 'Tiberium quoque Rhodi agentem coluerat: quod tunc patefecit in senatu, laudatis in se officiis et incusato M. Lollio, quem auctorem Gaio Caesari pravitatis et discordiarum arguebat.'

[2] p. 370.

[3] *Rom. Rev.* (1939), 486 f. (the history of T. Labienus and the libellous pamphlets of Cassius Severus).

[4] Belying entirely the pious prophecies of Velleius (II. 103. 4).

[5] II. 87: 'unde angusta et lubrica oratio sub principe qui libertatem metuebat adulationem oderat.'

and deed by his own past, and by the oppressive memory of Augustus. Sincere when he made profession of Republican principles, Tiberius was yet gradually driven to subvert those principles through failure, ill chance, or the needs of government.[1] In fine, the historian might have hit upon a strange but captivating idea: after, no less than before, Tiberius was the victim of Augustus.

Many things in Tiberius the historian could not but admire. The review of his administration down to the year 23 is all praise, except for the ruler's personal demeanour—'plerumque horridus'.[2] It is confirmed by what emerges elsewhere about his good qualities. The prince was imbued with a noble conception of the dignity of the Roman People in its relation to foreign states.[3] He had an exalted notion of a ruler's duty, above the fear of incurring enmity for the sake of the 'res publica' and disdainful of popularity.[4] At the same time it was invidious, he held, that the power of the State should intervene to make men better than they are.[5] Like an aristocrat, Tiberius set enduring fame as the goal, but deprecated extravagant forms of personal homage.[6] His constancy under the blows of fate, his stoical behaviour in the hour of bereavement recalled the Romans of old.[7] No kind of pretence or flattery deceived him, and he never forgave a disloyal friend. He liked freedom of speech; he respected tradition. While according a proper preference to blood and family, the heir of the patrician Claudii none the less insisted upon advancement for merit.[8] Nothing excited his anger more sharply than the subservience of senators or the sloth of *nobiles* who asserted pedigree as a mortgage upon state endowment: they outraged the honour of their own class, they brought into discredit the whole tradition of the aristocratic Republic.[9]

Above all, the penetration and ferocity of the man. Tiberius mingled sarcasm with serious arguments.[10] He produced his effects

---

[1] For the temperate and 'Republican' character of his rule see especially E. Kornemann, *Bayerische S–B, phil.-hist. Kl.* 1947, Heft 1. For the detrimental results of allowing free and unprepared discussions in the Senate, J. Crook, *Consilium Principis* (1955), 131 f.

[2] IV. 7. 1.

[3] II. 63. 2 f. (Maroboduus); 88 (a proposal to poison Arminius); III. 73. 2 (Tacfarinas).

[4] Tiberius is made to allude three times (twice in direct speech) to 'offensiones' incurred for the common weal (III. 54. 6; IV. 38. 1; VI. 15. 2).

[5] III. 53 f.; 69.

[6] IV. 37 f. He refused to let Livia be deified: 'sic ipsam maluisse'—so he asserted (V. 2. 1).

[7] IV. 8 (after the death of Drusus, a noble speech).

[8] IV. 6. 2: 'mandabatque honores, nobilitatem maiorum claritudinem militiae inlustris domi artes spectando, ut satis constaret non alios potiores fuisse.' For his promotion of *novi homines*, pp. 563, 589 f.

[9] II. 38 (M. Hortensius Hortalus). For adulation, below, pp. 573 f, 580 f.

[10] VI. 2. 4: 'Tiberius tamen, ludibria seriis permiscere solitus, egit grates benevolentiae patrum' (the proposal of the ridiculous Togonius Gallus, cf. p. 284).

either by grave and elaborate irony or by a single and demolitionary aphorism. Tacitus approves the eloquence of the Emperor in terms that fit his own style.[1] The verdict encourages speculation. The dignity and power of the Tiberian orations might furnish a clue to certain virtues that contemporaries admired in the consular orator.[2]

Tacitus builds up his Tiberius with careful and loving preoccupation. The process discloses more than he intended: 'odi et amo.' It is a literary or artistic infatuation, of a kind easily paralleled—and something more than that. Certain features in that Tacitean Tiberius, detestable on a superficial view, carried praise, not blame. Tacitus wrote for men of mature and pitiless understanding, as one of them, knowing the slippery paths of power and the devious recesses of human nature. How did a ruler survive for long years, save by deep counsels and dissimulation?

Tiberius Caesar showed consummate ability as a ruler—and he had need to be vigilant if he wished to introduce an unwonted freedom of debate. On his guard in small matters, he detected the traps laid by dishonest or adulatory senators. In the larger perils he was able to retrieve his own errors through craft and patience. Whatever the rights and wrongs in the quarrel between Germanicus and the legate of Syria, Cn. Piso (it is patent) was guilty of high treason for levying war. Piso was Tiberius' choice, and an old friend. Yet Piso had to be thrown over. The thing was managed. Discovering signal merit and loyalty in his minister Aelius Seianus, Tiberius committed himself imprudently. He drew back in time. Both factions were destroyed, that of Seianus after that of Agrippina. Tiberius Caesar survived.

Some of those who, writing about men and government, affect and advertise the highest moral ideals, are ready to concede that the people may be deceived for the people's good, at least intermittently. Others are more liberal in the indulgence they accord to authority— or more accurate in their diagnosis of behaviour. Tacitus was not compiling a manual of statecraft—he presupposes it all, and discreetly furnishes the material for subsequent compilers, or thinkers. Among the virtues requisite in the prince (given his predicament and his enemies) 'dissimulatio' will stand foremost. Tiberius Caesar cherished 'dissimulatio' as his favourite virtue: he was annoyed if it were seen through.[3] In his last hours, when bodily strength begins to collapse and life wanes, the Emperor's power of dissembling endures to the end.[4]

[1] XIII. 3. 2: 'validus sensibus aut consulto ambiguus.'
[2] For the speeches of Tiberius, pp. 283 f., 319; also App. 39.
[3] IV. 71. 3: 'nullam aeque Tiberius, ut rebatur, ex virtutibus suis quam dissimulationem diligebat: eo aegrius accepit recludi quae premeret.'
[4] VI. 50. 1: 'iam Tiberium corpus iam vires, nondum dissimulatio deserebat.'

So accurate and discriminatory is Tacitus' portrayal of Tiberius that it can be exploited to its own detriment or subversion. The other accounts that survive are defective, trivial, or miserable. Tacitus went to the documents, and he was a sceptical inquirer. Convention and tradition proved too strong for him.[1] Otherwise his Tiberius might have been wholly acceptable—less literary and more complex, closer to history, and in the end more tragic.

It is unprofitable as well as unjust to dwell exclusively upon the shortcomings of Tacitus. A graver charge involves many of his critics. Another age, disdainful of Tacitus in its writing of Roman history, often reproduces his defects without the compensating merits: it accepts patterns, of ancient origin or recently devised, and it is unduly deferential to consecrated beliefs.

The closing epoch of the Republic, the wars of the dynasts, and the establishment of the monarchy might have been interpreted as a chapter in the history of oligarchy at Rome. For oligarchy is the one thing that stands and endures when rulers come and go and names change, but not substance (and sometimes the empty names abide). Instead, the biography of one man, or two, or three. Most is known about Cicero, whose genius and fame created an epoch in the literature of the Latins. But Cicero was not an independent force in politics or the leader of a party. Caesar was that; and Caesar, having overthrown the Republic, emerged in act, if not intent, as an autocrat. But the power of Caesar was brief in duration—fresh wars were needed, rapid events, and a genuine revolution before monarchic rule could be established as a system and in permanence. The Caesar who in youth conceived the vast ambition, and saw clearly the path to the throne, is a literary figment, not unworthy of Cornelius Tacitus.[2]

It would have been better to build up Pompeius Magnus. Julius Caesar, until he became consul, pursued the normal career of a Roman *nobilis*. Pompeius from the outset was revolutionary and exorbitant—a private army raised in civil war, special mandates, and the consulate before he was even a senator, with great commands in the Empire thereafter, and the holding of *imperium* barely interrupted until war and battle deposed him. The last age of the Republic is the age of Pompeius Magnus.

Magnus might be rehabilitated under the rule of Caesar Augustus, likewise the Republic (certainly Cato, though Brutus and Cassius lay

---

[1] The excess of innuendo against Tiberius derives largely from the attempt to square the traditional concept of Tiberius with the results of his own researches.

[2] viz. the Caesar of Mommsen or of Carcopino.

under an official interdict), but Marcus Antonius was damned by foreign allies, the Egyptian woman, and the curse of civil war renewed. The victory of Caesar's heir seems as inevitable as it proved to be salutary.

When a narration about Caesar Augustus is allowed to take its beginning from the War of Actium, the harm is not irreparable: victory made him sole master of Rome and the world. The restoration of the Republic imparts error and distortion. So Caesar Augustus willed it, and historians conform. No more violence and usurpation. The years of tribulation are buried and forgotten: the First Citizen now governs through prestige, and by an authority which Senate and People have delegated.

By convention, the law and the constitution are held to determine the history and behaviour of the Roman People. The despot benefits. He exploited legal or public definitions—not always with extreme pedantry, and not always in an honest fashion. As a result the history of his reign tends to be interpreted in those terms, with juristic argumentation in the place of political analysis. The root or essence of power is neglected.

The Princeps could not hope to deceive men of the time about the nature of his predominance. Yet he might lay claim upon their complicity when he tried to expunge the recent past. Not anxious apologia —silence was safer. It was a good thing to forget the civil wars.[1] Many acquiesced, few resisted. The 'prudentes' at the funeral of Caesar Augustus expatiate on the career of the revolutionary adventurer and tyrannical Triumvir, violence and deceit from first to last. Tacitus (it might seem) is disproportionate, unjust, malicious. Yet equity and verisimilitude demanded that the unedifying origins of resplendent success should be mercilessly exposed. Men must have said those things.[2]

The 'prudentes' go on to censure the record of Augustus in the years of peace and principate.[3] They did not exhaust the theme. The historian, who proclaimed in his prologue that he would have very little to say about Augustus, discovered, before he was far forward with the Tiberian books, all manner of items that demanded elucidation or whetted his avid curiosity, with no propensity to benevolence. Notably the vicissitudes of individuals, calling to mind old scandals and discord in the dynasty.[4]

[1] As T. Labienus (no friend of the régime) once observed, 'optima civilis belli defensio oblivio est' (Seneca, Controv. x. 3. 5).

[2] That is not always allowed for by scholars who severely criticize the passage, e.g. H. Willrich, Hermes LXII (1927), 54 ff. On the other hand, the originality and boldness here shown by Tacitus in the hostile presentation of Augustus are perhaps exaggerated by F. Klingner, Bayerische S–B, phil.-hist. Kl. 1953, Heft 7, 21; 24.

[3] I. 10. 4: 'pacem sine dubio post haec, verum cruentam', &c.

[4] I. 53 (Julia); III. 24. 3 and IV. 71. 4 (the younger Julia); IV. 44. 3 (the son of Iullus Antonius).

There is something else—deliberate choice and design, revealed in the digressions. The author goes out of his way to show up the acts and institutions of the Augustan Principate. Discussing 'maiestas', he insists that it was Augustus who first extended charges of treason from deeds to words.[1] An excursus on the *praefectura urbis*, by introducing the name of Maecenas (who held no office), undermines and discredits the Republican and constitutional precedents which (it may be presumed) had been claimed to justify the innovation.[2] The laws of Pompeius Magnus are linked to the enactments of Augustus in his sixth consulate by a rapid and insidious presentation;[3] and, bold and subversive, Tacitus arraigns the whole moral and social programme of the Princeps, a failure when it was not deleterious.[4]

Tacitus is impelled to bring up forgotten facts, damaging parallels, and any uncomfortable truth. The other aspect had been advertised by tradition and the historians—abundantly. The benefits of the new order were manifest. The favourable tribute of Tacitus (some will object) is unduly brief. Yet it is not perfidious or grudging. It is monumental.[5]

Tacitus' account of that reign, had he survived to write it, would amply exhibit his virtues of dramatic presentation and political insight. A broad survey of the facts and resources of power covering Rome and Italy, provinces and armies, was requisite for introduction, and a sharp analysis of the Princeps' relations with the different orders in society. Tacitus excels in this technique. Not confining himself to the acts and performance of the government, he would unravel the complicated story of ambition and intrigue, of dissension and plotting. And especially the truth behind official professions and public attitudes. When, on January 13, 27 B.C., the Senate learned from the lips of Caesar's heir that Rome had now entered upon the full enjoyment of liberty and the Republic, that scene called for nothing less than the peculiar talents of Cornelius Tacitus.[6]

One of the essential Augustan ambiguities is the attitude of Caesar's heir towards Caesar. Though 'Divi filius', he seeks his legitimation in and from the Republic: like the Triumvir, the Dictator was better forgotten. The writers who most faithfully reflect governmental

---

[1] I. 72. 3.   [2] VI. 11. 2.   [3] III. 28. 1.
[4] III. 24. 2; 25; 28. 3 f.; 54. 2; 55. 1. Cf. p. 373.
[5] I. 9. 5, ending with: 'mari Oceano aut amnibus longinquis saeptum imperium; legiones provincias classis, cuncta inter se conexa; ius apud civis, modestiam apud socios; urbem ipsam magnifico ornatu; pauca admodum vi tractata quo ceteris quies esset.'
[6] As Gibbon observed in his third chapter, 'It would require the pen of Tacitus (if Tacitus had assisted at this assembly) to describe the various emotions of the senate; those that were suppressed, and those that were affected', &c. The historian could have spared the parenthesis.

opinion, namely Virgil, Horace, and Livy, agree in what they say (or do not say) about Caesar the Dictator.[1] The clearest testimony comes from Virgil. The parent of Aeneas, when passing in review the heroes of Rome from the beginning, names next after Romulus that Caesar who will establish the Golden Age, 'Augustus Caesar divi genus'.[2] Julius Caesar is banished from that context, to be introduced in another place, along with Pompeius. Both are warned against the sin of civil war—and Caesar is solemnly adjured to disarm before Pompeius.[3]

Though linked to Augustus by the ruler's filiation and nomenclature, 'Divus Julius' could be dissociated from persons and events, precisely because he had become a god. At the funeral procession of Augustus the ancestors were paraded in their *imagines*, also Romulus, the heroes of the old Republic, and the generals who augmented the dominion of Rome. Among them Pompeius Magnus—but not the conqueror of Gaul.[4]

Magnus, whatever the craft and violence of his career, ended on the side of the Republic. Favour to the memory of Magnus combined with doubts or silence about Caesar, and that suited Augustus very well. A tradition formed and prevailed. Livy was influential.[5] In the upper and middle classes there were sentimental Pompeiani who identified Pompeius and the Republic; and the aristocracy harboured genuine Pompeiani, the descendants of the dynast.[6] In the course of time even Marcus Antonius might earn some rehabilitation, but there was nobody to speak for Caesar. Emperors omitted his name when they held discourse on policy and precedents.[7]

Seneca saw no deception in the schematic contrast between Pompeius and Caesar.[8] Seneca's nephew in the epic poem made Pompeius out to be a sage as well as a patriot.[9] Moral and political doctrines or hostility towards the Caesars embellished steadily the fame of Magnus. Tacitus broke free. Already in the *Historiae* he was on the alert—'occultior non melior', that is Pompeius Magnus in the line of the dynasts whose alliances and quarrels overthrew the Republic.[10]

---

[1] *Rom. Rev.* (1939), 317 f.; *A Roman Post-Mortem* (Todd Memorial Lecture 3: Sydney, 1950), 12 ff.

[2] *Aen.* VI. 792.   [3] 834 f.

[4] Dio LVI. 34. 2 f.   [5] p. 140.

[6] pp. 259, 382, 385, 399, 404. Also *Rom. Rev.* (1939), 423 ff.; 496 f.; P. Grenade, *Rev. ét. anc.* LII (1950), 28 ff.

[7] Thus Claudius discussing the quaestorship (XI. 22. 6) and the *pomerium* (XII. 23. 2); also in *ILS* 212 (Lugdunum) where he ascribes a 'novus mos' to Augustus and Tiberius.

[8] W. H. Alexander, *Transactions of the Royal Society of Canada*[3], Section II, xxxv (1941), 15 ff.

[9] M. Rambaud, *Rev. ét. lat.* XXXIII (1955), 258 ff.

[10] *Hist.* II. 38. 1. As in *Ann.* III. 28, Sallustian studies saved him from any danger of idealizing Magnus.

He is more explicit in the *Annales* when he discusses Pompeius in the context of Augustan legislation. Magnus in his third consulate passed laws but broke them; his predominance rested on force and he lost it in war, with twenty years of anarchy ensuing. Not only that. Tacitus in this passage adapts a formulation that other writers had applied to the autocracy of Caesar.[1]

Tacitus mentions Julius Caesar very frequently, and never with dispraisal or malice. Banished by artifice or convention, the Dictator at length regains his place in the line of the Caesars.[2] The phenomenon is noteworthy. Time, the patent fact of monarchic rule, and the obsolescence of Republican affectations all contributed.[3] The epoch of Trajan felt the attraction of a Caesar who was also a conqueror; and the author of the *Annales* was guided by a familiarity with the western provinces, by an understanding of the world empire in its perspective and panorama, and by an extreme distrust of Augustan valuations.

---

[1] III. 28. 1: 'quae armis tuebatur armis amisit.' Compare Velleius II. 57. 1: 'laudandum experientia consilium est Pansae atque Hirtii qui semper praedixerant Caesari ut principatum armis quaesitum armis teneret.'

[2] Explicitly when the historian assesses the eloquence of those 'qui rerum potiti essent' (XIII. 3. 2).

[3] Republicanism ended in the year 98, cf. A. Alföldi, *Röm. Mitt.* L (1935), 13. Especially notable is Trajan's series of commemorative coins (c. 108), on which Caesar receives an honouring more varied and emphatic than Augustus. There are three types. One of the heads resembles Trajan more than it does Caesar. Cf. M. Grant, *Roman Anniversary Issues* (1950), 100; *Roman Imperial Money* (1954), 197 ff. Suetonius leads off with Caesar; and Appian some forty years later is emphatic that Caesar is the founder of the Roman monarchy (*proem.* 6).

XXXIII. THE CAESARS AND THE PROVINCES

ISTORIANS in all ages become liable through their profession to certain maladies or constraints. They cannot help making persons and events more logical than reality; they are often paralysed by tradition or convention; and they sometimes fall a prey to morbid passions for a character or an idea. Tacitus in his account of Tiberius betrays each and all of these three infirmities. From a fourth, the most insidious and pernicious, he is wholly exempt.

Historians know the verdict in advance, they run forward with alacrity to salute the victors and chant hymns to success. A chorus of hierophants or apologists acclaimed the Roman Caesars—but not uncontradicted, and not earning good fame. The Roman senator despised them. On his guard against specious or shabby concessions, he refused to condone violence because, having succeeded, it became respectable; and, if nothing short of authoritarian government ensured peace and stability, he accepted it without rejoicing or any subservience.[1]

The senator could never forget what had happened to the 'res publica'. The emperors paraded a legitimacy that was fraudulent or extorted. What the Principate gained the Senate lost: not power only, but privilege, honour, and dignity. By contrast, profit and advantage accrued to other orders, to knights and the common people, to the armies and the provinces. And the process went on. Change did not derive merely from the caprice or malevolence of a despot among the Caesars. A prudent and dutiful ruler, careful for the prosperity of the Empire, might be decisive, or a weak man carried forward by the zeal of his ministers. Good emperor or bad, the imperial authority grew and spread and encroached, everywhere.

The rancour of senators, muttered or petulant in the Curia but ferocious and malignant when they met privately together for talk, intrigue, and other diversions, created an unprepossessing image of the Caesar.[2] Further and freely elaborated after his decease, it became canonical for posterity. Equity recommends, and history imposes, a severe scrutiny of these traditional portraits. Revision cannot be avoided. There is only one question, how far ought it to go?

[1] *Hist.* I. I. I; *Ann.* I. I. I, cf. 9. 5: 'non aliud discordantis patriae remedium.'
[2] G. Boissier, *L'Opposition sous les Césars* (1875), 57 ff.

Two methods offer. First, the personality of each emperor. Apologia has been assiduous. Sometimes eloquent and ingenious, sometimes drearily pedestrian, while levelling the Roman Caesars and bringing them closer to the normal behaviour of men and citizens, it tends to rob them of colour, shape, and movement. A great wrong was done to the Republican Princeps to whom destiny awarded the inheritance of Caesar Augustus. That will be granted. The wrong has not been set right if the Tiberius who emerges from the cleansing waters is a negative and sanctified character.[1]

The youth to whom the misanthropic recluse (indifferent, fatalistic, or vindictive) consigned the charge of Rome and the world showed no promise or aptitude. Caligula possessed savage lucidity and a kind of frantic energy. Not much, however, will be redeemed if the ostensible lunacy is toned down.[2] Men could predict a cruel and capricious tyranny.[3] From his familiars at the court of his grandmother Antonia (oriental princes were among them), from the entourage of the old magician on the island, what lesson was Caligula to learn save craft, servility, and the future licence of illimitable power?

Claudius is more promising. If his character ever appealed to Cornelius Tacitus (which is more than doubtful), it did not long engage the historian's curiosity—and the ineptitude with which a Roman Emperor in a speech to the Senate mutilated a splendid theme was grotesque and unpardonable.[4] Redress has been forthcoming in generous measure, with amicable prepossessions in favour of a Caesar who acknowledged the teaching of Livy and was himself a voluminous writer; for a scholar and an historian ought to be treated with respect.[5] The doctrine enounced by Claudius about the progressive development of the Roman State through long ages was sound and sagacious, even if lacking in novelty; his edicts, though pompous and pedantic, show industry in the conduct of public business and a concern for justice and welfare.[6] The strange creature whom his family ignored or despised often responded to the demands, though not to the dignity, of the imperial office and his own ancestry.

[1] The rehabilitation of Tiberius, firmly started in the fifties of the nineteenth century by Ihne and Sievers, was prosecuted with success, but often went too far. For a healthy, but perhaps too hostile, reaction see H. Dessau, *Gesch. der r. Kaiserzeit* II (1926), 1 ff.; for a brief and temperate summing-up, M. P. Charlesworth, *CAH* x (1954), 652. Indeed the process might not have to depreciate the merits of Tacitus, cf. A. Garzetti, *Riv. stor. it.* LXVII (1955), 71.

[2] For the best attempt, see J. P. V. D. Balsdon, *The Emperor Gaius (Caligula)*, 1934.

[3] VI. 48. 2 (the vaticination of L. Arruntius). [4] *ILS* 212 (above, p. 319).

[5] A. Momigliano, *L'opera dell' imperatore Claudio* (1932; English trans., 1934).

[6] For examples, App. 40. On the other side, Nero's opinion—'multaque decreta et constituta, ut insipientis atque deliri, pro irritis habuit' (Suetonius, *Nero* 33. 1). Also the strong language which the edict about the Anauni (*ILS* 206) evoked from Mommsen, *Hermes* III (1869), 107 = *Ges. Schr.* IV (1906), 299.

On the other side, the defects and oddities in character and demeanour. Claudius cannot be acquitted of arrogance and petty rancour. Gluttony is attested, and a sensuality that was healthy in every sense of the term. He was vulgar, garrulous, and timid. There was a coarseness in his nature not exempt from the imputation of cruelty.[1] Claudius grows intelligible, but not at all amiable.[2]

Claudius cannot easily be dissociated from his ministers—or from his wives. Some will be impelled to defend the imperial freedmen or Vitellius the consular.[3] If Valeria Messallina cannot quite be rehabilitated, attempts have not been lacking to explain and palliate: she was a mere girl, only fifteen when she married her kinsman Claudius, only twenty-four when she perished.[4] Chronology does not fully substantiate the claim to indulgence.[5] No such plea is invoked for Agrippina, who avows a more robust criminality. All for power, yet all for her son, Agrippina deserves her reputation, worthy of the answer she gave to the astrologers who revealed Nero's destiny and her own— 'occidat dum imperet'.[6]

Not much need be said about the personality of Nero, no item where the credit and veracity of Cornelius Tacitus can be seriously impugned. He wrote of times within the reach of memory or of reliable testimony. What has been transmitted by Suetonius and by Cassius Dio shows a remarkable concordance—save that Tacitus omits the grosser enormities and suspends judgement where those authors are cheerfully or ignorantly asseverative.[7] The concordance has been ascribed to the influence of a single dominant source, used by all three.[8] A better explanation serves: the portrayal of Nero corresponds in large measure with the facts.

Claudius Caesar benefits from a partial redemption because he was addicted to scholarly pursuits. Nero was devoted to the arts, to music, and to the stage; and the Greek world cherished his memory with affection.[9] It is not so certain that the Greeks relished the living and ludicrous presence of their ostensible friend and patron, ever-victorious

[1] For his character and ailments see T. D. Ruth, *The Problem of Claudius* (Diss. Baltimore, 1916).

[2] Nothing in Tacitus' portrayal conflicts with the documents, or with the anecdotal material in Suetonius.

[3] e.g. V. Scramuzza, *The Emperor Claudius* (1940), 96 f.

[4] M. P. Charlesworth, *CAH* x (1934), 672; V. Scramuzza, o.c. 90.

[5] Messallina's mother was Domitia Lepida (*PIR*², D 180), a daughter of the consul of 16 B.C.; the son of Domitia Lepida by her second marriage was Faustus Sulla Felix (*PIR*², C 1464), consul in 52, presumably born about 20. Messallina, older than this Sulla, married Claudius shortly before 41.

[6] XIV. 9. 3.

[7] K. Heinz, *Das Bild Kaiser Neros* (Diss. Bern, 1948), 117.

[8] p. 291.

[9] M. P. Charlesworth, *JRS* XL (1950), 69 ff.

in the games and robbing their sanctuaries. Rome, in the upper and middle classes at least, soon lost all illusions about Nero.

Tiberius Caesar, though failing in his purpose and detested by the Senate, handed on the imperial power intact. Caligula impaired the fabric, but assassination was a quick remedy. The next transference was a process rather than an act. The weakness of Claudius Caesar enabled Agrippina and her allies to seize control of the government and hold a tight rein until her son was old enough to rule. The decease of Claudius, however caused or accelerated, is not an important phenomenon in history. Nero, when he emancipated himself from his counsellors, not only subverted a monarchy which they had striven to buttress with concord and benevolence but destroyed the dynasty itself, involving the world in war.

The second method investigates impersonally the policy of each emperor—foreign, provincial, and domestic. An evil man may be a sagacious ruler; an autocrat is not omnipotent; a tyrant or a fool may be guided by wise counsellors.

Tiberius Caesar in his management of foreign and military affairs reflected the qualities of his generalship in the field: caution and economy achieved more than impulse, adventure, or bloodshed. 'Plura consilio quam vi', the maxim worked even in the invasions of Germany.[1] After the great Augustan conquests in central Europe a pause was needed. But Tiberius would suffer no affront to the dignity of the imperial people. Even in the last years on the island he remained vigilant and prompt.[2]

Caligula meditated vast enterprises in Britain or Germany, but left to his successor only a legacy of disturbance. Mauretania had to be pacified and annexed. The measure was premature. So, perhaps, was the invasion of Britain, among the reasons being Caligula's recent increase in the size of the army and the new ruler's urgent need of military glory.[3] Britain proved much more tedious and difficult than anybody thought. Thrace, however, despite its previous history, turned out to be a peaceful acquisition; and, although anarchy pervaded the vassal kingdom of Armenia, it mattered very little. The reign closed with a favourable balance to its credit.

After a few years the ministers of Nero decided to embark on a vigorous policy in two regions—in Armenia, which Claudius was deemed to have neglected, and in Britain, where the legions had

---

[1] II. 26. 3. Cf., for policy in the East, VI. 32. 1: 'consiliis et astu res externas moliri.'

[2] Notably against a threat from Parthia (VI. 31 ff.).

[3] It appears that Caligula enrolled the two new legions XV Primigenia and XXII Primigenia, cf. E. Ritterling, P-W XII, 1244 ff. There must have been a needless (and perhaps dangerous) concentration of troops on the Rhine.

halted to consolidate their gains. The British revolt checked further advances for a long time. In the East, after vicissitudes and diplomatic contortions, a compromise ensued, satisfying the demands of honour and advantage. The arrangement survived the civil wars and was perpetuated by the next dynasty.[1]

For the provinces the Principate began under good auspices, promising at the least a firm order instead of anarchy, with a prudent and rational exploitation of the Empire. Tiberius Caesar declared that a good shepherd does not flay his flock.[2] Nobody could deny the excellence of Tiberius' management—except senators who resented guidance and control. At the trial of a proconsul Tiberius ordered a document to be produced and read. It contained instructions from Augustus to the Senate, evoked by the notorious crimes perpetrated in Asia by Messalla Volesus.[3] That prosecution took place a few years before the death of Augustus. The destined successor of Augustus was perhaps already insistent on justice; and so he continued in the sequel for most if not all of his long reign. Nothing indicates that metropolitan calamities affected the well-being of the provinces.[4]

Four years of Caligula revealed something of the havoc an irresponsible ruler might create, notably in Judaea.[5] With Claudius sound principles seemed to return, and many branches of the administration were favoured with the ruler's attentions. He was eager to make reforms on any pretext, and volubly benevolent. How far an emperor's influence was effective for good might depend less upon his aspirations and proclamations than upon the quality and behaviour of his agents.

There was another side to the reign—the Emperor's fears or stupidity artfully exploited, allegations of treason, the long string of judicial murders. Men of birth and distinction perished, and a large number of Roman knights as well.[6] The times of Claudius Caesar also got an evil name for rapacity, extortion, and traffic.[7] It is easy (and suspect) to put most of the blame on Messallina and her associates. The removal of Messallina did not modify the practices of the governing camarilla—and most of the personnel remained. None the less, Agrippina made a difference. The second half of the reign may

---

[1] p. 237.

[2] Suetonius, *Tib.* 32. 2. The remark was made to a Prefect of Egypt (Dio LVII. 10. 5).

[3] III. 68. 1. This scion of the patrician Valerii (*PIR*[1], V 96), was consul with Cinna Magnus in A.D. 5. For his murderous cruelty when proconsul of Asia, Seneca, *De ira* II. 5. 5.

[4] The other side was inertia and fatigue, cf. H. Dessau, *Gesch. der r. Kaiserzeit* II (1926), 90.

[5] For example, the attempt to erect his statue in the Temple at Jerusalem.

[6] Seneca, *Apocol.* 10. 3 ff.; 13. 4 ff. (sundry names); 14. 1 (thirty-five senators and two hundred and twenty-one knights).

[7] *Hist.* V. 12. 2: 'per avaritiam Claudianorum temporum'; *Ann.* XII. 7. 3: 'cupido auri immensa' (of Agrippina).

paradoxically have shown an improvement, since Agrippina and the freedman Pallas, though no less avid and corrupt, were more efficient.[1]

The period of happiness which for the Roman Senate dawned at the accession of Nero may thus have begun earlier for the provinces, and it lasted longer, for a decade or more. A rebellion broke out in Britain, it is true, provoked by greed and oppression.[2] The central government sent out an inspector and took measures to repair the damage, enjoining mercy and moderation upon the legates who came after Suetonius Paullinus.[3] No such remedies were applied to allay discontent in other provinces a few years later; and, when the governors took up arms against Nero, they exploited local grievances and punished the imperial tax officers.[4] Nevertheless the fiscal burdens of Gaul and Spain are not the true reason for Nero's fall.

The main problem that confronted the Caesars was not foreign or imperial but domestic. It lay in the relations between Princeps and Senate. Whatever the acts and policy of a ruler at the outset, each reign went wrong soon or late. It is not easy to apportion the blame: the reasons are multiple and complex. The inquiry comes round to human personality again. Nero's folly was perhaps more deleterious than his crimes and his vices.[5] He not only antagonized the Senate and made the generals go in fear for their safety—he neglected the armies. The legions had never seen their *imperator*. Nero designed an expedition to the eastern lands. He ought to have gone to the Rhine. Had the soldiers been passionately loyal instead of confused or apathetic, no general could have risked a proclamation, and the tyrant might have reigned for long years.[6] The catastrophe of a dynasty that had endured for a century took its origin from a sequence of accidents, and perhaps of misunderstandings.

An emperor might be loathed by the Senate but popular with plebs, army, and provinces; and a despot who made Rome marvel or tremble at his iniquities did not poison life everywhere. A sensible man could honourably serve the Commonwealth when he rendered obedience to

[1] Compare the testimonial of Tacitus, 'adductum et quasi virile servitium: palam severitas et saepius superbia; nihil domi impudicum nisi dominationi expediret' (XII. 7. 3).

[2] XIV. 29 ff., cf. App. 69.

[3] XIV. 39. 3 (Petronius Turpilianus); *Agr.* 16. 2 ff.

[4] Plutarch, *Galba* 4 (the oppressions of the ἀλιτήριοι ἐπίτροποι). Betuus Cilo, executed in Gaul on Galba's order (*Hist.* I. 37. 3), may have been a procurator: there is no warrant for Stein's statement 'homo sine dubio nobilis' (*PIR²*, B 124).

[5] C. Barbagallo, *La Catastrophe di Nerone* (Catania, 1915), 20: 'non dunque il delitto ma la inettitudine.'

[6] Rostovtzeff's account of the events of 68 and 69 is seriously defective. He underestimated the dynastic loyalty of the soldiers and made the strange statement that 'they desired the best Roman of the senatorial class to be *princeps*' (*The Social and Economic History of the Roman Empire* (1926), 85).

a tyrannical emperor. That lesson the *Agricola* conveyed for the instruction of the senatorial class. To the provinces it might be largely irrelevant what manner of master they loyally and inevitably acknowledged. Petillius Cerialis had recourse to the doctrine when defending the Roman domination before a convention of Gallic notables—the influence of good emperors issues in benefits far and wide, whereas the bad can do harm only in their near vicinity.[1]

That crime, vice, and folly at Rome coexisted with a stable order and prosperity abroad is not a secret reserved for penetrating inquiry or distant ages to discover. So elementary a truth lay almost beneath the notice of Cornelius Tacitus. Testimonials to tolerable government or the effusion of provincial gratitude will not safely be invoked for the personal rehabilitation of any one of the Caesars.

Over the wide world from Spain to Syria, from the northern rivers to the Libyan desert, there was very little government, good or bad, directed from the capital. Towns or tribes in the West, cities or vassal princes in the East intervene between the individual and Caesar or Caesar's mandatory.

Tiberius Caesar developed the habit of leaving governors in office for periods of inordinate length. Various interpretations have been given, says Tacitus. He hated to make any change; he was grudging and malevolent; for all his craft and judgement, the effort of selecting the right governor was a torment—while not looking for outstanding abilities, Tiberius feared incompetence and misrule.[2] The historian does not add what might seem obvious, the Emperor's care for the welfare of the subject population. That reason will be conceded proper emphasis.[3] It should not obscure certain disadvantages in the practice. A legate by long tenure might acquire a dangerous hold upon the affections of the troops.[4] Other governors might lapse by an easy declension into torpor or corruption.[5]

Furthermore, while Caesar's *provincia* was his own affair, Tiberius in the last period of his reign encroached alarmingly on the sphere of the Senate. He refused to permit a renewal of proconsuls for Asia and Africa, keeping the same men for six years.[6] That was

---

[1] *Hist.* IV. 74. 2: 'et laudatorum principum usus ex aequo quamvis procul agentibus: saevi proximis ingruunt.'

[2] I. 80. 2: 'causae variae traduntur: alii taedio novae curae semel placita pro aeternis servavisse, quidam invidia, ne plures fruerentur; sunt qui existiment, ut callidum eius ingenium ita anxium iudicium; neque enim eminentis virtutes sectabatur, et rursum vitia oderat', &c.

[3] F. B. Marsh, *The Reign of Tiberius* (1931), 157; M. P. Charlesworth, *CAH* x (1934), 648 f.   [4] VI. 30 (Lentulus Gaetulicus in Germania Superior).

[5] Ten years in Judaea was too much for the procurator Pontius Pilatus.

[6] Dio LVIII. 23. 5. M. Junius Silanus (*cos.* 19) was in Africa for that period (*ILS* 6236), P. Petronius (*suff.* 19) in Asia (*PIR*[1], P 198, citing coin evidence).

an affront to the Senate, and prejudicial to the most eminent of its members.

One of the earliest acts of Tiberius had been to remove two provinces from the portion of the Senate, namely Achaia and Macedonia. They were added to Moesia.[1] This vast complex, with Thrace demanding vigilance as well, was administered by Poppaeus Sabinus until his death twenty years later, and the arrangement subsisted for a further decade.[2] Another large imperial province was Hispania Citerior, embracing the refractory zone only recently subjugated. A consular legate saw to it, helped by the legates of three legions.[3] The duties of civil government cannot have been arduous.

Tiberius for all his reiterated protestations did not find it necessary to leave the capital and inspect the provinces.[4] He even detained at Rome for many years the consular legates he had appointed to Spain and Syria: the legionary commanders carried out their functions.[5] It was a remarkable anomaly. Personalities and court intrigues were perhaps in play, and some will discern the hand of Aelius Seianus or the secret apprehensions of Tiberius.[6]

The legate of Syria was the chief imperial mandatory in the provinces beyond the sea. It was his duty to keep an eye upon the vassal princes in a wide zone from Pontus down to Judaea; and he might have to conduct negotiations with the only power of any magnitude in the world—the Parthians. To choose the right man demanded careful thought in an emperor—especially if one of the young Caesars were perambulating the region.[7] Recent history demonstrated the danger of clash or complications. Moreover, the legions of Syria, distant from the capital and very powerful, could support a proclamation or decide the outcome of a crisis in the dynasty. Likewise the army in Spain.[8]

So far as known, Tiberius had nothing to fear from Aelius Lamia

---

[1] I. 76. 2; 80. I.

[2] VI. 39. 3. Sabinus had been governor of Moesia for twenty-four years. His successor was P. Memmius Regulus, *suff.* 31 (*PIR¹*, M 342).

[3] Strabo III. 166.

[4] IV. 4. 2. Hardly necessary: he had seen every region except Africa and Egypt.

[5] L. Arruntius (*cos.* 6) for Hispania Citerior (VI. 27. 3, cf. *Hist.* II. 65. 2; Dio LVIII. 8. 3, without the name), L. Aelius Lamia (*cos.* 3) for Syria (VI. 27. I). L. Piso, assassinated by a native in Spain in 25 (IV. 45), is surely not, as generally assumed (e.g. *PIR²*, C 292), the consular legate, but a praetorian, acting in the absence of the consular (cf. App. 63).

[6] F. B. Marsh suggested that this was Seianus' device, so that the provinces should not be in the control of men hostile to him (o.c. 191).

[7] Augustus had selected M. Lollius as guide and counsellor for Gaius Caesar, a crafty and pliable man. It turned out badly (cf. III. 48. 2; Velleius II. 102. I). Tiberius went to the other extreme—the notoriously intractable Cn. Piso (II. 43. 2).

[8] The memory and *clientela* of the Pompeii may still have been feared—and in fact the first successful proclamation was that of an aristocratic legate, Sulpicius Galba.

and L. Arruntius, the consular legates he kept at Rome.[1] Yet he had grounds for disquiet when fate robbed him of his son Drusus only four years after the death of Germanicus.[2] Provinces and armies required from time to time the presence of some member of the dynasty. Such was the lesson of Augustus' reign. There was nobody left now.

The personal relations of the Emperor with senators and governors, that was Tacitus' theme, not the general condition of cities, peoples, and provinces in the Roman dominions. His vision (it is often urged) was narrow and parochial, urban where it might have been imperial. A vast spectacle offered. The historian averted his gaze. He preferred court and capital to the panorama of the Roman world.[3]

A further inhibition. The experience of Tacitus (so some believe) was imperfect. He knew little, as he cared little, about the provinces; he ought to have gone more widely about the lands of the Empire; travel would enlarge a man's sympathies and abate his pessimism, with an escape from the miasma of metropolitan corruption into the pure atmosphere of provincial morality.[4]

Criticism of this order is itself narrow and parochial. It ignores the official career of Cornelius Tacitus from the military tribunate in one of the imperial legions down to the governorship of Asia. It also ignores the design (and the inevitable restrictions) of that kind of history which the Roman senator was writing.

To describe foreign countries and the customs of natives the annalists had a traditional technique. Sallust, Livy, and Tacitus all used it. But Roman writers did not rise to their opportunities. They were incompetent to take the further step, to stand outside their own nationality and depict the Roman People in its behaviour, structure, and institutions. Tentative approaches, it is true, had been

[1] The standard and traditional view assumed that Tiberius must have suspected Arruntius, cf. *Hist.* II. 65. 2: 'ob metum'. Arruntius, it is true, had the Pompeian connexion behind him (p. 382), but Aelius Lamia should not have been dangerous: 'genus illi decorum', says Tacitus (VI. 27. 2), not inappropriately, though he was the first consul of his family. Tiberius appointed him *praefectus urbi* in 32, in succession to L. Piso (Dio LVIII. 19. 5): he died the year after.

[2] It could be conjectured that Arruntius and Lamia had just been appointed when Drusus died in September, 23. That would not conflict with the 'decimum iam annum attineri' of Arruntius (VI. 27. 2, under the year 32; cf. Dio LVIII. 8. 3: πρὸ δέκα ἐτῶν, under 31). That there was a L. Piso in Spain in 25 (IV. 45. 1) need not (as Groag assumed, *PIR²*, A 1130) impugn the credibility of Tacitus, cf. R. Syme, *JRS* XLVI (1956), 21; and Tacitus, to judge by the reference in VI. 27. 2, must already have mentioned Arruntius' governorship (i.e. somewhere in Book V, presumably under the year 31). The beginning of Lamia's term in Syria cannot be discovered, nor is its duration recorded.

[3] For a short anthology of opinions see App. 70.

[4] G. Boissier, *Tacite* (1903), 184.

made. The antiquary Terentius Varro perhaps divined the problem.[1] Tacitus is capable of tracing change and evolution in a broad
sweep. His own studies in the annals of Roman eloquence pointed
the way. Not merely a sequence of names and prosecutions. The
historian discerned mutations of taste and the gradual impact of
political forces.

It took few words to show why the new order was accepted. Battle
or proscription cut down the men of spirit among the *nobiles*; for the
others, the victor held out honours and endowment, if they were
pliable. Stability won the safe allegiance of those who had done well
out of the Revolution. Nor was the Principate in any way unwel-
come to the provinces.[2]

No need to enlarge on that theme. Tacitus can also render slow
trends and changes in behaviour. He inserts a digression about wealth
and extravagance. Hasty reformers might clamour for legislation, and
the credulous were prone to magnify its efficacy. Tiberius Caesar had
strong doubts, and so had the historian who reproduces the Emperor's
masterly oration.[3] Tacitus in comment is careful to point out that
luxury flourished unabated through a century, from the War of
Actium to the fall of Nero. The standards prevalent in his own day
were very different. A diagnosis follows. Tacitus draws the contrast
(it was obvious enough). First, the princely display of the aristocracy
under the Julii and Claudii.[4] Next, the modest habits of the new men,
whose native parsimony endured despite opulence and success;[5] and
he concedes especial force to the personality and example of the
Emperor Vespasian. That was not all. The historian must pause and
interject a doubt whether it be not better to invoke cycles of taste
and conduct, changing with the times.[6]

Tacitus was aware that large factors operated in human history. To
describe them was not easy. The historian can illustrate social change
by means of a digression or a speech subsidiary to the annalistic
record,[7] but he cannot elevate it to the central theme in an exposition
that shall embrace not Romans only but the whole empire of Rome.

---

[1] In his treatise *De vita populi Romani*.

[2] I. 2. 1: 'nullo adversante, cum ferocissimi per acies aut proscriptione cecidissent,
ceteri nobilium, quanto quis servitio promptior, opibus et honoribus extollerentur', &c.

[3] III. 53 f.

[4] 55. 2: 'nam etiam tum plebem socios regna colere et coli licitum; ut quisque opibus
domo paratu speciosus per nomen et clientelas inlustrior habebatur.'

[5] ib. 3: 'et quamquam fortuna vel industria plerique pecuniosam ad senectam perveni-
rent, mansit tamen prior animus.'

[6] ib. 4: 'nisi forte rebus cunctis inest quidam velut orbis, ut quem ad modum temporum
vices ita morum vertantur.'

[7] III. 33 f. (the position of women); XI. 6 f. (barristers and their fees); XIII. 26 f. (freedmen); XIV. 20 f. (Greek games at Rome); 43 ff. (slaves).

A new form of literature would be requisite, not built upon narrative, and not dominated by the character and the vicissitudes of a few individuals.[1]

The *Annales* omit many subjects altogether, or accord only a perfunctory recognition. No systematic treatment explains the senatorial cursus, the development of equestrian posts, or promotion and command in the armed forces. The historian does not reveal how revenue and finance were managed. Agriculture, commerce, and industry throughout the world seem barely within his scope. He refuses to bother about the condition of the poor in town and country; and he is largely indifferent to organized manifestations of civic loyalty or devotion to the dynasty.[2] There is scarcely a word anywhere about town government and municipal politics in Italy and the western lands.

The list of omissions mounts and swells to a bulky indictment. No matter: Cornelius Tacitus was not compiling an encyclopedia. Some topics were taken for granted by the writer and by the reader. Others could be dismissed as petty or laborious. Others again were wholly refractory to literary presentation.

'Urbem Romam'. The *Annales* begin with a traditional and restrictive definition. As in the old days, it denied and excluded both Italy and the Roman dominions. When the Caesars ruled, Rome remained the seat and domicile of power, even if power was exercised by an imbecile or by a group at court. The Roman government is therefore the historian's subject. The main concern of the government is with the senatorial class and the armed forces, as Tacitus clearly reveals. The provinces hardly come into his narrative, for in normal times they are almost devoid of identity.[3] The true units were not the provincial territories (or agglomerates), but the communities, both in the East and in the West. Units, but not sovereign states. How then could they have a history?

In Italy, when Rome became the capital of the whole land, the towns did not forfeit local autonomy or civic pride. But Rome overshadowed them all and drained their vitality: the most energetic of the municipal aristocrats departed to the capital. Education or ambition took them away, private profit, or the service of the Roman

---

[1] That is to say, something more like Rostovtzeff's *Social and Economic History of the Roman Empire* (1926). That great work, however, would have benefited if the author had properly exploited Tacitus for the social history. Many of his generalizations are vague and vulnerable.

[2] That indifference has been more than compensated by the lavish attention accorded to the subject by a large number of scholars. In the view of Lucan (VII. 455 ff.) emperor-worship was the punishment (the severest possible) inflicted by the gods on Rome for the sin of civil war.

[3] The provincial *concilia* were probably not very important as a factor in history.

State. Local politics, whatever degree (or semblance) of fervour they evoked, were not other than local; and the purity of municipal morals (advertised rather than authentic) might not compensate for all that the towns harboured of narrow, trivial, and tedious. Cities grew and prospered. They decked themselves out with baths and amphitheatres and temples to Caesar. In an effusion of zeal the small towns copied forms and ceremonies from the capital.[1] Not all became any more vital —some decayed.[2]

In the last age of the Republic, Ulubrae beside the Pomptine Marshes got a proverbial name for empty desolation.[3] When municipal institutions spread their pattern over the western world, Ulubrae might be everywhere—not depopulation but life in death. The poet Martial proclaimed a depressing truth: nothing is baser than a municipal existence.[4] Few who had escaped cared ever to go back. Martial was one of those few, and he quickly repented. His native Bilbilis was a 'provincialis solitudo'.[5]

A senator's station and duties prescribed attendance at the capital when he was not abroad in the service of the State. Both residence and recreation tied him to the vicinity of Rome, with little leisure even to visit the Transpadana. Pliny saw his native Comum perhaps twice in a decade; and his elderly friends, when the active career ends, are discovered living at villas on the coasts of Latium and Campania. Similarly the senators from Spain and Narbonensis. Transferring family and domicile, they soon become indistinguishable from Italians. It is rare indeed that men of this rank deign to accept an honorary magistracy in their towns of ultimate origin.[6]

The biographer of Julius Agricola knew the good side of municipal and provincial life; and if, in the *Annales*, he uses words and notions that have a suspiciously conventional ring, he can also essay a dry unsentimental analysis.[7] The bad side (stagnation or corruption) was

[1] Thus Pisae in grief for the Caesars Gaius and Lucius (*ILS* 139 f.), Forum Clodii with sundry ceremonies of loyalty to Tiberius (*ILS* 154)—and, of course, obscure Heba (App. 67).

[2] For the whole question see the four pamphlets of W. E. Heitland, from *The Roman Fate* (Cambridge, 1922) to *Repetita* (1930); for a more kindly view, H. M. Last, *CAH* xi (1936), 456 ff.

[3] Cicero, *Ad fam.* vii. 18. 3; Horace, *Epp.* i. 11. 30. Ulubrae duly built a temple to Rome and Augustus (*ILS* 6274).

[4] Martial iv. 66. 1 f.

[5] Martial xii, *praef.* Quintilian had the good fortune to come back to Rome with Galba (Jerome, *Chron.* p. 186 H).

[6] Pliny's letters furnish negative evidence. The emperor Hadrian, however, accepted the office (*HA, Hadr.* 19. 1).

[7] iii. 55. 3—the 'domestica parsimonia' and 'pecuniosa senecta' of the municipal *novi homines*. The word 'pecuniosus' is not honorific, observe the only other instances in Tacitus, xiii. 6. 4; 52. 2 (p. 448, n. 6). For conventional language, xvi. 5. 1 : 'sed qui remotis e municipiis severaque adhuc et antiqui moris retinente Italia.'

generally too trivial to bother about. Local magnates exhibited patterns of honourable leisure. Nobody spoke of conceit or torpor.

Despite the design (and the dignity) of his writing, Cornelius Tacitus furnishes many items of value about social and economic history. They arise from specific episodes and are often tied to persons, they occur sporadically or in digressions.[1] Thus three incidents in the reign of Nero. Local rivalry between Campanian towns led to rioting at a gladiatorial show (natives against visitors), with many deaths.[2] At Puteoli an ugly feud split the two orders, and each blamed the other—the plebs out of hand, the magistrates and the better sort unbearably rapacious. Cassius Longinus, the famous lawyer, was sent to allay discord. Puteoli found Cassius too harsh. Two other senators, with a cohort of the imperial guard, established social harmony.[3] Tarentum and Antium had not been prospering. Nero tried to re-inforce their citizen body with some veteran settlers. The remedy failed. Tacitus assigns the reasons, calling up for contrast the military colonies of ancient days, when a whole legion went with its officers to form a community.[4]

In town and country plutocracy reigned, with all its attendant evils. The free population declined, to the advantage of alien and servile stocks. Hordes of slaves might minister to a single magnate in his mansion. Hence an urgent preoccupation—'totidem hostes quot servi'.[5] Even the freed slaves were a problem. A debate in the Senate under Nero brought out a majority in favour of revoking the liberty of freedmen deficient in respect towards their former masters. The Emperor was consulted. Nothing came of the matter. The historian, however, is careful to supply the arguments that must have been heard, for and against, in the privy council.[6]

Several years later a high dignitary, the Prefect of the City, was murdered by one of his slaves. Tacitus enhances the incident with a set speech from Cassius Longinus.[7] Cassius, a persistent champion of the 'instituta et leges maiorum', advocated a vengeance of traditional severity: slave households, like nations in their multitude, and

---

[1] Hence, sometimes, a clue to the author's special interests, or to the time of his writing.
[2] XIV. 17.   [3] XIII. 48.
[4] XIV. 27. 3. A *colonia* of just such a type, three thousand legionaries conducted by a *primipilaris*, was established at Cyrene in the last year of Trajan, as emerges from the inscription at Attaleia cited by L. Robert, *Bull. ép.* 1948, 201, under n. 289. For the full text, *JRS* XL (1950), 84. See also *PIR²*, G 100.
[5] Seneca, *Epp.* 47. 5. An abortive servile rising in south-eastern Italy caused great alarm at Rome: 'ob multitudinem familiarum quae gliscebat immensum, minore in dies plebe ingenua' (IV. 27. 2).
[6] XIII. 26 f. Hadrian, most humane in his legislation about slaves, was strict about freedmen—and so were succeeding rulers, cf. A. M. Duff, *Freedmen in the Early Roman Empire* (1928), 42.
[7] XIV. 43 f.

heterogeneous, with foreign religious cults or none at all, cannot be regimented save by terror. Cassius prevailed. Four hundred slaves were led out to execution.

A pair of incidents in the historian's own day had excited great alarm about slaves. A senator of praetorian rank was assassinated in the bath.[1] Then, in the summer of 105, a consul was found dead in his house—murder or suicide, it was not clear. A complicated discussion ensued, with a medley of opinions from senators about the punishment to be visited upon the dead man's household. Pliny, wishing to know whether he had adopted the right line, consults at inordinate length a reputable jurist of his acquaintance called Titius Aristo.[2] The teacher of Pliny's friend was a great master, Cassius Longinus.[3]

The historian is keenly aware of riches as a factor for power.[4] Impoverishment bears down the *nobiles*, while new men rise by the pursuit of gain; a procurator's opportunities are such that he will prefer not to be a senator;[5] and opulent men tend to have the advantage when honours or even military commands are awarded.[6] The wealthy were assiduously besieged, with avid expectancy for their last dispositions; and wills and testaments receive a strong and proper emphasis.[7]

The process of enrichment is seldom praised—and seldom specified, save as peculation or inheritance. The great wealth of the Volusii is not explained;[8] and the 'magnae opes innocenter partae' of a Cornelius Lentulus must remain enigmatic.[9] Nor will a senatorial annalist describe how senators got profit from exploiting the new methods in industry or agriculture. The encyclopedic curiosity of the elder Pliny duly notes the vineyards of Seneca at Nomentum near Rome;[10] but

---

[1] Pliny, *Epp.* III. 14 (Larcius Macedo).

[2] VIII. 14. 12 ff. The victim was Cn. Afranius Dexter, 'in domo sua exanimis inventus' (*Inscr. It.* XIII. 1, p. 196).

[3] *Dig.* IV. 8. 40. Pliny generously praises his attainments (*Epp.* I. 22). Apparently not a senator. It is relevant to Tacitus' treatment of the incident under Nero to observe that Hadrian had views of his own—'non de omnibus servis quaestionem haberi, sed de his qui per vicinitatem poterant sentire, praecepit' (*HA, Hadr.* 18. 11). Cf. *Dig.* XXIX. 5. 1. 28.

[4] The words 'opes' and 'pecunia' each take nearly five columns in the *Lexicon Taciteum* of Gerber–Greef.

[5] XVI. 17. 3 (Annaeus Mela, Seneca's brother).

[6] XIII. 6. 4: 'si ducem amota invidia egregium quam si pecuniosum et gratia subnixum per ambitum deligeret.' Cf. the 'pecuniosa orbitas et senecta' of Pompeius Silvanus, a proconsul of Africa (XIII. 52. 2).

[7] p. 543.

[8] Except by Nero addressing Seneca—'quantum Volusio longa parsimonia quaesivit' (XIV. 56. 1). Note, however, that Columella (I. 7. 3) quotes words of L. Volusius (*suff.* A.D. 3) about the science of agriculture. For the Volusii, pp. 302 f., 372.

[9] IV. 44. 1 (Cn. Lentulus, *cos.* 14 B.C.: *PIR*[2], C 1380).

[10] *NH* XIV. 51 (cf. p. 335).

no writer has revealed the suburban brick kilns that worked for the orator Domitius Afer.[1]

Similarly, the resources of towns and territories are cursorily indicated, rather than any specific products. The *Annales* (as extant) show few geographical digressions. All the more notable is the treatment accorded to Byzantium,[2] a city which, during the early Empire, hardly assumes the prominence that its site and history appear to warrant. Byzantium sent an embassy to ask Claudius for some alleviation of its burdens. Tacitus seizes the opportunity to review the past, from the foundation (mentioning the famous oracular injunction); he explains the wealth of Byzantium; and he adverts upon its value for the passage of generals and armies—irrelevant perhaps to the time of Claudius Caesar.[3]

At first sight the provinces are unequally presented in the *Annales*. The Balkan and Danubian lands appear to hold very little attraction. The author duly registers recurrent disturbances in the vassal kingdom of Thrace; but no names of places in Pannonia, Dalmatia, or Moesia occur, not even a legionary station.[4] Nor are the Greek regions much in evidence, except for proconsular Asia. Syria as a country commands scant interest. Egypt comes in, picturesquely, because it was honoured with a visit from Germanicus Caesar; but Alexandria, that great city, is named only twice.[5] And there is only one passage describing conditions in the land of Judaea.[6]

The missing books (VII to X) will have furnished ample compensation—factions at Alexandria and the strife of Greek against Jew. Also several episodes concerning Judaea: princes and the intractable people and the vicissitudes of the Roman procurators, not omitting Pontius Pilatus.[7] The historian had a goal before him—the final explosion under Nero.

For the rest, the provinces of Africa and Asia suitably detain the senator of consular rank. Africa offered welcome relief, with the Sallustian theme of Tacfarinas and nostalgia for the past—a proconsul still permitted, though for the last time, to take the acclamation of 'imperator', or a Roman patrician renewing after long centuries the fame of his ancestors, also for the last time.[8]

---

[1] *CIL* xv. 979–83, &c., cf. *PIR*[2], D 126.   [2] xii. 62 f.

[3] Hadrian spent the winter of 117/18 in this vicinity (p. 243). The sources of the Tacitean digression are Claudius Caesar and Sallust, cf. App. 40.

[4] Carnuntum could have been mentioned in xii. 29. Compare his previous work, where only Poetovio is named (*Hist.* iii. 1. 1).   [5] ii. 59. 2; 67. 3.   [6] xii. 54.

[7] Pontius Pilatus, and some of the events of his ten years' government, would be put in Book VII. L. Vitellius, the legate of Syria, ordered the procurator to go back to face an inquiry: he reached Rome shortly after the death of Tiberius (Josephus, *AJ* xviii. 89). Both Vitellius and his successor (P. Petronius) intervened at Jerusalem.

[8] iii. 74. 4 (Q. Junius Blaesus); ii. 52. 5 (M. Furius Camillus).

More typical of imperial Rome was the minor item. Tacitus explains how a proconsul of Africa, an old man, was able to baffle prosecution because of his wealth and the greedy hopes which it excited—and disappointed, for he outlived his rescuers.[1] Tacitus knew more about this man;[2] and he did not forget the trial of Marius Priscus, and the various impediments in the path of justice.

The author himself had held the *fasces* in Asia.[3] The warfare in Britain is generously narrated; and he knew in detail the distribution of the armed forces in the island.[4] Above all, Tacitus has abundant knowledge about the Gallic territories, the frontier zone, and the Germans who dwelt in freedom beyond the Rhine.[5]

Various reasons can be invoked: not merely the tastes of the author and his personal experience, but the historical role of each region. For long years in the long imperial peace many a province is barren of incident or action—no disturbance, not even a criminal proconsul or legate. Spain was a vast area, embracing three provinces. It bulked large in the wars of Rome, foreign and civil, from the Scipiones to its final pacification under Caesar Augustus. Yet Spain contributes hardly anything to the *Annales* except the assassination of one governor—and the prolonged absence of another.[6]

Towns and tribes and provinces lead a quiet indescribable existence, remote from history. When civil war comes, they enter the orbit of great events. Then will their power and resources be properly expounded. Though Tacitus writes mainly about Rome, palace and Senate, he does not lose sight of the large imperial themes. Some emerge rapid and dramatic in the narration, like the armies in Book I, and then recede. Others have to wait for a long time.

[1] XIII. 52. 2: 'valuitque pecuniosa orbitate et senecta quam ultra vitam eorum produxit quorum ambitu evaserat.'

[2] M. Pompeius Silvanus (*PIR¹*, P 495: left out of P-W XXI), *cos. suff.* 45, proconsul 53/54 (*IRT* 338). He emerges as one of the 'divites senes' in 69 (*Hist.* II. 86. 3). Vespasian gave him a second consulate c. 75. Tacitus could have seen and known this political relic.

[3] For details about Asia, Ch. XXXV.

[4] p. 395.   [5] Ch. XXXIV.

[6] IV. 45 (L. Piso); VI. 27. 2 (L. Arruntius). The other items are I. 78. 1 (a temple to Augustus at Tarraco); IV. 13. 2 (the condemnation of a proconsul of Baetica); 37. 1 (Baetica petitions to have a temple of Tiberius and Livia); XIV. 41. 1 (Pompeius Aelianus, a young senator from Spain); XIII. 46. 3 (Otho sent to Lusitania).

XXXIV. TACITUS AND GAUL

WAR or peace, the legions on the Rhine are a large part of imperial history. The *Annales* bring them on promptly, first in mutiny and then marching to a renewed invasion of Germany. With the recall of Germanicus Caesar, colour and drama depart—and there is no danger now, thanks to Roman diplomacy and native dissensions. A long tranquillity ensued.

Tacitus does not forget the armies. Sporadic items reveal what went on along and beyond the frontier—some subject tribe in revolt or a sudden incursion, brought into relation with general imperial policy (not always for praise), or with the conduct of Roman troops. And, above all, the quality of the commanders. When Domitius Corbulo came to the lower Rhine, he took vigorous action against the Frisii and the Chauci, until a dispatch from the Emperor Claudius told him to stop and withdraw. Corbulo obeyed, cursing the age he was condemned to live in: 'beatos quondam duces Romanos'.[1]

Corbulo found a use for the troops. He made them dig a canal. About the same time the legate of Upper Germany, Curtius Rufus, went in for mining operations in the land of the Mattiaci. Corbulo had been mentioned already in the *Annales*,[2] and his future glory is here foreshadowed. As for Curtius Rufus, Tacitus seizes the opportunity to insert some remarks about his paradoxical career (low birth, a miraculous prediction, an emperor's favour, and high promotion).[3] Curtius was followed by Pomponius Secundus, who dealt most ably with a raid of the formidable Chatti. Both Curtius and Pomponius are much more than mere names in the record of the Rhine armies. Tacitus links personality and event, skilfully adding an obituary notice in advance, both for the repulsive upstart (he was aggressive as well as servile, with no claim to renown) and for the general who would be remembered, not for a military exploit however laudable, but for literary talent and the social graces.[4]

Again, when the historian required material to expand uneventful annals at the beginning of Nero's reign, minor operations conducted by several legates (not all bellicose) came in useful. A full narrative is provided.[5] It illustrates the policy of the Roman government, which would not allow migrant tribes to settle near the bank of the lower

---

[1] XI. 20. I.
[2] Since he is here introduced with one name only, 'Corbulo' (18. 1).
[3] XI. 21 (p. 563).   [4] XII. 28. 2 (p. 338).   [5] XIII. 53–56.

Rhine; and the identity of the legates was of some interest to Tacitus.[1] The section closes with two local or extraneous episodes—a battle between two German tribes contending for the possession of salt springs, and a conflagration of mysterious origin that threatened to envelop and destroy the Roman city that had recently been founded in the land of the Ubii, Colonia Claudia Agrippinensium. These events are all registered under the one year 58.[2]

For towns, tribes, and forts on or near the Rhine Tacitus is impeccable, as indeed the *Historiae* abundantly show.[3] To account for that, the first thought might be a written source of superior accuracy; and those who make inquiry into the methods of Tacitus are drawn without fail to the elder Pliny, who was in service on the Rhine for the greater part of the period 47–58.[4] If much in what Tacitus wrote about the Rhineland derives from that author, a problem would still remain: his keen attention, his choice and precision of detail.

No Roman of any consequence lacked friends and informants, from equestrian officers to legates of consular rank; and many had personal or family links with the region, and with its past history. The Roman knight and procurator Cornelius Tacitus superintended the revenues of Gallia Belgica (along with the two Germanies), and kept the pay chest of both armies.[5] A man in that position would contract ties of friendship with local worthies at Colonia Claudia—and (much more important) with dynastic families in great peoples like the Treveri.[6] Nor would it be safe to dismiss from the reckoning certain undocumented posts or periods in the official career of the senatorial historian —the military tribunate, the command of a legion, even perhaps a governorship in the lower or the upper Germany (c. 101–4).[7]

One item at least that is preserved in the *Historiae* cannot come from any book published at Rome during the reign of Vespasian or in the early years of Domitian—the incriminatory revelation about Petillius Cerialis (a kinsman of the dynasty): when the insurgents captured his vessel on the Rhine, Petillius was absent that night because of a woman. Tacitus supplies the name: Claudia Sacrata from Colonia Claudia.[8]

The author of the *Historiae* is not content with an odd detail or the picturesque incident that will fill space. He has a general interest, and a deep understanding of the relations between Rome and the natives.

---

[1] In Germania Inferior, Pompeius Paullinus, succeeded by Duvius Avitus (p. 591); in charge of the upper army, the excellent L. Antistius Vetus (*cos.* 55).

[2] XIII. 57.   [3] p. 174.   [4] pp. 60, 127, 288 f., 292.

[5] Pliny, *NH* VII. 76 (p. 60).

[6] A Treveran nobleman, Julius Classicianus, was procurator of Britain under Nero (below, p. 456, n. 6).

[7] Ch. VI.   [8] *Hist.* V. 22. 3 (p. 175).

The speeches help. Addressing the Treveri and Lingones, Petillius Cerialis delivers a firm apologia for the Roman rule and expounds its advantages. The argument is powerful—without Rome there would be no defence from the Germans; Gaul in the past had always been the scene of 'regna bellaque'; protection cannot be had without arms, or arms without taxation; the only alternative to the Roman dominion is anarchy.[1]

At the same time the orator, as might be expected, adduces pleas of dubious validity. Affirming that there is no barrier between the Romans and the Gauls, he alleges that Gauls command Roman legions (which cannot have been normal).[2] More significant than the oration of Cerialis is an incident which in itself has little bearing upon the fortunes of war. Tacitus deliberately exploits it. He brings in the citizens of Colonia Claudia (mixed colonial and native stock) to speak in their own person. The town had neither resisted nor actively helped the insurgents. After a time a German tribe across the river, the Tencteri, made an appeal, based on liberty, honesty, mutual confidence, and a common origin: the Agrippinenses should pull down their walls, liberate the traffic between the two banks, and kill all Romans in their territory.[3] The arguments were patently spurious. The Agrippinenses in a diplomatic answer, while admitting kinship with the Germans, and not averse to certain concessions, deny that there are any aliens among them: native or veteran, they constitute a single and indivisible community.[4]

So far the military zone of the Roman frontier: the proper complement, it might seem, and the sequel, to Tacitus' own early treatise about the peoples of Germany. There is something else, a matter neglected or obscured because of the *Germania* and all the zeal and study which that opuscule has evoked. In short, the Gallic problem in the early Principate. One aspect of it is revealed by the speech of Petillius Cerialis. There was more to be said in the *Annales*.[5]

The Gaul which Julius Caesar had invaded, crushed, and conquered, remained tranquil on the whole. Yet the Roman government was

---

[1] IV. 73 f.

[2] IV. 74. I: 'ipsi plerumque legionibus nostris praesidetis, ipsi has aliasque provincias regitis: nihil separatum clausumve.' The only attested governor hitherto is Julius Vindex, holding Lugdunensis in 68. The words of the Roman general were interpreted much too literally by Ph. Fabia, *Rev. ét. anc.* XIV (1912), 285.

[3] IV. 64.

[4] IV. 65. 2: 'deductis olim et nobiscum per conubium sociatis quique mox provenerunt haec patria est.' Further, when impersonating Claudius Caesar, the historian emphasizes the native element in Roman veteran colonies (*Ann.* XI. 24. 3).

[5] The central portion of this chapter appeared, in a modified form, in the article 'Tacitus on Gaul', *Latomus* XII (1953), 25 ff.

vigilant and distrustful. The land was large and populous, with an old tradition of martial glory. The Gauls were a collection of tribes, not a nation; but the resistance to Julius Caesar had called forth a national spirit. It might still be very dangerous.

The invasions of Germany in the time of Caesar Augustus helped to support Roman rule in Gaul. Rome could claim to be the protector of the Gauls, their ally in a war which for the Gauls (who remembered Ariovistus and others) was a war of revenge. The chieftains of Gaul and the levies of Gaul marched with the Roman legions into Germany (and perhaps did much of the fighting).

But the conquest of Germany had been abandoned. The revolt of Arminius and the loss of three legions came as a sharp lesson to the Roman government—and might be an incitement to the peoples of Gaul. How was the Roman government to deal with the problem?

No legions were stationed in the interior. At first sight, a sign of confidence. In truth, there was a strategic reason. Under Tiberius eight legions stood along the Rhine, from Vetera (Xanten) to Vindonissa (Windisch, near Basle). They seem to face Germany, to repel attack or to resume the conquest of that country. But they face both ways—Gaul as well as Germany.[1] That, indeed, is the especial function of two of the four legions in the Upper German command, those at Argentorate (Strasbourg) and Vindonissa. There were hardly any Germans in Baden and in the Schwarzwald. The legion at Strasbourg is ready for war—but not against Germans. The legion will march by Saverne on Metz and Reims. As for the other legion, from Basle it is a short step, by the Gap of Belfort, to Dijon, in the strategic centre of the whole country. Any Gallic insurrection will be crushed with promptitude.

Gaul under the early Empire remained very much as it had been before. Though men come down from the old *oppida*, and cities are founded in the plain (thus among the Aedui the new town Augustodunum takes the place of Bibracte), though the cities themselves prosper, though commerce flourishes and education spreads, the social structure subsists unchanged. Gaul is still rural rather than urban. It is a land of tribes and tribal chieftains, of large estates, country houses—and much of the population living in serfdom or close to it.[2]

The evidence provided by Caesar in the *Bellum Gallicum* can be regarded as still valid. Caesar shows perfect examples of the Gallic

---

[1] *Ann.* IV. 5. 1: 'commune in Germanos Gallosque subsidium.' Almost one third of the legionary strength of the Empire.

[2] For the persistence of those conditions, K. F. Stroheker, *Der senatorische Adel im spätantiken Gallien* (1948), 38 ff.

baron. First, Orgetorix of the Helvetii—'longe nobilissimus fuit et ditissimus'.[1] This man had an establishment, a *familia*, of ten thousand men; and, in addition, a large number of 'clientes obaeratique'.[2] With the help of these retainers and dependants Orgetorix was able to do as he pleased and baffle the process of justice among the Helvetii.

Secondly, the Aeduan chieftain Dumnorix, the friend and ally of Orgetorix. The facts about Dumnorix are the classic text for dynastic marriages among the *principes* of Gaul. Dumnorix had extended his power far and wide, and he had not confined his operations to taking a wife from among the Helvetii, the daughter of Orgetorix. He had made his mother marry a 'homo nobilissimus ac potentissimus' among the Bituriges; and he had used his half-sister and his female relatives to contract matrimonial alliances in other tribes.[3]

By contrast, the old *provincia*, Gallia Narbonensis, which is organized on the municipal system. The population was mixed in origin, and perhaps not Celtic by predominance; hardly any of the tribes (except the Allobroges) had a national memory of wars against the Romans; by climate and products it was a Mediterranean region; there was a tendency to live in towns; and, Roman civilization supervening upon the Hellenic, the *provincia* might have grown and developed upon the Italian model even if no colonies had been established there of Roman veterans.[4]

'Italia verius quam provincia.'[5] So was Narbonensis designated. Facts confirm the phrase. The inhabitants of the Narbonensian province are recruited for the Roman legions, and even, at an early date, for the Praetorian Guard—but they are hardly ever found in the auxiliary regiments.[6] The young men of the municipal aristocracies enter the imperial service as officers in the legions and go on to financial posts as *procuratores Augusti*.[7] And, the next stage, these families produce Roman senators. A number are attested in the early Empire.[8] The first consul comes in the reign of Tiberius Caesar, in 35—Valerius Asiaticus from Vienna (which had once been a tribal

---

[1] Caesar, *BG* I. 2. 1.   [2] 4. 2.

[3] 3. 5; 9. 3; 18. 6 f.

[4] Compare the Transpadane zone—hardly any colonies, and the indigenous element very important (p. 620).

[5] Pliny, *NH* III. 31: 'virorum morumque dignatione, amplitudine opum nulli provinciarum postferenda breviterque Italia verius quam provincia.'

[6] There were two *alae* of Vocontii; but that community had an anomalous structure, unique in the *provincia*.

[7] *Agr.* 4. 1: 'utrumque avum procuratorem Caesarum habuit, quae equestris nobilitas est.'

[8] See Ch. XLIII. In 49 they received a special favour, being permitted to visit their homes without leave from the Emperor (*Ann.* XII. 23. 1).

capital, the city of the Allobroges).[1] The second follows quickly, Domitius Afer of Nemausus (in 39).[2]

Narbonensis therefore belongs with the civilized parts of Spain—and with the provincial zone of northern Italy, namely, Italia Transpadana. Climate and history, organization and government, everything separates Narbonensis from Tres Galliae.

To return, therefore, to Gaul properly so called (Tres Galliae).[3] The natives are not normally permitted to serve in the Roman legions, but only in auxiliary formations.[4] The chieftains command tribal regiments, but seldom occupy the position of *tribunus militum* in the Roman legions;[5] still less do they find employment as *procuratores* in the service of the Roman government.[6] The Gallic *principes* cannot expect to have access to the governing class of Rome, like the families from the *coloniae* and *municipia* in Narbonensis or in Spain—despite their wealth and education.

The facts about the social structure of Tres Galliae are plain and patent. On the one hand, the chieftains, dynastic families, great owners of property; on the other, a large population, tenants, or even serfs. Clearly not a land that was ready to be put on a level with the regions of town-government—Italy, Narbonensis, and the civilized parts of Spain.

What then was to be the destiny of Gaul? An important part of the Roman Empire, rich and populous, yet not integrated with the more vital parts and not contributing to the imperial administrative class. And Gaul might also prove troublesome.

---

[1] Revealed by *FO* IX, discovered in 1941 and first published in 1947 (*Inscr. It.* XIII. 1, p. 188). Previously his first consulate had been assigned to Caligula's reign—naturally enough.

[2] Afer's origin is attested only by Jerome, *Chron.* 179 H.

[3] In Tacitus and in other authors the term 'Galliae' normally and firmly excludes Narbonensis, being restricted to the Gallia 'quae Comata appellatur' (XI. 23. 1). Cf., for example, Quintilian VIII. 5. 15; X. 3. 13 (cited in App. 91). Therefore, in *Dial.* 10. 2, 'ex Hispania vel Asia, ne quid de Gallis nostris loquar', the emendation of Schulting, 'Galli⟨i⟩s' should be accepted. Perhaps also Bentley's, likewise, in Suetonius, *Nero* 40. 1. But 'Galliam suismet viribus concidisse' (*Hist.* IV. 17. 3, where Wurm and Halm emend) should stand: there is no ambiguity—and 'Galliae' has already occurred three times in the chapter.

[4] Fewer than a dozen Gallic legionaries can be discovered in the first century. Almost all of them form a single group in III Augusta: presumably levied in the abnormal conditions of 69 and subsequently sent away to Africa, cf. R. Syme, *Rev. ét. anc.* XXXVIII (1936), 184 ff.

[5] Dessau found only two legionary tribunes in the early Empire (*Hermes* XLV (1910), 12 f.), viz., the Aeduan Julius Calenus (*Hist.* III. 35. 2, cf. *ILS* 4659), and a Treveran (*CIL* XIII, 4030). Add *ILS* 7017 and *CIL* XIII, 11045; and *ILS* 2755 might be fairly early.

[6] Observe, however, Julius Classicianus, the procurator of Britain (*Ann.* XIV. 38. 3), whose wife is 'Iulia Indi f. Pacata' (*CIL* VII, 30+*AE* 1936, 3: Londinium)—presumably of the family of Julius Indus (III. 42. 3). Indus is Treveran, as is the insurgent Julius Classicus—'regium illi genus et pace belloque clara origo' (*Hist.* IV. 55. 1).

Trouble might originate either among the barons or among the depressed class. Like their ancestors, the Gallic nobles were proud and bellicose, rejoicing in splendour and display. Hence quarrels, extravagance, and debts. Their pride would be injured by the Roman rule—and they might envy the opportunities of the Narbonensians who had easy admittance to the Roman senatorial order. And they resented the burden of Roman taxation.[1]

Such were the grievances of the rich. Discontent among the country population threatened a social revolution that would easily and perhaps inevitably take the form of a national rising against foreign rule. And nationalism might be fanned by superstition.

There were Druids—but what are Druids precisely? The old priestly and aristocratic class of Druids known from Caesar seems to have faded out.[2] The nobles had quickly abandoned the traditional education, turning with eagerness to the dominant language and culture of the civilized world.[3] When that happened, the old religious and magical beliefs sank into the lower classes and retained their potency there. If the name of the Druids survived, it now adhered to village sorcerers and rural magicians.

In the past Gaul and the Druids had a grim notoriety for human sacrifices. With the Roman conquest, or very soon after it, that practice was abolished, as Strabo the geographer testifies;[4] and another writer notes that only an innocuous ritual survived as a symbolic vestige.[5] The reproach might still adhere, and perhaps the suspicion of dark rites in the remote places. Tiberius Caesar by official enactment extirpated Druidism utterly, so the elder Pliny affirms.[6]

Whether ritual murder among the Gauls was the true reason or

[1] III. 40.

[2] Caesar gives a full description of the Druids (*BG* VI. 13 f.), but no Druids occur anywhere in the narrative. Hence a topic for speculation, see, for example, M. Rambaud, *L'Art de la déformation historique dans les Commentaires de César* (1953), 328 ff. Cicero had converse with the eminent Aeduan Diviciacus (the brother of Dumnorix), whom he describes as a Druid (*De div.* I. 90).

[3] N. J. De Witt, *TAPA* LXIX (1938), 319 ff.

[4] Strabo IV. 198. There is no sign that Strabo's information is fresh news (that is to say, Augustan rather than Caesarian). Strabo was probably writing towards 1 B.C.: the few sporadic items added on revision in A.D. 18 or 19 are not relevant.

[5] Mela III. 18: 'manent vestigia feritatis iam abolitae, atque ut ab ultimis caedibus temperant, ita nihilominus, ubi devotos altaribus admovere, delibant.' Mela was writing precisely in 43 (cf. III. 49), but his sources are seldom up to date. There is no indication that he is referring to a recent cessation of ritual murders.

[6] Pliny, *NH* xxx. 13: 'Gallias utique possedit, et quidem ad nostram memoriam. namque Tiberii Caesaris principatus sustulit Druidas eorum et hoc genus vatum medicorumque.' Pliny was close to the event, and he knew Gaul. Suetonius, who assigns to Claudius the abolition of Druidism (*Divus Claudius* 25. 5), cannot compete. It is therefore unsound to admit his testimony to equal rank with that of Pliny.

only the inevitable pretext is another question.[1] The belief in witch-craft kept much of its strength.[2] And witchcraft might not be harm-less. It might operate as a subversive force among the credulous and fanatical population of the country-side, and, working upon social discontent, lend fuel to a nationalist insurrection against the Roman rule.

Tacitus does not report the enactment of Tiberius, and there is nothing about Gallic religion in the *Annales*. Britain had authentic Druids, with their murderous rites. Tacitus is careful to relate how Suetonius Paullinus attacked the island of Mona and destroyed the sacred groves.[3] He may have been proposing to say something about Gallic religion later on, when he came to the rising in 68.[4]

A striking proof of native superstition had been duly registered by Tacitus in the *Historiae*. In the year 69 a native prophet arose, claimed divinity, and gathered a 'fanatica multitudo' of eight thousand follow-ers among the country folk of the Aedui.[5] Furthermore, in the next year Druids emerge, and, incited by the burning of the Capitol, proclaim the imminent destruction of the Roman power.[6]

The Gallic danger now becomes clearer. A rebellious noble had allies among his own class and kin—but he could also summon a large following of clients and serfs in the rural areas.

On first inspection there is not much about Gaul and the Gallic problem in the *Annales*. The lost books would redress the balance. Above all, the missing climax of the risings in the West against Nero. The movement started in Gaul. The historian was ready for it. He planned the design long in advance. Three episodes prepare and foreshadow.

First, in the year 21, the insurrection of the Treveri and Aedui

---

[1] The humanitarian ideals of the imperial government are accorded undue (and almost exclusive) importance by H. M. Last, *JRS* xxxix (1949), 1 ff. It should be noted that Rome witnessed the burying alive of foreigners under supervision of the *XVviri sacris faciundis*, cf. Pliny, *NH* xxviii. 12: 'etiam nostra aetas vidit.' Presumably by order of Claudius Caesar; perhaps natives of Britain.

[2] Pliny affirms most positively that Claudius put to death a Roman knight from the Vocontii (in Narbonensis) because of a Druidic practice, the carrying of a serpent's egg (*NH* xxix. 54).

[3] xiv. 30.

[4] Tiberius' measure might in fact have been provoked by the Gallic insurrection of 21; and Tacitus may have been saving up Druids to the end, so as to have the parallel of religious fanaticism, Gaul with Judaea. British Druids (xiv. 30) are therefore a sign-post on the way—as also the Christiani at Rome (xv. 44).

[5] ii. 61. Tacitus applies 'fanaticus' elsewhere only to the Druids in Britain (*Ann.* xiv. 30. 2).

[6] iv. 54. 2: 'fatali nunc igne signum caelestis irae datum et possessionem rerum huma-narum Transalpinis gentibus portendi superstitione vana Druidae canebant.' Some scholars ignore, and others deny, the testimony of a Roman consular.

under Julius Florus and Julius Sacrovir.[1] It is generously narrated—
the pride of the chieftains, their grievances, and their plot. Gathering
clients and dependants in a great host but imperfectly equipped, they
seized as hostages the aristocratic youths being educated at Augustodunum.[2] The revolt spread; they won much sympathy, and some help
from other tribes, but were opposed among the Treveri by a rival
nobleman, Julius Indus. When it came to battle, the levies of Gaul
were shattered and dispersed by the legions.

The second scene exhibited amity and pageantry. Caligula entered
upon his third consulship at Lugdunum, where the delegates from the
peoples of Gaul met at stated seasons for homage and worship at the
Altar of Rome and Augustus. Caligula organized various festivals.
One was an oratorical competition—for Gaul had already much
renown in that field.[3]

The contest did not pass without discomfort or hazard for some of
the performers.[4] And the Emperor went on to vex and pillage the
native aristocracy. Calling for the tax returns of Tres Galliae, he noted
the great fortunes and ordered their possessors to be executed.[5]

Birth, wealth, and education, the noblemen of Gaul might conceive
the ambition to enter the Roman governing order. The next act shows
the next emperor as their friend and patron. Claudius Caesar was born
at Lugdunum.[6] In 43 he spent several months in Gaul.[7] In 48, when
the Emperor as censor was supplementing the roll of the Senate, a
group of the notables turned up with a petition.[8] No legal defect, it is
true, impaired the citizenship of the Gallic *principes*; and the Caesars,
by bestowing the *latus clavus*, could admit whom they pleased to the
career of honours.[9] Claudius Caesar intervened with a whole batch of
promotions—and, though the censor needed no decree of the Senate,

[1] III. 40–46. It cannot be assumed that other historians would have narrated the episode
so fully.

[2] 43. 1. A precious item. Also, for accuracy of detail, the 'vulgus obaeratorum aut
clientium' (42. 2, cf. Caesar, *BG* I. 4. 2), and the gladiators encased in iron—'cruppellarios
vocant' (43. 2).

[3] cf. App. 91.

[4] Suetonius, *Cal.* 20, cf. Juvenal I. 44.   [5] Dio LIX. 22. 3 f.

[6] On August 1, 10 B.C.—on the very day the Altar was dedicated, according to Suetonius
(*Divus Claudius* 2. 1). The ceremony probably took place in 12 B.C. (Livy, *Per.* cxxxix).

[7] Six months absent from Rome, sixteen days in Britain (Dio LX. 23. 1, cf. Suetonius,
Divus Claudius 17. 2).

[8] XI. 23. 1.

[9] H. F. Pelham, *Essays on Roman History* (1911), 152 ff. The plain truth has been obscured by those who, adopting or extending a pronouncement of Mommsen, assume that
there was a 'ius honorum' from which categories of Roman citizens in the provinces could
be debarred: thus A. Momigliano, *Claudius: the Emperor and his Achievement* (1934), 44 f.;
J. Carcopino, *Points de vue sur l'impérialisme romain* (1934), 170 f. Still more peculiar (and
confused) is V. Scramuzza, *The Emperor Claudius* (1940), 105: 'only one disability stood
against them: they were not Italians.'

he insisted on publicity.[1] He made the high assembly the witness and the accomplice of his action. The Senate listened and voted.[2]

That most of the Emperor's speech should be extant confers an adventitious interest both upon his remarks and upon the occasion. After explaining with much tedious erudition how the Roman Commonwealth grew and spread, Claudius comes at last to the senators from the towns of Italy and thence moves on to Narbonensis, with emphasis upon the city of Vienna, long since a home of senators.[3] An orator who had to prove his case, or a ruler who cared for honest approbation, might have made some allusion by name and quality to the excellent Narbonensians he could see on the benches before him. The orator Domitius Afer deserved a word and a compliment. Yet one town only is named, one family referred to. Vienna evoked the thought of Claudius' victim Valerius Asiaticus, to whom he alludes in bitter rancour.[4]

That is not the worst. Vienna has brought the imperial orator to the boundary between Narbonensis and Tres Galliae.[5] He leaps over it with fraudulent alacrity. What need for further argument, he says, since the House enjoys the honourable presence of Roman senators from Lugdunum?[6]

The argument is frivolous and fallacious. Lugdunum was a Roman colony, therefore of full citizen rank, and an integral part of the Populus Romanus. That it should be situated within the borders of Tres Galliae is only an accident of geography.[7]

The boundary between Narbonensis and Tres Galliae, on the other hand, is not an accident or the mere result of provincial divisions and administrative convenience. Gaul is a land of tribes; and, though the

---

[1] For the oration compared with Tacitus' version see pp. 317 ff.

[2] XI. 25. 1: 'orationem principis secuto patrum consulto primi Aedui senatorum in urbe ius adepti sunt. datum id foederi antiquo et quia soli Gallorum fraternitatis nomen cum populo Romano usurpant.' The Gauls had asked for 'ius adipiscendorum in urbe honorum' (23. 1), which ought to mean the *latus clavus*: cf. the charges against Fabricius Veiento, 'venditata ab eo munera principis et adipiscendorum honorum ius' (XIV. 50. 1). Tacitus eschews technical precision: the term *latus clavus* is admitted only in *Dial*. 7. 1 (used by M. Aper). However, the setting suggests that Gallic noblemen were adlected in 48, the Aedui in the first instance.

[3] *ILS* 212, col. ii, ll. 9 f.: 'ornatissima ecce colonia valentissimaque Viennensium quam longo iam tempore senatores huic curiae confert.'

[4] ib. 14 ff., cited above, p. 318. Claudius also referred to Asiaticus' brother.

[5] ib. 20 f.: 'iam enim ad extremos fines Galliae Narbonensis venisti.'

[6] ib. 26 ff.: 'quid ultra desideratis quam ut vobis digito demonstrem solum ipsum ultra fines provinciae Narbonensis iam vobis senatores mittere, quando ex Luguduno habere nos nostri ordinis viros non paenitet.' The reference has always been taken to mean Roman senators, citizens of the *colonia* Lugdunum. Claudius does not quite say so—note 'solum ipsum'. He meant himself. The Roman emperor is a member of the senatorial order. For the dearth of senators from Lugdunum, p. 630.

[7] cf. Seneca on the fire at Lugdunum, *Epp*. 91. 10: 'civitas arsit opulenta ornamentumque provinciarum quibus et inserta erat et excepta.'

magnates of Gaul possessed wealth and talent, the advantages of education, and a Latinity that may often have shamed the scholarship or accents of Italians and colonials, they were tribal chieftains still. The contrast with Narbonensis is clear and sharp. The *provincia* is a natural and organic continuation of that Italy which had absorbed the Etruscan, the Oscan, the Illyrian, and the Celt.

The·imperial orator evoked the past of Rome, kept silent about recent disturbances in Gaul, and argued that he was creating a salubrious precedent. How should his act be assessed? Not by mere numbers of the newly admitted (small perhaps in relation to the size of the Senate). A novel principle was enounced, abruptly. Tacitus thought that it mattered. No other author has noticed this transaction, for praise or blame or bare record, not even Seneca, who derides Claudius for his lavish extension of the Roman citizenship and mocks him for having been born at Lugdunum—'Gallus germanus'.[1]

That is not all. The historian defends the Emperor from his critics —and improves his case in various ways.[2] Imperial orations often omit relevant facts or valid arguments, as Tacitus knew.[3] His own version brings in the wealth of the Gallic notables and their fusion with the best things in civilization.[4]

The outcome ought to have been beneficial. Conciliation instead of distrust—and the *principes* of Gaul, clients of the dynasty hitherto, would henceforth, as members of the governing order, be bound in allegiance to Rome as well, and to the Empire.

Fate came out with the epilogue twenty years later, in perfect irony —the insurgent Julius Vindex, the governor of Lugdunensis. That accident justified the hesitations of Claudius' advisers in the privy council: a senator from Gaul was still a native dynast. And there soon followed, arising from a Roman civil war, the Batavian War, and blending with it, the 'imperium Galliarum', promoted by the chieftains of the Treveri and Lingones. Rome was merciless against rebellion. Civilis surrendered.[5] There is no sign that his life was spared. The fate of Julius Classicus is not recorded; Julius Sabinus went into

---

[1] *Apocol.* 6. 1, cf. 3. 2: 'constituerat enim omnes Graecos Gallos Hispanos Britannos togatos videre.' Also *De ben.* VI. 19. 2: 'quid, ergo, inquit, si princeps civitatem dederit omnibus Gallis?' Cassius Dio is fragmentary; but Suetonius devoted a whole chapter to the acts of the censorship (*Divus Claudius* 16).

[2] p. 318. For the contrary opinion about the merits of Claudius' speech, J. Carcopino, o.c. 180 ff.; F. Vittinghoff, *Hermes* LXXXII (1954), 362 ff.

[3] XII. 11. 1 (kings given to Parthia); 22. 2 (the marriage of Lollia Paullina to Caligula). Claudius in this speech ignored the role of Julius Caesar in the promotion of municipal senators, cf. R. Syme, *BSR Papers* XIV (1938), 8.

[4] XI. 24. 6: 'iam moribus artibus adfinitatibus nostris mixti aurum et opes suas inferant potius quam separati habeant.'

[5] *Hist.* v. 26 (where the text breaks off).

hiding, concealed and succoured by his loyal wife. Nine years later they were captured and put to death by order of Vespasian.[1]

The lesson was not lost. The next age does not show many senators from Tres Galliae.[2] Instead, the emperors continue to draw upon Spain and Narbonensis. The process spreads quickly to Africa and to the Greek East. Men from the cities of Asia become senators—and Galatians, of Celtic ancestry, the descendants of kings and tetrarchs.[3]

What impelled Julius Vindex will never be known. The Roman exploitation of Gaul was ever a cause of discontent, exacerbated no doubt by the operations of Nero's financial agents. If a legate in defence of the provincials came to a clash with the procurator, there was no need to ask which side the central government would support. A prudent governor would avoid such entanglements.[4] Perhaps the act of Vindex was hardly policy or even conspiracy, rather self-preservation. However it be, the protest against the tyranny of Nero at once and inevitably took the form of a native insurrection against the Roman power, recalling Julius Florus and Julius Sacrovir, chieftains of the Treveri and Aedui, who raised war in Gaul in the days of Tiberius Caesar.[5]

Julius Vindex was not only a Roman senator—he was the descendant of kings in Aquitania.[6] And Vindex did not stand alone. The notables were with him, bound by the ties of tradition, class, and family, and bringing their hosts of clients.[7] When the levies of Gaul began to muster, the Rhine legions saw the chance they had been waiting for. Not to invade Germany or repel a German invasion, but to intervene at need in Gaul was the main function of the army of Upper Germany. Loyal to Rome (and to Nero), the legate Verginius Rufus confronted and defeated the Gauls.[8]

The act of the insurgent had been hazardous, his plea ambiguous—

[1] IV. 67. 2; Dio LXV. 16. I f.; Plutarch, *Amatorius* 25. 770 d ff.

[2] There could have been sporadic senators before Claudius' censorship. Perhaps the parent of Julius Vindex (Dio LXIII. 22. 1²); perhaps M. Aper, whose military service in Britain (*Dial.* 17. 4) should fall in 43 (App. 91). After 70, note the parent of Tacitus' friend Julius Naso (Pliny, *Epp.* VI. 6. 3 f., cf. App. 92). And one is entitled to wonder about the consuls C. Julius Juvenalis, Q. Julius Balbus, and C. Julius Silanus (*suffecti* 81, 85, 92). For Gallic senators in the second century, J. Colin, *Latomus* XIII (1954), 218 ff.

[3] Ch. XXXVIII.   [4] Thus Agricola, when legate of Aquitania (*Agr.* 9. 5).

[5] And it looked even more so after the events of 69 and 70. H. Schiller assumed that Vindex was a Gallic nationalist and separatist (*Gesch. des r. Kaiserreichs unter der Regierung des Nero* (1872), 261 ff.). Mommsen, arguing against, took Vindex for a Republican (*Hermes* XIII (1878), 90 ff. = *Ges. Schr.* IV (1906), 333 ff.). Extreme views, which neglect the complexity of the situation.   [6] Dio LXIII. 22. 1².

[7] Josephus, *BJ* IV. 440: ἅμα τοῖς δυνατοῖς τῶν ἐπιχωρίων. A hundred thousand followers according to Plutarch, *Galba* 8.

[8] For Verginius' loyalty to Nero, which had to be toned down subsequently or covered up, cf. p. 179.

a Roman governor, but appealing for native support to dethrone a Roman emperor. The historian no doubt brought out the dilemma sharp and clear. A speech was the best device. Tone and tenor might be surmised. Not a mere denunciation of Nero the tyrant, the matricide, the mountebank, not anger and sorrow for the slaughter of Roman noblemen and the degradation of the Roman Senate. The Gallic leader would utter a stirring challenge to the pride, the renown, and the ancient valour of Gaul.[1]

The provinces of the West had a dual structure—tribal and municipal. It imparted a dual shape to the rising against Nero, and all but caused it to collapse. Julius Vindex had the levies of Gaul, but Galba drew his support from the towns in Spain (whether their origin was colonial or native). When Galba made his proclamation at Carthago Nova, he could not fail to call upon Senate and People, upon Roman dignity, tradition, and patriotism. The cause also found support in cities of Narbonensis. More perhaps for Galba than for Vindex. Vienna was against Nero, but cannot have intended to help a native revolt from Rome.[2] The *provincia* as a whole earns commendation for zeal and deference to the Roman Senate.[3]

The Gallic problem develops in four stages—Florus and Sacrovir, Caligula at Lugdunum, the oration of Claudius Caesar, and the insurrection of Vindex. Spain burst into history with one act, throwing into the contest its resources of men, money, and Roman sentiment. Book XVIII of the *Annales* must have told what was needed about the Empire. Constructed upon a general survey of armies and provinces, with a speech from Vindex and a speech from Galba, it would recall the broad scene, the rapid action, and the swift narration of the *Historiae*.[4]

Compositions like the exordium of the *Historiae* or the battle for Cremona find nothing to surpass them in any language. Nor can accuracy or equity be more than faintly questioned. Detractors prefer to pounce upon the *Annales*, which is not altogether just.[5] Tacitus

---

[1] Dio's speech of Vindex (LXIII. 22. 3 ff., in the summary of Xiphilinus) is miserable and unreal.

[2] It is the Lugdunenses (imperial and Neronian) who describe Vienna as 'sedem Gallici belli: cuncta illic externa et hostilia' (*Hist.* I. 65. 2).

[3] *Ann.* XII. 23. 1: 'egregiam in patres reverentiam.'

[4] That is, if in fact Tacitus lived long enough to write it.

[5] Thus J. S. Reid, whose attack on Tacitus ignored the *Historiae* (*JRS* XI (1921), 191 ff.). Reid states that Suetonius 'has a feeling for great imperial interests such as we can rarely trace in his more famous contemporary' (o.c. 194). That scholar cannot have been reading the *Nero* (which is all but silent on Parthia and Britain). Much of the matter is trivial, and the author is vague and careless about points of historical detail. See further, on the *Nero*, App. 77.

was dealing with a tradition already formed, a period mostly beyond the reach of verification. An historian ought rather to be challenged on his own ground, to stand or fall by his treatment of events within his own time and knowledge.[1]

The *Annales* are open to various indictments. Not all of the critics allow for the restrictions that bound the Roman historian, whether inevitable or self-imposed: they use anachronistic standards, or merciless rigidities of doctrine. In the preceding pages the graver charges have been investigated. Something has been said about subject and style, about veracity, penetration, and grasp. It remains to discuss the opinions and beliefs of Cornelius Tacitus. The inquiry bears upon his time and rank and origin. In the first instance, the *Annales* in relation to their date.[2]

[1] Suetonius, being merely an erudite compiler, becomes progressively less good as he approaches his own time.

[2] Ch. xxxv.

ISBN 0–19–	Author	Title
8143567	ALFÖLDI A.	The Conversion of Constantine and Pagan Rome
6286409	ANDERSON George K.	The Literature of the Anglo-Saxons
8219601	ARNOLD Benjamin	German Knighthood
8228813	BARTLETT & MacKAY	Medieval Frontier Societies
8111010	BETHURUM Dorothy	Homilies of Wulfstan
8142765	BOLLING G. M.	External Evidence for Interpolation in Homer
814332X	BOLTON J.D.P.	Aristeas of Proconnesus
9240132	BOYLAN Patrick	Thoth, the Hermes of Egypt
8114222	BROOKS Kenneth R.	Andreas and the Fates of the Apostles
8203543	BULL Marcus	Knightly Piety & Lay Response to the First Crusade
8216785	BUTLER Alfred J.	Arab Conquest of Egypt
8148046	CAMERON Alan	Circus Factions
8148054	CAMERON Alan	Porphyrius the Charioteer
8148348	CAMPBELL J.B.	The Emperor and the Roman Army 31 BC to 235
826643X	CHADWICK Henry	Priscillian of Avila
826447X	CHADWICK Henry	Boethius
8219393	COWDREY H.E.J.	The Age of Abbot Desiderius
8148992	DAVIES M.	Sophocles: Trachiniae
825301X	DOWNER L.	Leges Henrici Primi
814346X	DRONKE Peter	Medieval Latin and the Rise of European Love-Lyric
8142749	DUNBABIN T.J.	The Western Greeks
8154372	FAULKNER R.O.	The Ancient Egyptian Pyramid Texts
8221541	FLANAGAN Marie Therese	Irish Society, Anglo-Norman Settlers, Angevin Kingship
8143109	FRAENKEL Edward	Horace
8201540	GOLDBERG P.J.P.	Women, Work and Life Cycle in a Medieval Economy
8140215	GOTTSCHALK H.B.	Heraclides of Pontus
8266162	HANSON R.P.C.	Saint Patrick
8224354	HARRISS G.L.	King, Parliament and Public Finance in Medieval England to 1369
8581114	HEATH Sir Thomas	Aristarchus of Samos
8140444	HOLLIS A.S.	Callimachus: Hecale
8212968	HOLLISTER C. Warren	Anglo-Saxon Military Institutions
2115480	HENRY Blanche	British Botanical and Horticultural Literature before 1800
8219523	HOUSLEY Norman	The Italian Crusades
8223319	HURNARD Naomi	The King's Pardon for Homicide – before AD 1307
8140401	HUTCHINSON G.O.	Hellenistic Poetry
9240140	JOACHIM H.H.	Aristotle: On Coming-to-be and Passing-away
9240094	JONES A.H.M	Cities of the Eastern Roman Provinces
8142560	JONES A.H.M.	The Greek City
8218354	JONES Michael	Ducal Brittany 1364–1399
8271484	KNOX & PELCZYNSKI	Hegel's Political Writings
8225253	LE PATOUREL John	The Norman Empire
8212720	LENNARD Reginald	Rural England 1086–1135
8212321	LEVISON W.	England and the Continent in the 8th century
8148224	LIEBESCHUETZ J.H.W.G.	Continuity and Change in Roman Religion
8141378	LOBEL Edgar & PAGE Sir Denys	Poetarum Lesbiorum Fragmenta
9240159	LOEW E.A.	The Beneventan Script
8241445	LUKASIEWICZ, Jan	Aristotle's Syllogistic
8152442	MAAS P. & TRYPANIS C.A .	Sancti Romani Melodi Cantica
8142684	MARSDEN E.W.	Greek and Roman Artillery—Historical
8142692	MARSDEN E.W.	Greek and Roman Artillery—Technical
8148178	MATTHEWS John	Western Aristocracies and Imperial Court AD 364–425
9240205	MAVROGORDATO John	Digenes Akrites
8223447	McFARLANE K.B.	Lancastrian Kings and Lollard Knights
8226578	McFARLANE K.B.	The Nobility of Later Medieval England
8148100	MEIGGS Russell	Roman Ostia
8148402	MEIGGS Russell	Trees and Timber in the Ancient Mediterranean World
8142641	MILLER J. Innes	The Spice Trade of the Roman Empire
8147813	MOORHEAD John	Theoderic in Italy
8264259	MOORMAN John	A History of the Franciscan Order
9240213	MYRES J.L.	Herodotus The Father of History
8219512	OBOLENSKY Dimitri	Six Byzantine Portraits
8116020	OWEN A.L.	The Famous Druids
8131445	PALMER, L.R.	The Interpretation of Mycenaean Greek Texts
8143427	PFEIFFER R.	History of Classical Scholarship (vol 1)
8143648	PFEIFFER Rudolf	History of Classical Scholarship 1300–1850
8111649	PHEIFER J.D.	Old English Glosses in the Epinal-Erfurt Glossary
8142277	PICKARD–CAMBRIDGE A.W.	Dithyramb Tragedy and Comedy
8269765	PLATER & WHITE	Grammar of the Vulgate

8213891	PLUMMER Charles	Lives of Irish Saints (2 vols)
820695X	POWICKE Michael	Military Obligation in Medieval England
8269684	POWICKE Sir Maurice	Stephen Langton
821460X	POWICKE Sir Maurice	The Christian Life in the Middle Ages
8225369	PRAWER Joshua	Crusader Institutions
8225571	PRAWER Joshua	The History of The Jews in the Latin Kingdom of Jerusalem
8143249	RABY F.J.E.	A History of Christian Latin Poetry
8143257	RABY F.J.E.	A History of Secular Latin Poetry in the Middle Ages (2 vols)
8214316	RASHDALL & POWICKE	The Universities of Europe in the Middle Ages (3 vols)
8154488	REYMOND E.A.E & BARNS J.W.B.	Four Martyrdoms from the Pierpont Morgan Coptic Codices
8148380	RICKMAN Geoffrey	The Corn Supply of Ancient Rome
8141076	ROSS Sir David	Aristotle: Metaphysics (2 vols)
8141092	ROSS Sir David	Aristotle: Physics
8142307	ROSTOVTZEFF M.	Social and Economic History of the Hellenistic World, 3 vols.
8142315	ROSTOVTZEFF M.	Social and Economic History of the Roman Empire, 2 vols.
8264178	RUNCIMAN Sir Steven	The Eastern Schism
814833X	SALMON J.B.	Wealthy Corinth
8171587	SALZMAN L.F.	Building in England Down to 1540
8218362	SAYERS Jane E.	Papal Judges Delegate in the Province of Canterbury 1198–1254
8221657	SCHEIN Sylvia	Fideles Crucis
8148135	SHERWIN WHITE A.N.	The Roman Citizenship
9240167	SINGER Charles	Galen: On Anatomical Procedures
8113927	SISAM, Kenneth	Studies in the History of Old English Literature
8642040	SOUTER Alexander	A Glossary of Later Latin to 600 AD
8270011	SOUTER Alexander	Earliest Latin Commentaries on the Epistles of St Paul
8222254	SOUTHERN R.W.	Eadmer: Life of St. Anselm
8251408	SQUIBB G.	The High Court of Chivalry
8212011	STEVENSON & WHITELOCK	Asser's Life of King Alfred
8212011	SWEET Henry	A Second Anglo-Saxon Reader—Archaic and Dialectical
8148259	SYME Sir Ronald	History in Ovid
8143273	SYME Sir Ronald	Tacitus (2 vols)
8200951	THOMPSON Sally	Women Religious
8201745	WALKER Simon	The Lancastrian Affinity 1361–1399
8161115	WELLESZ Egon	A History of Byzantine Music and Hymnography
8140185	WEST M.L.	Greek Metre
8141696	WEST M.L.	Hesiod: Theogony
8148542	WEST M.L.	The Orphic Poems
8140053	WEST M.L.	Hesiod: Works & Days
8152663	WEST M.L.	Iambi et Elegi Graeci
9240221	WHEELWRIGHT Philip	Heraclitus
822799X	WHITBY M. & M.	The History of Theophylact Simocatta
8206186	WILLIAMSON, E.W.	Letters of Osbert of Clare
8208103	WILSON F.P.	Plague in Shakespeare's London
8114877	WOOLF Rosemary	The English Religious Lyric in the Middle Ages
8119224	WRIGHT Joseph	Grammar of the Gothic Language